WOMEN
and the
AMERICAN
EXPERIENCE

ABOUT THE AUTHOR

Nancy Woloch is the editor of *Early American Women: A Documentary History, 1600–1900* (1992); coauthor of *The American Century: A History of the United States Since the 1890s* (4th ed., 1992), with Walter Lafeber and Richard Polenberg; and coauthor of *The Enduring Vision: A History of the American People* (2d ed., 1993). She teaches history and American Studies at Barnard College, Columbia University.

CONTENTS

PREFACE

Over the past quarter-century, the study of women's history has surged from a cottage industry, ignored by most professional historians, into a thriving academic enterprise. Spurred by feminist revival and the zeal of a new generation of scholars, courses in women's history have multiplied and publication has mushroomed. Scholarship within the field has been both bolstered and challenged by research on adjacent terrains, such as family history and social history. Collectively, since the late 1960s, historians of women have pursued a major revisionist mission. Not only have they made women historically visible but, by focusing on women's experience, they have uncovered a lost dimension—a distinctive world—of women's work, values, relationships, and politics. To re-create this world, historians have developed new types of data, new sets of concepts, and above all a new perspective.

Traditionally, women have been somewhere in the background of history, if not literally behind the scenes. In women's history, the stage revolves. As women move into the spotlight, the conventional stuff of texts and tests—battles and treaties, elections and tariffs—recedes to the wings. Familiar phenomena do reappear, but invariably in a new light. Westward expansion and religious revivals, depressions and wars, urbanization and immigration, turn out to have had a different impact on women than on men. The pace of history shifts as well. Since most of the changes with which women are involved are long-term, incremental changes, a new time frame is needed; old divisions into political eras no longer suffice. Most important, a new cast of characters appears. The stage now fills with daughters and widows, housewives and midwives, congregants and missionaries, domestic servants and garment workers, clubwomen, settlement workers, and suffragists. Exploring their experience reveals a new spectrum of concerns: courtship customs and marriage options, fertility patterns and child-rearing practices, dower rights and property rights, female friendship and women's networks, gender consciousness and feminist consciousness.

This book is an introduction to the history of American women, based primarily on recent scholarship. It suggests the scope of the field, the types of questions that historians have asked, and the most important themes and issues that have emerged. The focus is on women's experience in family life, economic life, and public life, with attention to the pervasive impact of class and race. Of special concern are topics that recur throughout and give women's history its distinctive character. I am interested, for instance, in women's movement into relatively empty or new areas of vocational space; in the development of female association and the significance of women's institutions; and in women's strategies, individual and collective, for acting as agents of change. I am also interested in the ways in which women's experience illuminates more general phenomena and thereby alters our interpretation of history as a whole.

The chapters in this book come in pairs, each devoted to a broadly defined historical era. The first chapter of the pair is a narrative episode that concentrates on a particular individual or event, a segment of experience, that is discussed in some detail. The second chapter is a general historical survey of larger scope, a synthesis, concerning the era in which the event or experience occurred. The process of reading each pair should be something like examining a small section of a large painting or tapestry and then stepping back for a more panoramic view.

The alternation of episode and survey is not intended to separate the personal and political, which are commonly intertwined, nor to consider the experience of exceptional women apart from that of the aggregate. Rather, the goal is to illustrate the main themes of women's history in a given era by reference to the concrete and particular. My assumption is that close attention to a specific experience, even an exceptional one—whether Mary Rowlandson's captivity in 1676 or Jane Addams's invention of a career in 1889—reveals patterns and designs that pervade the larger picture as well and that these patterns are worth inspecting from different vantage points. Obviously, all the episodes also involve events or experiences that are significant in themselves. They provide an opportunity to examine women's efforts to gain leverage, exert influence, or assume control—to shape their own destinies and those of others, whether as family members or union members, institution founders or reformers.

My scheme of periodization is geared both to the long-term changes that affect women's lives and to the work that has been done in the field. The pairs of chapters in this book are divided into four large segments: colonial and revolutionary America (chapters 1–4); 1800–1860 (chapters 5–8); 1860–1920 (chapters 9–14); and America since the 1920s (chapters 15–22). Within each era, I have focused on those areas of women's history in which research and publication have been concentrated. In the period from 1860 to 1920, for instance, pairs of chapters are devoted to working-class women, to middle-class women, and to the suffrage movement; all three pairs cover the same chronological ground but each pair of chapters approaches women's experience from a different angle. On no topic is the story complete. Women's history is currently a lively area of exploration and new scholarship continually extends its terrain.

An unannotated synthesis of women's history is something like a stroll through a mine field. Since the whole subject is relatively recent and much of the research extremely recent (that is, published since the mid-1970s), there is little that can be considered "common knowledge." On the contrary, most of women's history is still uncommon knowledge. Moreover, it is very much the property of those researchers who have uncovered it. Each chapter of this book, in short, is informed by the work of many historians. In some cases, I mention my benefactors in the text. In general, I rely on the "Suggested Readings and Sources" that follow each pair of chapters and serve in lieu of footnotes. A word, therefore, about "Suggested Readings."

For each episode (the odd-numbered chapters), I cite major secondary sources and published primary sources. For each general chapter of synthesis (the even-numbered ones), I suggest, first, a survey or surveys of the topic at hand, if any exist; and second, the major books and articles that I have used, in more or less the same order in which the chapter is organized. Additional reading suggestions are included, along with some suggestions about published primary sources. When citing articles, I give the original publication data, that is, the book or journal in which the article first appeared; many articles cited have also been republished in anthologies. For suggestions about journals, reference books, surveys, anthologies, and sources of vital statistics, see the bibliographical note at the end of the book.

Since the first edition of this book appeared in 1984, women's history has held fast as the most rapidly growing sector of American history; the rate of productivity continues to accelerate. For the revised edition, I have sought, first, to keep pace with the past decade's torrent of research and publication. Second, the revised edition reflects increased attention to diversity and ethnicity; new or enlarged segments concern, for instance, the impact of colonization on Indian women, women's roles in southwestern Hispanic communities, black women's lives in the twentieth century, and women's recent experiences as immigrants. Third, a new pair of chapters at the end of the book covers contemporary women's history. Chapter 21, the episode, discusses the immediate response to Anita Hill in the few weeks during and after the Thomas/Hill hearings in 1991, and the issue of sexual harassment. Chapter 22, the synthesis, explores major themes of women's history since 1975—feminist debates, the workplace, the family, the new immigration, and women in political life. These chapters reflect what I construe as a mainstreaming of women's history; that is, many women's concerns have recently become national concerns. Chapters 21 and 22, therefore, focus on legal issues and public policy. Finally, the revised edition appears in both a single volume and a split edition. Volume I includes chapters 1–14 (1600–1920); Volume II includes chapters 9–22 (1860 to the present). The shorter volumes, we hope, are appropriate for courses devoted, respectively, to early or modern American history.

During the years this book was in progress, I collected many debts. For their comments on the book proposal, I thank W. Elliot Brownlee, Nancy F. Cott, Anne Firor Scott, and Susan M. Hartmann. For the first edition, I am grateful to Catherine Clinton for her generous comments; to Linda S. Auwers and Patricia Cline Cohen for their perceptive advice on the manuscript; to Mari Jo Buhle, Joan Hoff, Louise Kerr, and Judith Modell for their comments on part or all of the book; and to Debra Herman, who prepared the charts and graphs. I am especially indebted to my editors at Alfred A. Knopf, Dorchen Leidholdt, Jack Wilson, and David Follmer. It was a privilege to work with them.

For the second edition, I am most grateful to Nancy A. Hewitt, Duke University, for reading the manuscript and for her helpful suggestions. For their advice on revision, I am indebted to Sharon Z. Alter, William Rainey Harper College; Patricia Cline Cohen and Mario T. Garcia, University of California, Santa Barbara; Nancy A. Hewitt, Duke University; June Sochen, Northeastern Illinois University; Jane Turner Censer, George Mason University; and Pamela Neal Warford, University of Maine at Orono. I am also indebted to Allen F. Davis and

J. Stanley Lemons for their comments and corrections. My colleagues at Barnard have been a fount of assistance. I owe special thanks to Rosalind Rosenberg and Herb Sloan, as well as to Beth Bailey, Mark Carnes, Ellen Chesler, David Farber, Eileen Glickstein, Caroline Niemczyk, and Deborah Valenze. I am grateful to my editors at McGraw-Hill—Chris Rogers, David Follmer, and Peter Labella—for their support of this book. Many thanks to my outstanding supervising editor Elaine Rosenberg and to my copy editor Norma Frankel for their wonderful work. Finally, I would like to thank my husband Isser Woloch and my sons David Woloch and Alexander Woloch. To all of the above, my immense appreciation.

Nancy Woloch

WOMEN
and the
AMERICAN
EXPERIENCE

Mary Rowlandson's Captivity

"It was the dolefullest day that ever mine eyes saw," wrote Mary Rowlandson, wife of the Puritan minister at Lancaster. At daybreak on February 20, 1676, 500 Narragansetts, armed with hatchets, knives, and English guns, descended on the tiny village that lay on the edge of English settlement, thirty-five miles from Boston. Braced for attack, Lancaster's fifty or sixty families had abandoned their homes the night before and barricaded themselves in six "garrison" houses— those that were fortified with stockades. Their preparation, however, did not deter the Narragansetts. After burning the deserted homes, the Indians turned on the garrisons, climbing on roofs, shooting at the walls, bludgeoning villagers who ventured outside, and taking some prisoners. Amazingly, the first five strongholds were relatively unharmed. But the last of the garrisons, the Rowlandson house, was surrounded and besieged for two hours. And forty-two people were inside, among them forty-year-old Mary Rowlandson, her three children, two sisters, a brother-in-law, and eleven nieces and nephews.

"The house stood upon the edge of a hill," as Mary described the fateful scene. "Some of the Indians got behind the hill; others into the Barn, and others behind anything that would shelter them; from all of which places they shot against the House, so that the Bullets seemed to fly like hail." At last, the Indians set fire to the house, with flax and hemp dragged out of the barn, and the villagers inside knew their time was short. "Now is the dreadful hour come, that I have often heard of," Mary Rowlandson remembered thinking to herself. "Now mine eyes see it. Some in our house were fighting for their lives, others wallowing in their blood, the House in fire over our heads, and the Bloody Heathen ready to knock us on the head, if we stirred out." With one of her sisters, Hannah Divoll, and a group of the children, Mary tried to unlatch the heavy front door, "but the Indians shot so thick that bullets rattled against the House," and they were forced inside. The garrison's defenses seemed to have collapsed. Even six large dogs

1

that were supposed to protect it turned out to be useless. "None of them would stir," said Mary, "though another time, if any Indian had come to the door, they were ready to fly upon him and tear him down."

The treachery of the dogs, in retrospect, was significant. Devout Puritans had to rely on God alone, not on dogs or muskets—or men, for that matter. "The Lord hereby would make us the more to acknowledge his hand," Mary concluded, "and to see that our help is always in him." But for the villagers crowded into the Rowlandson garrison, God seemed far away from Lancaster. It was unbearable to remain in the flames and equally unbearable to abandon the house and be surely massacred. Finally, "Out we must go, the fire increasing, and coming along behind us, roaring, and the Indians before us, their Guns, Spears, and hatchets to devour us."

As soon as Mary went out the door, she was shot in the side, and her youngest child, Sarah, whom she was carrying, in the stomach and hand. Her brother-in-law, John Divoll, who had commanded the garrison, was shot in the throat and dropped dead at once, whereupon the Indians ripped off his clothes. Her nephew William Kerley broke his leg, "which the Indians perceiving, they knockt him on the head." Her older sister, Elizabeth Kerley, came running out of the house after William and Mary, and was killed at once. "I hope she is reaping the fruit of her good labours," wrote Mary, "being faithfull to the services of God in her Place." Soon Mary was surrounded by the bodies of neighbors and relatives who had been stabbed, hacked, and shot by the Indians. One townsman who had been hit on the head with a hatchet was still crawling up and down. "There were we butchered by those merciless Heathen, standing amazed, with the blood running down to our heels. . . . It is a solemn sight to see so many Christians lying in their blood, some here, and some there, like a company of sheep torn by wolves. All of them stript naked by a company of hell hounds, roaring, singing, ranting, and insulting, as they would have torn our hearts out. Yet the Lord almighty preserved a number of us from death."

Almost all of the men in the Rowlandson garrison had been killed on the spot. But twenty-four miserable Puritans, mainly women and children, were taken prisoner by the victorious Narragansetts, and Mary Rowlandson was among them, as were her three children, her sister Hannah, and six nieces and nephews. Still clutching her younger daughter, Sarah, Mary Rowlandson was pulled off in one direction by the "barbarous creatures," while her son, Joseph, was dragged away in another, her daughter Mary in another, and Hannah in yet another. "I had often before this said, that if the Indians should come, I should chuse rather to be killed by them then taken alive," Mary wrote, "but when it came to the tryal my mind changed; their glittering weapons so daunted my spirit, that I chose rather to go along with those (as I may say) ravenous Beasts, then that moment to end my days." Leaving Lancaster behind in cinders, Mary Rowlandson began eleven weeks as captive, slave, and hostage during King Philip's War.

Mary Rowlandson's captivity, like the war itself, was an outcome of decades of English expansion, a process in which she had long been involved. Her parents, John and Joane White, were part of the great Puritan migration that brought 10,000 people to Massachusetts Bay in the 1630s. By 1638, they had settled at Salem, the most populous town north of Boston. Mary had been born in Somersetshire, England, probably around 1635, and in Salem the family grew much larger. The Whites had nine children, six daughters and three sons, all of whom lived to be married—an astonishing survival rate. In 1653, the family left Salem for the frontier township of Lancaster, which had just been incorporated. John White, in fact, was its wealthiest founder. By moving to Lancaster, the Whites no doubt hoped to find land for their sons. The daughters found husbands.

Joseph Rowlandson, who came from Ipswich, was Lancaster's first ordained minister. Mary married him in 1656, and between 1657 and 1669, they had four children, the first of whom died in infancy. At the time of the raid, the Rowlandson's son, Joseph, was thirteen, Mary was ten, and Sarah was six. (Providentially, when the Narragansetts attacked, Joseph Rowlandson was in Boston, pleading for military protection for Lancaster, and thereby escaping almost certain death.) Other White daughters also married local men, forming a tight-knit clan. Mary's older sister Elizabeth married Henry Kerley, the town's chief military officer, who was in Boston with Joseph Rowlandson when Elizabeth was killed. Between 1657 and 1672, the Kerleys had seven children. Mary's younger sister Hannah married John Divoll, who defended the Rowlandson garrison until he was shot, and they had four children. Through their offspring, the White sisters imposed their genealogical imprint on the Massachusetts frontier. Weaving a tapestry of family names, often using those of their siblings, they populated Lancaster with Marys, Elizabeths, Hannahs, Sarahs, Johns, Henrys, Josephs, and Williams. When a child died, as had the Rowlandsons' first daughter, Mary, her name was given to a new arrival, perpetuating the ties of kinship.

The proliferation of Whites, Rowlandsons, Kerleys, and Divolls, and the incorporation of such towns as Lancaster, were part of the cause of King Philip's War. Since Mary's parents had arrived in Salem, the Puritan population had exploded. New villages had steadily been set up in rings extending westward from Boston, township adjacent to township, pushing the local tribes—Wampanoags, Narragansetts, Nipmucks—farther and farther into the interior. Lancaster, on the edge of Indian country, was a veritable symbol of English expansion. Before 1650, it had been just a fur trading post; by the 1670s, it was full of Puritan families. The Indians of southern New England, in fact, were now outnumbered. In 1676, when the Narragansetts invaded Lancaster, there were about 20,000 Indians in the region and twice as many English settlers.

While Mary White was growing up in Salem, there was relative peace with the local Indians, at least nothing like the fierce conflicts familiar to seventeenth-century Virginians. But during the summer of 1675, the tribes of New England suddenly turned hostile. Mobilized by Metacom (called Philip by the English), chief of the Wampanoags, they had started to raid Massachusetts towns, burning Swansea, besieging Brookfield, demolishing Deerfield. Although the precise cause of the war is still unclear, Philip and the English had long harbored mutual suspicions. Driven off their former land by four decades of settlement and threatened by still further expansion, the Indians had ample cause for attack.

Despite a successful English reprisal in the fall, the colonists had reason to fear new trouble, especially on the perimeter of settlement. Only a week or so before the Lancaster raid, Joseph Rowlandson and his brother-in-law Henry Kerley had embarked on their trek to Boston to warn the authorities, though to no avail. By the time companies from Marlborough and Concord reached the town, the Narragansetts had attacked and vanished. When Joseph Rowlandson finally confronted the remnants of his house and the rubble of Lancaster, he assumed that his wife and family had been slaughtered. But Mary Rowlandson had been carried off by the Indians on a perilous series of "removes" into the wilderness.

The first "remove" was barely a mile from Lancaster, where the Indians set up camp for the night and celebrated their victory. But the distance, for Mary, was far greater: She had entered an inferno and was surrounded by fiends. "The roaring, and singing, and danceing, and yelling of those black creatures in the night . . . made the place a lively resemblance of hell." Watching her captors stuff themselves with roast cattle, horses, sheep, hogs, and chickens, although all food was denied to the prisoners, Mary was overcome by a sense of loss, despair, and impending doom. "All was gone, my Husband gone (at least separated from me . . . and to my grief, the indians told me they would kill him as he came homeward), my Children gone, my relatives and Friends gone, our House . . . and home and all our comforts, within and without, all was gone (except my life) and [I] knew not but at the moment that might go too."

During the next few days her misery increased. Still starving, the ten English captives in Mary's group were forced to march westward through the snow. Wounded six-year-old Sarah, carried by a warrior, was weakening rapidly and kept moaning "I shall die, I shall die." At one point the Indians placed Mary and the child on a horse, which they promptly fell off, to the merriment of their captors. The prisoners were not fed until the third day out, when they reached Menameset, an Indian town on the Ware River. Here Mary was sold, by the Indian who had captured her, to Quinnapin, a Narragansett chief who had participated in the Lancaster raid. Quinnapin had three squaws, Mary observed, "living sometimes with one, sometimes with another." The oldest of the three offered Mary some food and a blanket and treated her with some compassion. But Mary's services were at once appropriated by Quinnapin's most recent wife, Weetamoo, a more aggressive personality and soon to become the special villain of Mary's captivity.

For the moment, however, Quinnapin and Weetamoo permitted Mary to care for Sarah, who, too weak to move, lay in her lap, moaning day and night. After a week, when it was clear that Sarah was dying, she and Mary were moved by their captors to a separate wigwam, "I suppose because they would not be troubled with such spectacles." Mary's wound was now healing, although her side had grown stiff and was difficult to move. But within a few hours Sarah was dead, of fever and starvation. Buried by the Indians, she was left behind. "I have thought since of the wonderful goodness of God to me," Mary said, "in preserving me in the use of my reason and senses, in that distressed time, that I did not use wicked and violent means to end my own miserable life."

Mary had cause to marvel at her own survival. Among her small group of captives, now numbering nine, seven were children. The only other woman was soon murdered. Young Ann Joslin, whose husband had been killed defending the Rowlandson garrison, was clearly the least fortunate of the Lancaster prisoners. In an advanced stage of pregnancy, encumbered with a two-year-old daughter, and barely able to travel, she had many complaints. "Having so much grief upon her spirit, about her miserable condition, being so near her time, she would often be asking the Indians to let her go home," Mary remembered. Annoyed by Ann Joslin's problems and grievances, her captors prepared a more grisly fate instead.

> Vexed about her importunity, [they] gathered a great company together about her, stripped her naked, and set her in the midst of them; and when they had sung and danced about her (in their hellish manner) as long as they pleased, they knockt her on the head, and the child in her arms with her . . . they made a big fire and put them both into it, and told the other Children that were with them that if they attempted to go home, they would serve them in the like manner.

Mary Rowlandson did not actually witness Ann Joslin's death, though she learned about it a few days later. By the time the gruesome event occurred, Mary had been separated from the other English captives, including "four young cousins and neighbors, some of whom I never saw afterward." Now utterly alone, with neither English child nor neighbor near, Mary took steps to protect her life. The first was prayer. She "earnestly entreated the Lord, that he would consider my low estate, and show me a sign for good, and if it were his blessed will, some sign of hope and relief." Within days, she was inundated with divine responses. Her son, Joseph, a captive nearby, was able to visit, and she learned that he had seen her daughter Mary, who had been captured by a "praying Indian" (one whom the English had converted to Christianity) and sold for a gun. Both of the children were well. On Mary's eleventh day of captivity, moreover, another sign was given. A pack of warriors, who had just raided Medfield, came riding into camp, with "outrageous roaring and hooping," laden with English scalps and a variety of plunder. Medfield, which was only twenty miles from Boston, had been taken completely by surprise and burned to the ground. But a generous warrior gave Mary a Bible he had taken, "a wonderful mercy of God to me in these afflictions" and definitely a token of divine concern. Mary ploughed her way through Deuteronomy until she read that "the Lord would gather us together and turn all those curses upon our enemies."

While relying on faith and seeking for signs, Mary also took practical steps to ensure her survival. Housewifery and trade, it seemed, were her second nature. During two decades of married life in Lancaster, Mary had become adept at sewing and knitting articles of clothing for her family. As a captive, she put her skills to good use. Weetamoo quickly discovered her talent with needles and as soon as Mary became a full-time servant, kept her busy knitting stockings. Before long, Mary extended her clientele, sewing and knitting all sorts of clothing, such as caps, shirts, and aprons, and trading them to the Indians for pieces of food or other useful items. Staving off starvation, Mary was able, simultaneously, to extend her influence. When rewarded with a knife for one piece of work, she cagily turned it over to Quinnapin in order to impress him with the value of her skill. Her talent at needlework was also useful for establishing a favorable rapport with Philip, leader of the uprising.

Philip had not been among the Indians who attacked Lancaster. But by March Mary's captors had made their way northwest to the forests of New Hampshire, where Philip had taken refuge. He had just sought aid from the Mohawks in New York and was on his way back to southern New England. It now became clear that Mary Rowlandson was an especially valuable captive. Philip invited her into his wigwam, and even offered her a pipe, which she rejected. An occasional smoker at home, where she used to enjoy a few pipes in the evening, Mary knew from experience that smoking was a tempting habit and "a bait for the Devil's Layes." But when it came to business transactions, she was quick to accommodate and recalled all the details.

"During my abode in this place, Philip spoke to me to make a shirt for his boy, which I did, for which he gave me a shilling: I offered the mony to my master, but he had me keep it: and with it I bought a piece of Horse-flesh. Afterward he [Philip] asked me to make a cap for his boy, for which he invited me to dinner." Not only was Philip hospitable—indeed, Mary found little to criticize in his conduct—but his patronage seemed to increase her trade. "There was a squaw who spoke to me to make a shirt for her [husband], for which she gave a piece of bear. Another asked me to knit a pair of stockings, for which she gave me a pound of Pease. . . . Then came an Indian and asked me to knit him three pairs of stockings for which I had a hat and a silk handkerchief. Then another asked me to make her a shirt for which she gave me an apron." Successful at barter, and able to recall all her transactions, Mary appeared to establish a lively business. But she also had to deal with her mistress, Weetamoo, and this was another matter.

Weetamoo was a formidable mistress. "A severe and proud Dame she was," said Mary, "bestowing in every day dressing herself neat as much time as any of the Gentry of the land; powdering her hair, and painting her face, going with Neck-laces, with Jewels in her ears, and Bracelets upon her hands." Weeta-moo was indeed gentry. Squaw sachem of the Pocasset, a status the English labeled "queen," she held higher status among the Indians than any white woman did among New Englanders. She was also Philip's sister-in-law and a strategic wartime ally. Their involvement began long before, when Philip married Weetamoo's sister and she married his brother Wamsutta, called Alexander by the colonists. But Alexander died, suspiciously, during a conference with the English. Weetamoo then married an Indian called Peter Nanuet, whom she soon discarded. At the outbreak of war, Philip convinced her that Alexander's death had been caused by the English, and Weetamoo became a loyal supporter. Throughout the past summer, she and the Pocasset had helped Philip and his warriors escape from the colonists. During the conflict, finally, Weetamoo em-barked on a third marriage, this time to Quinnapin, with whose tribe she now lived. Her alliances, indeed, appeared to unite three Indian tribes, Philip's Wampanoags, Quinnapin's Narragansetts, and her own people, the Pocasset.

During the period of Mary's captivity, Weetamoo was a working queen. "Her work," said Mary, "was to make Girdles of Wampom and Beads." This elite occupation distinguished her from the other Indian women, who at each "remove" were occupied collecting food. Weetamoo was also used to exercising authority, an authority Mary was forced to tolerate. The status of servant to which Mary had been reduced was, to be sure, a familiar one. Colonial households often included indentured servants, usually young, whose obligations were clearly defined. As mistress of the Rowlandson home, one of the largest in Lancaster, Mary had probably had servants herself, to help with the work in house and barn. After captivity, once roles were reversed, she resigned herself to her new status and managed to get along with her master, Quinnapin, extremely well. But living with Weetamoo, in a small wigwam, made conflict inevitable. Weetamoo, according to Mary, was a mean and devilish mistress; her specialties were threats and confrontations. When Mary refused to work on the Sabbath, Weetamoo threatened to break her face, though she never did. When Weetamoo found Mary reading the Bible, she snatched it out of her hand and threw it outdoors, where Mary retrieved it. When Mary complained that her load was too heavy, Weetamoo "gave me a slap in the face and bade me go; I lifted up my head to God, hopeing the redemption was not far off." As antipathy increased between servant and mistress, Mary grew less compliant; most of her contacts with Weetamoo ended in slaps, "knocks," or at least close calls. On one occasion, Philip's maid came into Weetamoo's wigwam with a child and asked Mary to make some clothing for it, out of her apron.

I told her I would not: then my Mistriss bad me give it, but still I said no: the maid told me if I would not give her a piece, she would tear a piece off it: I told her I would tear her coat then, with that, my Mistress rises up, and takes a stick big enough to have killed me, and struck me with it, but I stept out, and [she] struck the stick into the Mat of the Wigwam. But while she was pulling it out, I ran to the maid and gave her all my Apron, and so that storm was over.

Domestic squabbles were not the only experiences Mary and Weetamoo shared. Both were mothers and both lost children. Several weeks after Sarah Rowlandson's death, Weetamoo's child died as well. By this time Mary's hatred was adamant. She showed no sympathy whatsoever, just as none had been shown to her when Sarah died. "My Mistrisses Papoos was sick," said Mary, "and it died that night, and there was one benefit in it, that there was more room." There was also more food, since Mary took advantage of the occasion to attend a funeral feast, where she was treated to a choice dish of venison. "On the morrow, they buried the Papoos, and afterward, there came a company to mourn and howle with her; though I confess, I could not much condole with them." The break in routine provided, instead, more time to think of her own desperate plight and its probable cause: "I saw how in my walk with God, I have been a careless creature."

Throughout Mary's trials with Weetamoo, the Indians were constantly on the move, dragging their captives with them and burning their wigwams behind them. Crossing forests and forging rivers, in rafts and canoes, they made their way northwest, staying a few days at one camp, a few weeks at the next. Mary marched all the way on foot, often carrying a heavy load for Quinnapin and Weetamoo, "for when they went but a little way, they would carry all of their trumpery with them." An English expeditionary force of Massachusetts and Connecticut troops under Major Thomas Savage was in close pursuit, but the Indians still stopped to attack and plunder English villages. "It was their usual manner," Mary observed, "to remove when they had done any mischief, lest they should be found out." Watching groups of warriors depart for their raids, she formed her assessment of Indian character. That her captors were hellish, she had no doubt; in fact, "when they left for an attack, they acted as if the Devil had told them that they should gain a victory." Indeed, they seemed to rejoice "in their inhumane and many times devilish cruelty to the English." She also found them "unstable" and perpetual liars, since various Indians informed her from time to time that her son had been killed and eaten, or that her husband was dead or remarried.

Considering the nature of the Indian character, as it appeared to her, Mary was amazed that God enabled her captors to survive at all. A case in point was the fifth "remove," when Mary's group of Indians had to cross Miller's River in Massachusetts, a three-day ordeal, with the English army close behind. Hundreds of Indians had assembled for the crossing, Mary observed, for the most part squaws, many with papooses on their backs, as well as the aged, the lame, and the sick, and all of them carried the entirety of their possessions. Rafts for the crossing, moreover, had to be made on the spot. Since the Indians were so slow in transit, it should have been easy for the English army to overtake and overpower them, in Mary's view. But somehow, unfathomably, the English never caught up. Instead, when they reached the river, they gave up the chase and turned around. Low on supplies, Savage's troops were reluctant to penetrate the wilderness, or possibly they were waiting for reinforcements. But Mary was outraged. It was hard to believe that the English army was so incompetent as to miss this opportunity. "God," she concluded, "did not give them courageous activity to go after us; we were not ready for so great a mercy as victory and deliverance; if we had been, God would have found a way for the English to have passed this river, as well as for the Indians, with their squaws and children, and all their luggage." Her disappointment lingered on, however, and the army's mistake continued to irritate her. "But what can I say? God seemed to leave his People to themselves, and order all things for his own holy ends."

God's insistence on preserving the heathen was only one of Mary's obsessions in captivity. Another was her own hunger. From the first "remove" onward, food became a preoccupation. Since her mistress had no concern if she starved or not, she was usually left to her own devices. The first week of captivity, she ate almost nothing. "The second week, I found my stomach grow very faint for want of something; and yet it was hard to get down their filthy trash." By the third week, Mary was eating any scraps she could obtain, "yet they were sweet and savoury to my taste." Sometimes she went from wigwam to wigwam, begging and scrounging, to pacify her "wolfish appetite," although Weetamoo threatened to knock her on the head. But other of the Indians were helpful and generous. Surviving on pieces of bear, handfuls of nuts, or donations of peas, Mary observed, "So little do we prise common mercies when we have them in the full."

What amazed her most, however, was the Indian diet. Her captors ate things "that a Hog or a Dog would hardly touch; yet by that God strengthened them up to be a scourge to his People." Mary never saw an Indian die of hunger, even when their crops were destroyed and they were forced into flight, foraging in the woods in the middle of winter, "still did the Lord preserve them for his holy ends." They would consume acorns, weeds, and roots. They would pick up old bones, even if they were filled with maggots, "and cut them to pieces at the joynts . . . and then boile them. . . . They would eat Horses guts, and ears, and all sorts of wild Birds . . . also Bear, Venison, Beaver, Tortois, Frogs, Squirrels, Dogs, Skunks, Rattle-snakes; yea, the very Bark of Trees; besides all sorts of creatures, and provisions which they plundered from the English." Such a diet was food for thought. Clearly, God intended to punish the English by preserving their enemies and must have had cause. "Our perverse and evil carriages in the sight of the Lord have so offended him," Mary concluded, "that instead of turning his hand against them [the Indians] the Lord feeds and nourishes them up to be a scourge to the whole land."

But like the Indians, Mary Rowlandson was a survivor. While knitting, trading, traveling, begging, praying, interpreting signs, and outwitting Weetamoo, she was also able to bargain for her own release. Quinnapin, she gathered, would not be averse to letting her go since he stood to profit from whatever ransom the English would pay. As soon as she could, Mary begged him to send her back to her husband. Early in April, after crossing another freezing river, Mary learned that a letter had come from the English about redeeming the captives. Philip took her by the hand and said, "Two weeks more and you shall be Mistriss again." Correspondence between the English and the sachems continued for the rest of the month. A second letter, to arrange for a ransom, was brought by two Christian Indians whom Mary knew, Tom Dublet and Peter Conway. Now filled with hope, Mary still feared her captors were too irresponsible to complete the transaction. "There was little more trust to them than the master they served," in her opinion. But soon the sachems met to discuss her ransom, and Mary was asked how much her husband would be willing to pay for her redemption. The answer was crucial, and she had to do some swift calculation. "Now knowing that all we had was destroyed by the Indians, I was in a great strait; I thought if I should speak of but a little, it would be slighted, and hinder the matter; if a great sum, I knew not where it would be procured; yet, at a venture, I said twenty pounds."

She had hit upon a fair price. The twentieth "remove," which brought her back to the southern end of Lake Wachusett, not far from Lancaster, was to be her last. Here Mary was able to see her sister Hannah, although Hannah's owner, Sagamore Sam (a Nipmuck leader whose real name was Shoshanin) dragged her away. He was later hanged at Boston, Mary noted, with some satisfaction, since "The Lord requited many of their ill-doings." At last, on April 30—a Sunday, providentially—an English emissary arrived to complete the bargaining for Mary's redemption. This brave diplomat, John Hoar of Concord, had considerable experience with Indians, since he ran a workhouse-jail for them at home. Although Hoar had brought twenty pounds in goods, Philip demanded something more for himself—coats, shillings, seed corn, and tobacco. "I thanked him for his love," said Mary, now skillful at diplomacy herself, "but I knew the good news as well as the Crafty Fox."

The next few days produced a "remarkable change of Providence." While Hoar left to get the rest of the ransom, the Indians engaged in a spree of revelry, which featured an amazing dance. Four men and four women performed, among them Quinnapin and Weetamoo, accompanied by some singing and "knocking on a kettle." Mary, who described the scene with glee, gave special attention to the garish combination of English and Indian garb her master and mistress had concocted.

He was dressed in his Holland Shirt, with great Laces sewed at the tail of it, he had his silver Buttons, his white Stockins, his Garters were hung round with Shillings, and had Girdles of Wompom upon his head and Shoulders. She had a jersey Coat, and covered with Girdles of Wampom from the Loins upward: her armes from her elbows to her hands were covered with Bracelets; there were handfulls of Necklaces about her neck, and severall sorts of Jewels in her ears. She had fine red stockins, and white Shoos, her hair powdered and face painted red, that was always before Black.

To complete the evening, Quinnapin got roaring drunk, although this was the first time Mary had seen an Indian in such a state. He then went chasing off after his wives.

But the most remarkable scene of all occurred the next Tuesday, May 2, when John Hoar returned with more goods. The Indians convened to decide on Mary's release, although Philip, peculiarly, declined to attend. Since a unanimous decision would have been irrevocable, according to Indian custom, Philip may have tried to avoid one. Fortunately for Mary, the other Indians had no objections to letting her go. Instead they surrounded her with farewells, gifts, and requests, "and seemed much to rejoyce in it," Mary observed. "Some askt me to send them Bread; others some Tobacco, others shaking me by the hand, offering me a Hood and Scarfe to ride in; not one moving hand or tongue against it. Thus the Lord answered my poor desire."

When Mary rode away from the Indian camp that night with John Hoar, Tom Dublet, and Peter Conway, she had been a captive for eighty-three days. During that time, she had traveled about a hundred and fifty miles, mainly on foot, in hunger and servitude. Retaining her faith, even after her daughter's death, she had bartered and connived her way to survival, and finally bargained for her own release. "O the wonderful power of God that I have seen, and the experience that I have had," Mary exulted. "I have been in the midst of those roaring Lyons and Salvage bears, that Feared neither God, nor Man, nor the Devil, by night and day, alone and in company: sleeping all sorts together, and yet not one of them offered the least unchastity to me, in word or in action." Mary was not the only New Englander to comment on the Indians' lack of profanity or to marvel at their abstention from sexual assault on their captives. "Though some are ready to say, I speak it for my own credit," she added. "But I speak it in the presence of God and to his glory."

Freedom was disorienting and seemed to take on the quality of a dream, in which long-lost friends and distant scenes from Mary's earlier life suddenly reappeared. Her rescue party first stopped at Lancaster, now burned to the ground, "not one Christian to be seen, or one house left standing." The pilgrimage continued through Marlborough and Concord, where Mary was reunited with one of her brothers, Joseph White. She also met her brother-in-law Henry Kerley, "who asked me, if I knew where his wife was? Poor heart, he had helped to bury her and knew it not." The next day, election day, a Puritan holiday, the group reached Boston, where Joseph Rowlandson was waiting. The rest of Boston was waiting as well, for Mary's captivity had attracted much attention and her return was considered a diplomatic coup. While the governor and Council negotiated for her release, she learned, prominent Boston men, joined by Mrs. Usher, wife of a merchant and selectman, had raised funds for her ransom. And since the Rowlandsons were now refugees, without home, town, or funds, everyone was anxious to help them out. "I was before so much hem'd in with merciless and cruel Heathen," said Mary, "but now as much with pitiful, tender-hearted, and [com]passionate Christians."

Within a few weeks, the Rowlandsons had even more cause to rejoice. They were soon surrounded by redemptions on all sides, as word came in that generous New Englanders had contributed to the ransom of their relatives. A week after Mary was released, the Puritan authorities approached the Indians again and arranged for the return of her sister, Hannah Divoll. Then the Rowlandsons learned that their son Joseph had been ransomed in Dover, New Hampshire, for seven pounds and that their daughter, Mary, had had an even more providential escape. Mary had simply wandered away from her captors, somewhere in Rhode Island, and the governor of that colony reported that she was under his care. Young Mary's return was a singular item on her mother's mental charge account. "The Lord hath brought her in free-cost," said Mary Rowlandson, "and given her to me a second time."

But the deluge of signs connected with Mary's return was not yet over. By the fall of 1676, after her family was reunited, the uprising was quelled and the Indians defeated. And in the process, all of the enemies who had been involved in Mary's captivity came to violent ends. Quinnapin, like Sagamore Sam, was taken prisoner. He was executed in Newport, along with three other captives. Philip was betrayed by a deserter, and the English attacked his Wampanoag camp. When Philip tried to escape into the woods, he was shot and then beheaded and quartered. His captors took his head, as a trophy, back to Rhode Island. Philip's young son, for whom Mary had sewn various items, had been captured not long before. Because he was only a child, he was spared execution and sold into slavery in another colony. But Weetamoo met the most grisly end of all. When Increase Mather, the minister at Boston, collated his account of King Philip's War, he described Weetamoo's fate with relish.

In Mather's view, Weetamoo, squaw sachem of the Pocasset, was the most dangerous enemy, next to Philip himself, "in respect to the mischief that has been done." During the war, she had thwarted the English and aided Philip by supplying transportation, refuge, and manpower. Her death, therefore, was a major event. In August, twenty men from Taunton, in Plymouth, were out on a mission, collecting prisoners, when they came upon the body of a squaw. Unaware of its identity, they cut off the head and set it on a pole. Their Indian captives at once broke out into a wail, "a most horrible and diabolical Lamentation, crying out that it was their Queen's head." As Increase reconstructed events, Weetamoo, thus far successful in evading capture, had been trying to cross the Taunton River, to escape the English. Only a year before, she had supplied Philip with canoes at that very spot. But now, unable to find a canoe, she had set out on a raft, which collapsed; just before her beheaders arrived, she had drowned. "Now it is to be observed," said Increase, "that God himself by his own hand had brought this enemy to destruction." While young Mary Rowlandson had been given to her mother twice, Weetamoo had been twice executed, first by God, when she drowned in the Taunton, and then by the English.

Like other Puritan historians of King Philip's War, Increase Mather felt obligated to extract significance from every detail, such as Weetamoo's inability to find a canoe. To Puritans, the study of history, especially their own, was a study of God and his mysterious ways. It revealed his hand at work. And in such a calamity as the Indian uprising of 1676, all that occurred begged for analysis, especially since the cost of the war had been enormous. Two-thirds of New England's towns had been attacked, many of them, like Lancaster, burned and shattered. Crops were ruined, trade impaired, and one white man out of ten in Massachusetts had been lost in the fighting. In addition, many of the captives— among them miserable Ann Joslin and most of the Divoll and Kerley children— never returned. But according to the Puritan interpretation, the war had been a test of faith and finally, in victory, a sign of God's favor. Once the Indian menace was gone, the path was clear for unlimited expansion, which could be seen only as divine intent. Clearly, God had been on the Puritan side. No sign or token that supported this claim could be ignored, whether Weetamoo's death or Mary Rowlandson's providential return.

The story of Mary's captivity, in fact, provided many insights into God's motives. In all the chronicles of King Philip's War, which began to appear before the year was out, Mary Rowlandson's experience was invariably treated as a significant, indeed symbolic, event. In some accounts, such as that of Nathaniel Saltonstall, Mary was given a good deal of credit for admirable conduct under stress. "For being a very pious woman and of great Faith, the Lord wonderfully supported her under these afflictions," wrote the young Boston merchant, who rushed his story of the war to London for immediate publication, "so that she appeared and behaved herself amongst them [the Indians] with so much Courage and Majestic Gravity that none durst offer violence to her but (in their rude manner) seemed to show her some respect." Puritan ministers, however, gave less credit to Mary than to Providence. Telling the tale of the raid on Lancaster, the villainy of the Narragansetts, the grief of Joseph Rowlandson, and Mary's survival, the divines found the hand of God at work. To William Hubbard, the minister at Ipswich, who wrote a long and detailed history of the war, Mary's return was a "Smile of Providence" and an answer to prayer. Her redemption, he stressed, was accomplished by the "over-ruling hand of God," rather than by "any other Contrivence of Man's Policy." Increase Mather was even more astute at interpreting signs. He found it significant that Mary finally arrived in Boston, after her captivity, on a major Puritan holiday, election day. This, he said, was a "Token for Good," a sign of God's favor toward the community. Mather also revealed an important factor in Mary's favor: Mary Rowlandson was a minister's wife. "For by reason of her near relation to a *Man of God*," Mather pointed out, "much prayer had been particularly made on her behalf."

But Hubbard and Mather were not the only analysts of God's intent. The most riveting account of King Philip's War was soon produced by Mary Rowlandson herself. Mary wrote the narrative of her captivity sometime between her return and 1682, when it was published, anonymously, in Cambridge, Massachusetts. In the first edition, her editor apologized for a woman's entry into "publick view" but explained that in this special case it was fully justified. The author's exemplary piety and the special providence God had shown her surely warranted attention. Moreover, he claimed, the captivity narrative had almost a biblical quality, an Old Testament flavor, that had to be preserved for future generations. What Mary Rowlandson had produced, in fact, was a superlative piece of propaganda, substantiating the Puritan thesis: God *had* been on the Puritan side. In addition, unlike Hubbard and Mather, Mary had been on the front lines. Her story, based on firsthand experience, was packed with vivid images, terrifying scenes, and powerful emotions. Enormously popular, in England and America, Mary Rowlandson's narrative was printed again and again. By 1800, it had gone through over fifteen editions.

The Rowlandsons never returned to Lancaster. Although some of the families that survived the raid eventually went back, at least after a few years, most of the original residents dispersed to other New England towns. The Rowlandsons stayed on in Boston for a year, supported by the South Church, until Joseph took a new post in Wethersfield, Connecticut, a town near Hartford, where the family remained. Although Mary was now "Mistriss" again, as Philip had promised, her captivity could not be forgotten. During the months after her release, her thoughts kept returning to her weeks in the wilderness, to Sarah's death, Weetamoo's ferocity, the constant "removes," and the sense of being surrounded by enemies. "I can remember the time, when I used to sleep quietly without workings in my thoughts, whole nights together, but now it is other ways with me," Mary wrote. "When all are fast about me, and no eyes open, but his who ever waketh, my thoughts are upon things past, upon the awful dispensation of the Lord towards us."

While everyone was asleep, Mary Rowlandson pondered the strange ways of God: the way He enabled the heathen to survive on skunks and roots to persecute His people; the way He had stopped the English army at Miller's River, and turned it around; the way He had chosen a pious woman, a devout believer, to undergo this extraordinary ordeal, only to show His power and might, "in

THE

N A R R A T I V E

OF THE

CAPTIVITY AND RESTORATION

O F

Mrs. *Mary Rowlandſon*,

Who was taken Priſoner by the INDIANS with ſeveral others, and treated in the moſt barbarous and cruel Manner by thoſe vile Savages : With many other remarkable Events during her TRAVELS.

Written by her own Hand, for her private Uſe, and now made public at the earneſt Deſire of ſome Friends, and for the Benefit of the afflicted.

The title page of a 1773 edition of Mary Rowlandson's narrative. The Narragansetts in the woodcut are armed with hatchets and guns. Mary Rowlandson, who had no weapon, was likely to have been holding on to six-year-old Sarah. *(From Frederick L. Weis, ed.,* The Narrative of the Captivity and Restoration of Mrs. Mary Rowlandson, *Boston, 1930)*

returning us to safety and suffering none to hurt us." Distilling her experience, Mary was able to shape it into an affirmation of faith: "Before I knew what affliction meant, I was sometimes ready to wish for it," she admitted. "But now I see the Lord has his time to scourge and chasten me."

Affliction I wanted, and affliction I had, in full measure (I thought) pressed down and running over; yet I see, when God calls a Person to any thing, and through never so many difficulties, yet he is fully able to carry them through and make them see, and say they have been gainers thereby. . . . The Lord hath shewn me the vanity of these outward things . . . that they are but a shadow, a blast, a bubble, and things of no continuance. That we must rely upon God himself, and our whole dependence must be upon him.

2

⧸⧸⧸⧸

THE SEVENTEENTH CENTURY: A FRONTIER SOCIETY

The ships that brought the earliest settlers to Jamestown and Plymouth also carried a heavy load of social ideology. Along with their chests and trunks, cows and Bibles, English colonists imported firm ideas on how society should be ordered and authority distributed, in family, community, church, and state. Whatever their rank or sect, they knew that society was a living organism, its health dependent on that of its parts. They also knew that basic patterns of power, submission, and mutual obligation determined the nature of all relations, whether of child and parent, wife and husband, servant and master, subject and ruler, "inferiors" and "betters," or man and God. These patterns permeated their compacts, charters, contracts, sermons, and statutes, as well as accounts of personal experience, such as Mary Rowlandson's captivity narrative. Quickly incorporated in colonial institutions, they were used to impose a modicum of order on a shapeless terrain, and to establish an English mode of life.

The position of women was a vital thread in the ideological cloth, so fundamental it was hardly conspicuous, so axiomatic it needed no defense. The Englishwoman had a subordinate place in the social scheme that could be defined only by deficiencies and limitations; she had no innate assets to distinguish her from a man. On the contrary, God and nature had made her weaker, in wit, will, and physical capacity. First in transgression and tainted by original sin, "the woman is a weak creature not endued with like strength and constancy of mind," as English parsons told their congregations. Inferior of brain and morally suspect, she depended on man to protect her interests, ensure her submission, and see that she did as little damage as possible. In England, as in every civilized state on the face of the earth, her passivity and powerlessness, divinely ordained, were bolstered by law, upheld by the church, and sanctioned by custom.

On a personal level, the Englishwoman was, ideally, meek and obedient. Tradition provided her with secondary status in the family, where she served her husband, cared for her children, and worked in the household. "We cannot but think that the woman was made before the Fall that man might rule over her," advised a manual of *Domesticall Duties* in the 1620s. In church as at home, her role was limited. According to a conservative reading of Paul, she was "not to teach, nor to hold authority over the man, but to be in silence." Her place in public life was similarly circumscribed. Common law, evaded only by those with class and clout, ensured the submergence of the married woman's identity under that of her husband. As a "feme covert," she was unable to own property, bring suit, make contracts, or act as a legal individual. Silent in church, subservient at home, and dependent on men, the seventeenth-century Englishwoman occupied a recessive space, an inconspicuous niche. She was part of the background scenery for a busy stage on which men made laws, wars, empires, and history.

If subordinate status was the common denominator of English woman-hood, class provided many variations. Upper-class women in England (aristo-crats, gentry, or members of the mercantile elite) exerted authority over their inferiors and sometimes wielded power, especially when male relatives were absent or dead. Under such circumstances, they might inherit estates, run mano-rial courts, manage lands, and handle business affairs. Few were leisured or very accomplished, but wealth and rank provided leverage. Propertied families could, for instance, arrange marriage contracts that preserved a daughter's property for her heirs or gave her control over it. The wives of "middling" people—small merchants, artisans, shopkeepers, and richer yeomen—had fewer options and more work. Their lives were devoted to housewifery, an all-encompassing realm of production soon familiar to colonial wives. If married to craftsmen or shop-keepers, they also helped out in shops and workshops or, if on the land, managed some aspects of family enterprise, such as poultry or dairy. Poor women in England might be part of the "excess" population, displaced by enclosure, or else tied down to tenancy. They worked in the fields or hired out their services as unskilled agricultural laborers or domestic servants, earning half as much as men. Some went into prostitution, begging, thieving, or the poorhouse, from which, if young, they might be released to enter servitude in some new and unpopulated colony.

While the contours of the English class structure were lost in transit across the Atlantic and gradually replaced by new ones, the ideology of female subor-dination, far more basic to the social order, was transported intact and easily replanted in colonial soil. The purpose of settlement was not to tamper with traditional roles and institutions but to re-create them as soon as possible. As a result, like their sisters in England, women in the seventeenth-century English colonies were excluded from positions of power and authority, such as govern-ment or ministry. Their lives centered around the household, and they rarely entered the foreground of events—nor had they any intention of doing so. The visible women of the seventeenth-century colonies were usually those brought briefly into center stage by catastrophe or deviance—such as Indian captivity or witchcraft charges.

But while the ideology of subordination remained intact, women's roles were constantly affected by the hazards and needs of their new environment.

Not every housewife saw her home burned down by embattled Narragansetts, such as those who attacked at Lancaster or Medford, but all were living in a young society that bordered on the wilderness, an elongated frontier. Throughout the century, the English colonies had wealth of land, need for labor, paucity of women, and great dependence on the family as an agent of settlement. These frontier qualities affected the seventeenth-century woman's options without revamping her basic status: as "weaker vessel," subordinate of man, and marginal member of society.

A Necessary Good

Anne Bradstreet, daughter of a prominent Puritan family, was the eighteen-year-old bride of a young colonist, an assistant of the Massachusetts Bay Company, when she arrived in Boston harbor in 1630. Finding "a new world and new manners," she was initially overcome with dismay. "But after I was convinced that it was the will of God, I submitted to it." Whether women emigrated as family members—as did Anne Bradstreet and Mary Rowlandson—or were shipped off as indentured servants, they were rarely in control of their own destiny. They were also in a minority. The vast majority of new arrivals were men.

The *Mayflower* arrived at Plymouth in 1620 with 102 passengers, 28 of them women. At Jamestown there were at first no women at all. In 1625, three-quarters of the white people of Virginia were men, and by midcentury there were six men to every woman. Maryland, by the 1650s, had about 600 men and fewer than 200 women. There, too, the proportion of men continued to increase. Throughout the colonies, of course, the balance—or imbalance—of the sexes was always in flux. More settlers were constantly arriving, most of them men. New generations were born, which began to decrease the sexual disparities. Finally, colonists began to move off to the edge of settlement, which tended to drain some of the oversupply of men on the eastern seaboard. By 1700 or even earlier, in some parts of Massachusetts, the sex ratio started to approach equality. But as a rule during the first century of settlement, the balance of the sexes was always skewed and men outnumbered women—as they did not in England, where there were about ninety-one men to every one hundred women throughout the era of colonization.

Sexual disparity was greatest in the early Chesapeake, where it affected the process of settlement. Of the 75,000 white people who emigrated to Virginia and Maryland between 1630 and 1680, up to three-quarters were indentured servants who arrived as single individuals. Four out of five were men. Since women were in such a minority, few male servants found wives, and those who did married relatively late, after their terms of indenture had expired. These marriages were brief; a harsh climate and rampant disease shortened life expectancy. Four out of ten immigrants died within six years, often of malaria, typhoid, or dysentery. Chesapeake men might live to forty-eight and women to forty-four, about a decade less than in England. Under such circumstances, family life took on a tentative quality. Late in the seventeenth century, half of the spouses in one

Maryland County became widows or widowers within seven years. Of the four children who might be born to such couples, two died in childhood. Survivors, if orphaned, were left in the care of neighbors or relatives or put out to service by special orphans courts.

From the outset, Chesapeake denizens recognized the dire implications of female scarcity. As soon as men arrive in Virginia, one colonist reported, "they grow very sensible of the Misfortune of Wanting Wives." Early Virginians attempted one remedy: importing shiploads of women. Between 1620 and 1622 about 150 "pure and spotless" women disembarked and were auctioned off for eighty pounds of tobacco apiece or more to future husbands. Recent research reveals the social origins of some of these prospective brides. Of the fifty-seven women who arrived in 1621, median age twenty, most were daughters of artisans, tradesmen, and gentry, mainly from the London area; they came with recommendations from their kinfolk and acquaintances attesting to their good character and domestic skills.

In some rare instances, unmarried women gained title to tracts of land. In Maryland in the 1630s, two English gentlewomen, Mary and Margaret Brent, each held large feudal estates. Subsequently, the southern colonies made efforts to attract men *with* wives. By basing the size of land grants given to household heads on the number of household members, the Virginia and Maryland legislatures attempted to spur the migration of families. Still, the preponderance of male newcomers continued and increased; tobacco planters had a greater need for men than women as indentured labor. Female scarcity and the frequency of early death prevented the early Chesapeake population from reproducing itself. To maintain a labor supply, the region became dependent on new infusions of immigrants, primarily indentured servants and, later on, slaves.

The minority of women who arrived in the Chesapeake, almost all as indentured servants, derived several benefits from the region's unbalanced sex ratios. Because they were so vastly outnumbered, they had virtual certainty of marriage and far greater choice of spouse than poor young women left behind in England did. A female servant might even escape her full term of service by marrying a man who offered to buy out her contract and promote her to wife. Devastating death rates also affected women's opportunities. Chesapeake husbands who wrote wills often made their widows executors of their estates, a more liberal arrangement than practiced elsewhere. In the latter part of the seventeenth century, many husbands left their wives most or all of their property for life, despite the likelihood that these widows would remarry. But such gains for women reflected the region's serious problems—female scarcity and high mortality. Only at the end of the century, when a native-born population arose with higher immunity to disease and equal proportions of boys and girls, did life spans lengthen and sex ratios start to become more balanced. The Chesapeake population soon began to grow primarily through natural increase.

New England settlement provided a startling contrast. Indeed, the Puritan colonists held demographic advantages over both their southern neighbors and kinfolk left in England. Unlike new arrivals in the Chesapeake, who were mainly single individuals, most immigrants to New England arrived in family units. A salubrious climate extended life expectancy to sixty-five for men and slightly less for women. Marriages might last a quarter century or more, and large families abounded. Although the seventeenth-century New England wife did not have the ten or twelve children once thought to be the typical colonial brood, she might have six or seven—somewhat more than the average of the Whites, Rowland-sons, Divolls, and Kerleys, and more than the four or five children in the average English family. About 80 percent of infants survived to maturity. Reproducing themselves at a prodigious rate, New Englanders created their own labor force, and never depended on servants or slaves. Unlike seventeenth-century south-erners, they achieved a fairly balanced sex ratio quite quickly, which facilitated their population boom.

Dependent on the family as an agent of settlement, Puritan authorities took steps to see that all women married. In Salem, Massachusetts, where Mary Rowlandson's parents had settled, unmarried women were at first given their own land parcels. But this procedure was soon discontinued. No woman was expected to remain unmarried for long, nor did Puritan authorities wish to encourage the single state. "It would be a bad president [sic]," the Massachusetts governor told one applicant, Deborah Holmes, "to keep hous alone." The colo-nies needed productive families, not propertied spinsters. Women, moreover, were clearly "without which there is no comfortable living for men," as Puritan minister John Cotton proclaimed. "It is true of them what is wont to be said of governments, *That bad ones are better than none.*" According to Cotton, woman was not a necessary evil but "a necessary Good, such as it was not good that man should be without."

It is tempting to debate the relative advantages of Chesapeake women, who seemed to profit from their low numbers, and New England women, with their longer life expectancy and greater chance of stable family life. But as historian Mary Beth Norton points out, the contrast between these two extremes of seventeenth-century settlement obscure the commonality of female experience throughout the colonies. North or South, immigrant or native-born, virtually all white women in the English colonies married. Consequently much of a woman's life would be spent as the mistress of a family unit on a family farm.

In the colonies, as in England, lines of authority and submission within the family were clearly drawn—most clearly by Puritans, who constantly examined social theories. But the basic prerequisite for a happy home, wifely obedience, applied everywhere. "A true wife accounts her subjection [as] her honor and freedom," John Winthrop, Massachusetts Bay's governor, explained in 1645, "and would not think her condition safe and free, but in subjection to her husband's authority." At the end of the century, the same ideal prevailed, although expressed perhaps more plaintively. "Wives are part of the house and family," announced Benjamin Wadsworth, a New England minister, in 1712, "and ought to be under the husband's government." The head of the family, in a Puritan colony or any other, was expected to control its members. He wielded authority over wife and children, supervised finances, made family decisions, served as intermediary between family and community, and in more pious circles, provided the conduit through which God's blessings flowed.

The preoccupation of seventeenth-century authorities with the "Well Ordered Family"—the title of Wadsworth's sermon—appealed to colonists for several reasons. In seventeenth-century England, patriarchy was not only a domestic habit but a political and religious one; the family was a model for church and state. Every institution had its own hierarchy, with authority residing in the "head." The English Reformation, especially the rise of Puritanism, had increased the importance of the patriarchal family. Colonization did so even more. In the colonies, where the family served as an agent of settlement and a source of population, where the economy depended on the family farm, and where other institutions were new and precarious, domestic order was especially crucial. The colonial family was the very foundation of social cohesion and far too valuable to be ripped apart by internal discord.

Accordingly, colonial authorities frequently reiterated the principle of male authority and wifely submission. But for the same reason, colonial wives were protected within marriage to a greater degree than their English counterparts were, and beyond the dictates of common law. Since domestic unity was viewed as a public good, all colonies devised measures that encroached on the domain of the home. Such laws were intended to keep families intact, to protect family members from one another, and to prevent dependents from being thrown on public welfare as community charges. This was not a coherent, systematic policy, intended to enhance the status of women, but rather an amalgam of statutes and practices intended to maintain social order. Still, wives were sometimes beneficiaries.

Throughout the colonies, marriage was recognized as a civil contract based on the mutual consent of both parties. Husbands were compelled to support, and cohabit with, their wives; deserters could be hounded or errant husbands hauled into court for adultery or failing to provide. And in New England, where authorities kept an especially "watchfulle eye" over the home, "disorderly carriage" within it was likely to evoke reprimands. Statutes outlawed or limited physical abuse of wives. The Massachusetts Body of Liberties in 1641 prohibited wife-beating, "unless it be in his own defense upon her assault." A New England husband might be fined for "abusing his wife by kiking her of from a stoole into the fier," as was a man in Plymouth. Law enforcement of course did not end desertion, which was common, or eliminate domestic disorder. The violence that pervaded seventeenth-century life tended to flare up within the home as well as outside it. In the southern colonies, moreover, husbands were prevented by law only from inflicting permanent injury or death on wives—one of many factors that distinguished the lot of a southern woman colonist from that of a New England woman. Still, the colonial wife gained, in principle, some legal protection that her English counterpart lacked.

Colonial wives might also benefit from antenuptial and postnuptial contracts, which mitigated common law and were used in England only by the rich. The antenuptial contract enabled a woman to retain control over her own property; for example, that signed by a Plymouth woman in 1667 entitled her "to enjoy all her house and lands, goods and cattle, that she is now possessed of, to dispose of them at her own free will." Typically, widows who remarried signed antenuptial contracts. After Joseph Rowlandson's death, when Mary Rowland-son wed her second husband, one Captain Samuel Talcott, in 1679, she signed such a contract. The postnuptial contract reconciled a couple who had disputes or enabled them to separate but compelled the husband to support his family. Acceptance of such contracts, or equity practices, helped to preserve domestic peace and public order. They also served to keep wives and children off the public dole.

And in New England, some wives had a last resort. The Puritans, in their zeal to promote domestic unity, granted absolute divorce, with the right to wed again (divorce *a vinculo matrimonii*). The rationale was that once an unstable marriage was dissolved, the aggrieved spouse, usually a woman, would be free to remarry and establish a stable, harmonious family. This policy was a major innovation. In England, where marriage was a sacrament and indissoluble, only the wealthy, mainly men, were able to terminate their unions, through special acts of Parliament or ecclesiastical annulments. Elsewhere in the colonies, legal separations with property settlements (divorce *a mensa et thoro*) might be ar-ranged, but absolute divorce was rare, and in the southern colonies, nonexistent. In New England, however, divorce with remarriage was possible. Divorces were granted most frequently for such causes as desertion, bigamy, failure to provide, and adultery. They were granted more often to women than to men. Neverthe-less, far more women petitioned for divorces than received them. And overall, such divorces were few in number. Massachusetts granted some twenty-seven divorces between 1639 and 1692. Connecticut granted nine between 1665 and 1678, all for desertion. Women were petitioners in eight of the nine cases.

Women, however, were not the only beneficiaries of the colonies' concern with maintaining harmonious homes. Seventeenth-century laws and decisions also protected husbands from wives who ran up debts, waged attacks, or engaged in adultery, a crime against both husband and community. The most common offense committed by wives was verbal abuse. If seventeenth-century women were silent in church, they were verbally assertive outside it—at least according to court records. Apparently keen on local gossip, they were also considered liable to scold their husbands, slander their neighbors, and curse their enemies, thereby threatening the stability of home and community. Reports of women's verbal aggression were not peculiar to colonial America; such aggres-sion was noted frequently in English villages too. The hostile harangue may have been the Englishwoman's response to a world controlled by men, in which women had no formal power. In her study of Maryland slander cases, historian Mary Beth Norton points out that gossip, which could lead to defamation, was for the seventeenth-century woman a means of affecting the social order and "perhaps the most valuable and reliable means of advocating or protecting her own interests." But colonial courts made special efforts to check verbal aggres-sion.

New England women might be sanctioned for persisting in "scurrilous language and bad speeches," as was Bridget Oliver, hauled into the Essex County Court in 1678 for calling her husband "opproprious" names on a Sunday. In New Netherland, where Dutch law permitted married women a wide array of independent action, wives were sued for defamation and on a few occasions sued others for the same. A Virginia statute of 1662 provided ducking as a penalty for "brabling women [who] often slander and scandalize their neighbors," in order to relieve their spouses of "vexatious suits." Public order and domestic peace, it was decreed, were too valuable to be ruined by a loud-mouthed wife. The ideal of marriage, as expressed in a Virginia postnuptial contract reconciling an especially disputatious couple, was "to live lovingly together and behave themselves to each other as a good wife and husband ought to do." In this case, the wife had to promise to stop running off with the husband's money and to forswear "vile names."

Whatever legal improvements the seventeenth-century colonial wife might enjoy, moreover, did not revise the structure of the family or provide her with a power base within it. Since the "well-ordered" home was a patriarchy, the wife's role was always subordinate. Her obligation, as Benjamin Wadsworth explained, was to devote herself to husband and household, "to keep at home, educating her children, keeping and improving what is got by the industry of man." Although expected to be obedient, the wife was not a servant or child but more of a junior partner, with partial control over children and servants. But her clout as a parent was limited. Children were legally a father's possession. More to the point, he was likely to work in or around the home and was therefore an active participant in child rearing. Parenthood was a joint occupation, in which mothers had more responsibility but fathers had more authority. It was also an increasingly important one.

In these new colonies, with their scarcity of population and paucity of labor, child rearing took on new significance. Children formed a larger part of the population than in England, exceeding half the population in some colonies, and there were more of them per household. With the exception of the early Chesapeake, colonial reproduction was impressive. The colonial wife, who married several years younger than her English counterpart, at age twenty to twenty-three instead of twenty-five or twenty-six, spent up to two decades of her life bearing children and most if not all of her adult life raising them. In addition, she might have several pregnancies that ended in miscarriage or stillbirth. Despite the frequency of infant deaths (slightly over half of colonial infants could expect to reach adulthood), the mortality of children was lower than in England. A higher colonial survival rate may have fostered greater emotional investment in children on the part of parents. Still, since early death occurred so regularly, seventeenth-century family life had an aura of risk, loss, and impermanence.

The death of a child, such as that of the Rowlandsons' first daughter, was an expected event. So was the death of a spouse. In two-thirds of colonial marriages, one of the partners could be expected to die within ten years. The seventeenth-century mother who had her last child in her late thirties might well be dead or widowed before that child left home. Or she might die much earlier. One-fifth of adult deaths among women occurred in childbirth. When preparing the equipment for lying-in, as a 1663 pamphlet of advice for "teeming American women" counseled, "she might perchance need no other linen than a winding sheet." The drama of childbirth, the pivotal event of women's lives, was clearly a perilous one. It was, in addition, a public event, an all-female ritual, at which a group of women relatives and neighbors congregated, along with the ubiquitous midwife. On no other commonplace public occasion were women in control and men excluded or relegated to the sidelines.

Once the risks of childbirth were survived, seventeenth-century mother-hood was neither a power preserve nor an outlet for specific gender-linked abilities. Women were not believed to be endowed with any specific feminine attributes, such as a gift for passing on moral precepts to the young. Most seventeenth-century records of family life, such as the diary of Samuel Sewall, exemplary Puritan, give the impression that the father was the focal figure in child rearing. Sewall, for instance, was especially active in preparing his children for the possibility of early death or eternal damnation, a prospect that threw his daughter Betty into fits of weeping and months of melancholia. Still, wives had a special realm of control as parents, and this was the socialization of girls. Almost all education took place in the home, and the major thrust of this education was character formation and vocational training. Girls were supposed to absorb the personality traits valued in women, such as obedience, industry, piety, and the habit of silence—although the last may have been a fond hope. They were also supposed to learn the arts of housewifery, as were young servants and appren-tices who lived in the household for extended terms.

The relations of seventeenth-century mothers and daughters remain murky. Powerful images, such as those conveyed by Mary Rowlandson, of carrying dying Sarah through the wilderness, do not re-create the everyday interchange between mother and daughter within the early colonial home. But since daughterhood was primarily a long apprenticeship in housewifery, one can assume that daughters, like young apprentices, were at a disadvantage. After surviving early childhood, a period devoted to breaking the will and eradicating aggression, girls had to spend most of their time in the home, listening to, working for, and emulating, the parent or mistress, who herself fulfilled a subservient role even while in charge of children, apprentices, and servants. Although conflict between mothers and daughters rarely surfaced in colonial records, servitude was a status that was rarely trouble-free for either mistress or young servant. When Mary Dudley begged her stepmother, Margaret Winthrop, in 1636, to send her "a good lusty servant that hath skill in a dairy," the girl turned out to be "a great affliction," "insolent in carriage," and "insufferable," who abused her mistress with "reviling speeches and filthie language"—the standard weapon of female discontent.

The tiny size of the seventeenth-century house made such discord (whether between mistress and servant, parent and child, or husband and wife) especially intolerable. The Winthrop home in the 1630s, with its six rooms, lofts, and garrets, was relatively large, as was the Rowlandson "garrison" in Lancaster in the 1670s. But the ordinary dwelling in the new colonies was more likely to be one room—"the hall," which served for sleeping, eating, cooking, and working—or possibly two, plus whatever lean-tos and sleeping lofts were later added on. This limited space, inhabited by parents, children, and sometimes apprentices or servants, had little privacy in it; but the modern concept of privacy was alien to the seventeenth century. Private life, moreover, was difficult to distinguish from public life, especially since living and working were not separated. The seventeenth-century home was not removed from the family enterprise, usually a farm. Nor was it a haven from labor but rather its fulcrum. The household, for women, was an arena of production. The seventeenth-century wife was a "necessary good" not only as a wife and parent but also as a worker.

Housewifery and Trade

Household labor, like the ideology of subordination, was a common denominator in women's lives. The seventeenth-century housewife, in her confined living space, might be encumbered with equipment—cast-iron pots, enormous cauldrons, kettles, mortars, pestles, candle molds, salt barrels, and possibly a butter churn or spinning wheel. "Housewifery" meant the lifelong production of food, clothing, and household items; and the newer the region, the more rugged the job.

Commonly, the wife cooked and washed clothes over open fires. She planted vegetable gardens, milked cows, operated dairies, produced hard cider, pickled and preserved, and smoked and salted meat. When not feeding hens, pigs, children, and servants, or stitching shirts or knitting stockings (skills Mary Rowlandson put to good use), she made lye out of ashes, soap out of lye and animal fat, wax out of bayberries, tallow out of wax, candles out of tallow, and medicines out of weeds and herbs. Often she exchanged labor with neighbors, if she had any, to complete a job, such as berrying, or a product, such as a skein of thread. Spinning was the colonial housewife's prized vocation, as well as an important skill to be passed on to daughters and apprentices. Not every housewife possessed such a skill. In mid-eighteenth-century Massachusetts, for instance, only about half of households contained dairy equipment or spinning wheels. The 17th-century household was typically more primitive and the woman who ran it unlikely to have such special skills.

In addition to the basic tasks of housewifery, the colonial wife helped out in the family enterprise, whether shop, plantation, or frontier farm—a type of labor that merged into whatever she did at home. If married to a craftsman or shopkeeper, she assisted in shop or workshop. If married to a farmer, she might help in the fields, although outdoor work was increasingly relegated, if possible, to servants and slaves. Still, on the perimeter of settlement, as William Byrd discovered when exploring the North Carolina–Virginia frontier, a woman might "carry a gun in the woods, and kill deer, turkeys etc. and shoot down wild cattle, catch and tye hogs . . . and perform most exercises as well as men." Whatever the locale, her responsibilities were fairly well defined—especially in the case of the Maryland bride who was obliged by contract in 1681 to "Dresse the victuals, milk the Cowes, wash for the servants and Doe all the things necessary for a woman to doe upon the . . . plantation."

The necessity for work was easily absorbed into ideals of womanhood, which reflected the needs of family and community. If "obedience" was the prerequisite for a harmonious home, "industry" was vital to a productive one. For women as for men, idleness was frowned upon, hard work was a virtue, and physical labor was not regarded as a degradation, since so much of it was involved in housewifery alone. In New England, "idleness and sottish carriage" resulted in a summons to court and a fine or worse. Moreover, the work women did at home in the English colonies was familiar enough to wives of "middling" means in England. The economic value of housewifery, however, did not enlarge a wife's authority or enhance her status within the home. Wives had no control over the distribution of family resources and, in most cases, since common law applied, no control over their own possessions. Still, seventeenth-century roles had a certain fluidity. When a husband was absent, historian Laurel Thatcher Ulrich points out, the wife was expected to take over his position as household head and defender of family interests. Hiring hands, keeping accounts, or managing a farm, the spouse of an absentee husband assumed full authority as his surrogate.

"Industry," moreover, was a passport to active roles beyond the home, where women filled a wide variety of economic loopholes left by men. The colonies were so land-rich, labor-scarce, and sparsely inhabited that economic space was not yet firmly divided between the sexes, and woman's "place" was easily stretched to fill up whatever vacancies existed. This meant there was opportunity to earn income, by producing goods, providing services, or running a commercial venture. Again, this was not a coherent policy but a pragmatic, haphazard one, appropriate in a primitive economy with few skilled workers. Women in the colonies, as in England, were a marginal work force; their options contracted and expanded as the economy warranted. In seventeenth-century England, women's roles were contracting. There, too, women had commonly filled the interstices of economic space, as "spinsters" and "brewsters," healers and midwives, even carpenters and printers. But by the end of the century, the most profitable of these spaces had vanished and women were forced out of them by men's craft organizations and guilds. Specialization of labor eroded their economic options. In the relatively empty colonies, however, where men could easily acquire land, there was plenty of space in trades and services for women.

Like Mary Rowlandson throughout her "removes"—stitching and bargaining, trading items of clothing for pieces of bear or a knife, and finally arranging to trade herself—the colonial housewife had an eye for exchange. A skilled worker, she was also able to turn homemade goods into income. Housewives sold whatever surplus items they baked, brewed, preserved, spun, wove, or sewed, as well as such products as medicines or cosmetics. This type of trading was an easy extension of household industry, domestic enterprise enlarged. A housewife might also run a small shop out of her home, supplying her neighbors with hardware or needles or cloth or thread. In addition, married women frequently sold their services as nurses, midwives, and medical practitioners. These services, too, were extensions of their domestic roles and involved some facet of household skills. Finally, widows might replace their husbands—again an extension of their work in the family as helpers and assistants in family enterprise.

As a result, throughout the colonial era, widows could be found in a wide range of occupations and trades. Indeed, seventeenth-century propertied men often left their estates to the charge of their wives—a practice that declined in the eighteenth century. Widows, therefore, managed lands they had inherited, ran small businesses, and invested in large ones. Since they took over enterprises their husbands had started (sometimes temporarily until sons could replace them), widows commonly worked as shopkeepers, grocers, booksellers, tavernkeepers, or even, on occasion, as blacksmiths, butchers, gunsmiths. A dead husband could provide legitimate entrée to commerce, trades, and managerial roles.

The widow, in fact, as a single woman, or feme sole, had many rights under common law. Unlike the wife, or feme covert, whose legal identity was "covered" by that of her husband, the feme sole, whether spinster or widow, was a legal individual. She could own, buy, and sell property, sue and be sued, make contracts, administer estates, and hold power of attorney. The spinster, obviously, was quite a rarity in the seventeenth century, and the propertied spinster even more so. A leading example was Margaret Brent, a wealthy Catholic who arrived in Maryland in 1638 with her sister and two brothers. Since Maryland then offered 1,000-acre manors to anyone who transported and provided for able male workers, each of the Brents received huge land grants, run on the pattern of feudal estates.

As a proprietor, Margaret Brent reigned over a manorial court, speculated in land, sponsored the migration of other settlers, and served as agent and attorney for her brothers. She also spent much of her time in the Maryland courts, suing for debts that were owed her and acting on behalf of others as well. (There were only a few hundred people in Maryland at this time.) Before Governor Leonard Calvert died in 1647, he named Margaret Brent executrix of his will, and in this capacity she took over his affairs and settled his estate. To facilitate her task, she applied to the Maryland assembly for two votes, one as proprietor and the other as executrix. When her request was denied, she contested the legislature's authority by protesting "against all proceedings in this present assembly unless she may be present and have vote afores'd."

Brent's demand for votes was unique, just as her status as landed proprietor in a new colony was unusual. But other seventeenth-century women occasionally served in court, representing themselves, their absent husbands, and others. Although Maryland ended women's right to represent clients a decade after Margaret Brent's protest, other colonies permitted the practice. In New Amsterdam, for instance, where Dutch law allowed great latitude, the wife whose husband was away on a voyage could manage his land and serve as his attorney. She could also be licensed as a "feme sole trader," to keep his affairs alive in his absence or even, on occasion, during his presence. Not every colony distributed feme sole privileges with such largesse, but colonial assemblies were liberal in granting permission to unmarried or widowed women to run businesses. When the Massachusetts General Court, in 1692, provided that any single woman of good repute be permitted "exercise of any lawful trade or employment for a livelihood," with the permission of the selectmen, it confirmed a practice of long standing.

This latitude, of course, was in the community interest. A destitute spinster or widow, clearly, could be a drain on a locale's resources. After Mary Rowlandson's husband died in 1678, the Connecticut town in which the Rowlandsons then lived and where Joseph had served as minister, awarded her a pension for as long as she remained a widow. The grant was probably made in regard for her husband's position or perhaps in memory of her exceptional experience, and it continued only until 1679, when Mary remarried.

But towns and counties had no interest in supporting all women and children whose husbands or fathers had died or deserted. Enterprise on the part of the feme sole kept her off the public dole and enabled her to keep her family unit intact. It also provided the community with useful trades and services. The wealthy widow was especially welcome, since she would be able to invest her funds in local enterprises. In the seventeenth-century Chesapeake region, where women were so scarce, widows who outlived a succession of husbands, acquiring property with each marriage, created what has been called a "widowarchy."

The loss of a husband and the opportunity to enter the world of trade and commerce were hardly prospects women welcomed. Dinah Nuthead, one of the first women to run a print shop, inherited the business in 1695 at the death of her husband, who had been the public printer of Maryland. Nuthead had left her with the press, shop, and—although this was usually a profitable post—a great many debts. With the assembly's consent, Dinah Nuthead continued the business, which must have been a difficult task, since she was illiterate. She remarried as quickly as possible, a year later. Maria Van Rensselaer, who had been widowed in Holland in 1674, came to New York to administer the huge patronship of Rensselaerwyck, which covered 700,000 acres on both sides of the Hudson, because there was no available man in her family to take charge. Despite her grist mill, sawmill, and sales of wheat and furs to Dutch buyers, Maria had to struggle to keep the estate afloat. "Consider, dear brother," she wrote to her uncooperative brother-in-law in Holland, who was long on criticism but short on assistance, "whether to lose my health and in addition to lose my property and my dearest partner and to be left with six children and such an encumbered estate is not hard on me either." Still, she remained in control of the estate and dealt with its problems until her oldest son was able to take over.

The access of widows to trade and commerce might present problems for local authorities, especially in the case of taverns. New England towns were stringent about who received a liquor license and for what purpose, since taverns in busy seaport locales did not always cater to a genteel clientele. Usually permission to run a tavern or brew or sell liquor was encumbered with a proviso, such as that a man be hired to work on the premises, or that a woman "sell to none but housekeepers." Or a woman might be licensed to distill and retail liquor, "provided shee did not sell to any of the inhabitants of the town to drinke in her house." But some enterprising women—among them Alice Thomas, Boston tavernkeeper—evaded the rules. In the 1670s, Widow Thomas was accused of selling liquor without a license, receiving stolen goods, profaning the Sabbath, and sponsoring "frequent secret and unseasonable entertainment in her house to Lewd Lascivious and notorious persons of both sexes, giving them opportunity to commit Carnale Wickedness." Although Widow Thomas was fined, whipped, and imprisoned, she pacified the authorities by giving Boston a large contribution for the construction of a sea wall—and presumably returned to her tavern.

Not surprisingly, a high concentration of tradeswomen appeared in New Amsterdam, where liberal Dutch law permitted grants of feme sole trader privileges to married women. Here, Margaret Philipse, merchant and shipowner, pursued her vocation through several marriages. Born in Holland, she had arrived in New Netherlands in the 1650s as the sister of an indentured servant and soon married a wealthy trader. Before his death, she worked as an agent for Dutch merchants; and after she was widowed in 1661, she became a merchant and trader herself, shipping furs to Holland and selling the merchandise she received in New York. After marriage to another rich New Yorker in 1662 and the signing of an antenuptial agreement that left her part of her inheritance, Margaret Philipse continued her business as a feme sole trader. In this capacity, she established a shipping line between Amsterdam and New York and personally supervised her ship in transit—to the discomfort of those who worked on it, according to passengers who reported her "avarice" and "covetesnous."

The energy and enterprise of memorable femes soles, such as Margaret Brent and Margaret Philipse, however, are misleading clues to the status of women in the seventeenth-century colonies. Femes soles were able to engage in profitable activities because their services and self-support were good for the community, because there were few skilled workers and no organized guilds of craftsmen or professionals, and because economic space was expanding, not contracting. Most widows, however, did not run estates or shipping lines but survived on small dower rights or scratched out a living. Indeed, most colonists, male or female, merely scratched out a living; few had any wealth. The number of femes soles in commerce and trade, moreover, was far less than that of another type of single woman, the indentured servant, whose options and rights were minimal.

Servants and Slaves

The condition of servitude to which Mary Rowlandson was reduced during her captivity—living with Weetamoo, knitting her stockings, enduring "knocks," and hating her mistress with a passion—was familiar to anyone who had grown up in England or its colonies. During the seventeenth century, servitude was a common status. One-third of colonial households included indentured servants who worked for the family and were considered part of it. Unlike Mary Rowlandson at Lake Wachusett, servants were unable to estimate their value or return to freedom after eleven weeks. Still, colonial servitude was a temporary status, not a lifelong one. Indentured servants were a distinctive underclass of the young. They were all single, or allegedly so, and about a third were women, aged eighteen to twenty-five. Their labor was sold for four or five years or longer, in return for transportation to America and maintenance and support during their terms of indenture. Perhaps as many as half of women newcomers arrived in that status, the vast majority going at first to the southern colonies and later to the middle colonies.

Servitude was also a mode of upbringing and vocational training for native-born children, under the apprenticeship system. A colonial daughter could be apprenticed at eleven, twelve, or thirteen for a lengthy term—some indentures lasted up to ten years—during which time she provided her master and mistress with help and acquired useful skills. Orphans and the children of poor widows were similarly "bound out," sometimes at very young ages, to be reared and to work in other homes until age twenty-one. The families who took in such children were legally responsible for bringing them up and teaching them trades. Indeed, the length of service expected was repayment for the expense of child rearing. (Parents expected similar service from their own children.) While boy apprentices might learn cordwaining, tanning, or other trades, girls were trained in the domestic work. Like daughters, female apprentices were expected to acquire such useful skills as "spining, sewing, knitting, or any other manner of housewifery," and sometimes basic literacy ("to read the English tongue").

Indentured servitude, for the emigrant, lay somewhere between voluntary and forced labor. Even when a woman signed a contract of indenture voluntarily in England, promising "to oblige myself as a faithful and obedient servant . . . according to the Laws and Customes . . . in the said place," as did one young woman before embarking for Carolina in 1669, she ended up an ocean away, working under conditions more primitive and harsher than domestic servitude in England. Subject to physical abuse and a high mortality rate, she was also supposed to endure a long period of celibacy, since marriage was prohibited. Not all women servants volunteered for such an experience. Some were kidnapped, some were pardoned felons, and some were convicts, such as the "fifty lewd women out of the house of correction" who were shipped off to Virginia in 1692, along with "thirty others who walked the streets." The promotional literature that lured young women to the southern colonies (such as Maryland, where 85 percent of newcomers and almost all of the women among them were servants) promised that they would not have to do field work. But once installed on a remote farm in a far-off colony, servants had no control over the nature of their labor. Even domestic work in a newly settled region would have to be done under the most primitive conditions. In addition, the "Laws and Customes" regulating servitude were severe.

Servants who ran away or otherwise violated their terms of indenture were penalized by an extension of the term of service. The most common violation of which women were guilty was pregnancy. Servants were not free to marry until the indenture term ended since they literally did not own themselves. Although all servants were enjoined to avoid sexual relations, the brunt of the prohibition fell upon women; child bearing would deprive their masters of their services. In Maryland, one-fifth of women who were servants were hauled into court for "bastardy." In Pennsylvania, Carolina, and Virginia, pregnancy was penalized with an extension of the period of servitude. In Massachusetts, servants who had been "unfaithful, negligent, or unprofitable" were saddled with extended terms; and in cases of "bastardy," the alleged father (determined by questioning the woman servant in labor) was forced to support the illegitimate child. Such children might themselves be put into service for the entire period of their youth—as was young Hannah Woolery, a New Englander who was bound out at the age of two until she was twenty-one.

A recurrent problem, as a Virginia statute of 1692 suggests, was that "some dissolute masters have gotten their maids with child, and yet claim the benefit of their service." Although the guilt of the servant was not absolved in such cases, the law provided that the woman's extra term of service be sold to another master, with the profits of the sale going to the local parish. The term of extra service was too valuable to discard when it could be of use to the labor-scarce community. So was the labor of the Maryland servant whose master claimed that she had been absent for short periods over the years amounting, in sum, to 113 days. He was awarded 1,130 days of extra service. Conditions of servitude were increasingly regulated by legislation. Some of these laws limited servants, by prohibiting fornication and miscegenation, for instance. Other laws restrained masters and mistresses from excessive abuse. "Cruel Mistress prevent'd from having servants" a Virginia Court injected tersely in its records of 1680.

Once a term of indenture was up, a young woman servant was available for marriage and virtually assured of it in the southern colonies, where women were so greatly outnumbered. In fact, since she had no property or family, marriage was her only option. She was likely to become the wife of a farmer on a small, perhaps new, plantation, probably marrying at an older age than a free counterpart and therefore having fewer children—as was the case in seventeenth-century Maryland. But once the spouse of a landowner, she might herself become the mistress of servants. This leap in status would have been far less likely in England, where land was unavailable, men in a minority, and servitude usually a lifelong condition. The seventeenth-century colonial servant could at least look forward to upward mobility.

The same could not be said for the black woman servant or slave, since even in the early seventeenth century, before slavery became a legal institution, race was a more crucial determinant of status than gender. Hostile to blacks and short of capital, Virginians far preferred indentured servants to slaves; there were no more than 5,000 slaves in the North American colonies by 1675, compared to 100,000 in the British West Indies. Still, as early as the 1640s in Virginia, when many blacks were indentured servants, albeit serving longer terms than whites, court records began to mention sales for life and the inheritance by black children of the status of "perpetual servant." The value of black women as producers of more "servants for life" was suggested in the record of the sale of "one Negro girl named Jowan, aged about ten years" made to a Virginian in 1652, since he acquired "her issue and produce duringe her . . . Life tyme and their successors forever."

Even before slavery was established by law, black women servants were distinguished from white women servants in another way: They were used without qualm in field work. Once slave codes had been drawn up by all colonies in the 1660s, the distinction between black and white female labor was clear-cut. "A white woman is rarely or never put to work in the ground if she is good for anything else," Robert Beverly reported from Virginia in 1703, but "It is a common thing to work a woman slave out of doors." Moreover, while the white servant was forced to be celibate, or penalized if she was not, slavery introduced a different set of standards. Only in New England, where slaves were few and slavery mainly a domestic institution, were slave marriages legal and sexual mores required of slaves. Elsewhere, promiscuity among slaves was ignored. Criminal codes established for slaves provided no barrier to fornication or adultery, for which whites could be prosecuted, since slave marriages were not recognized in law. The only important issue at law was who was a slave, and this was quickly settled. In 1662, Virginia provided a model double-barreled statute that stated, first, that all blacks would inherit the mother's condition and, second, that "any Christian [that] shall commit fornication with a Negro man or woman, he or she offending shall pay double the fines imposed." Laws prohibiting miscegenation existed in all colonies by the mid-eighteenth century.

If the seventeenth-century woman slave had one thing in common with the white woman colonist, besides the value of her labor, it was that she was affected by an extremely unbalanced sex ratio. In the southern colonies, which provided the biggest market for slaves, men were in greater demand than women. Early slaveowners did not seem aware of the economic potential of a permanent, self-perpetuating labor force. Their immediate need was to raise as much tobacco as possible. The imbalance in southern slave sex ratios, moreover, was destined to get worse before it got better. Slave importation increased during the late seventeenth century, and the majority of new slaves continued to be men. In Virginia, male slave arrivals outnumbered female arrivals two or three to one. Southern Maryland's sex ratio (the number of men per hundred women) was 125 in 1650; it reached 180 by 1730. In some of the older, more densely populated eastern counties, slave sex ratios began to reach parity in the 1720s and 1730s. But in general, sexual imbalance in the Maryland and Virginia slave populations dwindled only in the late eighteenth century, when imports dropped and were exceeded by natural increase.

However, the black woman slave imported into the southern colonies, whether severed from African relatives or sent from a plantation in the Caribbean, had nothing to gain from being in a minority. Since most southern plantations were quite small—few had over twenty slaves and a majority of slaveowners had less than five—she was unlikely to form any type of permanent union. The black population, moreover, was thinly spread over large areas, which made finding a partner especially difficult. Nor did the excess of men in the slave population create circumstances conducive to family life. And this was only part of the slave woman's plight. Her life expectancy, like that of all southern immigrants, white and black, was short; lack of immunity to new diseases caused chronic ill health and early death. Few slaves could expect to reach old age (over fifty), although among those who did, at least in Maryland, women seemed to predominate, despite the larger male population. Finally, the child-bearing rate of immigrant slave women was extremely low. Indeed, seventeenth-century southern slave populations experienced a natural decline rather than an increase. In part, this is attributable to such factors as high adult mortality, poor health, and the relatively old age of female slave immigrants in terms of childbearing. But low black fertility in the early South has also been attributed to the desperate condition of new women slaves, their inability to adjust to slavery, and their alienation, depression, and morbid state of mind. Under such circumstances, presumably, the first woman slaves were reluctant to reproduce.

The northern slave was more likely to be a woman, since the most promising and desirable slaves were sold in the South. She was more likely than a southern slave to do domestic work rather than field work; to live in a town or village, which meant greater autonomy; to be hired out, which brought certain perquisites; and even to hold personal property—as was the custom in New York, where slavery was a peculiarly liberal institution. Such regional distinctions in the nature of slavery had far more impact on the status of the woman slave than did those provided by gender.

Finally, North or South, the woman slave, like the woman servant, played a vital part in the colonial economy by providing cheap labor. So, indeed, did the average colonial housewife and her daughters. The Native American woman played a similarly vital part in the Indian economy. Like the seventeenth-century colonial housewife, the Indian woman had multiple roles—as family member, community member, and productive worker.

Indian Women and Colonizers

When Mary Rowlandson spent eleven weeks with the Narragansetts, she saw her captors as an alien race of "murtherous wretches" with diabolic motives. Nonetheless, she was also, inadvertently, an acute observer of Indian life—from the funeral rites for Weetamoo's child to the role of Indian women as food gatherers, traders, and raft builders. Such data could hardly serve the same function as an anthropologist's field report. Mary Rowlandson's observations were filtered through a Puritan prism and, like those of other seventeenth-century colonists who had contacts with the Indians, were colored by her English assumptions. Still, colonial records, along with ethnographic evidence, have been used to reconstruct the role of Indian women during the first century of colonization.

By the time of King Philip's War, interaction with Europeans had drastically affected the life of coastal Indians in the Algonquian language group, which ranged from New England bands such as the Wampanoag and Narragansett down to the Powhatan in Chesapeake Bay. New England tribes, for instance, had almost been wiped out by epidemics of plague and smallpox by the 1630s. The remnant that survived, estimated at only about 10 percent of the original population, had been further affected by half a century of contact with colonists. By 1676, as the Rowlandson narrative suggests, local Indians were long accustomed to communicating and trading with the English, as well as to acquiring English weapons, clothing, and money—the items Philip demanded as ransom from

John Hoar. The process of colonization, which steadily eroded and weakened the position of all coastal Indians, also affected the roles of women in Indian society, roles that had been traditional for centuries.

The coastal Algonquians were an agricultural people who engaged in hunting and fishing, farming and gathering. As in English society, gender was the prime determinant of roles in Indian society, and this was evident in the sexual division of labor. Men were active in hunting, war, and diplomacy—or "international" relations, both among tribes and with the colonists. Women did almost all of the farming. They planted and harvested crops, work that centered around family garden plots and could be most easily combined with child rearing. In general, coastal Indians appear to have created a division of work roles not unlike that of the colonists, in which women engaged in domestic production or work that took place near where they lived, while men's work ranged farther afield, involved more danger, and required their absence from the village.

By the seventeenth century, however, at least in some places, women's work had become more vital to subsistence. In southern New England, for instance, agriculture had replaced hunting as the primary source of food. Indian women, who developed the wide variety of crops that evoked the interest of colonists, produced 90 percent of their tribes' food supplies. Much of their time was spent tending fields and in complex tasks of food processing—such as the pounding, drying, packing, and storing that made cornmeal available in the winter. Indian women also fished, gathered wild plants, produced household items, and participated in some stages of the hunting process, such as lugging the game home. They were, in addition, responsible for specific tasks in the Indian village, such as setting up and dismantling camp, which they must have done during Mary Rowlandson's frequent "removes."

The increased importance of women's agricultural work during the era of colonization did not necessarily generate higher status within the community. European colonization may well have increased the significance of the male sphere, since once settlement of coastal areas began, the realms of trade, diplomacy, and war became even more important. In any case, when seventeenth-century Englishmen observed Indian life, they not only described a sexual division of labor but painted a picture of female drudgery and male idleness. "The men bestow their times in fishing, hunting, warres, and such man-like exercises," wrote John Smith in 1607,

scorning to be seen in any woman-like exercise, which is the cause that the women be very painefull, and the men often idle. The women and children doe the rest of the worke. They make mats, baskets, pots, mortars, pound their corne, make their bread, prepare their victuals, plante their corne, gather their corne, bear all kinds of burdens, and such like.

An unequal division of labor continued to pervade colonists' accounts, down to William Byrd, a century later. "The little work that is done among the Indians is done by the poor women," said Byrd, "while the men are quite idle, or at most employ'd only in the Gentlemanly diversion of hunting and fishing." In colonial eyes, the Indian concept of gender roles was at best peculiar and in general unjust, and the status of Indian women a degraded one.

But the description of female degradation by such men as Smith and Byrd was probably unjust as well. Other accounts suggest more cooperation between the sexes as well as some crossing over of occupational lines. Roger Williams, an unusually acute observer, reported that Indian men and women often joined together for special tasks, such as breaking up a field, and older Indians of both sexes engaged in agricultural work, as did children. At least one group of Englishwomen, who had extensive opportunities to assess Indian life, also had a different reaction to the roles of Indian women. While seventeenth-century captives—among them Mary Rowlandson and her children—were taken for ransom, in the mid-eighteenth century, some New England tribes attempted to adopt captive women and children and transform them into band members. Many such "white Indians" preferred to remain with their tribes, or at least were returned only under force, and these women voiced special reasons for appreciating Indian life. Indian women's work was "not so severe," said one famous captive, Mary Jemison, their tasks "probably not harder than [those of] white women." In particular, Indian women were spared the labor of housewifery ("no spinning, weaving, sewing, stocking knitting"). In addition, they worked together, in village units not nuclear family units, and had control of their own realm of work, village agriculture.

Cooperative crop raising and food production were not the only activities of coastal Indian women. Even in wartime, they remained involved in trade. Like colonial housewives, Indian women were always engaged in internal trade—indeed, it was a staple of their day-to-day existence. Incessant exchange of crops and goods was a basic part of Indian social life and part of a tradition of reciprocity. When Philip met Mary Rowlandson, for instance, he at once proposed an exchange of clothing items for a dinner. Rowlandson, moreover, was already enmeshed in the Indians' system of barter and exchange. Although external trade, with English colonists, was dominated by men, colonial observers throughout the century mentioned women traders who sold skins to the colonists or English goods to the Indians. By the end of the century, coastal Indian women were themselves interested in acquiring English products, from needles and cloth to kettles and tea. Like the women Mary Rowlandson met during her captivity, they became customers for English clothing items—caps, aprons, handkerchiefs, stockings, and occasionally shoes, such as the ones Weetamoo wore during her celebratory dance.

Indian women were also as conscious of kinship relations as were the White sisters of Lancaster. Within Indian villages, the clan was the primary unit of social and political organization. Coastal Indians lived in extended lineal families and formed exogamous marriages—that is, marriages to members of other clans or bands. An example was the marriage between Weetamoo and Quinnapin (although multiple wives such as Quinnapin's were relatively rare). As a result, New England tribes were linked by intermarriage. Patrilineal kinship reckoning and patrilocal residence were customary among coastal Indians, as they were among the Narragansetts. But in some bands outside southern New England,

The first English colonist to depict coastal Indian women was artist John White, who arrived on Roanoke Island in 1585. In the many paintings and drawings that he brought back to England, White presented an extremely favorable impression of Indian villages, rituals, and everyday life, since his purpose was to attract settlers to Roanoke. He also attempted to dispel English visions of naked and immoral savages, as did the expedition's chronicler, Thomas Hariot. Indian women, Hariot reported, "cover themselves before the behynde, from the naval unto the midds of their thighes . . . with a deered skynne handsomely dressed and fringed." And unmarried women, dignified and virtuous, "lay their hands often uppon their shoulders, and cover their breasts in token of maydenlike modesty." Two years later, John White led an ill-fated contingent of 120 settlers to Roanoke and went back to England for supplies. When he returned in 1590, all of the colonists, including his daughter, had vanished, and to this day their fate is unknown. Above, a John White watercolor of an Indian woman and child, holding a doll in English dress, 1585–1587. *(The British Museum)*

kinship was determined through the mother's heritage, property descended through the female line, and married couples lived with the wife's family. These matrilineal, matrilocal arrangements, adopted by such tribes as the Iroquois and Delaware in the east and the Creek and Seminole in the south, increased female influence in family and village life. Even without them, Indian women commonly exerted a large degree of authority within the clan, where they supervised affairs of domestic life, such as marriage choices, and regulated the arrangements for farming.

Indian women's daily lives, unlike those of Englishwomen, were affected by a pattern of sexual segregation. Women of the New England tribes, for instance, customarily ate separately from men and during menstruation inhabited separate menstrual huts. In Indian culture, a tradition of female modesty and male sexual restraint prevailed. Colonists continued to be surprised, as was Mary Rowlandson, at the lack of vulgar behavior among the Indians, and even more so by the absence of sexual assault. Most seventeenth-century English captives held for ransom were women and children, whose reports confirmed Mary Rowlandson's observations and revealed as much about English expectations as they did about Indian men. One explanation for male sexual restraint, as historian James Axtell points out, was that Indian warriors had a tradition of continence in times of conflict, fearing that indulgence would bring misfortune. In addition, members of Indian tribes, usually related to one another, had stringent incest taboos. Captives may have been regarded as temporary band members, protected by the same customs that applied to Indian women. This was certainly true in the case of the mid-eighteenth-century captives studied by Axtell, who were indeed adopted as band members. Finally, the Indians may have regarded rape as an abhorrent crime under any circumstances, since it was the only capital offense punishable by the band as a whole, whereas murder, for instance, might be avenged by the victim's immediate family.

If colonists were surprised at the Indian custom of sexual restraint, they must also have been surprised by Indian women's occasional roles as tribal leaders or sachems. Throughout the seventeenth century, colonial accounts mentioned various women sachems among the coastal tribes—for example, the "Massachusetts queen" who in 1620 sold land to the English. Succession to a sachem's role was based on primogeniture (inheritance by the firstborn), but retention of that role depended on performance—that is, the ability to gain a band's respect. While the vast majority of sachems were men, some women, like Weetamoo, inherited tribal office; others replaced deceased male relatives who had been sachems. Conventionally, sachems were supported by food contributions made by their followers and were expected to give gifts of some sort to those followers in return. Weetamoo, as Mary Rowlandson observed, worked at making belts, rather than at food collecting, the work in which other Indian women were occupied.

By the time of King Philip's War, female band leaders had appeared in profusion. The Narragansett sachem Quaiapan, whose warriors had attacked Nipmuck villages in the 1660s, was later drawn into King Philip's War, during which she was killed. Another war leader was Awashonks, a Rhode Island sachem who joined Philip's cause for about a year and then negotiated a separate peace. A third was Weetamoo, who before Mary Rowlandson's captivity had commanded over 300 Pocasset male warriors. By the summer of 1676, however, their numbers had dropped to thirty, all of whom were killed or captured by the time of Weetamoo's death. Significantly, the three female sachems were at first reluctant to join the conflict and became involved either when their villages were attacked or, in Weetamoo's case, at Philip's insistence.

Access of Indian women to tribal office distinguished their roles from those of European women, and so did their authority in religious life. Among the Indians, women sometimes assumed roles as shamans, or priests, which meant that they ran medical practices, specializing either in natural cures, as herbalists, or in supernatural cures. To be sure, women practitioners were most active in those bands that lacked an established male priesthood. Also, many of these religious/medical practitioners were older Indians of both sexes. Nonetheless, in some cases women served as both shamans and warleaders, a powerful combination. To colonists, the supernatural influence of a religious practitioner held the greatest fascination. Among the Wampanoag and Delaware, for instance, shamans could communicate with the dead, find missing persons or things, and predict future events. Not surprisingly, one colonial observer, Daniel Gookin, described Wampanoag shamans as part physician and part witch or wizard, since the powers they claimed were like those the English attributed to the devil's servants.

Many aspects of women's roles among coastal Algonquian bands were later encountered among inland tribes, such as the Seneca and Iroquois, as well as among western plains Indians in the nineteenth century. Though Indian societies were typically characterized by male dominance and a sexual division of labor, women exerted varying degrees of authority, formal and informal, within their clans and tribes. Those seventeenth-century colonists who observed Indian life were most impressed with aspects of women's roles that seemed unusual or even bizarre, whether their extensive agricultural work or their leadership roles as sachems or shamans. Although Englishwomen never filled any public offices, they were hardly excluded from involvement in religious life. This involvement was greatest in the northern colonies, where sectarianism was rampant.

Prophets and Saints

The cutting edge of change in seventeenth-century women's history, blunt as it may have been, was somewhere along the northern seaboard, in towns, in trade, and especially in church—the only social institution beyond the family in which women might become "members." For such women as the White sisters of Lancaster, church membership was the only formal affiliation outside the home, their only title beyond that of daughter, sister, wife, and mother. Church membership also provided entrée into a religious community, which at Sunday sermons and weekly meetings offered a degree of respite from the patriarchal family. In women's experience, therefore, the church was something of a halfway house between domestic life and public life. Indeed, among English sects such as the Puritans or the Friends (Quakers) whose emigration had been spurred by religious motives, religion was a form of political life. To the extent that it was, a portion of seventeenth-century Quaker and Puritan women was highly politicized.

The growth of dissenting sects such as Puritanism in seventeenth-century England had a twofold impact on women's lives in colonial America. First, sectarianism put new focus on the family as a vehicle for the transmission of religious values. The Puritan, Quaker, or Separatist home in the colonies, as in England, became an arena for indoctrination and character formation, which placed further demands on parents and children. At the same time, sectarianism contained an expansive dimension for women as individuals. By recognizing their souls, it raised their expectations. Even if subordinate in family and community, women could enjoy equal access to intimacy with God, or equality of souls.

This sense of personal contact with divinity, whether based on "inner light," revelation, or simply faith, had further ramifications. It helped women endure bad experiences—such as the trials of emigration, for Anne Bradstreet, or the period of captivity, for Mary Rowlandson, or the commonplace deaths of infants and children. It also contained an inspirational impulse, a sense of spiritual individualism, that was pregnant with potential. Such spiritual individualism was usually difficult to transfer to "worldly" affairs, since equality of souls was at odds with the English belief in woman's inferiority and the need for her subordination. There was, however, one exception, and that was the unique role of the woman Quaker.

The Society of Friends was a minority sect, whose singular customs affected only its own communities, primarily in Pennsylvania and New Jersey, starting in the 1650s. But the egalitarian precedent of Quakers was significant, not least because it aroused such hostility among outsiders. In particular, the Friends provided a model of alternative roles for women that was, in the context of the seventeenth century, revolutionary. By discarding a professional ministry, Friends provided reprieve from clerical domination. By insisting on the equality of souls, they opened the field of prophecy, or ministerial roles, to women. Equally important, Quaker women created their own organizational structure, a groundwork for collective action, through which they exerted authority within the community.

According to the Friends, the restrictions on women imposed by Paul for "silence in church" did not apply to those who had established contact with God or found their "inner light." Spiritual rebirth also brought in its wake the power of prophecy, or access to the calling of lay minister or "public" Friend. As the founder of the sect, George Fox, had explained in England, the spirit of Christ could "speak in the female as well as in the male." A goal of the Friends, moreover, was "to liberate for the service of the Church the gifts of government which lay dormant and barren in both men and women." This extraordinary view had profound implications for women.

Of the fifty-nine public Friends who arrived in the colonies at the start of the Quaker migration, from 1656 to 1663, nearly half were women. Active proselytizers, these women traveled throughout the colonies, supported by their "meetings," to spread the word and make new converts. Believing that God protected them with an "armour of light," they presented a grave challenge to more orthodox sects such as the Puritans. Female militancy was even carried to martyrdom by an avid proselytiser, Mary Dyer, in the late 1650s. Banned from Boston and New Haven, and repeatedly expelled, Mary Dyer returned to Boston four times and was finally executed by the exasperated Puritans, since she refused to end her crusade. Several Quaker men had been hanged before her for the same reason.

Although most Quaker women were not public Friends, the society's organizational structure also provided singular opportunities. Women played an important part in Quaker "government" through women's meetings, which began in 1681 and were regularly scheduled in all locales where Friends settled. Here, women conducted discussions, drew up rules, kept records, managed finances, trained younger members, and contributed to Friends' regional meetings. In no other formal institution in the seventeenth-century colonies did women play such roles. One special function of the women's meetings was to keep in touch with sister Friends through circular letters that passed from one meeting to another. Another function, as expressed in a letter from English sisters, was "to prevent our Children from running into the world [the non-Quaker community] for husbands, or for wives." Through their meetings, Quaker women supervised the realm of Quaker marriage, exerted authority over family life, and transformed "equality of souls" into collective influence within the community of Friends.

In the view of Puritans, however, the Friends had carried reformation to an ungodly extreme, especially by supporting female prophecy. Giving women access to religious leadership, the Puritans believed, could only upset the natural order of society, sabotage domestic life, subvert government, and bring chaos in its wake. Even the most pious of Puritan women never enjoyed access to the ministry or to collective influence over the community. Rather, Puritan goals of social cohesion and domestic order made the submission of women, at home and outside it, especially vital. But in New England, Puritan women were granted a limited version of "equality of souls" since they could be accepted, after private, oral examination, as nonvoting church members, or saints. The tension in the roles of these female saints, an elite group, lay in their dual status, as saints and women.

Sainthood was an asexual status, even if women's temporal lives were subordinate. It required of women and men the same attitudes toward God— submission, obedience, meekness, humility—the very postures required of women by men in worldly affairs. Indeed, these same postures were required of *men* toward men of higher status; seventeenth-century society was hierarchical, and most men were utterly in control only within their own families. Accordingly, many of the same virtues were valued in both men and women. Even the character traits recommended by Cotton Mather, a leading exponent of womanhood at the end of the century, in his "Ornaments of the Daughters of Zion"— modesty, silence, obedience, industriousness, humility, thrift, and discretion—

were not overwhelmingly sex-specific. (Silence and modesty, admittedly, were not constraints that Puritan men imposed on themselves.) Departed women saints were praised at their funerals for prudence, industry, piety, and charity, as well as for poring over the Scriptures, taking notes at sermons, and "pious society and discourse."

These studious attributes were significant. New England women were more likely to be literate than were women in England or elsewhere in the colonies. As late as the 1750s, only one out of three Englishwomen was able to sign her name in the marriage register, and even fewer could do so in the seventeenth century. In the colonies, under half of seventeenth-century women were able to read at all, and far fewer to write. But Puritan women were at an advantage. Although most of their training was in housewifery, they often learned to read at home. A modicum of learning was desirable to promote piety and facilitate study of the Bible. Unlike obedience and submissiveness, however, learning had its limits.

Puritan authorities believed that women were innately weaker of brain and easily seduced by bad influences, especially if they strained their minds beyond reasonable limits and crossed the line between private piety and critical thought. The learned, illustrious woman, a phenomenon rare elsewhere in the colonies, might be most admired if she devoted her efforts to pious matters and kept her learning to herself, or at least confined it to the boundaries of the home. Women's writings were preferably private documents, not to be exposed to public view but to be read by themselves and family members. Anne Bradstreet, whose poems were published anonymously and not at her instigation in England, provided a model of such private writings in her "Religious Experiences," intended to convey "spiritual advantages" to her eight children. This personal narrative was written not for self-glorification but in humility, "not to sett forth myself but the Glory of God." It was, of course, never published in her lifetime. Mary Rowlandson's captivity narrative, so useful for Puritan propaganda, contained a similar disclaimer. Like Anne Bradstreet's poems, it was published anonymously.

Both Bradstreet and Rowlandson, moreover, used their learning for private benefit, not for public troublemaking or "medling" in the affairs of men. "Medling" was the crucial word. Conveying a sense of incompetence and illegitimacy, it was frequently used to describe the sort of intrusive, aggressive female behavior to which seventeenth-century men objected. The epitome of such behavior was the disruptive example set by Anne Hutchinson in the 1630s, at the very outset of the Puritan experiment. Described by John Winthrop as "a woman of fierce and haughty carriage," Hutchinson had been not merely a "medler" but an all too competent insurgent. Her intellectual power had led to extreme assertiveness, insubordinate action, and, worst of all, charismatic power over others.

Anne Hutchinson was a woman of status, the middle-aged wife of a landowner, merchant, and public official. She was also a fervent Puritan saint. Since her arrival in Massachusetts Bay in 1634 with her husband and fourteen of her children, she had created a base of support in Boston. While her services as a midwife gave her entrée into many homes, her talents as a theologian attracted even more attention. Soon sixty or eighty townsfolk, at first mainly women but later men as well, were gathering in the Hutchinson home to hear Anne Hutchinson's learned discussions of weekly sermons. Here, her "medling" became apparent. Anne Hutchinson attacked the pivot on which Puritanism uneasily rested by throwing her weight toward the Covenant of Grace (a conviction that redemption came solely through God's grace, regardless of an individual's efforts) and away from the Covenant of Works (the belief that good behavior, a righteous life, was a sign of salvation).

This was not a small or harmless error, since Anne Hutchinson compounded it by challenging the sanctity of ministers who opposed her. Worse yet, she held a powerful sway over her followers, a "potent party" of Bostonians who were people of substance—merchants, landowners, and their wives. After inquisition by the leading ministers and a trial for sedition before the General Court, Anne Hutchinson was convicted, excommunicated, and banished. At the end of her trial, she admitted divine revelation, which proved her undoing. Even a man to whom God spoke directly would have been in trouble. But Anne Hutchinson had long been a triple threat, as her judges informed her, to home, church, and state. She had assumed male postures—by dominating her husband and exerting authority over the community, by attacking the sanctity of ministers and usurping their roles, and by having no respect for the "fathers" of the community. Anne Hutchinson was guilty not only of heresy and sedition but of role reversal. As she was told at her trial, "You have rather bine a Husband than a Wife, and a Preacher than a Hearer, and a Magistrate than a subject."

Anne Hutchinson's career following her expulsion from Massachusetts in 1637 confirmed the suspicions of her judges. After moving to Rhode Island with her husband, younger children, and a sizable contingent of followers, she continued to get into political squabbles. In Rhode Island, she attacked the magistracy by questioning its authority. The family next moved on to New York, where Anne Hutchinson and her younger children, except for one, were killed by Indians in 1643. Puritans could view this massacre only as divine retribution for her errors. Even four decades later, during King Philip's War, when one of Anne Hutchinson's nephews was killed, Increase Mather concluded that the demise of the Hutchinsons (like Mary Rowlandson's redemption) was an "observable work of Providence."

But Anne Hutchinson's cause had great appeal for women, who formed a vocal part of the "potent party" that supported her. In the eyes of such women, dependence on God alone may have seemed preferable to dependence on intermediaries, whether ministers, magistrates, or husbands. Not surprisingly, Anne Hutchinson's example remained more than an unpleasant memory in New England. Some of her supporters, such as Mary Dyer, followed her to Rhode Island. Dyer, whom Winthrop described as "notoriously infected with error" and "very censorious and troublesome," later embarked on her career as a Quaker proselytizer. Other women supporters, who remained in Boston, fell under suspicion—among them Mary Oliver, who criticized ministers and magistrates and ended up in the stocks.

In the decade that followed, other women of status paid the price for "persistence in error" or pernicious "medling." Ann Eaton, the governor's wife in New Haven, who disavowed infant baptism, was excommunicated in 1644 for lying and stubbornness. Her daughter, Ann Hopkins, another governor's wife as well as a delver into theological matters, bore God's wrath more directly. She was driven mad, as John Winthrop explained, by too much reading and writing and attempting "to meddle in such things as are proper for men, whose minds are stronger, etc." Assertive behavior continued to be regarded as a threat, as illustrated in the contentious case of Ann Hibbens, wife of a prominent Boston merchant and former official. Brought to trial in 1641 for lying and slander, and excommunicated, Ann Hibbens was denounced for usurping the authority of her husband, "whom she should have obeyed and unto whom God put her into subjection." Female dissent or aggressiveness remained evils to be suppressed before they got out of hand.

New England Puritans were no different from other Englishmen, at home or in the colonies, in their low opinion of women's capacities or their belief in the need for female subordination. Nor were New England Puritans different from those left behind in England, who followed a divergent path but experienced some of the same problems with women. During the English Civil War (1642–1660), women of the more radical Puritan sects, carried away by their sense of equality in the eyes of God, held demonstrations, petitioned Parliament, and "medled" collectively in men's affairs. At the same time, during the years when Puritanism was on the rise and especially during the English Civil War, epidemics of witchcraft struck the areas in which English Puritans lived. Women's alleged defects—of wit, will, and moral fiber—had dual ramifications in seventeenth-century society. First, female interference in men's affairs, such as theology and government, was considered dangerous and subversive, as the Anne Hutchinson episode in Boston suggested. Second, due to their supposed moral weakness, women were seen as ready prey for seduction by fiends and likely candidates for careers in witchcraft, a low and malevolent form of assertiveness.

Invisible Furies

Witches were not unknown in the colonies, although there had never been large numbers of them. Still, seventeenth-century society was rural, agrarian, traditional, and superstitious. And witches had been found—mainly in New England, where villagers kept a close watch on one another and the devil's works were more easily recognized. By the end of the century, some forty towns had discovered several hundred witches in their midst.

As in England, accused witches were usually women (only one out of four was a man) of eccentric and cantankerous disposition who went about harming their neighbors, invariably after a quarrel or dispute. Or rather, their curses, threats, or unwelcome visits were followed by a variety of misfortunes, such as a cow's death or a child's illness. Margaret James, for example, was executed in 1648 for a malignant touch, suspicious medicines, and (at her trial) intemperate behavior and notorious lying. Ann Hibbens, long known for her "crabbedness" of nature, was executed in 1656 after an exceptionally contentious career. Susanna Martin was accused in 1669 of bewitching a neighbor, although not tried until 1692. The famous witch Glover, who caused fits in children, was one of several witches executed in the 1680s.

Though of diverse social origins, women charged with witchcraft were mainly from the lower ranks. They were also mainly women of middle-age with long histories of abrasive relations and involvement in community squabbles. Relatively few accused witches were executed; most were exonerated of the charges against them and returned to their places, however marginal, within the community. Moreover, convictions for witchcraft, and then even accusations, seemed to fall in the 1650s and 1660s. But the "invisible furies" of witchcraft reappeared in force in New England at the end of the century. Their arrival coincided with a period of unusual stress in eastern Massachusetts and the rebellion of a small group of teenage girls.

By the 1690s, coastal New England had undergone many changes, including transformation of Massachusetts from a Bible commonwealth to a royal colony. Less tangible changes had also occurred, such as a falling off of religious interest among men. During the early days of settlement, men and women became church members in family units and in roughly equal numbers. At midcentury, when the sex ratio in eastern towns first showed signs of evening out, the proportion of women saints began to rise; and it continued to do so after church admissions were liberalized in 1662. By the time of King Philip's War, over two-thirds of new church members in Massachusetts and Connecticut were women; and women continued to join in disproportionate numbers. While ministers bemoaned a communal loss of piety, to an increasingly feminized and therefore less significant flock, young men in New England were turning their attention to other pursuits.

One was land, which led them further away from the seaboard villages where earlier settlers had congregated. By the end of the century, the loss of men in more densely settled areas, where land was unavailable, probably left fewer men than women in some places. Another source of diversion was trade and commerce—or "temporal gain and worldly wealth"—which led men away from more pious concerns. By the late seventeenth century, enterprising New England men were either losing faith or else eastern New England was losing them. Both the inroads of "worldliness" and the impact of expansion affected the eastern town of Salem, which had recently divided into Salem Village, a rural, farming backwater, and Salem Town, where those who had profited from trade and commerce were concentrated. In 1692, animosity between village and town, farmers and merchants, old values and new profits, erupted in a confrontation between two marginal groups of women. One was the "accusors" or "afflicted"— a dozen or so young women and girls, including some servants. The other group was the accused witches, the majority of them older women, sometimes tainted by a degree of deviance or peculiarity, and some of their husbands and children.

During a single year, 115 local people were accused of witchcraft, three-quarters of them women, and 20 were put to death. Throughout the episode, women occupied center stage, from meetinghouse to courtroom to gallows. They played almost all the leading roles in the witchcraft trials—except those of the judges and a second string of witnesses, mainly men, who testified against the accused. What occurred in Salem was a role reversal of unique dimensions, in which the "afflicted" girls exerted authority over everyone else—ministers and magistrates, masters and mistresses, neighbors and enemies. With tales of sucking birds and barking dogs, and with perverse behavior that ordinarily would have led directly to the stocks, they gained attention routinely denied them and an outlet for aggressiveness that was impermissible in normal times. By describing specters that flew around the area biting and tormenting their victim or, alternatively, offering them land, goods, clothes, and wealth if they would sign the devil's book, the girls gave shape and voice to widely shared antagonisms and resentments. By identifying the specters, they directed retribution toward the most susceptible of villagers—ranging from suspicious neighborhood hags such as pipe-smoking, muttering Sarah Good or the already discredited Susanna Martin to the pious and respectable, if somewhat deaf, Rebecca Nurse.

It was no surprise that middle-aged women were the prime targets of witchcraft charges, since this had been the case in earlier episodes. Nor were the accusations hurled against them unusual. The youth of their accusers, finally, was not unique either. Many previous witches had also been identified by young, unmarried women, indeed teenage girls, one generation younger than the women they accused. The history of New England witchcraft, as historian John Demos suggests, seems to reveal a hidden theme in the lives of seventeenth-century women: intense hostility of younger women toward the power and control of older women. On the other hand, as also has been suggested, middle-aged women, often slightly deviant, may well have been merely the most vulnerable scapegoats—or stand-ins for the less assailable male authority figures. In any case, what distinguished the 1692 episode was its large scope, and the way it spread even beyond the bounds of Salem to neighboring areas. Another distinctive feature was the unity, and consequent influence, of the young accusors.

Under ordinary circumstances, young women were the weakest and most marginal of community members, always under the domination of others. Only two of the Salem accusors lived in homes with fathers present. The rest, subject to the directives of mothers, uncles, masters, and mistresses, may have felt particularly powerless. But once their witchcraft accusations held, these otherwise insignificant young women were able to exert life-and-death power over the entire community. Before the trials were over, they had gone beyond indicting immediate neighbors, traditionally the bulk of the "accused," to charge more distant and prominent citizens, including some ministers. Only after accusations reached outlandish proportions was "spectral evidence" called into question. By then the witchcraft trials had provided an unprecedented outlet for personal grievances and community tensions. They also brought the common mode of female aggression—the squabble, harangue, and verbal assault—out of the home and into the historical record.

In the wake of the trials, New Englanders attempted to guess the cause of the unprecedented outbreak of witchcraft—as historians have done ever since.

Two decades later, when the Massachusetts legislature exonerated all those accused of witchcraft, it simply reversed the charges, contending that "evil spirits" had in fact been behind the accusers. But in 1692, attention was directed toward evil influences outside the community. Cotton Mather, for instance, a prominent minister, was quick to spot the similarity between witchcraft practice and Indian religious/medical practice. A well-known authority on both possession and captivity, Mather suggested a link between heathen diabolism and "the prodigious war made by the spirits of the invisible world upon the people of New England." The inexplicable attack of witchcraft in Salem, he thought, "might well have some of its origins among the Indians whose chief sagamores . . . have been horried sorcerers and hellish conjurors and such as conversed with demons."

The experience of Indian captivity, to be sure, rarely produced an affirmation of faith such as that so persuasively described by Mary Rowlandson. Other captives, like Ann Joslin, did not survive to examine their experiences. Yet others, such as Mehitable Goodwin, a famous captive, saw their children and other relatives murdered. And some were ransomed from the Indians in far worse shape than when they were taken. Mather's case in point was loud-mouthed Mercy Short, aged seventeen in 1692. During the Salem trials, Mercy had been an effective "accusor," notably of unfortunate Sarah Good, with whom she had quarreled. Her "affliction" by specters continued afterward while Mather subjected her to a period of extensive examination.

Mercy Short had been captured by the Indians in 1690, when living with her family at the very edge of settlement, in New Hampshire near the Maine border. She had seen her parents and much of her family killed before being carried off on a long "remove" all the way to Canada with several of her brothers and sisters. Mercy was finally ransomed; but release from captivity did not bring her praise, glory, or a grand reception as it had Mary Rowlandson, the wife of an important man. Instead, now orphaned, Mercy Short became a household servant, a lowly position alleviated only by her notoriety at the witchcraft trials. Her testimony afterward, which Mather recorded, revealed an imagination, as he observed, that was "strangely disordered." It also revealed intense hostility, and not only toward Indians. Mercy Short objected to her servile condition, "Fatherless" status, and lack of options. Her remarks, while arguing with the specters of unseen witches, provided a demented counterpoint to Mary Rowlandson's submission to divine will.

What Mercy wanted, as the specters guessed, was security, status, wealth, and power. Since the marital prospects for an orphaned servant were poor, they offered her a husband. "Fine Promises! You'l bestow a husband on me, if I'l bee your Servant," Mercy responded. "An Husband! What? A Divel! I shall then bee finely fitted with an Husband: No I hope the Blessed Lord Jesus Christ will marry my Soul to Himself yett before Hee has done with me, as poor a Wretch as I am!" The specters also offered clothes, just as they had tempted other villagers with silks and leisure and the other accoutrements of wealth. But Mercy turned them down. "Fine Clothes! What? Such as Your Friend Sarah Good had, who hardly had rags to cover her!" After offering, next, eternal life, the specters turned to intimidation, and in response, Mercy voiced her objection, not uncommon to the teenage servant, to the authority exerted by older women:

> What's that? Must the Younger Women, do yee say, hearken to the Elder?—They must bee another Sort of Elder Woman than You then! they must not bee Elder witches, I am sure. Pray, do you for once Hearken to me—What a dreadful Sight are you! An Old Woman, an Old Servant of the Divel! You, that should instruct such poor, young Foolish Creatures as I am, to serve the Lord Jesus Christ come and urge me to serve the Divel!

Mercy's responses, while "insolent" and "abusive," Mather observed, were never "profane." Even more impressive, like any good dramatist, she based her performance on the situation with which she was most familiar: the domestic squabble.

Neither the experience of possession nor the attention it attracted brought the "afflicted" girls to the wealth, security, and status for which Mercy Short expressed a desire. Nor did their accusations bring them permanent reprieve from the control of the older generation. What the Salem episode provided was a rare, brief instance in which seventeenth-century women of any age acted in unison in public for any purpose. The witchcraft trials also threw a spotlight on "invisible" conflicts within the female community and on the "afflictions" of some of its younger members. The epidemic had struck at a time of stress, when the customary availability of land and excess of men had vanished, leaving young women, such as the "accusors," with limited options and negligible marital possibilities. By 1692, they had decreasing chances of escaping from the insignificant positions they already held, in their own homes, in other people's homes, and in the community. Fatherless Mercy Short, deserted by God in New Hampshire and tormented by shapes in Massachusetts, could well expect to be husbandless, landless, and powerless at home and outside it—a prospect that had not been faced by Mary, Elizabeth, or Hannah White when their family arrived in Lancaster in 1658.

During the early decades of settlement, between the Whites' emigration to Salem in the 1630s and the witchcraft trials of 1692, colonial women benefited from an unusual set of frontier circumstances. These circumstances improved their options, at least in comparison to their English counterparts of "middling" rank and below, without altering their subordinate status. During the eighteenth century, women's status remained subordinate. But modern impulses began to permeate their insular, traditional, backwoods world.

❧

SUGGESTED READINGS AND SOURCES

CHAPTER 1

Mary Rowlandson's captivity narrative has appeared in scores of editions since its first publication in Boston in 1682. The most recent is Alden T. Vaughan and Edward W. Clark, eds., *Puritans Among the Indians: Accounts of Captivity and Redemption 1676–1724* (Cambridge, Mass., 1981), pp. 29–75, an annotated version in modern English. For an older version, also annotated, see Charles H. Lincoln, ed., *The Narratives of the Indian Wars 1675–1699* (New York, 1913), pp. 107–168. Howard Peckham describes the Rowlandson captivity in *Captured by the Indians: True Tales of Pioneer Survivors* (New Brunswick, N.J., 1954), pp. 3–18. Douglas Edward Leach traces Mary Rowlandson's route through New England in "The 'Whens' of Mary Rowlandson's Captivity," *New England Quarterly,* 34 (September 1961), 352–363. David L. Greene documents Mary Rowlandson's second marriage (1679) and date of death (1710/1711) in "New Light on Mary Rowlandson," *Early American Literature,* 20 (Spring 1985), 24–38. Mitchell Robert Breitwieser questions Mary Rowlandson's adherence to the Puritan value system in *American Puritanism and the Defense of Mourning: Religion, Grief, and Ethnology in Mary Rowlandson's Captivity Narrative* (Madison, Wis., 1990). For the tradition of captivity accounts, see R. H. Pearce, "The Tradition of the Captivity Narrative," *American Literature,* 19 (March 1947), 1–20, and Vaughan and Clark, pp. 1–27.

CHAPTER 2

For women's place in English society during the era of colonization, see the early chapters of Sheila Rowbatham, *Hidden from History: Rediscovering Women in History from the 17th Century to the Present* (New York, 1976). Lawrence Stone, *The Family, Sex and Marriage in England, 1500–1800* (New York, 1979), is a gold mine of revelations about domestic life and women's roles.

There is no general survey of women's history in the seventeenth-century colonies. A useful overview is Carol Ruth Berkin, "Within the Conjuror's Circle: Women in Colonial America," in Thomas R. Frazier, ed., *The Underside of American History,* 3d ed. (New York, 1978), pp. 79–105. Mary Beth Norton assesses the implications of recent research in "The Evolution of White Women's Experience in Early America," *American Historical Review,* 89 (June 1984), 593–619. David Hackett Fischer compares women's roles among diverse groups of English colonists in *Albion's Seed: Four British Folkways in America* (New York, 1989).

The study of seventeenth-century women is weighted in favor of New England. For family life, see Edmund Morgan, *The Puritan Family: Religion and Domestic Relations in Seventeenth-Century New England* (New York, 1966), and John Demos, *A Little Commonwealth: Family Life in Plymouth Colony* (New York, 1970). Two contrasting studies of women's roles are Laurel Thatcher Ulrich, *Good Wives: Image and Reality in the Lives of Women of Northern New England 1650–1750* (New York, 1982) and Lyle Koehler, *A Search for Power: The Weaker Sex in Seventeenth-Century New England* (Urbana, Ill., 1980). For the contrasting experience of the first women colonists in the Chesapeake region, see David R. Ransome, "Wives for Virginia, 1621," *William and Mary Quarterly,* 3d series, 48 (January 1991), 3–18; Lois Greene Carr and Lorena Walsh, "The Planter's Wife: The Experience of White Women in Seventeenth-Century Maryland," *William and Mary Quarterly,* 3d series, 34 (1977), 542–571; and Lorena S. Walsh, "'Till Death Do Us Part': Marriage and Family in Seventeenth-Century Maryland," in Thad W. Tate and David Ammerman, eds., *The Chesapeake in the Seventeenth Century: Essays on Anglo-American Society* (Chapel Hill, N.C., 1979), pp. 126–152. Mary Beth Norton analyzes slander cases in "Gender and Defamation in Seventeenth-Century Maryland," *William and Mary Quarterly,* 3d series, 44 (January 1987), 3–39. Allan Kulikoff examines the lives of early southerners in *Tobacco and Slaves: The Development of Southern Cultures in the Chesapeake, 1680–1800* (Chapel Hill, N.C., 1986). For marriage patterns of Dutch women in colonial New York, see Joyce D. Goodfriend, *Before the Melting Pot: Society and Culture in Colonial New York City, 1664–1730* (Princeton, N. J., 1992), chs. 5 and 8. Steven Mintz and Susan Kellogg survey colonial family life in

Domestic Revolutions: A Social History of American Family Life (New York, 1988), chs. 1 and 2. Helena M. Wall finds similarities among colonies in *Fierce Communion: Family and Community in Early America* (Cambridge, Mass., 1990). For childbirth, see Catherine M. Scholten, *Childbearing in American Society: 1650–1850* (New York, 1985).

A classic study of women's legal status in the English colonies is Richard B. Morris, "Women's Rights in Early American Law," *Studies in the History of American Law with Special Reference to the Seventeenth and Eighteenth Century Colonies*, 2d ed. (Philadelphia, 1959), pp. 126–300. Puritan divorce policy is examined in D. Kelly Weisberg, "'Under Greet Tempttations Heer': Women and Divorce in Colonial Massachusetts," *Feminist Studies*, 2 (1975), 183–184. Roger Thompson discusses sexual crimes in *Sex in Middlesex: Popular Mores in a Massachusetts County, 1649–1699* (Amherst, Mass., 1986). N. E. H. Hull examines women criminals in *Female Felons: Women and Serious Crime in Colonial Massachusetts* (1987). For household production and other aspects of women's work, see Alice Morse Earle, *Home Life in Colonial Days* (New York, 1898), Alice Clark, *Working Life of Women in the Seventeenth Century* (New York, 1919), and Ulrich, *Good Wives*, part 1.

The standard work on indentured servitude is Abbott Smith, *Colonists in Bondage: White Servitude and Convict Labor in Colonial America, 1607–1776*, 2d ed. (New York, 1971). For the experience of the first generations of women slaves, see Winthrop D. Jordan, *White Over Black: American Attitudes Toward the Negro, 1550–1812* (Baltimore, 1973); Allan Kulikoff, *Tobacco and Slaves*, part III; and Russell Menard, "The Maryland Slave Population, 1658–1730: A Demographic Profile of Blacks in Four Counties," *William and Mary Quarterly*, 3d series, 32 (1975), 29–54.

For the impact of European colonization on American Indian women, see two suggestive, though contradictory, views of women's roles among Algonquian-speaking coastal tribes: Neal Salisbury, *Manitou and Providence: Indians, Europeans, and the Making of New England, 1500–1643* (New York, 1982), ch. 1; and Robert Steven Grumet, "Sunksquaws, Shamans, and Tradeswomen: Middle Atlantic Coastal Algonquian Women during the 17th and 18th Centuries," in Mona Etienne and Eleanor Leacock, eds., *Women and Colonization: Anthropological Perspectives* (New York, 1980), pp. 43–62. A splendid collection of primary sources on gender roles among Indians in the colonial era is James Axtell, ed., *The Indian Peoples of Eastern America: A Documentary History of the Sexes* (New York, 1981). Axtell describes the reactions of mid-eighteenth-century women captives to life among Middle Atlantic Indian tribes in "The White Indians of Colonial America," *William and Mary Quarterly*, 3d series, 32 (1975), 55–88. For anthropological sources, see Rayna Green's review essay, "Native American Women," *Signs*, 6 (Winter 1980), 248–267. There are many books of a general nature on the culture of American Indian women; for instance, Carolyn Neithammer, *Daughters of the Earth: The Lives and Legends of American Indian Women* (New York, 1977).

Mary Maples Dunn describes the unique role of Quaker women in "Women of Light" in Carol Ruth Berkin and Mary Beth Norton, eds., *Women of America: A History* (Boston, 1979), pp. 114–136, and Dunn, "Saints and Sisters: Congregational and Quaker Women in the Early Colonial Period," *American Quarterly*, 30 (Winter 1978), 582–601. See also Elisabeth Potts Brown and Susan Mosher Stuard, eds., *Witnesses for Change: Quaker Women over Three Centuries* (New Brunswick, N.J., 1989) and Jean R. Soderlund, "Women's Authority in Pennsylvania and New Jersey Quaker Meetings, 1680–1760," *William and Mary Quarterly*, 3d series, 44 (1987), 722–749. Qualities valued in Puritan women are suggested in Laurel Thatcher Ulrich, "Vertuous Woman Found: New England Ministerial Literature, 1668–1735," *American Quarterly*, 28 (Spring 1976), 19–40. Charles Lloyd Cohen describes female conversion relations in *God's Caress: The Psychology of Puritan Religious Experience* (New York, 1986). For Anne Hutchinson's career, see Emery Battis, *Saints and*

Sectaries: Anne Hutchinson and the Antinomian Controversy in the Massachusetts Bay Colony (Chapel Hill, N.C., 1962); and Lyle Koehler, "The Case of the American Jezebels: Anne Hutchinson and Female Agitation During the Years of the Antinomian Turmoil, 1636–1640," *William and Mary Quarterly,* 3d series, 31 (1974), 55–78.

Studies of witchcraft present vivid pictures of women's roles in seventeenth-century New England society. In *Entertaining Satan: Witchcraft and the Culture of Early New England* (New York, 1982), John Demos uses social science methods, psychological theory, and collective biography to analyze several decades of witchcraft accusations. See also Demos, "Underlying Themes in the Witchcraft Trials of Seventeenth-century New England," *American Historical Review,* 85 (June 1970), 1311–1326. Carol F. Karlson, who also examines witchcraft accusations, suggests a link between ideas about witchcraft and ideas about women; see *The Devil in the Shape of a Woman: Witchcraft in Colonial New England* (New York, 1987). Attention often centers on the witchcraft trials of 1692. Three different approaches are Paul Boyer and Stephen Nissenbaum, *Salem Possessed: The Social Origins of Witchcraft* (Cambridge, Mass., 1974), which analyzes social and political tensions in Salem; Chadwick Hansen, *Witchcraft at Salem* (New York, 1969), which contends that witchcraft induced psychosomatic effects in its victims; and Marion Starkey, *The Devil in Massachusetts* (New York, 1949), which points to hysteria among the young "accusors."

CHAPTER 3

∽∾∽

Eliza Pinckney and Republican Motherhood

When Washington toured the southern states in the spring of 1791, he hoped to evaluate candidates for federal appointments, just as he had recently done in the North. The mission was a difficult one. Distances were long, travel was tedious, and much of the scenery was extremely dull. "The most barren country I ever beheld," the President scrawled in his diary. Once out of Virginia, moreover, likely candidates were few and far between, except for such families as the Pinckneys and the Rutledges, who had urged the tour. In South Carolina, the Pinckneys became a focus of Washington's attention. On May 1, the President's party rose at dawn, rode four hours, and arrived at the steps of Hampton, a substantial plantation on the Santee River. This was the home of a wealthy widow, Harriott Horry, the only sister of the prominent Pinckney brothers.

Harriott Horry had inherited the plantation from her husband, a Huguenot planter and lawyer, who had died at the end of the Revolution. It had once been part of his first wife's dowry. During the war, Hampton had been used for patriotic purposes. It had served as a refuge for wives of men who were serving in the Continental army or in the Continental Congress. Now, in time for Washington's visit, Hampton had taken on a federal air. The great facade, impressive in both its size and its symmetry, had just been renovated by the addition of an enormous pillared portico. While a huge reception waited inside, the women of the Pinckney family lined up on the portico to meet the President, all arrayed in bandeaux and sashes that had been painted with Washington's portrait. Accompanied by her daughter and surrounded by nieces, Harriott Horry stood next to her distinguished mother, Eliza Pinckney, to whom Washington addressed some effusive remarks.

Although Washington neglected to include these remarks in his diary, there is little doubt about their content. The President had journeyed all the way to Hampton expressly to meet Eliza Pinckney and to compliment her on her success as planter, parent, and patriot. As everyone knew, her early experiments with indigo had made that staple a profit to the region. But even more important was her service to the nation. A widow for almost thirty-five years, Eliza Pinckney had brought up two remarkable sons. Charles Cotesworth and Thomas, now in their forties, had distinguished themselves in national service. Both had served as Revolutionary War generals, and both were signers of the Constitution. Charles Cotesworth had been an active participant at the 1787 constitutional convention, while Thomas served as governor of South Carolina. Such achievements, as the President told the assemblage at Hampton, could only reflect on their upbringing. By imbuing her sons with republican principles, Eliza Pinckney had made a monumental contribution. Through precept and example, she embodied the spirit of republican motherhood.

As Washington was well aware, the Pinckney sons were destined for outstanding careers in federal service. And as all of the family would have agreed, Eliza was responsible for both their success and their promise. A model of conduct, she had bound her sons to impeccable standards of virtue and piety, reason and moderation. A molder of character, she had skillfully combined unlimited trust with high expectations, and had seen those expectations fulfilled. A master of self-control, Eliza excelled also at social control. For decade after decade, she had carefully woven an intricate web of kinship and connection, linking child to parent, family to region, and citizen to state. By raising such prominent citizens—in fact, a founding family—she had indeed imbued maternity with political purpose.

But Eliza Pinckney's success as a mother was the outcome of training, talent, and opportunity. Before becoming an exemplary parent, Eliza had been an exemplary daughter and had thereby gained a special advantage. The crux of this advantage was her relationship with her father, George Lucas, whom she regarded as the most "indulgent" of parents. An ambitious major in the British army, Lucas was himself a colonial, the son of a prominent sugar planter and officeholder in Antigua. He was also a council member and landed proprietor there, when not off fighting the French and the Spanish. Devoted to empire, Lucas was also devoted to his oldest child. He imparted to her the precepts that shaped her character, advice that she would later transmit to her own three children.

Just as imperialism determined her father's career, so Eliza's youth ranged over the Empire. Born in the Indies in 1722, she spent much of her childhood at school in England. There she lived with an English family, the Boddicotts, who served as substitute parents. Mr. Boddicott was her father's London agent. When Eliza was fifteen, her English sojourn and formal education came to an end. War with Spain threatened, and her father moved the family from Antigua to Carolina. While two younger brothers, George and Thomas, remained with the Boddicotts to finish school, Eliza, her parents, and her younger sister, Polly, settled in 1737 on a plantation on the Wappoo River, not far from Charleston.

Eliza Lucas adored Carolina and summed it up with an imperial eye. The soil was fertile, the rivers navigable, the wildlife abundant, the winters pleasant, and the opportunities excellent, she wrote to her brothers in England. "The poorer sort are the most indolent people in the world or they could never be wretched in so plentiful a countryside as this." The Lucases, who were the "better sort," did very well. Wappoo, the Lucas plantation, was fairly small, only 600 acres, with no more than a few dozen slaves and some indentured servants, who were far more troublesome and often ran away. But Wappoo was only part of the land that George Lucas inherited from his father, who had invested in Carolina thirty years before. He also owned two large plantations on the Combahee and Waccamaw rivers, which produced pitch, tar, pork, and rice.

Although the Lucas's prospects in Carolina were good, Eliza's were better. The family had no sooner settled in when a combination of imperial strife and domestic circumstances transformed her life. The War of Jenkins's Ear erupted in 1739, and George Lucas, promoted to lieutenant colonel, returned to Antigua to become governor of that island. But the rest of the family remained at Wappoo, and Eliza was left in charge. Her mother, Anne, was an invalid and not up to the strain of managing either lands or household. Anne Lucas's health, like George's absence, provided their daughter with singular opportunity. While still a teenager, Eliza assumed her father's role as planter and proprietor, and her mother's role as mistress and parent. In these roles, she left behind a trail of achievements and a detailed record of them.

At seventeen, Eliza was managing all the Lucas lands. She was fully in charge of overseers, servants, slaves, planting, harvesting, finances, records, and the three-way trade between Carolina, the Indies, and England. She was also in charge of reporting to George Lucas, whose instructions she followed. Her letters to Antigua told of "the pain I had taken to bring the indigo, cotton, lucerne, and cassada to perfection . . . also concerning pitch and tarr and other plantation affairs." Exulting in her new authority, Eliza linked it to daughterly devotion. "I have the business of 3 plantations to transact [which] requires much writing and more business and fatigue of other sorts that you can imagine," she informed Mrs. Boddicott with her customary exuberance in 1740, "but least you should imagine it too burthensom to a girl at my early time of life, give me leave to assure you, I think myself happy that I can be so useful to so good a father."

Eliza was not only a competent manager but an innovative one. She constantly started agricultural experiments, on George Lucas's directions and on her own initiative, striving for products with economic potential. "I am so busy in providing for Posterity I hardly allow myself time to Eat or sleep," she told a friend. Cedar groves were filled with fruit trees, vines bore grapes, and oaks were planted so that in future years their valuable wood could be used for ships. Fig orchards were a special success, since the fruit could be dried and exported. "I own I love the vegitable world extreamly," said Eliza. But most impressive were the father-daughter efforts to raise indigo, since Carolinians grew mainly rice and needed new staples to export. Lucas sent Eliza seeds from the Indies, and after repeated setbacks, she produced her first crop in 1741. Three years later, Eliza was giving away seeds to her fellow planters; within a decade, indigo became a southern staple. Eliza Pinckney gained an impressive amount of local prestige.

But planting was not her sole pursuit. She also practiced her harpsichord, French, needlework, and writing. Her schedule itself was a source of pride. "I rise at five o'clock in the morning," she informed a friend, "read till seven—then take a walk in the garden or fields, see that the Servants are at their respective business. . . . The first hour after breakfast is spent at musick, the next is constantly employed in recolecting something I have learned, such as french or shorthand." Then she tutored young Polly, along with two black girls whom she hoped to train as school mistresses for the other slave children—an advanced educational scheme. The rest of the day was devoted to music lessons, sewing, visits, reading, and correspondence. Like most business people of the day, Eliza kept a "letter book," full of copies of outgoing letters, which provided the record of her early life. She also ordered books from England, making her way through Locke (a guide to conduct) and Vergil (a source of agricultural tips). Never idle, useless, or frivolous, Eliza became an addict of reason, which she manipulated with wit for her own amusement. When a local woman criticized her for rising so early, which might destroy her looks and make her old before her time, Eliza responded that getting up early only lengthened the day and thereby lengthened her life, since more of it could be spent awake.

Despite her intensive household routine, she also extended her dynamism into the community. Since her mother, Anne Lucas, was too frail to be active in social life or "vizeting," Eliza took over. She quickly made friends with the local elite and reported her success to Mrs. Boddicott. "We have six agreeable families around us, with whom we live in great harmony," she wrote. "The people live very Gentile and in the English taste." Sometimes she spent three or four weeks at the Charleston homes of prominent local women such as Mrs. Pinckney or Mrs. Cleland, the wives of council members. On such occasions, she visited with girls of her own age such as Miss Bartlett, the Pinckneys' niece. She also began an original form of social service. "I am engaged in the rudiments of the law," Eliza told the admiring Miss Bartlett. After learning "how to convey by Will, Estates, Real and Personal," she performed this service for poorer folk in the neighborhood who might be unable to send for a lawyer, because they either could not afford it or were dying too quickly. Although she claimed to defer to professionals, Eliza reveled in her newfound talent, especially when pressed into service as an executor. "I should begin to think myself an old woman before I am well a young one," she disclaimed, "having these weighty affairs on my head."

Finally, Eliza assumed her mother's role as parent by taking control of her younger siblings. Polly was well in hand, if not underfoot, at Wappoo and soon was sent to school in Charleston. But George and Thomas were still in England with the Boddicotts, and their nurturance had to be by letter—a task beyond Mrs. Lucas's strength or perhaps ability. Eliza energetically filled the breach and sent off missives of guidance, counsel, and exhortation, no doubt reinforcing similar letters sent by her father. Self-control, moderation, rationality—these were the Lucas keys to success, and Eliza was adept at both following and promoting them. When her brother George moved on to Antigua to become a soldier like their father, Eliza told him the goal of life was "to live agreeably to the dictates of reason and religion." She tried to guide his personal conduct, in face of the hazards of army life; he was not yet sixteen. "You are a soldier and Victory and conquest must fire your mind," she wrote from Wappoo, "remember then the greatest conquest is a Victory over your own irregular passions, consider this is the time for Improvement in Virtue as well as in everything else."

The tenets Eliza urged on George in Antigua had thus far served her well at home in Carolina. Moderation, reason, and self-control had gained her father's trust and favor. Moreover, all around her were signs of the trouble that ensued without them—the dire effects of excess, imbalance, and irrationality. These sometimes reflected sex-linked proclivities. Men, for instance, tended toward violence. They could be carried away by their own ferocity, in war and bloodshed, which were (Eliza thought) wickedness and folly. War kept her father abroad; bloodshed occurred close to home. In 1741, when Eliza was nineteen, one Captain Norberry, a local man and notorious brawler, engaged in a sword duel with Captain Dobrusee, who should have known better. Norberry seriously wounded his opponent and got himself killed, leaving his wife and three or four children to "lament his rashness," as Eliza reported to her father. While men might indulge in such useless brutality, there were excesses of a more feminine type that also tempted the soul. Mindless frivolity, hunger for luxury, subservience to whim, inconstancy of temper, and too frequent indulgence in card playing or dancing—all were decried by Eliza. Card playing and dancing were not bad in themselves, she believed, but immoderate love of them was a hazard. It tended, she felt, to "effeminate" the mind and make the rational faculties inactive.

Another hazard to rationality was religious enthusiasm, which afflicted men and women alike and induced a loss of self-control. The Lucases had no use for enthusiasm. While Eliza and her father respected piety and scorned disbelief, their goals were pragmatic. The right combination of reason and religion, as Eliza kept explaining to her brother, brought "cheerfulness in maturity, comfort in old age, and happiness to eternity." Even if there were no future state, she surmised, piety in itself was pleasant and profitable. But "enthusiasm" went beyond the pale. When religion was carried to excess by avid evangelists such as George Whitefield, who was then touring the southern colonies, it led only to misery and madness. This was demonstrated by several neighbors who, converted by Whitefield and brought to the brink, proceeded to lose their wits.

In 1742, Mrs. Le Brasures, a wealthy Carolina widow and a Whitefield disciple, so longed to get to heaven that she shot herself with a brace of pistols and gained immediate entry. The year before, Hugh Bryan, a local gentleman who was prominent in both the military and the magistracy, had become even more of a lunatic. After his conversion, he took to the woods, claimed to work miracles, tried to divide the waters with a wand, and finally prophesied a great slave uprising, which caused his neighbors extreme discomfort. When the madness wore off, he resumed his career; but his experience was instructive. "I hope he will be a warning to all pious minds not to reject reason and revelation and set up instead their own wild notions," said Eliza. The most heartrending case of all was that of her friend Mary Woodward Chardon, a young widow. Mary went mad from striving for perfection. "Being ever so good as woman could be," observed Eliza, "she would fain have been an angel before her time." Once, Mary had been cheerful, sensible, and vivacious, but during her first marriage she underwent a terrible change. When Eliza visited, Mary appeared to be insane. She sighed, sang, laughed maniacally, and made incoherent speeches. Mary, like Hugh Bryan, eventually recovered, and she married again. But her lunacy troubled Eliza, especially since it had no apparent cause.

Except for marriage. A bad alliance of "unequal" partners, as Eliza told Miss Bartlett, could only bring "an end to all human felicity." The choice of a husband clearly had to be made with great discretion, and in Eliza's case, by herself. Even her father, who realized her worth, was open to error. Lucas had proposed some profitable unions in 1740, when Eliza was eighteen, but the candidates were unattractive. Mr. L., a rejected nominee, was a case in point. "I must beg the favour of you to pay my compliments to the old Gentleman for his Generosity," she wrote to Lucas, ". . . and beg leave to say to you that all the riches of Peru and Chili put together if he had them, could not purchase a sufficient esteem for him to make him my husband." Eliza reconciled defiance with deference by insisting that the interests of father and daughter were mutual and complementary. "I am well aware you would not . . . make me a Sacrifice to Wealth," she told George Lucas, "and I am as certain I would indulge no passion that had not your approbation."

An acceptable passion soon evolved. In 1744, Charles Pinckney, much admired by Eliza, became suddenly available. The first Mrs. Pinckney, long sick and ailing, had finally died of an enlarged spleen. At this point, George Lucas was planning to move his family back to Antigua, so time was short. Within a few months, before Eliza could be swept away to the Caribbean, her engagement was announced. Pinckney, now forty-five and a childless widower, could only be considered an excellent catch. Educated in England, he was the first lawyer in South Carolina and a very successful one. A wealthy planter, he had seven plantations, some of them huge, and a beautiful town house on the Charleston waterfront. He was also politically prominent and a member of the Governor's Council. Pinckney more than fulfilled the ambitions of Eliza and George Lucas alike.

That Charles was no beauty was clear. The only portrait, one cherished by Eliza, showed him in repose, as was the vogue of the day, wearing a nightcap (he was bald) and afflicted by a double chin. But he was very intelligent and extremely personable, as Eliza had good reason to know. During the five years in which they were friends, she had been a constant visitor at the Pinckneys'. Ingratiating herself with them and their relatives, she had waged a campaign of flattery and attention. This was directed especially at Charles, who was willingly enmeshed in Eliza's net of praise and obligation. She borrowed books, involved him in literary discussions, encumbered him with messages for his wife and nieces, and probably declared her affection with unseemly ardor. In one oblique letter, she promised to heed the bounds of reason and religion and never to lose control again. The opportunity for marriage evoked her rapture. "I can indeed tell you that I have the highest esteem and affection imaginable for you," she wrote to Charles on their engagement, "that next to Him that formed it, my heart is intirely at your disposal."

A barrage of ecstatic letters flew forth at once to family and friends all over the Empire. Charles Pinckney, Eliza told her girlhood companions in England, was "a Gentleman of the Law and one of His Majesty's Council." He was also rationality and moderation personified, for she praised "his good Sense and Judgment, his extraordinary good nature and evenness of temper." With consummate skill, Eliza wrote too to the relatives of the first Mrs. Pinckney. But her major diplomatic achievement was her letter to her father, now battling the French in the Caribbean. Again, she suggested their mutual interest, asserted her will, and stressed her deference. She knew, she told George Lucas, "that it must be a great satisfaction to you as well as to myself, to know that I have put myself in the hands of a man of honour. . . . I thought it prudent, as well as infinitely agreeable to me to accept the offer; and I shall make it the whole Study of my Life to fix that esteem and affection Mr. Pinckney has professed for me, and consequently be more worthily your daughter."

The web was now more firmly knit. Lucas knew Pinckney from Carolina and admired his prestige. He included all of the indigo lands in Eliza's dowry and sent her advice on the married state. She should, as a wife, control the dominance she had previously exerted as daughter and planter. Eliza obligingly promised not to "act out of my proper province" or to "invade Mr. Pinckney's." Still, she continued to manage the Lucas lands and pursue her work with indigo, now on the verge of success. Her father, moreover, could not restrain himself from urging her on to new ventures. Still searching for staples, he exhorted Eliza to start experiments with flax and hemp and, in his usual enterprising manner, inundated her with instructions and assistance. From Antigua, he sent indentured servants who could weave and spin, advised her to arrange for construction of a wheel and looms, and suggested she have "a sensible Negro woman or two" trained to use them. Eliza also pursued her own experiments at Belmont, the Pinckney plantation, where she attempted to cultivate silk. She imported mulberry bushes and silkworm eggs, but the silk was never very profitable. However, it served a purpose. Slaves who could not do other work could be employed with winding and reeling, and so be saved from idleness.

Eliza's nurturant role was not confined to worms, crops, and the "vegitable world." In 1746, Charles Cotesworth was born, and his ambitious parents taught him his letters with special blocks before he could speak. Charles Cotesworth could read at three. But while he was learning the alphabet, tragic news arrived from the Indies. During the War of the Austrian Succession, George Lucas had been captured by the French and had died in enemy hands. Charles hid the letter relaying this news, but Eliza, then pregnant, found it and collapsed. Her father's death precipitated the premature birth and death of a second son and also induced the only depression of her life. Refusing to communicate with anyone— her mother, sister, brothers, or the Boddicotts—Eliza closed her correspondence and "letter book" for five years. During this time, two more children were born, Harriott in 1748 and Thomas in 1750.

When the children were small, Eliza assessed her commitments and goals. Each year on her birthday, she made a list of resolutions and memorized them, striving not for angelic perfection, like poor Mary Chardon, but a worldly equivalent. The resolutions were both a guide to conduct and a tribute to the ideals of George Lucas. Eliza vowed "To govern my passions, to endeavor constantly to subdue every vice and improve in every virtue . . . humility, charity, etc. etc." Throughout, she strove for harmony, self-control, and moderation. She was going to balance frugality and generosity, to avoid extravagance on the one hand and covetousness on the other, "to endeavor after a due medium." She would also perfect her relations to others, as wife, mother, daughter, sister, mistress, friend, and "universal lover of all mankind." The chief of these aims was to be a good companion to Charles Pinckney, "to contribute all in my power to the good of his Soul and to the peace and satisfaction of his mind," as well as to care for his health, interests, reputation, and children. As a mother, she intended "to set the children a good example, to give them advice, to carefully root out the first appearings and budings of vice, and to instill piety, Virtue, and true religion in them." The fulfillment of these vows was to occupy her life.

While Eliza pursued moderation and virtue, the economy thrived and so did the career of Charles Pinckney. In 1752, he was chosen chief justice of the colony by the governor; but the appointment never received royal confirmation. In fact, someone else, with better English connections, was given the job. The furious Pinckneys referred to Charles, forever after, as "the Chief Justice." But meanwhile a new opportunity arose. Charles was appointed commissioner of the colony, a middleman between the governor and legislature in Carolina and the Board of Trade in London. Still smarting over the chief justice debacle, the Pinckneys threw themselves into the new mission and set off for England with their three small children. This was a chance not only for Charles to further his career but for the boys to receive an English education, which was what their father intended for them anyway. It was also a chance for Eliza to resume old friendships. And finally, it enabled her to extend her web of contacts and connections in the heart of the Empire.

At this she excelled, at least for six years. But once again imperial conflict changed the family's plans. In 1758, threatened by the onset of the French and Indian War, Charles Pinckney decided to return to America, sell the Carolina property, and move somewhere safer. The Pinckneys left their boys at school in England under the charge of the Evance family, who served as guardians just as the Boddicotts had done for the Lucas children. Charles and Eliza then set off, with Harriott in tow, planning to be gone for two years. They never returned. Hardly a month in Carolina, Charles contracted malaria and died a few weeks later, in July 1758. "I have a tale to tell that will pierce your infant hearts," Eliza wrote to her sons in August. "You have mett, my children, with the greatest loss you could meet on earth your dear Father the best and most valuable of parents is no more." The boys were not the only ones to hear from Eliza. While her father's death had immobilized her for years, her husband's death was a spur to action. She was now responsible for the Pinckney future and reputation, at home and abroad.

A typical letter went off to Antigua. "The greatest of human evils has befallen me," Eliza told her mother and Polly before presenting her eulogy to Charles. Her only interest now, she announced, was her offspring. "Grant God that I may spend my whole future life in their Service and show my affection and gratitude to their father by my care of these precious remains of him." An onslaught of letters followed, week after week, to all the family's friends and contacts in Carolina, Antigua, and England. In each, Eliza announced the tragedy, enumerated Pinckney's virtues, and described the children's loss. Even the slaves were overcome with grief on their behalf, she revealed, "so strong did natural affection to their offspring work in these poor creatures." She also assessed the family plight.

This plight was extreme. Not only was Eliza widowed at thirty-six, but the separation from her sons was to last much longer than she ever anticipated. She was not to see the boys for fourteen years. They had to remain in England for their education, as Pinckney would have wished. Eliza could hardly disagree. Her own English education, she felt, was the most valuable gift her father had ever given her. Meanwhile, the war in Europe prevented her from joining them. Moreover, she was now in charge of all of Pinckney's extensive property and several hundred slaves. While the Pinckneys had been in England, the temporary caretakers, Charles's relatives, had hired incompetent overseers, and all the lands had gone to ruin. Eliza's job was now even greater than that she had assumed as a girl. The plantations had to be reorganized, new overseers hired, crops planted, and directions sent off to her London agent. Widowhood also left her in control of the children, and once again, her teenage experience was a great advantage.

By this juncture, all of the family of Eliza's youth was dead or dying. The Boddicotts had died in the early 1750s and the Lucas tribe soon after: Thomas in 1756, Anne in 1759, and George in 1760. The last letter to Polly went off in 1758. Eliza's efforts now centered on Harriott at home and the boys abroad, "the darlings of my heart, the subjects of my daily thoughts and nightly dreams," as she told a friend in England. Her career as a mother was, like her girlhood, an extremely well-documented one: it was carried out largely by correspondence. For over a decade, Eliza sent a barrage of letters to Charles and Tom and wove about them her intricate web of obligation and love. The boys were inundated with reminders and praise, affection and restraints. All she wanted, Eliza kept telling them (on the one hand) was to contribute to their advantage. But as she constantly wrote (on the other), all of her happiness depended on them. What Eliza Pinckney developed was a system of nurturance by remote control.

Her major goals were to inculcate the proper standards of virtue and piety, to impress the boys with their obligations to their parents and therefore the importance of their every act, and to make sure they fulfilled their father's expectations. While binding them irrevocably to the family goals, she also forged a chain of command that began with herself. The Pinckneys believed in a sort of moral primogeniture. If the character of the older son was perfected, the younger could imitate him. Therefore, while little Tom was urged to write, praised for his script, and showered with love, Charles Cotesworth, the older, bore the brunt of responsibility. "I will do all that I can," Eliza told him, "but on you, all must depend." Dangers to morals were ever present, just as they had been when her brothers were growing up in the 1740s. These dangers became crucial when Charles went off to public school at Westminster, a step that all Eliza's friends advised. He was now surrounded by the lures of a great city and the prospect of undesirable companions. "The morrals of Youth are little taken of" at public schools, Eliza wrote, but she met this hazard in her customary way. "I have so good an opinion of your sobriety and modesty," she told her son, ". . . that I may venture to trust you to Westminster, without running any risk of what must be fatal to me as well, as to your self, [viz.] corrupt principles."

Such warnings were not unique to Eliza. Other eighteenth-century mothers with similar goals, such as Abigail Adams and Mercy Warren, later sent the same sort of missives to sons at school abroad. But Eliza's predicament was extreme. Having lived in England for many years, she was well aware of the dangers to youth in foreign climes. One young man she had known, for instance, the son of important Carolinians, had neglected his study of law and become instead a complete degenerate. He was almost thrown into debtors' prison and was rescued only by his father's connections. The Pinckney boys, however, had no father to provide an example or protect their interests. This obligation fell squarely on Charles Cotesworth, and Eliza constantly reinforced it. "You must know the welfare of a whole family depends in great measure on the progress you make in Morral Virtue, religion, and learning," she told him. Fortunately Charles was up to the task. When he had finished Westminster and Oxford and begun his study of law, Eliza assured her son that he had lived to be twenty-three years old "without offending me once." They had not seen each other since he was ten.

But Eliza did not depend on Charles alone. She also had an endless web of English connections, a backup system of parental control. One mainstay of this system was her agent, George Morly, who covered her expenses and transacted all her business in England. Another was Mrs. Evance, the guardian, who was always on call. Eliza also utilized a succession of headmasters, Pinckney's associates, and her own innumerable friends. These, variously, visited the boys, took them in during school vacations, and reported back to Carolina. And to them Eliza sent off a steady stream of inquiries, directions, and gifts. Agent Morly received crates of turtles and ducks to distribute to Eliza's friends, although most of these creatures died en route. Headmaster Gerrard was sent a shipment of rice, which the boys preferred to bread, said Eliza. Dr. Kirkpatrick was thanked for his attention and low fees. Everyone was asked for advice about fencing lessons or changes of school. And all were inundated with Eliza's distinctive combination of gratitude, flattery, and new assignments.

These were extended even to strangers. When Charles and Tom entered school at Kensington, Eliza dispensed an impressive letter to headmaster Longmore, explaining the Pinckney heritage and imposing on him the awesome responsibility of parenting her sons. He alone was now responsible, she announced, for Pinckney morals, for the family future, and for "forming their tender minds to early habits of Virtue and Piety." But the brunt of the work fell on Mrs. Evance, whom Eliza implored for constant reports. "Pray let me hear as often as possible how they do, how they look, whether they grow, and say as much as you can about them," Eliza wrote. Mrs. Evance also received more onerous assignments. In 1760, Eliza dispatched the portrait of Pinckney-in-nightcap, which had to be framed and hung in the Evance parlor so the boys could see it during vacations. This was followed shortly, in a burst of either reverence or frugality, by all of Pinckney's clothes. Mrs. Evance was to have them altered for the boys, who were expected, most literally, to fill their father's place.

While the boys were in England, Eliza devoted herself to plantation business and nurturing Harriott. "I have an excellent soil to work upon," she wrote to a friend. And this was correct. Harriott began to follow in her mother's footsteps with uncanny precision. At nineteen she married Daniel Horry, then aged thirty-five. Like Charles Pinckney, Horry was a planter, lawyer, and childless widower, English-trained and very rich. Harriott moved to Hampton, his major plantation, and Eliza extended the chain of interdependent relationships. "If she makes you happy, I am content," she wrote to Horry from Charleston.

In the early 1770s, affairs of empire once again reshaped the family. When conflict between England and the American colonies brewed, both sons returned. Charles Cotesworth, who had finished studying law, was the first to arrive. Tom, who had also studied law, came soon after, following a stint at a French military academy. Both had been transformed from English students to American rebels. While they were in England, young Americans there had vigorously protested English decrees, beginning with the Stamp Act in 1765. At Oxford, in fact, Tom had been known as "the little rebel." Pinckney traditions also contributed to their politics. One component was the insulting "Chief Justice" episode of 1752. Another was Charles Pinckney's will, a document that covered all contingencies. Here Pinckney instructed his oldest son to devote his life to the cause of liberty and never to favor "wrong, oppression, or tyranny of any sort, public or private." Once her sons announced their allegiance to the colonies, Eliza, following their initiative (or so she claimed), became a rebel too.

During the war, her losses were severe, both personally and financially. Her father had been a British officer, in fact a royal governor. Her English friends had married generals, officials, and peers. Her formative years had been spent in England, where her friends and associates still lived. The Revolution shattered the transatlantic web of connections she had so carefully created and also damaged her property at home. When Charleston was besieged, Eliza lost much of her income. Crops were not grown, slaves did not work, livestock was appropriated, and her wood was cut down for British garrisons. Houses she rented were taken over by soldiers, plantations she leased were overrun, and her slaves in town were impressed into labor. But when Eliza assessed the impact of the war, its positive benefits outweighed her losses. First, Charles and Tom distinguished themselves as rebel soldiers. As she wrote to Tom when he was wounded, "While I have such children, dare I think my lot hard?" There was also another, less obvious benefit for women like herself who had experienced "great reverse of fortune" during the war. Before the Revolution, as Eliza saw it, she was well on her way to becoming a southern aristocrat. But the War for Independence and the losses she suffered had rescued her from this life of excess. After the Revolution, she was able to enjoy "contentment in mediocrity, and moderation in prosperity."

For the rest of her life, Eliza was able to pursue the goal of moderation and enjoy the success of her children. By the end of the decade, both of her sons had married well. Charles Cotesworth married Sally Middleton, the descendant of an early governor, in 1773. Sally's father owned twenty plantations and 800 slaves. In 1779, Thomas married Betsey Motte, and when she died, he married her sister. Harriott, soon widowed, was now in control of substantial property and became a planter. Eliza moved in with Harriott at Hampton and devoted herself to her grandchildren. Young Harriott and Daniel Horry could now be brought up in the Pinckney mold. Daniel, it turned out, was a difficult case, and as he grew older, Eliza's letters were full of reprimands ("An idle man is a burthen to society and himself.") She valiantly tried to weave around him the skillful web of obligation and affection that had worked so well with her own children. "Be assured, my dear Daniel," she told the boy, "No pleasure can equal that which a mother feels when she knows her children have acted their part well through life, and when she sees them happy in the consciousness of having done so." She only hoped that Harriott might have such joy, that Daniel would imitate his worthy uncles, that his conduct "in publick and private life may emulate the example they have set you."

Their example was increasingly difficult to emulate. After the war, Eliza's sons forged ahead in state and national politics. Best of all, they both became exemplars of the type of moderation Eliza hoped to develop in Daniel. From the time they were young, she had often warned her sons that the "heat of temper" usually produced "mischief and misfortune." This advice had borne political fruit. Charles and Tom had not become radical extremists, even during the stress of rebellion, but virtuous statesmen of moderate stripe. "Enthusiasm" had never been their style. And their stance had won them influence and prestige. "Now the power is in their hand," Eliza told Daniel. "Their reason moderates the violence." Moderation had also served her well. It enabled her to enjoy old age, a period of "subdued passions," harmony, and tranquillity. "I regret no pleasure that I can't enjoy, and I enjoy some that I could not have had at an earlier season," Eliza wrote to a friend. The primary pleasure was that of seeing her children succeed.

Soon after Washington's gratifying visit, Eliza, now dying of cancer, went to Philadelphia for medical help. Since Congress was in session, officials and their wives provided an endless parade of visitors. When Eliza died in Philadelphia in 1793, Harriott was with her although her prominent sons were far away. Tom was minister to England, and Charles Cotesworth was practicing law in Charleston. But Washington, at his own request, served as pallbearer at Eliza's funeral. The President was a final substitute, in the illustrious pattern of the Boddicotts and the Evances.

Eliza Pinckney's success as a parent soon bore results in the new republic. During the next decade, her sons went on to diplomatic triumph. After serving as minister to England, Tom negotiated a treaty with Spain that established the Florida boundary and provided for free navigation of the Mississippi. Two years later, in 1797, Charles Cotesworth served as the United States' commissioner to France and impressed his countrymen with American virtue, in the XYZ affair. ("No! No! Not a sixpence!" Pinckney was said to have told French agents who demanded American loans and bribes.) Later, both were appointed U.S. generals and both became Federalist presidential candidates. Besides their politics, the Pinckney sons seemed to have inherited other Lucas-Pinckney proclivities. Tom, for instance, became an experimental planter like Eliza. He developed a system of dikes to grow rice on vast marshlands inherited by his second wife.

Eliza's daughter, Harriott Horry, followed her example. Married just over a decade, Harriott spent the rest of her life as a widow and, like Eliza, was an excellent planter and businesswoman. She personally supervised her holdings, from Hampton, and earned a large income from rice cultivation. Her children's careers were also significant. The recalcitrant Daniel, to whom Eliza devoted so much attention, may have been unable to meet her standards. He escaped entirely and settled in France. But Eliza's granddaughter, young Harriott Horry, married a son of Governor John Rutledge, a longtime Pinckney associate, and had numerous descendants. One devoted her efforts to a biography of Eliza, published in 1896. According to Harriott Horry Rutledge Ravenel, Eliza Pinckney's achievements had political significance. Eliza had shown how colonial women fulfilled a great, if unexpected, responsibility: "to fit themselves and their sons to meet the coming change (self-government) in law and soberness, not in riot and anarchy, as did the unhappy women of the French Revolution." Once again, Pinckney moderation had taken on a political hue.

While Eliza Pinckney's career as parent and patriot was often reshaped by affairs of the world, from imperial wars to Federalist politics, its rhythm was set by private landmarks and personal relationships. In all of her roles—daughter and sister, wife and mother, widow and matriarch—Eliza had served as custodian and transmitter of property and values. The property, whether her father's or her husband's, was considerable. It determined her status and associates, life-style and authority. As planter and proprietor, Eliza improved it in order to hand it down to her sons.

But property was not all they inherited. Of equal importance were the virtues she promoted—reason, moderation, self-control—which molded their characters and shaped their politics. These were virtues to which both men and women could aspire; indeed, self-control and moderation had been Eliza's lifelong themes. As she wrote to her brother in 1740, "to live agreeably to the dictates of reason and religion, to keep a strict guard over not only our action, but our very thoughts before they ripen into action, to be active in every good word and work, must produce a peace and calmness of mind beyond expression." The way her children absorbed such ideals, and transformed them into political postures, would have gratified George Lucas—ambitious soldier, enterprising imperialist, and the most "indulgent" of parents.

4

THE EIGHTEENTH CENTURY: THE EVE OF MODERNITY

Eliza Pinckney hardly typified women in the eighteenth-century colonies. On the contrary, she was on the frontier of progress. Wealthy, literate, and cosmopolitan, she had unusual opportunity to shape the course of her own destiny. By adopting "rational" attitudes, keeping her "letter book," supervising her sons' upbringing, shaping their values, and insisting on their "virtue" and "piety," Eliza Pinckney assumed an extremely modern role, far in advance of most of her contemporaries. Her distinctive experience, however, is relevant to the course of women's history. During the second half of the eighteenth century, women were affected by a network of changes that slowly transformed their remote, insular, traditional society.

The inroads made by modern trends were not only gradual but selective and uneven. Traditional roles, for men and women, constantly re-emerged along the shifting frontier, in the rural backwater, and on the family farm, where over 90 percent of Americans lived. Modernity encroached in cities and towns on the eastern seaboard, spurred by the rise of a mercantile, propertied elite—as well represented by the English-educated, Charleston-based Pinckneys as by their northern counterparts. This privileged class, distinguished from neighbors with less wealth and culture, served as a vanguard of innovation. During the post-Revolutionary decades, many of the values and ideals it transmitted began to gain a larger audience.

The rise of class was only one way in which eighteenth-century society became more settled, stable, and in many ways more like England. As the seventeenth-century garrison mentality grew obsolete, enterprising colonists were able to shift their energies from mere survival to commercial profit. By the end of the century, the communal ethos of the earliest settlements had been replaced by a competitive one. The expanding population was also in flux. Unbalanced sex ratios, characteristic of the early frontier, began to fade or even vanish in the east, although they reappeared in more remote regions, where new communities were carved out. Like class distinctions, economic change and shifting sex ratios impinged on women's lives by altering, for instance, their domestic work and marital options.

For much of the eighteenth century, however, women remained in a traditional world of their own, relatively insulated from their changing environment. As dependent family members, most eighteenth-century women had little opportunity to function in either family or society as autonomous individuals. Unlike Eliza Pinckney, they had little control over the course of their own destinies and few contacts beyond the household. Whereas men might gather in both informal institutions such as taverns and formal ones such as colonial assemblies, women had no institutional involvements beyond family and church. They were rarely able to adopt "modern" attitudes—such as ambition, achievement, risk—as did those men who negotiated transatlantic shipments of lumber, tobacco, and slaves, or cut the salaries of royal governors in provincial legislatures, or surveyed tracts in remote woodlands for future speculation. Of course, not all men were able to adopt such attitudes either. But women were still in a world apart. Home-based, child-bound, and limited by law, they remained subordinate in private life and marginal in public life.

The era of the American Revolution provided a turning point in women's history. The Revolution did not destroy women's separate realm of life but, rather, threw it into convulsions. During the war years, women became involved, unavoidably, in the turmoil and conflict of public events. Called on to provide public services as well as to handle enlarged domestic responsibilities, women began to express themselves politically, sometimes in groups, often as individuals. Wives and housekeepers suddenly became boycotters and camp followers, petitioners and fund raisers, loyalists and patriots. Whether women were actually capable of taking a political stance, however, remained a moot point throughout the war. They could, of course, be convicted of treason. But even if praised for patriotism, a woman was not considered a citizen. The newly independent states recognized that married women were femes coverts, not autonomous beings, and therefore unable to voice any political will.

After the Revolution, women were only the most indirect beneficiaries of "independence." They gained no new legal codes or access to political life. By increasing men's political rights, the Revolution increased the extent of female exclusion. But during the first decades of nationhood, social changes that had been filtering into colonial society, especially into its upper echelons, began to emerge on a larger scale. The patriarchal family of the seventeenth century, with absolute power residing in the male "head," started to be replaced by a new type of family that was more private, more affectionate, and less authoritarian. Within the family, women and children began to assume enhanced roles as distinctive individuals. During the early days of the new republic, finally, women began to profit from a new image, a change in the way they regarded themselves and were regarded by others.

By 1800, some American women assumed a novel, distinctive cultural role. The "new woman" of the turn of the century (many of whose qualities had been exemplified by Eliza Pinckney considerably earlier) was no longer considered morally suspect, mentally dim, or potentially dangerous to those around her. She was no longer liable to be viewed as a loud-mouthed shrew, a meddling inter-loper, or a devil's accomplice, whose only salvation lay in silence, industry, and obedience. Rather, she might now be considered a rational individual and even a quasi-autonomous one—within the family circle. Here at home, she had been promoted from a "necessary good" to a custodian of values. In this role, she was capable of transmitting ideas, having a positive influence on her children, and playing a role in society at large.

Wives and Widows

For most of the eighteenth century, while modern impulses made selective inroads in colonial society, the role of women—like that of most farmers, back-woodsmen, servants, slaves, and artisans—lagged behind, locked into a tradi-tional mold. Whatever her locale or station in society, the contours of a woman's life were defined by her dependent role within the family. Her wealth and status depended on that of the men to whom she was related. Although she might be, through birth or marriage, the beneficiary of a great deal of property—as were Eliza Pinckney, Harriott Horry, and the inordinately rich Sally Middleton—she was far more likely to belong to a family of modest means and to spend her life on a family farm. Here her labor continued to be vital to family enterprise, although not necessarily highly valued in her own view or that of others. In either case, her career was most likely to be shaped not by her own achievements but by her relations to men and by the changing shape of her family, as its members were born, married, and died.

These were circumstances over which she had no control, with one major, all-important exception. This was her own marriage—a step so momentous it was rarely made without the advice and consent of parents, relatives, and friends. Acceptance of a proposal was the most significant decision to which she would ever contribute, perhaps the sole instance in which her judgment carried weight, and often the only occasion on which modern attitudes—such as risk or indi-vidualism—came within grasp. During the eighteenth century, daughters' lev-erage over their own marriage arrangements increased. Beyond this decisive moment, however, autonomy—the ability to shape her own destiny—usually remained beyond a woman's reach.

She had no control over the family locale, status, or property. Nor, in most cases, could she control the property she had brought with her to the marriage— as wives of loyalists such as Grace Galloway discovered during the Revolution, when property they had inherited was confiscated because of their husbands' political views. Although the eighteenth-century woman commonly expected to spend most if not all of her adult life bearing children and taking care of them, she had no legal control over her children—a serious disadvantage in the event that her marriage was a disaster. And even under the most favorable of circum-stances, she had no control over the number of children she bore, except by prolonging the nursing of one, which was likely to delay the arrival of the next, or by extended stays at a relative's home. Nor could she regulate the amount of her time that would be devoted to her children's upbringing. "When I had but one child my hands were tied," confided Esther Burr, wife of the president of the College of New Jersey to her friend Sally Prince in 1756, after the birth of her second child, Aaron, "but now that I am tied hand and foot how I shall get along when I have ½ dozen or 10 children I can't devise."

If inability to control fertility helped to lock women into traditional roles, so did lack of literacy. Very few girls had the advantage of a few years in school, as did Polly Lucas in Charleston or Eliza Lucas in England. Throughout the century, women's ability to read, and especially to write, consistently lagged behind that of men. Reading and writing, when taught at all, were taught separately; even women who learned to read, usually at home, did not necessarily learn how to write. Only a portion of late-eighteenth-century women could write their names on wills, for instance, and still fewer could write a coherent letter. Among New England colonists, whose literacy exceeded that of counterparts in other colonies, gender limited transmission of skills. Viewed as a craft and a vocational skill, writing was taught primarily by men and required mainly of boys. In Massachusetts in 1789, under half of the women were minimally literate, as opposed to about 90 percent of the men. Women elsewhere fared no better. Since communication through the written word became steadily more important, women's lagging literacy put them at a disadvantage. Besides their paucity of schooling and frequent inability to read or write, women were also confined to traditional roles, as men were not, by their common vocation, domestic work.

Whether the eighteenth-century woman lived in a bustling seaport or in the backwoods, whether she was married to a merchant or a farmer, she managed a household, where she was likely to work for all of her life. Traditionally, the household work of wives and daughters was a myriad of repetitive tasks, which though varied were continual. Washing, ironing, cooking, baking, sewing, knitting, preserving food, preparing food, whitewashing walls—the housekeeper spent her days carrying out an endless sequence of responsibilities, some seasonal, most perpetual. Her daughters were in training for the same role. When Abigail Foote, a Connecticut girl, recounted a day's activity in 1775, she captured both the tedium and the timelessness of household work in its typical locale, the family farm:

> Fix'd gown for Prude—mend Mother's Riding-hood—Spun short thread . . . carded two—spun linen—Worked on Cheesebasket, Hatchel'd flax with Hannah . . . Pleated and ironed—Read Sermon of Dodridge's—Spooled a piece—Milked the cows—Spun linen, did 50 knots—Made a Broom of Guinea wheat straw,
> —Spun thread to whiten—Set a Red dye . . . corded two pounds of white wool. . . . Spun Harness twine—scoured the pewter.

But domestic work began to change in some ways too. The eighteenth century brought new distinctions in the types of work women did at home, and the types of homes within which they worked. The frontier of housewifery was a new brick house in an eastern town, rather than a two-room cabin in a newly carved out settlement.

By midcentury, the urban housewife had more opportunity to buy some of the things her family needed—notably cloth and clothing items—than did her rural counterpart or less prosperous neighbor. In seaport cities and thriving market towns, a new dynamic was at work within the home. When goods were available for purchase, household production decreased as wealth and privilege rose. Specifically, spinning might be replaced by buying. The housewife's new role as purchaser was evident in the diary of Mary Vial Holyoke, a well-off Boston woman, in the 1760s. Like all housekeepers, Mary Holyoke was constantly busy with domestic routines. She preserved food, produced soap, stitched clothes, scoured rooms, maintained a garden, and even raised hens, ducks, and pigs. But she did not spin. And she was able to buy tea, milk, butter, candles, sheets, cloth, coats, and gowns.

Once urban women such as Mary Holyoke became able to purchase such

Although many eighteenth-century women learned to spin, only a few were trained at the loom. The skilled housewife in this primitive painting is weaving an elaborate pattern into her fabric. Her spinning wheel stands in its customary place, by the hearth. (*"At the Loom," anonymous, around 1795. Smithsonian Institute, Archives of American Art. Selected by Mary Beth Norton for Liberty's Daughters, Boston, 1980, p. 16*)

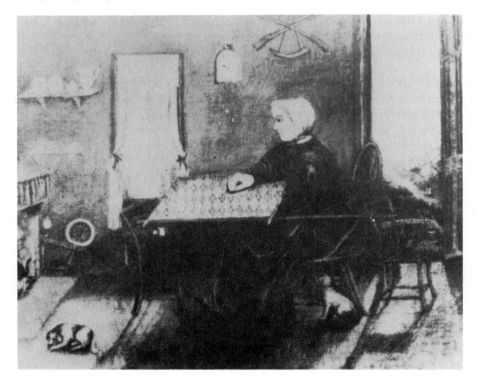

items, the seventeenth-century mode of housewifery symbolized by the wheel became increasingly a badge of lower status. In rural areas, however, wives and daughters continued to be surrounded by reels, spools, and knots of flax. Comparable distinctions appeared in the South. Mistresses of large plantations had to assume managerial roles, supervising the slaves who did household tasks—sometimes a large work force—and directing food and clothing production for the whole plantation. Slaveless neighbors, meanwhile, continued to milk cows, tend churns, and spin thread themselves.

Just as women could not control the encroachment of class distinctions or determine the nature of their domestic work, they had no control over the way their status might suddenly change, most commonly through the death of a husband. The eighteenth-century widow, who gained legal rights her married sister lacked, was also affected by changes in the class structure and economy. Although many widows may have felt, when bereaved, like "a walking Ghost"— as Eliza Pinckney did—few were able to assume the managerial roles taken on by Eliza or by Harriott Horry (a widow for virtually all of her adult life), both of whom chose not to remarry. Nor were they likely to be as young as these wealthy southern daughters who had married even wealthier older men. In all the colonies, a growing number of widows were able to live off holdings they inherited (as did Eliza Pinckney, by renting out plantations), but this was hardly the typical situation.

By midcentury in eastern Massachusetts, always in the forefront of social change, the widow was likely to inherit, by will or dower right, a third of her husband's estate. This meant, in most cases, a corner of the farmhouse in which she lived (perhaps now occupied by one of her grown children), the use of a well, a few cows, and a small plot of land, from which it was difficult or impossible to reap an income. She was also likely to remain single, not necessarily out of choice. The age of widows was rising; Massachusetts widows now tended to be middle-aged or older and therefore less marriageable. In addition, more densely settled eastern regions were constantly losing younger men who wanted land and moved away. These regions were likely to have an oversupply of unmarried women. Shifting sex ratios made the marriage market more competitive even for younger women, and the possibility of remarriage for middle-aged widows quite remote. For instance, in one eighteenth-century Massachusetts town, Hingham, about 14 percent of women who were widowed in their forties and fifties had remarried in the decades before 1760, but only 5 percent afterward. Younger women, widowed in their twenties and thirties, fared somewhat better in the marriage market, 57 percent remarrying before 1760 and 35 percent afterward. Nonetheless, in both cases chances of finding a new husband dwindled decade by decade. The widow was therefore increasingly likely to fall into the category of family or community dependent. Or if young enough, she might enter the ranks of working women, especially if she lived in a town or city or was able to move to one.

Although the proportion of self-supporting working widows (and, increasingly, spinsters) in the eighteenth century never exceeded 10 percent of the adult female population and was in most cases far less, they congregated in towns and cities. In Boston, as early as the 1740s, 13 percent of the 16,000 residents were widows, "almost all of them poor," according to the town's records. And in Boston as in other cities, these femes soles were likely to be active in business and trade. Such activism was in part a legacy of the past, a by-product of a labor-scarce society. But it also reflected, on a limited scale, the commercial spirit that pervaded eighteenth-century life. And it was visible, in a way that women's domestic work was not, through newspaper advertisements that proffered the services of seamstresses and starchmakers, boardinghouses and food shops.

As in the seventeenth century, some working widows managed trades inherited from their husbands, at least until sons could replace them, and were therefore found in every type of occupation—including that of mortician, blacksmith, and carpenter. But most working women were employed in trades connected to household production and in ventures they started themselves, usually catering to women clients. In Baltimore, 8 percent of the city's households were headed by women in 1796, and two-thirds of these women were widows, less than half of whom worked to support themselves. The rest were spinsters, almost all of whom worked. Although their number included the occasional printer, mill owner, and land speculator—vocations invariably inherited by widows—most of Baltimore's working women, like those elsewhere, entered the wide array of trades stemming from domestic work. And these became more specialized in nature. Women were not only seamstresses and laundresses but dyers, starchers, lacemakers, and mantua makers. As shop proprietresses, they dealt in china, groceries, pastries, dry goods, millinery, and hardware. As in other cities, they ran inns, boardinghouses, coffeehouses, and taverns. By now, in most towns, women held a majority of the liquor licenses. No licenses were needed to run "dame schools," attended by small children, or small boarding schools, where girls could learn drawing, writing, and needlework, or to sell homemade cosmetics or medicines, or to offer one's services as midwife, wet-nurse, or domestic worker. Married women who pursued vocations, like busy midwife Martha Ballard of Maine, may have depended on a retinue of female assistants. Ballard, who delivered some thirty to forty babies a year, utilized the services of her teenage daughters and later a succession of hired girls to help her with household tasks.

Two Boston shopkeepers of the late eighteenth century illustrate contrasting approaches, traditional and modern, to careers in trade. Benjamin Franklin's younger sister, Jane Mecom, was the last of her mother's ten children and the seventeenth of her father's, a soap and candle maker. She married a saddler at fifteen and became a mother of twelve children, most of whom died before maturity and the rest soon thereafter. After her husband became an invalid, unable to support the remnants of their brood, Jane Mecom took in boarders, a move of desperation more than enterprise. "Sorrows," she told Franklin, "roll upon me like the waters of the sea." When widowed, Jane Mecom opened a small millinery shop, with assistance from her brother, and imported fabric, ribbon, laces, and caps until imports were cut off by the Revolution. Since none of her children survived her, she spent her old age in relatives' homes, feeling like a "vagrant."

While Jane Mecom was victimized by successive disasters, domestic and commercial, the experience of Elizabeth Murray was characterized by increasing autonomy, influence, and an ability to manipulate her environment. An English emigrant, widowed when young, Elizabeth Murray ran a profitable millinery and cloth business, and converted her economic success into what she called "a spirit of independence." This was revealed in the increasingly stringent antenuptial contracts she signed with the last two of her three husbands and in the disposition of her estate, which she left to nieces whose upbringing and education she had supervised.

If Elizabeth Murray, like Eliza Pinckney, was able to affect her destiny and influence others, this was more the exception than the rule in the eighteenth century. Most women's lives were circumscribed by a series of barriers. Autonomy was precluded not only by a dependent role at home but by limited notions of women's capacities. Before the Revolution, the ideology of woman's "place" was rarely discussed. Since it was uncontroversial and unchallenged, there was little need to define or defend its perimeters. Rather, it rested on common assumptions that were widely shared by men and women alike.

Character and Capacity

During the eighteenth century, no one would deny that sex had an impact on character and capacity or that being female encompassed a spectrum of distinctive characteristics. A crucial distinction between the sexes was that "rationality" was believed to be in short supply among women. This belief was reflected even in the rhetoric of the day, which was loaded in favor of men. Like her contemporaries, Eliza Pinckney viewed "reason" as a masculine quality, although clearly one to which women might aspire, as she demonstrated herself. As a rational person, Eliza laid claim to what was called a "masculine mind," which meant intelligence. Similarly, she deplored activities, in men or women, that tended to "effeminate" the mind—that is, to make one vain, capricious, fickle, foolish, frivolous, or extravagant.

Throughout most of the century, in language and in life, femininity was defined by and associated with a core of inherent defects and disabilities. These defects appeared in popular advice tracts, published in England but reprinted in the colonies. The role of reason as a dividing line between the sexes was clearly set forth in Lord Halifax's *Advice to a Daughter* (1688), an English import with colonial sales throughout the century. Halifax conveyed a harsh view of women's capacities. "There is inequality in the sexes," he posited, "and . . . for the economy of the world, the men who were to be the law givers, had the larger share of reason bestowed upon them, by which means your sex is better prepared for the compliance that is necessary for the better performance of those duties which appear to be most properly assigned to it."

In Halifax's view of women's roles, "compliance"—a corollary of defective reason—was the crucial word. The woman who was pliable, flexible, patient, submissive, and resigned would be able to adapt to whatever type of husband she happened to get, even if he were a drunk, a scoundrel, or simply repellent. Aptitude for "compliance" was at once an innate trait and one that daughters and wives would do well to develop. By midcentury, an array of compensatory virtues had been added to the basic list of female defects and disabilities. In *A Father's Legacy to his Daughter,* a popular tract published in the 1770s, Dr. John Gregory attributed to women "softness and sensibility of heart." He also recommended cultivation of qualities that would gain men's affection and protection. Toward this end, a woman ought to be modest, cheerful, timid, delicate, tender, affectionate, graceful, and sympathetic. Innate or acquired, the "virtues" recommended in prescriptive literature were those that appealed to men.

Such imported advice tracts were no doubt inaccessible to the average colonial housewife, who would most likely have been unable to read them. Rather, they were manuals of upward mobility, destined for an audience of means and ambition who aspired to a high social status or the life-style of English counterparts. But the assumptions on which they were based—that women were weak and helpless, defective of reason, and dependent on men—were commonplace in the colonies. They were also shared by women, as is suggested in the journals and letters of the literate elite who produced such documents. During the second half of the century, women extolled the "softer" virtues in their private papers, but they also admitted to a medley of "foibles" and deficiencies.

One Virginia housewife, Elizabeth Foote Washington, left her unborn daughter a "legacy" in the form of a diary, on the grounds that "Daughters generally are attached to mothers, particularly if they lose them when they are young." Elizabeth Washington attempted to describe her dual role, as competent mistress and deferential wife. But had a daughter survived to read the legacy (none did), she would have confronted the spirit of resignation and inadequacy that pervaded it. "I am totally at a loss, in many respects," wrote Elizabeth, when her husband was sick and she had to deal with plantation accounts. "Indeed, I scarce know anything that goes on." A similar inability to grasp, cope, or control pervaded women's self-assessments. In her survey of the diaries and correspondence of late-eighteenth-century women, historian Mary Beth Norton finds that women habitually referred to themselves in self-deprecating and negative ways, as "weaker vessels," "imperfect," and "helpless." Bemoaning their lack of confidence and inarticulateness, they often belittled their domestic work, apologized for innumerable failings, and even referred to their own imbecility. Unlike Eliza Pinckney, who depicted herself as a model of positive qualities, including "rationality," literate eighteenth-century women, Norton reveals, tended to express low self-esteem.

This inferior self-image, like the negative assumptions that infiltrated language, reflected social reality. Women's roles *were* dependent, circumscribed, and, barring distinctions of class or race, interchangeable. The accused adulterer in Massachusetts who informed a woman witness, when caught in the act, that "One Woman was as good to him as another," expressed a pervasive belief about woman's place in traditional society. What one woman did might just as well be done by another, whatever their capacities. Although motherhood offered personal gratification, along with both social esteem and security, neither child rearing nor housewifery provided a sense of individuality within the home or outside it. There were two loopholes in these general rules, however, one traditional and one innovative; and some women were able to take advantage of them, especially toward the end of the century.

The traditional loophole was piety. Although women's capacity for rational thought was questioned, their piety was never in doubt. It had been effectively internalized, along with other passive qualities such as helplessness and resignation. But piety also had an activist facet. Churches remained the sole institution outside the home to which women had access; indeed, they often constituted a majority of congregants. Moreover, the liberating mood of the Great Awakening of the 1740s (which Eliza Pinckney disliked and which caused Mrs. Le Brasures to lose her wits) expanded their participation. Spates of revivals and a multiplication of sects spawned a diffusion of authority and a climate of excitement in which women were more likely to assert themselves. In some congregations, women were able to influence the admission of members and selection of ministers. And on some occasions, female practitioners, however irregular, were able to adopt leadership roles on the fringes of religious life. Throughout the 1760s, for instance, Sarah Osborn of Newport held religious meetings in her home for over 300 persons in the course of a week. Several women promoted new sects—as did Shaker leader Mother Ann Lee in the 1770s—or attracted large numbers of followers—as did revivalist Jemima Wilkinson in the 1780s.

Assuming such activist roles might involve anxiety, even among public Friends, who were often sent off by their meetings to prophesy in other communities. Quaker convert Elizabeth Ashbridge, an indentured servant in New York who later became a public Friend, was at first thrown into shock when she heard a woman preach. Public Friend Rebecca Jones was reduced "to the brink of the grave" when she felt the call to prophesy but finally, "in fear and trembling," gave herself up "to the Lord's will" and assumed her new role. Other activists expressed hesitancy to invade the public sphere. Although Sarah Osborn assumed an influential position in Newport, she was deferential to ministerial authority and "greatly distress'd" lest she "Move beyond my Line." Still she was able to supervise the conversions of marginal community members, such as local blacks and young unmarried women, "who were awakened to a concern for their souls and desired my assistance and advice." Indeed, the Revolutionary era seemed to inspire a surge of religious rebellion among women. Toward the end of the century, several female dissidents challenged their ministers; women members of smaller sects, such as the Free Will Baptists or Methodists, became prophets and lay preachers, and rampant enthusiasm disrupted long-established sects. In Philadelphia, Quaker matron Elizabeth Drinker reported that so many zealous women crowded the Yearly Women's Meeting of 1803, that some had to be turned away.

While piety provided women, on occasion, with an avenue of access to public influence, "friendship" served a different function. An innovative relationship, friendship enhanced private influence and self-esteem. During the eighteenth century, the meaning of the word "friend" was in transition. In traditional society, a "friend" meant an ally or connection, usually a family member. But by midcentury, the meaning had started to shift. As a friend—a status Eliza Pinckney added to her repertoire of roles in her resolutions of the 1750s—a woman was able to establish an effective link, as an autonomous individual, with someone who was not a family member, indeed, with a peer or equal. Often involving extensive "vizeting" and lifelong correspondence, friendship differed from traditional modes of social connection among the loose coalitions of relatives and neighbors that were typical of the seventeenth-century village. Indeed, it provided an escape hatch from authoritarian relationships within the traditional family. Friendship was a modern connection and, in the context of women's history, a political one. It also was a defiant connection, or at least one that required defense.

Eliza Pinckney, who increased her clout at home and abroad by cultivating circles of friends, defended friendship when she wrote to Mrs. Evance, to whom she had entrusted the care of her sons. Their very correspondence, she told Mrs. Evance, would "show how capable women are of both business and friendship." (The devoted Mrs. Evance was, of course, a business connection, an ally in the crucial task of child rearing.) Esther Burr defended friendship in the 1750s when she took issue with an obnoxious college tutor, Mr. Ewing, who had "mean thoughts of women." Ewing revealed his colors when he contended that "he did not think women knew what friendship was, they were hardly capable of anything so cool and rational as friendship," as Esther reported in the journal she kept to send to her best friend, Sally Prince.

The long-term Burr-Prince correspondence, however, was hardly "cool and rational." Rather, it was warm and affectionate. So was the correspondence between Susanna Anthony and Sarah Osborn, which went on for four decades. "O, my dear, my bosom-friend," wrote Susanna, "I feel my love to you to be without dissimulation." In the late eighteenth century, letters between woman friends adopted the same affectionate tone. Eunice Callender of Boston, for instance, addressed her cousin Sally Ripley as "the dearest Friend of my heart" throughout their three-decade correspondence. Educated young southern women carried on similar long-term correspondence, filled with effusive declarations. "I never knew how much I loved you," wrote Martha Lauren of Charleston in the 1770s to her friend Elizabeth Brailsford. "You have . . . imprinted on my soul your beloved image, in character so indelible that neither time nor absence can erase it." Nor would marriage end their relationships, young women announced. Matrimony, wrote Lucy Orr of Virginia to friend Polly in the 1780s, "is, I fear the bane of Female Friendship. Let it not be with ours, my Polly, if we should ever Marry."

Evidence of female friendship, concentrated at the end of the century, appears connected to the development of a literate female elite although similar bonds no doubt existed between women with less ability to express them in writing. In either case, friendship provided an independent, egalitarian connection, as well as a loophole of escape from traditional roles. The law, however, reinforced traditional roles, just as it reflected the negative assumptions about women's character and capacity that were so widely shared in the eighteenth century. On those occasions when a woman had to resort to law, whether she was a feme sole or a feme covert, she was likely to find that the law demanded dependence on men.

Legal Institutions

The legal status of eighteenth-century women derived from a combination of common law, equity practices, and provincial statutes, which varied from colony to colony, providing release from some common-law limitations and upholding others. As in the seventeenth century, there was no unity of policy among the colonies, although practices were fairly similar; nor was there unity of principle within them. The statutes enacted by provincial legislatures were not intended to enhance the position of women, or of men, but rather to protect community interests—by reducing public welfare obligations, for instance, or by increasing the ease of business transactions. Colonial laws often protected women's interests—by facilitating a woman's self-support if she were destitute, for example. But they rarely promoted her autonomy or independence. Almost inevitably, the approval of men—husband, judge, or legislature—was needed for the exercise of any legal "right."

All colonies, for instance, accepted antenuptial contracts; such acceptance apparently gave colonial women an advantage that most Englishwomen lacked. But these contracts were signed by only a minority of couples and only very rarely in a woman's first marriage. Through an antenuptial contract, parents of means might insist on keeping property in trust for a daughter and her heirs, thereby preventing the new husband from gaining control of it but not giving control to the daughter either. Wealthy widows, however, the more frequent beneficiaries of antenuptial contracts, might bargain for and insist on control over property they had inherited or acquired. In either case, the new husband's approval was needed. A married woman's control of property was not so much a legal option as it was a concession from a future spouse—and one not commonly given or requested.

Without benefit of special contracts, the real property a woman brought to her marriage, if any, went under her husband's control or management, just as her personal property, earnings, children, and person now belonged to him. A wife could bequeath her personal property, such as jewelry or clothing, to her heirs; but she needed her husband's consent to do so. Real property was another matter. Most colonies (Connecticut was an exception) prohibited a husband from alienating property that his wife brought to the marriage, without the latter's consent. But the wife was still at a disadvantage. She could be coerced into giving consent—for the sale of land, for instance. Or in the event that a scheming husband sold off her property without such consent, she would have to resort to law to fight the transaction, which was not the simplest of matters. Her position was yet more difficult if her husband was abusive or unfaithful or simply unable or unwilling to live with and support her, as he was obliged to do under common law.

Although common law clearly set forth the rights and obligations of husbands and wives, it provided no machinery for enforcement—which meant, in practice, that a married woman's fate depended much more on luck than on law. In most cases, if her marriage failed, her luck ran out. Absolute divorce, with the right to remarry, was available in the New England colonies. It was granted to only a small proportion of those who petitioned for it, men or women, and now to men more often than women. Moreover, it was never granted to women for the cause of adultery until the era of the Revolution. Other colonies sometimes granted divorce by individual legislative acts. But these could be, and often were, disallowed by the English Privy Council as "improper and unconstitutional." Most important, to obtain even a legal separation from an adulterer or criminal, a woman would have to be able to muster considerable support from others and exert a great deal of initiative. But men found it far easier to terminate an unsatisfactory marriage by the simple means of desertion—a mode of escape used by wives, too, but less often. Of the 229 petitions for divorce submitted in Massachusetts between 1692 and 1786, the majority were submitted by wives, and 65 percent of these were based on desertion or nonsupport. Only 37 percent of husbands cited desertion as a cause for divorce. And in all colonies, when a husband vanished through desertion, long-term absence, or death, the courts and legislature replaced him as the final arbiter of the woman's "rights."

The deserted wife was a special but not uncommon case, since she had no legal rights or property but was still unable to support herself as a feme sole in trade. Colonies might grant feme sole trader rights to such women, if requested, through private legislative acts. In 1718, Pennsylvania enacted a feme sole trader statute to cover such cases. But, as historian Marylynn Salmon shows, the law was enacted with extreme caution and with more concern for creditors than for wives. The statute made feme sole status available to wives of men who were absent for long terms (such as sailors) or who had deserted or gone bankrupt. It enabled them to engage in trade, support themselves, feed their children, and even assume liability for the debts their husbands had incurred. Deserted wives could thereby keep themselves off the public dole and, if need be, satisfy their husbands' creditors. South Carolina recognized feme sole trader status through two more liberal laws, in 1712 and 1744, that made married businesswomen liable for their own debts and enabled them to sue for debt.

Although widows, unlike deserted wives, automatically gained feme sole rights and could own property, sign contracts, and sue and be sued, their autonomy was also curtailed by law. Most colonies provided that a widow was assured of her dower right—a life estate in one-third of her husband's real property and a similar proportion of his personal property—if he died intestate. (Of course if he wrote a will, he could leave her more.) The real property, at any rate, could not be sold or bequeathed by the widow without special permission from a court or legislature. And in Pennsylvania, a widow could be deprived of even her dower right if her husband was in debt—an innovation unknown to common law. In any colony, moreover, a husband in his will could make retention of the dower right or whatever his wife was to inherit, whether much or little, contingent on her remaining single. In no case did the dower right provide the widow with control over the property; she received only a life interest in it, which might or might not be enough to sustain her, depending on the size of the estate. The legal system stood between the widow and autonomy, just as it did for the wife.

Colonial women's limited ability to own property or control capital severely curtailed their economic power. According to a study of probate records by historian Carole Shammas, men held at least 90 percent of colonial wealth. During the Revolution, when states confiscated Tory property, new problems arose involving dower rights and married women's property rights. Such problems were often solved with consideration for women's predicaments, though not by any alteration of law. Still, the Revolutionary era brought the beginning of change. Abolition of primogeniture, for instance, made all offspring equal to the eldest son as heirs—though all that daughters inherited still fell under their husbands' control. More important, in the post-Revolutionary years, most states enacted legislation that provided for absolute divorce in limited types of cases. But jurists discarded neither the doctrine of coverture nor insistence on female dependence. After the war, as before, English common law remained in effect.

Lawyers, moreover, continued to rely on Sir William Blackstone's *Commentaries* on English common law, published in 1765. This reference work provided a handy guide to the status of the feme covert—indeed a description so lucid that even the dimmest of attorneys could put it to use. As Blackstone explained, "The very being or legal existence of the woman is suspended during the course of marriage, or at least is incorporated and consolidated into that of the husband; under whose wing, protection, and cover she performs every thing." Blackstone's concise list of the feme covert's limitations was useful not only to eighteenth-century lawyers but to their successors. Coverture, as a state court asserted half a century after Blackstone, "is a civil disqualification at common law, arising from a want of free agency in the wife as much as from the want of judgement in an idiot." Only in the mid-nineteenth century, when states began to grant married women the right to possess inherited property, did the doctrine of coverture start to crack—and the proportion of total wealth held by men begin to decline.

Subordination of women was peculiar to neither the English legal system nor to Anglo-American society on the eastern seaboard. Patterns of sex hierarchy also characterized non-English communities, such as those of Hispanic settlers in the southwest, Indian tribes in the east, and slave societies, north and south. In each case, however, as in English society, elements of change impinged.

Diversity of Cultures

Distinctive social customs emerged in the non-English communities of North America, such as the Spanish settlements in the Rio Grande valley. By the start of the eighteenth century, about 3,000 Spanish settlers lived in towns like Santa Fe and Albuquerque, and on small ranches on the Rio Grande, along with some 15,000 Pueblo Indians. Until 1770, these remote northern settlements, linked to Mexico City only by yearly mule train, remained isolated from the rest of Spanish society. Within Spanish settlements, a complex status system prevailed. At the top was a tiny Spanish aristocracy that intermarried and owned most of the land. A peasantry of mestizo (mixed race) origins also considered itself Spanish; mestizos held small land plots and worked as wage labor. At the bottom of Spanish society, a large labor force of *genizaros,* or detribalized Indians (often prisoners of war), performed most of the physical labor, as household servants or farm workers.

Among the small group of Spanish aristocrats, historian Ramon A. Gutierrez contends, sex roles were sharply delineated. Men embodied the virtue of "honor" and exerted authority over family members and subordinates. Women embodied the equivalent virtue of "shame" *(verguena).* Expected to be shy and retiring, they were ideally pure before marriage and faithful afterward. This concept of feminine virtue applied only in aristocratic households, where women led isolated existences. Mestizo women, who worked on farms, had less secluded lives. *Genizaro* women, some of them slaves, were left out of the Spanish value system. One friar complained in 1734 that "an Indian does not care if you fornicate with his wife because she has no shame."

During the last quarter of the century, the isolation of northern "New Spain" diminished. Other European powers encroached in Texas, New Mexico, and California. Commerce with Mexico increased, the populations of Spanish settlements expanded, the authority of the church dwindled, and the rules that governed Spanish society loosened. Among aristocrats, according to Gutierrez, marriage for love and free choice of partners gained sway over arranged marriages, a change that was under way in Anglo-American society as well. Presumably young Spanish women in landed families experienced a slight increase in leverage, although the loaded Spanish value system remained in effect.

Indian women on the eastern seaboard, such as the Cherokee and Iroquois, may well have experienced a decline in status during the eighteenth century. Among southern Cherokees, for instance, contact with white settlers seemed to spur a process of female devaluation that continued into the 1800s. Originally, the Cherokees had been a matrilineal, matrilocal tribe that favored farming over hunting. The agrarian rhythms of women's lives determined tribal routines. But the disruption of war and trade with white settlers, historian Theda Perdue shows, made hunting (traditionally men's work) more important than farming (women's work). As early as 1725, Cherokees had become dependent on the deerskin trade with the English and accustomed to such items as European-style clothing, guns, and brass kettles. Women stopped making tools and utensils, deerskins became the currency, and men, imbued with new power because of the importance of trade, assumed dominant roles as household heads.

The deerskin trade dismantled the former balance in Cherokee culture. Hunting, no longer limited to the winter months, became a year-round activity. Trade encouraged acquisition of material goods, increased exploitation of the natural world, and diminished the value of women's agrarian roles. As hierarchy replaced harmony, an ethos of individualism replaced one of cooperation. Women also lost political powers they had formerly enjoyed, such as deciding the fate of captives (death or adoption into families). Local leadership councils, in which women had participated, declined in importance. Only Cherokee men met with colonial officials, and women lost their role in decision-making. In the second half of the century, conflict among Europeans completed the transformation that the deerskin trade had begun. The Seven Years' War (1756–1763) took a severe toll on the old Cherokee life-style; the invasion of Indian fields led to devastation and starvation. During the Revolution, some thirty Cherokee towns were destroyed, crops ruined, and Indian children sold into slavery.

By the end of the century, the Cherokee community had been permanently transformed. Cherokees now lived in isolated homesteads, not cooperative villages, and the nuclear family replaced the clan. Intermarriage of traders and Indians introduced class divisions. Female status became linked to family wealth, not clan well-being. Overall, once European values entered Cherokee life, women's influence and prestige diminished; decades of gradual anglicization took their toll. Well before Cherokee removal in the 1830s, according to Perdue, women had lost most of their power in the community. Iroquois women in the north seem to have experienced similar loss. When hunting territories were claimed by white farmers during the Revolution, Iroquois men became agriculturalists and the customary division of work roles dissolved. Iroquois women gave up their farming work, took responsibility solely for household labor, and lost status in their society. The same process may have occurred among other eastern tribes.

While the numbers of eastern Indians decreased in the eighteenth century, the institution of slavery enjoyed a period of phenomenal growth. Slave codes, the most innovative of provincial statutes, created a black subculture with different rules from those that applied in white society. Still, some of the factors that affected white women's experience—such as increasing parity of sex ratios and the development of a southern plantation aristocracy—had an impact on slave women, too.

Slave women on large plantations in stable areas, such as the Chesapeake or the Tidewater, had many advantages that new arrivals, frontier slaves, or women slaves with less privileged owners lacked. By the 1720s and 1730s, these older, wealthier regions had dense black populations, a high proportion of native-born slaves, and more balanced sex ratios. Women were able to find marital partners, establish relatively secure family lives, and develop networks of relatives on the same plantation or a neighboring one. Women stranded on small isolated farms—north or south—had less chance of finding appropriate marital partners or any at all. Moreover, despite the continued skewing of southern slave ratios in favor of men, a far larger proportion of slave women than white women were without partners. Still, despite the precarious conditions of slavery and lack of legal marriage, others managed to maintain long-term unions.

They also began to have more children. As slave society became more stable in eighteenth-century Maryland and Virginia, and as a native-born slave population developed, child-bearing rates rose markedly. Slave women in these settled regions now had almost as many children as white women, beginning in their late teens—a contrast to the very low fertility of immigrant slave women in the seventeenth century. By the early eighteenth century, as slavery became a self-perpetuating institution, the slave family became its distinguishing feature. And women served as the major bastions of slave family life—as reflected in plantation records, where slave genealogy was traced through mothers.

The development of a plantation aristocracy in older, stable areas also had an impact on the work roles of women slaves. Most women on large plantations worked in the fields, as they invariably did on small ones. But on sizable estates such as Hampton or Belmont, women might occupy preferable posts—such as dairymaid, poultrymaid, nurse, laundress, seamstress, or midwife, a pivotal job. These specialized vocations, which involved working in or around the house, not in the fields, were likely to be handed down from mother to daughter. But the woman slave's prospects of escaping field work were still limited. Only about 10 or 15 percent of slaves did so, and the majority were men, who might work not only as house servants but as artisans in a variety of trades or as slave overseers. Therefore, a higher proportion of women than men worked in the fields. Some were assigned to housework or other jobs only when too young or too old for field work, and others held alternate assignments according to plantation needs. "A stout able field wench and an exceedingly good washer and ironer," was the way a late-eighteenth-century Virginian evaluated a favored slave.

If the development of large plantations brought advantages to some women slaves, so did the era of the Revolution. Not only did the proximity of the British army encourage slaves to escape, but they did so in large groups that included family units and therefore women and children. (In ordinary times, women slaves, tied to their children and relatives, were less likely than men to become solitary fugitives.) Of the twenty-three slaves who departed from Thomas Jefferson's Virginia lands during the war, for instance, over half were women and girls, all but two leaving in family groups. In British-occupied New York City, similarly, a large proportion of fugitives who sought the protection of the British army when the city was evacuated were women and girls in family groups. Such opportunities for family escapes would not occur again in any numbers until the Civil War. Women who remained enslaved, however, may well have faced harder times. A new hiring-out system in the Chesapeake decreased family stability. Expanding cotton production in the lower South depressed living conditions and increased work demands.

The Revolutionary era, finally, reminded some groups of slaves, as it does students of history, of the contrast between colonial demands for self-determination and the slaves' lack of it. A particular grievance was the inability of slaves to establish the type of family life that all whites were free to enjoy. When a group of Massachusetts slaves sent a memorial to the legislature in 1774 petitioning for freedom, they stressed the incompatibility of slavery with family life. "How can a slave perform the duties of husband to wife or a parent to a child?" asked the Massachusetts petition. "How can a husband leave [his] master to work and cleave to his wife. How can the wife submit to her husband in all things?"

The upheavals of the Revolutionary era improved the lives of a minority of slaves, including the Massachusetts petitioners, when northern states abolished slavery. In the upper South, a spate of voluntary emancipation created a large free black population, a majority of which was female and mulatto. The Revolution left the legal status of most slaves, as of white women, untouched. But during the Revolutionary War, women were suddenly caught up in the turmoil of public events and drawn into new activities.

The Cradle of the Revolution

The era of the American Revolution, which epitomized shifts of power and authority, altered women's relations to public life and, on occasion, expanded men's views of women's capacities. The conflicts that began in the 1760s drew attention to women's household work and upgraded the value of their domestic contributions—as producers of homespun, boycotters of imports, and enthusiasts of the cause. The disruption of war, which shifted families to new locales and often removed men from the home, enabled or forced women to assume new authority. Finally, the war at home compelled women to become concerned about public affairs—a concern that was hard to avoid if one's town, for instance, was under siege. Most important, under the stress of the first modern revolution, women were suddenly assumed to be capable of sharing a highly valued and extremely rational political sentiment: patriotism.

Expressions of patriotism were novel and varied. There were some rare instances of women in battle—for example, male impersonator Deborah Sampson Gannett, who enlisted in the fourth Massachusetts Regiment and eventually received a pension for her service. (After her death, the pension was passed on to her husband, a curious example of role reversal.) But Gannett's role as a soldier was more a reflection of the primitive nature of the rebel army than of any new option open to women. During the Revolution, as in other eighteenth-century wars, women played a traditional role as camp followers. To Washington, who was desperately trying to create a professional army, the presence of female camp followers was a liability. "The Multitudes of women," he contended in 1777, "especially those who are pregnant or have children, are a clog upon every movement." What Washington appreciated, however, was one of the most modern roles women adopted during the war, and one that suggested the route that patriot daughters and granddaughters were later to follow into public life: raising money for the cause. In 1781, when he congratulated the Ladies Association of Philadelphia (a more elite group than the camp followers) on their fund gathering, he awarded its members "an equal place with any who have preceded them in the walk of female patriotism." The Philadelphia ladies had "embellished" the American character, Washington asserted, "by proving that the love of country is blended with those softer domestic virtues, which have always been allowed to be more peculiarly *your own.*"

Not only did the war throw a spotlight on "domestic virtue," but it imbued household work with political content. Once boycotts of English goods began in the 1760s, the spinning and weaving of cloth—activities usually relegated to less prosperous and rural homes—became transformed into patriotic acts. "I carded two pounds of whole wool and felt Nationaly," wrote Abigail Foote in her diary.

Urban wives and daughters began making clothes out of homespun. Later, during the war, they made blankets and shirts for the rebel army. Southern mistresses too turned to the wheel, once imports of English cloth ended. Women slaves were affected as well. Starting in the 1760s, they began to be reassigned to spinning. (Enterprising George Lucas had been foresighted when he advised Eliza, in the 1740s, to train some slaves to use the wheel and loom.) The stimulus to home manufacture provided by colonial boycotts also opened up a vocation. In urban areas and especially in New England households, women (and children) began producing cloth for income under the putting-out system, where manufacturers paid them by the piece. Finally, the boycotts of the 1760s drew attention to the role of urban women as family purchasing agents, when they refused to buy British goods.

Besides affecting women's household roles, the rebel cause sanctioned group activities for women. For over a decade, the gatherings of rebel women received publicity in the patriot press. Sometimes, women in groups created mob scenes—as did the 500 women who, Abigail Adams reported, harassed and hounded a Massachusetts merchant for hoarding coffee. More commonly, "association" took the form of sewing circles. Groups as large as sixty or seventy women or more convened to spin, weave, and sew. Women in association also passed resolutions not to patronize merchants who broke nonimportation agreements, took oaths renouncing marriage with men who did not support the patriot cause, and professed supportive sentiments. "We cannot be indifferent," declared a group of fifty-one North Carolina women, "on any occasion that appears to affect the peace and happiness of our country."

The chaos produced by war at home precluded indifference. It disrupted the livelihood of self-supporting women such as the small shopkeepers of Boston, many of whom had been put out of business when importation ceased. It created hardship for property owners such as Eliza Pinckney, whose income fell when rents were not paid and slaves refused to work. "They all do now what they please every where," she complained to her son Thomas in 1779. Most of all, the war disrupted families, which had mixed effects. In the absence of men, women were sometimes able to assume new authority and larger roles—for example, by taking over and managing farms and businesses. Many were unprepared for such responsibility, as was the case with those loyalist wives who, when pressing claims after the war, revealed that they knew little of their husbands' business affairs, earnings, debts, or even what property they owned. However, for patriots such as Abigail Adams, a great booster of women's capacity for domestic management as well as a master of egalitarian rhetoric, responsibility provided opportunity. "I find it necessary to be the directress of our husbandry," she wrote to her husband in 1776. "I hope in time to have the reputation of being as good a farmer as my partner has of being a good statesman."

Women's competent management of the home front, as historian Mary Beth Norton suggests, made some men pay more attention to their wives' roles—a new tack, since household work was customarily regarded as trivial and inconsequential. Christopher Marshall, a member of Congress in Philadelphia, who moved his family away from the besieged city, reported with pride in 1778 on

A British cartoon of "a society of patriotic ladies" determined to boycott British goods. Society members, depicted as either ferocious or simple-minded, are signing a petition not to buy tea or use British cloth "until such time that all acts which tend to Enslave this our Native Country shall be repealed." An attentive slave holds the inkwell, a child is forgotten under the table, and a dog desecrates the scenery. *(Mezzotint by Philip Dawes, 1775. Library of Congress)*

the labors of his wife, now a rural housekeeper in Lancaster. "From early morning until late at night, she is constantly employed in the affairs of the family," boasted Marshall. Mrs. Marshall baked, cleaned, tended the orchard, dried apples, made cider and cheese, and fed guests—activities that in ordinary times were likely to go unheralded. Another Philadelphian, Benjamin Rush, appreciated a change of a different sort that the war had made in his wife, Julia, who at the beginning of the Revolution "had all the timidity of her sex." During the war, Julia Rush became involved in fund raising, "distinguished herself by her zeal . . . and is now so thoroughly enlisted in the cause of her country that she reproaches me with lukewarmness."

Rush was not the only husband to assess his wife's avidity for the cause primarily in terms of its impact on himself. But the Ladies Association of Philadelphia, in which Julia Rush had worked, had greater impact on its members. Formed in 1780, the association attracted a core of prominent, well-off local women, including, for instance, the wife of the state's chief justice. They planned to collect from women and girls the money that would no longer be spent on extravagant clothes and to donate this sum to the rebel army. Dividing the city into districts, the women visited every home, in pairs, and amassed a substantial sum for the cause. ("People were obliged to give them something to get rid of them," complained loyalist Anna Rawle to her friend Rebecca Shoemaker.) They also spurred women in four more states to similar attempts. Proud of the "favor and affection found in this effort," according to one participant, the Philadelphia women offered proof that women were capable of sharing the rational sentiment of patriotism and able to act effectively on it.

Patriot women with less local clout may have had less opportunity for formal association during the war; and loyalist women, who often felt extremely isolated, still less. But neither was excluded from the discussion of politics—with husbands, relatives, visitors, and each other, sometimes in correspondence. Women were often ambivalent about entering the arena of political discussion, a male preserve, and even apologetic for going beyond their "province." Others apologized as a matter of form. "I've transgress'd the line . . . by dipping into politicks," wrote Sarah Jay, daughter and wife of politicians, in a letter to her family, although "politicks" were her preoccupation. Some women, such as Abigail Adams and Mercy Warren, wrote to each other constantly about politics, without apology. One New England woman, who later described the excitement she had felt "while rocked in the cradle of revolution," contended that the war era had inspired a lifelong interest in public affairs. Outspoken Eliza Wilkinson of South Carolina insisted to a friend in 1782 that political interest was within her province. Women had enough "sense" to voice opinions, she asserted, without being told that spinning and domestic affairs were "the only matters we are capable of thinking or speaking of with justness and propriety."

Even for those as politicized as Eliza Wilkinson, the Revolution brought about only negligible gains. Neither interest in politics nor avid patriotism transformed women into citizens. Women did not receive new legal codes or independence from coverture. On the contrary, after the Revolution, colonial equity practices such as antenuptial contracts or dower rights, which tended to mitigate common law to women's advantage, fell increasingly into disuse. Nor did women receive (or demand) the vote. Property ownership remained the basis for suffrage, and since married women owned no property, they had no free political will. Unmarried women were excluded too. The sole exception was in New Jersey, where for three decades an aberration in the suffrage law enabled unmarried women property owners to vote. This privilege came to an end in 1807, when women, boys, blacks, and other "irregulars" were finally excluded from the polls. The New Jersey precedent, ignored elsewhere, was unique. After the Revolution as before, as historian Linda Kerber points out, the family circle remained a woman's "state." From a legal and political point of view, the Revolution was a "conservative" one for American women.

But the apolitical status of women was not unique; nor was their apparent disinterest in altering it. Not all white men had access to voting or public office, either. In most states, those who owned little or no property (as did most women) were unable to vote. More important, most men who had the franchise had little interest in using it, rarely bothered to do so, and cultivated a grand indifference to politics. Few could afford to leave private concerns for public office, and those who did were constantly torn between civic obligation and the desire to return to farms and plantations, family life and provincial retreats. For women, as for the majority of men, the raised expectations incurred by "independence" existed more at a personal level than a political one.

During the postwar decades, these expectations started to surface in a private context, within the family. It would be rash to assume that a modern mode of marriage suddenly replaced the traditional one, or that an enhanced notion of womanhood immediately supplanted widespread convictions of female inferiority. Shifts within the private sphere were always far more gradual and less visible than authority shifts in political life. Some of the changes within the family, minimizing paternal power and giving more "liberty" to other family members, began before the Revolutionary era and accompanied rather than followed it. Other changes in domestic habits, despite the democratic rhetoric of the late eighteenth century, tended to start at the top of the social scale and only slowly filter downward. Still, during the last two decades of the century, new ideals of family life at least began to encroach and impinge. And in the process, women's status within the family began to rise.

The Pursuit of Happiness

During the eighteenth century, the analogy between the family and the state, an Anglo-American favorite, began to provoke new questions. In the wake of the English Revolution of 1688, when absolute monarchy fell out of favor, domestic patriarchy was also open to assault. "If absolute sovereignty be not necessary in a state, how comes it to be so in a family?" asked the English writer Mary Astell in 1706. "Is it not then partial in men to the last degree to contend for and practise that arbitrary dominion in their families which they abhor and exclaim against in the state?" During the era of the American Revolution, women of political bent could hardly avoid the same question or resist applying republican theory to domestic politics. "Emancipating all nations, you insist upon retaining absolute power over Wives," Abigail Adams wrote to her husband in 1776. "Do not put such unlimited powers into the hands of the husbands," she told John Adams while he was serving in the Continental Congress. "Remember all men would be tyrants if they could."

What Abigail Adams consistently advocated was a redistribution of authority within the family, a limitation of "absolute power over Wives," and the elevation of women to the status of partners and companions in marriage. During the 1780s and 1790s, when postwar exuberance was at its peak, just such ideals began to emerge in the new nation's magazines and journals, which flourished in cities such as Boston and Philadelphia.

The new, companionate ideal of marriage was one based on sympathy, affection, esteem, friendship, and mutual obligation, as opposed to the hierarchical mode of traditional marriage. Husband and wife were to be not only "the first and dearest friends of their partners," as described in a marriage guide of the late eighteenth century, but interdependent ones. The tyranny of the domineering patriarch and the obedience of the servile wife would now be replaced by complementarity, mutuality, and "reciprocal union of interest," as set forth in

Philadelphia's newly founded *Lady's Magazine* by a writer who identified herself as a "Matrimonial Republican." According to the Massachusetts essayist Judith Sargent Murray, in an anonymous article of the 1790s, the ideal marriage was an egalitarian one requiring "mutual esteem, mutual friendship, mutual confidence, *begirt about by mutual forbearance.*" In less egalitarian publications, such as Boston's *Gentleman's and Lady's Town and Country Magazine* in the 1780s, husband and wife were more likely to be engaged in a minuet of deference and good manners: "Acknowledging his superior judgement, [the wife] complies with all his reasonable desires, whilst he attempts to suit his requests to her inclinations."

The new ideal of companionate marriage was neither an invention of the republican press nor mere wishful thinking on the part of "matrimonial republicans." A less authoritarian type of marriage already prevailed among the propertied classes in England and was therefore familiar to members of the colonial elite, such as the Pinckneys. It was more likely to be found in the prosperous urban home than in the backwoods outpost, in the household with multiple separate rooms than in the two-room cabin. Its beneficiary was more likely to be the wife who was relieved of incessant domestic drudgery than the wife who was bound to reels, spools, churns, cows, and chickens. The pursuit of domestic happiness had been customarily a privilege of the family with a modicum of means. But during the prosperous post-Revolutionary decades, in the glow of independence, when other traditional benefits of privilege started to filter down, the companionate ideal of marriage began to find a wider audience. Moreover, it had important corollaries for the role of women in the new nation.

In the late-eighteenth-century version of companionate marriage, the wife enjoyed a higher status within the home. She could now be considered a rational being rather than a mental incompetent; an amicable companion rather than a shrew; a virtuous partner rather than a servile drudge who might even be "kiked into the fyre," as in seventeenth-century Plymouth. Her individualism was also enhanced. The replacement of compulsory obedience with voluntary affection made the "happiness" of the partners a vital component of marriage rather than merely a fortuitous by-product. The new stress on "affection" and "happiness" had great appeal to young women at the end of the century. Precocious Eliza Southgate, a Maine teenager, for instance, decided at first that marriage was not "absolutely essential to my happiness" but later chose a husband "calculated to promote my happiness." In private papers as in public journals, the language used to describe marriage seemed to be changing.

The ideal of happiness in marriage endorsed by Eliza Southgate may have had further ramifications. It appeared to be recognized in divorce proceedings in Massachusetts, where "loss of affection" was cited and accepted in several instances as cause for divorce. Although divorce was still a limited option, since the 1760s more people had applied for it in Massachusetts and Connecticut. A great proportion of Massachusetts applicants were women, and their petitions were increasingly successful. After the Revolution, moreover, several other states passed laws that made divorce more accessible. A grant of divorce was of course an attempt to preserve social order, not to promote female autonomy. The rise in women's petitions, however, suggests that women were promoting their own "independence." Increased access to divorce was the major legal advantage women gained in the new republic. And it was a limited gain, for absolute divorce remained rare. In most instances, the courts and state legislatures that ended marriages did so by granting separations and property settlements.

Integration of the companionate ideal with traditional marriage caused considerable confusion in Massachusetts divorce proceedings. This was reflected in the petition for divorce of one young man in 1781 who complained that he wanted his wife to be his "friend" and "in Subjection to me." He was probably using the term "friend" in its older sense, but still he pointed to a real problem. The very crux of companionate marriage was the replacement of patriarchal tyranny by benevolent leadership. Clearly, any shift in domestic politics limited the power of men. But men were still afflicted by what Abigail Adams called "the natural propensity in human nature to domination." The interweaving of authority and affection could be achieved only if wives adopted an attitude of deference, as George Lucas had advised Eliza Pinckney to do in the 1740s. If husbands had lost "absolute power," they still retained "superior judgement," and it was incumbent on wives to defer to it in order to preserve the companionate tone. Indulgent parents of the postwar era offered their daughters similar advice. "The happiness of your life depends now on continuing to please a single person," Jefferson told his daughter Martha on her marriage. "To this all objects must be secondary, even your love for me." Elizabeth Foote Washington was even more specific in the diary she kept in the 1790s for her unborn daughter. She had resolved never to argue with her husband, she revealed, since "husbands cannot bear to be thought in the wrong. . . . It was ever more pleasing to have my husband's opinion coincide with mine."

If the substitution of voluntarism for compulsion, deference for submission, and affection for obedience began to change the status of women in the post-Revolutionary family, it did even more for children. The parent-child relationship had been especially important in rebel rhetoric, which often conjured up the image of an adolescent society struggling to assert its independence from parental domination. In the new nation, children, like women, began to be viewed as individuals with distinctive characteristics and the capacity for reason. The late-eighteenth-century parent-child relationship was characterized by a decrease in paternal power, an increase in attention to children and their upbringing, and the substitution of suasion for domination. The modern parent hoped to inculcate values that would prepare the child for independence and, in this interest, to provide the proper combination of guidance and indulgence, love and restraint. The new mode of child rearing enhanced the authority of mothers, since they were as capable as fathers of providing or withholding affection (as opposed to property, which remained under the control of men). Not surprisingly, the messages imparted by notable parents of the late eighteenth century strove to elicit the same combination of love and deference that Eliza Pinckney had aroused, most effectively, in her sons thirty years before. "I have placed my happiness on your being good and accomplished," Jefferson told his eleven-year-old daughter in the 1780s, "and no distress which this world can now bring me could equal that of your disappointing my hopes." Abigail Adams, a memorable mother, was even more precise with teenage John Quincy, at school in England. "I would rather see you find a grave in the ocean you have crossed," she wrote, "than see you an immoral, profligate or graceless child."

The altered parent-child relationship was even more marked in diminishing parental control over children's marriages, another tilt in the family power structure, and one that had been in progress since midcentury. By the late eighteenth century, children were marrying when they wanted. Daughters might marry ahead of their older sisters, a new development; sons might marry before or without inheriting property from their fathers. Children were also marrying whom they wanted. Since marriages would now, ideally, be based on personal preference and compatibility, they were more likely to be arranged by the partners themselves, subject to parental objections, rather than arranged by parents, subject to the veto of the child. Eliza Pinckney's experience in the 1740s had included both patterns: In 1741 she had strongly opposed George Lucas's nominees; and three years later, confident of his approval, she had informed him of her own choice. By the end of the century, such independence in selecting partners was far more widespread than at the beginning. But it was likely to have a different impact on daughters than on sons.

Daughters could no longer depend on parents to act on their behalf, as George Lucas had attempted to do for Eliza, by initiating negotiations or bargaining over arrangements. They now had to rely on their own discretion and aptitude in what was turning out to be a more competitive market. Although an excess of men in the American population continued throughout the eighteenth century, western emigration, a man's option, was throwing sex ratios askew in the east. A steady exodus of young men unable to obtain land in more densely settled areas, to more remote ones, left a diminished pool of suitors behind. In Massachusetts, the bellweather of social change, there were only about 90 adult white men to every 100 white women as early as 1765. The scarcity of men was most pronounced in eastern towns and less evident, if it existed at all, in more sparsely populated western counties. Still, by the last decades of the century, the age of marriage in New England had risen, and so had the numbers of never-married women. Indeed, the proportion of spinsters in the female population, although small until now, would continue to increase for much of the nineteenth century.

During the colonial era, remaining a spinster had been a mark of opprobrium and hardly an attractive or viable option. It usually meant a dismal life of quasi-dependence, living in relatives' homes. But during the 1780s and 1790s, spinsterhood became an option—or at least more of a likelihood. The increase of spinsters in eastern regions may have reflected a rise in the autonomy of daughters, who had gained the right to refuse proposals, or a paucity of eligible candidates, or, most likely, a combination of both factors. Women's increased independence on the marriage market, however, was an ambivalent gain. It coincided with new demands of compatibility, fewer available men, less geographic mobility than men, and less leverage than men—who could choose whom to court. American daughters had little "liberty" to choose a husband, as eighteen-year-old Eliza Southgate observed in 1800, since they were unable to take the initiative. "It is true we have the liberty of refusing those we dont like," said Eliza, "but not of selecting those we do." In the marriage market, as in the commercial one, deregulation fostered competition, individualism, and high expectations. But it also brought a new set of risks and liabilities.

Under these more competitive circumstances, there was increasing stress on the personal qualifications and discretion of the candidate herself. A well-informed woman, "conscious of her nature and dignity," as Abigail Adams pointed out, would be more capable of "engaging and retaining the affection of a man of understanding." Such considerations, among others, contributed to a new interest in girls' education in the 1780s and 1790s and to the emergence of innovative "female academies"—schools that offered academic programs. The new academies reflected an improved image of women as rational individuals, capable of absorbing and transmitting ideas. They also reflected the new prosperity of ambitious Americans. A daughter's education, though not exorbitant, was nonetheless an investment—possibly one that served as a substitute for a dowry. "Independence," in the postwar decades, probably affected daughters more directly than wives and, especially, a small core of privileged daughters from eastern propertied families.

Fathers and Daughters, Mothers and Sons

Rationales for women's education had been utilitarian since 1692, when Cotton Mather described his feminine ideals in a sermon, "Ornaments for the Daughters of Zion." Education, said Mather, would enable a woman to better serve her husband and family and, by the same token, would prevent the degeneration of her character into what, it was feared, was its natural state: wickedness. The skills women needed, he contended, were training in housewifery, needlework, arithmetic, accounting, surgery, "and such other arts relating to business, as to do the man whom she may hereafter have, good and not evil, all the days of her life." The opening of female academies a century later elicited an equally utilitarian rationale. But it was based on a broader vision of women's roles—one that accepted female rationality and incorporated women into the ideology of the new republic.

Until the last decades of the eighteenth century, girls' education, when available at all, was rudimentary in nature and limited to the very well-to-do. Few families were able to provide much schooling for any of their children, and those who could provided it for their sons. Young children in towns and cities might be able to attend "dame schools" run by local widows or impoverished wives attempting to eke out a livelihood. Here, girls might learn some reading and spelling. By the 1750s and 1760s, well-off daughters might have a few more years at boarding or "adventure" schools that offered instruction in the "ornamentals," such as French, embroidery, drawing, and harpsichord; such schools might also teach writing or "cyphering," the rudiments of arithmetic. But this was hardly comparable to the secondary schooling available to boys. As a rule, whatever learning daughters acquired, they were likely to acquire at home. Even a girl as ambitious as Harriott Horry, who taught herself Latin and mathematics, could not receive the education provided for her brothers, since no local institution offered it.

The first years of nationhood, however, brought the beginning of change. Not only did opportunities for primary schooling increase, but some opportunities for girls' secondary education emerged along the eastern seaboard, catering to the daughters of families who could afford them. In some instances, New England boys' academies that sought to increase their rosters held special sessions for girls. More significant were the novel female academies. The Philadelphia Young Ladies Academy, born with the nation in 1787, was the leading example—probably a unique example, in fact, since few schools of the era could measure up to it. A complete academic program was provided at the academy. Classes, taught by men, included spelling, reading, writing, arithmetic, geography, rhetoric, and composition—that is, all subjects except the classics, a male preserve, and the sciences, although a series of lectures was held in this area. Over the next few decades, similarly ambitious institutions, some run by women, began to appear in towns and cities. During the 1790s, northern girls could attend a roster of academies in Philadelphia or Boston or small schools in New England towns, such as Sarah Pierce's Litchfield Academy. By the first decade of the new century, planters' daughters might be sent to board at northern schools or at female academies in Georgia or North Carolina. "You know how anxious I am that you should be Clever as well as good," a Virginia mother urged her daughter in 1801. "Take every advantage to improve your mind that falls in your way."

Ideally, the new schools were not only academic institutions but permanent ones, rather than temporary means of support for schoolmistresses, like the short-lived adventure schools. This, in turn, meant that they needed financial support from men in the community. Fathers paid the bills, served as trustees, and raised funds for school buildings. The Philadelphia Academy, significantly, was founded by prominent local men active in commerce, government, and the professions, many of them college graduates. The school's goals, accordingly, reflected the ideals of these well-off fathers. Academy education, according to one eminent trustee, was intended to inculcate neither pedantry nor frivolity, neither "excessive refinement nor extreme erudition," but rather the quality essential to republican womanhood—"a rational, well-informed piety."

Such moderate goals, reminiscent of those of Eliza Pinckney, held large but not universal appeal. The prospect of educated women was controversial, just as the notion of female rationality was recent. The most powerful eighteenth-century argument against education was not that girls were ineducable but rather that education would make them repulsive to men. Critics contended that learning would limit a girl's marital opportunities, unsuit her for domestic work, and turn her into an unfeminine monster. Such sentiments had been voiced in the 1750s by Esther Burr's unwelcome guest, the college tutor Mr. Ewing, who contended that education would make a woman "disgussful to all her acquaintance." Masculine minds and manners, as a minister confirmed in an 1801 Boston magazine, would not "inspire the tender passion." Female education, moreover, according to its critics, might even destroy family life. But defenders of women's education sought to show that the new nation needed educated women as wives and mothers. In the process, they attempted to fuse the modern notion of female rationality with women's traditional family roles.

Benjamin Rush presented this defense in his "Thoughts on Female Education," offered to the Philadelphia Academy on its opening. Education, Rush explained, would prepare a student to fulfill the role of wife in a companionate marriage, "to be an agreeable companion for a sensible man." It would enable her to assume responsibility for household management, even if servants were unavailable. Educated wives could take charge of family business, purchases, accounts, and upkeep. They could serve as "stewards and guardians of their husbands' property" and liberate men for profit-making ventures. Not only did family success depend on women's ability in household management, but in times of adversity, such as widowhood, the educated woman would be prepared with survival skills. She would also be able, in all circumstances, to assume responsibility for the training of her children—an argument that carried increasing weight in the new republic.

This argument had both private and public facets. It occurred to Jefferson as a father in the 1780s when supervising, from France, his daughter Martha's course of study. Jefferson's logic was unassailable: "The chance that in marriage she will draw a blockhead I calculate at about fourteen to one, and . . . the education of her family will probably rest on her own ideas and direction without assistance." (He was right, since Martha had twelve children, by a husband who was mad part of the time and in debt most of it.) But Rush, in his Philadelphia address, contended that educated mothers would also fill a civic role. Since every man now had an "equal share" in the country's liberty, it was necessary "that our ladies should be qualified to a certain degree, by a peculiar and suitable education, to concur in instructing their sons in the principles of liberty and government." Well-trained mothers, in Rush's vision, would be responsible not only for instructing daughters, whose upbringing had customarily been in their hands, but for shaping the values of their sons, who were likely to have a direct impact on the nation's success.

The vision of republican motherhood, as expressed by Rush and reiterated in the press, had a dual thrust. It included women in the new nation, at least on the periphery of political life. As value transmitters, they could serve as a link between founding fathers and republican sons, and provide the country with patriotic men. At the same time, republican motherhood confirmed female exclusion from political life, since it limited women to familial roles. Above all, it bolstered the social significance of motherhood. The assumption was that mothers *could* imbue their children with values and virtues, that they *could* have an influence over sons as well as daughters. The mother had gained an enlarged sphere of influence at home. While the republican press insisted that "virtue" was the backbone of the new nation, academy heads ceaselessly argued that virtue could be inculcated only by mothers. The goal of female education, the founder of a Georgia academy announced, was "to nurture and fix the principle

Idealized in portraiture, the republican mother imbued her offspring with virtue, piety, and patriotism. A Charles Willson Peale painting of Mrs. Richard Tilghman of Maryland and her sons, 1789. *(Maryland Historical Society, Baltimore)*

of virtue." Only mothers, contended the head of a Connecticut academy, could "plant the seeds of vice or virtue in their offspring." "Let the ladies of a country be educated properly" as Rush told his Philadelphia audience, "and they will form its manner and character."

Like Rush and the academy heads, other defenders of women's education proposed an enhanced social and civic role for mothers. But female education also served as the crux of a new eruption of raised expectations. After the Revolution, a rhetoric of female self-esteem emerged, along with a new contention: Education could be a remedy for female inequality. Author Judith Sargent Murray, who celebrated "excellency in our sex," expounded this view in a series of articles under the pseudonym "Constantia." Education, she contended, would eradicate women's sense of inferiority. An anonymous "aged matron of Connecticut," who published her own *Female Advocate*, continued the argument in 1801. Women, she asserted, had been deprived of education in order to keep them inferior and subject. A similar claim appeared in the salutatory address of a 1793 Philadelphia Academy graduate who launched an attack on "despotic man." Men, said Priscilla Mason, "denied us the means of knowledge and then reproached us for the want of it. . . . They doomed the sex to servile or frivolous employment on purpose to degrade their minds, that they themselves might hold unrivalled the power and preemptions they usurped." Throughout most of the eighteenth century, women had customarily described themselves in a self-deprecatory manner, with repeated reference to female weakness and foibles. The new assault on male "power and preemptions" and the celebration of "excellency in our sex" were a significant departure.

Education's role as a remedy for inequality was not solely an American theme. It was also the gist of Englishwoman Mary Wollstonecraft's *Vindication of the Rights of Women*, which appeared in 1792. Like academy defenders, Wollstonecraft contended that education would produce superior wives and mothers. She also decried the "false system of education" that prepared women only to appeal to men and left them in a "state of perpetual childhood." Her book, however, won little praise from American women. Even when readers accepted Wollstonecraft's conclusions, they usually condemned her life-style, deplored her premarital liaisons, or felt she denigrated feminine character. Several readers voiced appreciation. "In very many of her sentiments, she . . . *speaks my mind*," Philadelphia Quaker Elizabeth Drinker wrote in her diary in 1796. Young Eliza Southgate of Maine, in 1801, conceded to her diary that she admired the English author's sentiments, "prejudice set aside." Other women expressed disgust and abhorrence. The ideas voiced by Wollstonecraft, however, were not unlike those set forth by Judith Sargent Murray, whose essays appeared in Massachusetts journals in the 1780s and 1790s.

Murray, too, endorsed pragmatic arguments for women's education. "Felicity of families," she contended, depended on competent wives who could manage their time and accounts. But women's education, Murray asserted, would benefit self as well as society. Development of women's rational faculties would inculcate self-respect, self-confidence, and aspiration. The daughter addressed as a "rational being," Murray wrote in a 1784 essay, would develop "reverence of self . . . the glow of virtue . . . that elevation of soul, that dignity, which is ever attendant upon self-approbation." Such a daughter would not throw herself away on the first suitor who proposed; nor should girls be trained solely for marriage. Rather, "the art of economical independence should be placed within their grasp." To Judith Sargent Murray, women's education held the key to the future. As she wrote in 1798, "I expect to see our young women forming a new era in female history."

The graduates of the early academies did not fulfill all of the goals set forth for women in the heady 1790s. They did not gain entry into "the Church, the Bar, the Senate," as Priscilla Mason had hoped in 1793. Nor did they gain access to "all the emoluments, offices, honors, and merits" that men had usurped, according to the "aged matron of Connecticut" in 1801. For many students, the experience of independence provided by a few years of academy training was their first and last before becoming agreeable companions to sensible men, and virtuous mothers of patriotic sons. But academy graduates were soon to be prominent among those women who entered teaching, missionary work, and reform in the early nineteenth century. Expansion of primary schooling, meanwhile, affected women's status in the new nation. After the Revolution, female literacy began to rise; sometime between 1790 and 1830, the substantial literacy gap between men and women closed. Although academy training involved only a small group, increased literacy brought far greater numbers of women a step further into the modern world.

The major signs of a post-Revolutionary change in women's status, therefore, were a new ideal of companionate marriage, the new legitimacy of women's education, a new rhetoric of female self-esteem, and an enhanced regard for motherhood. These signs, it should be noted, were class-based. Republican womanhood, as historian Robert Gross observes, was a concept that "essentially served the interests of the emerging elite" and helped to "consolidate a middle-class gentry." The early decades of nationhood also brought the suggestion that women might serve a civic function. The role of the "republican mother," Linda Kerber points out, was a limited one. It provided a context in which "female virtues might comfortably coexist with civic virtue," and it appeared to reconcile politics and domesticity. But it was a role played solely in the home. Before the Revolution, women had been excluded from political life; afterward, they remained "on the periphery of the political community." It is possible, writes Kerber, "to read the subsequent political history of women in America as the story of women's efforts to accomplish for themselves what the Revolution failed to do."

Such accomplishments were a long way off. But by the end of the eighteenth century there were other omens of change that would affect women's roles. One was the start of female association, in the form of church-sponsored benevolent societies. Such societies, which first appeared in eastern cities around 1800, were to multiply during following decades. Another augury was the emergence of periodical literature and fiction catering to women readers. This genre was exemplified by a popular novel in 1794, Susanna Rowson's *Charlotte Temple*. A morality tale written by the founder of a prominent Massachusetts female academy, the book concerned, significantly, the evil consequences of seduction. Like female societies, women's literature was to burgeon in the years to come. A less visible sign of impending change was the beginning of a drop in family size, at least in some Quaker and New England communities, that had taken place between the Revolution and the turn of the century. This was a preview of the steady decline in the birth rate that would characterize the nineteenth century. A final preview of coming events was Samuel Slater's cotton mill in Pawtucket, Rhode Island. Started in 1791, the mill employed as its first operatives nine children under the age of twelve. During the next half-century, American manufacturing would draw thousands of women into paid employment.

If these omens were hardly noticed at the end of the century, another trend in American society caught the attention of two relentless commentators, Abigail Adams and Mercy Warren. "I deprecate that restless spirit, and that baneful pride, ambition, and thirst for power which will finally make us as wretched as our neighbors," Abigail Adams wrote to her sister, Elizabeth Shaw, in 1787. On the other side of the political fence, her longtime friend Mercy Warren, who became a Jeffersonian Republican, had a similar reaction to the ill effects of post-Revolutionary prosperity. According to Mercy Warren, changing standards of wealth and class had taken their toll on American values and virtues. "A sudden accumulation of property by privateering, by speculation, by accident or by fraud, placed many in the lap of affluence, who were without principle, education, or family," she recorded in her *History of the Revolution*, published in 1805. This sudden elevation in wealth, Mercy Warren contended, was accompanied by a descent into immoderation, avarice, tastelessness, and extravagance. Instead of the simplicity and elegance that had briefly characterized the new republic, the rising generation had acquired "a thirst for the accumulation of wealth, unknown to their ancestors." During the next half-century, republican motherhood, too, took on proportions that would have surprised its early proponents.

༺ঌৄৄ

SUGGESTED READINGS AND SOURCES

CHAPTER 3

Eliza Pinckney's letterbook, containing copies of her correspondence, is at the South Carolina Historical Society. For selections from the letterbook, see Elise Pinckney and Marvin R. Zahniser, eds., *The Letterbook of Eliza Lucas Pinckney 1739–1762* (Chapel Hill, N.C., 1972). The biography by Eliza Pinckney's descendant Harriott Horry Ravenel, *Eliza Pinckney* (New York, 1896), is based on the letterbook and other family papers. For the family history, see Frances Leigh Williams, *A Founding Family: The Pinckneys of South Carolina* (New York and London, 1978). Philip Greven, *The Protestant Temperament: Patterns of Child Rearing, Religious Experience, and the Self* (New York, 1977), and Linda K. Kerber, "The Republican Mother: Women and the Enlightenment, an American Perspective," *American Quarterly*, 28 (Summer 1976), 187–205, provide themes that are useful in interpreting the experience of Eliza Pinckney.

CHAPTER 4

For overviews of eighteenth-century women's lives, see Mary Beth Norton, *Liberty's Daughters: The Revolutionary Experience of American Women, 1750–1800* (Boston, 1980); Linda K. Kerber, *Women of the Republic: Intellect and Ideology in Revolutionary America* (Chapel Hill, N.C., 1980); and Ronald Hoffman and Peter J. Albert, eds., *Women in the Age of the American Revolution* (Charlottesville, Va., 1989).

Until recently, the major sources of information on eighteenth-century women were the works of historians of the 1920s and 1930s. See Elizabeth Dexter, *Colonial Women of Affairs* (Boston, 1931; first published 1924); Mary Sumner Benson, *Women in Eighteenth Century America: A Study of Opinion and Social Usage* (Port Washington, N.Y., 1966; first published 1935); and Julia Cherry Spruill, *Women's Life and Work in the Southern Colonies* (New York, 1938).

Much recent work on eighteenth-century women lies in the realm of family history, often in specialized local studies. On marriage and family life, see, for instance, Daniel Scott Smith, "Parental Power and Marriage Patterns: An Analysis of Historical Trends in Higham, Massachusetts," *Journal of Marriage and the Family*, 35 (August 1973), 419–428; Robert V. Wells, "Quaker Marriage Patterns in a Colonial Perspective," *William and Mary Quarterly*, 3d series, 29 (1972), 415–442; Nancy F. Cott, "Divorce and the Changing Status of Women in Eighteenth-Century Massachusetts," *William and Mary Quarterly*, 3d series, 33 (1976), 586–614; and Cott, "Eighteenth-Century Family and Social Life Revealed in Massachusetts Divorce Records," *Journal of Social History*, 10 (1976–1977), 20–43. For southern domestic life, see Daniel Blake Smith, *Inside the Big House: Planter Family Life in Eighteenth-Century Chesapeake Society* (Ithaca, N.Y., 1980); Allan Kulikoff, *Tobacco and Slaves: The Development of Southern Cultures in the Chesapeake, 1680–1800* (Chapel Hill, N.C., 1986); and Jan Lewis, *The Pursuit of Happiness: Family and Values in Jefferson's Virginia* (New York, 1983).

Philip Greven examines child-rearing attitudes and practices in *The Protestant Temperament: Patterns of Child-rearing, Religious Experience, and the Self* (New York, 1977). Alexander Keysser explores the plight of widows in his study of Woburn, Massachusetts, "Widowhood in Eighteenth-Century Massachusetts: A Problem in the History of the Family," *Perspectives in American History*, 8 (1974), 83–119. See also David Hackett Fischer, *Growing Old in America* (New York, 1977), chs. 1 and 2, and Lisa Wilson, *Life After Death: Widows in Pennsylvania, 1750–1850* (Philadelphia, 1992). Cornelia Hughes Dayton discusses sexual attitudes and social relations in "Taking the Trade: Abortion and Gender Relations in an Eighteenth-Century New England Village," *William and Mary Quarterly*, 3d series, 48 (January 1991), 19–49. For comparisons of male and female educational skills, see Kenneth Lockridge, *Literacy in Colonial New England* (New York, 1974); Linda Auwers, "Reading the Marks of the Past: Exploring Female Literacy in Colonial Windsor, Connecticut," *Historical Methods*, 13 (1980); E. Jennifer Monaghan, "Literacy Instruction and Gender in Colonial New England," *American Quarterly*, 40 (March 1988), 18–41; Joel Perlman and Dennis Shirley, "When Did New England Women Acquire Literacy?" *William and Mary Quarterly*, 3d series, 48 (January 1991), 50–67; and Patricia Cline Cohen, *A Calculating People: Numeracy in Early America* (Chicago, 1982).

Mary Beth Norton describes Elizabeth Murray's career in "A Cherished Spirit of Independence: The Life of an Eighteenth-Century Boston Businesswoman," in Carol Ruth Berkin and Mary Beth Norton, eds., *Women of America*, pp. 37–67. Kathryn A. Jacob examines women's roles in trade in "The 'Second Sex' in Baltimore," *Maryland Historical Magazine*, 71 (Fall 1976), 283–295. Laurel Thatcher Ulrich explores a midwife's experience in "Martha Ballard and Her Girls: Women's Work in Eighteenth-Century Maine," in Stephen Innes, ed., *Work and Labor in Early America* (Chapel Hill, N.C., 1988), pp. 70–105; "'The Living Mother of a Living Child': Midwifery and Mortality in Post-revolutionary New England," *William and Mary Quarterly*, 3d series, 46 (January 1989), 27–48; and *A Midwife's Tale: The Life of Martha Ballard, Based on her Diary, 1785–1812* (New York, 1990). Joan M. Jensen considers the work roles of rural women in the Philadelphia hinterland in the late colonial and early national periods in *Loosening the Bonds: Mid-Atlantic Farm Women 1750–1850* (New Haven, Conn., 1986). Carole Shammas draws connections between household furnishings and women's domestic roles in "The Domestic Environment in Early Modern England and America," *Journal of Social History*, 14 (1980), 3–24. See also Shammas, "Early American Women and Control Over Capital," in Hoffman and Albert, eds., *Women in the Age of the American Revolution*, pp. 134–154, and *The Pre-Industrial Consumer in England and America* (Oxford, 1990).

Marylynn Salmon assesses women's legal disabilities in *Women and the Law of Property in Early America* (Chapel Hill, N.C., 1986) and "Equality or Submersion? Feme Covert Status in Early Pennsylvania," in Berkin and Norton, eds., *Women of America: A History* (Boston, 1979), pp. 92–111. For inheritance law, see Toby L. Ditz, *Property and Kinship: Inheritance in Early Connecticut, 1750–1820* (Princeton, N.J., 1986) and Carole Shammas, Marylynn Salmon, and Michel Dahlin, *Inheritance in America: Colonial Times to the Present* (New Brunswick, N.J., 1977). Joan R. Gunderson and Gwen Victor Gampel stress practices benefiting women that differed from English practices in "Married Women's Legal Status in Eighteenth-Century New York and Virginia," *William and Mary Quarterly*, 3d series, 39 (1982), 114–134. Informative articles on inheritance law and women's legal rights appear in Hoffman and Albert, eds., *Women in the Age of the American Revolution*, cited above, parts I and IV.

Anthony F. C. Wallace describes the Revolution's effect on the Iroquois in *The Death and Rebirth of the Seneca* (New York, 1969). Theda Perdue assesses the impact of white settlement on eighteenth-century Indian women in "Cherokee Women: A Study in Changing Gender Roles" (Paper presented at the American Historical Association, San Francisco, 1989) and continues the story in "Cherokee Women and the Trail of Tears," *Journal of Women's History* (1989), 14–30. For Spanish settlements, see Ramon A. Gutierrez, "Honor Ideology, Marriage Negotiation, and Class-Gender Domination in New Mexico, 1690–1846," *Latin American Perspectives* 12 (Winter 1985), 81–104, and *When Jesus Came, the Corn Mothers Went Away: Marriage, Sexuality, and Power in New Mexico, 1500–1846* (Stanford, 1992). Elaine Forman Crane compares the impact of skewed sex ratios in New England and the Caribbean in "The Socioeconomics of a Female Majority in Eighteenth-Century Bermuda," *Signs* 15 (Winter 1990), 231–258.

Aspects of female religious experience are examined in Mary Beth Norton, "'My Resting Reaping Times': Sarah Osborne's Defense of her Unfeminine Activities, 1767," *Signs* 2 (1976), 515–529; Louis Billington, "Female Laborers in the Church: Women Preachers in the Northeastern United States, 1790–1840," *Journal of American Studies* 19 (1985), 369–394; and Ann Taves, ed., *Religion and Domestic Violence in Early New England: The Memoir of Abigail Abbot Bailey* (Bloomington, Ind., 1989). For the link between religious experience and female friendship, see Carol F. Karlsen and Laurie Crumpackers, eds., *The Journal of Esther Edwards Burr: 1754–1757* (New Haven, Conn., 1984). For Ann Lee's followers, see Stephen J. Stein, *The Shaker Experience in America* (New Haven, Conn., 1992). For the Society of Friends, see Jean Soderlund, "Women's Authority in Pennsylvania and New Jersey Quaker Meetings, 1680–1760," *William and Mary Quarterly*, 3d series, 44 (October 1987), 722–749, and Elaine Forman et al., eds., *The Diary of Elizabeth Drinker* (Boston, 1991).

The Revolution's impact on women is a subject of debate. In *Liberty's Daughters*, Mary Beth Norton offers an account of women's everyday lives and stresses the positive impact of the Revolutionary era. Linda K. Kerber, in *Women of the Republic*, concentrates on women's legal status and presents a more muted view of the Revolution's impact, which she sees as uneven. For a negative view, see Joan Hoff Wilson's argument that the Revolution bypassed women in "The Illusion of Change: Women and the American Revolution," in Alfred E. Young, ed., *The American Revolution: Explorations in the History of American Radicalism* (DeKalb, Ill., 1976), pp. 385–415. Joan R. Gunderson examines women's place in revolutionary rhetoric in "Independence, Citizenship, and the American Revolution," *Signs* 13 (Autumn 1987), 59–77. For women's predicaments during the war, see Mary Beth Norton, "Eighteenth-Century Women in Peace and War: The Case of the Loyalists," *William and Mary Quarterly*, 3d series, 33 (1976), 386–409, and Norton, "'What an Alarming Crisis is This': Southern Women and the American Revolution," in Jeffrey J. Crow and Larry J. Tise, eds., *The Southern Experience in the American Revolution* (Chapel Hill, N.C., 1978). The 1976 bicentennial spurred the publication of many books about women during the war, among them Linda Grant DePauw, *Founding Mothers: Women of the Revolutionary Era* (Chicago, 1975); Paul Engle, *Women in the American Revolution* (Chicago, 1976); and Elizabeth Evans, ed., *Weathering the Storm: Women of the American Revolution* (New York, 1975). For Abigail Adams, see Lynne Withey, *Dearest Friend: A Life of Abigail Adams* (New York, 1981); Paul C. Nagle, *The Adams Women: Abigail and Louisa Adams, Their Sisters and Daughters* (New York, 1987); Edith B. Gelles, "The Abigail Industry," *William and Mary Quarterly*, 3d series, 45 (October 1988), 657–683; and Gelles, *Portia: The World of Abigail Adams* (Bloomington, Ind., 1992).

For new attitudes toward women's education at the end of the eighteenth century, see Linda K. Kerber, "Daughters of Columbia: Educating Women for the Republic, 1787–1805," in Stanley Elkins and Eric McKitrick, eds., *The Hofstadter Aegis: A Memorial* (New York, 1974) and Ann D. Gordon, "The Young Ladies Academy of Philadelphia," in Berkin and Norton, eds., *Women of America,* pp. 68–91. Changes in women's status during the postrevolutionary decades are examined in Linda K. Kerber, "The Republican Mother: Women and the Enlightenment, an American Perspective," *American Quarterly,* 28 (Summer 1976), 187–205; Kerber, "The Paradox of Women's Citizenship in the Early Republic: The Case of Martin *v.* Massachusetts, 1805," *American Historical Review,* 97 (April 1992), 349–378; Patricia M. Alexander, "The Creation of the American Eve: The Cultural Dialogue on the Nature and Role of Women in Late Eighteenth-Century America," *Early American Literature,* 9 (1975), 252–266; Ruth H. Bloch, "American Feminine Ideals in Transition: The Rise of the Moral Mother, 1785–1815," *Feminist Studies,* 4 (1978), 101–126; Bloch, "The Gendered Meanings of Virtue in Revolutionary America," *Signs* 13 (Autumn 1987), 37–58; Jan Lewis, "The Republican Wife: Virtue and Seduction in the Early Republic," *William and Mary Quarterly,* 3d series, XVIV (1987), 689–721; and Linda Kerber et al., "Beyond Roles, Beyond Spheres: Thinking About Gender in the Early Republic," *William and Mary Quarterly,* 3d series, 46 (July 1989), 565–585. For changing trends in marriage and in its dissolution, see Merril D. Smith, *Breaking the Bonds: Marital Discord in Pennsylvania, 1730–1830* (New York, 1991).

Jane Rendall provides a comparative perspective in *The Origins of Modern Feminism: Women in Britain, France, and the United States, 1780–1860* (Chicago, 1985). Richard L. Bushman, *The Refinement of America: Persons, Houses, Cities* (New York, 1992), explores the rise of gentility in the late eighteenth century as reflected in material culture; see chs. 1–6. Lawrence Stone describes the rise of "companionate marriage" in eighteenth-century England in *The Family, Sex, and Marriage in England 1500–1800* (New York, 1979), ch. 8. Richard D. Brown provides an overview of changes in eighteenth-century society and attitudes in *Modernization: The Transformation of American Life, 1600–1865* (New York, 1976), chs. 3–5. For the emergence of the modern American family, see Carl Degler, *At Odds: Women and the Family in America From the Revolution to the Present* (New York, 1980), ch. 1.

CHAPTER 5

Sarah Hale and the *Ladies Magazine*

"I am an orphan; my parents died when I was very young and left me a small fortune," wrote "Althea" to the *Ladies Magazine*. But the small fortune, Althea revealed, caused great problems. An ardent suitor, George, who appeared to be bent on marriage, had turned his affection toward another. Althea's rival was not only beautiful but endowed with a very large fortune. And George had married her. Althea had been misled, deceived, and discarded. Her friends and relatives urged her to bring the "villain" to court and sue him for breach of promise. Reluctant to take this dire step, Althea appealed to the readers of the *Ladies Magazine*. What should she do?

Two issues later, replies began to appear, and the verdict was clear. Readers of the *Ladies Magazine* seemed overwhelmingly opposed to Althea's proposed suit against George. "Do not resort to any mercenary means for the purpose of binding up the wound of a broken heart," warned "E. E. N." Contending that it would be "unfeminine" to press such a suit in court, E. E. N. recommended that Althea "firmly and uncomplainingly bear this disappointment, thereby supporting the true delicacy of your sex." Other readers agreed, though for varied reasons. "Charity," for instance, had been similarly deceived by a man who married another, but her rejection had saved her from being the spouse of a drunkard. "He is now a poor pitiable creature; his wife proved a shrew and he became a sot," Charity wrote. "There are worse troubles than being a forsaken damsel or an old maid." But that was not all. A rich and eligible bachelor ("Miser") wrote in to point out that the very threat of suits for breach of promise had scared him away from marriageable young ladies permanently. And some women readers confirmed his point. "I am the mother of five marriageable daughters," wrote "xxxxx." Five years before, her eldest daughter, Frances Philomena, had recovered $2,000 in damages for breach of promise, and ever since then neither Frances (now "somewhat past her bloom") nor her younger sisters had had any suitors at all. "I have wished two thousand times," concluded their miserable mother, "that the money and the lawyer who advised the suit, were at the bottom of the Red Sea." A final correspondent told the same sad tale. Ten years earlier, "Lucy" had won a suit for breach of promise and now, a spinster of thirty-five, she had but one message for Althea. "If she sues for redress, I can assure her that she will never have another offer."

Althea's plea and the lively correspondence that followed all appeared in the *Ladies Magazine,* a Boston periodical, in the spring of 1830. And all of the letters were probably written by the magazine's editor, Sarah Hale. A widow in her early forties, Sarah Hale had been hired to edit the *Ladies Magazine* in 1828, when it first appeared. She had only "reluctantly engaged" on her new job, as she told her readers in the first issue, and with such "trembling" that she was hardly able to proceed. But since then she had acquired a loyal following. She had also created a most distinctive publication; for the *Ladies Magazine* was, as Sarah Hale claimed, "unprecedented."

Although many women's magazines were published in Boston in 1828, most if not all were compiled by men. "A magazine edited by a woman for women had never been conducted, so far as I know, either in the Old World or the New," Sarah Hale later contended. The *Ladies Magazine* was distinctive in another way, too. Unlike its competitors, a bevy of "miscellanies" full of pilfered prose, the *Ladies Magazine* was entirely original. Like the letter from Althea and the answers to it, most of its copy was written by Sarah Hale herself. But above all, the *Ladies Magazine* had a mission: "to make females better acquainted with their duties and privileges." Through its pages, for almost a decade, Sarah Hale would define the perimeters of "woman's sphere." She would also promote her doctrine of "influence"—the subtle, unobtrusive type of power that women might exert over others. At the helm of the *Ladies Magazine,* Hale would start to forge an identity for middle-class women.

The appearance of the *Ladies Magazine,* finally, was a turning point for Sarah Hale. Before 1828, she had been an impoverished widow, attempting to support her five young children by writing poems and selling hats. But afterward, as an editor, she began to rise to a prominent role in public life. Such a role was, ordinarily, far beyond the boundaries of sphere set forth in her columns, where readers were urged to devote themselves to "the chaste, disinterested circle of the fireside." Women's obligations, said the *Ladies Magazine,* were private, domestic, and interpersonal. But there were some exceptions, as Sarah Hale explained.

> It is only on emergencies, in cases where duty demands the sacrifice of female sensitiveness, that a lady of sense and delicacy will come before the public, in a manner to make herself conspicuous. There is little danger that such an one will be arrogant in her pretensions. These remarks may be considered as allusions to our own case.

As a self-supporting widow forced to embark on a career "foreign to the usual character and occupations of her sex," Sarah Hale was both deprived of and released from the domestic and private role that she exalted for her readers.

She had known this role well, however, before her life was interrupted by "emergencies."

Many aspects of Sarah Hale's early experiences would have been familiar to readers of the *Ladies Magazine*. Born in 1788, Sarah Buell grew up on a farm, as did most of her contemporaries. The Buell family had been in New England for six generations. When Sarah was born, the third of four children, her parents lived near Newport, New Hampshire, where the Buell children probably went to school. As a child, Sarah spent much time with a favorite brother, Horatio, only one year older. Horatio, who attended Dartmouth, shared his experiences with her over vacations. But after graduation, he moved away to a town in New York, where he practiced law and later became a judge. Ambitious and mobile, Horatio had left Sarah behind.

In 1806, the year her brother entered college, young Sarah Buell opened a small school, at which she taught for seven years. During this period, her family suffered one disaster after another. Her mother and sister died, on the same day, in 1811. Her remaining brother, Charles, left for sea and drowned. Her father, once a Revolutionary officer, opened a tavern in Newport, which failed within two years. In 1813, after this torrent of death, disappearance, and debacle, Sarah Buell married David Hale, a young lawyer with political prospects. Their five children were born between 1815 and 1822.

David Hale proved a model husband, a devoted father, and as thousands of readers would later learn from Sarah Hale's allusions to her early life, an ideal companion. He also was an active participant in community affairs and head of the local Masonic lodge. But Sarah Hale's marriage was ill-fated. A few days before the Hales' last child was born, David Hale died of pneumonia, leaving his widow to support the family. Sarah Hale, now thirty-four, wore black for the rest of her life. Her husband's death was its crucial event. She had lost not only her companion and provider but also her vocation, that of wife. In the years to come, she would re-create in print the home and role that David Hale, by his early death, had failed to provide for her in fact.

At the outset, Sarah Hale and her sister-in-law went into the millinery business, one of the few occupations that genteel but needy women might enter. While keeping homes and raising children, the two sisters dealt in "hats and new fancy goods." The venture soon failed. But throughout her interlude as a milliner, Sarah Hale wrote at a prodigious rate. A constant contributor to periodicals, the young widow became an aggressive entrant in literary contests and a poetry prize winner in a Boston magazine, the *Ladies Album*, which printed twenty of her pieces. In 1823, with the aid of her husband's fellow Masons, she published a book of poems, suggestively titled *The Genius of Oblivion*. This was followed in 1827 by a novel, *Northwood*. The book had been written, Sarah Hale explained in a later edition, "with a baby in my arms" and published "not to win fame, but support for my little children."

On the basis of *Northwood*'s success, Sarah Hale was invited by a Boston minister, Reverend Blake, Episcopal cleric and head of a secondary school for "young ladies," to edit a monthly magazine for women that he intended to start. The invitation, Sarah Hale later explained, was "unsolicited" and "unexpected," but she accepted immediately. In retrospect, the new opportunity seemed "an ordering of divine providence." By the spring of 1828, after the first few issues had appeared, it was clear that the *Ladies Magazine* would be a success. The first issue alone had won it a hefty subscription list of 600. At this juncture, Sarah Hale, now forty, left Newport behind. She moved her family to the cultural and commercial capital of New England.

Boston in 1828 was a thriving city of 60,000 and, like New York and Philadelphia, a center of publishing. Little capital was needed to start a magazine in the 1820s—just enough for a small press and a pair of scissors for cutting articles out of other magazines and using them again. Second-hand copy supplied three-fifths of the contents of the typical "miscellany" or "repository." Thousands of such magazines were started between 1825 and 1850 but died at almost the same rate they were born. Their average life span was less than two years. Subscription fees, the only source of income, were difficult to collect, and circulation was limited. It was rising rapidly, however, with the expansion of cities. A growing urban audience supported the publishing industry, and the majority of this audience was women. Many, like Sarah Hale, had recently moved to towns and cities, leaving their relatives and contacts behind in some rural village, like Newport, New Hampshire.

The idea of a women's magazine was hardly new with Reverend Blake. Since the 1780s, such periodicals had been printed for a small urban audience. By 1828, a multitude were available—not just the *Ladies Album*, to which Sarah Hale had contributed, but swarms of competitors—the *Portfolio*, the *Young Ladies Journal*, the *Ladies Mirror*, the *Ladies Museum and Weekly Repository*, and the *Bower of Taste*. Short-lived, they were filled with fashion plates, sentimental stories, and secondhand copy, usually clipped from English magazines. But the *Ladies Magazine*, the first of its type to last over five years, differed from its competitors. To Sarah Hale, such "miscellanies" were inappropriate to the needs of serious, responsible middle-class wives. The *Ladies Magazine* would not foster fashion or frivolity. It would, instead, devote itself to "the progress of female improvement." It would define for its readers their significant role in society, "awaken them to their sense of importance as women . . . aid them in their endeavors to perform their duties as women." The *Ladies Magazine* reader would be neither a household drudge nor an extravagant devotee of the latest styles. She would be a moral and spiritual exemplar.

The very first issue, which appeared in January 1828, revealed Sarah Hale's distinctive style. Fifty imposing pages of print, the *Ladies Magazine* was clearly an ambitious publication. But it also adopted a tone of deference. Sarah Hale's first column began with an appeal to men. Male relatives of female subscribers, she insisted, had nothing to fear from the *Ladies Magazine*. Not only would it make its readers better wives, mothers, daughters, and housekeepers, not only would it offer each subscriber "a means of agreeably beguiling the interval" while her husband was away at work, but it would leave male authority unimpaired and "domestic felicity" undisturbed. Gentlemen were invited to look through its pages to see for themselves.

The first issue could hardly have failed such inspection. The imaginative

"Letters" column had not yet been invented. But *Ladies Magazine* readers might delve into a "Sketch of American Character," designed to foster patriotic pride, or an essay denouncing the practice of dueling, or an article by a Boston minister, extolling the vocation of motherhood. "Most of the distinguished men on record received the seeds of their greatness from maternal culture," he declared. Readers also might encounter an appeal to support a Boston society for widows and orphans or a poem about the death of a child ("A Mother's Lament") or another about a girl gone mad ("The Harp of the Maniac Maiden"). Above all, they could read about Sarah Hale's favorite cause, "the granting to females of the advantages of a systematic and thorough education." The goal of such training, Hale explained, was neither to usurp male roles nor to encroach on men's prerogatives. Rather, it was to enable "each individual . . . to perfect the moral and intellectual character of those within her sphere."

None of the subscribers to the *Ladies Magazine* in 1828 needed to be told what "woman's sphere" was. The term was already in widespread use, especially by ministers, whose sermons and tracts often addressed female audiences. But in the *Ladies Magazine*, sphere would be celebrated relentlessly throughout. While men, more base, confronted the mundane world of business and commerce, government and politics, women, more moral, modest, virtuous, and benevolent, held superior status within the home. There, they could mold the character of their children and subtly, invisibly, uplift and improve the character of their husbands. Infiltration, not agitation, was the *Ladies Magazine* style. Its reader was not a wild-eyed reformer or aggressive interloper, seeking to invade the province of men or assert herself in public affairs. On the contrary, "Home is *her* world," as Sarah Hale assured subscribers in 1830. "We want patterns of virtue, of piety, of intelligence and usefulness in private life."

The distinctive nature of woman's sphere was thrown into relief by what lay outside it, "A society given over without reservation to the pursuit of wealth." Throughout the *Ladies Magazine,* Sarah Hale decried the failings of "this banknote world" and its mundane values—materialism, competitiveness, and acquisitiveness. Her readers were urged to maintain a "nobler sphere" of their own, "purer, more excellent, more spiritual." Under woman's control, said the *Ladies Magazine,* the home could be both a refuge from the commercial world and an antidote to it. "Our men are sufficiently money-making," Sarah Hale declared. "Let us keep our women and children from the contagion as long as possible." To be sure, "emergencies" sometimes intruded on women's lives, as they had on Sarah Hale's. But in other cases, "contagion" could be halted. As E. E. N. warned Althea, when telling her not to sue George, it was best to avoid "mercenary means" and thereby support "the delicacy of your sex."

Woman's sphere, clearly, was not merely a place or even a vocation but a value system. And its values, said the *Ladies Magazine,* reflected woman's distinctive character traits. In issue after issue, writing under the alias "P," Sarah Hale lost no opportunity to identify and exalt these traits. Women were imbued with "benevolent feelings," "amiableness of disposition," and "delicacy of moral sense." Compared to men, they had "more ardency of feeling, greater strength of attachment and superior purity of affection." And they were also equipped with intuition—an innate, feminine form of intelligence. "The female sex have long been the acknowledged possessors of a sort of mental quickness and intellectual acumen," as Sarah Hale explained in 1828, "which has enabled them to discern, or at least to recognise, those smaller springs of action that regulate the conduct of mankind, which, from their supposed insignificance, have escaped the notice of the grosser sex." Sympathetic and affectionate, moral and intuitive, a woman clearly had more in common with other women than with any member of "the grosser sex." As Sarah Hale contended in 1829, "the natural traits of her character are congenial with the emotion of friendship." Innately trusting and noncompetitive, she was unlikely to be "drawn aside," as a man might be, by "the silly struggle for honor and preferment." Above all, women were united by their feminine sensibility, as readers of the *Ladies Magazine* confirmed. "I feel as a Woman, I speak as a Woman, and I hope, I *understand* as a Woman," wrote "Cornelia" in 1830. ("Cornelia," of course, may well have been Sarah Hale.)

The nature of female sensibility was revealed in *Ladies Magazine* poetry and fiction. Although Sarah Hale intended the journal to serve as an outlet for female "effusions," she also intended to protect the modesty and anonymity of her contributors. Women authors of stories and poems, as of letters and essays, therefore, were usually identified, if at all, only by pseudonyms or initials. Some effusions, mainly unsigned, were contributed by professional writers—among them Catharine Sedgwick, Elizabeth Oakes Smith, and indefatigable Lydia Sigourney, the most prolific woman poet of the early nineteenth century and a friend of Sarah Hale's. Others were contributed by unknown aspirants such as "Inez" or "Lileth" or "A young lady from Boston." Over half of the *Ladies Magazine* was written by Sarah Hale herself. But just as her essays sought to exalt female character, so did the effusions. Full of sympathy, sentiment, and graveyard scenes, *Ladies Magazine* poetry and fiction was, in its way, devoted to "the progress of female improvement."

Almost all of the poetry fell into the category of consolation literature—pieces intended to bring comfort to mourners who, like Sarah Hale, had lost mother, husband, sister, brother, or, more frequently, children. Some poems took on a morbid tone, as suggested by "The Eye of the Dead," "Burial of a Motherless Infant," "The Departed," or "The Dying Girl." Others, such as "The Blind Mother and her Children," sought to evoke tears. Short fiction was more likely to invoke the theme of love, though preferably chaste, ethereal love—such as that (in one case) of brother and sister, "so pure in its indulgence, so holy in its effects upon the heart," or better yet, that of mother for child. In "The Mother," for instance, an aged parent, before expiring, told a stranger about the deaths of her first three children and the suicide of the fourth. The brother-loving sister also died, as did most *Ladies Magazine* heroines. Many effusions took the form of fictional obituaries; they gave long accounts of the dead woman's character and spared no graphic detail ("I have since seen her in her coffin and excepting that the bright eye was pressed down beneath its purple lid, there was no change in its countenance.") But the gallery of heroines, dead or alive, served an inspirational purpose. Their virtues had an uplifting effect on friends, family, and community;

the effusions conveyed a message. In almost every one, a woman exerted influence over all whom she encountered. And influence was a main theme of the *Ladies Magazine.*

"The government and the glory of the world" might belong to man, as Sarah Hale told her readers in 1832. "But nevertheless, what man shall become depends upon the secret, silent, influence of woman." The power of female influence was never fully defined: it was so awesome, it defied description. But clearly, the woman who exerted it was at an advantage, especially over men. "Inspiration springs up in her path—it follows her footsteps," Sarah Hale proclaimed in 1830. When man approached her, he did so "with an air, a reverence, and an affection which before he knew not he possessed." And influence over men, if exerted correctly, could bring tangible rewards. *Authority* over men must never be usurped, Sarah Hale warned, but

> still, women may, if they exert their talents and the opportunities nature has furnished, obtain an influence in society that will be paramount with authority. They may enjoy the luxuries of wealth, without enduring the labors to acquire it; and the honors of office, without feeling its cares, and the glory of victory, without suffering the dangers of battle.

The *Ladies Magazine* reader was not only to serve as a moral counterweight to the man who supported her and to provide him with refuge from the competitive world; she could also, if capable, share in the spoils.

To be effective, women's influence over men had to be so subtle as to seem unnoticeable. But over children it was more direct. Mothers, said the *Ladies Magazine,* could shape the minds and morals of the next generation, "the countless millions that will fill the continent." More important, as Sarah Hale pointed out, mothers had almost limitless opportunity to improve the character of men. ("Prudence and perseverance" should be used in child discipline, she recommended, since "injust and cruel mothers produce injust and cruel men.") But more important, the *Ladies Magazine* promoted a cause that had evolved when Sarah Hale was a girl. The educated mother, she insisted, would be best qualified to instill her children with virtue and piety, to raise sons who would be "polished pillars in the temple of our national glory." Women's education was hardly a new proposal. But in the *Ladies Magazine,* it found a vociferous advocate.

While the *Portfolio* and the *Ladies Mirror* published fashion plates and plagiarized essays, the *Ladies Magazine* became a chronicle of women's education. In her monthly column, Sarah Hale supported girls' academies, allied herself with women educators, and celebrated all their achievements. Readers might learn about the opening of Catharine Beecher's Hartford Female Seminary in 1828, about the anniversary of Emma Willard's famous Troy Female Seminary, or about the efforts of Mary Lyon, a Massachusetts educator, to raise funds to start a new female seminary. From Ipswich, Massachusetts, to Scottsboro, Georgia, Sarah Hale found academies and seminaries worthy of description in the *Ladies Magazine.* Her effusions promoted the cause as well. In "Confessions of a Husband," for instance, a man was bored by his ignorant wife and envied his neighbor, whose educated wife was a better companion and more efficient housekeeper.

Sarah Hale always expressed her position with deference. "We should solicit education as a favor," she exhorted her readers, "not exact it as a right." But contributors to the *Ladies Magazine* sometimes harbored egalitarian notions. It was unclear to "N. G. P.," for instance, that women were less intelligent than men, just because they had not yet had an equal chance to acquire "intellectual culture." "We must open to each indifferently the halls of academic learning," wrote N. G. P., "before the question of intellectual inferiority can be completely and satisfactorily settled."

A superior wife and mother, the educated woman had other advantages, as *Ladies Magazine* readers learned. She would also be prepared to support herself in "emergencies," when family members failed to do so. Fathers, for instance, could fail in business, husbands could die at the peak of their promise. In particular, the *Ladies Magazine* endorsed the vocation of teaching—an extension of woman's natural role as guardian of the young. Women, as Sarah Hale contended, had "many natural qualifications for the instruction of infants as men have not." In New England, by 1828, the woman teacher had already made inroads. Like Sarah Hale, many of the *Ladies Magazine*'s known contributors had been teachers, especially at girls' academies. In the 1830s, however, young women began to teach at common schools as well. The *Ladies Magazine* was supporting an innovation when it contended that women "might be advantageously employed in the business of education to a far greater extent than has been practiced." And since common schools were supported at public expense, woman teachers were needed more than ever, Hale explained: they could be paid less.

But women's influence need not end at the classroom. It could also extend into the community without violating the precepts of sphere, as Sarah Hale herself demonstrated. Throughout the years of the *Ladies Magazine,* she was an active participant in Boston women's associations and a vocal supporter of women's causes—causes that not only extended female influence into public life but, in Sarah Hale's case, served as a stepping stone to local prominence and upper-class contacts. During the early 1830s, *Ladies Magazine* readers learned about all of her projects.

They read about Sarah Hale's massive fund-raising drive to complete the Bunker Hill monument—a tribute to Revolutionary War heroes that men had started but failed to finish. Were all women in New England to contribute a pittance, Hale told her readers, they could succeed where men had failed. Female patriotism was exceeded only by female benevolence. Month after month, the *Ladies Magazine* constituency learned about associations run by Boston women of social standing to help poor women and children. They read about the Boston Society for Widows and Orphans, run by "a number of respectable ladies." They read about the Sabbath school movement, which provided a day of moral instruction for the indigent young. They heard a great deal about the new infant school movement, which sought to remove poor children from the contamination of vice, ignorance, and poverty at home and imbue them, at a tender age, with middle-class values. And they learned about Sarah Hale's favorite cause, the Seaman's Aid Society, a model of female benevolence. It was also a society that she had founded herself.

Organized in 1833, the Seaman's Aid Society was concerned not with Boston's sailors but rather with their abandoned wives, widows, and children. These innocent victims of male neglect were often left destitute, in chronic distress and depraved surroundings, when husbands and fathers departed for sea (as Charles Buell had done) for long periods or forever, leaving no provision for their support. Like the Bunker Hill monument drive, the society was an effort to step in where men had failed. It was also an avenue through which women of means and competence could help less privileged women who had been left in the lurch by negligent providers. Indeed, it would help such women to help themselves, since Sarah Hale favored self-support over charity. Under her leadership, the Seaman's Aid Society was transformed from a mere sewing circle into a veritable conglomerate of benevolence. Besides a clothing store and workshop, which employed fifty women to sew seamen's outfits, the society ran an industrial school for girls, an infant school, a Sabbath school, a free library, and a respectable boarding house. By underselling local sweatshops and driving disreputable boarding houses out of business, the Seaman's Aid Society fought the evils of the "bank-note world." It also mobilized female influence to provide homes, income, and uplift for unfortunate women and children.

While the perimeters of woman's sphere might be stretched to include such worthy activism, politics and public agitation were beyond the pale. Sarah Hale often brought them up in the *Ladies Magazine* to demonstrate the limits of "sphere." Public speaking, for instance, was abhorrent. Reformer Frances Wright, who gave lectures to mixed audiences of men and women in 1829, was denounced by a male critic as "a shameless and impious woman," and Sarah Hale agreed. Abolitionist agitation was also undesirable, since it entailed female interference in politics. While slavery was morally objectionable, Hale reminded her readers, it was best to combat it by "unobtrusive exertion of influence." Hale herself, for instance, supported the goals of the American Colonization Society and tried to raise money for a girls' school in Liberia. "Women's rights" appealed least of all. "The term . . . is one to which I have an almost constitutional aversion," Hale announced in 1833. "It is a kind of talisman, which conjures up to my mind the image of a positive, conceited, domineering wife, than whom scarce any object in nature can be more disgusting."

But if female violations of sphere were distressing, even more distressing were male assaults on feminine values, or indeed on women themselves. Although the *Ladies Magazine* remained deferential, the loyal subscriber could not help noticing that men, "the grosser sex," were at the root of most of the evils condemned in its pages. Althea's deceitful suitor, George, was only one of a series of troublemakers. Sometimes whole contingents were identified—Mormon men, for instance, who forced women to practice polygamy; or the mob of local men who attacked and burned a Catholic convent near Boston. This was "a wrong to women . . . at which every female heart must revolt," Sarah Hale declared. In issue after issue, moreover, the vice and abuse of men provided a persistent subtheme. Throughout *Ladies Magazine* essays and fiction, it was men, as a sex, who were duelists and drinkers, seducers and deserters, misers and misogynists, money-minded and violence-prone, "injust" and cruel. Constant vigilance, clearly, was needed to keep "the grosser sex" in line. Vigilance, however, was also needed to curb that distinctively feminine temptation, frivolity.

　　Sarah Hale opposed extravagance in dress and disliked the most popular feature of contemporary women's magazines: the fashion plate. Such illustrations encouraged slavish imitation of foreign styles and were therefore not merely frivolous but unpatriotic. For two years the *Ladies Magazine* resisted the plates. Then, in November of 1830, Sarah Hale began to give in, although not without a struggle. The first fashion plate, a horrendous engraving of an imported dress style, also revealed what appeared to be a decapitated head, decked out in a bizarre coiffure. This repulsive plate illustrated Sarah Hale's contention: fashion was absurd and imitation inane. Similar plates and critiques continued

Sarah Hale's first fashion plate, which appeared in the *Ladies Magazine* in November 1830, was intended to illustrate the foolishness of imitating European styles. Front and rear views of an elaborately coiffed head, hanging in mid-air, gave the plate a touch of the grotesque. (Ladies Magazine, *November 1830*)

for about a year. But in November 1831, the *Ladies Magazine* shifted gears and began to show fashions appropriate for "the calmer enjoyments of domestic life, elegantly illustrated." The next month, Sarah Hale capitulated completely. The *Ladies Magazine* would print plates of styles that were "elegant as well as useful." It did so until 1834, when Sarah Hale became part owner of the magazine and returned to her principles.

By that time, with or without the plates, the *Ladies Magazine* had more than proven itself. Subscriptions, probably several thousand of them, had been sold throughout New England, although Sarah Hale never boasted about her circulation. From month to month, readers eagerly awaited the latest effusions. They became accustomed to Sarah Hale's enthusiasms and opinions, as well as to her patriotic "sketches," book reviews, educational notices, and biographical essays (such as "The Mother of Washington"). They read her philosophical discourses, whether on "female character" or "the friendship of women." They looked forward to her distinctive "Letters" column, full of missives from husbands, bachelors, women in distress, and other characters Hale invented. And they were never allowed to forget that they were "gifted beings" whose influence on "the general mass of happiness or misery in the world is perhaps greater . . . than they can ever hope or believe." But the *Ladies Magazine* was not immune to the economic climate.

After a severe depression in 1834, subscriptions fell off and overdue subscription fees became hard to collect. By 1836, the magazine, almost nine years old, was in serious trouble. At year's end, Sarah Hale announced a momentous change. She had decided to "consolidate" with a Philadelphia competitor, *Godey's Lady's Book.* Its publisher, Louis Godey, had followed Hale's career and flattered her in his columns. In 1837, he bought her out. The *Lady's Book* gained both editor and subscription list—and some, though not all, of the *Ladies Magazine* tradition. Like David Hale's death and Reverend Blake's invitation, Louis Godey's offer was a turning point for Sarah Hale. She remained in Boston for the first few years of the merger, just as she had remained in Newport at the start of the *Ladies Magazine.* But in 1841, she moved to Philadelphia to join the *Lady's Book* and Louis Godey.

Godey, somewhat younger than Sarah Hale, had been born in New York in 1804 under humble circumstances. As a young man, he worked in a broker's office, cultivated literary ambitions, and ran a bookstore and circulating library. About the time that Sarah Hale moved from Newport to Boston, Godey left New York for Philadelphia, where he worked as a clerk and "scissors editor" at the *Daily Chronicle.* Like other aspiring entrepreneurs of the 1820s, Godey was anxious to strike out on his own. In 1830, he began to publish the *Lady's Book,* starting out with some secondhand plates and copy clipped from other magazines. The early *Lady's Book* was a conventional "miscellany," full of stolen material—just what the *Ladies Magazine* was not.

But Godey was also an innovator. He excelled at "embellishments"—illustrations, fashion plates, and songs with music. In April 1830, he introduced the colored fashion plate, which would become his hallmark. Eventually, scores of women were hired to color the *Lady's Book* plates by hand. In 1836, Godey branched out by starting a "family" newspaper and, soon after that, another women's publication, the *Ladies Dollar Newspaper*. With so many ventures in the works, it was opportune to hire an editor to take over the *Lady's Book*, as well as to join forces with his Boston competitor.

The business merger of Godey and Hale was a marriage of convenience with concessions and adjustments on both sides. The concessions, however, were significant, especially for Sarah Hale, who had sold out in more ways than one. "The *Ladies Magazine* . . . has lost its identity," an educational journal observed, "and, like many a 'better half,' assumed the name of a worse one." In return, Sarah Hale gained the largest reading audience in America, or, as Godey liked to put it, the widest circulation in the world. She also acquired the genial association of Louis Godey, who was to work harmoniously with her for the rest of their lives. And Godey was willing to make adjustments too.

From 1837 on, *Godey's Lady's Book* was no longer a conventional "repository." It now aspired to the status of a literary periodical, full of original essays, poems, and stories, similar to those that had appeared in the *Ladies Magazine*. After 1837, women's effusions, signed and protected by copyright, filled the *Lady's Book*. Besides Sarah Hale's addiction to original copy, Godey inherited some of her staff of "correspondents." And with the high fees he was able to pay, the *Lady's Book* could solicit contributions from a galaxy of male authors too. ("I am as usual exceedingly in need of a little money," wrote Edgar Allen Poe to Sarah Hale in 1844, as he sent in a story.) Neither Godey's fees nor the new array of contributors, except for Poe, won the *Lady's Book* great acclaim for literary merit. "The great marvel is that so many writers should have been able to produce so small an amount of literary matter," a New York newspaper commented in the 1840s. But the appeal of the *Lady's Book* lay in other channels.

Godey was solicitous and effusive toward his readers, the "fair lady subscribers." His sphere, however, was business, and his genius, publicity. A salesman and promoter, Godey was at home in the "bank-note world." He had much in common with his friend P. T. Barnum—another one-time newspaper man. The latter was starting to market freaks, stunts, and hoaxes to a growing audience. While Barnum's goal was paying spectators, Godey's was subscriptions, and his policy was to offend no one. There would, therefore, be no mention in the *Lady's Book* of anything outside the domestic realm—no reference to politics, public affairs, controversial issues, or religious disputes. These subjects, explained Godey, had no interest for "the fairest portion of creation." Sarah Hale regularly echoed these sentiments, explaining, as in 1841, that *Godey's Lady's Book* would not deal with politics or theology because "other subjects are more important for our sex and more proper for our sphere."

Woman's sphere, accordingly, was more rigidly defined in the *Lady's Book* than it had been in the *Ladies Magazine*. There, on occasion, Sarah Hale had dealt with politics and theology, if only to condemn antislavery agitation, Mormon polygamy, or anti-Catholic violence. In *Godey's Lady's Book,* however, such topics were ignored. Still, many of Sarah Hale's old concerns remained visible. She continued her support for women's education and endorsed many new ventures. To broaden the scope of the *Lady's Book* reader, she started, though rarely finished, ambitious series of historical essays. Persistently, she waged new campaigns, for patriotic goals—such as making Mount Vernon a national shrine. And throughout the pages of the *Lady's Book,* she reminded her readers that "the destiny of the human race is . . . dependent on the condition and conduct of women." The most distinctive features of the magazine, however, were not Sarah Hale's causes but her concessions: the embellishments.

In the *Lady's Book,* woman's sphere began to take on graphic shape and material substance. A major concession was, of course, the fashion plate, Godey's forte. Sarah Hale resisted, at the outset, by using the plate as a didactic tool ("Look at this plate, dear lady, and consider the influence of maternal example"). But within a year, colored plates were a prime feature, costing Godey $3,000 a year for the coloring, and more than that to import the plates from France. In addition to steel engravings, he experimented with mezzotints, woodcuts, and copper plates. In the 1860s, he introduced "extension" plates—a double-page spread that could display to advantage the enormous hoop skirts that had come into style. By now, fashion plates filled the first 24 pages of the 100-page *Lady's Book.* Sarah Hale's opposition to frivolity had been submerged in crinolines, bustles, hoops, and imported styles. The rather intangible virtues once espoused in the *Ladies Magazine* were now obscured by dress patterns, embroidery patterns, and crochet patterns, and by directions for making cloaks and mantelets, chemisettes and undersleeves. Despite Godey's fees to writers and Sarah Hale's inclinations, the *Lady's Book* became above all a fashion magazine.

The embellishments soon extended to the home. In 1849, a new, lavishly

Sarah Hale was known for her good looks and stylish, if unfrivolous, dress, as in this engraving made for *Godey's Lady's Book.* She wore black for the entirety of her fifty-year widowhood. *(© Virga Collection)*

illustrated feature, "Model Cottages," was introduced. Its engravings depicted huge and ornate Victorian dwellings, with gothic towers, lacy grillwork, mansard roofs, bay windows, and a combination of verandas, porticoes, and balconies. "Model Cottages" was followed by "Cottage Furniture" to fill up these mansions: elaborate draperies, canopied beds, upholstered sofas, and carved rosewood chairs covered in satin demask. Clearly, not all readers of *Godey's Lady's Book* would be able to live in such ornate homes, so lavishly furnished, any more than they could afford the yardage needed for the fashions featured in the magazine. Many articles, accordingly, offered less expensive tips on home decor. But the *Lady's Book* reader was still a potential consumer. Testimony to her purchasing power came in 1852 when Godey began a shopping service that would choose and forward "bridal wardrobes, bonnets, dresses, jewelry," to any part of the country.

The shopping service was only one of several public relations devices that Godey introduced to increase sales. He also took advantage of the "exchange" system, whereby the magazine received free publicity in local newspapers in exchange for subscriptions; the "premium," a small gift to new subscribers, which might be a subscription to another of Godey's publications; and the "club subscription," which meant a reduced price for a number of copies sent to the same address. Such offers drew an enthusiastic response from readers, though hardly the sort of correspondence that the *Ladies Magazine* had published in its "letters" column. "Mr. Godey i write A few lines to you A boute your Magazine," wrote Mary Ann Hoover from Indiana in 1845. "i will try to gite A Clobe up if i can." While Sarah Hale bargained with contributors, ebullient Louis Godey dealt with subscribers. And in his cheerful monthly column, he exulted over sales.

In 1837, when the *Ladies Magazine* had been absorbed, *Godey's Lady's Book* had had 10,000 subscribers. Two years later, Godey was able to announce that his subscription list exceeded "the combined number of any three monthly publications." But circulation had barely started to grow. While the *Ladies Magazine* had been limited to New England readers, the *Lady's Book* attracted a national audience. "From Maine to the Rocky Mountains, there is scarcely a hamlet, however inconsiderable, where it is not received and read," Godey proclaimed in 1841, "and in the larger towns and cities, it is universally distributed." In 1849, circulation reached 40,000 ("an edition unprecedented in this or any other country"), and at the end of 1850, it was 70,000 (twice that of any competitor, Godey announced). Finally, unscathed by the panic of 1857, the magazine reached an all-time peak. In 1860, it had a record-breaking 160,000 subscribers—thousands more than its nearest rival. The production staff grew as well. In 1851, Godey revealed, as many as 150 women were employed to color fashion plates and bind the pages of the *Lady's Book* together. Louis Godey, observed a New York magazine, "keeps almost as many ladies in his employ as the Grand Turk."

During the 1850s, as circulation mounted, the *Lady's Book* assumed a shape and style that had little in common with the long-defunct *Ladies Magazine*. "When this magazine is taken in a house, no other is wanted," a flier for the

January 1856 issue proclaimed. But the list of upcoming articles contained only one, "Maternal Counsels to a Daughter," that recalled Sarah Hale's old style. This was accompanied by "How to Make Wax Flowers and Fruit," "How to Make a Bonnet," "New Styles of Illuminating Windows and Lamp Shades," and "Poetry and History of Finger Rings." Monthly features now included "Embroidery," "Model Cottages," "Dress Patterns," and "Godey's Invaluable Receipts." Fiction had been completely discarded. All of the articles, moreover, were overshadowed by the tissue-thin fashion plates. "In this as in all other departments, we defy imitation or rivalry," Godey proclaimed. In addition, the *Lady's Book* promised the newest designs for window curtains, broderie anglaise, bonnets, caps, cloaks, evening dresses, fancy articles, headdresses, robes de chambres, carriage dresses, brides' dresses, mantillas, walking dresses, riding habits, morning dresses, as well as patterns for children's clothes, and "Needlework of All Kinds."

While the *Lady's Book* reached its peak of circulation, Sarah Hale's reputation also reached new heights. Her name became, literally, a household word, known to every reader who pored over the magazine's dress patterns and fashion plates. Women readers, moreover, bought more than the *Lady's Book*. During the 1830s, while struggling to keep the *Ladies Magazine* afloat, Sarah Hale had embarked on a profitable sideline, writing and editing books for women. In the 1840s and 1850s, women readers purchased her etiquette books, children's books, and housekeeping manuals. Above all, they bought her gift books—genteel collections of poems and stories, heavy with engravings and elaborately bound in leather and silk. Tangible tokens of female friendship, gift books were expensive but very popular. Sarah Hale's New York publishers, Harper and Brothers, could hardly keep up with the growing market. Woman's sphere had become a lucrative enterprise.

Since fame, success, or any kind of public notice remained beyond woman's sphere, the *Lady's Book* regularly printed Sarah Hale's disclaimers. "The wish to promote the reputation of my sex and my country were the earliest mental emotions I can recollect," she disclosed. If she had made a name for herself, against her inclinations, it had been done only to support her children. "The Mother, not the Author, has been successful." Sarah Hale's most distinctive success, however, was neither the massive circulation of the *Lady's Book* nor the steady sales of her gift books and housekeeping manuals. It was, rather, the brief existence of the *Ladies Magazine*, bent on "the progress of female improvement."

In the *Ladies Magazine* of the early 1830s, Sarah Hale had attempted to provide a secure and significant social niche for her middle-class readers, safe from the perils of the "bank-note world" and immune to its base commercial values. Woman's sphere, said the *Ladies Magazine*, was a "nobler" one, attuned to female values and character, "purer, more excellent, more spiritual." It was a power base from which influence could emanate while moral superiority was preserved, uncorrupted. The *Ladies Magazine*, however, had a limited audience and a short life span. In the *Lady's Book*, which won a readership of thousands, woman's sphere began to be submerged in possessions—in fashions and mansions and embroidered upholstery. The salesmanship that brought Sarah Hale the largest circulation in the country was not unrelated to the commercialism she had decried back in Boston.

"I am a young man, and have been several years in pursuit of a wife," wrote "Coelebs" to the *Ladies Magazine* in October 1833, "but cannot yet find a girl who equals the standards of excellence I have, in my own mind." Although the women he considered had a smattering of accomplishments, they also seemed to have low attention spans and frivolous interests. "When I see young ladies devoted entirely to fashion, and following the most absurd modes, sacrificing their comfort, and often their health, to appearances, I cannot but fear they will never exercise much reason—and with an unreasonable wife, what happiness can be expected?" the young man asked. After analyzing the defects of all the available candidates, Coelebs went on to explain his standards. Like many contributors to the "Letters" column, his views were amazingly similar to those of the editor. "I admire understanding in a woman," Coelebs confided to the readers of *Ladies Magazine.* "I want one whose eye will flash with intelligence when she hears a learned allusion, whose smile of approval will cheer me on to mental exertion." Sympathy and congeniality were also high on his list. "I do not want a wife to amuse, but to improve me . . . one in whose judgment I can confide. Such a one I have not yet found." Moreover, quite a few of his eligible friends found themselves in the same predicament. "But I am not quite in despair," Coelebs concluded. "I think there has been within the last two or three years, an important change in the opinion of society respecting female education."

6

PROMOTING
WOMAN'S
SPHERE, 1800–1860

The era of *Godey's Lady's Book* differed from the one in which Sarah Hale had grown up. During the first half of the nineteenth century, the nation was transformed by massive economic growth. As America started to industrialize, home production shifted to workshop and then to factory. Productivity, trade, and commerce increased. Transportation improved, markets grew, income rose, and the urban population tripled. By midcentury, almost a fifth of Americans lived in towns and cities, many of them recent migrants. The nation's inhabitants seemed to be in constant motion. While more and more joined the swirl of population around urban areas, others filled up vacant land, east and west, transforming wilderness into territories, territories into states, and by the 1840s, crossing the continent to settle the Pacific coast.

The tremendous mobility of early-nineteenth-century Americans was not only geographic but social. Economic expansion opened new avenues of upward mobility. Income and advancement beckoned in land speculation, business investment, and the professions. Opportunity to rise in the world was accompanied by the extension of suffrage to virtually all free white men, by the development of common schools, and by outbursts of evangelism that democratized even prospects for salvation. New attitudes arose to suit these expanding options. Americans now lived by an ethos in which ambition, initiative, and achievement counted for more than social origin. The new egalitarian order, observers agreed, was one in which wealth and status were always in flux, where change and risk were the only constants. A man of humble background could hope to succeed as Louis Godey had. But he could just as easily fail, as had Sarah Hale's father Gordon Buell, by starting an enterprise that collapsed.

Under such shifting, precarious circumstances, a new middle class began to emerge, visible first in the urban and industrializing Northeast. Always expanding, the new middle class had no fixed boundaries or stable membership.

Americans could fall out of it as rapidly as they rose into it. But it did have some recognizable characteristics. Middle-class Americans had rising incomes, expectations, and living standards. They provided a market for consumer goods—for clothing, furniture, books, and magazines. They supported churches, schools, and voluntary associations. Most of all, the middle class had a new type of family life. The doctrine of "woman's sphere," as promoted by Sarah Hale in the *Ladies Magazine* and *Godey's Lady's Book,* reflected changes in the middle-class home.

The Home and the World

When the *Ladies Magazine* first appeared in 1828, a transformation in domestic life was well under way, at least in the commercial, urbanizing Northeast. During colonial days, when most families lived on farms, the household was a productive unit. All family members engaged in work to sustain it, work that was done in or near the home. As part of the family labor force, women and children were subordinate to paternal authority. But during the early nineteenth century, as a market economy developed, old patterns of life started to vanish. Some men who once would have been farmers or craftsmen now worked outside the home to earn the income that supported it. Their homes were no longer centers of production, nor did family members work together for family sustenance. Within the emerging middle class, "home" became a private enclave, a retreat from the "world" and a refuge from commercial life. And within the home, women assumed a distinctive role.

The middle-class wife, like the *Ladies Magazine* reader of 1828, remained at home while her income-earning husband went to work outside it, in office or store, business or profession. While the man ventured forth into the world, the woman at home gained an independent realm of her own, one that was no longer constantly under male domination. Domestic life was now under female control. Nor was the wife tied down to wheel and loom, hearth and dairy. Once home manufacture shifted to workplace, the woman at home took responsibility primarily for housekeeping, child rearing, and moral and religious life. Within her own domestic space, however, she gained both a new degree of autonomy and a new degree of authority over others.

The doctrine of sphere, as expounded in the *Ladies Magazine, Godey's Lady's Book,* and countless other publications, celebrated the new status of the middle-class woman, along with her distinctive vocation, values, and character. It also described an unspoken bargain between middle-class women and men. While men were still heads of families, their real domain was now in the world—a world of business, professions, politics, and money making. Family status depended on their earned income and public roles. Women were expected to devote themselves entirely to private life, to the "chaste circle of the fireside," and to maintain an alternate world with separate values. But their roles at home also helped to define family status. Moreover, within the home, they had gained new clout and respect. The bargain was based on mutual gain. If men had the opportunity to rise in the world, women had the opportunity to rise in the home.

The middle-class woman's role was of course a dependent one. Her author-ity expanded only as the family's productive functions contracted, and those functions contracted only when family income went up. Rising income was at the center of woman's sphere. Only with substantial support could a married woman adopt the nonproductive role once reserved for the very wealthy or the antieconomic attitudes propounded by the *Ladies Magazine.* In reality, few women could completely escape either home production or physical work. Middle-class women and those who aspired to that status remained active albeit unpaid contributors to the family economy through household labor. Indeed, unpaid labor, historian Jeanne Boydston points out, was now largely, though not exclusively, "the province of women." Most women, moreover, were only re-mote beneficiaries of the middle-class bargain. In rural areas, on farms in New England, in the South, and in the Midwest, traditional ways of life persisted. Household production continued, women and children remained part of the family labor force, and paternal authority as head of that labor force remained in effect, if not entirely intact. A woman's influence did not increase if a family was poor, or if she was not attached to a dependable, income-producing man. In many cases, the perquisites of woman's sphere—influence, autonomy, and authority—were little more than shared aspirations.

Nor were women of any class able to ignore worldly concerns. Within the middle class, woman's sphere was as precarious an ideal as its counterpart for men—the opportunity to rise in the world. The early-nineteenth-century family was likely to be in both financial and geographical motion. Income rose or fell according to personal fate and twists and turns of the economy such as the depression that diminished *Ladies Magazine* subscriptions in 1834. Buffeted by panics or elevated by good fortune, Americans faced the possibility of downward mobility at every turn. The "vicissitudes" were particularly precarious for women, who had little ability to determine family finances. When a husband died or a father failed in business, consequences could be dire. Shifts in family fortune, moreover, were usually linked to shifts in locale, to constant waves of internal migration—from rural areas to towns and cities, or from crowded areas to vacant land. Hardly insulated by sphere, early-nineteenth-century women continually adapted to new homes, communities, associations, and economic situations. The very concept of "woman's sphere," many historians contend, is misleading and must be modified or qualified, if not discarded.

But in important ways, many antebellum women could identify with woman's sphere because their everyday patterns of life and work increasingly differed from those of men. Even on the family farm, that most traditional of settings, men were now attuned to the market economy while women's respon-sibilities remained tied to the household economy. In towns and cities, differ-ences between male and female work patterns were even more marked. During colonial times, as historian Nancy Cott points out, the work of both men and women was closely tied to the land. It was seasonal, discontinuous, and task-ori-ented. But during the early nineteenth century, as the economy changed and as wage labor replaced family labor, male work patterns became oriented to time, not task. Whatever a man did for a living—laborer, businessman, tradesman, or clerk—he now had a clearly defined working day. His work, accordingly, became separated from the rest of life. Household work, however, remained in a time warp of task orientation. Women's workday expanded and contracted to fit the jobs at hand, whether the washing of clothes, baking of bread, or care of children—activities that all merged into life. In short, women's work and home-bound world remained premodern, whereas men's was changing. A distinctive rhythm of labor and life-style also defined woman's sphere.

Finally, a broad spectrum of women could hope to benefit from the new importance now attributed to their shared vocation. In traditional society, household work and child care had never drawn much acclaim. During the early nineteenth century, however, they were found to have social significance, to contribute to the well-being of society at large. Woman's sphere was in fact a new social space, one that had not been recognized before. On the one hand, it was an enclosed, limited, private space. On the other, it was an improvement over having no space at all. Woman's sphere, according to popular literature, encompassed a now important social institution, the home. It linked all women together in a valuable vocation—domesticity and child rearing. It fostered a positive consciousness of gender, one that had not existed in the colonial era. And it impelled a redefinition of female character, one appropriate to the middle-class woman's elevated domestic status.

During the early nineteenth century, the home took on new significance, material and emotional. By midcentury, the middle-class home had become a substantial place, with pantries and drawing rooms, mirrors and pianos, and at least some of the items featured in *Godey's Lady's Book*—upholstered sofas, elaborate furniture, carpets, and draperies. Its center was no longer the hearth, where colonial women did much of their work, but the parlor, where the family assembled. Since middle-class Americans had not only far more possessions but rising standards of neatness and cleanliness, "housework" quickly replaced "housewifery." Even with hired help, the middle-class woman remained industrious, since home maintenance and management was now a more elaborate procedure.

The middle-class home was also viewed as an emotional space, a refuge from the competitive world, and a source of stability and order in a society that seemed to be losing both. And it was now under feminine sway. Increasingly, the home was idealized as a bastion of feminine values, of piety and morality, affection and self-sacrifice—commodities that were in short supply outside it. Literature directed at women, especially, lost no opportunity to define the home as a feminine fief. "The family state . . . is the aptest earthly illustration of the heavenly kingdom and woman is its chief minister," educator Catharine Beecher declared in her *Treatise on Domestic Economy* in the 1840s. "The duties of the woman are as sacred and important as any ordained by man." By midcentury, the home was depicted as an insulated, privatized, feminized shrine. "Our homes—what is their corner-stone but the virtue of a woman, and on what does social well-being rest but in our homes?" asked *Godey's Lady's Book* in 1856. "Must we not trace all other blessings of civilized life to the doors of our private dwellings? Are not our hearthstones guarded by holy forms, conjugal, filial and

A metaphor for the privacy of family life, "woman's sphere" was depicted in popular literature as a calm and isolated retreat. Here, the middle-class homemaker devoted herself to an endless circle of domestic tasks and cultural pursuits, centering around child care. The floral motif was ubiquitous. Frontispiece from Caroline Howard Gilman, *The Housekeeper's Annual and Lady's Register* (1844). *(Library of Congress)*

parental love, the corner-stone of church and state, more sacred than either, more necessary than both? . . . . Oh! spare our homes."

While the middle-class home expanded in size and significance, the family itself grew smaller. Americans were having fewer children. In 1800, the national birthrate had been the highest in the world; but during the next few decades it rapidly fell, a process that would continue for the rest of the century. The mother of 7.04 in 1800 became the mother of 5.92 in 1850 and 3.56 by 1900. Although the decline was national, it was uneven. During the early nineteenth century, large families were still the rule in most agricultural regions, along the newly settled frontier, and among immigrants and blacks. Rural fertility, in fact, also fell, but urban fertility was consistently lower. The most precipitous drop was among the new middle class in towns and cities.

As the family began to shrink, however, the value attached to motherhood rose. Though post-Revolutionary rhetoric had suggested such mounting signifi-cance, during the early nineteenth century, it increased dramatically. Once household production waned, child raising became the family's central focus and purpose. In the middle-class home, children were no longer family workers but rather *what* the family produced. More time was devoted to their upbringing, more resources to their education, more effort to instilling the values and traits that would keep them in the middle class. The increased importance of child rearing contributed to an authority shift in the family. Paternal power dropped a notch as maternal affection became the main psychological force at home. The mother was now the primary child rearer, the crucial dispenser of values and former of character. She could "generate those moral tendencies which cover the whole of existence," as a minister wrote in the *Ladies Magazine.* "Her character is felt throughout the intricate workings of society." In the 1830s, when the publishing industry began an era of rapid expansion, the mother's significance received extensive publicity.

Innumerable tracts and stories—like those in the *Ladies Magazine*—paid tribute to the mother of Washington. In prints and etchings, a new iconography of motherhood developed. Magazines featured scenes of mothers at home, surrounded by children, in affectionate poses. Literature directed at women celebrated motherhood as the ultimate opportunity for self-sacrifice and, simultaneously, the ultimate role of female power. "How entire and perfect is this dominion over the unformed character of your infant," *Ladies Magazine* author Lydia Sigourney exuded in her *Letters to Mothers* (1838). No opportunity was lost to celebrate the social utility of motherhood. It was mothers, as Lydia Maria Child declared in her popular *Mother's Book* (1831)," on whose intelligence and discretion the safety and prosperity of our nation so much depend." Nor was the expansion of maternal influence just rhetorical. By midcentury, it began to be recognized even in the law. Northern states started to alter the tradition of paternal custody in cases of separation and divorce. Courts began to consider the "good of the child" and "parental fitness." "The father's custodial right is not an absolute one," stated an 1852 treatise on marriage law, "and is usually made to yield when the good of the child . . . is the chief matter to be regarded." Southern courts, too, began to award custody to the mothers of young children. Women did not gain equal custody rights, to say nothing of preference, until the end of the century. But adulation of motherhood still had some legal ramifications.

While celebrations of woman's sphere stressed the significance of domestic roles and maternal influence, they also suggested a new and positive consciousness of gender. The polarity of spheres that segregated middle-class men and women was not without an emotional bonus. Since women shared a common vocation and values, they did have more in common with one another than with men, as Sarah Hale contended in the *Ladies Magazine.* And they profited from long-term, intense relationships with other women—relationships that continued for decades, despite marriage and geographical separation, often in the form of lengthy visits and correspondence. Such correspondence, as historian Carroll Smith Rosenberg contends, reveals that "Women's sphere had an essential dignity and integrity that grew out of women's shared experiences and mutual affection." Within their self-contained female world—noncompetitive, empathetic, and supportive—women valued one another and thereby gained a sense of security and self-esteem. "Women, who had little status and power in the larger world of male concerns, possessed status and power in the lives of other women."

Historians disagree as to whether an intimate mother-daughter relationship lay at the heart of this female world, or whether the peer relationship was more important. In either case, early-nineteenth-century middle-class women assumed centrality in one another's lives, depended emotionally on one another, and appreciated their same-sex connections and friendships. The role of friendship as an outlet for shared "sentiments" emerges in the New England letters and diaries analyzed by historian Nancy Cott. Men, in these documents, were usually remote, distant figures, often without names. Or they might be referred to, with muted sarcasm, as "the Lords of Creation," an expression favored by Sarah Hale in the *Ladies Magazine*. But affection among women was explicit. Friendship provided an opportunity to exchange "reciprocal views and feelings," wrote Eliza Chaplin to Laura Lovell in 1820. "To you I unfold my whole heart without apology." "I do not believe that men can ever feel so pure an enthusiasm for women as we can feel for one another," *Ladies Magazine* author Catharine Sedgwick revealed to her diary in 1834. "Ours is nearest to the love of angels."

The positive consciousness of gender suggested by personal documents reflected a new assessment of female character. According to the doctrine of sphere, character traits, like social roles, were gender specific. Men were expected to be competitive, assertive, individualistic, and materialistic so as to be able to make their way in the world. The woman at home needed a compensatory set of character traits. Dependent and affectionate, she was also pious, pure, gentle, nurturant, benevolent, and sacrificing. Such "softer" virtues had been filtering in throughout the eighteenth century, especially in advice tracts aimed at the upwardly mobile. But during the early nineteenth century, the softer virtues became accepted as innate. Women, moreover, compared to men, were believed to have a firmer grip on religion and morals, a stronger claim to piety and purity, a positive sense of moral superiority. In traditional society, women were not assumed to be superior to men in any way. Now, piety and purity provided some leverage. They also led to a new set of bargains between women and men.

Piety and Purity

Early-nineteenth-century ministers provided a vital bolster to the doctrine of woman's sphere. They opposed those forces antithetical to women's interests—materialism, immorality, intemperance, and licentiousness. They helped to formulate a new definition of female character. Christian virtues—such as humility, submission, piety, and charity—were now primarily female virtues. Most important, ministers confirmed female moral superiority. Women might be the weaker members of society, but they were now assured that they exceeded men in spiritual fervor and moral strength.

Religion was also one of the few activities beyond the home in which women might participate without abdicating their sphere. Their participation in the churches was in fact vital. Women formed the majority of congregants. Accordingly, female piety, and even activism, won ministerial applause. "We look to you, ladies, to raise the standard of character in our own sex," announced New England clergyman Joseph Buckminster in an 1810 sermon. "We look to you for the continuance of domestick purity, for the revival of domestick religion, for the increase of our charities, and the support of what remains of religion in our private habits and publick institutions." Under such circumstances, a mutually dependent relationship developed between Protestant clerics and their middle-class female parishioners. Both saw themselves as outsiders in a society devoted to the pursuit of wealth, as allies who strove for morality in a competitive world. It was no accident that women's publications such as the *Ladies Magazine* counted on ministers for articles exalting the character of women. Ministers in turn depended on women for their loyal support.

Despite clergymen's fears of dwindling authority, religion was not on the wane. Protestantism flourished during the early nineteenth century. The Second Great Awakening of the first quarter of the century was surpassed by the great evangelical crusades of the second. Presbyterians and Congregationalists attracted members in New England, fiery waves of revivals swept over New York State, westerners flocked to camp meetings on the frontier, and Baptists and Methodists made gains nationwide. According to some estimates, formal church membership tripled. Throughout all this fervor, women remained prominent. Their affinity for piety became evident in a spate of revivals at the start of the century. The Second Great Awakening marked the beginning of the new alliance between women and ministers as well as of their unstated bargain: clerical endorsement of female moral superiority in exchange for women's support and activism.

Female converts outnumbered male converts three to two in the Second Great Awakening in New England, and women formed the bulk of congregations thereafter. They played an equally prominent role in revival-swept western New York. By 1814, for instance, women outnumbered men in the churches and religious societies of bustling Utica, and they could be relied on to urge the conversion of family members. A mother's conversion, ministers learned, could lead to those of her children and husband; a daughter's conversion might soon create a pious family. The most zealous activists of these early revivals, significantly, were women of the new middle class—the wives and daughters of men who worked outside the home. Church membership boosted upward mobility. But female religiosity also moved down the social scale, to wives of artisans and farmers, just as it spread to other regions. On the midwestern frontier, it was women who could be counted on to form congregations, join religious societies, and demand Sabbath observance. Piety had become female property. When Englishwoman Frances Trollope investigated American society in the 1830s, she claimed that she had never seen a country "where religion had so strong a hold upon the women, or a slighter hold upon the men."

If religion had a hold on women, however, they in turn had a hold on the clergy. Through weight of numbers, women gained a genuine influence in

Protestant churches that they lacked elsewhere. They contributed, for instance, to a softening of doctrine: The old idea of infant damnation had little appeal to American mothers. Ministers, accordingly, granted that Christian nurture could outweigh original sin. Discarding predestination as an axiom, ministers now suggested that mothers, not God, were responsible for their children's souls. The "feminization" of religion and of child rearing went hand in hand. Ministers bolstered the authority not only of the pious mother but of any pious woman, even the once insignificant daughter. Evangelical magazines, for instance, celebrated female influence in tales of dying daughters who, to the end, sought the conversion of relatives and friends. Social weakness, even fatal illness, was no obstacle to spiritual strength.

While ministers accorded women a new degree of influence, religious commitment offered other advantages. It also provided a community of peers outside the home, among like-minded women in church-related associations. The passivity of the convert, once she was united with her sisters, could be transformed into activist zeal. Early-nineteenth-century women provided the constituency for a multitude of societies formed under clerical auspices. They joined Bible and tract societies, which distributed pious literature, and Sabbath school unions, such as those endorsed in the *Ladies Magazine,* and missionary societies, which raised funds for pious endeavors. They formed charitable associations to aid the indigent and maternal associations to foster Christian motherhood. Through voluntary religious groups, women gained one another's company, new routes to participation in the world, and clerical approval. "While the pious female . . . does not aspire after things too great for her," a minister told a women's charitable society in 1815, "she discovers that there is wide field opened for the exercise of all her active powers."

In many ways, the evangelical Protestant experience was loaded with potential for women. Conversion encouraged introspection and self-attention. Cooperative efforts in church groups inspired a conscious sense of sisterhood and mutual interest. And clerical assurance of moral superiority supported a new degree of authority over others. But religious activism also had built-in limitations; clerical support meant clerical control. In the heat of revivals, as female piety assumed new significance, ministers warned women to avoid leadership roles as, for example, revivalists. Their piety was to be limited to the private role of personal persuasion; "influence" was contingent on acceptance of limits. As long as a woman kept to her "proper place," a tract society pamphlet explained in 1823, she might exert "almost any degree of influence she pleases." This was part of the implicit bargain between clergymen and women parishioners. It was also a fundamental tenet espoused by Sarah Hale in the *Ladies Magazine.*

If piety became a vital component of female character, so did purity, a word with several meanings. One was passionless, or lack of sexual feeling. According to the doctrine of sphere, the sexes were distinguished by features that were not merely different but opposite. Lust and carnality were male characteristics, or liabilities. Women, less physical, more spiritual, and morally superior, were indeed closer to "angels." This was a new development. In traditional society, women, like men, were assumed to be sexual beings. Since weaker of will, they were assumed to be even more lustful, licentious, and insatiable than men. But around the time of the Second Great Awakening, purity became a female bargaining point. Like piety, it was now a prerequisite for influence. Sermons often warned that if purity gave way, all of the perquisites of sphere were lost. "Let her lay aside delicacy," a minister held in 1837, "and her influence over our sex is gone."

Though ministers were the first authorities to endorse the female virtue of purity, they were not the only ones. By midcentury, the medical profession also confirmed that passionlessness was an innate and commendable female characteristic. "The majority of women (happily for them)," physician William Acton stated in a much-quoted medical treatise, "are not much troubled with sexual feeling of any kind." Some doctors dissented. But in medical manuals aimed at the middle class, midcentury physicians usually emphasized the debilitating effects of sexual indulgence, recommended infrequent intercourse, opposed contraception, and confirmed female asexuality. They also assured women that their physical health, and social roles, were determined by their reproductive organs. Doctors explained that the uterus was linked to the female nervous system, and that any malfunction affected the entire body, causing a gamut of ailments—headaches, backaches, indigestion, insomnia, and nervous disorders. Woman's unusual physiology, indeed, determined her emotions, character, and vocation. "Mentally, socially, spiritually, [woman] is more interior than a man," a Philadelphia physician concluded in the 1860s. "The house, the chamber, the closet, are the centers of her social life and power."

Like other components of woman's sphere, purity encompassed both sanctions and benefits. The sanctions were stressed in the advice literature directed at middle-class women. Etiquette manuals, for instance, counseled prudent behavior that would serve to deter male advances. "Sit not with another in a space that is too narrow," warned the *Young Ladies Friend*. Magazine fiction offered tales about girls who lacked discretion, were consequently victimized by male predators, and ended up ruined, impoverished, ostracized, or dead. Such proscriptions reflected significant changes in courtship customs, since incidence of premarital pregnancy sharply declined—from a high of almost 30 percent of first births in the late eighteenth century to a new low of under 10 percent in the mid-nineteenth century. This precipitous drop, historians contend, suggests the acceptance by both young men and women of a new ideology of sexual restraint. Convictions about female purity imposed limitations not only on women but on men as well.

Purity was also a code word for a new degree of female sexual control within marriage. During the early nineteenth century, when the fertility of white women began to decline, the shrinking family became a hallmark of the new middle class. It may also have represented the new clout of wives within middle-class homes. Now imbued with moral superiority, wives gained a right of refusal, an escape from "submission," and power to limit the frequency of sexual relations. They also gained more control over the number of children they had. Available methods of family limitation (beyond folk remedies and patent medicines) were abstinence, as recommended in medical literature, and withdrawal, which was condemned; abortion was also a possible last resort, at least until later in the century when it was outlawed. Although abstinence was not the sole effective means of curbing births, it probably was in widespread use. And female purity was probably an ideal on which middle-class men and women agreed, an asset for the family that wanted to rise in the world—a family in which children were no longer economic assets but, rather, liabilities. In the early nineteenth century, sexual restraint appeared both to serve family goals and to enhance women's autonomy within the home.

Convictions about female purity also affected women's relation to the medical profession. Connections between women and doctors were hardly as clear-cut as the unstated bargain between women and ministers. Physicians were a far newer source of authority. Medicine became a recognized profession only after the turn of the century. By the 1820s, all states except three had laws requiring medical practitioners to be licensed, and most licensing laws required graduation from medical college. As a result, medical practice excluded women, and midwifery, once a female monopoly, began a slow decline. In rural areas and on the frontier, and also among the urban poor, midwives continued to deliver babies. The rural midwife, indeed, remained in business into the twentieth century. But the urbanizing East set the trend for the future. During the early nineteenth century, middle-class mothers in towns and cities turned to physicians. No longer a public female ritual, childbirth became a private event with two main participants, a woman and a male professional.

The physician's new role in childbirth brought both loss and gain. The entourage of women relatives and friends who had once played a supportive part gradually vanished. But middle-class women seemed to appreciate the use of the forceps (the physician's prerogative) as the means of a faster delivery with less suffering. Mothers, indeed, became the doctor's prime constituency, since a successful obstetric practice paved the way for a profitable family practice. Moreover, with the rise of the medical profession, female ill health assumed new visibility.

Middle-class women of the early nineteenth century were distinguished by their debilitating illnesses—nervousness, anemia, hysteria, headaches, backaches. The marked rise in female illness may have been connected to physical causes—such as the spread of venereal disease—or psychological ones. Women's dependent status could have had debilitating effects on their health. Sickness might also have had a positive function, providing reprieve from domestic work. In any case, physical fragility became a female liability. When Catharine Beecher surveyed women's health across the nation in the 1850s, she concluded that sick women outnumbered the healthy three to one. Reporting from one Illinois town, Beecher gave her version of the terrible state of women's health: "Mrs. H. an invalid. Mrs. G. scrufula. Mrs. W. liver complaint. Mrs. S. pelvic disorders. Mrs. B. pelvic deseases very badly. Mrs. B. not healthy. Mrs. T. very feeble. Mrs. G. cancer. Mrs. N. liver complaint. Do not know one healthy woman in the place." If all the facts and details of women's diseases were known, Catharine Beecher claimed, "It would send a groan of terror and horror over the land."

Even when chronically ill, women did not completely trust their doctors.

The professionalization of medicine did not ensure its competence. At midcentury, as historian Regina Morantz explains, medicine was in a state of crisis. "Heroic" medicine—bleeding and enormous doses of dangerous substances—was being discarded, but it had not yet been replaced by anything better. Not only were well-trained doctors unlikely to be very effective, but few were well trained. During the 1830s, any profit-minded doctor could open a medical college and, however lax its standards, produce hundreds of graduates to be licensed. Not surprisingly, middle-class women sought alternatives.

One set of alternatives were nonmedical remedies or fads—Grahamism (diet reform), water cures, animal magnetism, or phrenology. The *Ladies Magazine*, for instance, ran many features on phrenology, complete with huge charts of the human skull. Middle-class women also took refuge at spas, joined ladies' physiological societies, where health and medicine were discussed, and accepted the views of health reformers. The latter usually favored preventive measures that would preclude the need to resort to physicians at all—such as exercise, fresh air, baths, and cereals. The medical columns of *Godey's Lady's Book*, written by doctors, endorsed similar measures. Women also turned to irregular practitioners—unlicensed dispensers of remedies and advice, who might well be women. Dr. Harriot Hunt, for instance, went into practice in Boston with her sister in the 1830s, after an apprenticeship with other irregulars. Opposed to the "heroic" methods of the licensed profession, which rejected her, she prescribed homeopathic, preventive measures and became interested in the psychological causes of women's ailments. An even less regular practitioner, Mary Gove Nichols, once a contributor to the *Ladies Magazine*, became a water cure therapist and health reformer, catering, like Hunt, to a female clientele. Although not committed to the idea of female passionlessness, these leading irregulars were committed to the protection of women from male depravity.

Another response to the professionalization of medicine appeared in *Godey's Lady's Book*. Women, wrote Sarah Hale, should be allowed to enter the medical profession in order to minister to women and children. Her argument for women doctors depended on the sanctity of sphere. Propriety and morality dictated that women should be examined by women. The woman physician, moreover, would raise the moral tone of the profession and open to women new avenues for practicing their altruism, benevolence, and sympathy. Through the entry of women into medicine, woman's sphere would be not destroyed but preserved. Hale lent strong support to Elizabeth Blackwell, the first woman medical college graduate and licensed woman physician. Like Hunt and Nichols, Blackwell hardly subscribed to the doctrine of female asexuality. She did, however, crusade against prostitution and obscenity, and supported the moral purity movement.

The doctrine of woman's sphere, and its redefinition of female character, could therefore be used as a bargaining tool. Piety, purity, and moral superiority could be mobilized to increase women's authority at home and demand more influence outside it. The doctrine of sphere could also be used to bolster other demands, such as that for "advanced" education. Although only a small proportion of Americans had any education beyond the primary level, an increasing number of them were women. Sending a daughter to an academy or seminary was now a perquisite of the expanding middle class.

Academy and Common School

By 1828, when the *Ladies Magazine* first appeared, rapid development of female literacy was closing a great divide that once had separated the sexes. The movement to establish common schools, starting in the 1820s, accelerated this process. By midcentury, over half the nation's school-age white youth were enrolled in schools, 90 percent of them in primary school. Even where common schools existed, education was often sporadic, with short terms and irregular attendance. There were also profound regional variations. In New England, over 75 percent of school-age boys and girls attended school, and in the South, less than half of this percentage. In all regions, girls were slightly less likely than boys to be enrolled in school at all. But by 1850, at least half the nation's women could read and write—a tremendous advance over the eighteenth century. And in New England, always ahead of the rest of the nation economically and culturally, literacy was almost universal. During the early decades of the century, New England women took the lead in expanding opportunities for women's education.

Since the late eighteenth century, daughters of well-off families might be sent to female academies, although contrary to the ambitious goals expressed in the wake of the Revolution, such schools did not always fulfill academic criteria. Their offerings often stressed those "ornamentals" that were supposed to enhance girls' chances for matrimony. Benjamin Rush's vision of a "peculiar and suitable education" had not yet materialized on a large scale. By 1820, however, an outgrowth of female academies or "seminaries" appeared in New England, and between 1830 and 1860 similar schools spread over the Northeast, Southeast, and Midwest. Although clearly connected to the rising income and ambitions of middle-class families, the very existence of such schools also signified a rise in women's status, especially to advocates of "female improvement." "Perhaps no experiment," as Sarah Hale announced in the first issue of the *Ladies Magazine*, "will have an influence more important on the character and happiness of our society than granting to females the advantages of a systematic and thorough education."

Some of the early New England schools were carryovers from the late eighteenth century—such as Sarah Pierce's Litchfield Academy, begun in her home in 1792 and incorporated in 1827. But most were new ventures. Often schools for young women were run by ministers, like Reverend Blake, who invited Sarah Hale to edit the *Ladies Magazine*. Others were administered by women, such as Emma Willard, whose Middlebury Female Seminary opened in 1814, or Catharine Beecher, who started a female seminary at Hartford in the 1820s, or Zilpah Grant, who was invited to run a female academy at Ipswich in 1828. These pioneer educators wanted to establish and endow academic institutions that went beyond the ornamentals but, at the same time, provided a type of secondary education appropriate to woman's separate sphere and special destiny. Advanced education, they contended, would improve women's performance as housekeepers and mothers. It would enable them to enlarge their moral influence in society. And it would increase their social utility by preparing them to teach, a function for which they were naturally endowed.

When Emma Willard appealed to the New York legislature in 1819 for the endowment of a female institution of advanced study, she summarized this pragmatic rationale. The classes offered at a female academy, Willard assured the legislators, would be "as different from those appropriated to the other sex, as the female character and duties are from the male." Suitable instruction for young women, she contended, would be "First, moral and religious; second, literary; third, domestic; and fourth, ornamental." Such a curriculum, Willard explained, would make graduates better homemakers. It would equip future mothers for the upbringing of sons who would later govern. Finally, if "women were properly fitted by instruction, they would be likely to teach children better than the other sex." Unlike "Constantia" in the 1780s and 1790s, Willard did not promote education as a remedy for inequality or a route toward "reverence of self." Instead, she posed the argument in terms of social utility. Advanced education, crafted to women's needs, would enable them to be "the greatest possible use to themselves and to others."

Although Willard failed to win funds from the New York legislature, she fared better with the citizens of Troy, New York, who contributed enough to open a female seminary in 1821. The first endowed institution for women, the Troy seminary became a model of the new type of women's school, much as the Philadelphia Academy had been a few decades earlier. Within a decade, it had 300 students and provided an enormous range of instruction. Besides the required female courses—moral philosophy and domestic science—and the ornamentals, which were optional, the school taught science, mathematics, history, and languages. Like similar institutions that followed, the Troy seminary catered to a special clientele—the daughters of the ambitious middle class. It also became a model teacher training institute, whose graduates fanned out to staff other schools. And it continued to stress its utilitarian goals. The purpose of knowledge, as Willard's sister, educator Alma Phelps, told Troy students in 1830, was to make them "better daughters, wives, and sisters; better qualified for usefulness in every path within the sphere of female exertions."

Like Emma Willard, Mary Lyon capitalized on the new regard for women's sphere. A teacher at the Ipswich Academy, Lyon began a campaign in 1833 to found an endowed institution of higher learning for women, one that would rescue young women from "empty gentility" and prepare them for enlarged social roles. "Our future statesmen and rulers, ministers and missionaries must come inevitably under the moulding hand of the female," Lyon declared. When Mount Holyoke Seminary opened in 1837, Lyon introduced high academic standards, a selective admissions policy, and curricular offerings similar to those at men's colleges. But the seminary also promoted specifically feminine roles. Students performed domestic chores, contributing at once to the school's support and to their own preparation for domesticity. Most important, Mount Holyoke fostered an extreme emphasis on piety, since Mary Lyon conducted regular revivals among her students. A graduate, according to the 1839 catalogue, was expected to be "a handmaid to the Gospel and an efficient auxiliary in the great task of renovating the world." Not only did the school train and support hundreds of missionaries, but it also produced a corps of what Mary Lyon called "self-denying female teachers," who took up posts at other seminaries and common schools.

Many of the ambitious schools established in the 1820s and 1830s, unlike the Troy seminary and Mount Holyoke, failed to secure permanent endowments. Catharine Beecher's Hartford Female Seminary, where the ornamentals were replaced by domestic economy, failed for lack of financing within a decade. The much respected Ipswich Academy, known for its religious piety and teacher training, capsized. Nor did most institutions meet Willard's and Lyon's high academic standards. Virtually any type of school for girls could proclaim itself an "academy" or "seminary" and, endowed or unendowed, make a bid for paying clientele of varying ages, usually by stressing a domestic or religious course of study. Critics assailed female academies for their superficial curricula— long lists of course offerings with little serious content. Still, by midcentury, no

Envisoned by Mary Lyon as a "residential seminary to be founded and sustained by the Christian public," Mount Holyoke Female Seminary was chartered in 1836 and opened its doors to eighty students the following year. Funds to erect the red brick Georgian building were raised by Lyon, who solicited her first donations from Massachusetts housewives. N. Currier lithograph, 1836. *(Culver Pictures)*

state lacked at least a small cluster of women's institutions for "advanced" study. The female academy provided a crucial experience in the lives of its middle-class students, an interlude in which they spent a few years in the company of peers. "The union which subsisted among us bound our hearts with no feeble ties," a New England alumna wrote to a classmate in 1822. It also became a spawning ground for women teachers, who found employment at other academies and common schools.

The seminary's goal of teacher preparation was most timely. Expansion of common schooling created a national teacher shortage. Not only were few men available for the growing number of low-paid, low-status teaching posts in common schools but, as school boards discovered, young women teachers were anxious to serve and would do the same work for half of men's salaries or less. As a result, after 1830, the young woman teacher made steady inroads into primary education. In New England, for instance, young women began to teach common school summer sessions, attended only by girls in the 1820s. By the 1830s, they had begun to replace men in winter sessions at the common schools, teaching both boys and girls. During the next two decades, women teachers extended their domain to the rest of the East and to the Midwest. "As the business of teaching is made more respectable," an Ohio school superintendent observed, "more females engage in it and wages are reduced."

Advocates of women's education always cited low cost when explaining the virtues of the female teacher. Emma Willard had stressed this point when she appealed to the New York legislature in 1819, and Sarah Hale reiterated it in the *Ladies Magazine*. When Catharine Beecher appealed to Congress in the 1850s for appropriations for women's teacher training, she put the case concisely:

> To make education universal, it must be at moderate expense, and women can afford to teach for one-half, or even less, the salary which men would ask, because the female teacher has only to sustain herself; she does not look forward to the duty of supporting a family, should she marry, nor has she the ambition to amass a fortune.

But cost was not the sole consideration, according to women educators. Women, they contended, would make superior teachers. "Nature designated our sex for the care of children," Emma Willard claimed. "If men have more knowledge, they have less talent at communicating it," argued Harriet Beecher Stowe, once a teacher at her sister's Hartford Seminary. "Nor have they the patience, the long-suffering, and gentleness necessary to superintend the formation of charac-ter." Capitalizing on the precepts of woman's sphere, supporters of the female teacher relentlessly argued that women excelled as guardians of youth. By midcentury, such arguments, combined with the powerful factor of low cost, had made an impact. "It is the *manner* and the very weakness of the teacher that constitutes her strength," a New York State committee of educators concluded. In addition, unlike men, women teachers were "much more apt to be content with, and continue in, the occupation of teaching."

The lot of the woman teacher was not only low-paid but difficult. The woman moving to a new post in a rural area usually boarded with the families of her pupils. In the classroom, she had to confront all ages of children, including large and unruly teenage boys. School boards often worried about her competence in such circumstances, but her low cost outweighed any reservations. Since cheap labor was needed, the teaching profession was rapidly feminized, at least in the East. By 1860, one-quarter of the nation's teachers were women but in Massachusetts, always a harbinger of future trends, almost four-fifths of the teaching force was female. At midcentury, one out of five Massachusetts women had taught at some point in their lives. "It seems as if the daughters of New England have a peculiar faculty and love for this occupation," observed traveler Frederica Bremer in the 1850s. "Whole crowds go hence to the western and southern states where schools are daily established and placed under their direction."

Since the 1830s, New England educators had placed seminary graduates in teaching jobs in other states. But in the 1840s, Catharine Beecher transformed teacher training and placement into a crusade. At this point, Beecher had already established her female seminary at Hartford and had also founded the Western Female Institute in Cincinnati. When the institute failed Catharine Beecher enlarged her goals to national scope. She began a campaign to raise funds for the recruitment and training of teachers who would be sent west to staff the common schools, and for the establishment of teacher training schools around the nation. Beecher's goal was "the elevation of my sex by the opening of a profession for them in the education of the young." Common schools might take advantage of the low-cost, readily available female teacher but Beecher intended to use the schools to enlarge the scope of female influence.

Catharine Beecher envisioned the creation of a distinguished profession for women, a profession equivalent to the noble vocation of motherhood but, at the same time, comparable to the male professions of law, medicine, and ministry. For those who must earn a living, teaching surpassed exploitation in the textile mills. It was preferable as well to the frivolity of the wealthy, which served no function. For those thrown into financial straits, it provided a respectable means of self-support. And if only a temporary vocation, teaching prepared young women for "happy superintendence of a family." The teaching profession, Beecher claimed, could unite women of all classes and all regions in a great common mission. According to her biographer, Kathryn Sklar, Catharine Beecher viewed the teaching profession as a national benevolent movement, similar to the missionary movement—a crusade that would extend female influence across the continent.

Catharine Beecher threw her energies into this crusade with enormous assertiveness. Under the auspices of two groups she created, the Board of Popular Education and the American Women's Educational Association, she began a round of speaking tours and fund raising. Crossing the country, Beecher coopted male collaborators, selected sites for western training schools, sought recruits for "missionary teachers," and cultivated the influential. Mobilizing the work force of a voluntary benevolent association, she rounded up boards of managers, supportive clergymen, and committees for teacher recruitment. Sarah Hale, for instance, lent her support by serving on the board of the American Women's

Educational Association and giving it publicity in *Godey's Lady's Book*. In 1847, seventy New England women were sent west, after a month of training with Beecher, to meet the challenge of frontier schools. Almost 400 soon followed. Catharine Beecher also managed to establish a group of western training schools, although few survived the era. By the Civil War, she had done much to convince the nation that woman was "the best as well as the cheapest guardian and teacher of children in the school as well as in the nursery."

Like Sarah Hale, Catharine Beecher campaigned for "the elevation of my sex" and female influence. Like Sarah Hale, she promoted the values of woman's sphere by leaving it to make her way in the world. And like Sarah Hale, finally, she used the medium of print to wage her campaign and earn an income. Although both Beecher and Hale were unusually successful in the book market, they were not alone. During the early nineteenth century, women rose to prominence as the authors of popular literature. They also became the major part of the American reading public.

Readers and Authors

From the 1820s onward, a huge barrage of printed matter conveyed the values of woman's sphere to a growing female audience. Periodicals such as the *Ladies Magazine, Godey's Lady's Book,* and their competitors were only one facet of this vast outpouring. Sermons and religious tracts provided boundless tributes to female piety. Didactic manuals on housekeeping, marriage, manners, and child rearing confirmed the significance of domesticity. Gift books filled with stories and poems similar to those in the *Ladies Magazine* catered to feminine sentimentality. And a mass of popular novels written by women for women readers demonstrated the force of female influence. During the antebellum decades, in short, an unprecedented amount of literature was directed at and bought by women. Never before had so vast a literate female audience existed, nor had women authors ever been so welcome in the literary marketplace. And never before had the technology existed to mass produce what they wrote.

By 1830, when *Godey's Lady's Book* appeared, a major transformation in publishing was under way. The wooden hand press of colonial days was replaced by an iron press, a machine press, and then a steam press. The rest of the business connected with publishing, from paper making to typecasting and typesetting, became mechanized as well. Stereotyping and electrotyping improved the mass production of text and engravings. By the 1850s, a decade of advance in the industry, the assembly line had been adapted to publishing, and the work place had shifted to the urban factory in New York, Boston, and Philadelphia. The nation's annual book production, over 12 million volumes at midcentury, was five times as much as it had been in 1820. The transformation of the industry was symbolized in 1853 when Harper and Brothers, Sarah Hale's New York publisher, built two seven-story buildings in which thousands of books a year could be produced.

While technology now provided for the mass production of books and magazines, prosperity and literacy created an enormous middle-class female market. Women readers were buying gift books such as Sarah Hale's *Flora's Interpreter* or *The Ladies Wreath* at the rate of sixty new titles a year. By the 1850s, *Harper's Magazine* estimated that four-fifths of the reading public were women— to whom culture had been relegated, along with religion, morality, child care, and other nonprofit activities. Vast profits were available, however, to those who could capitalize on the female market, as did Louis Godey and the Harper brothers. At least a portion of those profits were available to successful authors as well. Publishing was a field in the "bank-note world" in which women's talents were in demand and in which female influence was tangible.

During the 1830s and 1840s, when "home" and "mother" became central themes in popular culture, a steady stream of publications explained the role of the middle-class woman, her conduct, character, and new significance. Figures of authority such as ministers had always defined ideal roles and continued to do so. Antebellum clerics, historian Karen Halttunen points out, directed many conduct manuals at young men who left rural homes to work in cities. Professional men also produced much of the advice directed at women. Marriage guides such as physician William Alcott's *The Young Wife* (1836) gave directions in every area from "submission" to "moral influence on the husband." Ministers produced innumerable guides to wifehood and child rearing, and contributed steadily to women's periodicals. But professional men were no longer the sole authorities. Women now assumed a prominent place among the advice givers and image makers, both in the periodical press in innumerable *Ladies Friends*, *Companions*, *Mirrors*, and *Caskets* and in manuals for wives, mothers, homemakers.

Especially prominent were the group of New England authors who had contributed, usually anonymously, to the *Ladies Magazine* and went on to develop their own followings. Like Sarah Hale, they combined cautionary injunctions with celebrations of female influence. Advising attitudes of deference and politesse that signified rising social status, they also supported a new degree of female clout. In *Home* (1835), for instance, Catharine Sedgwick offered fictionalized tracts on domestic life that idealized the new middle-class family. In a succession of parlor scenes, father and mother joined together to surmount domestic crises and demonstrate wise, compassionate modes of child rearing. Caroline Gilman, another *Ladies Magazine* contributor, established a reputation with her fictionalized *Recollections of a Housekeeper* (1834)—a trough of advice on all responsibilities from managing servants to pacifying husbands ("Reverence his *wishes* even when you do not his *opinions*"). Enterprising Lydia Sigourney produced a steady stream of conduct guides such as *Letters to Young Ladies* (1835) and *Letters to Mothers* (1838). Counseling stoicism, patience, and "passive" virtue, Sigourney celebrated power and control. "You have . . . taken a higher place in the scale of being," she informed mothers. "You have gained an increase in power." But while women authors had to share the advice field with professional men, they had a monopoly over the realm of housekeeping manuals.

The first housekeeping manual was probably Hannah Barnard's *Dialogues on Domestic and Rural Economy* (1820). Directing her advice at farm women, Barnard used fictional characters such as "Lady Homespun" and "Uncle Thrifty" to impart techniques of household production. Lydia Maria Child reached a far wider audience with *The Frugal Housewife* (1829), which went through thirty-three editions before its last printing in 1870. Throughout the antebellum decades, it made its way to New England farms and remote frontier cabins, providing household hints, recipes, and above all, advice on thrift. "How to Endure Poverty" was a particularly useful chapter for women thrown into financial distress by the vagaries of economic life. In this "land of precarious fortunes," they might suddenly have to do all their own housework on a minimal budget. This was indeed Lydia Maria Child's predicament, since her husband, a sometime lawyer, editor, reformer, and farmer, was downwardly mobile and she had to become a "frugal housewife" herself.

If Lydia Maria Child failed to connect housework and influence, Catharine Beecher more than made up for it. Beecher's monumental *Treatise on Domestic Economy,* first published in Boston in 1841, was frequently adopted in the classroom. It was reprinted annually through 1856 and revised and republished thereafter, with supplements written by the author and her sister Harriet. Unlike Lydia Maria Child, Catharine Beecher did not limit herself to the constraints of frugality but instead created a new profession: the domestic economist. The encyclopedic *Treatise* covered every conceivable aspect of domestic activity, from infant care to kitchen plumbing. The homemaker could learn about health and hygiene, basic physiology, suitable meal hours, appropriate home furnishings, the importance of regular domestic routines, and even the appropriate design of an eight-room house, complete with physical plans. In Beecher's hands, the role played by women at home became a highly skilled and multifaceted vocation, easily comparable to any profession filled by men. Domestic responsibility, Beecher contended, united all women, whatever they did, in a great and glorious mission.

> The woman who is rearing a family of children; the woman who labors in the schoolroom; the woman who, in her retired chamber, earns, with her needle, the mite, which contributes to the intellectual and moral elevation of her Country; even the humble domestic, whose example and influence may be moulding and forming young minds, while her faithful services sustain a prosperous domestic state;—each and all may be animated by the consciousness, that they are agents in accomplishing the greatest work that ever was committed to human responsibility.

But antebellum women readers provided a market for more than tracts, treatises, and periodicals. They were also the major audience for novels. Fiction had long had a female following. Since the late eighteenth century, women readers had been warned against its corruptive influence, but such warnings had little impact. Men might assume all the major roles in government, politics, and business; but in the realm of popular fiction, women assumed important roles, which appealed to women readers. Through the pages of long, sentimental novels, fictional heroines, often orphaned and impoverished, rose from obscurity to authority through talent, ingenuity, virtue, and benevolence. Triumphing over adversity, they overcame the perils created by men who were less than ideal—deserters, philanderers, gamblers, drinkers, profligates, inept speculators, or financial failures. In the world of the popular novel, as in the *Ladies Magazine*, heroines exerted influence. And so did their authors. As early as the 1820s, women wrote a third of American novels; by midcentury, women authors had captured the market.

During the 1850s, while the circulation of *Godey's Lady's Book* surged, an insatiable female reading audience kept the presses rolling and sentimental fiction selling in huge editions. While Melville went out of print and Thoreau's library was filled with his own books, all returned unsold by his publisher, women dominated the literary market. Susan Warner's *Wide, Wide World* (1850) went through fourteen editions in two years, and Elizabeth Stuart Phelps's *The Sunny Side* (1851) sold 100,000 copies. Novels by Sarah Payson Willis and Elizabeth Oakes Smith went through dozens of printings, while Mrs. E. D. E. N. Southworth, a prolific hack, earned over $10,000 a year from serial publication of her melodramatic Gothic romances. Harriet Beecher Stowe broke all records in 1852, when *Uncle Tom's Cabin* kept eight presses working day and night; 300,000 copies sold within the first year.

Harriet Beecher Stowe adhered to many of the rules for feminine fiction. She presented an endless array of domestic scenes, and featured an innocent, virtuous, dying child-heroine. But she also violated a tradition of noncontroversy by delving into "politics." Women authors, as Sarah Hale once contended in the *Ladies Magazine*, could not choose their themes at will, as could "the Lords of Creation." In fiction as in life, they were obliged to avoid "the agitation of political questions" and depict instead "domestic scenes and deep emotions." In *Woman's Record* (1853), an encyclopedia of distinguished women from the Creation to the present, Sarah Hale judged her competitors by how closely they clung to her precepts. Unlike Harriet Beecher Stowe, most best-selling authors featured domestic scenes and deep emotions, and in the process celebrated feminine values, character, and influence.

Susan Warner's overwhelmingly popular *Wide, Wide World*, for instance, elaborated on female aversion to the crass, mundane world beyond the home. Ellen Montgomery, a pious heroic little girl, is forced to confront the base domain of commercial life when her father loses a lawsuit and collapses financially. Interested only in the Bible and good deeds, virtuous Ellen rejects the values of the world and after innumerable risks and rebuffs is adopted by rich relatives. Elizabeth Oakes Smith's *Bertha and Lily* (1854) celebrated female moral superiority. Since childhood, talented Bertha has served as the "conscience" for her whole neighborhood and has been revered by all. In later life, however, she runs into difficulties. During the course of the novel, she rejects Nathan Underhill, the repentant father of her long-lost illegitimate daughter—the saintly child Lily, now a foundling in an almshouse—and marries an adoring young minister. But Bertha is superior to her spouse and soon usurps *his* role as spiritual guide for the entire town. Woman, proclaims the oracle Bertha, is "closer to the spiritual manifestations of being. . . . She will live in nearer relation with the divine. . . . She will do great works but in a womanly way."

Not all women's novels satisfied the criteria posited for feminine fiction. Sarah Payson Willis, for instance, wrote a best-seller of 1855, *Ruth Hall*, that violated all the canons. The story of an ambitious woman writer, *Ruth Hall* abandoned woman's sphere with such vigor that Sarah Hale refused to review the book. Orphaned, widowed, impoverished, and victimized, Ruth at the outset has much in common with other heroines. But she triumphs over adversity by discarding conventional virtues completely. On the contrary, she becomes aggressive and shrewd and finally achieves overwhelming literary success, spurred on by a desire for fame and financial rewards. Although *Ruth Hall* enjoyed sensational sales, most reviewers condemned her creator as "not sufficiently endowed with female delicacy" and accused her of defiling the "sacredness" of the home "for the sake of profit." The woman author, in fiction as in life, was expected to be a defender of sphere, not an interloper in the male world of ambition and financial success.

Like Ruth Hall, women who achieved success in literary sales were assertive and prolific entrepreneurs who needed income. If single, like Catharine Sedgwick, they supported themselves. If widowed, like Sarah Hale, they supported their families. If married, they earned the bulk of their families' incomes, as was the case with Harriet Beecher Stowe, Lydia Maria Child, Elizabeth Oakes Smith, and Lydia Sigourney. Like Sarah Hale, however, most women authors denied their role in the marketplace and affirmed, instead, their femininity. They contended variously that their work was divinely inspired, that creative and domestic urges were inextricably linked, or both. Far from being ambitious, they only gradually became inured to seeing their work in print. Caroline Gilman's first published lines made her feel "as alarmed as if I had been detected in man's apparel." Sarah Hale assumed her role as editor only with "trembling" and later assured her readers that "The Mother, not the Author has been successful." Susan Warner, according to her sister, wrote her best-selling novel "on her knees." While denying that they had invaded the male preserve of commercial enterprise, however, women authors succeeded in popularizing feminine values, celebrating domestic influence, and feminizing the literary marketplace.

They were also able to earn income without appearing to leave the home, to adhere to the limits of woman's sphere while capitalizing on it. As literary critic Ann Douglas points out, publishing enabled women authors "to be unobtrusive and everywhere at the same time." But authors were not the only women involved in the "bank-note world." The same long-term changes that created the publishing industry also provided new roles for women in manufacturing.

Factory and Mill

"You want to know what I am doing," wrote sixteen-year-old Mary Paul from Lowell, Massachusetts, to her widowed father in Claremont, New Hampshire, in 1846.

I am at work in a spinning room tending four sides of warp which is one girl's work. The overseer tells me that he never had a girl get along better than I do. . . . I have a very good boarding place, have enough to eat. . . . The girls are all kind and obliging. The girls that I room with are all from Vermont and good girls too. . . . I get along very well with my work. . . . The usual time allowed for learning is six months but I think I shall have frames before I have been in three as I get along so fast. I think that the factory is the best place for me and if any girl wants employment, I advise them to come to Lowell.

Factory work was not Mary Paul's life vocation. Before entering the mills, she had worked as a domestic in Bridgewater, Vermont, not far from where she had grown up. During the next four years, she moved in and out of mill work at Lowell. After leaving the mills, Mary Paul cared for her father in New Hampshire, started a coat-making business with another woman in Vermont, worked at an associationist community in New Jersey, and found a job as a housekeeper in New Hampshire. Finally, after twelve years of self-support, she married the son of her former boardinghouse keeper at Lowell and settled down in Lynn, Massachusetts. By the late 1850s, Mary Paul was a New England housewife. But by working a few years at the Lowell mills, like thousands of other young New England women, she had participated in a major development, the shift of production from household to work place.

This shift did not affect the majority of women who worked for pay. The largest numbers of women wage earners in the early nineteenth century labored as domestic servants, laundresses, and seamstresses—work that was low-status and "invisible," since it was performed either in one's own home or in someone else's. Moreover, it was usually work performed for other women. Domestic service was in transition, as historian Faye Dudden has shown. Early in the century, the typical domestic worker was the "hired girl," a neighbor's daughter who worked for and lived with a local family, as did Mary Paul before she turned to factory work. The hired girl helped with household chores and home production, working along with her mistress. By midcentury, the hired girl had been replaced by a domestic servant, often an immigrant woman, whose work was more specialized and whose relationship with her employer was more formal, distant, and decidedly unequal. Free black women in northern and southern cities also did domestic work. Some earned livings by providing services for other women, such as hairdressing or dressmaking; more often, they took in work at home, such as washing, ironing, or sewing.

Domestic servants, laundresses, and seamstresses were not the only home workers. Many farm wives were drawn into the commercial economy: Rural Pennsylvania women, for instance, processed milk into butter to be sold to the Philadelphia market. Middle-class women, too, when thrown into need, might engage in paid work at home, by taking in boarders, by sewing, or by selling goods they made to other women—as did Sarah Hale during her short foray into the millinery business. Most manufacturing work was also done at home. Under the putting-out system, entrepreneurs distributed work on garments, hats, books, and other items to women at home who were paid by the piece. The women who colored *Godey's Lady's Book* fashion plates in the 1830s, for instance, were home workers, as were young New England women who made straw hats and the women who worked in the urban garment industry. But the factory hand such as Mary Paul, although hardly the typical female wage earner, was the most novel. By 1828, nine out of ten New England textile workers were women.

Since thread and cloth had once been produced in self-sufficient households, it is often assumed that women who became mill hands followed their "natural" productive work outside the home. To an extent this is true. Once textile work moved to the factory, it became more difficult for New England farm girls to contribute to family income by spinning or weaving at home. Prices paid for homemade cloth fell, and the amount of homemade goods dropped accordingly. However, it was not solely an affinity for making thread or cloth—or beer, cigars, or shoes—that lured women into factory work. Employers too had an affinity, for cheap, tractable labor. Women, moreover, were hired only when other labor was scarce and when there was no competition from men for the jobs they did. In the printing trades, for instance, which mechanized and unionized early, women were quickly excluded from the best jobs and hired only at the bottom rung. At Harper's big New York factory, a few hundred young women worked as binders, gatherers, stitchers, gilders, letters, and folders; but only men worked as printers. Manufacturing was not a wide-open field.

The rationale for hiring women workers was not that they were cheap, tractable, and available, but that manufacturing work was good for them and good for the country. In the new nation, land-rich and labor-scarce, the employment of women in manufacturing would free men for farming and, later, for business, while saving women "from poverty and idleness," as mill owners contended in the 1820s. Similar arguments were used by champions of women's welfare such as Mathew Carey, Sarah Hale's Philadelphia publisher and occasional contributor to the *Ladies Magazine.* An advocate of women's employment in manufacturing, Carey contended that such work prevented young women from spending their time perniciously or burdening their parents. It taught them "habits of order, regularity, and industry, which pave a broad and deep foundation of public and private usefulness." Female employment, in the mouths of advocates, became a combination of social welfare, poor relief, and education.

American industry had been stirred into life during the War of 1812, when imports of manufactured goods were curtailed. According to government reports of 1822 and 1832, women worked in over 100 industries, from beer and nails to gunpowder and lumber. By midcentury, when only about 10 percent of adult women worked for pay, women formed one-quarter of the labor force in manufacturing, with the largest numbers employed in the cotton textile, men's clothing, and shoe industries. Each had been transformed over the past half-century. Tasks became more specialized, machinery was introduced, and production shifted from household to factory. But in each industry, these changes had a different impact on women workers.

The urban garment industry, centered in New York, Boston, and Philadelphia, customarily used the putting-out system. Seamstresses employed in the manufacture of cheap, ready-made men's clothing worked at home and in small tailor shops, hand-stitching garments cut by skilled tailors. The labor market for seamstresses was extremely crowded. Cities burgeoned with women in need of income—married, unmarried, widowed, and deserted—who competed for piece work. If regularly employed, they earned half the income of female factory operatives; the going wage for piece work was that offered by the almshouse, which supported women on work relief. Irregular, ill-paid employment made their condition precarious. "The wages paid to seamstresses who work in their own apartments . . . are utterly inadequate to their support, even if fully employed," Mathew Carey observed in Philadelphia in 1829. They are often unemployed—sometimes for a whole week together, and very frequently one or two days in each week. In many cases no small portion of their time is spent in seeking and waiting for work. The introduction of the sewing machine in the 1840s transformed the garment industry, but not to the advantage of homebound seamstresses. As the scale of production increased, the need for workers declined, and much of the labor shifted to factories, where it was done by men. The homebound seamstress now had to buy or rent a machine as well as to compete with skilled tailors.

The sewing machine also affected the shoe industry of eastern Massachusetts, where women had long been employed. Even before mechanization, shoemakers had divided the craft between men and women. One part of the process, the sewing of uppers, was turned over to wives, widows, and children, who labored at home as stitchers and binders. By the 1830s some 15,000 New England women worked in boot and shoe production under the domestic system. When sewing machinery arrived in the 1850s, work shifted to factories, but the sexual division of labor continued. This proved an advantage for many women employees, historian Mary Blewett contends. Not only did they profit from their group experience in central shops, but their virtual monopoly over the stitching process meant increased leverage in the industry. Sexual division of labor in shoemaking, Blewett concludes, "rewarded the skills and experience of some female industrial workers, which they used to control the work process."

The textile industry followed another pattern. Textiles were first manufactured under the putting-out system, with spinning and weaving done in the household. After the power loom was introduced in 1814, more and more work shifted to mills, which soon peppered the New England countryside. Half the textile labor force worked under the "family system," introduced in the original cotton "manufactury" founded by Samuel Slater in Pawtucket, Rhode Island, in 1791. Slater hired entire families, often English immigrants, under annual contracts. His system was used in New England, the middle Atlantic states, the Midwest, and part of the South. But the "boardinghouse" system, introduced by Francis Cabot Lowell in Massachusetts in 1821, employed only women and gave the New England mills a new image.

Within five years, Lowell transformed a New England farm town into an industrial center of six mills. He also attracted a unique labor force. Young, unmarried farm girls from all over New England flocked to Lowell and other mill towns. Like Mary Paul, they moved into and out of mill work, some staying a few months, some a few years, and some longer. All weighed the attractions of mill work against the alternatives—teaching, sewing, and domestic work—which paid less. "There are very many young ladies at work in the factories that have given up milinary dressmaking and school-keeping for to work in the mill," mill worker Malenda Edwards wrote to her cousin Sabrina Bennett from Nashua, Massachusetts, in 1839. Like Mary Paul and Malenda Edwards, all of the mill workers lived in company-run boardinghouses under the supervision of widowed matrons. Here they were subject to elaborate codes of company rules, such as curfews, room cleaning, and compulsory church attendance. But Lowell's paternalistic system provided an unusual combination of opportunities: income, independence, and community.

The income was not earned easily. "At five o'clock in the morning the bell rings for the folks to get up," Mary Paul told her father. "At seven they are called to the mill. At half past twelve we have dinner, are called back again at one and stay until half past seven." The twelve- to thirteen-hour workday may not have been longer than the workday on a farm, although it seemed so at the outset. "I was so sick of it, at first, I wished the factory had never been thought of," Malenda Edwards wrote to Sabrina Bennett. "But the longer I stay, the better I like [it]." What mill workers appreciated was their female community. They engrafted friends made at Lowell or Nashua onto networks of friends and relatives from home. Mill operatives also organized a great array of activities. They ran lending libraries, benevolent associations, debating clubs, missionary societies, Sabbath school unions, and the company-sponsored *Lowell Offering*, where their writings were published. According to Harriet Robinson, a "graduate" of the mills, the workers discussed dress reform, phrenology, Grahamism, and the Mexican War. They subscribed to *Godey's Lady's Book* and brought Lydia Maria Child's *Frugal Housewife* back to their farm-bound mothers.

Most important, the mill girls enjoyed their autonomy. Whether banking their wages, supporting their parents, or paying off family mortgages, they had become independent wage earners. "Don't I feel independent!" wrote Anne Appleton to her sister Sarah in the 1840s. "The thought that I am living on no one is a happy one indeed to me." "It was like a young man's pleasure in entering upon business for himself," concluded former mill worker Lucy Larcom. "Girls had never tried that experiment before and they liked it." Nor was mill work viewed as permanent. The time spent as an operative was, ideally, a profitable interlude between a rural past and a middle-class future—as wife, mother, student, or teacher. Lowell's "boardinghouse" system and the labor force it attracted fused factory work and respectability.

Lucy Larcom and Harriet Robinson, who immortalized their Lowell experiences in vivid memoirs, celebrated this fusion. Daughters of widows who worked as dormitory supervisors, both had spent their youth in the mills as "bobbin girls," and both went on to careers. Larcom moved west, attended college, taught school, and returned to New England as an author. Robinson, who married, became an advocate of antislavery and woman suffrage. For both, the mills had provided advantages without the odium of working-class identification. "Lowell might well have been looked upon as a rather selective industrial school for young people," Larcom claimed. "We were happy in the knowledge that, at the longest, our employment was only temporary." For Robinson, mill work was a "preparatory school" for life. In *Loom and Spindle,* she too celebrated income, independence, and impermanence. The best part of the factory experience, Robinson explained, were the workers themselves: industrious, moral, religious, frugal, supportive of each other, full of self-respect, and capable of "self-cultivation." Not only did they serve as cultural emissaries to the countryside, bringing home "new fashions, new books, new ideas," but they were, in addition, upwardly mobile: "No one could tell the difference in *church* between the factory girls and the daughters of some of the first families in the city." Some mill girls married into the best of families, Harriet Robinson contended, ensnaring professional men. Others went on to academies and professional work. For those less mobile or less marriageable, the mills still served an important purpose.

> From a condition approaching pauperism they were at once placed above want; they could earn. . . . They were no longer obliged to finish out their faded lives mere burdens to male relatives. . . . For the first time in this country woman's labor had a money value. She had become not only an earner and a producer, but also a spender of money, a recognised factor in the political economy of her time.

The unique opportunity provided by the mills was short-lived. By the 1840s, when Lowell reached its peak as a tourist attraction, the operatives were complaining of long hours, wage cuts, and speed-ups, as well as of a decline in housing conditions. "I never worked so hard in my life," Mary Paul wrote to her father in 1848. "The company pretends they are losing immense sums every day and therefore they are obliged to lessen the wages, but this seems perfectly absurd to me." Although the women at Lowell had organized earlier, in 1834, when their Factory Girls Association protested wage cuts and blacklists, the panic of 1837 wiped out their efforts. In 1845, however, the Lowell workers organized a Female Labor Reform Association led by Sarah Bagley, an energetic campaigner who had worked in the mills for a decade. The labor reformers agitated for a ten-hour day, allied themselves with the New England Workingmen's Association, and petitioned the Massachusetts legislature to investigate mill conditions. Dismissing the *Offering* as a company organ, they stated their grievances in a new publication, the *Voice of Industry.* Mill operatives, complained the *Voice,* now had to "tend three or four looms, where they used to tend but two . . . the pay is not increased to them, while the increase to the owners is very great." In 1846, the *Voice* issued ominous warnings:

> Be assured that if you do not live to witness it, the time is not far distant when those who labor in the mills will (as is the case with many now) earn barely enough to purchase the necessities of life by working hard thirteen hours a day; recollect that those who worked here before you, did less work and were better paid for it than you are, and there are others to come after you.

An engraving of workers at power looms in a New England textile mill in 1839. By the late 1830s, real wages in the mills declined, the workday was lengthened, and mill hands were urged to increase productivity. The operative who once tended one or two looms might now be tending five or six. *(Culver Pictures)*

The militant rumblings of the *Voice* did not sit well with the new generation of manufacturers, whose predecessors had wanted, two decades before, to "save respectable women from poverty and idleness." By now, mill owners had discovered a more tractable labor force—Irish immigrants, both men and women. Throughout the 1840s, the number of native New England women in the mills dwindled, and by midcentury, the Lowell experiment was no longer an attractive option. The prospect of temporary industrial work as an avenue to upward mobility had vanished. But for those who had worked in the mills at their peak, the experience was a transforming one. Mill operatives married later and had fewer children than peers left behind on the farm. Nor did they return to their farms; instead, they tended to settle in towns and cities. Like Mary Paul, they became middle-class housewives.

New England textile workers were not the only early nineteenth-century women to leave the countryside for towns and cities. Between 1800 and 1860, the number of "urban" places—with residents numbering a few thousand or more—multiplied tenfold, and waves of newcomers swelled the populations of older cities. Simultaneously, the pace of westward expansion increased. The lure of land had led settlers west for decades, beyond the Appalachians and then beyond the Mississippi. At midcentury, families embarked on the long overland trip across the Great Plains to Oregon and California. For many women in transient circumstances—migrants, immigrants, pioneers—the middle-class notion of woman's sphere was likely to be a remote ideal or irrelevant. Similarly, for the majority of women who lived in rural areas, the perquisites of woman's sphere were minimal.

City and Frontier

Most antebellum urban migrants were fairly poor people who had been forced into motion by changing conditions. Young folk from farming communities, artisans whose crafts were vanishing, day laborers in need of jobs, widows seeking self-support, all settled in the working-class neighborhoods of eastern cities. So did immigrant families, primarily from England, Ireland, and Germany. These new city residents faced chronic insecurity. For working-class people, employment was precarious. Only a narrow line separated the "respectable" or "worthy" poor from the destitute. Women faced a special insecurity, for they might well descend into abject poverty if deprived of male support. Destitute female heads of household, like those observed by Mathew Carey in Philadelphia, often became pieceworkers and seamstresses in tenements, laboring for less-than-subsistence wages and facing frequent bouts of unemployment. Under such deprived conditions, the experience of many urban women had little connection with middle-class visions of domesticity.

The identity of antebellum working-class women, historian Christine Stansell contends, was rooted not in the home but in the city neighborhood. For the New York women whose lives Stansell examines, "home" was likely to be a piece of an attic, basement, stable, or shed. Domestic furnishings were few, private space unimportant, and physical labor arduous. Indeed, "the poorer the family, the heavier was women's work." Beyond coping with clogged chimneys, smoking stoves, and flooded cellars, working-class wives' main task was to obtain water, fuel, and food, a job that kept them on a constant round of errands. To survive, women spent much of their time outside the home, in a bustling population of neighbors, lodgers, peddlers, and shopkeepers; scavenging children also contributed to family upkeep. "Laboring women made their lives as wives and mothers on the streets as much as by the hearthside," Stansell points out.

Working-class women's life in the tenements and on the street drew them into a community of women. Heavily involved in the lives of neighbors and acquaintances, they were usually gossiping, borrowing, lending, providing services, or seeking them. Women's involvement with one another ranged from solicitude and cooperation to disputes, fracases, and other outbursts of hostility; serious fights evoked curses, name-calling, physical aggression, and occasionally small mob actions, usually in disputes over tenancy, noise, racial conflict, or sexual impropriety. When visiting working-class neighborhoods, representatives of charitable organizations cited "conditions which others of refinement would find intolerable" and strove to impose middle-class values, which working-class women tended to resist.

Region, too, diluted the impact of woman's sphere. The sense of community shared by poor women in city neighborhoods became more rare in rural outposts. On southern farms as on the western frontier, homes were likely to be remote if not isolated; traditional forms of household production continued; and contact with other women was difficult to maintain. For women, the family farm was never the frontier of opportunity, especially when it had been removed to some remote place. Not surprisingly, women's attitudes toward their experience as pioneers often reflected more deprivation than advantage.

Westward-bound women in the early nineteenth century were the wives and daughters of farmers and tradesmen, as well as of army men, Mormons, and missionaries. Their numbers included some unattached women, ranging from the schoolteachers Catharine Beecher sent to the Midwest to the prostitutes who settled in California mining camps. But for the most part, women moved west as members of families, not of their own volition. Westward treks were initiated by men in search of economic advancement and often struck women family members, in the words of one diarist, as a "wild goose chase." Migrating families usually covered irretrievable distances, ensuring separation from all prior connections. Women migrants lost their friends and relatives, churches and homes; comfort, companionship, and community vanished. They also lost the benefits of eastern society, where women were held in higher esteem, enjoyed one another's company, and had more influence within the family. For the woman migrant, moving west seemed to mean moving backward in time, away from the benefits of modern life and into a harsh frontier world, where they would have to play traditional roles.

Such sentiments were suggested by women who crossed the Great Plains in the 1840s and 1850s and recorded their experiences in diaries and letters. The overland trek to Oregon and California, in women's eyes, seemed a double battle. Not only was it a struggle against hardships and hazards—storms, insects, snakes, cholera, dysentery—but also a struggle to maintain the higher status that women had achieved in middle-class homes. Wives and daughters on the overland trail, historians John Faragher and Christine Stansell contend, did not view their westward journey as an opportunity for equality but as an all-male enterprise; along the trail, male dominance was omnipresent. Under such circumstances, female influence diminished. "Men on the plains . . . were not so accommodating, nor so ready to wait upon women, as they were in the most civilized communities," observed Lavinia Porter, who traveled by ox team to California.

Although the traditional sexual division of labor often broke down en route, women's access to men's work, such as driving wagons or livestock, in addition to their traditional jobs of laundering and cooking, hardly seemed a step forward. Rather it seemed a violation of feminine roles. In addition, women on the trail experienced an overwhelming sense of loss. They missed their homes and all that went with them—personal possessions, domestic routines, and female companionship. When they were able to enjoy the company of other women along the trail, such relationships were treasured. When wagon trains separated and newfound friends disappeared, desolation increased. Women migrants were often left with the sense that they had lost the benefits of "civilization" itself. After crossing the Missouri, Margaret Chambers felt "as if we had left all civilization behind us." To Phoebe Judson, "each doomed step . . . carried us farther and farther into a desolate, barren country."

When they arrived at their destinations, in the Midwest or Far West, women migrants had to confront a new set of circumstances. Home, on the frontier, was not a model cottage but rather, at first, a hut, tent, or gravel-floored cabin. Everyday life was likely to be similar to that in colonial times. In midwestern farming communities, the family was once again the basic work unit; wives and children formed part of the labor force. Like colonial women, midwestern farm wives tended animals, raised gardens, ran dairies, and produced most of their families' food, cloth, and clothing. In newly settled regions, author and reformer Eliza Farnham reported from the Midwest at midcentury, women performed many types of work "of which they are released in the older regions by the greater perfection of machines . . . and the presence of a larger portion of their own sex." In the frontier farming community, men dominated both private and public life. But women struggled to maintain kinship and friendship networks and to re-create familiar institutions—home, school, church, and association. Sabbath observance took on crucial significance. "What opportunities these days of rest a home present to the wife and mother," Sarah Hale once exclaimed in an etiquette book. Sharing such views, frontier women united to form congregations and demand Sabbath observance. When Sunday was ignored, they mourned its absence. "The Sabbath is little regarded and is more a day for diversion than devotion," one of Catharine Beecher's teachers reported from the Midwest. "Those days of social communion and prayer at Hartford I shall never forget."

The battle grew more difficult in the Far West. Here the proportion of women dropped sharply—for instance, only 8 percent of the California population was female in 1850. But the challenge to female moral superiority increased. Sabbath desecration remained a symbol of the obstacles that women faced. As Harriet Behrins, whose husband had been struck by "gold rush fever," wended her way to church, she passed gambling halls, marching bands, and bulls on their way to a fight. "A longing for the refined home life which I had left behind me would pull on my heart strings," she recounted. Others complained of lack of female companionship; of lawlessness, vice, and impiety; and of unkempt characters. Full of transitory miners, adventurers, and outright criminals, the Far West of the 1850s seemed masculinized beyond redemption. "There is little in California society . . . to engage the higher order of female intelligence," Eliza Farnham warned eastern women. Overall, the commentary of many women pioneers supports a recent, critical interpretation of western history. Far from being a triumphant achievement, some historians contend, the conquest of the West represented a moral failure and a white man's adventure, one that exploited the environment, native peoples, and members of pioneer families. For frontier women, westward expansion frequently meant lives of isolation, exhaustion, and endurance.

The experience of Hispanic women on the Mexican borderland, however, suggests that frontier conditions could have different impacts on different female populations. The western frontier for antebellum Americans overlapped the

A watercolor by Alexander Barclay in 1853 depicts a New Mexico Woman returning from the river with a tub of washed laundry. It also illustrates Hispanic women's everyday dress on the southwestern frontier. *("Theresita Suaso of New Mexico, 1853." Watercolor by Alexander Barclay. Courtesy of The Bancroft Library)*

northern frontier for Mexicans, who in 1821 declared their independence from Spain and established a republic. Until the late 1840s, when the United States claimed New Mexico, Arizona, California, and parts of Texas, these territories formed the northern edge of Mexico. Here, frontier conditions may have mitigated the tradition of female subjugation that characterized Spanish society in more settled areas to the south, and also altered the traditional sexual division of labor. Hispanic frontierswomen, historians point out, engaged in a wide variety of paid occupations, as bakers, weavers, venders, craftswomen, farmers, and ranchers. Some gender barriers that existed in central Mexico vanished. A number of California women, for instance, received land grants in their own names, and New Mexico women commonly ran business establishments.

Hispanic women also inherited a legal tradition that enabled wives to maintain property separate from that of their husbands, as well as their maiden names, and that gave them easy access to court, where they could sue and be sued. Unlike American frontier communities, where men invariably outnumbered women, in Mexican communities such as Santa Fe and San Antonio, and in other Texas and New Mexico towns, women slightly outnumbered men—probably because the latter often met violent deaths. Living conditions hardly exceeded those of American frontier people. In California, the well-off might have adobe homes of three or four rooms, but most families lived in single rooms, sparsely furnished; cooking was done outdoors. At midcentury, growing affluence brought the well-off more possessions, such as mirrors, clocks, and pianos, and improvements such as glass windows, planked floors, and indoor fireplaces. But as Americans penetrated and then occupied the Hispanic borderland, women lost the independent life-style they had created during the era of the Mexican frontier.

White Women in the Antebellum South

If the benefits of woman's sphere seemed difficult to retain in the West, the South was even more recalcitrant. Here, as in the North, the feminine ideal—promoted in sermons, speeches, and periodicals—stressed piety, innocence, submissiveness, intuition, compassion, and self-abnegation. But the southern ideal had a regional flavor. Unlike northern celebrations of women's roles, such as Sarah Hale's *Ladies Magazine* or Catharine Beecher's *Treatise on Domestic Economy*, the antebellum southern ideal was shaped mainly by men. It did not depend on an exodus of middle-class men from home to workplace, for as historian Elizabeth Fox-Genovese points out, the South escaped the middle-class revolution that was transforming northern society. Nor did it reflect a female gain of influence within the home. Instead, the southern ideal was an integral part of the proslavery defense.

As this defense reached a crescendo in the 1850s, the southern feminine ideal become more shrill and exalted. Women might be viewed as capricious, delicate, dependent, and adored—as George Fitzhugh, the southern social theorist, described them in a proslavery defense of 1854. But above all, they were subordinate. Fitzhugh depicted a hierarchical system of rights and allegiances, in which femininity carried little real weight. "Women, like children, have but one right, and that is the right to protection," he wrote in *Sociology for the South*. The right to protection involved the obligation to obey. "If she be obedient, she stands little danger of maltreatment." Fitzhugh expressed extremist views and spoke only for himself. Still, while northern middle-class women made new claims to influence and authority, the South resisted changes that might erode patriarchal power.

Southern women were less likely to be affected by rhetoric than by the region's agrarian life-style. During the early nineteenth century, agrarianism became more firmly entrenched, as cotton and slavery expanded into the fertile Southwest. Although westward expansion opened up new routes of social mobility, it did little to change white women's roles. In Virginia as in Mississippi, most southern women lived in rural areas, where work routines resembled those of colonial times.

On small family farms, where most white southerners lived and worked without slaves, women retained traditional roles in farming and in household production: the spinning, weaving, sewing, making of lard, keeping of gardens, feeding of poultry, hoeing of corn. On small plantations with slaves, planters' wives were relieved of outdoor work, but household production continued. Southern townswomen, too, engaged in productive labor well into the nine-teenth century, historian Suzanne Lebsock reports; city living retained a "barn-yard ambiance." Only on substantial plantations with large numbers of slaves did women assume managerial roles. The wife of a big planter might be respon-sible for the upkeep of a large labor force. She supervised plantation accounts, the distribution of rations, slave health and housing, and a range of productive activities—from the making of clothes to the butchering of hogs. But the grand plantation mistress represented only a tiny proportion, less than 5 percent, of southern women.

Even for the privileged, the rural nature of southern life limited opportunity for communication, association, and education. Mail arrived infrequently, visit-ing provided the sole entertainment, and the company of others often required special effort and travel. Although women in towns might form a charitable association, like the well-to-do Petersburg, Virginia, women who joined forces to start an orphan asylum, the southern woman's institutional affiliation was likely to be limited to church membership. Educational options existed only for daughters of wealthier families. A southern academy movement had emerged in the Revolution's wake; some female academies won special mention in the *Ladies Magazine.* The goals of southern academies (like many northern ones) were usually to turn out more marriageable graduates. Common school systems barely existed. By midcentury in the Southeast, only 35 percent of school-age white girls (and 40 percent of white boys) were in school at all. In New England, by contrast, these percentages were doubled. Not surprisingly, almost 25 percent of southern white women over twenty (and almost 15 percent of white men) were completely illiterate.

Meager education helps explain the paucity of literary contributions among antebellum southern women. Another factor was their exclusion from public life; as Fitzhugh proclaimed, "Woman naturally shrinks from the public gaze," and in this case, ideal and reality coincided. Women who achieved prominence in letters were usually transplanted northerners. There were rare exceptions, such as Louisa McCord of Charleston, whose political articles and translations of economic treatises were published in leading southern journals. But McCord, as described by *DeBow's Review,* was a "brilliant anomaly." As a rule, literate southern women confined their self-expression to correspondence and diaries. Like Mary Chesnut's famous Civil War diary, an artful revision of her wartime records, these antebellum diaries dispensed with the effusive language used by men to exalt women's status. Diarists often expressed, instead, their grievances.

Among the significant motifs in this private literature were women's hostility to slavery and anger at miscegenation—a subject that evoked painful soliloquies. The sexual relations of white men and slave women, diarists contended, ruined marriages and morals and destroyed family harmony. "Southern women are I believe all at heart abolitionists," contended a Georgia matron, Gertrude Ella Thomas, in her journal for 1858, after a long digression on the subject. "I will stand to the opinion that the institution of slavery degrades the white man more than the Negro and exerts a most deleterious effect upon our children. . . . The happiness of homes is destroyed but what is to be done?" Like the planter's wife who told English author Harriet Martineau that she was "the chief slave of the harem," southern diarists also compared their position to that of slaves. Citing the harassment and responsibility that slave management involved, some expressed a desire to free themselves from the institution of slavery, especially from the obligations it entailed. "I believe my servants are going to craze me," wrote Alabama diarist Sarah Gayle in 1835.

But planters' wives' objections to slavery have to be qualified. When southern women complained of slavery, they usually did so on a pragmatic basis rather than a moral one. Stressing the need for reform, not abolition, they rarely opposed slavery in principle or in the abstract, historian Fox-Genovese concludes. Experienced matrons, historian Catherine Clinton points out, "generally groaned over the evils of *slaves* rather than the curse of slavery." Similarly, anger about illicit interracial sex was usually directed at women slaves instead of unfaithful husbands. Planters' wives and daughters were also well aware that their financial security and social status rested upon slave property, which compounded their ambivalence. (In some instances, sons inherited land while daughters inherited slaves.) Most important, whatever the objections of plantation mistresses toward either slaves or slavery as an institution, they were nonetheless free women in a slave society. Disadvantages of gender, historians agree, were far exceeded by the privileges of both color and class.

For slave women, the same generalization appeared to apply, though in reverse. In many ways, the woman in slavery had more in common with enslaved men than with free white women. The condition of slavery as a system of labor precluded the kind of distinctions between the sexes so carefully drawn in white society, just as it precluded the social segregation by sex that came to characterize the experience of white women. Not only did all slaves work, but all were property that could be sold, mortgaged, hired out, bequeathed, and inherited. Slave status as property inevitably affected gender roles. It was impossible for slave men to be dominant in the same way that white men were, or for women to assume the same type of subordinate roles that white women did. One result, some historians have suggested, was that there was more sexual equality in slave society, by default, than in free society. Another result, one stressed by northern women reformers, was that gender became yet more of a liability: slave women were deprived of the perquisites of womanhood. After 1830, once women in the

North began a spate of activism in benevolence and reform, the plight of the woman in slavery became a prominent concern.

പ്ര

SUGGESTED READINGS AND SOURCES

CHAPTER 5

Although Sarah Hale is invariably mentioned throughout the literature on nineteenth-century women, there are no recent biographies. Two antiquated studies are Ruth E. Finley, *The Lady of Godey's* (Philadelphia, 1931), which is sprightly, admiring, and somewhat garbled, and Isabelle Webb Entrekin, *Sarah Josepha Hale and Godey's Lady's Book* (Philadelphia, 1946), which is thoroughly annotated but uncritical and tedious. For a lucid interpretation of Hale and her work, see Ann Douglas, *The Feminization of American Culture* (New York, 1977). Hale's achievements as an editor are suggested in Lawrence Martin, "The Genesis of *Godey's Lady's Book*," *New England Quarterly*, 1 (January 1928), 41–70, and Frank Luther Mott, *A History of American Magazines, 1741–1850* (New York, 1930), 348–351 and 580–594. See also *The Ladies Magazine* (Boston) 1828–1836 and *Godey's Lady's Book* (Philadelphia) 1837–1877. Representative Hale publications are *Traits of American Life* (Philadelphia, 1835); *Woman's Record; or, Sketches of All Distinguished Women* (New York, 1853); and *Manners; or Happy Homes and Good Society All the Year Round* (Boston, 1867).

CHAPTER 6

Historians of the 1960s and 1970s debated whether the early-nineteenth-century doctrine of "woman's sphere" represented loss or gain. For a negative view, see Barbara Welter, "The Cult of True Womanhood, 1820–1860," *American Quarterly*, 18 (Summer 1966), 151–175, an analysis of prescriptive literature that identified character traits valued in women; Gerda Lerner, "The Lady and the Mill Girl: Changes in the Status of Women in the Age of Jackson," *Mid-Continental American Studies Journal*, 10 (Spring 1969), 5–15, which stresses the disparity between women's place and opportunities for men; and Mary P. Ryan, "Mothers of Civilization: The Common Woman 1830–1860" in *Womanhood in America* (New York, 1975), pp. 137–191. A more positive view is suggested in Nancy F. Cott's pivotal book, *The Bonds of Womanhood: "Woman's Sphere" in New England, 1778–1835* (New Haven, Conn., 1977), which analyzes the liabilities and benefits of sphere; Kathryn Kish Sklar, *Catharine Beecher: A Study in American Domesticity* (New Haven, Conn., 1973), which discusses the development of domestic ideology; Daniel Scott Smith, "Family Limitation, Sexual Control, and Domestic Feminism in Victorian America," in Mary Hartman and Lois Banner, eds., *Clio's Consciousness Raised* (New York, 1974), pp. 119–136, which posits a female gain of autonomy within the family; and Carroll Smith-Rosenberg, "The Female World of Love and Ritual," *Signs*, 1 (Autumn 1975), 1–29, an exploration of women's relationships in a sexually segregated society. This essay is reprinted in Smith-Rosenberg, *Disorderly Conduct: Visions of Gender in Victorian America* (New York, 1985).

Recent studies further explore women's domestic lives and social experience. Most of Carl Degler, *At Odds: Women and the Family from the Revolution to the Present* (New York, 1981) concerns women's roles in the nineteenth-century family; chs. 7–11 on the demographic transition and sexuality are of prime interest. Lee Virginia Chambers-Schiller considers the lives of unmarried women in *Liberty, A Better Husband: Single Women in America, The Generations of 1780–1840* (New Haven, Conn., 1984). Ellen K. Rothman examines changing modes of romance in *Hands and Hearts: A History of Courtship in America* (Cambridge, Mass., 1984). Michael K. Grossberg presents the legal history of domestic issues from courtship to custody in *Governing the Hearth: Law and the Family in Nineteenth-Century America* (Chapel Hill, N.C., 1985). Steven Mintz and Susan Kellogg describe the rise of the middle-class family, 1770–1830, in *Domestic Revolutions: A Social History of American Family Life* (New York, 1988), ch. 3. Christine Stansell examines the experience of urban working-class women in *City of Women: Sex and Class in New York, 1789–1860* (New York, 1986). Mary P. Ryan's local study, *Cradle of the Middle Class: The Family in Oneida County, New York, 1790–1865* (New York, 1981), devotes attention to women's roles in home, church, economy, and community, and discusses their contribution to class identity; see especially chs. 2 and 5. Karen Halttunen, *Confidence Men and Painted Women: A Study of Middle-Class Culture in America, 1830–1870* (New Haven, Conn., 1982), analyzes the rituals, manners, and postures of the upwardly mobile. Jeanne Boydston explores the connection of household labor and industrialization in *Home and Work: Housework, Wages, and the Ideology of Labor in the Early Republic* (New York, 1990). Richard L. Bushman discusses the diffusion of gentility in *The Refinement of America: Persons, Houses, Cities* (New York, 1992), chs. 7–12. Stuart M. Blumin examines the process of class formation in *Emergence of the Middle Class: Social Experience in the American City, 1760–1900* (Cambridge, Mass., 1989). For an illuminating study of class development in England, see Leonore Davidoff and Catherine Hall, *Family Fortunes: Men and Women of the English Middle Class, 1780–1850* (London, 1987).

Ann Douglas posits an alliance between women and ministers in *The Feminization of American Culture* (New York, 1977). Barbara Leslie Epstein, *The Politics of Domesticity: Women, Evangelism, and Temperance in Nineteenth-Century America* (Middletown, Conn., 1981), examines the role of religion in the development of feminine consciousness; see ch. 2. Women's religious involvement is further discussed in Barbara M. Welter, "The Feminization of American Religion, 1800–1860," in Mary Hartman and Lois Banner, eds., *Clio's Consciousness Raised* (New York, 1974), pp. 137–157; Nancy F. Cott, "Young Women and the Second Great Awakening," *Feminist Studies,* 2 (Fall 1975), 15–29; Mary P. Ryan, "A Woman's Awakening: Evangelical Religion and the Families of Utica, New York, 1800–1840," *American Quarterly,* 30 (Winter 1978), 602–623; Epstein, *The Politics of Domesticity,* ch. 2; Louis Billington, "Female Laborers in the Church': Women Preachers in the Northeastern United States, 1790–1840," *Journal of American Studies,* 19 (1985), 369–394; and Ann M. Boylan, *Sunday School: The Formation of an American Institution, 1790–1880* (New Haven, Conn., 1988).

For changes in sexual ideology and practice, see in addition to Smith, "Family Limitation" and Degler, *At Odds,* above, Nancy F. Cott, "Passionlessness: An Interpretation of Victorian Sexual Ideology, 1790–1850," *Signs,* 4 (Winter 1978), 219–236; Linda Gordon, *Woman's Body, Woman's Right: A History of Birth Control in America* (New York, 1976), part I; Charles Rosenberg and Carroll Smith-Rosenberg, "The Female Animal: Medical and Biological Views of Woman and her Role in Nineteenth-Century America," *Journal of Social History,* 60 (September 1973), 332–356; John S. Haller and Robin Haller, *The Physician and Sexuality in Victorian America* (Urbana, Ill., 1974); Daniel Scott Smith and Michael Hindus, "Premarital Pregnancy in America, 1640–1971: An Overview and Interpretation," *Journal of Interdisciplinary History,* 5 (Spring 1975); and G. J. Barker-Benfield, "The Spermatic Economy: A Nineteenth-Century View of Sexuality," *Feminist Studies,* 1 (1972), 45–74. For relationships between women, see, in addition to Smith-Rosenberg, "The Female World of Love and Ritual," William Taylor and Christopher Lasch, "Two 'Kindred Spirits': Sorority and Family in New England, 1839–1846," *New England Quarterly,* 36 (1963), 25–41.

Women's roles as patients and practitioners are examined in Regina Markell Morantz-Sanchez, *Sympathy and Science: Women Physicians in American Medicine* (New York, 1985); Mary Roth Walsh, *"Doctors Wanted: No Women Need Apply": Sexual Barriers in the Medical Professions, 1835–1975* (New Haven, Conn., 1977); Ann Douglas Wood, "The Fashionable Diseases: Women's Complaints and Their Treatment in Nineteenth-Century America," *Journal of Interdisciplinary History,* 4 (Summer 1973), 25–52; Regina Markell Morantz, "The Perils of Feminist History," *Journal of Interdisciplinary History,* 4 (Spring 1974), 649–660; Morantz, "Making Women Modern: Middle-Class Women and Health Reform in Nineteenth-Century America," *Journal of Social History,* 10 (1976–1977), 490–507; and Susan E. Cayleff, *Wash and Be Healed: The Water-Cure Movement and Women's Health* (Philadelphia, 1987). For the beginning of the midwife's demise, see Catherine Scholton, *Childbearing in American Society: 1650–1850* (New York, 1985). Judy Barrett Litoff traces the history of midwifery into the twentieth century in *American Midwives: 1860 to the Present* (Westport, Conn., 1978). For a history of childbirth, see Judith Walzer Leavitt, *Brought to Bed: Childbearing in America, 1750–1950* (New York, 1986). Sylvia D. Hoffert explores mothers' leverage in *Private Matters: Attitudes Toward Childbearing and Infant Nurture in the Urban North* (Urbana, Ill., 1989).

On women's education, see Thomas A. Woody, *A History of Women's Education in the United States* (New York, 1929), vol. 1. This massive tome has not yet been replaced. See also Barbara M. Cross, ed., *The Educated Woman in America* (New York, 1965); Polly Welts Kaufman, *Women Teachers on the Frontier* (New Haven, Conn., 1984); Anne Firor Scott, "The Ever-Widening Circle: The Diffusing of Feminist Values from the Troy Female Seminary," *History of Education Quarterly,* 19 (Spring 1979), 3–25; Maris A. Vinovskis and Richard M. Bernard, "Beyond Catharine Beecher: Female Education in the Antebellum Period," *Signs,* 3 (Summer 1978), 856–869; Vinovskis and Bernard, "The Female Schoolteacher in Antebellum Massachusetts," *Journal of Social History,* 10 (March 1977), 332–345; and Keith Melder, "Woman's High Calling: The Teaching Profession in America, 1830–1860," *American Studies,* 13 (Fall 1972), 19–32. For the Beecher family, besides Sklar, *Catherine Beecher,* see Jeanne Boydston, Mary Kelley, and Anne Margolis, eds., *The Limits of Sisterhood: The Beecher Sisters on Women's Rights and Women's Sphere* (Chapel Hill, N.C., 1988).

Nina Baym surveys women's literary output in *Women's Fiction: A Guide to Novels By and About Women in America, 1820–1870* (Ithaca, N.Y., 1978). Ann Douglas assesses the influence of literary women and indicts female sentimentalism in *The Feminization of American Culture,* above. Mary Kelley, *Private Women, Public Stage: Literary Domesticity in Nineteenth-Century America* (New York, 1984), studies the careers of women authors. Jane Tomkins, *Sensational Designs: The Cultural Work of American Fiction, 1790–1860* (New York, 1985), defends the sentimental novel. David S. Reynolds discusses the rebellious role of women writers of the 1850s in *Beneath the American Renaissance: The Subversive Imagination in the Age of Emerson and Melville* (New York, 1988), ch. 12. Martha Saxton, *Louisa May: A Modern Biography of Louisa May Alcott* (New York, 1977) is an engaging book. Articles of interest include Ann Douglas Wood, "Mrs. Sigourney and the Sensibility of Inner Space," *New England Quarterly,* 45 (1972), 163–181; Wood, "The Scribbling Women and Fanny Fern: Why Women Wrote," *American Quarterly,* 23 (1971), 3–24; Mary Kelley, "A Woman Alone: Catharine Maria Sedgwick's Spinsterhood in Nineteenth-Century America," *New England Quarterly,* 51 (1978), 209–225; and Kirk Jeffrey, "Marriage, Career, and Feminine Ideology in Nineteenth-Century America: Reconstructing the Marital Experience of Lydia Maria Child," *Feminist Studies,* 2 (1975), 112–125.

Thomas Dublin examines women's experience in the textile mills in *Women at Work: The Transformation of Work and Community in Lowell, Massachusetts, 1826–1860* (New York,

1979) and *Farm and Factory: The Mill Experience and Women's Lives in New England 1830–1860* (New York, 1981). For mill workers' publications, see Benita Eisler, ed., *The Lowell Offering: Writings by New England Mill Women (1840–1845)* (Philadelphia and New York, 1977) and Philip S. Foner, ed., *The Factory Girls: A Collection of Writings on Life and Struggles in the New England Factories of the 1840s* (Urbana, Ill., 1977). Mary H. Blewett explores the sexual division of labor and its ramifications in *Men, Women, and Work: Class, Gender, and Protest in the New England Shoe Industry, 1780–1910* (Urbana, Ill., 1988). Joan M. Jensen examines the work roles of rural Pennsylvania women in *Loosening the Bonds: Mid-Atlantic Farm Women, 1750–1850* (New Haven, Conn., 1986). For paid domestic work, see Faye E. Dudden, *Serving Women: Household Service in Nineteenth-Century America* (Middletown, Conn., 1983). Urban women wage earners are discussed in Stansell, *City of Women,* above; David Montgomery, "The Working Classes of the Pre-Industrial American City, 1780–1830," *Labor History,* 9 (Winter 1968), 3–27; and Sharon Harley, "Northern Black Female Workers: Jacksonian Era," in Sharon Harley and Rosalyn Terborg-Penn, eds., *The Afro-American Woman: Struggles and Images* (Port Washington, N.Y., 1978, pp. 5–16. Timothy J. Gilfoyle depicts a facet of the urban economy in *City of Eros: New York City, Prostitution, and the Commercialization of Sex, 1790–1920* (New York, 1992). Alice Kessler Harris integrates labor history with economic and social developments in *Out to Work: A History of Wage-Earning Women in the United States* (New York, 1982). For further sources on women in the labor force, see the suggested readings for chapter 10.

The growing literature on women in the West includes John Mack Faragher, *Women and Men on the Overland Trail* (New Haven, Conn., 1979); Julie Roy Jeffrey, *Frontier Women: The Trans-Mississippi West, 1840–1880* (New York, 1978); Glenda Riley, *The Female Frontier: A Comparative View of Women on the Prairie and the Plains* (Lawrence, Kans., 1988); Riley, *Women and Indians on the Frontier, 1825–1915* (Albuquerque, N. Mex., 1984); Sandra L. Myres, *Westering Women and the Frontier Experience, 1800–1915* (Albuquerque, N. Mex., 1982), and Lillian Schlissel, Byrd Gibbens, and Elizabeth Hampsten, *Far From Home: Families of the Westward Journey* (New York, 1989). For collections of western women's writing, see Lilliam Schlissel, ed., *Women's Diaries of the Westward Journey* (New York, 1982) and Christiane Fischer, ed., *Let Them Speak for Themselves: Women in the American West, 1849–1900* (New York, 1978). Articles of interest include John Mack Faragher and Christine Stansell, "Women and their Families on the Overland Trail to California and Oregon 1842–67," *Feminist Studies,* 2 (1975), 150–166, and Faragher, "History from the Inside Out: Writing the History of Women in Rural America," *American Quarterly,* 33 (Winter 1981), 537–557. Bibliographical articles include Sandra L. Myres, "Women in the West" in Michael Malone, ed., *Historians and the American West* (Lincoln, Neb., 1983), and Elizabeth Jameson, "Toward a Multicultural History of Women in the Western United States," *Signs,* 13 (Summer 1988), 761–791. The experience of early-nineteenth-century Hispanic women is examined in Janet Lecompte, "The Independent Women of Hispanic New Mexico, 1821–1846," *Western Historical Quarterly,* 12 (January 1981), 17–35, and David J. Weber, *The Mexican Frontier, 1821–1846: The American Southwest Under Mexico* (Albuquerque, N. Mex., 1982). For recent historical interpretations of westward expansion, see Richard Bernstein, "Unsettling the Old West," *New York Times Magazine* (March 18, 1990), pp. 34ff; Larry McMurty, "How the West Was Won," *New Republic* (October 22, 1990), 32–39; and Patricia Nelson Limerick, *The Legacy of Conquest: The Unbroken Path of the American West* (New York, 1987).

For antebellum southern women, see Elizabeth Fox-Genovese, *Within the Plantation Household: Black and White Women of the Old South* (Chapel Hill, N.C., 1988); Suzanne Lebsock, *The Free Women of Petersburg: Status and Culture in a Southern Town, 1784–1860* (New York, 1985); Catherine Clinton, *The Plantation Mistress* (New York, 1982); Jean E.

Friedman, *The Enclosed Garden: Women and Community in the Evangelical South, 1830–1900* (Chapel Hill, N.C., 1985); Jane Turner Censer, *North Carolina Planters and Their Children, 1800–1860* (Baton Rouge, La., 1984); Sally G. McMillen, *Motherhood in the Old South: Pregnancy, Childbirth, and Infant Rearing* (Baton Rouge, La., 1990); and Carol Bleser, ed., *In Joy and in Sorrow: Women, Family, and Marriage in the Victorian South* (New York, 1991). An older account is Anne Firor Scott, *The Southern Lady: From Pedestal to Politics, 1830–1930* (Chicago, 1970), ch. 1. The studies above express diverse views about the nature, impact, and roots of southern patriarchy; historians often contrast the interpretations of Clinton and Fox-Genovese. For explorations of southern character and society, see William R. Taylor, *Cavalier and Yankee: The Old South and American National Character* (New York and Evanston, Ill., 1957); Bertram Wyatt-Brown, *Southern Honor: Ethics and Behavior in the Old South* (New York, 1983); and Steven M. Stowe, *Intimacy and Power in the Old South: Rituals in the Lives of the Planters* (Baltimore, Md., 1987). A recent edition of Mary Chestnut's diary, a revised account of her wartime experience, composed in the 1880s, is C. Vann Woodward, ed., *Mary Chestnut's Civil War* (New Haven, Conn., 1981). For the original Civil War diary, see C. Vann Woodward and Elizabeth Muhlenfeld, *The Private Mary Chesnut: The Unpublished Civil War Diaries* (New Haven, Conn., 1984).

CHAPTER 7

❧❧❧

Frances Wright at Nashoba

In November 1825, a thirty-year-old Scotswoman used part of her inheritance to buy 320 acres of marshy swamp in western Tennessee from two friends of Andrew Jackson, who had recently sold the land to them. Five years before, it had belonged to the Chickasaws. Uncleared, untamed, and bordering on Indian country, the tract lay thirteen miles northeast of Memphis, a tiny river port. It was an outpost in the wilderness. But Frances Wright, who arrived at this desolate spot in the middle of the winter, had unusual ambitions. Here in these remote backwoods, which were "still inhabited by bears, wolves, and panthers," she was going to create a model community that would pave the way for the gradual emancipation of the southern slaves. "I have made the hard earth my bed, the saddle of my horse my pillow," she reported, "and have staked my life and fortune on an experiment having in view moral liberty and human improvement."

By the time she founded Nashoba, Frances Wright was already known on two continents as an ardent admirer of everything American and a friend of the famous. After an earlier voyage to the United States, she had written an enthusiastic travel account that was well received by American readers and English liberals. Her reputation was excellent and her career promising. She also had means. The legatee of an ample fortune, Wright had been orphaned at two and brought up in England, along with her younger sister, Camilla, by a maternal aunt. Her early years were pervaded by "the heart solitude of orphanship." But at age sixteen, she became entranced with America and its history, and "from that moment on, my attention became rivetted on this country as upon the theatre where man might first awake to the full knowledge and exercise of his powers." Wright's passionate interest in America soon transformed her into a literary celebrity and generated a chain of events that ultimately led to the Tennessee backwoods.

154

In 1818, she made a two-year voyage to the United States accompanied by Camilla, her constant companion. The expedition only reinforced her avid enthusiasm. Once back in London, in 1821, she published her favorable impressions in *Views of Society and Manners in America,* which was widely admired and translated into three languages. Frances Wright now became well known as an author. She used her prominence to gain the attention of notable older men, with whom she had a talent for forming attachments. The most important was the Marquis de Lafayette, admired hero of the American Revolution, with whom she established a correspondence. Lafayette was then sixty-four and twenty years widowed. Within a few months, amazingly, Frances and Camilla Wright moved in with him at his family estate in the Seine-et-Marne and remained there for the better part of two years.

Lafayette was both a living link with American history and a major conquest. Their friendship, as Wright told him, was "of no ordinary character," a view that was shared by all of his relatives, who were anxious to get rid of her. But Frances Wright was tenacious, and whenever they were apart, she besieged him with letters. "My friend, my father, and if there be a word more expressive of love, and reverence, and adoration, I would fain use it," she wrote to him during one of his absences from home. "I am only half alive when away from you. . . . I put my arms around the neck of my paternal friend and ask his blessing." Her goal, it turned out, was to be adopted by Lafayette, along with Camilla—a scheme that threw his descendants into a panic. Frances Wright was undaunted. When Lafayette took off on a triumphal tour of America in 1824, Frances and Camilla Wright followed.

This second voyage had far different consequences than the first. While shadowing Lafayette all over the United States and stirring up gossip, Frances Wright gained access to most of the prominent statesmen—Madison, Monroe, and Jackson—who turned out to greet him. She met Thomas Jefferson, with whom she managed to hold private discussions at Monticello. She also traveled extensively on her own, this time in the South, and became obsessed with the "pestilence" of American slavery, "the extent of its demoralizing influence . . . the ruin with which it threatened this country . . . its sin, its suffering, its disgrace." When Lafayette returned to France, his "bien aimée Fanny, la tendre fille de ma choix" remained behind. Not only had she given up hope of becoming an adopted Lafayette, but she had developed a scheme to bring slavery to an end.

Wright's ambitious proposal, for gradual and compensated emancipation, was published in the leading antislavery journal, Benjamin Lundy's *Genius of Universal Emancipation,* in September 1825, only two months before Wright bought her Tennessee tract. It was a long-range plan. If slaves would work for five years, earn back their purchase price, and learn a trade to support themselves, they could then be freed and colonized—in some foreign place such as Texas, California, or Haiti. Such a plan would have to be carried out at first on a small scale, at an experimental community somewhere in the South. And Nashoba, on the southern frontier, was to be the pioneer experiment—to prove that gradual emancipation would work.

Wright's goals for the backwoods plantation were very specific. She in-

tended to get at least fifty slaves—contributed, she hoped, by enlightened planters, or else by purchase. Each would be charged with his price, plus interest and
the cost of his upkeep, which he would then work off, by the hour, on a credit
system. Meanwhile, all of the slaves would undergo a "moral, intellectual, and
industrial apprenticeship," to be prepared for the responsibility of liberty. Older
slaves would learn a trade, and children would be educated at a community
school. At the end of five years, all would be rewarded with freedom and
colonization. "The prejudice whether absurd or to the contrary against the
mixture of the two colors is so deeply rooted in the American mind," Wright
wrote to English friends, "that emancipation without expatriation (if indeed that
word be applicable) seems impossible."

The source of Wright's inspiration for Nashoba is unclear. She had long
been convinced, since her first American voyage, that immediate emancipation
without preparation would be bad for the nation and worse for the slaves. "Poor,
lazy, and ignorant," they would soon become "vicious," she predicted. She was
surely influenced by Jefferson, who thought that emancipation had to be gradual,
compensated, and agreeable to the "prevailing opinion" of southern planters.
Never hesitant, Wright invited him to join her at Nashoba, but Jefferson declined
the offer, explaining that he was eighty-two, "with one foot in the grave and the
other uplifted to follow it." Her plan, he granted, had an "aspect of promise." Or
perhaps she was inspired by Lafayette, who had once attempted a similar plan
of emancipation on his plantation in French Guiana. By her own account, she
had been especially impressed by the Rappites, a religious sect whose thriving
cooperative communities in Pennsylvania and Indiana she had visited. But most
probably she had been spurred into action by a new connection, the famous
Scottish industrialist and philanthropist Robert Owen. Then in his fifties, Owen
had just arrived in America himself.

An extremely successful textile manufacturer and free-thinking socialist,
Robert Owen was a boundless source of idealism and enthusiasm. Convinced
that competition was at the root of all evil, he had come to the United States in
1824 to buy out an Indiana Rappite community and establish his own. New
Harmony was to serve as a model of a better society. Owen wanted to prove his
belief that character could be molded by the environment and that the environment could be perfected by a system of "cooperative labor"—in which competition was eliminated and surplus wealth was spent for the public good. New
Harmony, of course, had no connection with any plan for freeing the slaves.
Robert Owen excluded blacks from the community. A few of his followers felt
that cooperative labor could somehow be harnessed to the goal of emancipation,
but no one had tried it. Frances Wright was the first to do so.

By early 1826, when the Tennessee experiment got under way, Wright was
both carried away with the promise of her scheme and sure of her own ability to
carry it out. She was certain that she was the only individual, "with the exception
of the beloved General," who could undertake such a venture. Her sex was no
handicap, she informed her friends. If violence arose, she explained, it could be
an advantage. On the other hand, it made little difference. "The mind has no sex
but what habit and education give it," she had written to Lafayette a few years

before, "and I who was thrown in infancy upon the world like a wreck upon the waters have learned, as well to struggle with the elements as any child of Adam." The elements were to be a major concern at Nashoba, as its residents soon learned. Another concern was the residents themselves, both free and slave.

Besides Camilla, Wright had collected an assortment of associates during her travels around the country. All would contribute their labor, and, in some cases, property to the model commune. And all were young men—of liberal beliefs, opposed to slavery, and very much taken with Frances Wright. Richeson Whitby was a Quaker follower of Robert Owen whom she met at New Harmony. James Richardson was a fellow Scot and former medical student whom she found in Memphis. And George Flower, a young Englishman, was by far the most promising. It was he who helped Wright choose her Tennessee tract. A fervent advocate of equality, Flower had extensive communitarian experience and, most important, practical knowledge of farming, which the other associates lacked. George Flower brought his wife and three children with him to Nashoba; but this was an error never repeated. Wives and children did not adapt well to the Tennessee wilds.

By the time the associates gathered at Nashoba, slaves had begun to arrive as well. The first family to get there was donated by Robert Wilson, a generous planter, who escorted Lucky, who was pregnant, and her five young daughters all the way from South Carolina to Nashoba. At this point donations ceased, and Frances Wright had to buy the slaves for Nashoba herself. "In view of the moderate size of my fortune, and since I have to run the risks of possible loss," she wrote to English friends, "I am limiting myself to the sum of twelve thousand dollars which . . . will suffice to establish a good plantation worked by six men and four women whom I am buying at Nashville for four to five hundred dollars each." She bought only eight, and some cost as much as $1,500. But in March 1825, Willis, Jacob, Grandison, Redrick, Henry, Nelly, Peggy, and Kitty arrived by steamboat at Memphis. By this time, Frances Wright had bought adjoining tracts as well, enlarging Nashoba to almost "two thousand acres of pleasant woodland, traversed by a clear and lovely stream."

The stream was the wretched Wolfe River, which ran through the place. Near its banks, associates and slaves set up two double-roomed cabins, one for whites, one for blacks, and went about clearing the thickly covered land. Within a year, Nashoba had a vegetable garden, a five-acre orchard, fifteen acres of corn, and two of cotton. A helpful New York Quaker contributed supplies, and the associates distributed tasks among themselves. George Flower was overseer, Camilla Wright attempted to set up a school, and James Richardson took care of bookkeeping and correspondence. Frances Wright and Richeson Whitby worked in the fields, along with the slaves, digging trenches, uprooting tree stumps, breaking up boulders, and fighting off malaria. Wright was ecstatic. "Here I am at last, property owner in the forests of this new territory," she reported. "I have traveled the length and breadth of this territory two times, doing forty miles a day on horseback, through unbroken country, spending the night in cabins open to the air on all sides, or in the woods themselves. . . . Even I am beginning to find an unaccustomed joy in life."

The obstacles at Nashoba, however, were enormous. One was the work force. More slaves arrived and there were soon about thirty, almost half of them children. But none of the slaves shared Wright's enthusiasm for Tennessee or for her scheme of cooperative labor. As Frances Wright had observed at the outset, "there is nothing more difficult than to make men work in these parts." Another obstacle was the soil, which was muddy, and the climate, which was terrible. The commune was covered with ice in the winter, drowned with rain in the spring, scorched in the summer, and at all times extremely damp. Although Wright had hoped to avoid "the unhealthy miasma of the swamps," she had fallen right into it. The moisture-ridden air was full of mosquitoes that transmitted diseases throughout the community. George Flower's children got sick at once and had to be sent away, followed by Camilla, who had to recuperate for spells. Frances Wright was soon affected as well. Since she worked in the fields, she often suffered from sunstroke, chills, and fever and was forced to spend much of her time recovering, in Memphis or New Harmony.

It was during a visit to New Harmony at the end of 1826 that Frances Wright was inspired to enlarge the scope of her experiment. Nashoba was almost a year old but it was still a desolate outpost in the forest, populated mainly by unhappy slaves. Robert Owen's Indiana community, in contrast, was a huge and bustling center of activity. Owen had already thrown the bulk of his considerable fortune into land, buildings, shops, and a "school of industry." Moreover, some 900 people, led by a contingent of idealistic reformers, many of them friends of Wright's, were already embarked on creating a new social order. In December 1826, Owen made the nature of the new order more precise. In a formal "Declaration of Mental Independence," he condemned the "trinity of evils" that afflicted humanity. These evils were private property, organized religion, and marriage, none of which would exist in the improved society he intended to create. Robert Owen's "Declaration" had a powerful influence on Frances Wright, who was already an avid Owenite. She returned to Tennessee convinced that Nashobans too should strive for sexual and religious liberation. She now decided to alter the community's goals by adding Robert Owen's principles onto the original plan for freeing the slaves.

Not only would Nashoba set an example of gradual emancipation, Frances Wright announced to her colleagues and slaves on her return, but it would now become, like New Harmony, a pilot project for world reform. From this point on, the backwoods plantation would provide a haven for congenial spirits from around the world who could join in the search for liberty, happiness, and the "emancipation of the human mind"—which meant, in Owenite lingo, freedom from marriage, religion, and economic competition. New recruits were invited to contribute property or such services as gardening, trades, teaching, or nursing. Children would attend a racially integrated school. Slaves, meanwhile, would continue to perform those tasks "their habits render easy," that is, the heavy work. Wright completed the transition by divesting herself of ownership and turning Nashoba over to ten trustees including Lafayette, Robert Owen, and one of Owen's sons, Robert Dale, an ambitious young man who worked at New Harmony. Wright herself became a "resident trustee."

What Frances Wright envisioned was a "city of refuge in the wilderness" where free-thinking liberals like herself could escape the evils of society and establish their own communal utopia. "I have devoted my time and fortune," she informed a potential recruit, "to laying the foundation of a society where affection shall form the only marriage, kind feelings and kind action the only religion, respect for the feelings and liberties of others the only restraint, and union of interest the bond of peace and security." But unlike New Harmony, Nashoba was supposed to be both a haven for liberals and, at the same time, an experiment in gradual emancipation. It was, according to utopian John Humphrey Noyes in a study of early American socialist communities, a "two story commonwealth . . . a Brook Farm plus a Negro basis."

At the outset, of course, the new ideals made little impact on the community's prospects. Nashoba continued to be a slave plantation run by a handful of "residents." No new recruits appeared. The slaves continued to clear the land, pick away at the uncooperative soil, and build new cabins, under duress. But George Flower, the most capable of the resident trustees, became suspicious of Nashoba's new ideology and left. When Owen's son, Robert Dale, who was infatuated with Wright and thrilled at being made a trustee, arrived at Nashoba in 1827, he was appalled. The place was a wreck. Robert Dale Owen found "second rate land, and scarcely a hundred acres of it cleared; three or four squared log houses and a few cabins for slaves, the only buildings." And the slaves were working "indolently" under the incompetent management of Richeson Whitby.

Frances Wright now turned her attention to the work force. She established the custom of giving weekly lectures to the slaves on Nashoban morals and philosophy. The lectures were intended to explain the new Owenite goals and to "develop their sense of individual responsibility," which was clearly lacking. The slaves, from the start, were recalcitrant and churlish, rather than anxious to work off their purchase price and expenses through cooperative labor. Moreover, their ranks were pervaded by disgruntled individuals and troublemakers—such as Redrick, who was contentious, and Dilly, a vociferous complainer, and Willis, who was always defending her. The evening sessions were supposed to improve their behavior. James Richardson dutifully recorded the proceedings in his community log, the "Nashoba Book."

May 7, 1827

Met the slaves this evening. Frances Wright endeavored to explain to them the powers with which she had invested the trustees.

Dilly and Redrick were reprimanded for exchanging abusive language, instead of laying their respective complaints before us.

Willis was made to retract the threat which he had uttered of avenging with his own hands the wrongs of Dilly.

James Richardson continued to record community meetings in his "Nashoba Book." But Frances Wright and Robert Dale Owen went off to Europe for the rest of 1827, to hunt down recruits. Wright was as ambitious here as in

Tennessee. She focused her efforts on Mary Wollstonecraft Shelley, in whom she was sure she had found a model Nashoban. Mary Shelley was not only a brilliant author, the child of distinguished parents, and the recent widow of a famous husband but also, Wright decided, a kindred spirit. In a slew of letters, Wright stressed the virtues of Nashoba, her compassionate outlook, and her need for friendship. "I too have suffered, and we must have done so to feel for the suffering," she told Mary Shelley. "I have greatly pitied and greatly dared. . . . Yet I do want one of my own sex to commune with, and sometimes to lean upon in all the confidence of equality and friendship. . . . Delightful, indeed it is to aid the progress of human improvement. . . . But still the heart craves something more, ere it can say, I am satisfied."

While Frances Wright pressed her case with Mary Shelley, Camilla Wright and James Richardson were left in charge at Nashoba. Here they assumed the enormous obligation Wright had imposed, of welding Owenite ideals onto the original plan for gradual emancipation. Richardson now used the nightly sessions to explain to the slaves the need for freedom from the evils of private property, religion, and marriage. The slaves, however, were largely indifferent to the new ethos. Since the outset they had been unable to distinguish between forced labor at Nashoba and forced labor elsewhere. They were now unable to imbibe the spirit of a new "school of industry"; vocational training seemed to involve only more compulsory work. In addition, their conduct was getting worse. The Nashoba slaves, Richardson recorded, were always behaving "in a riotous manner," acquiring food on the sly, slipping treats to the children, bickering among themselves, and complaining about the rules.

James Richardson and Camilla Wright therefore imposed new rules. Slaves were not to receive extra food or clothing from anyone, resident or visitor. They were not permitted to eat, except at community meals. They were not to use the swing until their habits were "more refined than at present." Finally, Camilla announced, the children would be removed from parental control and placed under the care of Mademoiselle Lalotte, a free black woman from New Orleans who had just arrived with her own children. All communication between slave parents and children would henceforth cease, except with special permission. The adult slaves might be recalcitrant and disorderly, but the two Nashoba residents hoped at least to prepare the children for emancipation.

Once the new rules went into effect, James Richardson's "Nashoba Book" became a record of the slaves' resistance. The adult slaves were unable to tolerate separation from their children. Willis was reprimanded for interfering between Lalotte and one of his children, Dilly for giving food to one of hers. Willis complained that Mademoiselle Lalotte beat a child of his and preferred her own, who were light in color, although Richardson explained that "distinctions of rank" at Nashoba were never based on color. Finally, Dilly lashed out at Camilla and grumbled to everyone about "having so many mistresses." Richardson was forced to reiterate to the slaves that "they can get rid of these masters and mistresses in no other way than by working out their freedom when they will be transformed into masters and mistresses themselves." Within a few days, however, Dilly's complaints were overshadowed by the outrageous Redrick, who now forced his attentions on the slave Isabel. Richardson recorded the incident in his "Nashoba Book."

June 1, 1827

> Met the slaves at dinner time—Isabel had laid a complaint against Redrick, for coming during the night of Wednesday to her bedroom uninvited, and endeavoring without her consent, to take liberties with her person. Our views of the sexual relation had been repeatedly given to the slaves; Camilla Wright again stated it, and informed the slaves that, as the conduct of Redrick, which he did not deny, was a gross infringement of that view, a repetition . . . ought, in her opinion, to be punished by flogging. She repeated that we consider the proper basis of the sexual intercourse to be the unconstrained and unrestrained choice of *both parties.* Nelly having requested a lock for the door of the room in which she and Isabel sleep, with the view of preventing the future uninvited entrance of any man, the lock was refused, as being, in its proposed use, inconsistent with the doctrine just explained; . . . which will give to every woman a much greater security, than any lock can possibly do.
>
> Maria tried to hang herself for jealousy of Henry which we would not support her in.

James Richardson was not through with the subject of sexual emancipation. Two weeks later he moved in with Josephine, Mademoiselle Lalotte's teenage daughter, a "provisional" community member. He carefully recorded the new domestic arrangement in his "Nashoba Book."

Sunday evening, June 17th 1827

> Met the slaves—James Richardson informed them that, last night, Mam'selle Josephine and he began to live together; and he took this occasion of repeating to them our views of color, and of the sexual relation.

Although such a liaison was by no means unique, Richardson's next move was. He had the "Nashoba Book" published in Lundy's *Genius of Universal Emancipation* and, in so doing, revealed the novel nature of the community. The journal's readers, alarmingly, were unable to understand the benefits of free love at the Tennessee experiment and tended to see, instead, immorality, depravity, and vice. To one correspondent, Nashoba sounded like a "great brothel." The resident trustees rushed to their own defense. Camilla, who had just married Richeson Whitby, denounced the institution of marriage. And Frances Wright, who returned from Europe, hastened to uphold Nashoba and its principles.

Wright's "Explanatory Notes" on Nashoba, published in newspapers in Memphis and New Harmony, explained the new ideals she had introduced at the commune with unusual clarity. Nashobans, she stated, were striving for "moral liberty." This meant that women had to be freed from the tyranny of matrimonial law, which was founded in religious prejudice and bound them to servitude. Defending "unlegalized connections" and the rights of unmarried mothers, Wright announced that the institution of marriage would be excluded from Nashoba. Organized religion would be banned as well, along with obsolete moral codes that generated vice and sexual repression.

> Let us look to the victims . . . of those ignorant laws, ignorant prejudices, ignorant code of morals, which condemn one portion of the female sex to vicious excess, another to as vicious restraint, and all to defenceless helplessness and slavery, and generally the whole of the male sex to debasing licentiousness, if not to loathesome brutality. . . . Let us not attach ideas of purity to monastic chastity, impossible to man or woman without consequences fraught with evil, nor ideas of vice to connections formed under auspices of kind feelings.

Moreover, Wright proclaimed, Nashoba would pursue yet another path in the quest for utopia: racial amalgamation. The Tennessee commune would now become a "cooperative colony," where free blacks and whites could be admitted as members and live together while their children were educated to be equal. The color barrier could not be erased in one generation, she prophesied, but it could in the next. At Nashoba, she declared, equality would be assured "without regard to sex or condition, class, race, nation, or color." Her hope was that "brotherhood be embraced by the white man and the black, and their children gradually . . . blend into one their blood and hue."

The goals of the "Explanatory Notes" surpassed anything ever proposed or endorsed by Frances Wright's mentors. Neither Lafayette nor Jefferson, for instance, had ever defended racial amalgamation. Nor had Robert Owen. Frances Wright's new principles were especially unnerving to those who had once looked with favor on her humanitarian aims. "Her views of amalgamating the white and black populations [are] universally obnoxious," James Madison wrote to Lafayette. So were "her notions on the spirit of religion and marriage." The crisis created by Redrick and Richardson, in short, appeared to be insurmountable. But scandal was not the only problem that Nashoba faced.

By 1828 the community had severe financial problems as well. Very little could be grown on the dismal plantation. Cooperative labor had never made a profit and debts were mounting. Finally, despite Frances Wright's efforts to explain the virtues of the Tennessee commune, few new recruits had arrived to contribute either their labor or their property. Ever since the original residents had come to Nashoba in 1825, only two free adults had ever ventured into it of their own accord, Robert Dale Owen and Mademoiselle Lalotte. No one else had been attracted to the "city of refuge in the wilderness." But during the winter of 1828, when the community was reaching its nadir, an old friend of Frances Wright's suddenly appeared. At this singularly inopportune moment, the English author Frances Trollope, who had just arrived in the United States, decided to look into the possibility of staying at Nashoba.

Frances Trollope had her own reason for embarking on an American sojourn: bankruptcy. Her husband was unable to support his family in England. In addition, she wanted to write a book about American society and needed somewhere to live, with her five children, while Mr. Trollope set up a business in Cincinnati. Nashoba, she discovered, was not the spot. "The forest became thicker and more dreary looking every mile we advanced," she recalled. "One glance sufficed to convince me that every idea I had formed of the place was as far as possible from the truth. Desolation was the only feeling—the only word that presented itself." As far as Frances Trollope was concerned, the climate was awful, the forest impenetrable, comfort nonexistent (the cabins had no roofs), and Nashoba intolerable. But Frances Wright was totally unaware of the "savage aspect of the scene," said her friend. Her mind "was so exclusively occupied by the object she had then in view, that all else [was] worthless or indifferent to her." Wright's enthusiasm, concluded the last recruit, was that of the "religious fanatic."

Frances Trollope spent only ten days at Nashoba and then made a hasty exit, moving her family on to Cincinnati. After she left, the community's goals were once again revised. "Co-operation," wrote Frances Wright, "has well nigh killed us all." This was all too true. By the spring, the free Nashobans were themselves dispersing. James Richardson and Josephine had already decamped. Robert Dale Owen left in May. Camilla Wright and Richeson Whitby soon took off for New Harmony. Finally, by June of 1828, Frances Wright alone was left at Nashoba, with some thirty-odd slaves, the ramshackle cabins, and the uncleared forests. Perhaps, during these weeks, she began to feel, as Frances Trollope put it, "the favourite fabric of her imagination fall to pieces beneath her feet."

But Frances Wright was unable to face failure. As Nashoba's potential shrunk, her goals for reform expanded. "She was now aware," Wright explained in her memoirs, written in the third person, "that, in her practical efforts at

"The only word that springs to mind is desolation," wrote English author Frances Trollope, who arrived at Nashoba in December 1827. Accompanying her was a young French artist, Auguste Hervieu, who was intrigued by the new community and hoped to teach art there. Hervieu left Nashoba as soon as he saw it, but not before making a sketch. *(From Frances Trollope,* Domestic Manners of the Americans, *ed. Donald Smalley)*

reform, she had begun at the wrong end." Slavery, clearly, was only one form of evil pervading American society. Inexplicably, the most democratic and egalitarian nation in the world had lost sight of its own purpose. It had become ridden with class, dominated by ministers, tyrannized by prejudice, and oppressive to women. An "individual experiment" such as Nashoba, Wright concluded, was useless until the "collective body politic" was reformed. It was not the slaves, in short, who had to be prepared for freedom, but the rest of Americans as well. At this crucial juncture, a new mission became clear. Frances Wright decided to become a public reformer and to shift her energies from the failing commune to the nation's growing cities, where the "popular mind" might be swayed. This meant full-scale entry into public life, a realm of experience reserved for men.

In the summer of 1828, Wright left Nashoba and its slaves in the care of a hired overseer and moved on to New Harmony. Her campaign was two-pronged. With Robert Dale Owen, who was still enthralled, she ran the former New Harmony newspaper, retitled the *Free Enquirer*. And at her own expense, for Wright still had half her inheritance intact, she began a lecture campaign to alter American sentiments. In her new role as lecturer, Frances Wright became the first woman to address mixed audiences of men and women from a public platform. As a lecturer, she caused, said Frances Trollope, "an effect that can hardly be described." This was not surprising, since Wright's goals in reform were to spread the ideals that had just failed to make headway at Nashoba—free thought, sexual emancipation, and "mental independence."

During the summer, while Willis, Dilly, Redrick, and the others worked on in Tennessee, Wright began her public lectures in Cincinnati and then moved on to the East. By 1829, she had made her base in New York and formed a new commune of sorts, composed of former Nashobans and New Harmonyites. Besides young Robert Dale Owen and Camilla Wright, now separated from Whitby, the "free enquirers" included Robert Jennings, an Owenite whom Wright had tried to attract to Nashoba, and Phiquepal D'Arusmont, an educational reformer who had run the "school of industry" at New Harmony. At first Frances Wright rented downtown theaters for her public addresses; but soon she bought a former Baptist church on Broome Street, which the free enquirers rebaptized the Hall of Science. This novel institution was used for lectures, debates, a secular Sunday school, editorial offices, and a reform-minded bookstore, which sold the works of Tom Paine and Mary Wollstonecraft. The free enquirers were emissaries of the Enlightenment, bent on reviving the age of reason in a nation captivated by evangelism.

The crux of the excitement, however, was Wright's lecturing career. By taking to the lecture platform, she had broken all rules of decorum, crossed a rigid sexual boundary, and struck a raw nerve. The lectures were free and attracted large crowds. Auditors often had to be turned away for lack of room. A tall and imposing figure, Wright was an eloquent and effective orator. She came to the podium dressed in white and armed with the Declaration of Independence, to which she frequently referred. One admirer, reformer Orestes Brownson, remembered "her graceful manner, her tall, commanding figure, her wit and sarcasm, her apparent honesty of purpose." But public speaking was

Published by J Akin Phila.

A DOWNRIGHT GABBLER,
or a goose that deserves to be hissed —

Frances Wright's public lectures in 1828–1829 were at first received with curiosity, but once she attacked the clergy, newspapers published hostile critiques, angry letters, and uncomplimentary cartoons, including this one of a lecturing goose. *(New-York Historical Society)*

viewed as unnatural for a woman. Even Lafayette disapproved. Opponents heckled and turned out the lights, while Wright was denounced from the pulpit and in the press, as an infidel, free lover, and "female monster whom all decent people ought to avoid."

"She ceases to be a woman," said the *New York American*. "A bold blasphemer and a voluptuous preacher of licentiousness," said the *Commercial Advertiser*. One critic portrayed her as a goose in a dress. Another exclaimed that she wanted "to vitiate public morals and . . . turn the world into a universal brothel." Sarah Hale declared in the *Ladies Magazine* that even attending a Wright lecture was "not to be thought of." A review reprinted in a Quaker journal summed up the criticism launched against Wright. "The dogma inculcated by this fallen and degraded fair one, if acted upon by the community, would produce the destruction of religion, morals, law, and equity, and result in savage anarchy and confusion." Frances Wright was not deterred. "The storm has run high," she wrote to a friend. "Truly I have felt in this world like some being fallen from a strange planet among a race whose senses and perceptions are all different from my own."

Wright's lectures were devoted to Nashoban ideals, only slightly revamped for public consumption. She had no creed, she told her audiences, nor any proof of God's existence. In her speeches and in the *Free Enquirer*, which she used as a battering ram against clerical influence, Wright denounced the clergy as servants of superstition who were trying to enhance their own power, especially through religious revivals. Her primary object, she stated, was "to overthrow priestcraft, to hasten the down fall of the clergy, to empty their coffers, to sap their influence, to annihilate their trade and calling, and render the odiousness of their profession apparent to all eyes—even, if possible, to their own."

Another of her goals was to correct "the neglected state of the female mind, and the consequent dependence of the female condition." On the lecture platform, Frances Wright became a vocal exponent of women's rights. Women should be provided with equal educational opportunities, she asserted, and should be equal under law. They should control their own property after marriage and be the beneficiaries of easier divorce laws. The marriage contract, she insisted, was but one part of a defective legal system, based on common law, which had no place in the United States. Although Wright's opinion of the marriage contract gave ammunition to her critics, she attempted to avoid the inflammatory thrust of the "Explanatory Notes," which had explained too much.

However novel it may appear, I shall venture the assertion, that, until women assume the place in society which good sense and good feeling alike assign to them, human improvement must advance but feebly. . . . How many, how omnipotent are the interests which engage men to break the mental chains of women, . . . to exalt rather than lower their condition, to multiply their solid acquirements, to respect their liberties, to make them their equals, or wish them even their superiors. . . .

There is a vulgar persuasion, that the ignorance of women, by favoring their subordination, insures their utility. Tis the same argument employed by the ruling few against the subject many in aristocracies; by the rich against the poor in democracies; by the learned professions against the people in all countries.

But Frances Wright's ultimate panacea, and the cornerstone of her proposals, was educational reform, a distinctively Owenite solution. Throughout 1829, while the slaves of Nashoba endured their last few months of cooperative labor, Wright campaigned for the most grandiose of her utopian schemes, the "guardianship system" of education. This was a plan to wipe out inequality of class and sex and to regenerate society. According to Wright's scheme, each state would be divided into townships, where the government would establish boarding schools for all the children of the district. At the age of two, the age at which

Frances Wright had been orphaned, children would leave home to live at the schools, where their parents could visit them but not interfere with their education. At school, there would be complete equality and uniformity of routine, although children with bad habits would have to be separated from the rest. Under such a system, students could be imbued with the spirit of free inquiry, trained in the physical sciences, liberated from dogma and superstition, and prepared to "perfect the free institutions of America." They would also, of course, be spared the prejudices and opinions—especially the religious opinions—of their parents by the simple expedient of removing them entirely from the home.

The "guardianship system" was reminiscent of the separation of parents and children at Nashoba. It was also entirely at odds with the esprit of American womanhood, the idealization of motherhood, and the cult of domesticity that had developed in the early nineteenth century. But Frances Wright had acquired a different base of support. This came from New York craftsmen and the short-lived Workingmen's party, with which the free enquirers were soon embroiled. One of the earliest American labor movements, the party had emerged in 1829, right after a depression. Its members supported humanitarian reforms, such as the ten-hour day, and opposed imprisonment for debt, capital punishment, the banking system, and professional aristocracies. Most important, they advocated a system of public education. There were no free schools in the city, other than charity schools run by benevolent women's associations and religious societies for the children of the poor. The workingmen were therefore receptive to guardianship, the free enquirers, and Frances Wright.

The battle for guardianship, however, turned out to be a lost cause. It contributed to disputes between factions in the Workingmen's party, which soon collapsed. Frances Wright's entry into New York political life was no more successful than the experiment at Nashoba. But her penetration of the public sphere was now complete. Within a few years, since the purchase of the Tennessee land, she had left her mark on communitarianism, antislavery, free thought, educational reform, and the incipient labor movement. She had also spent much of her money, ruined her reputation, violated all codes of respectability, and provided a unique, if notorious, example of sexual emancipation. "Simple minded men were out of their wits," recalled one listener, author Elizabeth Oakes Smith, "lest their wives should learn from her example . . . to question male supremacy."

Frances Wright's public career and her hopes for guardianship came to a sudden end in 1830—along with Nashoba, which she had been financing ever since she left it. In the middle of her New York campaign, Wright returned to Tennessee and told the slaves she intended to free them. She also explained that their color would eternally preclude their equality in the United States. In Haiti, however, they would meet only equals. And in January 1830, Wright chartered a ship, the *John Quincy Adams,* which sailed from Boston, and embarked on the six-month voyage to Haiti and back. Accompanied only by Phiquepal D'Arusmont, who served as her business manager, she escorted the Nashobans, eighteen adults and sixteen children, to Haiti and freedom. The Haitian president gave them land and repaid Wright in coffee for the cost of their transportation.

A unique experiment, Nashoba had failed in its role as a pilot project for gradual emancipation and world reform. Frances Wright's pastoral vision of 1825, a community filled with "beautiful wooded pastures and retiring walks extending over meadows," had never materialized. The interracial school had never been started. Troops of recruits had never appeared. Instead, the community had been buffeted by changing policies, abysmal administration, a terrible climate, hostile public opinion, and the abortive attempt to combine cooperative labor and slavery. It was also a financial disaster. The slaves never earned back their purchase prices on the credit system but rather became indebted to Nashoba for their upkeep. Frances Wright had invested, and lost, half her fortune. But the community's failure had spurred her into an even riskier venture, public agitation for social reform. And she had succeeded in emancipating over thirty slaves. "Her whole heart and soul were occupied by the hope of raising the African," summed up Frances Trollope, who retained her original sympathy for her old friend. "Even now I cannot recall the self-devotion with which she gave herself to it without admiration."

The final fate of the backwoods plantation was intricately bound up with Frances Wright's subsequent career, a career full of reversals and ironies. After the end of Nashoba, the failure of "guardianship," and the near dissolution of the Workingmen's party, Frances and Camilla Wright returned to Europe as abruptly as they had descended on America only five years before. The two sisters settled in Paris, where Camilla died in 1831. Frances Wright then married Phiquepal D'Arusmont, the educational reformer who had managed her lecture tours and accompanied her to Haiti. A daughter, Sylva, was born soon after. But the D'Arusmonts' marriage, which lasted for twenty years, was not a successful one. Nor could Frances Wright adjust to retirement from public affairs. Within a decade, the couple was arguing over control of her property, which supported the family; over the upbringing of their daughter; and over Frances Wright's desire for an independent life.

In 1835, Wright returned to the United States, where she attempted to resume her role as a lecturer and reformer, though with little success. She was forbidden to speak in Philadelphia, met violence in New York, and needed an "escort" to appear in public. Leaving D'Arusmont and Sylva behind in France, she finally settled down in Cincinnati, where she spent the rest of her life in relative obscurity. There she wrote her memoirs and proposed new schemes for gradual emancipation and universal reform. She also traveled to Europe and to Haiti, where she visited her former slaves. To admirers from the labor movement, Wright retained all of her old enthusiasms. A workingman who visited her in the 1840s reported that she was still denouncing "King Craft," "Priest Craft" and "Law Craft," as well as advocating a free, state-run school system. But to old associates from the "free enquirer" era, such as Orestes Brownson, she appeared to be "the wreck of what she was in the days when I knew and admired her."

D'Arusmont, meanwhile, traveled back and forth to Paris and finally remained there to educate their daughter. By the late 1840s, after Frances Wright inherited the entirety of her family's fortune, relations between the D'Arusmonts deteriorated yet further in a battle over Frances Wright's property. To retain control of it, she finally obtained divorces, in Tennessee in 1850 and in Ohio in 1851. At the time of their divorce, D'Arusmont accused her of treating her husband and child only as "appendages" to her personal existence. He retained custody of their daughter Sylva. After Frances Wright's death in 1852, the Nashoba land was inherited by Sylva, who ultimately turned it into a private estate and lived there. But Sylva, who had been alienated from her mother, inherited none of Frances Wright's proclivity for free thought, women's rights, or universal reform. In later life, she became a devout Episcopalian and an opponent of woman suffrage. Her two sons became ministers.

After 1830, the American public quickly forgot about Frances Wright, her Nashoba experiment, and her ambitious schemes for reforming the "public mind." Wright had been accurate when she described herself as a "being fallen from a strange planet among a race whose senses and perceptions are all different from my own." A missionary of the Enlightenment, an admirer of Thomas Paine and Mary Wollstonecraft, of Thomas Jefferson and Robert Owen, she had attempted to promote free thought and "free enquiry" in a nation captivated by religious enthusiasm. Contending that "the mind has no sex," she had assaulted the bastion of public life, at a time when Americans believed that women were innately domestic beings whose mission was to care for home and family. Frances Wright's commitment to ending slavery and improving the status of women was not unique, however, as the next decades were to prove. Her example was remembered in the late 1830s, when abolitionist women began addressing mixed audiences from the public podium to promote the cause of emancipation. It was recalled again after 1848, when a new generation of women reformers mobilized to demand women's rights.

8

❧

BENEVOLENCE, REFORM, AND SLAVERY, 1800–1860

When Frances Wright first appeared on the lecture podium in 1829, no woman in America had yet attempted to assume such a leadership role in public affairs. But American women were not uninvolved in enterprises beyond the home. During the early nineteenth century, middle-class women in northern towns and cities formed female societies devoted to charitable and humanitarian ends. Through voluntary associations, women created their own networks outside the home, developed experience in organization and tactics, and made a distinctive contribution to benevolence and reform. The "female society" provided a stepping-stone from domestic life to public life.

The voluntary associations in which women participated between 1800 and 1860 were initially formed to pursue religious goals, with clerical approval. Missionary, charitable, and tract societies, which erupted and multiplied in the early 1800s, enabled middle-class women of pious bent to assist and uplift the deprived and depraved. But the habit of association had militant potential. By the 1830s, northern women formed associations not only for a vast array of benevolent goals but also for broader ones—peace, temperance, abolition, and moral reform. They worked not merely to ameliorate social ills but to eliminate them. Far fewer women were involved in reform than the untold numbers committed to benevolent works. But their activism raised new questions about women's role in public life. By midcentury, the stage had been set for the beginnings of a women's rights movement and a frontal attack on the limitations of sphere.

The tradition of female association was not a national one. It began in the urbanizing Northeast and made its way west but weakened in the South. In the North, a number of circumstances combined to facilitate it. During the early nineteenth century, an era of evangelical fervor, women were prominent, at least by numbers, in Protestant congregations. Ministers depended on their fund-raising, support, and good works. Also, the expansion of towns and cities made increasing numbers of middle-class women accessible to one another and provided a field for their activism. The poor and impious in urban areas, it appeared, could only profit from women's assistance and control. As in the churches, these women were filling a social vacuum, not invading a territory occupied by men. After 1830, once the tradition of female association was well established, an outburst of reform opened new options and broadened the arena of women's involvement.

A final contributing factor, throughout the early nineteenth century, was an expanding middle class. Although excluded from business and politics, middle-class women held a positive sense of their roles and responsibilities as women. Benevolence and reform were not merely the most appealing routes to public life for such women but the only ones. Within the scope of the female association, they extended the skills they already had, in household management, care for the young, concern for the afflicted. They capitalized on their obligations as bastions of piety and guardians of morals. They also created new roles that were parallel or complementary to those of the men in their families— the minister, lawyer, tradesman, and entrepreneur. Excluded from official channels of authority, middle-class women created their own. In so doing, they carved out and occupied a public space midway between the realms of domesticity and politics.

Origins of Association

The groundwork for entry into public life was laid in the first three decades of the nineteenth century by the founding of female societies for pious purposes. Bible and tract societies, missionary societies, charitable societies, maternal societies, and Sunday school associations—all arose in the wake of religious revivals. The emotional upheavals of the Second Great Awakening and the fervor generated by leading evangelists such as Charles G. Finney left converts with a sense of commitment and mission. Since women were bastions of piety in their congregations and a proven success as domestic evangelists (awakening male relatives to the need for salvation), ministers encouraged their formation of associations. The model for such activism had in fact been established by Englishwomen in the evangelical sects, which lent it a certain legitimacy. Moreover, female societies would extend the Protestant empire and keep the funds flowing. Following the trail of revivals, women's benevolence peppered the East, moved westward with migrants, and spread as far as the territories.

Whatever their titles, early female associations delved into the same type of activities: fund-raising, charity, uplift. At one of the first, the Boston Female Society for Missionary Purposes, formed in 1800, members congregated at regular meetings to sew and knit goods for sale. The proceeds were dispensed for a multitude of causes: to prepare young men for the ministry by supporting their education, to fund missionaries to the heathen in the West, and to assist the locally indigent with clothes, food, spiritual inspiration, and donations to their churches. Society members engaged in the vital tactic of "visiting" the poor with such assistance, and distributed religious publications along with their charitable contributions. "Visiting," indeed, was the crucial word in voluntary benevolence. It led out of the home and into the homes of others. As women's associations multiplied, they developed more specialized goals—such as care for orphans, widows, or destitute mothers. They also created a gamut of institutions, such as schools, asylums, refuges, and workshops, to aid and redeem the worthy poor.

Voluntary benevolence was by no means a female monopoly. Women's societies were often absorbed as "auxiliaries" into large, male-dominated, national, nonsectarian federations—such as the American Bible Society, Tract Society, Home Missionary Society, or Sunday-School Union. On other occasions, female societies spawned auxiliaries and statewide unions of their own. And sometimes they just sprang up independently, as was the case with maternal societies—the most informal of voluntary associations. Members of maternal societies met monthly or biweekly to share methods for raising pious offspring, a generation of committed Christians. Since the only prerequisites for membership were piety and motherhood, rather than time, funds, or local clout, maternal societies involved a broad social range of women, especially from rural and small-town constituencies. They emerged wherever a few women congregated— in the countryside, in cities, even on the frontier. Their evangelical goals and stress on activism in the home were well within the confines of women's sphere.

But women's voluntary associations assumed an especially activist role in urban life, primarily in the expanding commercial towns of the Northeast and Midwest and in the older seaports. Growing cities were a challenging field of conquest, since poverty and vice were more proximate. Here benevolent women made their most aggressive attempts to assist the indigent, reform the deviant, combat impiety, and provide employment for poor women. Such efforts created a new frontier of social welfare, at first through "visiting" and then through institutions, supported by subscription. Sunday schools, for instance, were formed to impart spiritual values to children of the poor. By the 1820s, hundreds of such schools had been started, enrolling almost 50,000 children and staffed and managed by benevolent women. Female associations also ran charity schools, infant schools, orphan asylums, and a gamut of homes, shelters, and refuges for women in need. Such efforts even appeared in southern cities. In 1812, forty-six Petersburg, Virginia, women signed a petition to start a female orphan asylum that would protect the most vulnerable of poor people, parentless girls, "forlorn and helpless," from economic need and sexual hazards.

Often the tactic of visiting spawned new goals and institutions. This was the case with one of the earliest charitable associations in New York, formed by fifteen women in 1797. Its founder and director, Isabella Graham, a devout Presbyterian widow, and her board of managers provided food and help for worthy widows with families. By 1816, the Society for the Relief of Poor Widows with Small Children supported 202 widows and 500 children. Each manager was responsible for a district, as well as for making sure that the poor widows in her charge did not beg, sell liquor, own property, behave immorally, or have living husbands. The goals of the managers soon expanded. Raising funds by subscription and by lottery, the society turned its attention to the poor widows' children, to prevent them from "growing up in habits of idleness and its native consequence, vice." The society eventually supported three Sunday schools in poor districts, two Sunday schools for adults, and a charity school for poor widows' children. It also ran a tailor shop and a spinning shop, where poor widows made flax. Isabella Graham's daughter, Joanna Bethune, who married a rich merchant and served as a society officer, carried these goals still further and became a dynamo of benevolence. She founded an Orphan Asylum Society, a Female Sabbath School Union, an Infant School Society, and a Society for the Promotion of Industry, which employed 500 women.

As the efforts of Graham and Bethune suggest, female benevolence might encompass not merely charity but also the creation of institutions with a distinctly economic, compensatory thrust—to provide both jobs and relief for working women who were unable to subsist. The Boston Seaman's Aid Society, directed by Sarah Hale, was one example. It began by providing work for women bereft of male support and ended up with a small nonprofit business, a vocational training program, a school, and a residence. Significantly, the Seaman's Aid Society originally had a religious affiliation, but quickly became a secular venture. Another secular model was the Providence Employment Society, which began in the 1830s. Here well-to-do women from prominent families tried to correct the ills of an economic system that victimized poor seamstresses. The society, run by a board of directors and supported by subscription, was in effect a small garment business and model employer. It paid good wages, which kept up with inflation. Board members, who defined sphere to suit their own purposes, developed a rationale for extending their managerial roles from home to civic work: As women, they understood "what female work is and what female suffering means."

Like the Providence Employment Society and the Seaman's Aid Society, women's benevolent associations usually adopted a corporate structure. They drew up constitutions, elected officers, held formal meetings, and wrote minutes, reports, and tracts. The main business at hand was the soliciting, managing, and dispensing of funds. An unmarried woman might best serve as treasurer, so that no husband could control the money. The association provided a variety of other positions for its leaders as well—director, board member, manager, corresponding secretary, or the all-important "visitor." Enterprising women often had overlapping memberships, just as the voluntary societies of a locale developed overlapping constituencies. The boards of directors who ran such associations were often no strangers to the business world. They came from families of means and were related to men who were active in banking, manufacturing, and commerce.

Whether women managed institutions, taught in Sunday schools, solicited funds from local housewives, or visited in the poorer parts of town, the voluntary association provided an outlet for their skills, a community of peers, and a foothold outside the home. It also provided an avenue for extending female values into the community. Through association, women transformed moral superiority into a social calling. They legitimized the tactics that were used to achieve benevolent goals—fund-raising, tract distributing, and "visiting." Most important, they made the female society acceptable. The tradition of association provided a conduit through which more volatile currents would later flow.

There was of course an ambivalent thrust to voluntary benevolence. The progress it achieved was unconscious and insidious, just as "visiting" was covertly aggressive. Often pious and devout, the thousands of women involved in such societies sought to fulfill a mission rather than to tamper with the boundaries of woman's sphere. Benevolent associations united such women in common cause but never challenged the roles they were assigned by custom, convention, and clergymen. They opened avenues to social activism but were also a means of class identification. Leadership roles in voluntary benevolence were confined to the "haves," who were able to help those with little or nothing. Not surprisingly, Sarah Hale was an inveterate officer of women's groups that fell into the benevolent category—not only the Seaman's Aid Society but a grand array of missionary associations.

More liberal, critical spirits, such as Harriet Martineau, Lucy Stone, and Sarah Grimke, decried the defects of benevolent efforts. They cited the inanity of raising funds for male divinity students when women had no access to higher education, or of distributing tracts and Bibles instead of campaigning against slavery. "Men like to see women pick up the drunken and falling," Susan B. Anthony once observed. "That *patching business* is 'woman's proper sphere.'" Lydia Maria Child, however, argued that the evangelical sects, and the female societies they spawned, transformed their participants. They had "urged upon women their prodigious influence and consequent responsibility," said Child in 1841. "They have changed the household utensil into a living energetic being." After 1830, some of the energy unleashed by benevolence was harnessed to humanitarian reform as well.

There were two main links. First, voluntary benevolence promoted the visiting not only of homes but of public institutions—first almshouses, and then asylums, hospitals, jails. The increase of such institutions, indeed, provided a new social space to which benevolent women gained entry. By the 1830s, for instance, women were regular presences at prisons where they sought to "commiserate and alleviate the condition of the inmates," as a New York minister proclaimed. Prison reform soon became a female cause. Access to the incarcerated might also create new callings. When Dorothea Dix discovered her vocation in 1841 she was teaching a Sunday school class for women at the East Cambridge jail. Here she found the insane mixed in with the rest of the inmates—vagrants and prostitutes. For the next two decades, Dix investigated public institutions and deluged state legislatures with "memorials" appealing for funds to expand the care for the insane. Her mission as a reformer built on the groundwork laid by voluntary benevolence.

Second, voluntary benevolence capitalized on the gender consciousness associated with woman's sphere. It evoked empathy for female victims—the widowed, the abandoned, the "friendless female" destined for prostitution. It spurred disdain for their oppressors—the deserting spouse, the underpaying employer—and for all social evils attributable to men. War, drink, licentiousness, all left in their wake a trail of miserable women—the soldier's widow, the drunkard's wife, the victim of seduction. By the 1830s, when associations were formed to obliterate specific evils, women became involved in female societies for peace, temperance, and antislavery, which were run under the aegis of men's organizations. They also joined societies for moral reform, which were not.

Moral Reform

Moral reform, a women's crusade, was a drama played out in the 1830s and early 1840s, with a cast of thousands. Moral reformers intended not only to abate social ills through charitable works but also to make basic changes in thought and behavior, primarily those of men. The movement was both a benevolent, fund-raising one and a militant pressure group. Within its ranks, urban and rural women united to extend their moral superiority beyond the home with considerable vigor and aggression.

Their overall platform was to erase the double standard of sexual morality and impose a single standard of moral purity on all Americans, male and female. This involved a gamut of subsidiary planks, in part domestic and in part social. Within the home, children were to be given a pious upbringing and moral education. Outside it, moral reformers assumed ambitious goals. They wanted to end prostitution and to punish and ostracize seducers, adulterers, and lechers. They also intended to reform fallen women, to give them support, employment, and moral uplift, and to prevent the downfall of others. And running throughout the moral reformers' aims was a perfectionist streak: to obliterate licentiousness from the minds of men and to drive vice from the face of the earth.

The movement began in New York City in 1834, at a church meeting of middle-class women, following a five-year siege of Finney revivals. It also came on the heels of the Magdalen Society, a brief and abortive attempt by a young divinity student, John McDowell, to reform New York prostitutes and save young men from corruption. The New York Female Moral Reform Society, with Mrs. Finney as its first president, picked up where McDowell had left off. Indeed, the society hired him as an agent. But the female society altered the tenor of his cause. It was now fallen women who were to be saved.

During the 1830s, moral reform expanded geographically at a rapid rate, spawning auxiliaries in profusion and attracting large numbers of women. When the Boston Female Moral Reform Society was formed in 1835, seventy women were involved in its founding, and hundreds more soon joined rural auxiliaries. In 1837, the New York society had 250 auxiliaries and 15,000 members. In western New York, local societies gathered as many as 100 to 200 members each. By 1840, the New York society transformed itself into a national one, the American Female Moral Reform Society, and claimed 555 auxiliaries. The movement had swept through New York and New England and yet further west, absorbing local groups, spurring the formation of others, reaching city, town, and rural backwater. The society now held annual conventions and regional meetings; vice-presidents were posted in strategic cities; correspondents among groups addressed one another as "sister." And at least two periodicals expounded the cause. A successful weekly journal, the *Advocate of Moral Reform,* begun in New York in 1835, had 20,000 subscribers within a few years. A Boston-based counterpart, the *Friend of Virtue,* filled a similar function.

Although the moral reform movement began with clerical endorsement and help, as did all evangelical groups, this was no ladies' auxiliary. It was a women's campaign. Significantly, by the late 1830s, moral reform societies hired only women as their agents, bookkeepers, and institutional staff. Moral reform was also a specifically female reaction to urbanization and the perils of migration, as historian Mary P. Ryan contends. The mobility of the early nineteenth century brought in its wake a youthful migrant population—apprentices, clerks, seamstresses, factory girls—who left home, boarded out, and moved beyond the reach of parents and ministers. The weakening grip of traditional authority left no one in control in the moral arena and paved the way for manifold abuses, from seduction to prostitution. The vacuum of moral authority was one that women were ready to fill. And the cause attracted a broad range of activists: the well-off church-going matron who had long resided in a city or town; the migrant mother who had just moved in and feared for the welfare of her children; the rural correspondent of the *Advocate,* ever on the lookout for abuse. Moral reform offered a way to improve the environment, protect the young, help less fortunate women, and exert authority over men—or, as the *Advocate* put it, in a strident moment, "to control masculine behavior as he dictates hers."

Moral reform was distinguished not only by its widespread appeal but by its innovative tactics. At the outset, the New York society hired male agents to proselytize among fallen women in almshouses and jails. But the members of the executive committee soon took over the "visiting" themselves. In New York, in Boston, and wherever they could, moral reformers presented themselves at brothels, where they sang hymns, offered prayers for the fallen, searched out runaway daughters, and noted—and threatened to reveal—the identity of patrons. Moral reformers also assaulted their state legislatures, in Boston and Albany. Here they petitioned and lobbied for laws that would make seduction a crime. Such laws were passed in Massachusetts in 1846 and in New York in 1848. A third battle front was institutional. At first, activists tried to reform prostitutes through prayers, conversion, moral education, and location of alternative employment. Then they founded homes and refuges to redeem the fallen and protect the helpless. The New Yorkers opened a House of Reception, a prostitutes' refuge. The ambitious Bostonians founded a Home for Unprotected Girls, a Refuge for Migrant Women, and an Asylum for the Repentant. Both groups set up employment services to place the reformed in domestic jobs, preferably in rural areas where they would be out of harm's way.

Finally, the executive committees of moral reform societies actively investigated alleged instances of immorality, or even sought them out. Visiting took on a new and aggressive dimension. In the expanding industrial town of Utica, a fulcrum of revivals and reform in western New York, "visiting committees" went into less prosperous parts of town, where they solicited data on sexual offenses within the home. The Utica reformers also waged a petition campaign against prostitution and supported the legal prosecution of seducers. Altogether, moral reformers battled the enemy on a number of fronts: in brothels, in state legislatures, and in the courts; in their own homes, in other people's homes, and in "homes" they established themselves (although the last had a meager clientele).

The *Advocate*, meanwhile, discussed the dangers of licentiousness and printed letters from rural correspondents exposing seducers and lechers. When called to task for the assertiveness of their campaign, as well as its impropriety, the editors took the offensive: "Why should we be castigated as Amazons . . . when we wish to unite to take measures for the protection of our own sex?" New York reformers, who increasingly empathized with the prostitutes they assisted, became concerned with the low wages paid to working women, the role of poverty as a cause of prostitution, and the plight of women who were destitute or in prison. "The fallen and the falling . . . are our sisters by way of a common humanity," the *Advocate* proclaimed.

But the newspaper's militant stance was short-lived. By 1845, moral reform was retreating from the more aggressive aspects of its campaign. The *Advocate* urged readers to pursue their domestic goal, moral education of the young, and to maintain their vigilance within the home. New York reformers gave up their visits to brothels and were drawn into related causes, such as prison reform. Local societies disbanded and ended their far-flung campaigns. Clearly there were limits to the extension of moral superiority beyond the home. These limits were sometimes suggested by the clergy and sometimes established by the reformers themselves. The Boston society, significantly, promised in 1839 to confine its activism only to women. The Utica society splintered in 1845 over the issue of whether it was proper to hold a public discussion of sexual matters in a nearby college town. It was difficult, in short, for moral reformers to combat lechery, seduction, and prostitution without violating their own propriety and respectability.

During its decade of activism, however, moral reform involved a broad range of middle-class women. It also served as a link between voluntary benevolence and more radical causes. The Boston society, for instance, was connected with the maternal society movement, which permeated New England. Many of its leaders also belonged to the more controversial Boston Female Antislavery Society, founded in 1832. The New York branch drew heavy support from the Tappan brothers, whose largesse also financed the early abolitionist campaign. Future women's rights advocates, too, belonged to moral reform societies. Susan B. Anthony joined such a society in New York, and Lucretia Mott was an officer of one in Philadelphia. Finally, the moral reformers' demand for a single standard of sexual morality would remain a major plank in women's campaigns for the rest of the century.

But the feminist thrust of moral reform, like the life span of the movement, was limited. This became clear in 1838 when the *Advocate* published a piece by abolitionist Sarah Grimke, certainly the most controversial woman in public life at that time. Like Frances Wright, Sarah Grimke had violated propriety by speaking to "promiscuous" audiences of men and women from the lecture platform, and like Wright, she had invoked the ire of the clergy. Her remarks to the moral reformers were much, or too much, to the point. "Men have endeavored to entice, or to drive, women from every sphere of moral action," she told *Advocate* readers. Deploring clerical domination, Grimke exhorted the moral reformers to "rise from the degradation and bondage to which we have been consigned by men." But *Advocate* readers took offense. They were unwilling to defy ministers and unable, in the end, to defy the limits of sphere. Moral reform illustrated both the radical potential of female association and its limitations. It ended up back in the home.

The abolitionist movement, which emerged at the same time as moral reform, had far different consequences. Abolitionism catapulted women into "politics" and evoked bitter disputes over their role in public life—the very type of controversy the moral reformers tried to avoid. But like moral reform, abolition was an outgrowth of evangelical Protestantism. It evolved in the wake of revivals and employed evangelical techniques. Also, to women caught up in the cause of the slave, abolition was itself a moral reform and therefore especially appropriate as an arena for female activism.

Women in Slavery

When Frances Wright proposed her plan for gradual emancipation in 1825, she denounced slavery from the "natural rights" standpoint of the Enlightenment, citing the need for "moral liberty and human improvement." American women of the 1830s and 1840s assaulted slavery from another angle. They became committed to abolition not as Enlightenment egalitarians but rather as nineteenth-century women, imbued with sympathy for suffering, concern for other women, and a sense of moral responsibility. Women, as Sarah Grimke declared, were obliged to attack "moral pollution" of all sorts. In their petitions and addresses, tracts and conventions, abolitionist women asserted their special proclivity for the cause. They also assumed, as their particular target, the degradation of the woman slave.

From the 1820s onward, all slaves were affected by the hardening of slavery as an institution. The expansion of cotton into the new, fertile lands of the Southwest, the rising value of slaves, the growing fear of rebellion and outside interference, and a universal tightening of the slave codes made slavery at once more permanent and more oppressive. The need for labor in new states—Alabama, Mississippi, Louisiana, and later Texas—increased the likelihood of sale and separation. Sometimes whole plantations were moved to the Southwest. But young adults, like those at Nashoba, were more likely to be sold to meet labor demands. Frances Wright, ironically, began her experiment in gradual emancipation just when slavery became more profitable and entrenched. In all states, emancipation became more difficult, if not impossible. Slave codes, now strictly enforced, prohibited gatherings and curtailed the most minimal of liberties.

Slave women, like slave men, worked mainly in the fields, under the gang system or the task system, usually in all-female groups. They were found in all kinds of agricultural work—the sowing, picking, and packing of cotton; the hoeing and milling of corn; even in lumbering and construction work. Northern schoolteacher Emily Burke, who taught in Georgia in the 1830s and 1840s and described life on a large plantation near Savannah, observed slave women engaged in every facet of labor, from fence building to plowing. "When I beheld such scenes, I felt culpable in living in ease and enjoying the luxuries of life," said Burke, "while so many of my own sex were to drag out such miserable existences merely to procure those luxuries enjoyed by their masters." Middle age brought no relief. Women who performed the most strenuous physical tasks, such as plowing, were probably past their child-bearing years. Untrained in the more skilled and valued crafts (blacksmiths, carpenters, masons) women might escape field work if assigned to work in the house as cooks, nurses, seamstresses, or maids. But the division between house and field was clear-cut only on the larger plantations, and probably no more than 5 percent of slaves attained the status of "house servant." Women slaves were also hired out. By 1860, about 5,000 worked in cotton and woolen mills, sugar refineries, tobacco plants, and other industries.

Whatever their work, women slaves were valued less as laborers than men; their prices were uniformly lower. But if able to produce more slaves, their value rose. Since slave children, as a Georgia overseer observed, might be considered "part of the crop," the woman who already had one or two children and was assumed to be capable of having more was a profitable investment. Having children was also an advantage to the slave, since it helped to secure her family unit, perhaps even preventing the breakup of her marriage by sale. Slave codes always provided that children of slaves belonged to the mother's master. Although a few states enacted laws to prevent the sale of young children apart from their mothers, such laws were not uniformly or widely enforced. Former slaves who recounted their life stories viewed the separation of mothers and children as a major crime of slavery. "The domestic hearth, with its holy lessons and precious endearments is abolished in the case of a slave mother and her children," wrote Frederick Douglass. Abolitionist women saw the slave as deprived of the right of maternal love. If not thwarted by separation, such love could be used as a weapon against the mother. "You can do anything with a woman when you've got her children," said Cassy, a slave in *Uncle Tom's Cabin* who was driven to immorality and self-mutilation.

Black fertility was high and did not begin to fall until the 1880s. Typically, slave women began having children in their late teens (as did Southern white women). A slave woman was customarily released from field work for a month before and after delivery and was usually allowed to leave the field a few times a day to nurse her infant, who might be left in the care of another child or an aged slave. She also prolonged nursing as long as possible, even for several years. The combination of child-bearing and forced labor probably resulted in a high miscarriage and stillbirth rate and in other health problems. The English actress and abolitionist Fanny Kemble, when stranded on her husband's Georgia plantation in the 1830s, investigated the conditions of her women slaves with persistent questions and recorded her findings. "*Sally*, Scipio's wife, has had two miscarriages and three children born, one of whom is dead. She came complaining of incessant pain and weakness in her back," Kemble wrote. "*Charlotte*, Renty's wife, had had two miscarriages, and was with child again. She was almost crippled by rheumatism." Kemble was especially impressed by the high birth and infant mortality rates, and the serious ailments endured by slave women, compounded by the strain of field labor.

> *Sarah*, Stephen's wife; this woman's case and history were alike deplorable. She had had four miscarriages, had brought seven children into the world, five of whom were dead, and was again with child. She complained of dreadful pains in the back, and an internal tumor which swells with the exertion of working in the field; probably, I think, she is ruptured. She told me she had once been mad and had run into the woods . . . but was at last tracked and brought back . . . and was severely flogged. . . . I suppose her constant childbearing and hard labor in the fields at the same time may have produced the temporary insanity.

Hardly one of these women, wrote Kemble, "might not have been a candidate for a bed in a hospital, and they had come to me after working all day in the field."

Although Sarah had attempted to escape, women were less likely than men to become fugitives. Still, there were exceptions. A $40,000 reward was offered for Harriet Tubman, who had escaped from Maryland as a young woman (her husband refused to accompany her) and became the most famous conductor on the underground railroad. She was said to have returned to the South nineteen times to lead over 300 slaves to freedom. If not often fugitives, slave women participated in all forms of resistance. They were as likely as men to join in the sick-outs, slowdowns, theft, and sabotage that were routine forms of protest, as well as in its most dire form, arson. Above all, they were vital participants in what has come to be regarded as the ultimate conspiracy, the preservation of the slave family as refuge from the dehumanizing aspects of slavery.

According to recent studies of slavery, the two-parent family was very much the ideal and the strength of family ties pervasive, as suggested by the tremendous efforts of family members to reunite after emancipation. Even under slavery, separated couples made valiant efforts to keep in touch; escapes were often motivated by a desire to reunite with wives, husbands, or children. Slave marriages were universally respected in the slave community unless a couple was separated, either voluntarily, by "divorce," or involuntarily by sale. Still, under slavery marriage was extralegal and at the owner's discretion. For instance, the success of a "broad" or "abroad" marriage—a union between slaves on different plantations—depended on the cooperation of owners, who often gave it only reluctantly; interplantation visits promoted freedom of movement, desired by slaves but not by masters. Marriage, moreover, might be formal, casual, or nonexistent. Owners usually found it useful—to improve morale, discourage escape, and prevent what appeared to be promiscuity and depravity.

Within marriage, slave women attempted to assume a supportive role in

Under slavery, women typically worked for their owners as field labor. Pictured are slaves picking cotton. *(Schomburg Center for Research in Black Culture, New York Public Library)*

their relations toward their husbands. If the condition of slavery minimized gender distinctions, slaves tried to restore them in their private lives. Similarly, women also assumed dual work roles, both as plantation workers and as cooks, housekeepers, and caretakers within their own families. Private domestic work represented freedom to slaves, compared to work that was done for their owners. The desire to assume traditional roles within marriage and family would emerge again after emancipation. Still, under slavery, marriage and family life were always precarious. In records of the Union army and the Freedmen's Bureau, former slaves reported that a third of prior marriages had been broken up by "force," that is, by masters. All family relationships were vulnerable, since they might be abruptly terminated by the death of an owner, the liquidation of an estate, the claims of creditors, or the hiring out or sale of a spouse.

Slaves both accommodated to and resisted the impact of slavery on family life. Not solely dependent on nuclear families, they usually depended on kinship networks extending into the slave community, networks that included spouses, parents, children, uncles, aunts, cousins, even distant relatives. They managed to perpetuate African customs, such as not marrying their first cousins, a prohibition not observed by their owners. They also used naming practices to preserve kinship ties. Although planters traced slave lineage through mothers and rarely recorded fathers' names in slave registers, slaves strove to perpetuate family ties by naming sons after fathers, though not daughters after mothers. Children of both sexes were often named after other relatives, including deceased siblings (a practice that had evidently faded in white society). Through family networks, kinship customs, naming practices, and, sometimes, long-term unions, slaves preserved the family as the primary institution of the slave community.

But undoubtedly the most important efforts to preserve the slave family, on a day-to-day basis, were those made by women. Since much recent literature on slavery underrates the crucial role that women played in family life, historian Deborah Gray White offers a corrective. Slave families, she contends, were matrifocal: In their roles as mothers, women were the focus of familial relationships, and more central than fathers to the family's continuity and survival. Moreover, White points out, women in slave society "identified and cooperated more with other slave women than with slave men." Citing a number of factors, such as the independence women derived from the absence of property considerations in conjugal relationships, the "abroad" marriage, the ability of female slaves to supplement the diet of family members, the work done by women in groups, the supremacy of the mother-child bond over all other relationships, and the high degree of female cooperation and interdependence, White underlines the distinctive role that women assumed in slave communities: "Slave women did not play the traditional female role as it was defined in nineteenth-century America." Nor did slave families fit into the patterns established by white society.

Some owners were oblivious of the distinctive patterns of slave family life. Others tried to regulate and supervise all aspects of slave life, including the realm of moral behavior. Within the slave community, however, a standard of sexual morality different from that of white society prevailed. Extensive sexual freedom was permitted and accepted before marriage. The purity of women, in white terms, was not an overwhelming concern. Nor was premarital pregnancy or childbirth thought to be irreconcilable with eventual monogamous marriage. No stigma was attached to the "outside child" born before or even outside of marriage. But slaves took a severe view of philandering after marriage and often regarded adultery, especially female adultery, as a violation of their social code. At the same time, the slave community had a more lenient attitude toward marital breakups. There were no economic reasons under slavery to continue a union that had failed. As a result, "divorce," a rarity in white society, might be commonplace in slave society. When abolitionist editor James Redpath interviewed slaves in the 1850s, he asked one woman why she had left her husband for another man, and she replied, "I didn't like him and I neber did." From a white viewpoint, the customs and morals of the slave community were a world apart.

Women abolitionists, however, were concerned primarily about one aspect of sexual morality, the exploitation of slave women by white men. Historians suggest that white male sexual license did not exist on the plantation to the extent that it did in antislavery literature. On the plantation, the degree to which slave women were sexually exploited by white men was limited by strong slave resistance as well as by a strong current of white disapproval. But white assumptions about "loose" slave morals made it possible for some Southerners to simultaneously condemn and condone white male relations with women slaves. Whatever the countervailing pressures, coercive sex was still an integral part of slavery, one that affected slave women far more directly than men. As historian Catherine Clinton points out, "Denial of sex to male slaves cannot be equated with the force of sex to which female slaves were subjected." Under slavery, the threat of sexual exploitation remained a major gender distinction. The impact of such exploitation emerged in a book written by Harriet Jacobs, a fugitive who assumed the name of Linda Brent. Brent's *Incidents in the Life of a Slave Girl* (1861), edited by abolitionist author Lydia Maria Child, was a saga of brutality and lechery covering, in the author's words, "twenty-one years in that cage of obscene birds." The incidents centered around Brent's exploitation by her master, who began to pursue her when she was fifteen. "The slave girl is reared in an atmosphere of licentiousness and fear," Brent explained. "The lash and foul tongue of the master and his sons are her teachers."

> He told me I was his property: that I must be subject to his will in all things. My soul revolted against the mean tyranny. But where could I turn for protection? . . . The mistress, who ought to protect the helpless victim, has no other feelings towards her but jealousy and rage. The degradation, the wrongs, the vices, that grow out of slavery, are more than I can describe. . . .
>
> O virtuous reader, you never knew what it is to be a slave; to be entirely unprotected by law or custom; to have the laws reduce you to the condition of a chattel, entirely subject to the will of another.

Using the language of moral reform, Linda Brent analyzed the evil of slavery as an agent of perversion: "It makes the white fathers cruel and sensual; the sons violent and licentious; it contaminates the daughters, and makes the white women wretched. And as for the colored race, it needs an abler pen than mine to describe the extremity of their sufferings, the depths of their degradation."

To women in the abolitionist movement, such sentiments struck resonant chords. Throughout the decades of the antislavery crusade, abolitionist women voiced paramount concern about the oppression of women in slavery. According to their arguments, all slaves were deprived of basic human rights, but women slaves were additionally deprived of the inviolable rights of women. One aspect of this deprivation was revealed in the remarks of former New York slave Sojourner Truth at a women's rights convention in 1851. When a clergyman alleged that since women were weaker than men they were unable to be trusted with equal rights, Sojourner Truth entered the debate. "The man over there says women need to be helped into carriages and lifted over ditches and have the best place everywhere," she retorted, according to the chairwoman's account.

Nobody helps me into carriages or over puddles, or gives me the best place—and ain't I a woman? I have ploughed and planted and gathered into barns, and no man could head me—and ain't I a woman? . . . I have borne thirteen children, and seen most of 'em sold into slavery, and when I cried out with my mother's grief, none but Jesus heard me—and ain't I a woman?

America's answer to the woman slave, abolitionist women stressed, was "no." Under slavery, women were deprived of legal marriage, male protection, and maternal rights, and subject to every type of degradation. "The Negro woman is unprotected by either law or public opinion," wrote Lydia Maria Child in her pioneer antislavery tract of 1833.

She is the property of her master, and her daughters are his property. They are allowed to have no conscientious scruples, no sense of shame, no regard for the feelings of husband, or parent; they must be entirely subservient to the will of their owner, on pain of being beaten as near to death . . . or quite to death, if it suits his pleasure.

Just as southern women objected to the sexual availability of the woman slave, so antislavery women objected to her vulnerability, her powerlessness against male owners. "We should be less than women," asserted members of an Ohio Female Antislavery Society in a petition to Congress, "if the nameless and unnumbered wrongs of which the slaves of our sex are made the defenceless victims, did not fill us with horror . . . the soul formed for companionship with angels, is despoiled and brutified." To abolitionist women, slavery gave licentious men total power to ruin "the sanctity and glory of woman." In addition, as Sarah Grimke pointed out, male power under slavery ruined white women as well as black. The southern white woman, she contended, who "looks upon the crime of seduction and illicit intercourse without horror . . . loses that value for innocence in her own [sex] which is one of the strongest safeguards to virtue."

By voicing such arguments, women in the antislavery movement used gender to justify their antislavery commitment. Their inherent responsibility as women, they insisted, was to effect the salvation of women in bondage. "They are our sisters," Angelina Grimke told a women's antislavery convention in 1837, "and to us as women they have a right to look with sympathy for their sorrows, and effort and prayer for their rescue." Again, as women, antislavery activists contended, they had special reason for their activism. "Women can do more than men for the extension of righteousness," exhorted antislavery agent Abby Kelley, "because they have not, from the customs of society, been so much perverted, and hence their moral perception is much clearer." Appealing to the women of Massachusetts, the Boston Female Antislavery Society made the same point. "As *wives* and *mothers*, as *daughters* and *sisters*, we are deeply responsible for the influence we have on the human race," the society declared. "We are bound to urge men to cease to do evil and learn to do good."

There was yet another link between gender role and antislavery commitment, one that Lydia Maria Child had expressed in her antislavery tract of 1833. "The comparison between women and the colored race is strong," she wrote. "Both are characterized by affection more than intellect; both have a strong development of the religious sentiment; both are exceedingly adhesive in their attachments; both comparatively speaking, have a tendency to submission; and hence, both have been kept in subjection by physical force and considered rather in the light of property, than as individuals." Sympathetic toward the woman slave or empathetic toward a subject race, hundreds of northern women gave their support to the antislavery cause. Although the abolitionist movement was dominated by men, the influence that women exerted surpassed their expectations.

Abolition and the Woman Question

As soon as the antislavery crusade began in 1831, when William Lloyd Garrison first published the *Liberator* and formed the New England Antislavery Society, women joined the fold. Female antislavery societies began to form throughout New England in 1832. By 1838, over 100 such societies had been created. Their spread followed a route familiar to revivals—all over New England, into the major eastern cities, through the towns of western New York, and out to the Midwest, where Ohio became a hotbed of antislavery agitation. Female societies fell at once into the traditional pattern of auxiliaries and devoted their efforts, at first, to fund-raising for the cause.

But women abolitionists soon embarked on new and more controversial tactics. They spearheaded a militant petition campaign, organized national conventions, and spoke on public platforms as antislavery agents. This meant addressing "mixed" or "promiscuous" audiences—a feat no one had attempted since Frances Wright. Such activism evoked a formidable controversy over woman's proper place, a dispute in which the cause of women and slaves became intertwined. As women defended their roles as abolitionists, they mobilized the conventional rhetoric of benevolence to attack restrictions based on sex. In 1837, a national women's antislavery convention resolved: "The time has come for woman to move in that sphere which providence has assigned her, and no longer remain satisfied in the circumscribed limits which corrupt custom and a perverted application of Scripture have encircled her."

From the outset, this radical cause brought its supporters into the spotlight of public attention and removed the cloak of respectable anonymity that covered women's benevolence. Abolition, to be sure, drew on a narrower constituency. Members of female antislavery societies often came out of reform-minded environments and from families where husbands or fathers were abolitionists as well. Many activists had already liberated themselves from the rigors of orthodox Calvinism and adopted more liberal creeds. Moreover, a significant proportion of abolitionist women were Quakers, with their own long tradition of egalitarianism and a proclivity for relying on conscience, whatever the consequences. Even Quaker meetings, however, castigated women who adopted the cause. Many left their meetings, if only temporarily, to follow "the divine summons" of abolition, as it was described by a Rhode Island Quaker, Elizabeth Buffum Chace. Becoming an abolitionist meant risking social ostracism, loss of reputation, and outright persecution. The rewards were a sense of personal regeneration, the support of new peers in the movement, and an ennobling sense of commitment. According to Chace, "The antislavery spirit grew and prospered in proportion to the difficulties in the way."

The difficulties became clear in 1833 in the cases of Lydia Maria Child and Prudence Crandall. When Child, a successful author, published an *Appeal in Favor of That Class of Americans Called Africans*, which denounced slavery and defended racial equality, she met ostracism, ridicule, and loss of income. Her book sales plummeted. The same year, a young Quaker schoolteacher in Canterbury, Connecticut, admitted a black student into her hitherto successful female academy. After the other students had been withdrawn, Prudence Crandall reopened her academy as a school for black girls, a move that aroused the ire of the citizens of Canterbury. Crandall was arrested three times and eventually convicted under a new state law that prohibited the instruction of out-of-state blacks. Finally the townsfolk vandalized her school. She closed it and vanished into the West. Throughout her ordeal, Prudence Crandall received support and funds from the newly organized abolitionists in New York and Boston, who transformed her isolated instance of defiance into a cause célèbre.

The opprobrium experienced by Child and Crandall was familiar to women who founded female antislavery societies, such as Maria Weston Chapman in Boston and Lucretia Mott in Philadelphia. The Boston society was started in 1832 by Chapman and twelve other women, the Philadelphia society in 1833 by Mott and a few Quaker associates. Like other auxiliary groups, they both profited at first from male assistance (the Philadelphia society was presided over by a man, a black dentist). Both embarked on the traditional spectrum of activities familiar to voluntary benevolence. The women raised funds for the *Liberator* and for the American Antislavery Society. They held "antislavery fairs" where homemade articles were sold. They also distributed tracts, invited lecturers to address them on the evils of slavery, supported male agents who spoke for the cause, and embarked on charitable works among local blacks—"visiting" black areas and opening black schools.

But in the context of abolition, these once acceptable activities were no longer innocuous. When the Boston Female Antislavery Society invited a prominent English abolitionist, George Thompson, to address it in 1835, the meeting was disrupted by the threats of a hostile mob and adjourned. Moreover, female antislavery societies soon exceeded their scope as local auxiliaries and united their efforts in a massive petition campaign to Congress, demanding an end to slavery. Not only did women succeed at the arduous door-to-door canvass for signatures, but the petition campaign evoked a sense of shared purpose among female societies. In 1837, abolitionist women organized a national network of volunteers to solicit signatures and set up regional offices in major cities. They also began to hold national conventions, formed an Antislavery Society of American Women, and elected a slate of officers that brought the local leadership to prominence.

The unity evoked by petitioning was quickly disrupted, however, by a controversy that divided the abolitionist crusade. In 1836, the American Anti-slavery Society proposed that women be hired as antislavery agents. The first women agents, Sarah and Angelina Grimke, became at once the first southern women to become known in public life and the first women since Frances Wright to address "promiscuous" audiences of men and women. Public speaking on behalf of abolition placed them, irrevocably, at a crucial frontier, a juncture at which demands for racial and sexual equality were linked.

Like Frances Wright, to whom the Grimkes were invidiously compared, the sisters were very much "outsiders" who burst upon the scene of northern reform with a singular clarity of mission. Daughters of a prominent, slave-owning South Carolina family (their father and brothers were judges, lawyers, legislators), they had been virtual exiles from the South since 1830, when they settled in Philadelphia. Longtime opponents of slavery, they had passed through a sequence of conversions—from Episcopalianism to Presbyterianism to Quakerism. They then became members of the Philadelphia Female Antislavery Society, a commitment that meant discarding their affiliation with the Friends. The barrage of conversions seemed impelled by its own velocity. For the Grimkes, conscience, like Wright's irrepressible egalitarian streak, knew no bounds, and the outcome was much the same.

The Grimkes began to lecture on abolition in New York in 1836, speaking to women's meetings. But their next lecture tour in New England, sponsored by the Boston Female Antislavery Society, drew men as well. As southerners, members of a slave-owning family, and women, the Grimkes were the most exotic and controversial of antislavery agents. Their engagements attracted crowds in the thousands, made new converts, and spawned new societies. Moreover, since their innovative roles evoked opposition, the Grimke sisters became adept in defending not only the slave but also themselves.

The reaction to the Grimkes reached a peak in 1837, when their "obtrusive and ostentatious" behavior drew the wrath of the Massachusetts clergy, who denounced them for assuming "the place and tone of man as public reformer." Such activism was unnatural, the ministers contended. Indeed, by describing the victimization of slave women, the Grimkes lost "that modesty and delicacy . . . which constitutes the true influence of women in society." In conclusion, the clergy urged the agents to return to "the appropriate duties and influence of women." Sarah Grimke responded with her *Letters on the Condition of Women and the Equality of the Sexes,* a scriptural analysis and a militant response to male domination. Like Lydia Maria Child, Grimke drew a parallel between the condition of women and that of slaves. She also demanded for women equal education, pay, and rights—above all the rights of a "moral being." "Men and women are CREATED EQUAL. They are both moral and accountable beings," said Sarah Grimke. "All I ask our brethren is that they take their feet from off our necks and permit us to stand upright on the ground which God destined for us to occupy."

While Sarah Grimke responded to the clergy, Angelina Grimke took on an equally formidable adversary, Catherine Beecher. Like the ministers, Beecher objected to the Grimkes' invasion of public life and explained her views in an 1837 tract. Woman held "a subordinate relation in society to the other sex," Catherine Beecher declared, and should confine her activities to "the domestic and social circle," though this did not mean that "her influence should be any less important or all pervading." In her published reply, Angelina Grimke insisted that female influence should be exerted in the same way as male influence. If ministers could address "promiscuous" audiences, so could women. "It is a woman's right to have a voice in all the laws and regulations by which she is to be governed, whether in church or in state," Angelina Grimke told Catharine Beecher.

The Grimkes' stance offended those abolitionists who felt that women who made a spectacle of themselves by lecturing in public could only damage the cause. This conservative view won favor among many clerically oriented women who were active in organizing and petitioning, such as those in New York and about half the Bostonians. The Grimkes' major defense came from Garrison, who announced in the *Liberator* in 1838: "As our object is *universal* emancipation, to redeem women as well as men from a servile to an equal condition—we shall go for the rights of women to their utmost extent." Garrison, like Sarah Grimke, drew an analogy between women and slaves—it was impossible to advocate the rights of one and deny the rights of the other. For those defending "human rights" there was no other choice.

The controversy over women's roles in antislavery soon caused abolitionists to divide into factions. In 1839, the dominant New England branch cracked into opposing camps, aggravated by a women's petition campaign to permit racial intermarriage in Massachusetts. In 1840, the Boston Female Antislavery Society split and so did the national organization. The Garrisonians nominated antislavery agent Abby Kelley to the business committee of the American Antislavery Society, imported several hundred New England women to attend the annual convention in New York, and won their point, on women's votes. Conservatives withdrew and formed their own antislavery society. Later that year, the "woman question" crossed the Atlantic and disrupted the World Antislavery Convention in London. After 1840, the abolitionist crusade ran on two tracks.

The divided movement of the next two decades had an important impact on women's history. The Garrisonians provided a setting in which women could participate in all facets of reform, a context in which women's rights as reformers were recognized. By the same token, they severed themselves permanently from politics and from all institutional outlets for effecting emancipation. The Grimkes, meanwhile, had retired in 1838 to work with Angelina's new husband, abolitionist Theodore Weld, on his massive compendium of antislavery testimony. Garrison regarded this retreat from the fray as desertion. But the Grimkes' efforts were followed by others. Abby Kelley lectured indefatigably throughout the 1840s and recruited new women agents, including Lucy Stone. Many were soon to throw their energies into women's rights. Confronting hostile audiences and angry mobs, on behalf of the slaves, was a radicalizing experience. "We have good cause to be grateful to the slave," said Abby Kelley. "In striving to strike his irons off, we found most surely, that we were manacled ourselves."

The split within abolition, however, did not prevent more conservative women from continuing their work in the cause. Nor did it have much impact in the West, where female societies proliferated throughout the 1840s, fanning outward from Ohio to Illinois, Michigan, Minnesota, and Wisconsin. In St. Cloud, Minnesota, outspoken editor Jane Swisshelm, who felt unable to commit herself to either of the factions in abolition, published an antislavery newspaper, the *Visitor*, that gained, she claimed, thousands of votes for the Free Soil party. In Michigan, Laura Haviland, who formed the first antislavery society in the territory in the 1830s, opened a racially integrated academy, worked as an operative on the underground railroad, and engaged in missionary work among blacks. Like many abolitionist women, including Elizabeth Buffum Chace in Rhode Island and Lucretia Mott in Pennsylvania, Haviland became a professional visitor on behalf of the cause. Whether working with fugitives, canvassing for signatures, soliciting funds, or addressing conventions, women in antislavery gained training in tactics and a spirit that "grew and prospered in proportion to the difficulties in the way."

Black women too were active in the abolitionist movement. Four black women participated in the founding of the Philadelphia Female Antislavery Society, including three members of the prominent Forten family, one of whom served as an officer. Several black women joined the Boston Female Antislavery Society in the early 1830s. But hostility to slavery did not necessarily mean that whites endorsed association with blacks; racial segregation prevailed throughout the North. When the Fall River (Massachusetts) Female Antislavery Society urged black women to join in 1835, opposition among members was so strong that the society almost disbanded. The 1837 convention of antislavery women condemned "those societies that reject colored members," but black women usually formed their own female antislavery societies.

Nor were blacks, male or female, at first used as antislavery lecturers. But once they were, women were often on the podium. Former slave Sojourner Truth proved a popular speaker with antislavery audiences, starting in the 1840s, as did Harriet Tubman in the 1850s. By then, other black women abolitionists also had active lecturing careers. The best known were relatives of prominent black male abolitionists, such as Sarah Remond of Massachusetts, sister of lecturer Henry Remond, and Frances Ellen Harper, niece of another important abolitionist, who spoke on behalf of the Maine Antislavery Society. The first woman antislavery lecturer, in fact, was a black Bostonian, Maria Stewart, who made several speeches to mixed audiences in the early 1830s. Her public appearances did not seem to evoke any controversy at all, as the Grimkes' did a few years later.

Abolitionist women described their commitment and careers as quasi-religious experiences. They recounted veritable conversions to the cause, conversions that were often preceded by some inspirational event, such as coming upon a coffle of slaves being sold or hearing a Garrisonian address. The most influential conversion was undoubtedly that of Harriet Beecher Stowe, who first developed antislavery sympathies in Ohio in the 1830s. Attuned to the patriotic and providential, she felt "the heroic element was strong in me. . . . It made me want to do something, I know not what . . . to make some declaration on my own account." Her moment of truth did not occur until 1850 when, while taking communion, the vision of Uncle Tom's death scene came upon her. After the initial vision, and much research in antislavery literature, the rest of the novel rushed in upon her "with a vividness that could not be denied." Later, Stowe explained that she had written *Uncle Tom's Cabin* as "an instrument of God." Attempting to induce a national conversion in sentiment, Harriet Beecher Stowe became the most successful antislavery "visitor" of all, reaching over 300,000 homes.

Unlike Sarah and Angelina Grimke, Harriet Beecher Stowe never joined an antislavery society or spoke on any public platform. She was, on the contrary, a model exerter of "influence." The divided abolitionist movement provided an arena in which women could participate on different levels. By far the greatest number of women who opposed slavery filled the role of "domestic evangelist"; they empathized with Uncle Tom, mourned the death of little Eva, and promoted antislavery views among family members. A more activist group of women joined antislavery societies and, in the context of female associations, became propagandists, fund-raisers, petitioners, and visitors. Finally, within the small but embattled Garrisonian faction, women became antislavery agents, public speakers, and converts to the doctrines of "human rights." After 1840, division within the abolitionist ranks neither handicapped the movement nor limited women's attachment to the cause.

The Garrisonians did raise new questions about women's rights in public life. They were not the only reformers concerned about women's rights and roles. During the ferment of the 1840s, even before a formal women's rights movement emerged, women's status in society had become a focus of attention.

Communitarian Alternatives and Legal Rights

"Many women are considering within themselves what they need and what they have not," wrote Margaret Fuller in her transcendental tract, *Woman in the Nineteenth Century* (1845). A celebration of female potential, Fuller's tract catered to women's rising expectations and captured a sense of impending change. Stressing the imperative to remove "every arbitrary barrier that hindered woman's progress," Fuller asserted that "What woman needs is not as a woman to act or rule but . . . as a soul to live free and unimpeded." The means for attaining such a liberated state were varied, including "a much greater range of occupation than they now have, to raise their latent powers." But above all, Fuller recommended psychological independence from male domination.

> I would have Woman lay aside all thought, such as she habitually cherishes, of being taught and led by men. . . . Men do *not* look at both sides, and women must leave off asking them, and being influenced by them, but retire within themselves,

and explore the groundwork of life, till they find their peculiar secret. Then, when they come forth again, renovated and baptised, they will know how to turn dross into gold.

Margaret Fuller's tract was a version of one of the "conversations" she had held for Boston women in the early 1840s. Here she had sought to fill her listeners with intellectual self-reliance and a boundless sense of possibility. Mystically vague and much like a sermon in tone, Margaret Fuller's *Woman* met a more appreciative reception than had Frances Wright's "Explanatory Notes." Still the nineteenth-century reader might well have wondered how she could reach the status of "a being of infinite scope" within traditional marriage, which Fuller described as a flawed institution, or how she could achieve Fuller's goal of a "ravishing harmony of the spheres" in a society split into male and female compartments. But during the 1840s, an era when all institutions were called into question, reformers became absorbed with such problems. One set of answers was provided by those men and women who retreated from the world into the haven of communities.

Since the 1820s, when New Harmony and Nashoba were founded, utopian communities had attempted to provide models of alternative societies that improved on worldly society. Some communities were formed by religious sects—such as the Shakers and Mormons. The Oneida community, led by John Humphrey Noyes, was also sectarian in origin. Others were nonsectarian— among them the transcendentalist communities such as Brook Farm and the rash of Fourierist associations that sprang up in the 1840s. Religious or secular, communitarian experiments had two characteristics that linked them to Nashoba and New Harmony. Most rejected, to a greater or lesser extent, the values of capitalist society and attempted to replace them with some variant of socialism. And most attempted to offer alternative ways in which men and women could live together, within or outside the bounds of marriage. As a result, communitarians provided new visions of women's roles.

Shaker communities, for instance, relieved women of sexual oppression by excluding both marriage and sexual relations. These celibate communities, which had existed since the Revolutionary era, experienced their greatest period of growth in the 1840s, when the attraction of communitarian life reached its peak. In particular, the Shakers provided an alternative role for women that had considerable appeal; the Shaker "families" that peppered the Northeast, encompassing some 6,000 souls, attracted more women than men. Within each Shaker "family," or community, a rigid system of sexual segregation prevailed: Shaker men and women lived, ate, worked, and worshiped separately. To one observer, physician Harriet Hunt, the Shaker "family" offered an asylum from the "perversions of marriage" and "the gross abuses which drag it down." Rejoicing in the role of Shaker women as ministers, elders, and medical practitioners, Hunt concluded that "the equality of women . . . is recognized in every department of Shaker life." But her enthusiasm was not universal. When Abba Alcott, the overworked wife of universal reformer and free spirit Bronson Alcott, inspected a Shaker community, she found that the men had "a fat, sleek, comfortable look," while the women were stiff, awkward, and reserved. "There is servitude some-where, I have no doubt," Alcott told her journal. "Wherever I turn, I see the yoke on women in some form or other."

Transcendental communities, such as Brook Farm, did not discard mar-riage as an institution. But they attempted to create what Margaret Fuller called a "harmony of the spheres," an atmosphere in which men and women were equal participants in community life. At Brook Farm, a specific goal was to free women from domestic drudgery by dividing all menial work, indoors and outdoors, among community members. "Our womenfolk had all the rights of our men-folk," one enthusiastic resident claimed. "They had an equal voice in all our public affairs, voted for our offices, filled responsible positions, and stood on exactly the same foot as our brethren." Such noble goals inspired Brook Farm women. "The very air seemed to hold more exhilarating qualities than any I had ever breathed," a young woman resident claimed. At Fourierist communities, which multiplied in the 1840s, similar enthusiasm prevailed. Women appreci-ated the Fourierists' attempt to give equal credit to the labor of both sexes. "Both men and women have the *same* pay for the same work," former mill operative Mary Paul wrote to her father from a New Jersey association. "There is more equality in such things according to the work, not the sex."

While celibate Shakers and idealistic transcendentalists were able to live in harmony with their eastern neighbors, the Mormons were not. By the 1840s, the Mormons had removed themselves as far as possible from the "world" to the remote haven of Utah. The Mormon custom of "plural marriage," more than any other religious tradition, necessitated their retreat. To outsiders, polygamy was anathema and an insult to womanhood. But Mormons defended it as an improve-ment on women's conventional roles. "Plural marriage," they contended, gave every woman in the community the opportunity for a husband, a home, children, and entry into heaven with the man of her choice. Men, to be sure, ran the Mormon community, just as they dominated public life elsewhere. But each plural family was its own female community, with all aspects of marriage, from domestic work to sexual relations, divided among two or more wives. Mormon women, like Mormon men, defended the sect and claimed that it improved their status within both family and community.

Mormons were not alone in seeking to alter the institution of marriage. So did John Humphrey Noyes and his controversial community at Oneida, New York. The Oneida experiment ultimately involved about 300 people and lasted for four decades, long after other utopian ventures had collapsed. Noyes created both a successful socialist economy and alternative roles for women that seemed to outsiders as offensive as those of the Mormons, if not more so. At Oneida, monogamy was prohibited. Under "complex marriage," which Noyes intro-duced, all the Oneidans were married to one another. This was far from free love, as critics charged, but rather a highly regulated system involving community approval of successive unions, behavior control through "mutual criticism," public application for parenthood, communal child rearing, and a new variant of motherhood. Noyes's son, for instance, remembered visiting his mother once or twice a week.

The economic, social, and sexual policies at Oneida were connected. While socialism inhibited acquisitiveness and selfishness, complex marriage eliminated men's possession or ownership of women, as well as parents' possession of the communally raised children. An original type of egalitarian, Noyes also developed new techniques of sexual relations intended to satisfy the sexes in equal measure while preventing conception. The "amative" and "procreative" faculties, he contended, were separate. Noyes insisted, too, that less licentiousness existed under complex marriage than in conventional marriage, a view that won little credence outside Oneida. Significantly, those sects that provided alternatives to conventional marriage—Shakers, Mormons, and Oneidans—transformed sexuality from a private concern to a public, or community, concern. They also prided themselves on the elimination, containment, or diffusion of male licentiousness and the enhancement of opportunities for women.

Since communities had limited followings and, in most cases, limited life spans, they had little impact on women's lives beyond their boundaries. Out in the "world," communitarians were considered either harmless eccentrics or hopeless degenerates, depending on their sexual arrangements. In the "world,"

Communal child rearing was a distinctive feature of the Oneida community in western New York; founder John Humphrey Noyes objected to the "gloom and dullness of excessive family isolation." Since all labor, including household labor, was socialized, Oneida women might work in the community factory, in domestic industries, or in the cooperative kitchen, school, or child-rearing facility. Here, parents gather to overlook the "children's hour." (Frank Leslie's Illustrated Newspaper, *September 13, 1873*)

however, new efforts emerged to change women's status. During the 1840s, a campaign began to redress the legal disadvantages of married women—a cause that Frances Wright had advocated in her lecture tour of 1829–1830.

The law had always discriminated against wives. In all states, married women remained legal possessions, rather than legal persons. Under coverture, they had no control over their real or personal property, no rights to their own earnings, no contract rights, and no guardianship rights over their children, although northern courts began to treat mothers with greater lenience. There remained, however, loopholes to coverture. Under equity law, for instance, a wife could acquire a "separate estate." To do so, she needed a written conveyance, perhaps a prenuptial contract or some other document, that stipulated her assets, their source, and the degree of control she might exert over them. A variant of the separate estate was the trust, in which a third party controlled the wife's estate. While other aspects of equity law fell into disuse, the separate estate rose in popularity. In her study of Petersburg, Virginia, women, historian Suzanne Lebsock notes that instances of separate estates, while rare until 1820, increased markedly thereafter. The object of such devices, she points out, was not to empower women but to keep property in the family—and out of the hands of husbands' creditors.

But separate estates required special arrangements, and affected only a minority of wives. Grievances about their legal status permeated women's writings. "I had lived twenty years without the legal right to be alone one hour, to have exclusive right of one foot of space," complained abolitionist Jane Swisshelm, a supporter of married women's property reform, who sued her husband for property she had inherited. Marriage, claimed Mary Lyndon, the heroine of an autobiographical novel by Mary Gove Nichols, had "turned me into a thing," with no claim over either property or child. When an improvident husband wasted his wife's inheritance, spent her earnings, or sold her furniture, she had no other choice, as author Elizabeth Oakes Smith expressed it, than to "go down with the ship."

During the 1840s, efforts to improve the legal status of married women met with some success. Propertied legislators appreciated measures that would preserve their estates, if inherited by daughters, from disintegration in the hands of sons-in-law. Mississippi enacted the first Married Women's Property Law in 1839. A similar bill had been proposed in 1836 in Albany, where a women's pressure group was formed. Under the leadership of Ernestine Rose, a Polish-born follower of Robert Owen who had just emigrated from England to New York, women petitioned and lobbied for an end to the most blatant disabilities of feme covert status. Married women, they contended, should be allowed to retain ownership of their property, keep their own earnings, and enjoy joint guardianship over their children.

In 1848, the New York legislature passed a minimal bill providing that married women could retain control over their real and personal property, and other states enacted similar measures. An 1860 New York law gave married women the right to their own earnings. By 1865, twenty-nine states had enacted some form of married women's property law, and the process continued for the rest of the century. The passage of such legislation made the equity loophole of "separate estates" available, in theory, to everyone.

Still, the significance of married women's property laws has to be qualified. First, their impact depended on the state courts, where judges often retained an affection for common law. In New York, for instance, where several pioneer statutes were enacted, superior court judges interpreted the new laws conservatively, thus vitiating their intent. A second qualification involves the motives behind the statutes. Their enactment reflected not so much a new respect for wives as a changing economy, one that required investment capital and a spirit of risk. The married women's property acts can be viewed as part of a larger effort to promote commercial ventures by providing buffers against insolvency: Like separate estates, the laws protected property not only from husbands but also from husbands' creditors. Married women's property acts therefore "represented the demands of an acquisitive and propertied middle class," historian Norma Basch contends. But the campaign for marital property reform "also encompassed a constellation of ideas that extended beyond class interest to gender interest," Basch points out. "In the context of the nineteenth century, the right of wives to own property entailed their right not to be property."

The battle against legal inequities continued after 1848 under the banner of the women's rights movement. The new crusade, like the Garrisonian camp of abolition from which it sprang, took on a perfectionist hue. It identified a new, pervasive root evil to be exterminated, and it mobilized a battery of disparate grievances that until now had been unconnected and diffuse. It was, in fact, a combination of multiple inequities, rising expectations, and abolitionist expertise that thrust the new movement into existence.

The Women's Rights Movement

When women's rights advocates attempted to draft a manifesto for their first convention at Seneca Falls in 1848, they felt, said Elizabeth Cady Stanton, "as helpless and hopeless as if they had been asked to construct a steam engine." The "Declaration of Sentiments" that resulted mobilized a battery of grievances that women had voiced for two decades and transformed them into a cohesive program of reforms. Identifying the enemy as the "absolute tyranny" of man, the declaration enumerated "his repeated injuries and usurpations." Women had been excluded from higher education, profitable employment, the trades and commerce, the pulpit, the professions, and the franchise. They were deprived of property rights, denied guardianship of their children, and victimized by the double standard. Moreover, their oppression had an insidious psychological dimension. "[Man] has endeavored, in every way that he could, to destroy her confidence in her own power, to lessen her self respect, and to make her willing to lead a dependent and abject life," the declaration stated. After a dozen resolutions demanding redress, the declaration culminated in an assertion of women's right to the vote—an ultimate invasion of the public sphere.

The new call to arms of 1848, and the movement it began, was directly a product of the abolitionist crusade, where most of its leaders had been initiated into activism. From the abolitionists, the early feminists inherited a geographical circuit, a mode of agitation, a human rights ideology, and even a small constituency. They were also the legatees of decades of activism in benevolence and reform and of female efforts to rescue female victims—of poverty, slavery, prostitution. In this case, to be sure, the agitators and the victims were the same. The women's rights movement was at once an evangelical crusade that aimed at a massive "awakening," a humanitarian rescue mission, and a modern pressure group. Unique in the context of antebellum reform, it challenged the assumptions on which social space was divided. But the women's rights movement was distinguished primarily by its unseverable link with Garrisonian antislavery.

The new movement was led by a network of women formed in the crucible of abolition, joined by other experienced reformers. Elizabeth Cady Stanton, married eight years to a prominent abolitionist, had been thrown into inspirational antislavery circles before moving with her family to Seneca Falls in 1847. She had participated in a local Female Antislavery Society, attended the World Antislavery Convention in London with Lucretia Mott, and campaigned in New York for a Married Women's Property Act. Lucretia Mott, a public Friend since 1817, had a long career as a stalwart of causes—moral reform, temperance, and abolition. An active Garrisonian, she had spent the past decade lecturing on religion and antislavery. Whether fresh from the abolitionist lecture circuit, like Lucy Stone and Abby Kelley, or the property rights campaign, like Pauline Wright Davis and Ernestine Rose, or the temperance crusade, like Susan B. Anthony, women's rights activists were already active in public life in one way or another. "I was a believer and advocate of the doctrine long before I became so publicly, "recalled Elizabeth Oakes Smith, a longtime reformer, "for I could not smother aspiration nor could I be a mere household woman."

These advocates brought with them not only experience in reform and an acute sense of "woman's wrongs" but an eagerness to discard the hallmarks of female benevolence. The first to go was the religious impulse that pervaded the majority of women's voluntary associations. Most women's rights advocates had experienced some form of "deconversion" from the rigors of orthodox Protestantism. Converts to the notion of universal salvation, many had moved into more liberal sects or a humanitarian secularism of their own devising. Others were Friends. Moreover, as Garrisonians, many were skeptical of clerical authority and disdained the "perverse application of the Scriptures" in regard to women. "The pulpit has been prostituted," Lucretia Mott told a women's rights convention in 1854, "the Bible has been ill-used." Elizabeth Cady Stanton, who claimed she had narrowly escaped conversion as a girl, at the hands of Charles G. Finney, eventually became as anticlerical as Frances Wright.

The new movement also discarded formal organization. Although women's rights associations sprang up as far west as Wisconsin, there were no elaborate networks of female societies, no state or national organizations, no battalions of officers, agents, managers, and visitors. There was, rather, a spontaneous informality. Individuals or contingents took off on speaking tours or petition campaigns quite independently, while an informal, shifting series of

committees organized conventions. The conventions were staged almost annually, along the abolitionist circuit. They passed resolutions and engaged in debate
with the male opponents who regularly appeared. They also drew public attention, which was overwhelmingly negative. The new cause was surrounded by
hostility and derision and mocked in the press. According to Elizabeth Cady
Stanton and Susan B. Anthony, women's rights leaders were "wholly unprepared to find themselves the target of the jibes and jeers of the nation." But
conventions also provided an opportunity for supporters, drawn mainly from
antislavery ranks, to reiterate and refine the sentiments expounded in the 1848
resolutions.

The women's rights convention at Salem, Ohio, in 1850, the only one from
which men were excluded, provided one such opportunity. Issuing a call to the
women of the state, the Ohio reformers passed twenty-two resolutions, in which
political and economic grievances were reduced, in stages, to psychological
dependence and female complicity:

> Resolved, that while we deprecate thus earnestly the political oppression of
> Woman, we see in her social condition, the regard in which she is held as a moral and
> intellectual being, the fundamental cause of that oppression.
> Resolved, that amongst the causes of such social condition, we regard the public
> sentiment which withholds from her all, or almost all, lucrative employments, and
> enlarged spheres of labor.
> Resolved, that in the difficulties thus cast in the way of her self-support, and in her
> consequent *dependence* upon man, we see the greatest influence at work in imparting to
> her that tone of character which makes her to be regarded as "the weaker vessel". . . .
> Resolved, that we regard those women who content themselves with an idle,
> aimless life, as involved in the guilt as well as the suffering of their own oppression. . . .

The Ohio reformers, like those at other conventions, had two targets. One
was the state legislature, which, engaged in rewriting the state constitution,
rejected their petition for suffrage. Another was women-at-large, "involved in
the guilt as well as the suffering of their own oppression." A basic dilemma of
the movement was that women were not aware of the need for rights. Lucretia
Mott confronted this problem in an 1849 speech, where she used images of
bondage and confinement, inertia and paralysis, to describe the psychological
enemy:

> [Woman] has been so long subject to the disabilities and restrictions, with which
> her progress has been embarrassed, that she has become enervated, her mind to some
> extent paralyzed; and like those still more degraded by personal bondage, she hugs her
> chains.

The conferring of rights, equal opportunities, and the vote, Mott concluded,
"shall raise her from this low, enervated, and paralyzed condition." Women's
rights, like abolition, was a humanitarian rescue operation. The vote was a means
to emancipation, not an end in itself.

Suffrage, however, proved an unwieldy weapon with which to penetrate the perimeter of sphere, and women's rights activists were ambivalent about it. At Seneca Falls, the demand for the vote was the only resolution that failed to evoke unanimous approval. It was passed, by a small majority, only as a result of the concerted efforts of Elizabeth Cady Stanton and Frederick Douglass. Many women who signed petitions demanding legal rights in the 1840s, as in New York, refused to endorse petitions for suffrage. Most Americans believed that women were not entitled to vote precisely because of their dependent status, a status that women's rights advocates deplored but had to acknowledge. To others, the demand for suffrage symbolized the extreme and unwarranted belligerance of its advocates. "I don't believe woman is groaning under half so heavy a yoke of bondage as you imagine," Lucy Stone's sister wrote to her in 1846. "I am sure I do not feel burdened by anything man has laid upon me, to be sure I can't vote, but what care I for that, I would not if I could." For Garrisonians such as Lucretia Mott, who believed that "political life abounds in outrage," the issue was especially difficult. "Far be it from me to encourage women to vote or take an active part in politics in the present state of the government," she stated. However, Mott also asserted that "[woman's] right to the elective franchise . . . should be yielded to her, whether she exercise that right or not."

The early feminists' dual allegiance—to radical abolition, which rejected the corruption of politics, and women's rights, which demanded access to it—also posed a liability. The women's rights movement was unable to sever itself from the abolitionist crusade because of its leaders' dual commitment, their dependence on other abolitionist women for support, and finally the endorsement of prominent Garrisonian men. While faced with virtually unanimous hostility outside abolitionist circles, women's rights campaigners won unconditional support from the advocates of human rights. Besides Garrison and Frederick Douglass, an eloquent and loyal spokesman for women's demands, other stalwarts contributed their endorsements as well. Wendell Phillips and Gerrit Smith (Elizabeth Cady Stanton's cousin) supported the cause, as did Samuel May, Thomas Wentworth Higginson, William H. Channing, and Henry Clarke Wright, who had been a staunch backer of the Grimkes. This interesting contingent, composed mainly of liberal ministers, had also escaped from orthodoxy into the more hospitable parlors of Unitarianism and Universalism, antislavery and nonresistance. The women's rights movement's most visible, unified group of backers, significantly, were dissenting clerics within the ranks of radical abolitionism.

What this support was worth, however, is questionable. The mingling of reforms was not necessarily an advantage. On the one hand, it made the cause of women's rights inaccessible to a potential constituency of women who did not share the radical abolitionist stance of its leaders. And on the other, as historian Ellen Dubois contends, advocates of the cause were restrained by the dual affiliations of their leaders, "which kept them from the mobilization of women around a primary commitment to their own vote." Until the slave was free, the women's rights movement was restricted by its dependence on an antislavery base. Critics were able to attack the movement, as in *Harpers* in 1853, both for its friends (its "intimate connection with all the radical and infidel movements of the day") and for its deviance ("a peculiar enormity of its own . . . a deficit of both nature and revelation").

While women's rights advocates were able to make limited gains in the area of legal rights, they made no headway in enlarging their tiny constituency. Their tactical successes and failures were best illustrated by the Stanton-Anthony campaigns in New York State in the 1850s. Throughout the decade, activists assaulted the state legislature with an unrelenting petition campaign, demanding further redress in married women's rights (control of their own earnings, joint guardianship rights of children, improved inheritance rights of widows) and suffrage. While Anthony mobilized volunteers and organized the campaign, Stanton, now the wife of a state senator, addressed a joint judiciary commitee in Albany to press the case. By 1860, when New York finally passed the most comprehensive married women's property law yet enacted, fourteen other states had passed some form of improved legislation as well. Suffrage demands were ignored.

Other tactics backfired. One was an attempt to enlarge the base of support for women's rights by extending it to temperance—a reform movement dominated not only by men but by ministers. Within the crusade against drink, the Daughters of Temperance fulfilled a conventional auxiliary role, unable to participate in conventions or hold office in the male-run national organization. When New York feminists created a State Women's Temperance Association in 1852, 500 women withdrew from the national temperance movement, attended a convention of the new association, and elected Elizabeth Cady Stanton president. But the membership soon splintered and disbanded over Stanton's radical proposal that drunkenness should be cause for divorce. Indeed, Stanton's proposals for liberal divorce laws were unpopular even among advocates of women's rights. A joint feminist-abolitionist invasion of the World Temperance Convention the following year, when activists used the Garrisonian ploy of nominating a woman to the business committee, resulted in ignominious defeat. The temperance movement remained under ministerial sway. The women within it were unwilling to abandon clerical support in favor of a feminist alliance or to support Stanton's insistence that women had the right "to be present in all Councils of Church and State."

The temperance women's reaction resembled that of the moral reformers in 1838, when Sarah Grimke's remarks in the *Advocate* evoked dismay. The contrast between moral reform and the women's rights movement is significant. While moral reform, balanced on the brink between benevolence and aggression, was able to evoke the commitment of thousands, it was ultimately hamstrung by its own ideology. Women's rights, isolated on a new frontier between evangelical reform and politics, lacked the widespread support that moral reform had enjoyed. Devoted to stimulating conversions in "sentiment," women's rights advocates were unable to harness such sentiments effectively. They succeeded, however, where the moral reformers had failed, by integrating a barrage of demands and fortifying them with the human rights convictions they brought with them from abolition. Their antebellum triumph was ideological rather than tactical.

The women's rights movement culminated decades of women's encroachment into the public sphere, beginning with the pious, evangelical voluntary societies of the early nineteenth century. As historian Keith Melder has shown, women's benevolence gradually became more independent and innovative, as it veered away from religious goals and began attacking specific evils (prostitution, drink, slavery) that victimized women. The tactics of women's societies similarly shifted from fund-raising and visiting to petitions, conventions, and public speaking. The more radical and assertive the cause, the greater the tendency to discard clerical authority and to view the limitations of sphere as illegitimate. In the women's rights movement, attacks on sphere were finally reformulated into a demand for total autonomy. As a women's rights convention resolved in 1851, "the proper sphere for all human beings is the largest and highest to which they are able to attain."

Throughout these decades, the voluntary association provided a framework in which women could function outside the home and collectively exercise what Abbey Kelley called their "clearer moral perception." The Civil War and the vast economic changes that followed wiped out both the evangelical and perfectionist impulses that gave antebellum movements their particular character. The heritage that remained was threefold: the tradition of female association, the extension of women's influence through benevolence and reform, and the newborn ideology of women's rights. In the postwar years, all three reemerged—in women's clubs; in temperance work, settlement work, and labor reform; and in the movement for woman suffrage. Between 1800 and 1860, women succeeded in appropriating and feminizing a portion of public space. Their postwar activism in public life was "visiting" writ large.

SUGGESTED READINGS AND SOURCES

CHAPTER 7

William Randall Waterman's biography, *Frances Wright* (New York, 1924), remains a reliable source. Celia Morris Eckhardt provides the most recent interpretation in *Fanny Wright: Rebel in America* (Cambridge, Mass., 1984). See also A. J. G. Perkins and Theresa Wolfson, *Frances Wright, Free Enquirer: The Study of a Temperament* (New York, 1939), and Richard Stiller, *Commune on the Frontier: The Story of Frances Wright* (New York, 1972), a lucid and accurate narrative. Two useful articles are Edd Winfield Parks, "Dreamer's Vision: Frances Wright at Nashoba (1825–1830)," *Tennessee Historical Magazine*, 2 (January 1932), 75–86, and O. B. Emerson, "Frances Wright and Her Nashoba Experiment," *Tennessee Historical Quarterly*, 6 (December 1947), 291–314. A recent edition of Frances Wright's *Course of Popular Lectures* (New York, 1972) includes her short autobiography. See also Wright's *Views of Society and Manners in America*, ed. Paul R. Baker (Cambridge, Mass., 1963). The classic history of Owenism in America is Arthur Bestor, Jr., *Backwoods Utopias: The Sectarian and Owenite Phases of Communitarian Life in America* (Philadelphia, 1950).

All of the important Nashoba documents were published in the *New Harmony Gazette* (New Harmony, Ind., 1825–1828) and in the *New Harmony and Nashoba Gazette, or*

The Free Enquirer (New Harmony, Ind., 1828–1829). Wright's articles on reform are in *The Free Enquirer* (New York, 1829–1835). Some of the letters quoted in this chapter are in the Lafayette Collection, University of Chicago Library, and in the Percy Bysshe Shelley and Mary Wollstonecraft Shelley journals in the Duke University Library.

CHAPTER 8

Keith Melder surveys women's activism in benevolence and reform in *Beginnings of Sisterhood: The American Women's Rights Movement 1800–1850* (New York, 1977). Deborah Gray White explores the distinctive experience of slave women in *Ar'n't I a Woman? Female Slaves in the Plantation South* (New York, 1985).

For the development of female voluntary benevolence, see Melder, "Ladies Bountiful: Organized Women's Benevolence in the Nineteenth Century," *New York History*, 48 (1967), 231–254. Urban benevolence and social reform are examined in the following works: Barbara J. Berg, *The Remembered Gate: Origins of American Feminism, The Woman and the City 1800–1860* (New York, 1978); Nancy A. Hewitt, *Women's Activism and Social Change: Rochester, New York, 1822–1872* (Ithaca, N.Y., 1984); Lori D. Ginzburg, *Women and the Work of Benevolence: Morality, Politics, and Class in the Nineteenth Century* (New Haven, Conn., 1990); Susan Porter Benson, "Business Heads and Sympathizing Hearts: The Women of the Providence Employment Society, 1837–1858," *Journal of Social History*, 12 (Winter 1978), 301–312; Ann M. Boylan, "Women in Groups: An Analysis of Women's Benevolent Organizations in New York and Boston, 1797–1840," *Journal of American History*, 71 (December 1984), 497–523; and Boylan, "Timid Girls, Venerable Widows, and Dignified Matrons: Life Cycle Patterns Among Organized Women in New York and Boston," 1797–1840," *American Quarterly*, 38 (Winter 1986), 779–797.

Carroll Smith-Rosenberg assesses the moral reform movement in "Beauty, the Beast, and the Militant Woman: A Case Study in Sex Roles and Social Stress in Jacksonian America," *American Quarterly*, 23 (October 1971), 562–584. Mary P. Ryan examines moral reform in upper New York State in "The Power of Women's Networks: A Case Study of Female Moral Reform in Antebellum America," *Feminist Studies*, 5 (Spring 1979), 66–86. I have also used Marlou Belyea's paper, "Put Down the Libertine, Reclaim the Wanderer, Restore the Outcast: The New England Moral Reform Society," given at the Berkshire Conference on the History of Women, Bryn Mawr College, 1976. Estelle B. Freedman examines the prison reform movement in *Their Sister's Keepers: Women's Prison Reform in America, 1830–1930* (Ann Arbor, Mich., 1981).

For women in slavery, besides Deborah Gray White, *Ar'n't I a Woman?* (above), see Eugene Genovese, *Roll, Jordan, Roll: The World the Slaves Made* (New York, 1972); Elizabeth Fox-Genovese, *Within the Plantation Household: Black and White Women of the Old South* (Chapel Hill, N.C., 1988), ch. 3; Jacqueline Jones, *Labor of Love, Labor of Sorrow: Black Women, Work, and the Family, from Slavery to the Present* (New York, 1985), ch. 1; Angela Davis, "Reflections on the Black Woman's Role in the Community of Slaves," *Black Scholar*, 3 (December 1971), 3–15; and Catherine Clinton, *The Plantation Mistress* (New York, 1983), ch. 11. Herbert Gutman examines slave strategies for family preservation in *The Black Family in Slavery and Freedom, 1750–1925* (New York, 1976), part 1. For documents, see Dorothy Sterling, ed., *We Are Your Sisters: Black Women in the Nineteenth Century* (New York, 1984), part 1; Gerda Lerner, ed., *Black Women in White America: A Documentary History* (New York, 1972), parts 1 and 2; Willie Lee Rose, ed., *A Documentary History of Slavery in North America* (New York, 1976); John Blassingame, ed., *Slave Testimony: Two Centuries of Letters, Speeches, Interviews, and Autobiographies* (Baton Rouge, La., 1977); and *Six Women's Slave Narratives*, int. by William L. Andrews (New York, 1988). The authoritative edition of Linda Brent's narrative is Harriet A. Jacobs, *Incidents in the Life of a Slave Girl: Written by Herself,* ed. Jean Fagan Yellin (Cambridge, Mass., 1987).

For women's roles in the abolitionist movement, see Melder, *Beginnings of Sisterhood,* chs. 5 and 6; Blanche Hersh, *The Slavery of Sex: Feminist Abolitionists in Nineteenth-Century America* (Urbana, Ill., 1978), and Jean Fagan Yellin, *Women and Sisters: Antislavery Feminists in American Culture* (New Haven, Conn., 1990). See also Judith Wellman, "Women and Radical Reform in Upstate New York: A Profile of Grass Roots Abolitionists," in Mabel E. Deutrich and Virginia Purdy, eds., *Clio Was a Woman: Studies in the History of American Women* (Washington, D.C., 1980), pp. 113–127; Gerda Lerner, *The Grimke Sisters from South Carolina: Pioneers for Women's Rights and Abolition* (New York, 1967); Lerner, "The Political Activities of Antislavery Women," in *The Majority Finds its Past: Placing Women in History* (New York, 1979), pp. 112–144; Elizabeth Ann Bartlett, ed., *Sarah Grimke: Letters on the Equality of the Sexes and Other Essays* (New Haven, Conn., 1988); Dorothy Sterling, *Ahead of Her Time: Abby Kelley and the Politics of Antislavery* (New York, 1992); Edmund Fuller, *Prudence Crandall: An Incident of Racism in Nineteenth-Century America* (Middletown, Conn., 1971); and Frederick B. Tolles, ed., *Slavery and "The Woman Question"* (London and Haverford, Pa., 1952), which contains Lucretia Mott's diary of 1840.

For divisions in the antislavery movement see Aileen S. Kraditor, *Means and Ends in American Abolition: Garrison and His Critics on Strategy and Tactics* (New York, 1969). Black women's roles in antislavery are discussed in Rosalyn Terborg-Penn, "Discrimination Against Afro-American Women in the Woman's Movement, 1830–1920" in Sharon Harley and Rosalyn Terborg-Penn, eds., *The Afro-American Woman: Struggles and Images* (Port Washington, N.Y., 1978), pp. 17–27; Janice Sumler Lewis, "The Forten-Purvis Women of Philadelphia and the American Antislavery Crusade," *Journal of Negro History,* 66 (Winter, 1981–1982), 281–288; and Dorothy Sterling, ed., *We Are Your Sisters,* part II. See also Bert Loewenberg and Ruth Bogin, eds., *Black Women in Nineteenth-Century America: Their Words, Their Thoughts, Their Feelings* (University Park, Pa., 1976). Angela Davis discusses the antislavery and women's rights campaigns in *Women, Race, and Class* (New York, 1983), chs. 2 and 3.

On Margaret Fuller, see Paula Blanchard, *Margaret Fuller: From Transcendentalism to Revolution* (Cambridge, Mass., 1978), and Charles Capper, *Margaret Fuller: An American Romantic Life,* vol. I (New York, 1992). For utopian communities, see Louis J. Kern, *An Ordered Love: Sex Roles and Sexuality in Victorian Utopias—The Shakers, the Mormons, and the Oneida Community* (Chapel Hill, N.C., 1981); Lawrence Foster, *Religion and Sexuality: Three American Communal Experiments of the Nineteenth Century* (New York, 1981); Foster, *Women, Family, and Utopia* (Syracuse, N.Y., 1991); Carol A. Kolmerton, *Women in Utopia: The Ideology of Gender in the American Owenite Communities* (Bloomington, Ind., 1990); and Barbara Welter, "The Feminization of American Religion, 1800–1860," in Mary Hartman and Lois Banner, eds., *Clio's Consciousness Raised* (New York, 1974), pp. 137–157. The New York State Married Women's Property Acts of 1848 and 1860 are discussed in Norma Basch, *In the Eyes of the Law: Women, Marriage, and Property in Nineteenth-Century New York* (Ithaca, N.Y., 1988). Lori D. Ginzburg suggests a trend away from evangelism in "'Moral Suasion Is Moral Balderdash': Women, Politics, and Social Activism in the 1850s," *Journal of American History,* 73 (December 1986), 601–622.

The antebellum women's rights movement is assessed by Ellen Dubois in *Feminism and Suffrage: The Emergence of an Independent Women's Movement, 1848–1869* (Ithaca, N.Y., 1978), ch. 1. See also Eleanor Flexner, *Century of Struggle: The Woman's Rights Movement in the United States* (Cambridge, Mass., 1959), ch. 5 and 6, as well as useful document collections such as Aileen Kraditor, *Up From the Pedestal: Selected Writings in the History of American Feminism* (Chicago, 1968), and Alice Rossi, ed., *The Feminist Papers* (New York,

1973), part 2. Women's rights advocates provided their own document collection in Elizabeth Cady Stanton, Susan B. Anthony, and Matilda Joslyn Gage, eds., *History of Woman Suffrage* (New York, 1881), vol. I. For selections from *HWS,* see Mari Jo Buhle and Paul Buhle, eds., *The Concise History of Woman Suffrage: Selections from the Classic Work of Stanton, Anthony, Gage, and Harper* (Urbana, Ill., 1978). The memorial of the Salem, Ohio, women's rights convention of 1850 is reprinted in Gerda Lerner, ed., *The Female Experience: An American Documentary* (Indianapolis, Ind., 1977, and New York, 1992), pp. 342–347. For excerpts from women's rights journals, see Cheris Kramarae and Ann Russo, eds., *The Radical Women's Press of the 1850s* (New York, 1990).

Abolitionist and feminist memoirs include Elizabeth Buffum Chace's reminiscences in Malcolm R. Lovell, ed., *Two Quaker Sisters* (New York, 1937); Maria Weston Chapman, *Ten Years of Experience* (Boston, 1842); Ednah Dow Cheney, *Reminiscences* (Boston, 1902); Lucy Newhall Colman, *Reminiscences* (Boston, 1891); Laura S. Haviland, *A Woman's Life Work, Labors, and Experiences* (Chicago, 1889); Georgiana Bruce Kirby, *Years of Experience* (New York, 1887); Mary Gove Nichols, *Mary Lyndon; or, Revelations of a Life* (New York, 1855), a fictionalized account; Mary Alice Wyman, ed., *Selections from the Autobiography of Elizabeth Oakes Smith* (Lewiston, Maine, 1924); Elizabeth Cady Stanton, *Eighty Years and More* (Boston, 1898); and Jane Swisshelm, *Half a Century* (Chicago, 1880).

CHAPTER 9

The Shirtwaist Strike of 1909

On the morning of November 24, 1909, 18,000 New York garment workers walked off their jobs at 500 of the city's shirtwaist shops. "From every waistmaking factory in New York and Brooklyn, the girls poured forth, filling the narrow streets of the East Side, crowding the headquarters at Clinton Hall, and overflowing into twenty-four smaller halls," reported an official of the waistmakers' union. "It was like a mighty army, rising in the night, and demanding to be heard." Although the size of the waistmakers' uprising was unexpected, rumblings of protest had been heard since early fall. Over the previous six weeks, during walkouts and lockouts at several downtown shops, picketing factory girls had been intimidated by guards, attacked by thugs, harassed by streetwalkers, undermined by strikebreakers, and arrested by police. By November, however, the strike had won support from a coalition of unionists, socialists, and upper-class reformers. Drawing the attention of the press and the sympathy of the public, it threw a spotlight on the shirtwaist worker.

Four out of five of the striking waistmakers were young women, most of them under the age of twenty-five. Some, such as sixteen-year-old Pauline Newman, had earned wages since they were children. Newman had begun work at the Triangle factory in 1901. Others, such as Russian-born immigrant Esther Lopetkin, had only recently arrived in New York. A few, such as teenage Clara Lemlich, an experienced worker at the Leiserson factory, earned as much as $15 a week. But many were "beginners," lucky to get $3 or $4 a week from the subcontractors who employed them. Typically, the shirtwaist worker was either foreign-born or the daughter of immigrants. She lived at home with her family in one of the Lower East Side tenements that housed the Jewish and Italian immigrant communities. Marching in front of her shop throughout the extremely snowy winter of 1909–1910, singing songs of protest and risking arrest, she won admiration for her spirit and tenacity. "Into the foreground of this great moving picture comes the figure of one girl after another as her services are needed," an observer recorded.

> With extraordinary simplicity and eloquence she will tell before any kind of audience, without any false shame and without self-glorification, the conditions of her work, her wages, and the pinching poverty of her home and the homes of her comrades. Then she withdraws into the background to undertake quietly the danger and humiliation of picket duty . . . no longer the center of interested attention but the butt of the most unspeakable abuse.

Humble and eloquent, the striking waistmaker of 1909 became a symbol of the New York garment worker. The clothing trade, dependent on a huge supply of immigrant labor, was the city's largest industry. It had been growing for three decades; sweatshops and factories produced first ready-made men's clothing and then women's clothing. Like other types of manufacturing, clothing production, once a facet of "housewifery," had gone through several intermediary stages in the progression from home to factory. By the 1880s, the New York garment industry was divided between the "inside shop," where garments were made entirely in the factory, and the "outside shop." Under this system, garments were precut in the factory, but contractors, or middlemen, arranged to have the pieces sewn together in the tenement homes of workers. Here entire families worked on clothing—spilling over from room to room, out into halls, and onto rooftops. Riding downtown on the Second Avenue Elevated, through the Lower East Side, a passenger could peer into rows of tenement windows and see garment workers of all ages bent over their machines. The experience, to one rider, was like passing through "an endless workroom where vast multitudes are always laboring."

Man, woman, or child, the sweatshop wage earner could expect to work up to eighty-four hours a week in the busy season, usually in the fall and winter, and to be laid off when panic struck or when business was slow. During the summer, over half of clothing workers might be unemployed. Still, the garment industry supported the immigrants, as long as several family members were able to find work. By the turn of the century, 65,000 women, most of them young and single, were employed in the clothing business. One out of four worked in the men's garment industry, or "cloakmaking"—a rubric that included suit, coat, and shirt manufacturing. The rest worked in the newer women's clothing trade. By 1909, New York produced most of the nation's ready-made women's clothing, including the latest and most popular item, the shirtwaist.

The shirtwaist business was a relative newcomer to the garment trade. Starting only in the 1890s, waistmaking developed rapidly after 1900. Its growth was connected to another development, the rise of the woman office worker. The shirtwaist was the emblem and uniform of the new white-collar woman wage earner—the salesgirl, stenographer, switchboard operator, and office clerk, as well as the schoolteacher. Similar to a man's shirt, but of thinner cloth, the shirtwaist was usually pleated in front, with a row of tucks, and buttoned in the back. The shirtwaist dress, made by the same manufacturers, combined the blouse with a long dark skirt. Even the fashionable "Gibson Girl," whose portrait had filled the pages of popular magazines since the 1890s, often wore a shirt-waist.

Since waistmaking was a new branch of garment production, it took place entirely in factories rather than in the tenement sweatshops. By 1909, there were about 600 waist- and dressmaking shops in New York—many of them small operations, with as few as ten workers, and some very large, with several hundred workers. Between 35,000 and 40,000 labored in the shirtwaist industry, four out of five of them young women. Two-thirds of waistmakers, including all of the men, were Russian Jews. Up to one-quarter of the work force were Italian women, and a small proportion were native-born white women. An even smaller proportion, possibly a few hundred, were black women—probably employed only in the rush season, since blacks as a rule were excluded from industrial work, except in a menial capacity or as scabs.

The one-fifth of the waistmaking trade that was male held the most skilled and highly paid jobs, as was customary in the garment business—usually as cutters, the elite of the work force. Women workers (and sometimes children, although child labor had recently been outlawed in New York State) were trimmers, tuckers, operators, and finishers, most of them paid by the piece. Many were employees not of factory owners but of subcontractors, who were them-selves employees of the shop manager. The subcontractor, or "inside contractor," was paid a lump sum to complete a load of work in the factory, on machines loaned or rented from the owner. He would then assemble a group of young women to do the job, for as little as possible and as quickly as possible, so that he could earn a profit on his contract.

Subcontracting, which affected about one-quarter of the waistmakers, was one of the major abuses of the industry, as the strikers made clear in 1909. There were other abuses as well. The fifty-six- to fifty-nine-hour week—8 a.m. to 6 p.m. weekdays and part of Saturday—could be extended to include nights and weekends during the busy season, without any hope of overtime pay. Waistmak-ers recalled that employers often posted signs: "If you don't come in on Sunday, you needn't come in on Monday." Workers could expect to be fined or sent home for half a day if they came in late, and to be penalized for errors in their work. Their employers charged them for needles, thread, electric power, chairs, and lockers. Such charges were commonplace in the garment industry, which in its early days had insisted that operators supply their own machines as well. In addition, many waistmakers felt subject to various forms of subterfuge, such as not being paid at all if they lost the minuscule "ticket" given out for completing a batch of piecework. Others were concerned about safety hazards. In the Triangle Company lofts, for instance, located on the top floors of a tall building, the doors to stairways were customarily locked to prevent employees from leaving with pieces of fabric. Finally, like all workers in the garment industry, waistmakers were subject to seasonal vagaries of the trade, fluctuations of the economy, and layoffs or wage cuts such as those caused by the serious depression of 1908–1909.

But whatever their grievances, almost no one expected the shirtwaist workers to organize successfully or to call a general strike. There were good reasons for such doubts. One was that labor organization in the garment trade had always been feeble and ephemeral. Since the 1880s, there had been a succession of small and passionate strikes but few victories, and those were soon dissipated by new depressions. In 1890, for instance, a desperate six-month walkout of cloakmakers had finally ended with an acceptable contract, albeit one that specifically excluded "female cloakmakers." But victory vanished in the panic of 1893, when thousands of garment workers lost their jobs. When the shirtwaist strike began in 1909, there were no strong, permanent unions, except perhaps that of the highly skilled cutters. An organization for employees who worked on women's clothes, the International Ladies Garment Workers Union (ILGWU), an offshoot of the Cloakmakers Union, had been started at the turn of the century but did not yet amount to very much. Still, a special subdivision of the union, Local 25—the Ladies Waistmakers Union—had been created in 1906 in the hope of organizing the shirtwaist workers.

Started by thirteen shirtwaist workers—seven women and six men—Local 25 was led by men, who held all the offices and were also a bare majority on the sixteen-member executive board. Organization had thus far been a losing proposition. Before the strike began, Local 25 had 100 members, $4 in its treasury, and modest expectations. Not only did labor organization have a dismal record in the garment trade, not only were most unions guilds of craftsmen rather than industrywide organizations, not only did all clothing workers lack bargaining power under any circumstances, but the obstacles in organizing women workers such as those in shirtwaist manufacturing were commonly regarded as insurmountable.

No one was more aware of these obstacles than members of the Women's Trade Union League, recently organized by reform-minded women. Hoping to spur working women to join unions, the WTUL encountered many problems. Some were logistical. Women workers were unable or unwilling to attend union meetings, always held at night, when they were expected to be at home. Union men often met in "halls," in the back of saloons, as Mary Anderson, a WTUL organizer, later explained, "or in questionable districts, dirty and not well-kept," where young working women refused to go. The women were also dismayed by "large groups of men, playing cards and hanging about." A far more basic obstacle, according to the WTUL, was the woman worker herself. She did not expect to spend her life as a factory hand and tended to see herself primarily as a family member rather than as a member of the working class. "Women are at a disadvantage," said league officer Alice Henry, "through the comparative youth and inexperience of many female workers, through the want of trade training [that is, a lack of skills], through the assumption, almost universal among girls, that they will one day marry and leave the trade, and through their unconscious response to public opinion which disapproves of women joining trade unions." Public opinion, in fact, doubted that women belonged in factories at all, a sentiment shared by male workers and, in particular, by male trade unionists.

All of these obstacles made an impact. At the turn of the century only about 3 percent of women in industry were organized, and in New York after 1900 women's membership in unions declined. The 1908 depression caused yet further slumps, along with layoffs and wage cuts in the garment industry. But wage cuts also provoked signs of upheaval. These first appeared in July 1909, when 200 employees of the Rosen Brothers Shirtwaist Company went on strike for higher wages. Their victory in August—a 20 percent wage hike and union recognition, a vital goal in labor protests—spurred activism elsewhere in the trade. At the outset, shirtwaist manufacturers had little cause for alarm since it was the slow season. Even if some of their workers were rash enough to strike, there was still a large supply of unemployed, nonunionized workers available for hire. But the vigor of the first few groups of strikers had unanticipated repercussions, far exceeding the expectations of waistmakers, their employers, or their unions.

In September, the strike spread to the Leiserson and Triangle shirtwaist companies. Both were in the Washington Square area, once a fashionable residential enclave but now full of lofts and businesses. At both factories, workers who had never been organized rushed to join Local 25 and go on strike. At Leiserson, 98 workers were arrested for picketing and most of them were fined. Paying the fines used up whatever funds the local had been able to collect. At Triangle, even more people were involved; 150 workers, 90 women and 60 men, who had been tricked by their employers into admitting union membership, were suddenly told that there was no more work for them to do. "The girls took their discharge without suspicion," recounted WTUL officer Alice Henry,

but the next morning they saw in the newspapers advertisements of the company asking for shirt-waist operators at once. Their eyes opened by this, the girls picketed the shop ... the company retaliated by hiring thugs to intimidate the girls, and for several weeks the picketing girls were being constantly attacked and beaten. These melees were followed by wholesale arrests of strikers, from a dozen to twenty girls being arrested daily.

Within a few weeks, 500 waistmakers were on strike at the Triangle Company, along with another contingent at the nearby Diamond Waist Company, to which the Triangle owners had sent their uncompleted orders. Meanwhile, the strike scenes around Washington Square began to attract attention. These now had a standard retinue of participants. First, there were the hired factory guards, called "gorillas" by the waistmakers and "thugs" by the WTUL. The guards were assigned by factory owners to patrol the streets in front of the shops, break up picket lines, and enable scabs to enter factories. Then there were the young women strikers carrying their signs. (Men on strike did not picket, since all agreed that women would be more effective on the line. Also, it was hoped, violence would be minimized.) Third, crowds of local residents gathered at each site, many of them prostitutes who appeared to bear a great animosity toward the waistmakers. According to the women on strike, the prostitutes had merely been paid off for their services. Finally, there were the inevitable police, who had long been known for their antipathy to strikers. The police appeared regularly to make arrests and to cart off picketers—some of whom had been beaten in the "melees"—in their patrol wagons and deposit them in the magistrate's court. There the strikers were charged with assault, intimidation, or disorderly conduct.

During these early weeks of protest, several thousand striking workers, never before union members, signed up with Local 25. In October, imbued with confidence, the local began to consider a general strike throughout the shirtwaist industry, with demands for a 10 percent wage increase for all waistmakers and recognition of the union as their bargaining agent. The ILGWU was less enthusiastic, and in its role as parent of the fledgling local, counseled caution: General strikes were extremely risky and rarely successful. But Local 25 won support from other sources, including the United Hebrew Trades Union, the Socialist party, and most important, the New York branch of the Women's Trade Union League. The WTUL's well-off activists were already providing strikers with aid and funds. They were also ready to transform the strike from a minor protest, ignored by the public and not well known even among garment workers, into a major event.

The WTUL was a new arrival on the labor scene. Founded in 1903 by a coalition of upper-class reformers and women unionists, mainly the former, the league's goal was to spur the organization of working women. Its task, according to a WTUL report, was "largely educational." Unable to form unions itself, since most of its members were not employed, the league's main function was to influence others, namely women wage earners and male trade unionists. Toward this end, it tried to carve out a niche for itself as backseat adviser to the American Federation of Labor (AFL), the leading national coalition of unions. Here, the opposition of male union leaders to the organization of women had to be erased. More important, in the league's view, the timidity and inertia of women wage earners had to be eradicated as well. The woman in industry would be trained in organization, leadership, and, indeed, citizenship. As league officer Alice Henry explained, the trade union, like the public school, could become an effective agent of "Americanization." If young and powerless women workers—underpaid, exploited, and often recent immigrants or their daughters—were encouraged to form and join trade unions, they could be transformed into assimilated citizens.

Like many upper-class reform efforts, the WTUL was modeled after an English example. Like fellow reform movements of progressive stripe, it had a distinctly parental thrust. But the league was also a pioneer attempt to bridge the chasm between working class and leisure class, a self-conscious alliance of women wage earners and upper-crust activists, or, in WTUL terminology, "allies." The hope that wage-earning women would soon take on leadership roles in the league, even replacing the dominant allies, gave the WTUL a singular mission. It planned to reform itself. A small degree of interclass alliance had already been achieved in the New York branch of the WTUL, presided over by Mary Dreier, daughter of a wealthy businessman and sister of the WTUL national president. Although most members of the New York WTUL were well-off women, two notable labor organizers of working-class origin were both very active in the league. Leonora O'Reilly, a collar worker at thirteen, had risen in the ranks of the Knights of Labor; and Rose Schneiderman, a Russian Jewish immigrant and former cap sewer, was also prominent in the labor movement. A compelling spokeswoman, Schneiderman occasionally referred to fellow league members as the "mink brigade," but her loyalty was unquestionable. Committed to trade unionization, wage earners and allies alike saw in the waistmakers' troubles a great opportunity for the New York league to prove its mettle. Adept tacticians and publicity agents, WTUL members used their considerable talents to shape the events of the strike.

At the first signs of protest in the fall, the New York league mobilized its troops and swung into action. Forty-eight well-off volunteers (allies) descended on strike scenes to accompany the picketing waistmakers. They planned to serve as witnesses in case of arrest, to mitigate violence by their presence, and if that failed, to complain about it, both at police headquarters and in magistrate's court. Once on the scene, league volunteers—"some of whom were plainly women of leisure," according to Helen Marot, secretary of the New York league—"became convinced of official prejudice in the police department against strikers." Moreover, unable to resist joining the picketers, socially prominent allies were themselves arrested. League member Mary Johnson was arrested on October 23 in front of the Leiserson shop, and then on November 4, league president Mary Dreier. Although both were released, their arrests made good copy. Soon reporters from the New York dailies were drawn to the tumultuous scenes in front of New York's shirtwaist factories. As they covered the strike, they began to present a sympathetic view of the picketing waistmakers.

One *New York Sun* reporter, McAlister Coleman, ventured downtown to watch a picket line form in front of the Leiserson shop, and he described the scene to his readers. Clara Lemlich, an organizer of Local 25, led the striking girls. Lemlich had first been arrested in 1908 for disorderly conduct while distributing boycott leaflets. Singing working-class songs in Russian and Italian, the strikers marched in pairs around the factory entrance.

Of a sudden, around the corner came a dozen tough-looking customers, for whom the union label "gorillas" seemed well-chosen.

"Stand fast, girls," called Clara, and then the thugs rushed the line, knocking Clara to her knees, striking at the pickets, opening the way for a group of frightened scabs to slip through the broken line. Fancy ladies from the Allen Street red-light district climbed out of cabs to cheer on the gorillas. There was a confused melee of scratching, screaming girls and fist-swinging men and then a patrol wagon arrived. The thugs ran off as the cops pushed Clara and two other badly beaten girls into the wagon.

I followed the rest of the retreating pickets to the union hall, a few blocks away. There a relief station had been set up where one bottle of milk and a loaf of bread were given to strikers with small children in their families. There, for the first time in my comfortably sheltered, Upper West Side life, I saw real hunger on the faces of my fellow Americans in the richest city in the world.

Not only could the WTUL draw attention to the strike and evoke compassion from reporters such as Coleman, but as Local 25 was well aware, the league could also provide the money to continue the strike and enlarge it. Now out of funds, the local was glad to cooperate with the wealthy women so determined to assist it. Joining forces, union and league called a mass meeting on November 22 at Cooper Union to discuss the possibility of an industrywide strike. Three

American Federation of Labor president Samuel Gompers addressing the mass meeting of shirtwaist strikers and sympathizers at Cooper Union, where a general strike was called. *(Brown Brothers)*

thousand waistmakers gathered at the well-known hall to receive encouragement from a galaxy of labor activists, including socialist lawyer Meyer London and New York WTUL president Mary Dreier. But most of the speakers cautiously hedged on the major issue. A general strike, AFL president Samuel Gompers told the audience, was only a last resort when all other courses of action had failed. Suddenly, the meeting was galvanized by Clara Lemlich of the Leiserson factory, just released after one of her arrests, who interrupted a labor leader's speech. Lemlich gave an impassioned plea in Yiddish for a general strike. "I am a working girl, one of those striking against intolerable conditions," she told the assembly. "I am tired of listening to speakers who talk in generalities. What we are here for is to decide whether or not to strike. I offer a resolution that the strike be declared—now." Pandemonium then swept the hall. When the chairman of the meeting finally could be heard again over the enthusiastic cheers, he asked the crowd to take an old Jewish oath, affirming commitment to the general strike. Thousands of hands shot up in the air, as the audience swore, "If I turn traitor to the cause I now pledge, may this hand wither from the arm I raise."

Local 25 had expected that as many as 5,000 waistmakers would join the general strike. But the response was astounding. By the end of the first day, 20,000 workers had gone on strike, rushing in droves to join the union. Within a week, in the league's estimate, 30,000 factory employees had joined the strike. According to the New York league's secretary, Helen Marot, about 20,000 strikers were Russian Jewish women, 6,000 were Russian Jewish men, 2,000 were Italian women, and 1,000 were native-born women who, she contended, struck out of "sympathy" with the immigrants. Within a few days, the massive walkout had affected almost all shirtwaist manufacturers and brought production to a virtual halt. This was the waistmakers' moment of triumph. Many of the smaller shops signed contracts with the union, boosting wages between 12 and 20 percent and providing for union recognition. Under these conditions, about half of the striking waistmakers returned to work at over 300 of the factories by the end of November. On November 27, 160 of the remaining shirtwaist manufacturers, including those who owned the largest enterprises, formed their own organization, the Association of Waist and Dress Manufacturers of New York. The manufacturers association refused to sign agreements recognizing the union, declared their opposition to the strikers' demands, and began hiring new employees. With thousands of waistmakers still off the job, Local 25 now directed its attention toward the holdout manufacturers.

Meanwhile, the WTUL, whose members were labeled "uptown scum" by the factory owners, raised its volunteer force of allies to seventy. It also increased its activities. The league ran the union headquarters, established an information bureau, set up relief stations where food was distributed, made regulations for picket lines, kept account of arrests and convictions, and prevailed on important lawyers to defend accused strikers. An intermediary between the pickets and the public, the WTUL threw much of its energy into an impressive public relations campaign. While the union circulated leaflets among the strikers—in Yiddish, Italian, and English—the league staged a huge march on City Hall. Led by three recently arrested waistmakers and three allies, the marchers presented the mayor with a petition of grievances against manufacturers and the police. The New York WTUL also edited special editions of the *New York Evening Journal* and the *New York Call*—the latter a socialist paper that gave the strike coverage for its duration. Finally, league members, accompanied by striking waistmakers, were sent out to address women's groups on the virtues of the cause. "Wage-earner" Rose Schneiderman and waistmaker Pauline Newman traveled around New York and New England, speaking to women's clubs, colleges, and union meetings, collecting support and donations. Wellesley students raised a fund for the strike, and Vassar students appeared on the picket line. Back in New York, letters poured into the newspapers sympathizing with the strikers. The press also commented on the female solidarity evoked by the strike. A Brooklyn paper marveled at "the earnestness with which many prominent women have joined hands with the girls . . . in marked contrast with the aloofness of men of wealth when there is a strike in which only men are involved."

Especially keen on fund-raising, the New York WTUL lost no time recruiting any women of wealth who voiced an interest in the cause. One was Anne Morgan, sister of banker J. P. Morgan, who had told the *New York Times*, "When you hear of a woman who presses forty dozen skirts for eight dollars a week, something must be wrong." The New York league immediately placed Anne Morgan on its executive board, and she joined the picket line. Another recruit

After a general strike was declared, the New York Women's Trade Union League opened a strike headquarters where "allies" arranged publicity and raised funds to pay the fines of arrested waistmakers. The three young women at the left are wearing shirtwaists. *(Museum of the City of New York)*

was Alva Belmont, society leader and outspoken suffragist, who had joined the picketers when the strike began. The shirtwaist workers had drawn her sympathy, she told the press, because of her interest "in women everywhere and of every class." The league made her, too, an executive board member and head of a fund-raising committee, and, as a result, reaped a new barrage of publicity.

No one could have had less in common with the immigrant waistmaker. Alva Belmont had broken into society's higher realms in 1875 by marrying a Vanderbilt, grandson of the commodore, and fighting her way to social power. As a Vanderbilt, Alva supervised the construction of a Newport mansion and a $3-million château on Fifth Avenue. Known in society for her lavish balls and large ambitions, she married her daughter to the duke of Marlborough. After divorcing her husband for adultery in 1895, she immediately married Oliver Belmont, son of banker August Belmont. When her second husband died in 1908, Alva Belmont threw her energies into the suffrage movement. Within a year, she had organized her own Political Equality Association to crusade for the vote. She then turned her energies to the shirtwaist workers. Throughout December 1909, Alva Belmont generated a series of events to promote the cause—or rather, causes, since she informed the press that the battle for suffrage was clearly linked to that of the strikers.

Contributing her own automobiles, Alva Belmont organized a motorcade to circulate through the Lower East Side and galvanize support for the strike. Next, under the auspices of the Political Equality Association, she sponsored an enormous rally at the Hippodrome, a huge meeting hall. Eight thousand suffragists, unionists, socialists, and others turned out for the December 5th meeting, which was chaired by the rector of the Holy Trinity Church. A retinue of public figures and WTUL activists appeared on the podium, as well as a contingent of striking waistmakers. Among the speakers was Anna Howard Shaw, president of the National American Woman Suffrage Association, who supported the strike as an individual, since her organization refused to take a stand. The audience also heard from the WTUL's Leonora O'Reilly, who wept as she described the oppression of the woman garment worker. The shirtwaist strikers packed the gallery, and several took the floor. But not all of their supporters were unequivocally enthusiastic, about either Alva Belmont or the Hippodrome rally. Socialist Theresa Malkiel, an especially critical spirit, voiced her objections in *The Diary of a Shirtwaist Striker*, published in 1910 as a piece of party propaganda. Many of the girls came without dinner to the Hippodrome meeting, Malkiel claimed, and most "had to walk both ways in order to save the car fare."

Although Malkiel was skeptical about Alva Belmont's commitment to the working class, there was no question about Belmont's clout with the upper class. On December 15, she carried her assault to the Colony Club, the most exclusive women's club in the nation. Club members, according to one New York newspaper, could "count their fortunes in seven figures." Here Alva Belmont produced a pageant of a fund-raiser. Mary Dreier and Rose Schneiderman of the New York WTUL addressed the meeting, along with John Mitchell of the United Mine Workers, followed by a lineup of waistmakers, who adeptly presented their case. One of the strikers told of how her employer covered the face of the clock to get more time out of the workers, another of a priest who visited her shop to warn the Italian girls that if they struck they would go to hell. Others told of fines, loss of work in the off-season, and other abuses common in the trade. "We work eight days a week," a young waistmaker told the clubwomen. "This may seem strange to you who know that there are only seven days in the week. But we work from seven in the morning till very late at night, when there's a rush, and sometimes we work a week and a half in one week." The startled assemblage contributed $1,300 to the strikers. Similar engagements enabled the New York WTUL to contribute at least one-fifth of the $100,000 strike fund and an additional $29,000 in bail money.

Bail money was needed. Between November 22 and Christmas 723 striking waistmakers were arrested. One magistrate told a shirtwaist worker who testified against a strikebreaker: "You are on strike against God and Nature, whose prime law it is that man shall earn his bread in the sweat of his brow." He sent her to the women's prison at Blackwell's Island, along with other waistmakers. Some strikers—among them shop leader Esther Lopetkin, who was arrested many times—vowed to go to prison rather than use up the union's funds. Lopetkin found, nonetheless, that her fine had been paid with WTUL funds. The WTUL also supplied the press with photographs of picketers being dragged off the line or sentenced to the workhouse. Meanwhile, the strike spread. Those shirtwaist manufacturers who had held out against union recognition, unable to complete their orders, had sent to Philadelphia waistmaking shops to have them filled. Union leaders followed at once, with great success.

On December 20, two-thirds of Philadelphia's 15,000 waistmakers, almost all of them women, went on strike. WTUL members from New York and Chicago arrived at once to coordinate the event with the ILGWU's Local 15. The league opened an office, held meetings, arranged publicity, and raised funds—the same tactics that had worked so well in New York. Mary Harris ("Mother") Jones, for decades an intimidating power in labor organization, joined other union leaders at a large rally for the strikers, sponsored by the WTUL and held at the Philadelphia Opera House. Clubwomen contributed aid and funds. WTUL allies served as witnesses, the Equal Suffrage Association protested police brutality, and society leader Mary Rodgers Biddle investigated the plight of arrested strikers. Bryn Mawr students rushed into Philadelphia to join the waistmakers on the picket line. One, when arrested, was told by the judge, "It is women of your class, not the actual strikers, who have stirred up all this strife."

The ethnic background of the Philadelphia strikers resembled that in New York: Eighty-five percent were Jews, the rest Italians and Poles. WTUL members were well aware that their efforts were far better received by the Jewish women, who appeared to have a proclivity for organization. The Italians, said New York WTUL secretary Helen Marot, "were a constantly appearing and disappearing factor." In both New York and Philadelphia, Italian women had joined the strike in proportionally small numbers and needed special encouragement to remain off the job. The majority of Italian women kept going to work, throughout the winter, often accompanied to and from their shops by members of their families. The league tried to understand their position. "The Italian girl is guarded in her home," concluded WTUL officer Alice Henry, and therefore very difficult to organize. In contrast, "The Russian Jewish girls brought a spirit of fearlessness and independence . . . militant determination and enthusiasm . . . remarkable gifts of intellect and powers of expression."

Distinctions among women workers, according to the WTUL, were not only ethnic but racial. Hardly any black women had been accepted in the shirtwaist labor force, to say nothing of the union, before the strike. Their participation in the strike was accordingly minimal. WTUL publicists pointed to black women who were devoted union members in New York and Philadelphia—specifically, one in New York who was secretary of her shop organization and two in Philadelphia who were active picketers. It was clear, however, that black women were hired during the strike as strikebreakers. While supporting the admission of black women to the union, the WTUL deplored the hiring of black women as scabs. Similarly, the New York Cosmopolitan Club, an association of blacks and whites devoted to improving race relations, urged black women not to break the strike. But the black press in New York took a different view. "Why should Negro working girls pull white working girls' chestnuts out of the fire?" asked the *Age*, a black weekly, in January 1910. Contending that black women were excluded from employment in the shirtwaist industry, the *Age* urged them to take the jobs while they could get them, the strike notwithstanding.

What interested the WTUL more than race or ethnicity, which turned out to be delicate problems, was women's potential as unionists. The most gratifying part of the shirtwaist strike, in the view of Helen Marot, secretary of the New York WTUL, was that women had proved uncompromising.

> Working women have been less ready than men to make the initial sacrifice that trade union membership calls for, but when they reach the point of striking they give themselves as fully and instinctively to the cause as they give themselves in their personal relationships. . . . The shirt-waist makers strike was characteristic of all strikes in which women play an active part. It was marked by complete self-surrender to a cause, emotional endurance, fearlessness, and entire willingness to face danger and suffering.

"Self-surrender" was probably the crucial phrase in Marot's analysis, for she elaborated on this point. Patrolling the streets in midwinter, hungry and coatless, the young girls had shown "a spirit of martyrdom." Their meetings, in fact, had taken on a "spirit of revival," Marot observed. "Like new converts, they accepted the new doctrine in its entirety." The core of the "doctrine" the strikers embraced was, of course, the union's demand for closed shop and union recognition. And the waistmakers' devotion to these new tenets soon took on proportions that neither the league nor the union officials had anticipated.

During December, the manufacturers association managed to establish individual agreements with some employees in a few shops. But since thousands of strikers remained on the picket line, arbitrators were called in. On December 23, the manufacturers association and Local 25 officers finally settled on a contract that answered some of the complaints strikers had been voicing. The manufacturers conceded that they would reduce the workweek to fifty-two hours; provide free needles, thread, and appliances; institute several paid holidays; rehire all strikers; and not discriminate against union members. But the contract ignored strikers' demands for union recognition and the closed shop, or union shop—one that hired only union members. Instead, the manufacturers agreed to welcome statements of grievances and to "take necessary steps to correct such grievances as upon investigation are found to exist and [to] welcome conferences as to any differences which may hereafter arise and which may not be settled between the individual shop and its employees." Four days later, the strikers overwhelmingly rejected the contract their union leaders had approved. "The contention of the striking employees is that they can only enforce their demands if they have the backing of the union," explained a social worker for the University Settlement who had undertaken an investigation of the strike. "The contention of the . . . manufacturers is that the recognition of the union would mean disastrous interference with their business through the union representatives."

In Philadelphia, the strikers rejected a similar settlement. In both cities, clearly, the waistmakers' militance, once mobilized by the strike, exceeded that of their union officers. The shirtwaist workers had become intransigent—at least in the view of union officials, whose support for the strike now fell markedly. The enthusiasm of WTUL allies also showed signs of faltering. After a last flurry of publicity early in January, the formidable Alva Belmont seemed to retire from the fray. Indeed, public opinion appeared to shift in favor of a settlement, now endorsed by labor notables, league officials, and the *New York Times*. Only the

Socialist party remained staunchly in the waistmakers' camp. Socialist Theresa Malkiel reflected the party line in her *Diary of a Shirtwaist Striker* by referring to a turncoat union officer as a "serpent."

As support waned, chances of a settlement that would please the strikers also seemed to shrink. By the end of January, factory owners who had held out against union recognition were able to get assistance in filling their backlog of orders from smaller manufacturers who had reopened. Those strikers who remained on the line appeared more pinched and frozen than ever. Throughout the winter they had given up their $2 a week in strike benefits to support the men on strike with families at home. On February 6, Local 15 in Philadelphia signed a settlement providing for a shorter workweek and other benefits but leaving the issue of union recognition up to future negotiation. The Philadelphia strikers drifted back to work. Finally, on February 15, Local 25 in New York signed agreements with some of the larger manufacturers. The shirtwaist strike, it declared, was over.

All in all, settlements had been made in New York, shop by shop, with 339 shirtwaist manufacturers, 300 of whom had agreed to recognize the union (they had done so in November, at the outset of the strike). According to the league's Alice Henry, at least 100 of these shops were "lost" during the next year, in part because they had never been made union shops. A majority of strikers had won concessions in terms of wages, hours, and working conditions. But some of the largest employers, who settled last, never agreed to either union shop or union recognition. And over 100 manufacturers had failed to sign any labor agreements at all. In mid-February, while New Yorkers bought sheet music for a new popular tune, "Heaven Will Protect the Working Girl," the last of the strikers returned to their factories, many without contracts. The workers at Triangle, which had signed no agreement with Local 25, were among the most severely affected. Some straggled back to their old jobs, working fifty-nine hours a week. Others were not rehired; scabs who had taken their places during the strikes were kept on instead. Nothing had changed at the Triangle Company, except that some of the amenities that had been provided for strikebreakers during the winter, such as chairs and snacks, vanished.

Neither union leaders nor the New York WTUL activists were ready to regard the strike as a failure, however. At the AFL convention in 1910, Samuel Gompers paid a gallant tribute to the militant waistmakers. The shirtwaist strike had shown, he said,

the extent to which women are taking up with industrial life, their consequent tendency to stand together in the struggle to protect their common interest as wage-earners, the readiness of people in all classes to approve of trade union methods in behalf of working women, and the capacity of women as strikers to suffer, to do, and to dare in support of their rights.

Moreover, despite their failure to achieve all of their goals, the shirtwaist workers had stimulated organization in the garment trades. At the strike's end, the membership of Local 25, once tiny, stood at 20,000. By 1914, the ILGWU was one of the largest unions in the AFL. Even before that, other garment workers had begun to profit from the militant spirit the waistmakers had shown. A series of "great strikes" broke out in the clothing industry. In 1910, 60,000 cloakmakers (men's garment workers) went on strike and achieved far more than the waistmakers of 1909. Three-quarters of the cloakmakers were men. The settlement they won, negotiated by some of the nation's most eminent lawyers, included a "protocol"—a compulsory arbitration board that would settle disputes without strikes. Later used in other labor settlements, the protocol provided a formula for union recognition. The cloakmakers were the first real beneficiaries of the waistmakers' militance.

Another beneficiary was the WTUL, which could only look on the strike as a success. It had affirmed the league's role as an ally of the woman wage earner. League members had been able to prove that the WTUL was, in Alice Henry's words, "no dilletante society but absolutely fair and square with the labor movement." The strike had also provided what Henry called "an educational lesson on a grand scale." Not only had the WTUL made its imprint on the labor front, but, as Henry explained, "the strikers gained much better terms than they could have done unassisted." In addition, the WTUL had certainly fostered the unionization of women, in return for which Local 25 presented it with a silver cup. The ILGWU elevated the league's own Rose Schneiderman to its executive board. Finally, the New York branch of the league doubled its own enrollment. By 1911, it was second in size only to the enormous Chicago branch of the sisterhood. Gratifyingly, many new members were "wage earners," including the impressive Clara Lemlich, who was placed on the New York WTUL's executive board.

Uniting the upper-class woman and the working woman in common cause was, in fact, a crucial achievement. One of the WTUL's major tenets was that women who worked at home without pay ("allies") and women who worked in lofts and factories ("wage earners") shared the same interests. Both were earners and producers, Alice Henry contended, "both should be integral parts of the labor movement." League members assured one another that during the strike, by coming to the aid of their "sister women who are out there in the world of work struggling for a living," allies had demonstrated the "sisterhood of women." "The strike seemed at times to be an expression of the women's movement rather than the labor movement," said Helen Marot. "This phase was emphasized by the wide expression of sympathy which it drew from women outside the ranks of labor."

Not everyone shared this view. Socialist Theresa Malkiel, in her *Diary of a Shirtwaist Striker,* voiced suspicion of sisterhood that claimed to cut across class lines. The socialist stance during the strike had never been identical with that of the league. Moreover, socialist women, who had been active in the strike as speakers, organizers, demonstrators, and relief workers, resented that most of the credit for success went to the WTUL. Some, of course, had seen the interclass alliance among women as a hopeful sign, since social classes should be abolished anyway. But in her *Diary,* Malkiel expressed qualms about the motives of wealthy women who had aided the strikers.

I shouldn't wonder their conscience pricks them a bit—they must be ashamed of being fortune's children while so many of the girls have never known what a good day means. The rich women seem to be softer than the men; perhaps it's because they ain't making the money, they're only spending it.

By the middle of February 1910, the Triangle Company was back in business. Returning to the top floors of the Asch building near Washington Square, ex-picketers found the same hazards to which they had objected before the strike. Doors were locked between the floors to prevent the workers from walking out of the lofts with goods, and no fire escapes or sprinkler systems had been provided. A year later, the company's negligence had tragic results. On March 25, 1911, a WTUL member was walking down Fifth Avenue "when a great swirling, billowing cloud of smoke swept like a giant streamer out of Washington Square and down upon the beautiful homes in lower Fifth Avenue." Fire had broken out in the Triangle lofts, quickly spreading from floor to floor, igniting piles of material and turning the lint-ridden air into roaring flames. But since the one open exit was blocked by fire and other doors to the lofts were locked, many of the 500 Triangle waistmakers were trapped. As a result, 146 women died in the flames or when they jumped out of windows, falling ten stories to sidewalks below or dropping onto the spikes of an iron fence.

"This is not the first time that girls have been burned alive in the city," WTUL leader Rose Schneiderman told a mass meeting at the Metropolitan Opera House after the Triangle fire. "Every year thousands of us are maimed." But charity gifts to the relatives of dead or injured waistmakers would not be enough, Schneiderman told the assemblage of public officials, unionists, and sympathizers.

I would be a traitor to those poor burned bodies if I came here to talk good fellowship. We have tried you good people of the public and we have found you wanting. . . . Every time the workers come out in the only way they know how to protest against conditions which are unbearable, the strong hand of the law is allowed to press down heavily upon us. . . . I know from my experience it is up to the working people to save themselves . . . by a strong working class movement.

10

WOMEN AT WORK,
1860–1920

The waistmaker of 1909 was the product of a half-century of economic change. Between the Civil War and World War I, rapid industrialization and urbanization transformed the American landscape. Higher rates of immigration, increased internal migration, and the last stages of westward expansion compounded their impact. All of these factors shaped women's lives and the work that they did, in the home and outside it. A major event was the entry of large numbers of women into the paid labor force, not only as domestic servants—the largest single category of women workers—but also as factory workers, white-collar workers, and professionals.

Some of the changes in women's paid work were propelled or accelerated by the Civil War. Far more important were the growing economy, which provided new jobs in factories and offices, and the rise of cities, where they were located. During the late nineteenth century, the quick clip of industrialization shifted ever larger portions of work from farm and household to business and workplace, and in the process, technology opened new options. Better machines reduced the need for skilled labor and increased the need for cheap labor, which women traditionally provided. At the same time, cities expanded. The national population doubled betwen 1860 and 1910, but the urban population doubled every decade. By 1920, a majority of women lived within range of paying jobs.

Paid employment, of course, did not represent the bulk of women's contributions to the economy. Domestic labor remained women's major occupation. Much of the nondomestic work that women did at home, moreover, was "invisible" because it was unpaid and did not show up on the census rolls, as was the case with female labor on family farms. The farmer's spouse, whether a sharecropper's wife or a pioneer on the Great Plains, labored a lifetime without pay or recognition as a working woman. Western settlement both extended the life of household production and increased the need for additional unpaid female labor. Other types of work done at home for pay, like taking in sewing, laundry, or boarders, also went unrecorded. Wage labor, however, was in retrospect the wave of the future. During the late nineteenth century, the numbers of wage-earning women rose, the work they did changed, and the nature of the female labor force changed as well.

Part of the story is told by statistics. In 1860, women were 10.2 percent of the free labor force. Almost one out of ten free women over the age of ten earned wages, in a limited range of jobs such as servant, seamstress, teacher, or mill operative. The slave labor force included about 2 million women workers. The next census reflected black women's entry into the paid labor force. In 1870, 13.7 percent of women worked for pay, and 14.8 percent of the nation's workers were women. At this point, the numbers of women wage earners started to surge. By 1910, one out of five wage earners was a woman and one out of four women over fourteen held jobs. (One out of four children between the ages of ten and fourteen was employed as well.) According to the 1910 census, the numbers of working women had just about tripled since 1870.

The types of work women did also changed. Immediately after the Civil War, as before it, most women wage earners were servants. In 1870, for instance, seven out of ten women workers were servants. Women continued to dominate domestic work and related types of menial labor. But the proportion of women workers hired as domestics fell steadily as other types of jobs opened up—in factories, offices, stores, and classrooms. Most of these were "new" jobs, that is, jobs provided by the growing economy, not jobs once held by men. Throughout the era, a sexual division of labor curtailed female employment. In industry, women were hired for unskilled or semiskilled work and concentrated in certain industries, such as those that produced cloth, clothing, food products, and tobacco products. In the growing white-collar sector, as in the professions, women entered a small range of jobs, such as teachers, nurses, office workers, or salesclerks. By the turn of the century, both teaching and clerical work were clearly feminized—that is, dominated by women. By World War I, more women worked in white-collar jobs than as domestics.

Finally, the woman worker was defined by her age as well as by her occupation. Like the shirtwaist worker of 1909, the typical woman wage earner was urban, young, and single. According to a Labor Bureau survey in 1880, for instance, the female work force in cities was 90 percent single, 4.3 percent married, and 5.6 percent widowed; three out of four employed women were age fourteen to twenty-four, and nine out of ten were native-born daughters of immigrants. An exception to this profile was the black woman worker, who was more likely to be older and to work after marriage. Among white women workers, too, thousands of older women—mainly single, widowed, deserted, or divorced—entered the labor market. But the typical woman wage earner was now the "working girl." The youth of the female work force meant that the woman worker tended to view wage earning as a temporary phase, since she planned to marry and leave the job market. It meant that she was more apt to contribute to family income than to support her own independence. It also meant that her work experience would differ from that of a male contemporary. Since women were seen as perpetual newcomers to the work force, they were invariably expected to take the lowest-level jobs at the lowest pay.

Women's acceptance of low wages was their special asset on the labor market. It was also one of many factors that favored their rapid entry into the work force. First, a majority of men could not earn a living wage, which spurred the employment of women family members. Second, employers welcomed low-cost female labor, unless pressured to do otherwise. Third, low-wage, unskilled jobs multiplied as business and industry expanded. Fourth, urban populations bulged with potential women workers, including waves of immigrants and rural migrants, white and black. Finally, throughout the late nineteenth century, the marriage rate dropped and the proportion of single women in the population rose. Family size shrank, the birth rate fell, and educational opportunities increased, especially for middle-class women. The conjunction of these factors created a climate in which women's employment should have increased even more than it did.

But the forces that spurred women's entry into the labor force were mitigated by cultural forces stacked against it. The economic push toward employment was counteracted by a pull toward the hearth, by a middle-class domestic ideal. Most Americans, women included, shared the conviction that a woman's place was at home, supported by men, raising children, keeping house, and bolstering family life. As Theodore Roosevelt wrote around the turn of the century, "If the women do not recognise that the greatest thing for any woman is to be a good wife and mother, why, that nation has cause to be alarmed about its future." Widely endorsed and vigorously defended, the domestic ideal affected the experience of women wage earners as much as it did women at home.

The story of women who worked for pay was largely the story of those excluded from the domestic ideal by age, class, race, or need, although it still determined their options and expectations. This story began around the era of the Civil War. The war enabled some women to prove their capabilities, opened jobs to others, and forced many more into self-support. It also freed almost 2 million black women and deposited half their number on the free labor market.

Civil War and Women's Work

The Civil War affected women's work, in the long run, by spurring productivity and business incorporation, which would later expand the labor market. It had immediate effects as well, though these were different North and South. Among Union women, the war opened up new jobs and new routes to civic involvement, which stimulated the next generation of middle-class reformers and professionals. It also provided models of the large-scale corporate-style associations that women would form in the postwar decades. During the war, under the aegis of male-run organizations—such as the U.S. Sanitary Commission, religious commissions, and freedmen's aid societies—a galaxy of women agents, volunteers, and nurses contributed to the Union effort. Exhilarated by their new roles, women celebrated their contributions for the rest of the century. "At the war's end," nurse Clara Barton claimed in 1888, "woman was at least fifty years in advance of the normal position which continued peace would have assigned her."

Though Barton's claim was a vast overstatement, other contributors to the Union effort shared her view. Through work with refugees, freedmen, and the wounded, women war workers, paid and unpaid, found a gratifying entry into public service. Ministering to the "boys" in the wards, serving as teachers of former slaves, rolling bandages, or visiting camps, they became participants in national affairs. The Sanitary Commission, which involved thousands of women at the local level, urged a fusion of public service and domestic ideals. According to its literature, which adopted a rhetoric of affection and instruction, the Commission was "a great artery that bears the people's love to the army." Memoirists of war work, too, often viewed the Union, and its army, as an extended family. But their maternal spirit cloaked new aggression.

Western agents of commissions—such as Annie Wittenmyer of Iowa, Laura Haviland of Michigan, Mary Livermore of Illinois, and "Mother" Bickerdyke of Ohio—were good examples. Exceeding their authority, they excelled at manipulating officers and denouncing incompetents. Resigned to such "prima donnas of benevolence," Sanitary Commission officials conceded that women surpassed men as fund-raisers and supply collectors. Other women challenged the Sanitary Commission's domestic ideology and stressed their involvement in national affairs. In either case, to women war workers, their efforts were a source of inspiration. The woman in the war, concluded Mary Livermore, "had developed potencies and possibilities of which she had been unaware and which surprised her, as it did those who witnessed her marvelous achievement."

While providing a need for service, paid and volunteer, the war era also offered Union women other opportunities. They took over men's jobs in teaching, a field women had already entered, and assumed for the first time positions as clerks in government offices and stores. Such opportunities were born of necessity. Women needed work, and in this instance, employers needed women workers. Nursing, however, was the major occupational battlefront of the war. Like other types of "progress" for women, this too depended on need: Male nurses were in short supply. Nursing also exemplified the back-door approach to a field monopolized by men, medicine. To gain acceptance, nursing pioneers created a domesticated vocation, one that combined menial services with medical ones. The main prerequisite was a capacity for self-sacrifice and solicitude, rather than training or expertise. The highest nursing post of the war, in fact the only major federal appointment won by a woman, went to Dorothea Dix, a leading spirit of benevolence, which was deemed a more important qualification than experience in medicine. Many women war workers referred to themselves as "nurses," whatever their functions or responsibilities.

Some 3,000 women on both sides of the war served as nurses, most without training or skills, many without pay, and all inspired by the British example set by Florence Nightingale in the Crimean War. Union nurses were more organized than their Confederate counterparts. Originally part of a relief program started by New York women in 1861, the preparation of nurses was soon taken over by the quasi-official Sanitary Commission, which coordinated relief efforts and staffed hospitals, and by the surgeon general, to whom Dix was responsible. Only a minority of women nurses served under Dix as paid appointees. Most were self-appointed volunteers, who stationed themselves in hospitals. But all found that wartime nursing fused medical care and domestic service. New York nurse Sophronia Bucklin, a former schoolteacher and a Dix appointee, wrote an inspired account of her war work, full of mangled limbs and medical emergencies. The bulk of her time, however, like that of other nurses, was spent as housekeeper, since she was also expected to cook, clean, and do laundry for her patients.

Despite the fusion of menial and medical, Civil War nursing met with great resistance, especially from army doctors and officers who disliked the influence of women in the wards and tried to curtail, disparage, or demean it. Women were unfit as nurses, it was argued, because they were variously too weak, annoying, refined, or imprudent, and in any event incapable of dealing with the bodies of strange men. In response, women stressed their traditional roles as caretakers of the sick and feeble at home. "The right of woman to her sphere, which includes housekeeping, cooking, and nursing, has never been disputed," Sanitary Commission agent Jane Hoge argued. The most effective argument in favor of nursing, ultimately, was that women had already done it. After the war, nursing veterans administered hospitals, wrote textbooks, and founded training programs. The 1870 census listed only about 1,000 nurses, including midwives; the two vocations were lumped together for the rest of the century. Three decades later, among 12,000 nurses, nine out of ten were women. Hospital nurses, like other types of household help, commonly worked twelve-hour days and lived in the hospitals where they were employed. To compound the fusion of menial and medical, the 1900 census listed nurses in the category of "domestic and personal service."

Like women in the North, Confederate women formed patriotic societies, sent supplies to the front, and nursed the wounded. But their wartime work was often less voluntary and their hardships greater. Compared to the North, the South faced higher inflation, more severe shortages, and a far larger loss of manpower: four out of five eligible southern men served in the Confederate army, as opposed to about half in the Union. With white men away at the front, many women managed farms and plantations, where supplies dwindled, equipment crumbled, and productivity fell. Yeomen's wives met scarcity and deprivation. Plantation mistresses faced other problems: In the absence of husbands and overseers, they had to take charge of slaves. "Go ahead [and] deal with the Negroes [just as if] they were yours and you had to controll them the balance of your life," a soldier from Georgia wrote to his wife in 1861. Such assignments proved difficult, since slaves grew restive, as evidenced in theft, malingering, sabotage, and mounting audacity. Ironically, women confronted slave administration just as the institution of slavery began to crumble. Moreover, historian Clarence L. Mohr contends, southern women had trouble assuming authority, for they were products of a culture that reserved leadership roles for men. Such a heritage, he suggests, "left many women ill-prepared to take control of an isolated enterprise during the prolonged absence of a spouse." In some instances, weary mistresses rebelled. "You may give your Negroes away," one exasperated Texas wife wrote to her husband in 1864. "I cannot live with them another year alone."

The Civil War affected women's work by a final factor, its casualties. Over a million men were killed or wounded, more than in any other American war before or since. These casualties created a generation of widows, spinsters, and wives with disabled husbands, and enlarged the pool of women in dire need of income. For many postwar women, such as those living off meager widow's pensions and those who would never marry at all, the problem was self-support. Most had few skills to market outside the home beyond sewing. So many seamstresses sought work during and right after the war that wages fell for all forms of needlework. The war's demographic impact on women was perhaps the most far-reaching and long-lasting. But the problem of self-support, though national in scope, had its most severe impact on the postwar South. The Confederacy had suffered disproportionate casualties—almost one out of five white men under forty-four had died in the war—and the consequences affected women's lives through the turn of the century and beyond.

The southern states after the war were a world in which women were in excess by the thousands, historian Anne Firor Scott points out. In 1870, for instance, women outnumbered men by 36,000 in Georgia and 25,000 in North Carolina. In 1890, the ex-Confederate states claimed more than 60,000 war widows, many of whom had to support themselves. Much of the income-producing work done by women, such as managing farms and plantations, went unrecorded by the census, though Scott assumes it was widespread. White middle-class women who needed income often became teachers; postwar expansion of public education made jobs available, since prerequisites were minimal. Working-class women labored in local factories—binderies, box factories, cigarette factories, and textile mills. In 1890, more than two out of five southern textile workers were women (and almost one out of four was a child). By the end of the century, single women in southern towns and cities, like their counterparts in the North, took work in stores and offices—as typists, bookkeepers, cashiers, and saleswomen. One woman commented in the 1890s that more "well-bred" women were at work in the South than anywhere else in the world.

This entry into the job market, however, was both involuntary and unanticipated. Eliza Frances Andrews, author of a famous war memoir and subsequently a newspaper editor and educator, explained that she found it necessary to earn a living in the 1870s "though wholly unprepared either by nature or training for a life of self-dependence." Widows and spinsters seeking work, another woman wrote, had "come to the front, forced there by other movements which they neither anticipated nor are responsible for nor fully comprehend." For postwar southern white women, employment was less a sign of progress than an index of need. An irony of defeat was that southern black women entered the labor force at the same time. The war had freed 1.9 million slave women, and as many as half their number soon became wage earners.

The Black Experience

Although many white married women in the late nineteenth century were able to realize the cultural ideal of caring for homes and families as a long-term career, without resort to the paid labor force, a large proportion of black women were not. From emancipation onward, black women worked for pay in disproportionate numbers. At any given time, moreover, a far greater proportion of black married women than white married women were employed. Almost all were hired as agricultural workers or domestic servants. The black working woman, moreover, was a symbolic figure. She was part of a syndrome of black life in which shared ideals—of family farms, land ownership, and female domesticity— became increasingly unrealistic. These ideals emerged with vigor, however, at the time of emancipation.

During the Civil War and immediately afterward, the freedmen's desire to reconstitute their families was paramount. This was evident in the massive rush of newly freed slaves to legalize and sanctify marriages, to locate missing family members, and to establish stable family lives, with two-parent households. Some newly freed blacks traveled from state to state searching for their husbands or wives or advertised for them in newspapers. The man who walked over two months, covering 600 miles, to find his wife and children, the women who broke off relationships with white men, the couples who attempted to resolve marital tangles that had developed under slavery—all illustrated both the vulnerability of the family under slavery and its survival despite slavery. So did the huge marriage ceremonies that followed emancipation, sometimes in camps of contrabands and often involving sixty or seventy couples. Legal marriage and a stable household were commonly viewed as the major privileges of freedom. A basic component of the black ideal of family life, significantly, was female domesticity.

"When I married my wife I married her to wait on me," a freedman told his former master, soon after the war, when denying permission for his wife to work in the "big house." "She got all she can do right here for me and the children." This new sense of "woman's place" was widespread. "The women say that they never mean to do any more outdoor work, that white men support their wives, and that they mean that their husbands shall support them," an Alabama planter reported in 1865; some months later he noted that black women still wanted "to play the lady . . . 'like the white folks do.'" Plantation managers voiced similar complaints about black women's refusal to work and the consequent loss of field labor. Clearly, free blacks viewed women's work in a white person's house or field as a badge of slavery. As a point of pride, many determined that black wives would do neither.

Freedwomen may not have been universally anxious to "play the lady" since, as historian Leon Litwack points out, it is not clear that newly freed black women were overly impressed with white women. Still, domesticity had obvious appeal as a perquisite of freedom. Unquestionably, the theme emerged on all sides. American Tract Society pamphlets, circulated among southern blacks and aimed at "Young Women," "Young Men," and "Married Folks," reiterated it.

Freedman's Bureau literature offered "plain counsels" to becoming a "true woman" and adopting an appropriate role in the home. During Reconstruction, the committed white souls who worked among freedmen, under various auspices, avidly promoted white ideals. Their efforts resembled subsequent ones, in the 1880s and after, to assimilate and Americanize other groups, whether the remnants of Native American tribes or immigrants and their children. But the ideal of female domesticity drew support from blacks as well. Black newspapers urged "development of a womanly nature" as a means of "elevating and refining" the race.

A related perquisite of emancipation may well have been an enhanced sense of male supremacy, or so it seemed to white women teachers who worked with the freedmen. According to Laura Towne, a northern white teacher on the Carolina Sea Islands soon after the war, black men believed in their right "just found, to have their own way in their families and rule their wives—that is an inestimable privilege." Towne reported that black leaders urged freedmen "to get the women into their proper place," and observed that "the notion of being bigger than women generally, is just now inflating the conceit of the men to an amazing degree." Massachusetts teacher Elizabeth Botume made the same point in 1869. Male supremacy and female labor, she noted, were not incompatible. "Most of the field-work was done by the women and girls; their lords and masters were much interrupted in agricultural pursuits by their political and religious duties," Botume reported. "When the days of 'Conventions' came the men were rarely at home; but the women kept steadily at work in the fields."

Although the shared ideal of female domesticity outlasted the early days of emancipation, it proved increasingly fragile. Despite the formation of stable two-parent families, southern black men had difficulty earning enough to support them. "My wife takes in washing and goes out to work," said a Richmond working man in 1867, "and so we get by." Reporting on southern black women in 1878, black writer Frances Ellen Harper found an increasing number of wives at work. "In some cases, the Southern woman is the mainstay of the family, and when work fails for men in large cities, the money which the wife can obtain by washing, ironing, and other services, often keeps pauperism at bay." Former antislavery lecturer, clubwoman, and feminist, Harper liked success stories about black women who owned land, ran businesses, and formed charitable enterprises; but she reserved her greatest praise for those who contributed to family support. During the 1870s, the numbers of black women wage earners rapidly increased. Although most married black women did not work for pay, a black wife was seven times as likely to work as a white one. Female domesticity was not the only black ideal to be endangered or abandoned in the late nineteenth century (widespread landowning never materialized either), but it was a major one.

By the end of Reconstruction, half of black women over sixteen were in the paid labor force, and many other black women worked alongside sharecropper husbands or took in work. In 1890, according to the first census that distinguished workers by race, almost a million black women were employed—37.8 percent in agriculture, 30.83 percent as domestic servants, 15.5 percent as laundresses, and

The family was the basic work unit for the majority of former slaves who remained in the South as farmers and sharecroppers, as well as for those who migrated west. The Nebraska family above poses in front of its sod cabin in 1888. *(Solomon D. Butcher Collection, Nebraska State Historical Society)*

a minuscule 2.76 percent in manufacturing. In 1900, about one out of every five white women, but more than two out of every five black women, worked for pay. More revealingly, over a quarter of black married women were wage earners but only 3.26 percent of white married women. Unlike the typical white woman worker, the black woman worker was likely to be married. If rural, she was employed in farm work; if urban, in domestic work or related services. She was rarely able to get work in industry except at the most menial levels. She might be a cleaning woman in the cotton mills, for instance, or a tobacco stripper—labor that involved carrying 30 pounds of the weed in sacks to and from the backless benches where she sat to pull it apart. There were occasions too, as in 1909, when black women were hired as strikebreakers; but this was hardly steady work. As a rule, the work black women *were* able to obtain, whether in field or household, was similar to the work once done by slaves. It was also work that other women attempted to avoid. As social worker Mary Ovington observed in 1900, the black woman got "the job that the white girl does not want."

If the black woman worker had one thing in common with the white wage-earning woman, it was the growing likelihood that she lived in or moved to a city. Most black migrants moved to southern cities. But even before the massive black urban migrations of the World War I era, indeed, before the nineteenth century was out, the lure of jobs drew southern black women to northern cities in greater numbers than black men. Among immigrant groups in northern cities, men were always in a majority, but women predominated among black urban migrants. In New York in 1890, for instance, there were eighty-one black men for every 100 black women. Such discrepancies in sex ratios could not be explained even by the standard undercount of black men in census reports. Black women dominated the ranks of early urban migrants because they were always able to get jobs, as men could not, in the growing market for domestics—as cooks, laundresses, scrubwomen, and maids. In New York in 1910, for example, four out of five black working women held domestic jobs. By the first decade of the twentieth century, the steady migration of southern blacks to northern cities had already begun to break up black families and communities. A prominent black woman in Chicago, Fannie Barrier Williams, was inundated with supplications from southern mothers, she reported in 1907, begging her to find jobs "domestic or otherwise" for their daughters to save them from becoming servants in the South. In the World War I era, when black migration surged, the black press was filled with letters from women job applicants anxious to take on work of any sort that would enable them to move north.

In southern cities, an oversupply of female labor was always available for domestic jobs. "We have no labor unions or organizations of any kind," a middle-aged domestic in a southern city reported in 1912. "If some Negroes did here and there refuse to work [for low wages] there would be hundreds of other Negroes right on the spot ready to take their places and do the same work." The glutted southern labor market for black women made their position worse than that of northern counterparts. But North or South, black women needed to work for the same reason. Throughout the era, prejudice precluded job security for black men. It limited their options for steady employment, excluded them from most types of industrial work, confined them to unskilled work, and often made jobs unavailable at all, especially in cities. Even employed black men were often unable to support whole families on their low earnings, especially if their employment was seasonal. But black women were usually able to find some sort of menial work, on farms or in households, to supplement or provide family income. According to economist Claudia Goldin, the black working wife "was purchasing a substantial insurance policy against her husband's being unemployed."

The black working woman might also head a male-absent family, although this was not typical. Local studies suggest that between 70 percent and 90 percent of postbellum black families were two-parent families. But the proportion of black families headed by women was always higher in urban areas than in the rural South, and higher in southern cities than in northern ones. In northern cities, there were more female-headed families among blacks than among other ethnic groups, native-born or immigrant. In Philadelphia in 1880, for example, about 25 percent of black families were headed by women, compared to 14 percent of native-born white families and even smaller proportions of Irish or German families. (When only families of equal economic status were considered the differences dwindled or vanished.) In Boston, female-headed households appeared to be more common in the black community than in the Irish community, especially as exposure to urban life increased; city-bred blacks had less stable families than southern migrants. In 1880, among second-generation families with children, 16 percent of Irish families and almost twice that proportion of black families were female-headed. In New York's black neighborhoods in 1905, the proportion of women that headed male-absent families was twice as high as that among women in the Jewish and Italian communities, with all proportions rising as women aged. Although historians have reached no final conclusions about the origins of the black female-headed family, those who work with postbellum data generally contend that it emerged not as a legacy of slavery but as a response to the conditions of urban life. Among the factors considered are imbalanced sex ratios, high black male mortality, a general level of poverty, black male unemployment or underemployment, and the ability of black women to find work and support themselves. The last factor is of special interest, since in some cases studied, working women appear to have been the "deserters," or instigators of marital breakup, not their husbands.

Although the black working woman was not likely to head a male-absent household, her status differed from that of white counterparts in another way. There was, within black communities, acceptance and support for wives who worked outside the home. This reflected in part the need for and frequency of paid work. Indeed, since slavery's end, a majority of black women had contributed to family support—whether or not the census reflected all of their efforts. (That is, the sharecropper's wife and the woman who took in washing or sewing were not likely to be counted as wage earners.) Moreover, women's work was not as strongly opposed by the domestic ideal, since in many black families this ideal had never been realized. Excluded from the benefits of capitalism, the black family in the late nineteenth and early twentieth century could neither indulge in fantasies of domestic femininity as a way of life nor share the confidence in the future held by white families, both native-born and immigrant.

Assessing the differences between black and immigrant families around the turn of the century, historian Elizabeth Pleck concludes that black women's paid labor was "a means of coping with long-term income inadequacy." Cultural support for the working mother, she contends, was related to the black family's lack of hope in the future. What hope there was, as Pleck points out, was concentrated in children, and this factor too spurred the wage earning of married women. Since Reconstruction, black mothers had avidly supported their children's schooling, as Frances Ellen Harper observed, while fathers would have been willing to let the matter drop. Mothers, Harper contended in the 1870s, "are the levers that move in education. The men talk about it, especially about election time . . . but the women work most for it." Such insistence on education persisted through the turn of the century. A major distinction between black and immigrant families around 1900 was that black mothers, bent on keeping their children in school, felt obliged to work. In many immigrant families, youngsters were apt to become wage earners and contribute to family income.

By preserving this hope for their children's future, over a quarter of black mothers sacrificed the domestic ideal and came to represent its antithesis. The immigrant woman who worked outside the home, though also a contributor to family income, was more likely to be a daughter than a mother. In this status, she was less likely to exert influence over other family members. But since she expected to be only a temporary wage earner, she was able to retain a grip on domestic ideals.

Immigrants, Cities, and Working Girls

By the time of the Civil War, immigrant women were part of the labor force. The largest immigrant group at midcentury, the Irish, had settled in eastern cities. Young Irishwomen entered domestic service, and quickly became a feature of middle-class northeastern homes. In the 1880s, the first waves of new immigrants arrived. While Scandinavians customarily migrated to the Great Plains to carve out homesteads on the last frontier, southern and eastern Europeans—Poles, Jews, Slavs, Italians—settled in eastern and midwestern cities and industrial towns. They soon constituted substantial percentages if not majorities of urban populations. Although the new immigrants came from diverse origins, ranging from the Pale of Settlement to the Sicilian village, and although they identified only with members of their own ethnic group, they were united by a common cultural tradition. The family was the pivot of the new immigration, its cultural center and economic hub. The immigrant family formed a wage-earning unit, and the work of immigrant women was determined by their family roles.

A standard feature of the urban immigrant family was the wife who remained at home. Even in cases where married women had worked outside the home (usually seasonally) in their old countries, new immigrant families were averse to living off the wages of wives and mothers. Married women, therefore, rarely took on full-time jobs, although they often took in piecework or boarders. Italian and Jewish women in New York's immigrant communities, for instance, made artificial flowers, chains, and garments at home, utilizing the hands of available family members. In all immigrant communities, a surplus of single men who boarded with families created a need for paid housekeeping services. By 1900, one out of every five urban homes housed boarders. Women at home thus often contributed to family earnings. The income earned by immigrant fathers, indeed, rarely sufficed to support a family. Employment on railroads, in mines, and in factories was both irregular and poorly paid. The immigrant breadwinner never knew when he would next be laid off, which made family support a precarious venture. Unmarried children, therefore, were also expected to contribute to family income.

In Boston, New York, Chicago, and industrial towns across the Northeast, the daughters of immigrant parents sought employment in whatever work was available near their homes—factory work, mill work, domestic work. In Chicago at the turn of the century, for example, half of Italian women aged fifteen to nineteen worked for pay outside the home. New York's garment industry depended on the low-paid labor of young, single immigrant women such as Pauline Newman and Clara Lemlich. Providing a bridge between Old World patterns and the new environment, the working daughter played a special role in family acculturation and in the economy. Throughout the late nineteenth century, the majority of women who entered the labor force were young, unmarried immigrants or the daughters of immigrants.

The work patterns of urban immigrant women, both mothers and daughters, usually depended on a combination of local opportunities, family traditions, and ethnic attitudes toward women's work. In Pennsylvania steel mill towns, for instance, there was little opportunity for female employment outside the home; in cotton mill towns, options rose, and in large urban areas, opportunities were varied. The types of work women did also varied from one ethnic group to another. At mid-century, for instance, in New York's sixth ward, almost half of Irish women under fifty worked outside the home. Most of this group were young, unmarried women who took jobs as domestic servants or in related work. Wives and mothers earned income by caring for boarders. In the Italian community of Buffalo, New York, a half century later, both mothers and daughters avoided work that took them away from home or family. Married or unmarried, women might take in piecework at home or take on seasonal work, on farms or in canneries, but only as members of family groups. Significantly, whatever women did to contribute to family income, even within the tradition-bound Italian family, their work did not necessarily disrupt ethnic patterns, challenge male leadership, or alter the balance of power within the family. Instead, the immigrant family adjusted its economy to the new urban environment.

The ranks of urban women wage earners also included young native-born women who left rural areas and migrated to cities in search of employment. As early as the 1870s, the native-born working girl made an appearance in fiction—in Louisa May Alcott's *Work* (1873). Alcott's heroine, Christie Devon, a model of pluck and determination, was "one of that large class of women . . . driven by necessity, temperament, or principle out to the world to find support." Christie found an episodic series of jobs, as servant, seamstress, hired companion, and, briefly, in the theater, which Alcott viewed as an unwholesome environment. Two decades later, Theodore Dreiser's controversial novel *Sister Carrie* (1900) presented a more passive type of urban migrant. Still, Carrie Meeker followed the same episodic trail in search of work, from factory to store to theater, teetering on the line between wage earning and immorality. These fictional experiences seemed to reflect fact. For most late-nineteenth-century working girls, as for Christie Devon, paid work was both irregular and interchangeable; it shifted from shop to mill to factory to unemployment in rapid succession. Many urban migrants, like Carrie Meeker, who lived apart from their families or employers were considered "women adrift." One-fifth of women wage earners in 1900, women adrift sometimes ventured into jobs as chorus girls or dance hall hostesses. This "sexual service sector," historian Joanne Meyerowitz suggests, was part of the urban economy. Whatever her job, the "working girl" became a feature of the city scene, along with its mansions, lodging houses, factories, and tenements. She could be recognized by her outfit, which a turn-of-the-century writer described as "coarse woolen garments, a shabby sailor hat, a cheap piece of fur, a knitted shawl, and gloves."

For Alcott's heroine, as for the next generation of working women, domestic service was often the only job option. At the turn of the century, the million women in domestic service—maids, laundresses, cooks, companions, waitresses, and nurses—were 26 percent native-born, 19 percent daughters of immigrants, 28 percent foreign-born, and 27 percent black. For white workers, servitude was a last resort, since the domestic workweek was about 50 percent longer than a week of factory work, with irrregular hours and rare days off. Young women who had a choice usually preferred factory work to domestic work because of the lack of free time, the drudgery, the boredom, and especially the low status associated with domestic service. A 1902 reporter concluded that Massachusetts women would turn to shoe factories, textile mills, department stores, and restaurants rather than resort to domestic work, even if they earned less. In 1903, a New York settlement worker explained that "only the less desirable girls and new arrivals go willingly into this work." Yet many women had no choice. In midwestern cities, young Scandinavian immigrants often became domestic servants. In the Far West, as cities absorbed Chicano communities, Mexican American women frequently took domestic work to contribute to family income. In the 1880s and 1890s, Mexican American women around Los Angeles entered the labor market as domestics and laundresses, as well as fruit canners and farm laborers.

Like the factory girl, the female lodger, and the rural migrant, the prostitute was also a by-product of urbanization—one that generated much anxiety. She appeared wherever men congregated, whether in Civil War army camps or western mining towns. In Virginia City, Nevada, where men outnumbered women three to one in 1875, for instance, one woman in twelve was a prostitute. The prostitute also appeared in eastern cities and metropolises, despite vigorous efforts of reformers to lower her numbers and eliminate her vocation. The urban

Unlike the antebellum "hired girl," who helped a neighbor's wife with her work, the turn-of-the-century servant performed specialized functions, whether sweeping, scrubbing, baking, serving, preparing food, caring for children, or accepting a calling card. The seven young women below posed for a photographer in Black River Falls, Wisconsin, in 1905. *(State Historical Society of Wisconsin)*

prostitute had much in common with her wage-earning sisters insofar as she was likely to be young, poor, and in many cases recruited from their ranks. *Why* she had entered prostitution evoked special concern. Surveying the conditions of working women in the 1870s, the Massachusetts Labor Bureau concluded that low pay drove women into vice and that "the root of the evil will not be reached until women's wages will supply them with the necessities of life, elevating them above the clutch of sin." But economic need was not the only cause cited. Sometimes the prostitute appeared to be the victim of a network of urban perils that included villainous seducers, active recruiters, and the low quality of city life. Sometimes she seemed the victim of unfortunate family circumstances, notably lack of male support. And sometimes she seemed the victim of her own low threshold of resistance to what was described, variously, as temptation, attraction, and adventure. The woman in question was not the Chinese prostitute, impressed into service in West Coast cities, or the black urban prostitute, North or South. She was the young white woman, native-born or immigrant daughter, the possible victim of the dread "white slave trade," who became the target of surveys, investigations, and remedial efforts.

One of the first surveys of urban prostitutes was made just before the Civil War at New York's Blackwell Island, the women's jail to which some convicted shirtwaist strikers were sent in 1909. When William Sanger, the prison physician, asked what had led the 2,000 women surveyed into the trade, one out of four answered "inclination." Sanger suspected, however, that "other controlling influences" were at work. Giving more credence to such answers as "destitution" and "seduced and abandoned," he also cited "the low rate of wages paid to women." Three out of four prostitutes surveyed had been previously employed, most in domestic work and the rest making such items as clothes, hats, umbrellas, or flowers. Subsequent investigators too found that only a narrow occupational line separated the streetwalker from the servant, pieceworker, and factory girl. In 1889, on the basis of a government survey of almost 4,000 prostitutes in major eastern and midwestern cities, the commissioner of labor, Carroll D. Wright, concluded that prostitutes were often recruited among girls of the "industrious classes." Almost a third of those surveyed had entered the trade directly from home. The rest had been previously employed in a cross section of women's occupations. Half had been domestic servants; the other half were drawn from the ranks of cloakmakers, dressmakers, shirtmakers, boxmakers, milliners, mill girls, salesgirls, cashiers, switchboard operators—indeed, every trade open to urban women.

Women who investigated prostitution in the first decades of the twentieth century stressed the urban evils that led girls astray. Middle-class reformers and professionals, they saw the prostitute as a victim of city life and male predators. Dorothy Richardson, who studied the lot of working women in 1911 by joining them, found factories to be a recruiting ground for the cities' red-light districts. In 1903, New York settlement worker Frances Kellor noted networks of aggressive recruiters ready to prey on newly arrived immigrants. Girls who were "homeless, friendless, penniless," she said, were often unable to "resist temptation . . . attractively presented." In Chicago, Jane Addams cited a combination of urban temptations, female gullibility, and the hazard of seduction. "A surprising number of country girls have been either brought to Chicago under false pretenses or have been decoyed into an evil life very soon after their arrival," she wrote in 1912. City girls too could be "decoyed" by dubious men who took them to disreputable places, such as dance halls, saloons, and vaudeville shows, and supplied them with drink. Rural or urban, said Addams, the girl who loved pleasure and adventure "could be easily recruited to a vicious life."

Yet another cause, the paucity of profitable alternatives, was suggested by a Philadelphia prostitute in the progressive era, in a correspondence she maintained with Boston philanthropist Fanny Howe. Although she had been half-heartedly looking for work, wrote Maimie Pinzer, "I don't propose to get up at 6:30 to be at work at 8 and work in a close stuffy room . . . until dark, for $6 or $7 a week. When I could . . . spend an afternoon with a congenial person and in the end have more than a week's work could pay me." Ironically, prostitution had become a last frontier of female free enterprise. According to historian Ruth Rosen, the progressive era prostitute *could* expect to earn about five times the income of the typical woman wage earner, such as a factory worker. Unlikely to see herself as a passive victim, she often viewed her trade as an avenue to upward mobility. Those prostitutes who responded to investigators' questionnaires also mentioned "bad family conditions" as a motive for entering the trade. Many reported a background of broken, troubled, and estranged families, with a history of incest, alcoholism, and economic crises. "Since prostitutes differed little from other women in the working class, except for a higher incidence of family instability," Rosen concludes, "the lack of family or good family relations may have been an important factor in many women's decision-making. Most women, whatever their class, who lacked the support of a family economy, found survival difficult on the wages paid for 'women's work.'"

By World War I, the campaign against prostitution effectively closed down urban red-light districts, driving both prostitutes and the industry that lived off them underground. The prostitute had become more menace than victim. But the woman who became a "factory girl," spending twelve hours a day stitching, packing, or bottling, was often seen as a social hazard as well.

Women in Industry

By the turn of the century, 5 million American women earned wages and one out of five women was employed, a quarter of them in manufacturing. Although women were only 17 percent of the industrial work force, their numbers had vastly increased; there were four times as many women in industry in 1900 as there had been in 1870. This female labor force was primarily white, urban, and young. Three out of four women workers in industry were under twenty-five, and three out of four were foreign-born or daughters of foreign-born parents. About half worked in the manufacture of cloth and clothing, including shoes, gloves, hats, stockings, and collars. Indeed, women were a majority of garment workers. But sizable contingents held jobs in other manufacturing as well—in tobacco factories, where they were 38 percent of the employees, and in canneries, bookbinderies, twine- and box-making factories, packing plants, and commercial laundries.

The woman factory worker was distinguished by her unskilled work, her low pay, and her concentration in a limited segment of industry. In every type of manufacturing in which they were employed, female workers held "women's jobs," that is, the ones that required the least training and that could be learned quickly. The garment industry was a good example. As in waistmaking, the most highly skilled work—the cutting of fabric—was reserved for men. Most other work was only semiskilled, and women were easily trained as machine opera- tors, trimmers, and finishers. The same formula applied elsewhere. In breweries, men were brewers and young women were bottle washers. In the preparation of baked foods, such as cookies and crackers, men were bakers and women were boxers or "cracker-packers." In bookbinding, men were eligible for four-year apprenticeships to become skilled craftsmen, while women held lower-level jobs. Not surprisingly, unskilled women workers earned less than male workers in the same industries. In 1899, for instance, a man employed in industry could expect to earn $597 a year, and a woman $314. Moreover, the skilled woman worker, one who had learned a trade or craft, could expect to earn about half as much as a nonunionized man doing the same work. Finally, women tended to be concentrated in certain industries such as textile and garment manufacturing or food processing. Indeed, women crowded the industries that employed them, which ensured that wages would remain low.

But, as in the early days of the textile industry, the clustering of women workers in industries that were seen as extensions of household production did not mean that women had followed their inclinations for spinning, weaving, sewing, or brewing out of the home and into the factory. Obviously, by 1900, most women had not followed household production anywhere. On the con- trary, any form of mechanization that spurred the shift from home to workshop to factory, whether in textile, garment, or food production, tended to open an area of employment to men. The sewing machine, for instance, brought male workers into garment production more than it lured women from hearth to workplace. Clearly, women workers were concentrated in textile mills, hoisery plants, glove factories, and shirtwaist shops because of their exclusion elsewhere. Large numbers of women were not hired in heavy industry, in foundries or mines or oil rigs, or in the production of machines or shipbuilding or construction. Nor were they welcomed in *any* skilled trade or craft, such as typography, welding, molding, or electrical work, at the insistence of men who were already employed in such occupations. The prospect of replacement by cheap female labor did not appeal to late-nineteenth-century craftsmen. Nor was it always a viable option for employers. The temporary expectations of young women workers made it expedient for factory owners to hire them to do low-level, unskilled jobs in which one worker could easily replace another. And due to the abundance of young woman applicants, plenty were available for whatever work was open to them.

Once she was hired, whether in garment shop, bottling plant, shoe factory, or laundry, the turn-of-the-century woman worker was likely to confront the same problems that men did—long hours, dismal working conditions, and occupational hazards, which varied according to industry. The sixty-hour, five-and-a-half-day week was commonplace, and every industry had its rush season, which often meant a fourteen-hour day. When Rose Schneiderman got her first job as a cap maker in the 1890s, doing piecework, she was expected to work from eight until six, stitching linings in golf caps and yachting caps, which brought in, with hard work, about $5 a week. As in other parts of the garment trade, working women had to buy their own machines; they paid them off on the installment plan and lost them entirely if, for instance, a factory burned down. Although the waistmakers of 1909 were saved from even worse working conditions by a New York law of 1897 that limited sweatshop labor, women workers were still subject to the inevitable hazards of factory life—standing, stooping, lifting, and hauling, as well as heat, dust, dampness, noise, monotony, and exhaustion.

Two constant complaints were unsanitary facilities and lack of fresh air. When the Massachusetts Labor Bureau investigated the conditions of needle-work employees in the 1890s, it found women stuffed into unventilated attics and basements, "packed like sardines in a box." Women employed in commercial

Throughout the early twentieth century, documentary photographer Lewis Hine exposed the evils of industrial life. As a reporter for the National Child Labor Committee, a pressure group founded by settlement leaders and other progressive reformers, Hine investigated working conditions in coal mines and canneries, textile mills and garment factories. His commentary and photographs, many of women and children workers, were published in committee literature and reform-minded journals. Below, garment workers in a sweatshop on New York's Lower East Side in 1908, a year before the shirtwaist strike. *(International Museum of Photography, George Eastman House)*

laundries, such as those in San Francisco, worked days and nights in steam-filled rooms, ironing one shirt a minute, dripping with sweat, and breathing ammonia. Investigating the work of bottle washers in a Milwaukee brewery in 1910, Mary Harris ("Mother") Jones reported that they were "condemned to slave daily in the washroom in wet shoes and wet clothes, surrounded with foul-mouthed, brutal foremen. . . . The poor girls work in the vile smell of sour beer, lifting cases of empty and full bottles, weighing from 100 to 150 pounds."

That Mother Jones, celebrated agitator and mine workers organizer, protested the lot of women workers was much in character. Daughter of Irish immigrants, wife of an ironmolder, sometime teacher and seamstress, Mother Jones had entered the labor scene in the 1870s after losing her husband and children to a yellow fever epidemic. In the outspoken role she fashioned for herself—defender of working men, mobilizer of wives, protector of children, and patron saint of the miners—Jones earned her reputation as "mother of the laboring class." "She fights their battles with a Mother's Love," explained a reporter who trailed Mother Jones on a march to protest child labor in 1903. "[She] sacrifices herself for them, complains of no hardship." Mother Jones's maternal aggression was a unique contribution to the labor struggle. Like the working men she organized, she believed that women and children should be protected from the abuses of industrial life. Neither, she contended, should work in mills, mines, and factories. But Mother Jones was not the only woman to investigate the plight of women workers.

During the progressive era, several middle-class women embarked on similar assignments. Some—among them Elizabeth Butler and Mary Van Kleeck—conducted scholarly inquiries into conditions of women's wage earning in various industries. Vassar historian Lucy Maynard Salmon extensively questioned servants and employers for a major study of domestic employment. Others sought to study female labor by joining the work force themselves. These middle-class reporters intended to serve, as one of them put it, as "a mouthpiece for the woman labourer," on the assumption that women workers were unable or unwilling to speak for themselves. They also hoped to discover and reveal the mentality of the woman worker.

Toward this end, in 1903, Bessie Van Vorst and her sister-in-law, Marie Van Vorst, assumed the roles of undercover agents in working-class territory. Marie worked in a Massachusetts shoe factory and then as a spooler in southern cotton mills. Adopting a disguise and an alias, Bessie Van Vorst spent nine months in various factory jobs, and finally worked as a bottler in a Pittsburgh pickle factory. Her job was to stuff the pickles into jars, cork, label, load, and haul. Although critical of working conditions and of discrimination against women workers, Van Vorst also criticized the workers themselves. First, women workers did not seem to be especially ambitious or adept; indeed, Van Vorst herself was immediately recognized by her forewoman as an unusually bright and able worker. Moreover, she contended, there were significant differences in motivation between male and female workers, even in the same plant. All of the men in the pickle factory were "breadwinners," whereas the women were only in part self-supporting. Some contributed to family income, others worked only for "pin money" or to buy themselves clothes. Van Vorst's working girls were hardly committed, whether to pickle bottling, personal advancement, or proletarian causes.

Another undercover woman investigator, Dorothy Richardson, also adopted the role of a "working girl," living in a cheap New York boardinghouse and finding jobs in local factories. Like the Women's Trade Union League (WTUL), Richardson decided that working women would have to unionize before their lot would improve. But like Bessie Van Vorst, she was also critical of the working girls' attitudes. The young woman wage earner, said Richardson, was "relatively undeveloped as a wage-earning unit." Indeed, she failed as a wage earner because she had "an instinctive antagonism to her task" and was unable to cope with factory life. If she was exploited, it was because she had never learned to "work," only to "be worked," and because of some vital defect in her character. "At the present time," said Richardson, "there is nobody so little concerned about her condition as the working woman herself . . . apathetic, patient, long suffering."

The alleged problem of apathy, passivity, and disinterest to which Richardson pointed had many implications. Because of these qualities, the woman factory worker was seen as both a victim and a menace—to herself, to other workers, and to society at large. Because she was easily exploited, she was always associated with the lowering of wages in whatever industry she entered and with the consequent demeaning of the work that she did. Even more to the point, it was widely suspected that she displaced male workers by her willingness to work for less. New machinery, moreover, seemed to enhance her opportunities. In most instances, of course, machinery simply provided more work for men. But in some trades, such as the shoe industry, mechanization enabled more women to move into factory jobs. Between 1870 and 1910, the proportion of shoe workers who were women increased fivefold. Shoemaking was, by now, no longer a craft but an assembly-line process, in which machine operators could be quickly trained.

The "progress" of women in industry therefore seemed linked, inexorably, to the degradation of work and the unemployment of men. The woman worker, through no fault of her own, was in a double bind. Government reports on women in industry reflected this bind. "A generation ago, women were allowed to enter but few occupations," said the commissioner of labor in 1889, "but now there are hundreds of vocations in which they can find employment." Explaining the "vast extension of opportunity," the commissioner presented low wages as a female advantage. "Whenever any industrial occupations are simplified to such an extent that the weaker person can perform what was done of old by the stronger one, the cheaper labor comes in." Women may have lowered wages in the industries they entered, he pointed out, but they earned more than they could before. "In so far as women have displaced men, they have taken advantage of opportunities which were not open to them before such displacement. . . . They are now earning something where formerly they could earn little or nothing."

A special commission's investigation at the turn of the century also supported the theory that women displaced men in industrial jobs. And in her 1910 report on the condition of women and children wage earners for the U.S. Senate, labor historian Helen Sumner assessed the shift of women's work from home to factory with ambivalence. From one point of view, women had advanced by entering industry. "Their unpaid services have been transformed into paid services . . . their ranges of possible employment have increased." On the other hand, the woman wage earner was a liability, a source of problems as well as a sign of progress. "The story of women's work in gainful employments is a story of . . . long hours, low wages, unsanitary conditions, over work, and the want on the part of the woman of training, skill, and vital interest in her work," concluded Sumner. "It is a story of monotonous machine labor. . . . It is a story, moreover, of underbidding, of strikebreaking, of the lowering of standards for [male] breadwinners."

The working woman had not really displaced men, as government reports contended. Rather, most women wage earners filled gaps in the expanding industrial sector by taking "new" jobs—unskilled jobs that men had never held, jobs that multiplied in profusion. Nor is it clear that women wage earners lowered the standards for male "breadwinners," since women were concentrated in certain industries and job categories. By entering the work force, however, they did increase the labor supply and thereby contribute to a general lowering of wages for all workers. By the same token, immigrant men, who entered the work force in yet larger numbers, contributed even more to the lowering of wages. In fact, since women were crowded into certain industries, they tended to lower wages for each other more than for male workers.

But the threat posed by the "factory girl" to the male "breadwinner" was still very real. Not only were women willing to work for low wages, not only were they available in large numbers, but they were usually passive and tractable as employees. Regarding industrial work as a temporary occupation, young women did not seem to see themselves as permanent members of the labor force and were less likely than men to start protests, strikes, or labor organizations. This only increased their threat to the working man. As a result, local and national unions, run by skilled men, tended to view the woman worker with suspicion.

The Union Experience

Although women workers participated in many labor protests in the post-Civil War era, these strikes—of cigar makers, seamstresses, laundresses, and textile workers—were usually local actions and responses to particular situations, rather than efforts to establish permanent labor organizations. Nor were they very successful. Women textile workers in Fall River, for instance, who protested wage cuts and struck three mills in 1875, mobilized effectively and persuaded men to join them. But eight months later, the starving strikers returned to work, accepted wage cuts, and signed oaths not to join a union. Strike leaders were blacklisted. Another factor compounded the impotence of women workers in labor confrontations. National crafts unions, formed and run by skilled male workers, did not welcome women. In 1890, only two national unions admitted women and the vast majority of women workers were unorganized. By the turn of the century, only 3.3 percent of women in industry were in unions; and during the next decade, their numbers dropped. The surge of organization among garment workers after the shirtwaist strike of 1909 began to turn the tide, but union membership rose very slowly. In 1920, women were 20 percent of the work force but under 8 percent of organized workers.

Unions not only lacked interest in organizing women but also consistently tried to exclude them, both from their ranks and from the work force entirely. Unionists had their own rationale. According to male craftsmen, female labor in industry was, variously, a temporary phenomenon, an unfortunate necessity, a capitalist plot, and an insult to women. It was also, explicitly, a threat to themselves. To the skilled worker, who felt his job endangered by cheap female labor, the woman worker took on an aura of menace. "Wherever she goes," a union leader told a government commission in 1900, "she is reducing [man's] wages, and wherever large numbers of women are employed in any occupation, the point will be reached where woman gets as much as a man by making man's wages as low as a woman's." To the working man, the entry of women would drive down wages for everyone in an industry and even drive men out of the work force. Moreover, craftsmen associated the very arrival of women workers with the introduction of machines that foreshadowed their own obsolescence.

As a result of these fears, by no means unjustified, union men supported the domestic ideal. "Woman was created to be man's companion," argued an official of the National Labor Union in the 1860s, "to be the presiding deity of the home circle . . . to guide the tottering footsteps of tender infancy." The policy of the NLU, made up of skilled craftsmen, set the tone for labor's stance in the decades to come. First, the NLU leaders put the blame for female competition not directly on women but on the employers who hired them—"the worst enemies of our race, the shylocks of the age, the robbers of women's virtue." Second, the Union argued that women should get equal pay for equal work. This was an earnest but double-faced plea. Were women to receive equal pay, there would be less reason to employ them at all. In that event, men—who were preferable as workers—would get all the jobs, and women would be excluded from the labor force.

Unorganized women workers could not contest this barrage of arguments. But throughout the late nineteenth century, spokeswomen from feminist and labor ranks disputed the reality of the domestic ideal and defended women's need to work. "The old idea, that all men support all women, is an absurd fiction," reformer and writer Caroline Dall claimed in 1860. In 1869, when Susan B. Anthony urged women typographers (who had been excluded from the typographers union) to break strikes, she stressed the right of women to earn wages. "I perfectly agree that women should be married," she answered a unionist who claimed that woman's true role lay outside typography. "The real fact of life is that women have to support themselves." The leading woman organizer of the Knights of Labor, Leonora Barry, echoed the argument. "I believe it was intended that man should be the breadwinner," she wrote in 1889. "But as that is impossible under present conditions, I believe women should have every opportunity to become proficient in whatever vocation they choose."

The Knights of Labor, which was active in the 1870s and 1880s, was an exception in the unionist crusade against women workers. This national union had 50,000 women members and 113 all-women locals. Moreover, it attempted to organize unskilled women workers, blacks, and immigrants. The Knights' Woman's Bureau was headed by Barry, an Irish immigrant, widowed mother, and former hosiery worker from upstate New York. When she retired in 1889, after a successful career, Knights of Labor president Terence B. Powderly resented her departure with much the same rage that Garrison had voiced against the Grimkes when they left the fold in 1837. As she left, Barry recommended the abolition of the bureau she had run. "The time when we should separate the interests of the toiling masses on sex lines is past," she explained. But Leonora Barry's hopes for the unity of labor made little headway. After 1886, moreover, the Knights of Labor lost influence, and the American Federation of Labor surged to the forefront of union leadership.

Representing skilled workingmen, native-born and nativist, the AFL grew steadily from the 1890s to the 1920s, when it had over 4 million members. An exponent of the domestic ideal, the AFL adopted a position toward women that was, in practice, profoundly ambivalent, as labor historian Alice Kessler-Harris has shown. To the AFL leadership, women were weak, helpless, and easily exploited and therefore a dangerous threat to workingmen. Committed to extracting equal pay for women, the AFL wanted to make them less desirable as employees and get them out of the labor force. The federation hired a few women organizers, such as Mary Kenny in 1892 and Annie Fitzgerald in 1908, but its primary goal was to protect male members. As a result, it urged women to organize, on the one hand, and to stay home, on the other.

This "double-edged sword," as Kessler-Harris calls it, was waved by AFL leaders with consummate skill. One tactic was to deny the need of women to work. "In our time, and at least in our country, generally speaking," AFL president Gompers told the *Ladies Home Journal* in 1905, "there is no necessity of the wife contributing to the support of the family by working." Patently false, such statements also evaded the fact that daughters rather than wives filled up the ranks of women in industry. An even more effective technique was to depict the working class as a huge family. "It is the so-called competition of the unorganized, defenceless woman worker, the girl and the wife, that often tends to reduce the wages of the father and husband," said Gompers. The working woman, as an AFL spokesman told a government commission in 1900, "is competing with the man who is her father and husband, or who is to become her husband." In unionist rhetoric, the working girl became a saboteur of the home. "Is it a pleasing indication of progress to see the father, the brother, and the son displaced as the breadwinner by the mother, sister, and daughter?" asked a craft union leader in the *American Federationist* in 1897. He then answered his own question with a devastating tirade:

The growing demand for female labor is not founded upon philanthropy . . . it does not spring from the milk of human kindness. It is an insidious assault upon the home; it is the knife of the assassin, aimed at the family circle. . . . We can no longer afford to brush away with an impulse of mock gallantry the terrible evil that is threatening the land, the community, the home.

The hostility of male unionists to female labor, as epitomized by the AFL, was effective. Unable either to organize or to stop working, women sometimes formed "protective associations," which were mutual benefit societies rather than unions or bargaining agents. In the 1880s, women reformers created a network of "Working Girls' Clubs," which sought to supply a wholesome environment and foster self-improvement. But these were not unions either, and they faded away in the 1890s. Meanwhile, since barred from most skilled work, women continued to gravitate toward the textile industry and the garment trade. The shirtwaist strike of 1909 reflected this gravitation. Indeed, the clothing industry provided a prime exception to women's inability to organize, as demonstrated by the waistmakers. But two factors made the shirtwaist strike and the organization of women garment workers unique. One was the personnel. A large proportion of garment workers were Jewish immigrant women who were able to capitalize on a sense of ethnic solidarity and a tradition of militancy. These pervaded the non-wage-earning sector as well. In 1902, for instance, Jewish housewives had organized effective boycotts of kosher meat markets in New York and other eastern cities. Another factor was the New York branch of the WTUL and its well-to-do "allies," eager to demonstrate female solidarity. Successful in this effort, the league mobilized impressive support for the waistmakers. Although defeated in its ultimate goals, the shirtwaist strike inspired further labor activism. It also provided what league members called a "training ground" for women who later became organizers.

The training ground theme was prominent, since the WTUL saw itself as an educator. The league hoped not only to spur women's unions but also to train working-class women for labor leadership. It made strides on both counts. By 1910, women workers had been organized in a variety of trades, including bookbinding, tobacco manufacture, laundries, and some textile mills, and a dozen national unions were admitting women. But the extent of organization was never adequate. As a result, the WTUL eventually sponsored a combination of vocational training and protective legislation.

Protective laws were intended to ensure the welfare of working women by limiting their hours, raising their wages, and providing improved working conditions. To advocates, such laws would serve as a substitute for unionization, offering women the benefits that unions had failed to provide. Although only nominally supported by male unions, the laws also offered an ideal way to achieve goals long endorsed by the AFL. By limiting working hours and insisting on minimum wages, protective laws could take away the woman worker's major assets—cheapness and exploitability. Moreover, protective laws could also be used to keep women out of all kinds of work that might be viewed as injurious to their health, morals, or reproductive capacity. As a craft union leader in the cigar industry observed in 1879, "We cannot drive the female out of the trade but we can restrict [her] through factory laws." Protective legislation signified both the failure of women's unionization and the tenacity of the domestic ideal.

Curiously, a state supreme court invalidated one of the first such laws, an 1881 statute banning women from working in places that sold alcohol. The law, said the court, violated the state constitution by depriving women of a vocation open to men. But subsequent laws were upheld. Massachusetts led the way with an 1887 law limiting women's working day to ten hours, and during the 1890s, other states followed. By 1914, twenty-seven states regulated women's working hours, and by the 1920s, fifteen states had minimum wage laws. Between 1908 and World War I, a peak of progressive achievement, many states enacted new protective laws or made earlier measures more rigorous. Besides regulating wages or hours or both, such laws might prevent women from working at night, carrying heavy weights, working in dangerous places, such as mines, or in morally hazardous places, such as bars. Indeed, many trades were now found unsuitable for women. The growth of protective legislation was propelled by the 1908 Supreme Court case of *Muller* v. *Oregon,* a case concerning a woman laundry worker whose employer was arrested for forcing her to work overtime in violation of the state's ten-hour law. The woman herself was not a party to the case. Contending that "sex is a valid basis for classification," the Court upheld the Oregon law and thereby endorsed protective legislation. As an AFL columnist contended in 1900, "female labor should be limited so as not to injure the motherhood and family life of a nation."

The enactment of protective legislation had several effects. In many cases, the laws *did* protect women's health, improve their working conditions, limit their hours, and raise their wages—the goal of reformers who supported them. (To be sure, in states that limited working hours without the benefit of minimum wages, women workers lost ground.) Protective laws also narrowed women's employment opportunities—the goal of male unionists and concerned citizens, who feared the effect of women's work on society. As a result, the laws provoked an ideological feud among politicized women that continued through the 1920s. Socialists, for instance, who strove for class unity, thought that *all* workers, not just women, should be protected by law. Some feminists, who denied that sex was a valid basis for classification, decried the laws. As Susan B. Anthony had explained early on, they set women apart from men. Social reformers—such as the earnest advocates in the WTUL—devoted to women's welfare, supported the laws in order to protect women workers from exploitation. And women unionists, ever pragmatic, supported them too, though as something of a last resort. Labor leader Fannia Cohen, for instance, who criticized unions for not treating women equally, endorsed protective laws in the 1920s. "Considering that women are not as yet organized into trade unions," she contended, "it would be folly to agitate against such laws."

With or without the laws, in fact, male bastions within the industrial work force successfully resisted feminization. This was not the case elsewhere on the labor market. During the late nineteenth century, as business and trade expanded, women moved into other categories of new jobs, in offices and stores. A cut above domestic and factory work, such white-collar jobs drew middle-class women into the labor force. But like her counterpart in industry, the white-collar worker tended to be young, temporary, and crowded into her occupation.

Office, Store, and Classroom

The feminization of clerical work and teaching by the turn of the century reflected the vast growth of business and public education. It also reflected limited opportunities elsewhere. Throughout the nineteenth century, stereotyping of work by sex had restricted women's employment. Since job options were limited, any field that admitted women could attract a surplus of applicants willing to work for less pay than men would have received. The entry of women into such fields—whether grammar school teaching or office work—drove down wages. This in turn spurred male workers to seek more profitable opportunities elsewhere. The low status of occupations dominated by women resulted from the low pay that accompanied feminization.

Domestic work was the ultimate feminized occupation. It was such undesirable low-paid work that men never sought it and women tried to avoid it as well. By 1900, more women were employed in offices, stores, and classrooms than as domestics. The feminization of clerical work and teaching had much in common. Both fields provided new jobs—that is, business and public education were areas of rapid expansion. In both the private sector and the public sector, the cheaper labor of women made them desirable employees. Both fields employed native-born women, not immigrant daughters, especially at the outset. Indeed these new jobs attracted new women into the labor force—middle-class young women with the requisite skills. Positions were refused to those whose accent or appearance might be inappropriate. In neither field, finally, was there organized opposition to the hiring of women such as that provided in industry by male craft unions. The feminization of teaching and office work did *not* threaten large numbers of men with the loss of desirable, permanent jobs. Men did not view grammar school teaching or clerking as prime arenas for achievement. They were more like *rites de passage*, or first jobs, for young men on their way up to better things. By 1900, expanding opportunities for men reduced their interest in low-paid clerkships or grammar school posts. The combination of better male options elsewhere and the growth of business and education paved a golden path for female employment.

Women first took office jobs during the Civil War, when worthy widows of Union officers received posts in government offices, at lower pay than the men they replaced. Jobs opened up in the private sector, too. During the 1860s, for instance, women bookkeepers were hired at one-third the pay of men. By the 1870s, women *were* competing with men for office jobs in the private sector as clerks and stenographers, with considerable advantages. Not only could they be hired at half men's pay but also they had no expectations of constant promotions and higher salaries, as men did. Since office bureaucracies grew rapidly, few men were deprived of work. Improved technology, meanwhile, created new jobs for women. The introduction of the typewriter, a term also used for the person who typed on it, proved a special boon. By the 1890s, the new machines were widely used. Business schools now trained women as "typewriters," stenographers, and bookkeepers. (The steno-typist had far more skills than the worker she replaced, the copyist.) Half the nation's women high school graduates completed business programs. By 1890, a majority of high school graduates *were* women, which provided a large pool of potential employees.

Women's entry into office work took on huge proportions. In 1870, women were only about 3 percent of office workers, but by 1890, they were 17 percent. During World War I, women became omnipresent as clerks, stenographers, copyists, typists, and bookkeepers. They also worked as sales clerks in retail stores—another outpost of business expansion. Between 1870 and 1900 the number of women sales clerks multiplied tenfold. Finally, rising options in commerce and trade were again enhanced by improved technology, namely, the telegraph and the telephone. Although men, or rather boys, were the first phone operators, women who would work for half their pay soon held a share of the jobs. By 1890, all daytime operators were women.

Like other women wage earners, those at typewriters, switchboards, and store counters tended to be young and to view themselves as temporary wage earners. But since they were better educated than women in industry, they considered themselves as an elite among women employees. An office worker might earn no more than a skilled garment worker, but the work itself was more regular, "dignified" and desirable. Women viewed the world of commerce as a new frontier of female employment. The editor of the New York *Business Woman's Journal* reminded her readers in 1889 to acquire proper manners so as not to "destroy the good opinion women had earned" and to "make a place for others." As more young women entered office work, the field was reshaped to suit domestic ideals. A sexual division of labor in business transformed office work into service work—or "women's work." A man entering business was expected to be ambitious, aggressive, and competitive, so as to rise in the ranks; but not so the woman office worker. She was expected instead to be neat, clean, agreeable, and useful to others—qualities that would later suit her for home life as well.

In teaching, women had made inroads even earlier. By the Civil War, one out of four teachers was a woman, who earned at most half the salary of a male teacher. When the army advertised for teachers in southern freedmen's schools in 1865, it offered half pay for the same positions as men. Nonetheless, women dominated the ranks of freedmen's teachers and took over many jobs in the common schools as well. After the war, the availability of women candidates willing to work for low pay and the vast growth of public education ensured rapid feminization of the teaching profession. In 1870, 90 percent of professional women were teachers, and two out of three grammar school teachers were women. The proportion of teachers who were women expanded most rapidly in the 1870s and continued to grow thereafter. By the turn of the century, two out of three professional women were teachers and three out of four teachers were women. In cities this percentage was even higher.

The teacher's status as a "professional" has to be qualified. During the late nineteenth century, the young woman teacher was likely to have no more than a sixth- or eighth-grade education herself. She taught, as a rule, only at the primary school level; secondary education was dominated by men. The quality of her preparation and the nature of her work were illustrated in the experience of future suffrage leader Anna Howard Shaw in Michigan during the Civil War.

Shaw's first job was not too different from those of most young women teachers, especially in rural areas, for the rest of the century. "When I was fifteen years old I was offered a situation as schoolteacher," she wrote in her memoirs.

By this time the community was growing around us with the rapidity of these western settlements, and we had nearer neighbors whose children needed instruction. I passed an examination before a school board consisting of three nervous and self-conscious men whose certificate I still hold, and I at once began my professional career on the modest salary of two dollars a week and my board. The school was four miles from my home so I "boarded round" with the families of my pupils. . . . During the first year I had about fourteen pupils, of varying ages, sizes, and temperaments, and there was hardly a book in the schoolroom except those I owned.

As Shaw's experience suggests, even young women of modest means could aspire to teach, since little training was required—but only if they were single. Like other working women, teachers were expected to leave their jobs at marriage, and school boards often mandated that they do so. Beyond spinsterhood, prerequisites were few, at least until the twentieth century, when teachers began to be required to have special training and pass licensing exams. But since teaching was the only profession women could enter in any numbers, college graduates flocked to it also. During the 1880s, when the first generation of women graduated from college, teaching absorbed two out of three of those who sought employment.

Finally, teaching was an opportunity for black women, to whom other white-collar occupations were closed. The establishment of a black public school system in the South drew black women into the classroom. By the turn of the century, they were the mainstays of impoverished rural primary schools throughout the region; black school systems were so underfunded that their teachers received only a fraction of what white teachers earned. The preparation of black teachers was as varied as that of white contemporaries. At one extreme was the example of Susie King Taylor, who had received some rudimentary training as a slave and supported herself through Reconstruction as a teacher. At the other was that of distinguished educators such as Fannie Jackson Coppin, also born a slave, who graduated from Oberlin College in 1865 and went on to head the "female department" of the Philadelphia Institute for Colored Youth. During the progressive era, women teachers played a special role in the black community. Some, such as Lucy Lainey, Nannie Burroughs, and Mary McLeod Bethune, founded educational institutions, often supported by black and white philanthropy. These schools were a source of pride; the South had few black secondary schools. In addition, teaching provided more black women than men with professional work or at least skilled vocations. As a result, black families went to greater efforts to educate daughters than sons, reversing the priorities of white families.

When suffrage leader Carrie Chapman Catt assessed women's progress in the professions in 1900, she proclaimed that "No occupation illustrates more clearly the immensity of the changes wrought than teaching." Although Catt pointed out that higher positions in the field were reserved for men and that women teachers always received lower pay, her emphasis was on progress—on the "rapidity with which conditions have changed in the last fifty years . . . the constantly increasing demand of women for work, the decrease of prejudice against the woman worker . . . the opening of nearly all occupations to women." In 1903, Charlotte Perkins Gilman similarly celebrated women's advances over the past century as "a phenomenon unparalleled in history." Never before, announced Gilman, "has so large a mass made as much progress in so short a time."

From the penniless dependent to the wholly self-supporting and often other-supporting business woman, is a long step, but she has taken it. She who knew so little is now the teacher; she who could do so little is now the efficient and varied producer; she who cared only for her own flesh and blood is now active in all wide good works around the world. She who was confined to the house now travels free, the foolish has become wise and the timid brave.

Such celebration, however, rested on a distorted vision of women in the past as variously idle, inactive, dim, meek, or ineffective. It also ignored the strange ambivalence of women's employment. For the vast majority of white wage-earning women, "progress" meant movement into new, exploitative types of work, whether in industry, classrooms, or offices. This was work that became underpaid when women assumed it and work that was assumed, for the most part, by the least powerful members of society—young women and poor women. Black women, meanwhile, and white women as well continued to take even less desirable work as domestic servants or in related menial jobs. In either case, the woman wage earner was less liberated by her employment than proletarianized, though reluctant to assume a working-class identity. The pattern of female employment set before 1900, finally, continued to characterize the labor market for decades to come. In the early twentieth century, as in 1860, women's low rank as workers reflected the pervasive belief that their true vocation was at home. A cultural emblem, the domestic ideal relegated women wage earners to second-class status in economic life.

The domestic ideal also affected the roles of middle- and upper-class women, who were better able to capitalize on it. During the late nineteenth century, while thousands of women entered the bottom realms of the labor market, women also entered colleges, the professions, and large, new women's associations. A generation of organizers and institution builders, they expanded the boundaries of "home" to include the nation.

ᥱᔦᓕ

SUGGESTED READINGS AND SOURCES

CHAPTER 9

For the WTUL version of the shirtwaist strike, see Alice Henry, *The Trade Union Woman* (New York, 1915); Helen Marot, "A Woman's Strike: An Appreciation of the Shirt-waist Makers of New York," *Proceedings of the Academy of Political Science* (New York, 1910), pp.

122–125; and "The League and the Strike of the Thirty Thousand," *Annual Report of the Women's Trade Union League of New York, 1909–1910* (New York, 1910). Charles S. Bernheimer, *The Shirtwaist Strike* (New York, 1910), was written by a University Settlement social worker while negotiations were in progress. Theresa S. Malkiel, *The Diary of a Shirtwaist Striker* (New York, 1910), a socialist account, criticizes the WTUL role in the strike. The *New York Call*, a socialist weekly, gave the strike sympathetic coverage (November 24, 1909–February 15, 1910).

　　Several recent histories describe the strike: Philip S. Foner, *Women and the American Labor Movement* (New York, 1979), ch. 18; Barbara Meyer Wertheimer, *We Were There: The Story of Working Women in America* (New York, 1977), ch. 16; and Meredith Tax, *The Rising of the Women: Feminist Solidarity and Class Conflict, 1880–1917* (New York, 1980), ch. 8. For the history of the garment trade and the early years of the International Ladies Garment Workers' Union see Louis Levine, *The Women's Garment Worker* (New York, 1924). Nancy Schrom Dye examines the role of the New York WTUL in *As Equals and Sisters: The Labor Movement and the Women's Trade Union League of New York* (Columbia, Mo., 1980). An older history of the WTUL is Gladys Boone, *The Women's Trade Union League in Great Britain and the United States* (New York, 1942). For the disaster at the Triangle shirtwaist factory, see Leon Stein, *The Triangle Fire* (New York, 1962).

CHAPTER 10

Alice Kessler Harris provides an overview of women's roles in the labor force in *Out to Work: A History of Wage-Earning Women in America* (New York, 1982), chs. 4–8. See also Robert Smuts, *Women and Work in America* (New York, 1959); Barbara Meyer Wertheimer, *We Were There: The Story of Working Women in America* (New York, 1977); Julie A. Matthaei, *An Economic History of Women in America* (New York, 1982); Lynn Y. Weiner, *From Working Girl to Working Mother: The Female Labor Force in the United States, 1820–1980* (Chapel Hill, N.C., 1985); and Claudia Goldin, *Understanding the Gender Gap: An Economic History of American Women* (New York, 1990).

　　For primary sources, see W. Elliott Brownlee and Mary N. Brownlee, eds., *Women and the American Economy: A Documentary History* (New York, 1976), and Rosalyn Baxandall, Linda Gordon, and Susan Reverby, eds., *America's Working Women: A Documentary History from 1600 to the Present* (New York, 1976). Collections of articles on working women and labor organization include Milton Cantor and Bruce Laurie, eds., *Class, Sex, and the Woman Worker* (Westport, Conn., 1977), and Ruth Milkman, ed., *Women, Work, and Protest: A Century of U.S. Labor History* (Boston, 1985).

　　Mary Elizabeth Massey surveys women's roles in the Civil War era in *Bonnet Brigades: American Women and the Civil War* (New York, 1966). For recent research, see Catherine Clinton and Nina Silber, eds., *Divided Houses: Gender and the Civil War* (New York, 1992). The origins of nursing are discussed in Susan M. Reverby, *Ordered to Care: The Dilemma of American Nursing, 1850–1945* (Cambridge, Mass., and New York, 1987); Ann Douglas, "The War Within a War: Women Nurses in the Union Army," *Civil War History*, 18 (1972), 197–212; and Jane E. Schultz, "The Inhospitable Hospital: Gender and Professionalism in Civil War Medicine," *Signs*, 17 (Winter 1992), 363–392. Jeanie Attie explores women's response to the ideology of the U.S. Sanitary Commission in "Warwork and the Crisis of Domesticity in the North" in Clinton and Silber, eds., *Divided Houses*, pp. 247–259. The experience of Confederate women is examined in George C. Rable, *Women and the Crisis of Southern Nationalism* (Urbana, Ill., 1989); Ann Firor Scott, *The Southern Lady* (Chicago, 1970), chs. 4 and 5; and Drew Gilpin Faust, "Altars of Sacrifice: Confederate Women and the Narratives of War," *Journal of American History*, 76 (March 1990), 1200–

1228. Clarence Mohr discusses women's work on plantations in *On the Threshold of Freedom: Masters and Slaves in Civil War Georgia* (Athens, Ga., 1986), ch. 7. For women's work in the freedmen's schools, see Henry L. Swint, *The Northern Teacher in the South* (Nashville, Tenn., 1941), and Jacqueline Jones, *Soldiers of Light and Love: Northern Teachers and Georgia Blacks, 1865–1873* (Chapel Hill, N.C., 1980).

Jacqueline Jones surveys black women's experience in this era in *Labor of Love, Labor of Sorrow* (New York, 1986), chs. 2–5. Leon Litwack examines the impact of emancipation in *Been in the Storm so Long: The Aftermath of Slavery* (New York, 1979). Sociologist Susan A. Mann explores the transition from slave labor to sharecropping in "Slavery, Sharecropping, and Sexual Equality," *Signs,* 14 (Summer 1989), 774–798. For the black family after slavery, see Herbert M. Gutman, *The Black Family in Slavery and Freedom, 1750–1925* (New York, 1977); Gutman, "Persistent Myths About the Afro-American Family," *Journal of Interdisciplinary History,* 6 (Autumn 1975), 181–210; Frank F. Furstenberg, Jr., Theodore Hershberg, and John Modell, "The Origin of the Female-Headed Black Family: The Impact of the Urban Experience," *Journal of Interdisciplinary History,* 6 (Autumn 1975), 211–234; and Elizabeth Pleck, "The Two-Parent Household: Black Family Structure in Late Nineteenth-Century Boston," *Journal of Social History,* 6 (Fall 1972), 1–31. For urban migration, see Florette Henri, *Black Migration: Movement North, 1900–1920* (New York, 1976); Elizabeth Pleck, *Black Migration and Poverty, Boston, 1865–1900* (New York, 1979); and James Grossman, *Land of Hope: Chicago, Black Southerners, and the Great Migration* (Chicago, 1989). Black women's roles as wage earners are discussed in Claudia Golden, "Female Labor Force Participation: The Origin of Black and White Differences," *Journal of Economic History,* 37 (March 1977), 87–108, and Elizabeth Pleck, "A Mother's Wages: Income Earned Among Married Italian and Black Women, 1896–1914," in Michael Gordon, ed., *The American Family in Social and Historical Perspective,* 2d ed. (New York, 1978), pp. 490–510. For black and white women in poverty, see Jacqueline Jones, *The Dispossessed: America's Underclasses from the Civil War to the Present* (New York, 1992), which focuses on the outmigration of Southerners in the twentieth century.

For women's work on family farms, see Nancy Grey Osterud, *Bonds of Community: The Lives of Farm Women in Nineteenth-Century New York* (Ithaca, N.Y., 1991), and Deborah Fink, *Agrarian Women: Wives and Mothers in Rural Nebraska, 1880–1940* (Chapel Hill, N.C., 1992). Women's work roles in the post-Civil War West are discussed in Sandra L. Myres, *Westering Women and the Frontier Experience, 1800–1915* (Albuquerque, N. Mex., 1982); Lillian Schlissel, ed., *Western Women: Their Land, Their Lives* (Albuquerque, N. Mex., 1988); and Glenda Riley, *A Place to Grow: Women in the American West* (Arlington Heights, Ill., 1992), section 4. For Mexican American women's labor in the late nineteenth and early twentieth centuries, see Sarah Deutsch, *No Separate Refuge: Culture, Class, and Gender on an Anglo Hispanic Frontier in the American Southwest, 1880–1940* (New York, 1987); Albert Camarillo, *Chicanos in a Changing Society: From Mexican Pueblos to American Barrios in Santa Barbara and Southern California, 1848–1940* (Cambridge, Mass., 1979); and Mario T. Garcia, "The Chicana in American History: The Mexican Women of El Paso, 1880–1920: A Case Study," *Pacific Historical Review,* 49 (May 1980), 315–337.

David M. Katzman examines household servants from 1870 to World War I in *Seven Days a Week: Women and Domestic Service in Industrializing America* (New York, 1978). For prostitution see Ruth Rosen, *The Lost Sisterhood: Prostitution in America 1900–1918* (Baltimore, Md., 1982); Marion S. Goldman, *Gold Diggers and Silver Miners: Prostitution and Social Life on the Comstock Lode* (Ann Arbor, Mich., 1981); Barbara Meil Hobson, *Uneasy Virtue: The Politics of Prostitution and the American Reform Tradition* (New York, 1987); Anne M. Butler, *Daughters of Joy, Sisters of Misery: Prostitutes in the American West, 1865–1890* (Urbana, Ill., 1985); Timothy Gilfoyle, *City of Eros: New York City, Prostitution, and the*

Commercialization of Sex, 1790–1920 (New York, 1992); and Lucie Cheng Hurata, "Chinese Immigrant Women in Nineteenth-Century California," in Carol Ruth Berkin and Mary Beth Norton, eds., *Women of America: A History* (New York, 1979), pp. 223–244. Estelle Freedman discusses the treatment of prostitutes in *Their Sisters' Keepers: Prison Reform in America 1830–1930* (Ann Arbor, Mich., 1981). See also Marc Thomas Connelly, *The Response to Prostitution in the Progressive Era* (Chapel Hill, N.C., 1980), and Ruth Rosen and Sue Davidson, eds., *The Maimie Papers* (Old Westbury, N.Y., 1977).

Recent studies of immigrant and working-class women include Virginia Yans McLaughlin, *Family and Community: Italian Immigrants in Buffalo, 1880–1930* (Ithaca, N.Y., 1977); Hasia R. Diner, *Erin's Daughters in America: Irish Immigrant Women in the Nineteenth Century* (Baltimore, Md., 1983); Elizabeth Ewen, *Immigrant Women in the Land of Dollars: Life and Culture on the Lower East Side, 1880–1925* (New York, 1985); Judith E. Smith, *Family Connections: A History of Italian and Jewish Immigrant Lives in Providence, Rhode Island, 1900–1940* (Albany, N.Y., 1985); Kathy Peiss, *Cheap Amusements: Working Women and Leisure in Turn-of-the-Century New York* (Philadelphia, 1986); Sydney Stahl Weinberg, *The World of Our Mothers: The Lives of Jewish Immigrant Women* (Chapel Hill, N.C., 1988); and Susan A. Glenn, *Daughters of the Shtetl: Life and Labor in the Immigrant Generation* (Ithaca, N.Y., 1990). See also Daniel Walkowitz, "Working Class Women in the Gilded Age: Factory, Community, and Family Life Among Cohoes, New York, Cotton Factory Workers," *Journal of Social History,* 5 (Summer 1972), 464–490; Carol Groneman, "Working-Class Immigrant Women in Mid-Nineteenth-Century New York: The Irish Woman's Experience," *Journal of Urban History,* 4 (May 1978), 255–274; and Tamara Hareven, "Family Time and Industrial Time: Family and Work in a Planned Corporation Town, 1900–1924," *Journal of Urban History,* 1 (May 1975), 365–389. For documents, see Maxine Seller, ed., *Immigrant Women* (Philadelphia, 1980).

Alexander Keyssar examines women's role in the labor market in *Out of Work: The First Century of Unemployment in Massachusetts* (Cambridge, England, and New York, 1986), ch. 4. Leslie Woodcock Tentler discusses early-twentieth-century working-class women in *Wage-Earning Women: Industrial Work and Family Life in the United States, 1900–1930* (New York, 1979). Joanne J. Meyerowitz explores the lives of urban migrants who lived apart from families and employers in *Women Adrift: Independent Female Wage Earners in Chicago, 1880–1930* (Chicago, 1988). Studies of women industrial workers include Joan M. Jensen and Sue Davidson, eds., *A Needle, A Bobbin, a Strike: Women Needleworkers in America* (Philadelphia, 1984); Susan Levine, *Labor's True Woman: Carpet Weavers, Industrialization, and Labor Reform in the Gilded Age* (Philadelphia, 1984); and Patricia A. Cooper, *Once a Cigar Maker: Men, Women, and Work Culture in American Cigar Factories, 1900–1919* (Urbana, Ill., 1987). For the late nineteenth-century shoe industry, see Mary H. Blewett, *We Will Rise in Our Might: Workingwoman's Voices from Nineteenth-Century New England* (Ithaca, N.Y., 1991), part 2.

Alice Kessler Harris analyzes the obstacles to women's labor organization in "Where Are the Organized Female Workers?" *Feminist Studies,* 3 (Fall 1975), 92–110, and in "Organizing the Unorganizable: Three Jewish Women and Their Unions," *Labor History,* 17 (Winter 1976), 5–23. See also James Kenneally, "Women and Trade Unions, 1870–1920: The Quandary of the Reformer," *Labor History,* 14 (Winter 1973), 42–55; Carole Turbin, "And We Are Nothing But Women: Irish Working Women in Troy," Berkin and Norton, eds., *Women of America,* pp. 203–222; and Meredith Tax, *The Rising of the Women,* cited above. Joanne Reitano describes working girls' clubs in "Working Girls Unite," *American Quarterly,* 36 (Spring 1984), 112–184. Philip S. Foner surveys post–Civil War labor organization in *Women and the American Labor Movement from Colonial Times to the Eve of World War I* (New York, 1979), chs. 8–27. For protective laws, see Susan Lehrer, *Origins of*

Protective Labor Legislation for Women, 1905–1925 (Albany, N.Y., 1987); Judith A. Baer, *The Chains of Protection: The Judicial Response to Women's Labor Legislation* (Westport, Conn., 1978); and Joan Hoff, *Law, Gender, and Injustice: A Legal History of U.S. Women* (New York, 1991), ch. 6. Ann Schofield examines gender ideology among unionists in "Rebel Girls and Union Maids: The Woman Question in the Journals of the AFL and IWW, 1905–1920," *Feminist Studies* 9 (Summer 1983), 335–358.

For women's roles in office work and sales work, see Cindy Sondik Aron, *Ladies and Gentlemen of the Civil Service: Middle-Class Workers in Victorian America* (New York, 1987); Margery W. Davies, *Women's Place Is at the Typewriter: Office Work and Office Workers, 1870–1930* (Philadelphia, 1982); Lisa Fine, *The Souls of the Skyscraper: Female Clerical Workers in Chicago, 1870–1930* (Philadelphia, 1990); and Susan Porter Benson, *Countercultures: Saleswomen, Managers, and Customers in American Department Stores, 1890–1940* (Urbana, Ill., 1986). Stephen H. Norwood examines unionization in *Labor's Flaming Youth: Telephone Operators and Worker Militancy, 1878–1923* (Champaign, Ill., 1991).

The woman worker received much attention from women scholars and reporters of the progressive era. See, for example, Edith Abbott, *Women in Industry: A Study in American Economic History* (New York, 1909); Helen Sumner, *History of Women in Industry in the United States* (Washington, D.C., 1910), part of a massive Bureau of Labor study of women and children in the work force; Alice Henry, *The Trade Union Woman* (New York, 1915); and Theresa Wolfson, *The Woman Worker and the Trade Unions* (New York, 1926). Margaret F. Byington examined women's roles in working-class families in *Homestead: The Households of a Mill Town* (Pittsburgh, Pa., 1910). Foundations and endowments supported studies of wage-earning women, such as Mary Van Kleeck's studies for the Russell Sage Foundation, *Women in the Book Binding Trade* (New York, 1913) and *Artificial Flower Makers* (New York, 1913); and Elizabeth Butler, *Women and the Trades: Pittsburgh 1907–1908* (New York, 1909). For the accounts of investigators who impersonated working-class women, see Mrs. John Van Vorst and Marie Van Vorst, *The Woman Who Toils* (New York, 1903), and Dorothy Richardson, *The Long Day: The Story of a New York Working Woman* (New York, 1905). Social worker Mary Ovington, a founder of the NAACP, explored black women's experience in *Half a Man: The Status of the Negro in New York* (New York, 1911).

Autobiographies of prominent women in the labor movement include *The Autobiography of Mother Jones*, ed. Mary Field Parton (Chicago, 1925); Rose Schneiderman, *All for One* (New York, 1967); Agnes Nestor, *Woman's Labor Leader: The Autobiography of Agnes Nestor* (Rockford, Ill., 1954); and Mary Anderson, *Woman at Work* (Minneapolis, Minn., 1951). For the immigrant experience, see Mary Anton, *The Promised Land* (New York, 1912); Rose Cohen, *Out of the Shadows* (New York, 1918); and Elizabeth Hasonovitz, *One of Them* (New York, 1918).

CHAPTER 11

The Founding of Hull-House

"It has always been difficult for the family to regard the daughter otherwise than as a family possession," Jane Addams wrote in 1898, a decade after her escape from home. "But where is the larger life of which she has dreamed so long?" The conflict between the daughter's ambitions, her desire for a "larger life," and her family's demands produced the major crisis of Jane Addams's career, a crisis that held her immobile for almost a decade. Between 1881, when she graduated from college, and 1889, when Hull-House was founded, Jane Addams was caught in a limbo of inactivity and dependence, afflicted by "nervous depression and a sense of maladjustment." The crisis was resolved only when she deserted her family—primarily her stepmother, but also her sisters, brother, and stepbrothers—and moved to Chicago with her friend Ellen Starr. A few months later, they set up a home on the second floor of a dilapidated mansion and created a new vocation.

Settlement work, which meant moving into an urban slum and providing services for the neighborhood residents, was a two-way street of mutual benefits. Obviously, it helped the urban poor, mainly the foreign-born and their children, who received the settlement's services. At the same time, it resolved the problem of the young educated woman, the college graduate, who had no purposeful way to participate in "life," no outlet in which to apply her training, and no way to escape her family's clutch. Replacing what Addams called "the family claim" with a larger, public one, settlement work fused an activist social role with what appeared to be conventional feminine tendencies. (Well-off women, after all, had always helped the poor.) But the "larger life" of which Jane Addams once dreamed in a vague and inchoate way during the 1880s had other distinctive characteristics. It was a life that melded traditional charity with intellectual challenge. It was a life in which she could assume a dominant, leadership role. Finally, it was a life that permanently excluded family demands, both the demands of marriage and, alternatively, the demands that could be imposed on a maiden aunt for the rest of her days. In fact, the settlement itself replaced the family—with a vibrant community of friends and admirers, much like the women who had been in Jane Addams's college class, all of them embarked on a noble enterprise, a vital mission.

A sense of mission reflected Jane Addams's education and her upbringing. Born in 1860 in Cedarville, Illinois, she was the youngest child of a prominent family headed by a much-admired father. Businessman, banker, and Republican politician, John Addams was well known locally as an Illinois state senator. Jane's mother, Sarah, died when she was two, but six years later, a stepmother, Anna Haldeman, took over management of the large family—Jane had three older sisters, an older brother, and two new stepbrothers. Profoundly attached to her eminent father, Jane absorbed John Addams's high ideals and impeccable standards. She also profited from his belief in women's education. John Addams had long endorsed a nearby girls' school, the Rockford Seminary, attended by his older daughters before they got married. More ambitious than her sisters, Jane wanted to attend one of the new, prestigious eastern women's colleges, especially Smith, which opened its doors in the 1870s. But she was ultimately persuaded to put in a year at Rockford, closer to her home and family. Entering the Rockford Seminary in 1877, Jane completed a full course of study there, as her sisters had not. Moreover, she found school a completely invigorating and satisfying experience—an experience she transformed into that of the "college girl." At Rockford, nestled away in another small Illinois town, Jane saw herself as part of the first generation of college women, a cohort she soon came to represent and epitomize.

Rockford was not quite a college when Jane Addams entered, although it was to achieve collegiate status soon after her graduation. But in 1877, it was still in the indeterminate state of "seminary," much like Mount Holyoke, after which it was modeled. Mount Holyoke became an accredited college only in 1888. Rockford viewed itself as a western version of the Massachusetts school. Since its first class entered in 1849, it had built up a reputation as the leading girls' seminary of the area, patronized by families such as the Addamses. The daughters of well-off farmers, businessmen, and eminent citizens might go to school there for a few years before marriage or teaching or missionary work, to which Rockford gave special emphasis. The school's head, Anna Peck Sill, like her prototype, Mary Lyon, was determined to elicit religious conversions and to steer her students into foreign missions. This emphasis was not entirely lost on Jane Addams who, though resistant, later created her own version of mission. But she found other aspects of Rockford life even more to her liking. From 1877 to 1881, she reveled in the identity, activity, and community it provided.

Jane's class at Rockford, no more than two dozen girls, of whom seventeen graduated, viewed themselves as pioneers. The novelty of "college" life, the sense of enjoying "the highest privilege of our time," was inspirational, perhaps all the more so since Rockford was not yet formally a college. Jane's classmates felt an unusual sense of kinship and sorority, both with each other and with girls who were students at eastern schools. Adopting the class name of "breadgivers," they corresponded with their counterparts at Vassar and Smith, introduced rites and rituals like those at the eastern colleges, and cultivated the spirit of innovators. A spirited participant in class events, undeterred by either the rigid school schedule or the requirement that students perform domestic chores, Jane Addams seemed to excel in all facets of Rockford life. Her grades were excellent, she relished her studies in Greek and science, and she joined in the endless discussions about religion that Rockford fostered. She also joined the literary society, edited the school magazine, contributed innumerable essays, excelled at debates, and gave public addresses at many academic ceremonies.

The Rockford experience spurred self-confidence in other ways too. Jane Addams made herself felt as a student leader, admired and sought after by both classmates and faculty. At Rockford, in fact, she began to show the amazing force of personality that would characterize the rest of her life. She developed only one extremely close friendship, with another small-town girl of intellectual bent, Ellen Gates Starr, who was slightly older. When Ellen left Rockford after a year to teach school, they continued the friendship through an intense, devoted correspondence. Jane Addams was somewhat more distant from her classmates (she liked to be called "Miss Addams"), but she retained her role as center of attention as well as an active contributor to the Rockford ethos. This ethos evoked in her all sorts of ambitions—to achieve, excel, influence, serve, and do something significant. Such ambitions were enhanced by her class's sense of contributing to progress and its ceaseless concern over women's roles. At a college debate, Jane championed woman's "potent influence in the age in which she lives," while retaining "the old idea of womanhood—the Saxon lady whose mission it was to give bread unto her household."

Could serving the family and exerting "potent influence" be successfully meshed? At Rockford, as at other early women's colleges, the experience of college was often at odds with college goals, which were themselves ambivalent. Rockford trained its students "to give oneself fully and worthily for the good of others." At the same time, it gave them a chance to study academic subjects, write essays, speak in public, and participate in a women's community. Above all, the school treated its students as valued individuals. It was not quite clear what this type of training was supposed to do, nor what the highly educated woman was supposed to do with her education. Nor was it clear in what ways she was supposed to be different from either her non-college-trained mother or from the male college student of the same generation. But if the purpose of college was vague, the experience was concrete. For Jane Addams, as for hundreds of young women in the 1870s and 1880s, the experience provided a purpose of its own. And it was an experience that she was, eventually, unready to give up.

Many of Jane's classmates at Rockford moved on to marriage, as her older sisters had done, but marriage was a possibility Jane Addams never considered. Instead, during her last days at school, she was full of alternate plans—to attend Smith for a year, to get a degree, to travel in Europe, to study medicine. As soon as she left Rockford and returned to Cedarville, however, she got sick, although her health had been good during her college years. Her illness made departure for Smith less likely. It also marked the start of a downward spiral that soon developed its own momentum. Within a few weeks, just when Jane had started to recover, her father died, most horribly and unexpectedly, of a ruptured appendix. This changed her psychological landscape unalterably. "The greatest sorrow which can ever come to me is past," she wrote to Ellen Starr. "I will not write of myself or how purposeless and without ambition I am." "I shall never be disappointed in you," Ellen wrote back. But Jane Addams became more and more disappointed in herself.

After setting forth in the fall to enroll in the Philadelphia Women's Medical College, accompanied by her stepmother, Anna Haldeman Addams, she got sick again and dropped out of school after a month. There seemed to be something wrong with her spine, the recurrence of an illness that had plagued her childhood. Instead of becoming a doctor, Jane Addams became a patient. Her attentive family provided her with one of the best-regarded remedies of the day, Dr. S. Weir Mitchell's rest cure. This was a special treatment for nervous and "invalid" young women, who, unlike their energetic mothers, were exhausted, depressed, and unable to function. The treatment involved lying in bed for months without company, activity, books, or "stimulation." Jane Addams appeared to survive this enforced passivity fairly well, just as she next survived an operation by her stepbrother, an Iowa doctor, to improve her spine. But she never returned to medical school, and her loss of identity increased. Within a year, she had embarked on a course of false starts, setbacks, sickness, and increasing despair. "Failure in every sense," she wrote in her private notebook.

As the Rockford days receded further and further into the distance, Jane Addams's sense of purposelessness and failure mounted, despite Anna Haldeman Addams's attempts to find remedies. The next attempt was a grand tour of Europe, on which Jane and her stepmother embarked in 1883 with a small party of women friends, trailing from hotel to museum to cathedral to resort. The trip was a success, but it was more of a holding action than a cure. By 1886, Jane was living at home in Baltimore, where Anna had moved to accompany her son George who studied at Johns Hopkins. Here Jane attended teas and lectures, helped Anna entertain, visited charity wards, and cast about for some significant activity. She still felt without "purpose and ambition," as she kept writing to Ellen Starr, now teaching at a fashionable girls' school in Chicago. "I am filled with shame that with all my apparent leisure I have nothing at all to do." Further education by now seemed out of the question. Missionary work, the Rockford goal, had never appealed to her. Teaching, another option, was no more attractive; she had been invited to teach at Rockford, but she gave up after a day. None of the options seemed to cater to the special qualities she had exemplified to her classmates, such as leadership. Nor did remaining in her stepmother's household, subject to what Jane later described as "the family claim."

The family claim offered two options, neither attractive. One was marriage. Anna Haldeman Addams was especially anxious that Jane marry her younger son, George, and pressed her to do so but without any luck. All of the other women in Jane's family had married and had children, except for her sister Martha, who died at seventeen. Jane's mother, Sarah, who had migrated to Illinois as soon as she was married in 1844, had had eight children, three of whom died. Her own death, at age forty-nine, had come just after a ninth child was born and died. Jane's forceful stepmother, Anna, an attractive widow steeped in culture, had had four children, of whom two survived to see her married to John Addams in the 1860s. Jane's oldest and favorite sister, Mary, fifteen years her senior, was married to a not-too-successful Presbyterian minister and had four small children. They lived in a series of Illinois towns. Her next sister, Alice, seven years older than Jane, had married Anna's oldest son, Harry Haldeman (this family preferred insiders to outsiders) and also had a child. But Jane Addams, the youngest child and only college graduate, chose spinsterhood. Although an unspoken choice, it was also a choice she had made early on, perhaps at Rockford, when she became the confidante of Ellen Starr, whose support and affection surpassed what any man could offer.

The rejected option of marriage—or of marrying her own stepbrother and becoming, like Alice, a double daughter—was only one part of the family claim. There were also the roles into which she had fallen, of quasi-invalid daughter and spinster aunt. The first, encouraged by attentive Anna Haldeman Addams, seemed to serve some function as ballast for other family members. The second increased as the family expanded. By the time Jane Addams graduated from Rockford, there were already several households, many nieces and nephews, and plenty of need for a female relative to be available, as Jane sometimes was, as helper and companion. Her family cared for her too, of course. In fact, since Jane had become ill, as her sister Alice later said, she thought "it was her due to be waited upon and petted . . . to be cared for and catered to." But the family needed repayment in kind. Mary was often sick, her children needed attention, and her husband was continually unhappy with his work. He changed posts often, which meant that Mary was always moving the household to another town. Anna also made demands. And Jane's older brother Weber, who lived with his family near Cedarville, had a mental breakdown in 1883, which meant that Jane had to step in, handle his affairs, and arrange for his care. Between 1881 and 1889, while Jane Addams was floundering for purpose or sunk in depression, she was alternating between her two familial roles. It was only during a second European trip, made with Ellen Starr and another friend in 1887–1888, that her undefined but multiple ambitions began to form and fuse.

"It is hard to tell just when the very simple plan which afterward developed into the Settlement began to form itself in my mind," Jane Addams wrote in 1910.

It may have been even before I went to Europe for the second time, but I gradually became convinced that it would be a good thing to rent a house in a part of the city where many primitive and actual needs are found, in which young women who had been given over too exclusively for study might restore a balance of activity along traditional lines and learn of life from life itself; where they might try out some of the things they had been taught.

According to Addams's reminiscences, she had been "irresistibly drawn to the poor quarters of each city" during her second European trip and was finally converted to a new course of action while watching a bullfight in Madrid in 1887.

In this unlikely setting, inspiration fell upon her with the shock of recognition so familiar to true believers. But Jane Addams's moment of inspiration probably occurred some months later, in the spring of 1888, in London, where she threw herself into a final binge of serious searching. During this last leg of the voyage, her quest for purpose grew so desperate that she even attended a missionary conference. She also visited Toynbee Hall, a pioneer settlement in London's East End, a notorious slum. The first mission of its type, Toynbee Hall was run by a group of young university men of radical bent, who were determined to bridge the enormous rift between social classes. Toynbee Hall was the final impetus that threw Jane's disparate motives and ambitions into shape.

That Jane Addams described her inspiration for Hull-House in terms of a conversion was not surprising. Although religious experience, in the old sense, had become as rare as the spinning wheel, the need for such an experience remained—an experience that followed a period of intense misgivings, depression, anguish, and even physical misery; an experience that imposed purpose and identity, that justified or even necessitated a radical departure. By 1888, Jane Addams had had enough of the anguish and was ready for the radical departure. After revealing her new idea to Ellen Starr and eliciting Ellen's ardent approval and support, Jane Addams's conversion experience was complete. She returned to America with

... high expectations and a certain belief that whatever perplexities and discouragement concerning the life of the poor were in store for me, I should at least know something at first hand and have the solace of daily activity. I had confidence that although life itself may contain difficulties, the period of mere passive receptivity had come to an end, and I had at last finished with the everlasting "preparation for life," however ill prepared I might be.

Such high expectations were not unfounded. The settlement idea provided a solution to two major problems, public and private, simultaneously. An American settlement, along the lines of Toynbee Hall, spanning the gulf between rich and poor, was both a timely and an attractive plan. Jane Addams was not the only one to hit on such a plan. A few years earlier, a group of Smith College graduates, also inspired by Toynbee Hall, had formed an association to start a settlement. Their venture, called the College Settlement, opened in New York about the same time that Hull-House was founded in Chicago. The need for both was manifest. During the past decade, urban populations had exploded. And in the cities, the poor and foreign-born had become far more numerous and far more visible. Middle-class Americans had, as yet, no positive way of confronting this immigrant invasion, but some sort of action was imminent. Even American clerics, often a bastion of reaction, were veering away from theological concerns and turning their attention to urban social problems. By the 1880s, the settlement's moment had arrived. The social settlement was also a timely solution to Jane Addams's problem, not least of all because the settlement effort was going to be a joint one. Although the whole project was Jane's idea, and she was to remain its driving force, she embarked on the plan with the companionship and devotion of her old friend, Ellen Starr. "Let's love each other through thick and thin and work out a salvation," she wrote to Ellen before moving to Chicago.

Chicago was both a natural choice of locale for the two Illinois women and a natural site for their new venture. The city was at an optimal period in its growth, which had been phenomenal. When Jane Addams was born in 1860, Chicago was just a small lakeport city with a little over 100,000 residents. After the Civil War, railroads, factories, stockyards, and immigrants transformed it at a breathtaking rate. During the 1880s, while Jane Addams was floundering for purpose, the city doubled in population, in part by absorbing some nearby towns in 1889. By 1890, there were over a million residents, four out of five of them foreign-born or the children of immigrants. The nineteenth ward, on the west side, where Jane Addams and Ellen Starr decided to establish a settlement house, symbolized Chicago's expansion. Once a fashionable suburb, it had been overrun by newcomers, mainly the poor and immigrants, while former residents, the "older" families, had moved up and out.

The search for the right house, on which the two women embarked in 1889, was no simple matter. Fortunately, Jane Addams had ample funds. Her father had left a large estate, and she had inherited at least $50,000 in stocks and property. This provided a financial base on which to build. Ellen Starr had less

Even as a young woman, Jane Addams exuded an aura of authority, one that impressed her college classmates, the Chicago Woman's Club, and subsequently, the Hull-House staff. By the 1890s, she was able to describe herself, in matriarchal terms, as the "grandmother" of American settlements. *(1896 portrait, Jane Addams Memorial Collection, University of Illinois Library, Chicago)*

money but many connections in Chicago society. For almost a decade, she had taught at Miss Kirkland's, a fashionable girls' school, and had gained access to a number of prominent families. Using these contacts and making new ones, the two women canvassed Chicago explaining their project—to businessmen, philanthropists, ministers, missionaries, charity groups, and community leaders. Through their impressive skill at publicity and appeals, they won much approval. Their major coup was to gain the support of the Chicago Woman's Club, an elite institution that admitted just one new member a year to its very select ranks. Club members wielded considerable influence, since their families owned most of Chicago, and these wealthy women were anxious to contribute funds and assistance. Not only did the enthusiasm of the Chicago Woman's Club give the settlement idea the blessing of the city's upper class, but in 1889 the club also chose Jane Addams as its sole new member. By the end of the year, Jane Addams and Ellen Starr had rented a floor in an old building in the nineteenth ward and moved themselves in with all their possessions, including Jane's heirloom silver. The silver was significant. No temporary venture or trial run, the settlement would be a permanent home.

Once an elegant mansion, Hull-House had been built at midcentury by a wealthy real estate man and was now owned by his niece. It was in ill repair when Addams and Starr first saw it, containing, significantly, an office, a warehouse, and a saloon. The house was on South Halsted Street, at the corner of Polk Street, in the center of Chicago's nineteenth ward. Stockyards lay down the street in one direction, shipyards in another. The once suburban neighborhood, with its small wood-frame houses, each now filled with several families, provided a varied and exotic clientele. The ward was filled with immigrant colonies, surrounding Hull-House on all sides. Ten thousand Italians filled the immediate area around Halsted and Polk. To the south lived the Germans, the Russian and Polish Jews, and the Bohemians. Irish and French-Canadian colonies lay to the north. Toward the west were patches of English-speaking nonimmigrants—often "men and women of education and refinement," according to Addams, who had "come to live in a cheaper neighborhood because they lack the power of making money, because of ill health, because of an unfortunate marriage." The nineteenth ward was not only a composite of ethnic groups but also a panorama of urban ills. As a slum, in fact, the ward was almost as promising as London's East End. When Hull-House residents summed it up in 1895, they rated the area east of Halsted as the poorest in Chicago and the district south of Polk as "one of the most openly and flagrantly vicious in the civilized world."

Many of the Jewish and Italian immigrants, and their children, worked in tenement sweatshops, in basements, stables, and shanties, without water supplies or fire escapes. Health hazards abounded. Streets were dirty, lighting was poor, paving was bad, and residences were unsanitary. Religion and education were weak. The nineteenth ward had 50,000 souls, seven churches, two missions, ten parochial schools, no public schools, and most impressive of all, by Addams's count, 255 saloons. "There is no doubt that the saloon is the center of the liveliest political and social life of the ward," Jane Addams stated in 1892, and this situation presented a special challenge. The saloon, a male bastion, was a major competitor to the settlement house. Even more competition was provided by the political machine (city aldermen from the ward were often saloonkeepers) with influence over the entire neighborhood. When Jane Addams and Ellen Starr opened their doors to their neighbors in September 1889, inviting the local Italians in for a cultural evening, they hardly seemed likely to take on such formidable foes. But the founder of Hull-House already had an extraordinary array of goals.

The settlement house was going to provide an alternative to the saloon as a gathering place and to the political machine as a giver of favors. It would offer a meeting place to the neighborhood residents, and recreational activities to lure them in—clubs, classes, social evenings, ethnic celebrations. It would provide social services exceeding those of the ward bosses. It would open a door to culture and refinement by exposing the immigrants of the nineteenth ward to the best in American life, to works of art, fine language, and "beautiful surroundings." It would teach American values—that is, those of the middle and upper classes—to the poor, the working people, the new arrivals, and their children. And finally, it would serve as an intermediary between social classes. The settlement would funnel middle-class efforts and funds into the ward; indeed, its success depended on the contributions and goodwill of well-off Chicagoans. At the same time, it would funnel out an understanding of the "submerged tenth" that the settlement workers were going to acquire.

Even more overwhelming than this array of goals was the rapidity with which Hull-House achieved success. Unable to function as a daughter, Jane Addams excelled as an administrator. Within only a few years, the settlement sprawled all over the Hull-House mansion with an endless gamut of activities. By the early 1890s, 1,000 people of the ward attended Hull-House programs each week, over 90 volunteers contributed their efforts, and a group of "residents," mainly young women, had established themselves in the expanding house with Addams and Starr. For the residents, the settlement was not only an innovative fusion of private life and vocation but an interesting change from familiar types of female benevolence. Earlier generations of charitable women had emerged from their own homes to "visit" the poor—armed with uplift, prayers, advice, food baskets, cast-off clothing, religious tracts, and various donations. In the settlement house, however, the visited became the visitors, and their benefactresses became the hosts. When Jane Addams, who was often called on to describe the new institution, assessed the inroads it had made by 1892, a mere three years after it had been founded, she set forth a model of settlement work that had already inspired imitators in Chicago and in other cities.

Reflecting both the needs of the ward and the talents of the residents, the Hull-House program was an amalgam of clubs, classes, and services that constantly expanded, as did the house itself; it absorbed a house next door, which had once been a saloon. The saloon was transformed into a gymnasium. The forty or so programs involved, overwhelmingly, women and children, the most numerous of the visitors. First, there was a kindergarten and a day nursery, the latest vogue of social service, which soon had an enormous waiting list. Then there was a succession of youth clubs catering to every age and interest, from afterschool clubs for games, stories, gymnastics, sewing, or singing, to the Young Citizens club for older boys or the Hull-House Columbian Guards. Teenagers belonged to youth clubs, which provided literary evenings followed by a social hour. Local mothers learned about nutrition and household management at special classes or joined the more selective Hull-House Woman's Club, which involved "the most able women in the neighborhood" and met weekly, as did its elite model, the Chicago Woman's Club. There was an even larger men's club, but it met only once a month. Throughout the day and night, the gymnasium and the drawing room were used for club meetings and other functions, and in the evening, a new barrage of adult programs was available to those who worked during the day. The settlement organized a chorus, a concert program, a debate club, university extension classes, an art gallery, a reading room, and the Working People's Social Science Club, where, as Addams described it, political theories could be uncorked and deodorized before they exploded. From the outset, Hull-House was a bustling center of activity.

In addition to the clubs, each of which elected officers and required dues, Hull-House immediately threw its energies into a wide variety of community services, ferreting out the neighborhood's needs and rivaling the ward bosses in meeting them. The settlement, said Addams, served as an "information and interpretation bureau" for newly arrived immigrants and sometimes as a labor bureau, finding jobs for the unemployed. It channeled the services of outside professionals—ministers, priests, doctors—into the community and established a visiting nurse service. It served as a middleman between nineteenth ward denizens and city institutions—hospitals, asylums, charity groups, and county agencies. It arranged for ambulances, relief workers, and "fresh air" summers for children. It ran a public bath facility, a diet kitchen for invalids, a coffeehouse for profit, and a cooperative boardinghouse, the Jane Club, for working girls. It provided a meeting place for women's unions—bookbinders, shoemakers, shirtmakers, and cloakmakers. It worked as a pressure group on the ward's behalf, first by sending out its own corps of residents to report on poor sanitary conditions and then by campaigning for city services, even challenging the leading ward politician for authority over garbage collection. "One function of the settlement to its neighborhood," said Jane Addams in 1892, "somewhat resembled that of the big brother whose mere presence in the playground protected the little ones from bullies." No longer the protected youngest child, Jane Addams had found a far more appealing role.

If Hull-House quickly succeeded in setting an astonishing pace of activity, it also provided Jane Addams with the sense of exhilaration and community that had been missing since her days at Rockford. On a personal level, especially, the settlement was the ultimate fusion of solutions. It offered home, work, family, friends, activity, and mission, all in one. It enabled Jane Addams to establish a home for herself that insulated her forever from a lifetime of family obligations. It was a home over which she had complete control, one in which she took the place of both John Addams and Anna Haldeman Addams. It was also a home that in many ways re-created the luminous days at Rockford, full of challenge and enthusiasm, significance and sorority. And at the center of that life, at its vital core, was a world of women not unlike the world of college—a world that Jane had missed since 1881.

By 1895 there were twenty residents, and of those who had been there over six months, fifteen were women and two were men. The young women residents were usually college graduates and typically women from well-off families, who wanted to put their culture and education to use. Most important, they formed a sort of family, much as Jane's college class had done. Residents lived in a dormitory-like arrangement and ate in a common dining room, with Jane Addams at the head of the table, dishing out soup for a growing contingent of family members. She also entertained a coterie of admirers and distinguished guests— from the University of Chicago, other settlements, eastern cities, and abroad. Not only a family, Hull-House quickly became something of a salon. But above all, it was a community dominated by educated women who, like the students at Rockford, established their own cooperative style and communal identity. Even settlement terminology, like that of the college, was distinctive; it was quasi-professional and quasi-familial. The residents, including the "head resident" (rather than president or director), addressed one another often as "dear sister." The

A model settlement, Hull-House was also a pioneer in communal living. The large family of residents, who usually lived in upstairs apartments, convened at meal time in the common dining room. This tradition continued for decades. Below, the Hull-House dining room around 1930. Jane Addams is seated at the head of the middle table. Longtime associate Alice Hamilton is to her right. *(Jane Addams Memorial Collection, University of Illinois Library, Chicago)*

head resident was often called "Lady Jane," although some of her intimates began to call her, in corporate fashion, "J.A."

As in any family, the founding members were most important. The residents who arrived in the first few years formed an inner circle, a Hull-House network, forever identified with Jane Addams and the Chicago settlement. For some of these college-educated, professional women, settlement residency was a training ground for other types of public service. But even after they moved on, Hull-House remained their base of operations. All of the inner circle, moreover, had experiences in some way akin to that of Jane Addams. Julia Lathrop, whose mother was a Rockford graduate, had gone to the school herself briefly before attending Vassar. Arriving at Hull-House the year it was founded, Lathrop remained at the settlement for twenty years and later became the first head of the federal Children's Bureau. Florence Kelley, daughter of a Republican politician, was a Cornell graduate. She joined Hull-House in 1891 and left in 1898 to become head of the National Consumers' League and prominent throughout progressive reform. Alice Hamilton, who went to medical school at the University of Michigan and Johns Hopkins, founded the field of industrial medicine and eventually taught it at Harvard. Arriving at Hull-House in 1897, she remained in the settlement for over a decade. Early in the twentieth century, finally, the inner circle was enlarged by Grace and Edith Abbott, whose mother had gone to Rockford. Both had been graduate students at the University of Chicago. Edith Abbott later taught there, while Grace Abbott became head of the Immigrants' Protective League and later followed Julia Lathrop to the Children's Bureau. By the second decade of the twentieth century, Hull-House had its own network of distinguished alumnae.

Like the inner circle, some Hull-House residents stayed on for extended terms. Others, like most settlement workers elsewhere, stayed for shorter ones. But their ranks kept expanding at an almost unbelievable pace. By the early 1900s, there were up to seventy residents. Those who left were quickly replaced by an unending supply of able young women (and some men), well-off and well educated. Financial means was almost a vital prerequisite. Residents were not only unsalaried but had to pay for their room and board. There were exceptions, of course, such as Ellen Starr, who had always been self-supporting. Starr's Hull-House work was funded by a special donation. But Ellen Starr's career was a special case in another way as well.

Her role as cofounder quickly faded into the background, since Jane Addams was clearly the pivotal personality of the settlement as well as its major fund-raiser. Moreover, once the support and approval Starr provided for Addams in the early days were replaced by those of the Hull-House community and outside admirers (and this was fairly soon, since Addams's reputation expanded with astonishing speed), Ellen Starr was replaced in her role as Addams's closest friend and favored colleague by a wealthy younger woman. In 1890, twenty-year-old Mary Rozet Smith, a graduate of Miss Kirkland's, where Ellen Starr had taught, arrived at Hull-House to supervise the kindergarten. Within five years, Mary Rozet Smith became Jane Addams's constant companion and treasured intimate. Devoted to Addams, Mary Smith lived with her for forty years, making many donations to the settlement and serving on its board of trustees. "I miss you dreadfully and am yours 'till death," Jane Addams wrote when they were separated. Ellen Starr became radicalized and an activist in the labor movement, though she continued to live in Hull-House for most of her life as well. Any alliance with Jane Addams seemed to be a permanent one. Addams, meanwhile, as head of both the Hull-House family and a national settlement movement, achieved as much of a leadership role as her father ever had.

In her public persona, beyond the Hull-House family, Jane Addams quickly carved out a unique niche in American life and extended her influence in ever-widening circles. "I find that I am considered quite the grandmother of American settlements," she commented in 1893, when only thirty-three years old. As rapidly as Hull-House programs filled up the Hull mansion and adjacent buildings, so did Jane Addams's reputation blossom, first as Chicago's most eminent woman and then as a national model of benevolence. Jane Addams, said an Atlanta newspaper in 1908, was "synonymous with all that is charitable, ennobling, public-spirited, and good." Addams's skill as Hull-House spokes-woman and publicity agent greatly enhanced her reputation. Since the settle-ment's success depended as much on the contributions of the rich as on the participation of the poor, Addams spoke continually at public forums, to college audiences and women's groups, and cajoled benefactors, most of them wealthy women.

In this she was inordinately successful. One big donor, for instance, was Helen Culver, who owned the Hull-House building and much of the surround-ing area. Piece by piece and year by year, she gave it over to the settlement. Another was Louise Bowen, a rich Chicagoan who joined the Hull-House Woman's Club in 1893 and began to finance adjoining buildings for a variety of clubs. Soliciting funds and dispensing a philosophy of settlement, Jane Addams served as a crucial link between the settlement movement and its wealthy backers, to say nothing of an admiring public. By the first decade of the twentieth century, the settlement house had become an urban fixture, settlement work a woman's vocation, and Jane Addams its leading practitioner. Soon she was widely recognized not only as the matriarch of the settlement movement but also as America's leading woman citizen. Reporters referred to her as "The Lady Abbess of Chicago," "The Only Saint America Has Produced," and "The First Lady of the Land."

Addams's triumph was both institutional and personal; it was hard to separate the two. By 1910, Hull-House had expanded into a huge complex of buildings and adjuncts, covering an entire city block. Nationally, settlements had multiplied, now numbering in the hundreds. Their residents not only exerted local clout but also filled the front ranks in progressive reform. Investigating sweatshops, working conditions, and public school systems, they had become an important pressure group for industrial safety laws, welfare laws, child labor laws, protective laws, compulsory education, and juvenile courts. Jane Addams and Hull-House were at the center of the crusade. At the peak of her influence, between 1900 and World War I, Addams won innumerable honorary degrees, published an inspirational autobiography, reached a national audience through the big-circulation magazines, served as a leader of women's organizations, and threw her weight into the woman suffrage campaign. She attained the pinnacle of her political success in 1912, when she seconded the nomination of Theodore Roosevelt for President at the Progressive party convention and was greeted by a torrent of cheers and applause. Throughout the progressive era, Jane Addams was a living link between past and present, embodying the virtues of Victorian womanhood while simultaneously providing a model of female leadership in public life.

As a philosopher of settlement, too, Addams performed a unique function. After 1895, when a board of trustees began to supervise Hull-House affairs, Addams devoted more and more time to her public role, as resident intellectual and reformer. Settlement workers were not just philanthropists, as she took great pains to prove, but also social scientists, bent on understanding and explaining the problems that separated class from class or generation from generation. In her role as explicator, Addams adopted a calm, studious, almost ministerial tone, supporting her generalizations with little parables from the settlement experience. Her audience would understand the great divide separating the "submerged tenth" from the middle class and would learn, as she had, why homes in the slums were rarely spotless and neat, why the working girl spent most of her income on clothes, or even why the ward boss, the arch enemy of Hull-House, was able to win the gratitude of his constituents. Addams's writings, tolerant and unsentimental, were peopled with an endless cast of characters—with the German washer-woman, who carried water up and down two flights of stairs; with her daughters who had "fallen victim to the vice of the city"; with the working man who regarded his children as his "savings bank" because of the money they could earn. Her readers met the old woman who had become an opium addict; the local Italians, "with their petty lawsuits, with their incorrigible boys, with their hospital cases, with their aspirations for American clothes"; and the overworked girls who were attracted to dance halls, streaming along the Chicago streets, with "the self-conscious walk, the giggling speech, the preposterous clothing."

But Jane Addams was more than a mediator between social classes. She also took on the role of mediator between generations. As agile as a minister at combining personal anecdotes with discussions of general problems, Jane Addams could never ignore her own experience. And she could never forget the overwhelming crisis she had gone through in the 1880s, the conflict between her own vague ambitions and her family's demand that she remain a "possession." By the 1890s, she was already transforming her personal experience into a common experience—one shared, she contended, by a whole generation of young women. The "subjective" need for the social settlement, Addams told her national audience, was just as valid as the city's need. It rescued young women from the "family claim" and provided entrée to a "larger life."

By 1900, few of the Addamses were in a position to grasp the import of Jane's experience. During the 1890s, while Hull-House thrived and stepmother Anna aged, some of Jane's siblings died or disintegrated. Sister Mary, whose husband had turned out to be a failure, died in 1894. Jane Addams contributed to the support of Mary's children. Stepbrother Harry Haldeman and sister Alice had never appreciated Jane's career. Harry disliked Hull-House, and Alice, who had always thought Jane usurped more than her share of attention, felt she should contribute more to family support. George Haldeman had had a nervous breakdown shortly after Hull-House was founded. Brother Weber Addams, also a depressive, spent long periods in mental institutions. In many ways, Jane Addams was the psychic survivor of a sinking ship. But the conflict between the daughter and the family—the impossible problem that had used up her twenties—was not, she insisted, solely a personal problem. Rather, it was a social problem. One nub of the problem was that sons were treated as individuals whereas daughters were viewed only as family members. Another was that colleges fostered women's individualism but society gave them nothing to do with it. Left out in limbo, the college woman was unsuited to daughterhood but unprepared for life.

"From babyhood the altruistic tendencies of . . . daughters are cultivated," Addams wrote. "They are taught to be self-forgetting and self-sacrificing, to consider the good of the whole before the good of the Ego. But when all this information and culture show results, when the daughter comes home from college and begins to recognise her social claim to the 'submerged tenth,' and to evince a disposition to fulfill it, the family claim is strenuously asserted." While Addams's writings were usually upbeat, hinting that all problems could be resolved by compromise and compassion, her thoughts about the returning daughter were singularly depressive. Enclosed by the family claim, the daughter was likely to be "restless and miserable," "consumed by vain regrets and desires." "I have seen young girls suffer and grow sensibly lowered in vitality in the first years after they leave school," Addams wrote. The young woman "finds 'life' so different from what she expected it to be. She is besotted with innocent little ambitions, and does not understand this apparent waste of herself, this elaborate preparation, if no work is provided for her."

The son was in a different position, since he was automatically considered a "citizen" and expected to make his way in the world. "The family claim is urged much less strenuously in his case," said Addams, "and as a matter of authority, it ceases gradually to be made at all." Once women were given a college education, however, the "family assumption" about their roles and obligations, she contended, should be considered as invalid as it was for men. The college, in fact, was several steps ahead of both family and society. "Modern education recognises women quite apart from family or society claims and gives her the training which for many years has been deemed successful for highly developing a man's individuality and freeing his powers for independent actions."

Whether this type of education was appropriate for women was a moot point, however. In Addams's view, it raised women above the family claim but did not prepare them for the social claim. The college fostered women's individualism and nurtured their ambitions. But "it trained women almost exclusively for intellectual accumulation; and it did not provide a definite outlet for this training." In her autobiography in 1910, Addams wrote:

I gradually reached a conviction that the first generation of college women had taken their learning too quickly, had departed too suddenly from the active, emotional life led by grandmothers and great-grandmothers; that the contemporary education of young women had developed too exclusively the power of acquiring knowledge and of merely receiving impressions; that somewhere in the process of "being educated" they had lost that simple and almost automatic response to the human appeal.

By the turn of the century, 85,000 young women attended college, but their higher education, Addams felt, tended to bury them "beneath mere mental accumulation" without preparing them "in the line of action." Few would be able, as she had done, to transform a personal problem into a public solution.

12

THE RISE OF
THE NEW WOMAN,
1860–1920

Jane Addams exemplified the New Women of the 1890s, who integrated Victorian virtues with an activist social role. By plunging into a "larger life," Addams discarded an old persona, that of the dutiful daughter and neurasthenic invalid, and transformed herself into a public figure of national repute, admired and emulated. Like Addams, the New Woman had an enhanced sense of self, gender, and mission. Vigorous and energetic, she was likely to be involved in institutions beyond the family—in college, club, settlement, or profession. During the last decades of the nineteenth century, women's culture began to assume a public shape.

The New Woman reached her stride in the progressive era, although she had antecedents in the 1870s and 1880s. Decidedly middle-class, if not upper-class, she was usually a town or city dweller, the wife or daughter of a business or professional man, and better educated than average. Perhaps she was even a college graduate, a possibility that increased year by year. She was more likely to be single than was any other group of women at any time, before or since, in American history, even more so if she had been to college. If unmarried, she might be employed outside the home, most likely in a profession dominated by women, mainly young women, such as teaching or library work. If she never married, she might maintain her own home, possibly with another woman, rather than live with a relative. If and when she married, she usually gave up salaried work and devoted herself to household and family. Both, however, had been reshaped, much to her advantage.

By the turn of the century, the middle-class home had lost most of its productive functions (no one mourned their passing) and had become a unit of consumption, for which the homemaker was responsible. She also had to meet increasingly stringent standards of housekeeping, though usually with domestic help. But home was emptier, with men at offices and children at school for ever-increasing periods of time. Within the home, the middle-class wife was in firm control, albeit over a diminished domain. She had assumed "all authority and management of home and family," as women's columnist Dorothy Dix told her readers in 1898, since the husband "doesn't want to be bothered about it." If she had fewer children than her mother or grandmother, as was likely to be the case, she was "fully responsible for their mental and physical well-being." And she had come to reign supreme "in the matter of society," as Dix emphasized. "She dominates it and runs it." More powerful at home, the New Woman was also likely to be more active outside it.

During the late nineteenth century, woman's sphere expanded visibly, especially through the vehicle of the single-sex association, which women used to penetrate public affairs. Indeed, through a massive spate of institution-building, late-nineteenth-century women created a separate space in public life. The middle-class woman was usually involved in some sort of voluntary society, whether a church group, a literary discussion circle, or a welfare project. Or she might be involved in some special interest group such as an alumnae association, a mothers' club, or the temperance movement. By the 1890s, the women's club had become a standard feature of the urban scene. In organization, women assumed an aggressive stance and a distinctive identity. Unlike men, they entered public life as cooperators, not competitors. Moreover, they took special pride in gender. As temperance leader Frances Willard contended, women were more civilized and refined than men, they stood on a higher step of the evolutionary ladder, and they shared feminine goals and impulses, which gave them more in common with one another than with men. Her contemporaries seemed to share such views. Their special mission in public life was to purify, uplift, control, and reform; to improve men, children, and society; to extend the values of the home. "The home does not stop at the street door," said Marion Talbot, dean of women at the University of Chicago in 1911. "It is as wide as the world into which the individual steps forth. The determination of the character of that world and the preservation of those interests which she has safeguarded in the home, constitute the real duty resting upon women."

The New Woman's ventures beyond the street door evoked controversy. The "woman question" pervaded the late nineteenth century. Should a woman attend college, where she might ruin her health or lose her mind, or enter a profession, where she would risk her feminine identity, or leave the home for innumerable club meetings, or speak in public to groups of strangers? These were vexing questions, to say nothing of whether or not she should be able to vote. Women responded to such challenges by citing the values of home. A cover for self-assertion and a rubric for a feminine value system, "home" was a code word with many meanings. It was sometimes a euphemism for Anglo-Saxon superiority; foreigners, for instance, had to be taught the values of the middle-class home. It sometimes stood for female control over male sexuality, as in the crusades against drunkenness and prostitution. And it was sometimes part of a campaign against business run rampant, since the goals of many women's groups in the progressive era were to remedy some evil of industrial capitalism—whether to end child labor, protect women workers, or get the impurities out of milk.

Despite her frequent assaults on industrial evils, the New Woman was herself the product of industrialization, which removed productive labor from middle-class homes and made her long for something to do. She was the product of urbanization, which brought her into contact with other women and also into contact with the "other half" or "submerged tenth." She was a product of prosperity, whether her father's wealth, as in Jane Addams's case, or her husband's income, or the large fortunes that were used to endow private colleges or support settlements. She was the product of an old ideology, which gave her first claim on rectitude, made her a guardian of culture, and legitimized the single-sex association. She was the product of recent history, specifically of the Civil War era, which provided an example of women's talents for public service, whether in local sewing clubs or in the ranks of the Sanitary Commission. Finally, she was a product of the middle-class family, where her "influence" reached an all-time peak.

Shrinking Families

While the nation expanded and urbanized, the family changed too. It became smaller, more companionate, and longer-lived. As life expectancy rose, parents could expect to reach old age, marriages were expected to endure longer, and children were expected to survive to maturity. There were fewer children per home as well. The fertility rate continued its century-long plunge, dropping to 3.56 children per woman in 1900, and kept on falling. All of these changes contributed to, or were symptoms of, women's changing role at home, especially in the native-born, middle-class home. The late-nineteenth-century American family, such as that of Jane Addams, was a closely knit, highly supportive, and extremely demanding institution. It was also a family in which the wife and mother had gained influence and authority, status, and control.

The link between rising status and falling fertility was hardly a sudden development. The declining birthrate was part of a long-term transformation that had started in the late eighteenth century, when patriarchal power began to be replaced by a new ideal of mutual affection and companionship in marriage. The shift from the traditional family to the modern one meant a rise in the status of women (and children). Over the course of the nineteenth century, as historian Daniel Scott Smith hypothesizes, women acquired "an increasing power over sex and reproduction within marriage" and experienced "a great increase of power and autonomy within the family." Smith calls this development "domestic feminism." During the late nineteenth century, women consolidated their gains. If fertility is an index of female status, the companionate family had become much more than an upper-class ideal. Birthrates dropped not only in cities but also in rural areas, not only in the more densely populated Northeast but in all regions, although more slowly in the South. There were some significant variations, however. Black fertility did not begin to decline appreciably until the 1880s. Immigrant families also had more children than native-born Americans, although the disparity decreased in the second generation. Falling fertility was most pronounced in the native-born middle-class white family, especially as women's educational levels rose.

In the last quarter of the nineteenth century, the native-born middle-class white woman could expect to have about three children, to live long past fifty, and to survive the departure of the last child from home. A quarter of the women who married between 1880 and 1910 had two children or less, as did 40 percent of those who lived in the middle-Atlantic states or in some midwestern states. The woman who married in the first decade of the twentieth century could expect to spend at least five years less caring for children than had her counterpart a century earlier and to live at least ten years longer. Such changes had tremendous implications for middle-class children and mothers. Child-care standards rose as the number of children per home declined and each child could receive more attention. In some ways this was a mixed blessing; the middle-class youngster might expect to have less freedom and independence than one who was part of a great brood. But wives and mothers profited. They had less drudgery, better health, more energy, and more free time, which could now be devoted to outside activities. Although the increased leisure of the middle-class wife was often decried, wives were not the principal decriers.

Most important, the shrinking family was a change to which women contributed. The fall of the nineteenth-century birthrate cannot be correlated with any improvement in birth-control techniques, since effective new methods did not become widespread until the 1920s. Moreover, throughout the nineteenth century, contraception and abortion were condemned by a wide range of women, from feminists to free love advocates to pious churchgoers, since both encouraged the sexual exploitation of women. Continence and abstinence, however, remained effective methods of birth control. Historians suggest that women were able to exert control over men by decreasing the frequency of sexual relations, thereby both avoiding pregnancy and increasing their power at home. Nineteenth-century women, historian Carl Degler contends, may well have wanted to "minimize or deny their own sexuality" in order to press for greater autonomy in marriage. Long periods of abstinence were the trade-off for greater individualism. According to this hypothesis, the late-nineteenth-century middle-class wife was both more autonomous and more inviolate than any of her predecessors. The acme of female autonomy and sexual control in marriage was probably in the first two decades of the twentieth century.

If late-nineteenth-century married women gained in autonomy by minimizing sexual "indulgence," this was not because they saw themselves as asexual. Ideas about female sexuality were in transition. The old idea that women were asexual, or markedly less sexual than men, persisted to an extent in medical and popular literature. But there was debate on the subject within the medical profession, and this was reflected in marriage manuals. By the end of the century, female sexuality appears to have been a common assumption. Women, however, were unlikely to view their own sexuality as identical with that of men. This distinction emerged in a pioneer survey of sexual attitudes devised by a woman physician, Clelia Mosher, in the 1890s. The Mosher survey was given to a group of forty-five middle-class married women over a thirty-year period. These women, to be sure, were hardly typical. Almost two out of three were college educated, as were only 2 percent of all American women in 1890. Their responses, however, may have represented those of the New Woman. Respondents sometimes voiced a high opinion of marital sex—"the most sacred expression of our oneness," one woman commented. But they also voiced a marked desire for "temperance" and "moderation" in sexual activity. One-third of respondents thought that sexual intercourse was not a "necessity" for either sex, and over half indicated that they engaged in it more than they would have preferred. On an average, the woman surveyed had sexual relations once a week and would have preferred to do so once a month.

The driving theme of women's history in the late nineteenth century was neither to achieve any new type of sexual "freedom" nor to avoid sex, but to assert control over their own sexual lives. Historian Linda Gordon uses the term "voluntary motherhood" to describe women's demands for continence and abstinence. During the late nineteenth century, both feminists and advocates of "social purity" voiced such demands. To suffragists of the 1870s, for instance, who defended "enlightened motherhood" or "self-ownership," control of sexual relations within marriage was a vital goal. "Woman must have the courage to assert the right to her own body as the instrument of reason and conscience," wrote suffragist Lucinda Chandler, who published her views in a gamut of women's journals in the 1870s. Proponents of social purity shared such views. Their statements revealed the same connection between female autonomy and abstinence. "If women had their own way in the matter, this physical intercourse would take place at comparatively rare intervals," wrote social purity advocate Elizabeth Evans in an 1875 tract. "As woman becomes more free and wise and self-sustaining, she will demand the same purity of man that she has always demanded of herself." Physician Elizabeth Blackwell, who contended in the 1890s that "passion commands" the same "vital force" in women as in men, similarly advocated social purity. Favoring "restraint" over "indulgence," middle-class women were committed to exerting sexual control and expanding their autonomy at home. The late nineteenth century was an era of raised expectations, both of men and of marriage.

One tangible sign of raised expectations in marriage was the divorce rate, which in the late nineteenth and early twentieth centuries grew to what historian William L. O'Neill calls "critical dimensions." During the 1890s, the divorce rate shot up with unparalleled speed—at a rate three times as great as the rate of population increase. And it doubled again in the first two decades of the twentieth century, without any major change in the divorce laws. In 1880, there was one divorce for every twenty-one marriages; in 1900, one for every twelve marriages; and by 1916, one for every nine marriages. Throughout the era, most demands for divorce came from women, to whom about two-thirds of divorces were granted. Such women rarely rebelled against marriage but rather against mates who failed to meet traditional ideals. In her study of Los Angeles divorces in the 1880s, historian Elaine Tyler May finds that wives applied for divorce if their husbands failed to support them, forced them into the labor force, or violated the purity of domestic life by bringing drinking, gambling, and revelry into the home. (Husbands complained if wives left conjugal, maternal, or domestic obligations unfulfilled, indulged in excessive leisure pursuits outside the home, or admitted to premarital adventures.) Divorce had few public advocates; most contemporaries viewed the increase in divorce as an augury of the family's dissolution and a sign of "unwholesome individualism." Historians, however, view the phenomenon as part of the rise of the companionate family and a reflection of higher expectations of marriage, notably among women.

Another sign of raised expectations was that a smaller proportion of Americans married at all. Of women who were born between 1835 and 1855, between 7 and 8 percent never married. In Jane Addams's generation, born 1860 to 1880, between 10 and 11 percent of women never married, and in the next generation, the percentage was only slightly lower. More important, during the late nineteenth century, the spinster, once a marginal member of society, suddenly moved from the periphery of history to center stage. During Jane Addams's lifetime, single women became the advance troops of New Women; they assumed highly visible leadership roles in the professions, reform, and women's education. Jane Addams was not an isolated example but part of a large cohort of never-married women leaders, including Lillian Wald in the settlement movement, Frances Willard in the temperance movement, Anna Howard Shaw in the suffrage movement, M. Carey Thomas in women's higher education, and all of the Hull-House inner circle except Florence Kelley, who was divorced. During the progressive era, when women's impact on public life reached a new high, more single women were at the peak of their careers, in proportion to all women, than at any other time, before or since.

The decision not to marry reflected a combination of rising expectations and falling opportunities. Not only did middle-class women expect more of marriage, but they also faced a scarcity of eligible men. Nationwide, the loss or incapacitation of men in the Civil War was eventually mitigated by the rise of a new generation. Increased immigration helped also, since 60 percent of the immigrants arriving between 1880 and 1920 were men. But this did little to enhance the marital options of native-born middle- and upper-class women. The crunch was particularly acute in the East and in cities. In 1880, for instance, there were 50,000 more women than men in bellwether Massachusetts. That same year in Providence, a typical eastern city, there were 93 men to every 100 women. The greatest scarcity struck at the twenty- to twenty-nine-year-old group, where there were only 86 men to every 100 women. Similar discrepancies in numbers in countless eastern towns and cities were likely to take their toll in the marriage market. The brunt of the impact fell on young women with the highest status, standards, and educational levels, who were likely to have the fewest options of all.

In the view of middle-class women, there was a decline not only in the quantity of eligible men but in their quality. Or, as expectations of marriage rose, so did perceptions of male liabilities. These were reflected in an extremely popular speech given by Mary Livermore hundreds of times across the country in the 1870s and 1880s. Livermore advised parents to train their daughters for self-support because opportunities for good marriages were diminishing.

The men who were not killed off by drink, vice, or overwork were not necessarily going to make "good or competent husbands," Livermore warned. They were likely to be invalids or deserters, unambitious or dissolute—in any event, hardly viable candidates for companionate marriage. The extremely protective, close-knit, late-nineteenth-century family itself may have contributed to men's inadequacies. In Jane Addams's family, for instance, none of the young men measured up to John Addams, a self-made man who rose to success in business and politics. Both Jane's brother, Weber, and her stepbrother George, the only known applicant for her hand, had nervous breakdowns. Her brother-in-law, Mary's husband, was a professional failure. Similarly, close-knit, protective families may have left young women ill-prepared for the competitive marriage market.

Finally, the single middle-class woman of the late nineteenth century had improved options—for higher education, for professional employment, and for establishing supportive relationships with women outside the family. In the experience of Jane Addams and others, such options made spinsterhood not only a viable option but a preferable one. First, an educated woman had to choose between marriage and a career; many chose the latter. Second, many preferred the company of women to that of men. "The loves of women for each other grow more numerous each day, and I have wondered much why such things were," Frances Willard wrote in 1889. "That so little should be said about them surprises me for they are everywhere." Female couples might establish same-sex households or "Boston marriages," based on romantic friendship. Single women in leadership roles often formed long-term relationships with other women, such as that of Jane Addams with Ellen Starr and then Mary Rozet Smith. Frances Willard, Lillian Wald, and M. Carey Thomas, all heroic figures to their constituencies, had similar relationships with women who contributed either labor or funds to their respective causes. As historian Blanche Wiesen Cook points out, women's institutions, such as the woman's college or the settlement house, could provide life-long support groups for the women who lived in them. In the context of such institutions, some women maintained lesbian ties and many created surrogate families in which they could depend on other women for "emotional sustenance and political support."

One factor that contributed to such relationships was that women occupied a separate sphere in public life, a sphere dominated by single women. Another was that women thought themselves morally superior to men, and single women such as Jane Addams even more so. Their contemporaries agreed. In a 1906 contest run by a local newspaper for "the best woman in Chicago," one of many popularity contests that Jane Addams won, the competition was limited to single women because, as the editors explained, "Unless the married woman ignores the wishes of her husband, it is difficult for her to achieve the same degree of goodness the unmarried woman does." Demographic liabilities, higher expectations, preferable alternatives, and a personal sense of superiority all contributed to the rise of the single woman in the late nineteenth century. So did the advent of the college-educated woman, who probably had the highest expectations of all.

The College Woman

Jane Addams's invigorating experience at Rockford from 1877 to 1881 represented a major advance of the late nineteenth century. When midwestern land-
grant colleges began to admit women during the Civil War and when Vassar
opened its doors in 1865, they raised the expectations of all American women.
Relatively few attended college at the outset, but their proportion of the college
population rapidly rose. In 1870, when 1 percent of college-age Americans
attended college, 21 percent were women. But by 1910, when about 5 percent of
college-age Americans attended college, 40 percent were women. Unanticipated
and relatively unhampered, the sudden increase in the number of college women
had wide ramifications. Significantly, women made inroads in higher education
by cracking the barrier of sphere at one of its weakest links.

The vast upsurge of women college students was in part a result of the rapid
growth and feminization of secondary schooling. By 1900, when only 7 percent
of Americans went to high school, a large majority were women, as were 60
percent of high school graduates. Boys were more likely to go to work than finish
secondary school. A similar phenomenon occurred in higher education. After the
Civil War, opportunities for college education expanded rapidly, a result of
federal largesse and of the large fortunes now available for endowing private
institutions. But male interest in college degrees did not keep up with the
enormous expansion of college places. Middle-class young men found more
opportunity in business than in professions requiring a liberal arts education. As
a result, there was a vacuum of space in higher education, which women students
surged to fill. "While the education for men has outgrown the old college
system," an early president of Vassar explained, "that for women has just grown
up to it." According to historian Patricia A. Graham, academia was seen as
outside "the mainstream of industrial capitalism" in the late nineteenth century.
College education may have been a frontier for women, but for men it was a
retreat from the "real" world of business. More of a backwater than a male
bastion, the college was therefore open to increasing numbers of women students. This development was most visible at coeducational colleges and state
universities, where, by 1880, the majority of women students were enrolled.

Higher education for women began in the 1830s at Oberlin where women
students followed the "ladies course," received special degrees, and entered
men's classes only with special permission. Women were admitted to Oberlin in
order to improve education for men—by raising the tone of campus life and
preventing the growth of vulgar customs that "so frequently deprave" the
all-male college. Oberlin's regard for female influence had little impact on other
antebellum schools. But during the Civil War, when Congress funded higher
education through the Morrill Act, a new spurt of coeducation began. By 1870,
eight state universities, mainly in the West and Midwest, admitted women,
whose tuition fees were more in demand than their influence. Women students
were accepted with caution by administrators, and often with hostility by fellow
students ("bitter indignation" according to a Wisconsin alumnus). But they
formed a pool of ready applicants when men were scarce. Their brothers were

either serving in the war or, afterward, bound to farms or entering business. During the 1860s and 1870s, moreover, coeducational institutions multiplied rapidly. In 1867 there were twenty-two coeducational colleges and universities and by 1900 almost five times as many.

Although new land-grant colleges welcomed women because doing so cost less than creating separate institutions for them, coeducation also had ideological support. Liberal reformers of the 1860s and 1870s—notably, the small contingent of women suffragists and their male allies—endorsed it with enthusiasm as a route to social equality and an antidote to "sexual polarization." "In a mixed school, as in a family, the fact of sex presents itself as an unconscious healthy stimulus," minister Thomas Wentworth Higginson wrote in the suffragist *Woman's Journal* in 1870. "It is in the separate schools that the healthy relation vanishes and the thought of sex becomes a morbid and diseased thing." Elizabeth Cady Stanton, another avid supporter, told an 1870 suffrage convention that coeducation would lead to "more congenial marriages," a major feminist goal. Similar idealism pervaded some of the early coeducational institutions, such as Cornell and Wesleyan, which saw themselves as egalitarian experiments. But beyond a small group of administrators and liberal reformers, coeducation did not win widespread support. At Wesleyan, for instance, where 8 percent of the students had been women since 1873, a vast majority of male students opposed coeducation. In addition, coeducational colleges were usually of lower quality than elite all-male colleges and later women's colleges. Few were able to draw on the large private fortunes available to single-sex schools. Finally, women had much to gain from the all-woman institution.

To the new generation of women educators and college founders, the true frontier of women's education was not at the coeducational college, public or private, that needed women to fill up space. It was at the women's college, which, like Vassar, would admit women students through the "front door," not the "side door." At the women's college, said Bryn Mawr's M. Carey Thomas, "everything exists for women students and is theirs by right not by favor." To be sure, at the elite male colleges, on which Vassar and Bryn Mawr were modeled, women were not admitted even through the side door, which was justification enough for establishing women's institutions. Other prominent women's colleges, such as Barnard (1889), were established in affiliation with leading men's colleges only after the trustees of those schools vigorously rejected the admission of women. Though controversial at the outset, the women's college soon won acceptance as the superior institution for women students. At the same time, it enabled women to establish a separate sphere in higher education, one where women were in control and where women could be employed. Finally, it reflected an ambivalence about women's roles that pervaded society at large.

Vassar, the first well-endowed, strongly academic women's college, was followed by sister schools that opened in the 1870s and 1880s—such as Wellesley in 1875, Smith in 1875, and Bryn Mawr in 1884. Coordinate colleges, or women's colleges affiliated with men's universities, included Barnard (1889) and Radcliffe (1894). Mount Holyoke, which was accredited in 1888, had already served as a model for a variety of women's schools, some of which, like Rockford, also became colleges. Significantly, Vassar regarded itself in the early years as an "experiment." This experiment was twofold. First, Vassar had to prove that women ("the daughters of our most affluent and aristocratic families," according to a dean) were capable of undertaking an academic education as stringent as that for elite men. Second, Vassar had to prove that they could do so without ruining their health or going insane. According to informed opinion, higher education posed even more of a threat to women's health than sweatshop, cotton mill, or canning plant. As Dr. Edward Clarke's influential *Sex in Education* (1873) explained, mental activity drew blood from the nervous system and reproductive organs. Higher education, contended the Boston physician, could cause mental collapse, physical incapacity, infertility, and early death. This line of reasoning continued through the turn of the century in various guises. It was feared, for instance, that college would produce generations of invalids who would never marry or who would have no children or only puny, sickly, nervous children— while immigrant women raised healthy hordes. The women's colleges therefore had a complex mission: not only to educate women but to do so without ruining health, sacrificing femininity, or contributing to "race suicide." The spirit of experiment cultivated at Vassar and its sister schools was both defensive and ambitious, and the institutions it inspired were innovative.

One innovation was an academic curriculum in the arts and sciences similar to that at the best men's schools—in line with Matthew Vassar's dictum that woman had "the same intellectual constitution as man" and with M. Carey Thomas's conviction that women and men had "the same love of abstract truth." Initially, some colleges ran preparatory departments to bring applicants up to par. Administrators were also prepared to cover all other contingencies. As Vassar stated, the college provided women with a liberal arts education "but one adapted to their needs in life." The most significant special program was a stringent course of physical activity, to ensure health as well as to make college women physically superior to noncollege women. The curriculum also included traditional female courses—such as the arts, music, and in some cases, domestic science (although Bryn Mawr eschewed the last). Finally, the women's college offered a familial environment. College was more than a course of study, it was a surrogate home. Part of the college experience was the common dormitory, the meals in the common dining room, and at some colleges, such as Wellesley and Mount Holyoke, the requirement that students perform domestic tasks, such as serving meals. Besides this multifaceted program—academics, physical education, homelike atmosphere, and domestic service—the women's colleges were, like their male counterparts, exclusionary societies. They therefore developed their own rites and rituals, such as those imitated by Jane Addams's class at Rockford.

The personnel and goals of women's colleges were also distinctive. Physicians (often women) were kept in residence because of the colleges' overriding interest in health. Many if not most professors were women as well, though Wellesley alone established the tradition of a woman college president and an all-female faculty. At the outset, women professors were supposed to be not so much academic specialists as role models. Always unmarried, they were usually young, since there was not yet an older generation of educated women on whom the colleges could call. One example of such a role model was Alice Freeman Palmer, a University of Michigan graduate, who became a high school principal at twenty-two, a Wellesley history professor at twenty-four, and president of the college at twenty-six. Palmer looked like one of her students throughout her seven-year reign; she retired to marry in 1888. The desirability of role models such as Alice Freeman Palmer was connected to the often ambiguous goals of the women's college. The purpose of college was not primarily advanced learning, as a Smith dean explained, or to produce women who could compete with men, but for "ennobling women as women."

Vagueness of goal enabled college administrators to hedge their bets as the situation demanded. The colleges contended, variously, that women were the intellectual equals of men; that they needed special programs to survive the rigors of higher education; and that they were being trained to serve both family and world. Graduates would be able "to fill every womanly duty at home and in society," as at Vassar, or to do the "work of life for which God has made them, in any place to which in His providence they may be called," as at Smith. Women's colleges shared the assumption that women exerted influence in society and that educated women could do so better than others. It was difficult to explain precisely how academic training would serve such ends, but this was hardly the colleges' fault. It was equally difficult to cite the purpose of a liberal arts education for a business-minded man. There was, however, a residual conflict between femininity and "intellect" that college administrators avoided confronting, except at Bryn Mawr. Here, M. Carey Thomas opted for intellect and refused to offer domestic science, hygiene, child study, or "sanitary drainage." "Of all things, taking care of children seems most utterly unintellectual," she observed in a college speech. But, not completely consistent, Thomas was willing to shift gears in order to promote Bryn Mawr's success. In 1901, she contended that college women married better than noncollege women, were healthier, rarely died in childbirth, bore healthy children, and made "efficient housekeepers as well as wives and mothers."

If the stated goals of the women's colleges were understandably ambivalent, the college experience was specific. It provided community, sorority, identity, and purpose. It instilled vigor, enthusiasm, and confidence. College, after all, consisted of a group of favored, privileged individuals who devoted themselves to self-improvement. This alone was an enormous boost to self-esteem. College also provided a new type of socialization, since it was a community beyond the bounds of home—no matter how much the women's colleges made their dormitory common rooms resemble the parlors of upper-class households. M. Carey Thomas recognized this process of socialization when she required that Bryn Mawr students live at the college and avoid frequent visits home, where they would fall under the influence of their mothers. Fathers, who paid the bills, were aware of it too. When Sophonisba Breckinridge of Lexington, Kentucky, entered Wellesley in 1884, her mother wrote her the household news and agonized with concern for her health, but her father, a lawyer and soon-to-be congressman, was full of advice. "It is a double and very hard lesson you are

Rigorous science courses distinguished the curriculum of the elite late-nineteenth-century woman's college from those of its antecedents, the academy and seminary. Above, a Wellesley class of the 1880s meets in the physics laboratory, the first to be established in a woman's college. *(Wellesley College Archives)*

unconsciously learning," he wrote, "the individual insignificance of each of us when put out of our circle . . . and the difference between our home, & any place else." Overflowing with pride in Sophonisba's accomplishments, William Breckinridge urged her, above all, to continue. "If I die, you will have to make your own living," he wrote in 1885, "& if I live you may have to do so anyhow."

What to do after college, however, was a problem—for Sophonisba Breckinridge, as for Jane Addams and their fellow graduates. Many felt alienated when deprived of the identity and community of college—"as if I had been flung out into space," one graduate contended. The college experience was an end in itself, leading nowhere. There seemed to be no purposeful role for college-trained women. Instead there was something of an abyss between college and "life." Moreover, the options were loaded. "I hang in a void midway between two spheres," wrote a Radcliffe alumna of 1900 a decade later. "A professional career . . . puts me beyond reach of the average woman's duties and pleasures," she said, but "the conventional limitations of the female lot put me beyond reach of the average man's duties and pleasures." Left in limbo, few late-nineteenth-century graduates could follow Jane Addams's path of complete severance from "the family claim." As historian Joyce Antler shows, families sometimes aided the adjustment after college by supporting career aspirations and new interests. Emily Talbot, for instance, joined her daughter Marion, a Boston University

Whereas the new women's colleges provided liberal arts curricula, most black educational institutions offered vocational programs. Tuskegee Institute in Alabama, founded in 1881, was a model. At Tuskegee, women students divided their time between the academic division and the industrial division, where they learned such trades as dressmaking, housekeeping, horticulture, upholstery, millinery, or laundry work. Margaret Murray Washington, a Fisk graduate and wife of Tuskegee founder Booker T. Washington, served as director of girls' industries and dean of women. Above, a Tuskegee domestic science class around the turn of the century. *(Library of Congress)*

graduate, in forming the Association of Collegiate Alumnae (ACA) in 1882, so that the small retinue of women graduates might perpetuate collegial ties and share common concerns. A thriving organization, the ACA later became the American Association of University Women. Many families, however, exerted a "claim" as strong as that of the Addamses. "My life since college has been very quiet at home," a Wellesley alumna wrote for the classbook of the class of '97. "At present I am living with my father and keeping house for him. . . . I have very little strength and haven't been able to undertake anything beyond my class in Sunday school." "All my plans for a 'career' have been knocked to atoms," wrote another, who cared for her mother. "You can put me down as still alive, though."

If alumnae were troubled by postgraduate trauma, society was more concerned about their low rate of marriage. Although a bare majority of late-nineteenth-century women college graduates married, they married later than noncollege women. Also, fewer married. More than 90 percent of the female population married in the late nineteenth century, but the proportion among college graduates was far lower. Of 8,000 women graduates in the 1880s, only 5,000 were married, and marriage rates were lowest among alumnae of prestigious, single-sex eastern women's colleges, where academic standards were most stringent. By 1890, only 25 percent of Bryn Mawr graduates had married; perhaps they were limited by Thomas's advice to marry college men who were willing to form intellectual rather than sexual alliances. Between then and 1908, 45 percent of Bryn Mawr graduates and 57 percent of Wellesley graduates married. Surveying three decades of Vassar alumnae in 1895, Frances Abbott Sweeney found that among the first four classes, 63 percent had married within twenty-five years. But less than 38 percent of the 1,085 Vassar women in her survey had married; the rate was lowered by single members of recent classes who were still in the long interim period between graduation and possible alliances. The link between higher education and single status would decline only when the proportion of women attending college vastly increased.

Women's influx into college also had an impact on higher education, where there was something of a backlash. By 1900, coeducational institutions found that their female populations had surged. The proportion of women students leapt from 25 percent to 50 percent at the University of Chicago, for instance, in its first decade of life. Some colleges, such as Wesleyan in 1909, simply ended female admissions. Others, such as Chicago, developed curricula to attract more men. Large state institutions relegated women students to normal schools or home economics programs within the universities. Private colleges that had admitted women or were under pressure to do so formed special women's branches, or coordinate colleges, to segregate their women students and keep them out of the way—as at Tufts, for example. Such measures preserved a college's appeal for male applicants. The specter of encroaching feminization continued to hover over academic life, and spurned special tactics to combat it.

Finally, the option of college education had widespread ramifications for women. College women were a new elite, and their advent affected roles on all fronts—home, work, and "world." One of the most visible results was the entry of college-trained women into professional work. By the turn of the century, when 17 percent of all alumni were women, college graduates dominated the ranks of professional women. This was little threat to the established male professions but led instead to the rapid development of "women's professions," specially suited to the needs and talents of college alumnae.

The Professional Woman

The professional woman was a contradiction in terms, since professions had developed in order to exclude irregular practitioners, notably women. At the turn of the century, experts viewed women and professionalism as being at opposite poles. As psychologist G. Stanley Hall explained in 1905, professionalism meant specialization, which was alien to the female brain. The man, said Hall, tends "by nature to *expertise* and *specialization* without which his individuality would be incomplete." The woman, "less prone to specialization," and by inference less of an individual, would clearly make a second-class practitioner, especially if she tried to crack a male bastion such as the ministry or law. During the late nineteenth century, the male bastions remained relatively secure, although women made gains in medicine. But women professionals emerged in great numbers in teaching, nursing, library work, and social work, and in relatively large numbers in academic life. These "women's professions" were either old vocations that had already been feminized and were now uplifted to the status of professions, or new vocations that were shaped and staffed by educated women. Between 1870 and 1930, the proportion of women in professions was twice as high as that in the work force. In 1890, for instance, when women were only about 17 percent of the work force, 36 percent of all "professionals" were women.

Women's professions were created both by the college experience and by the resistance of traditional "male professions" to women. The ministry, for instance, was virtually impenetrable. Pioneers such as Antoinette Brown Blackwell, the first woman ordained as a Congregationalist minister, or Olympia Brown, the first woman Universalist minister, or formidable Anna Howard Shaw, both minister and physician, did not clear paths that others could follow in any numbers. All three, significantly, were more active in the suffrage movement than in the ministry. Their clerical roles were usurped on a grand scale, moreover, by an extraordinary irregular practitioner, Mary Baker Eddy. Eddy created the new creed of Christian Science, attracted hundreds of thousands of followers, and at her death in 1910 left behind a wealthy, permanent institution. Eddy's contribution was not unlike that of Jane Addams. Capitalizing on accepted female virtues (in her case, intuition and spirituality), she created a unique way for well-off women, the bulk of her followers, to defeat neurasthenia and physical complaints, the lingering vestiges of Victorian womanhood. Carving out a new terrain in spiritual welfare, Mary Baker Eddy was an astounding success. But as a profession, the ministry rejected women.

There was no hope for irregular practice in law. The legal profession was highly organized and the courtroom, like the saloon, was a male citadel. The first woman lawyer was admitted to the bar in Iowa in 1869, but this was hardly the beginning of a stampede, since each state could decide on its own requirements for bar admission. In Illinois the same year, Myra Bradwell, a lawyer's wife, Sanitary Commission veteran, and suffragist, was denied admission to the bar; the Illinois Supreme Court declared that the "hot strife of the bar, in the presence of the public" would destroy femininity. When Bradwell took her case to the U.S. Supreme Court, it confirmed in 1873 that the delicacy and timidity of the female sex "unfit it for many of the occupations of civil life." Bradwell was not admitted to the Illinois bar until 1890.

Like Myra Bradwell, who read law with her husband, women lawyers were often trained in relatives' offices, although law schools began to admit small numbers of women in the 1890s. Once licensed, the woman lawyer, with rare exceptions, was excluded from courtroom practice and limited to office work.

Sometimes she found employment with a government agency or women's organization, or else she followed another career. Myra Bradwell, when excluded from the bar, edited a law journal and printed legal forms. Sophonisba Breckinridge, the first woman admitted to the Kentucky bar, in the 1880s, after studying law with her father, found it impossible to establish a practice and moved on to academic life. Other licensed graduates simply gave up. By 1910, there were almost 9,000 licensed women physicians but only 1,500 women lawyers. In 1920, only 3 percent of American lawyers were women.

Medicine, however, was at the lower end of the male professional scale. Since its status was most shaky and its organization least rigorous, women's medical colleges blossomed. Not surprisingly, in the 1880s, Jane Addams turned immediately to medical school as a first attempt to enter "life." Like Jane Addams, women students usually attended women's medical colleges, but by the 1890s several major medical schools, public and private, admitted women. By the turn of the century, women were 10 percent of medical students, and by 1910, they were 6 percent of the medical profession—a peak figure that soon declined. Unlike women lawyers, women doctors and also women dentists were able to establish practices. Treating mainly women and children, they charged less than male competitors, and often worked out of offices in their homes. Significantly, a high proportion of women physicians in the late nineteenth century combined marriage and career. According to historian Regina Morantz, some 30 to 40 percent of women doctors were married, perhaps four times as many as other professional women.

During the late nineteenth century, some women physicians created new institutions, but these were short-lived because, if successful, they were taken over by men. Women's medical colleges were soon absorbed by men's schools, and women's hospitals, such as Elizabeth Blackwell's New York Infirmary, soon vanished. Nor did women physicians control any medical field; male physicians dominated gynecology and pediatrics. In the early twentieth century, Alice Hamilton created the field of industrial medicine, a field that sprang in large part from her Hull-House residency. Though this never became a women's field either, Hamilton's experience at Hull-House was significant. The settlement house, and subsequently social welfare work, became havens for women professionals who had few outlets in private practice. The Hull-House inner circle, for instance, was formed by women professionals—physicians, lawyers, academics. Many settlements also ran visiting nurse services to provide medical care for neighborhood residents. Traipsing over the rooftops lugging her medical bag, the visiting nurse was a model practitioner of a women's profession, a vocation that was something of a halfway house between public service and professional expertise.

Women's professions depended on, and were shaped by, a vast outpouring of women college graduates. By the turn of the century, droves of college women became teachers, librarians, settlement workers, and, in smaller numbers, academics. Nurses, still counted as domestics in the census, were not often college women. Still, they could no longer be trained on the job but had to attend special nursing schools and thereby laid claim to professional status. Until 1920, however, hospitals employed only student nurses, at minimal rates, and nursing school graduates competed with untrained nurses for home-care jobs. Teaching, the major outlet for college alumnae, was gradually transformed. The college graduate began to replace the old breed of nineteenth-century teacher—a teenager with a grade school education. College women, boasted M. Carey Thomas in 1907, had driven out women without degrees. With a growing pool of educated women available, states began to impose standards, give licensing exams, and require advanced training. This was a gradual process that went on, state by state, from the 1880s through World War I.

Although women's professions, such as teaching, nursing, library work, and social work, developed in various ways, they had much in common. Each defined itself by extending woman's sphere, that is, by suggesting that women were naturally inclined and equipped to care for the young, sick, or poor, or to serve as guardians of culture, or to guide young women on the path to adulthood. Women's professions were usually practiced in places that could be defined as homelike—whether hospital, schoolroom, library, college, or settlement. They were professions in which the practitioners dealt primarily if not exclusively with other women, with children, and with persons in need. They were also alternatives to marriage, substitute routes for fulfilling female missions. The woman professional was either a young college graduate, filling an interlude between school and marriage, or a lifetime spinster. Most important, she was paid less—both less than a man in the same line of work, who might well rise to an administrative post, and less than a man in a male bastion like law. The most distinguishing mark of the woman professional was that she was almost always a salaried employee, often in the public sector, rather than a free-wheeling entrepreneur. For women, profession meant service not profit.

The librarian, as historian Dee Garrison has shown, was a superb model of the woman professional. The public library, funded by taxes and donations, proliferated in the late nineteenth century. It needed low-paid, well-educated workers, and women college graduates needed appropriate work beyond the classroom. Woman's role as guardian of culture was easily extended to the library, where she could welcome guests and assist them. The reading public was composed mainly of other women, who had the most time to consume culture, and children. The children's reading room was clearly a natural spot for the educated woman. Other library users were at least expected to be quiet and relatively harmless. Under these circumstances, women quickly filled all the lower-level library posts, while men surfaced in the top ones. And women could be employed at half the pay men would have earned. The relatively few men in the field welcomed them. "They soften the atmosphere, they lighten our labor," said a male librarian in 1877, "and . . . they are infinitely better than equivalent salaries will produce of the other sex." By 1880, the profession of librarian was feminized.

Like the librarian, the woman professor was needed at a new institution. She was mainly employed at the women's college, where, in some cases, she competed with men for jobs. She also found work at the coeducational schools, if only "to look after the discipline and home life of women students," as M.

Carey Thomas explained in 1901. Since the numbers of women students shot up rapidly, there was a sudden demand for her services. Women were 36 percent of all faculty members in 1880, and about 20 percent from 1890 to 1910. Unlike Alice Freeman Palmer, the woman academic usually made a lifetime commitment to spinsterhood. She often found at the women's college the same type of surrogate family Jane Addams created at the settlement. If she worked at a coeducational university, she was well advised to carve out a niche in a newly created academic area—such as the indefinite space encompassed by social science, domestic science, and social welfare.

Marion Talbot, for instance, who earned a B.S. degree at MIT in 1888, became an instructor in domestic science at Wellesley but was hired in 1892 by the innovative University of Chicago as a professor of sociology. At Chicago, Talbot became an avid supporter of women's equality in academic life. Her career, however, hung midway between social science and domestic science. Soon dean of women and then head of the department of household administration, Talbot rose to prominence as an officer of the American Home Economics Association and an authority on household management. Her friend Sophonisba Breckinridge, also lured to Chicago, became an instructor in her department, while earning both a law degree and a Ph.D. in political science. A part-time Hull-House resident, Breckinridge soon taught at Chicago's new School of Civics and Philanthropy, where social workers were trained, and became its dean. By creating new disciplines, women academics created space for themselves in academic life.

Few universities were as hospitable as Chicago, but women were able to create academic fiefs in other places as well. Ellen Richards, a Vassar graduate, became the first woman student at MIT, where she earned a B.S. degree in chemistry in 1873. Three years later she established a "woman's laboratory" at MIT, which specialized in applying chemical analyses to the home. Subsequently a professor of "sanitary chemistry," Ellen Richards also became an authority on household management, a leading light of the Home Economics Association, and an advocate of scientific careers for women. A model woman professional, although married, Richards was able to fuse woman's special terrain of domesticity with science—an effort that won the support of male colleagues. "Perhaps the fact that I am not a Radical or a believer in the all powerful ballot for women . . . and that I do not scorn womanly duties, but claim it as a privilege to clean up, is winning me stronger allies than anything else," she contended. It was not only lack of stridency that led to success. The New Woman was least threatening and most welcome if she occupied a sex-specific niche, such as the field of household management, or was contained in a women's profession where she was unlikely to compete with men.

By the turn of the century, women's professions filled an importance new space in the nation's occupational hierarchy. Not only did they provide vocations for growing numbers of educated women but, by creating a lower-level professional caste, they helped define the distinctive qualities of male professions: high status, profit, and expertise. But professional work was not the only new space to be filled by women. During the late nineteenth century, middle- and upper-class women also edged into public life in new, large women's associations that defined their own territory.

Clubwomen and Crusaders

The late nineteenth century saw a proliferation of women's associations, which splintered, multiplied, federated, and expanded at an energetic pace. The basic units of this outburst, the temperance society and the women's club, arose spontaneously and won adherents rapidly. Temperance gained momentum in the 1880s, and the club movement in the 1890s. Like the settlement, these associations had many functions. They enabled thousands of conventional middle-class women to learn from others, share female values, and work toward common goals. Combining self-help and social mission, they created an avenue to civic affairs, or what temperance leader Frances Willard called "the home going forth into the world." Not only did they give wide exposure to female "influence," but they invigorated their members and politicized their leaders. And they created a separate space for women in public life.

The women's club and temperance movements were both reminiscent of the commissions of the Civil War era—those massive federations of volunteer bandage rollers, supply collectors, fund-raisers, and organizers. Some of their alumnae, such as Mary Livermore and Annie Wittenmyer, who held high positions in commission work, threw their efforts into the new women's groups. But whereas the memorable Sanitary Commission had been run by men, the new associations were led by women. Moreover, unlike the majority of antebellum female societies, often formed under clerical auspices, they were secular associations. A separate network of women's charitable and missionary societies continued to maintain religious affiliations. In form, the women's club and temperance movements imitated various male models. Women's clubs, like men's clubs, had formal meetings, followed parliamentary procedures, elected officers, wrote minutes, and read reports. After federation, in 1892, their delegates attended national conventions, debated issues, and passed resolutions. Almost from the outset, the tightly organized temperance movement resembled a women's political party. But like the women's colleges, both movements were also agents of education and socialization. They saw themselves as training ground for public life. Through association, in the company of peers, home-bound matrons could learn to pursue common interests with vitality, enthusiasm, and self-assurance.

Both the women's temperance movement and the first women's clubs sprang up in the decade after the Civil War. The temperance campaign began in Ohio in the early 1870s with a women's crusade to close down saloons through prayers and harassment. Since antebellum days, the saloon had been a powerful symbol, an enemy of women and an insult to the sanctity of the home—because the men who sought companionship in the saloon might spend all their wages, lose their jobs, abuse their wives, victimize their children, or desert their families entirely. The women's crusade of Ohio was quickly successful in small towns, although less so in larger ones, where riots were barely averted. The Ohio saloons that were closed soon reopened, but the revulsion they aroused had long-term repercussions. In 1873, the Women's Christian Temperance Union was formed in Chicago. First led by Annie Wittenmyer, the WCTU surged to prominence after 1879, when Frances Willard took the helm. One-time college president (of the Evanston College for Ladies, a short-lived adjunct of Northwestern) and an organizational genius, Willard dominated the temperance movement for the next two decades and changed its style and direction. She transformed the union from a midwestern prayer group into a militant army of national scope.

A potent politician, Frances Willard attracted converts through nationwide speaking tours. By 1890, the WCTU had 160,000 members, including many in the South, each ready to "bless and brighten every place she enters and enter every place" (the political slogan was one of Willard's fortes). By 1911, with 245,000 members, the WCTU was the largest single women's organization ever. Size was not Willard's only achievement. She also enlarged the WCTU's single goal of temperance into a master plan for reforming the human race, especially the male half of it. As historian Barbara Leslie Epstein has shown, no small degree of sex antagonism spurred much of nineteenth-century female activism, from the early waves of revivalism through the energetic temperance crusade. Under Willard's direction most of the WCTU's energies still went toward ending the production, sale, and consumption of alcohol, and to urging state temperance laws. But the cause now had a larger thrust: to erase all evils for which men were responsible, from prostitution to political corruption. Under Willard's direction, the WCTU became a vocal pressure group for the protection of women and the improvement of society.

By 1889, when Hull-House was founded, the WCTU was an administrative masterpiece. Willard called it "a branch of social science and religious activity" but it bore more resemblance to a political movement. Her policy of "Do everything" meant that all WCTU members did something—whether in local societies, autonomous state federations, or the huge national federation, which held an annual convention complete with delegates, banners, flags, and music. Wearing her badge, a white ribbon to symbolize the purity of the home, the WCTU member might also work for one of the union's many departments. Each was a propaganda arm for a cause, such as peace, labor reform, social purity, health, or city welfare work. Unless she had unusual powers of resistance, the temperance advocate was likely to find herself opening kindergartens or Sunday schools for the poor, or visiting prisons and asylums, or embarked on some other campaign in which female virtue might prevail over lesser standards. The WCTU member might even be converted to woman suffrage, a cause that Willard endorsed with fervor; she believed that the ballot was "the most potent means of social and moral reform."

A model of the nineteenth-century woman politician, like Jane Addams a decade later, Frances Willard excelled at strategy and alliances. She was able to mobilize women to manipulate men, the ultimate target of most WTCU campaigns. The union's success was in its size, stamina, and centrality to women's politics. It established temperance as a cause around which women would rally for decades. It drew middle-class matrons, most of quite conservative bent, out of their homes into meetings, conventions, and crusades. Providing its members with what Willard called "a nobler form of social interchange" than the visits and calls of a bygone era, it also spurred some of them into the suffrage camp. Though many temperance advocates had little interest in suffrage, others went on to leadership roles, even in the South, where until now women had not been involved in either social reform or public life. To Mississippi suffragist Belle Kearney, in 1900, the WTCU was "the golden key that unlocked the prison door of pent-up possibilities."

Women's clubs similarly drew women into association, at first mainly for cultural purposes, but later to support an agenda of civic reform. Like the WTCU, women's clubs educated their middle- and upper-class members while providing an avenue to public affairs. Less embattled and more exclusive than the WTCU, the clubs had a wide range of potential adherents. At the outset, their goals were vague. The first model for a women's club, Sorosis, established by journalists and other career women in New York in 1868, described itself as "an order which shall render the female sex helpful to each other and actively benevolent in the world." Its organizer was energetic Jane Croly, mother of four, newspaper columnist, and avid exponent of women's involvement in public affairs. The New England Woman's Club, formed the same year, intended to serve as "an organized social center for united thought and action." Its leading spirits were Caroline Severance, wife of a banker, mother of five, and veteran antebellum reformer, and well-known author Julia Ward Howe. Members were Boston professional women and reformers. Significantly, the two pioneer women's clubs were established at the same time and in the same cities as the two pioneer woman suffrage societies. Some women participated in both. The club movement, however, was far more contagious.

During the 1870s, some women's clubs adopted decidedly feminist agendas, though most kept their purposes cultural, convivial, and general. But vagueness of stated goal served the motivating drive behind club formation, which was simply the desire to associate. This appeared to be unquenchable. Throughout the 1880s and 1890s, women's clubs proliferated, some splitting off from larger ones, others arising on their own. By the time the General Federation of Women's Clubs was established in 1892, there were almost 500 affiliate clubs and over 100,000 members. By the end of the century, women's clubs had 160,000 members; and by World War I, over a million. Throughout these decades, as historian Karen Blair points out, the women's club movement served a special purpose. It enabled middle-class women to enter public life without abandoning domestic values and without adopting the aggressive stance associated with either the temperance crusade or the more highly politicized movement for woman suffrage.

But women's clubs were a step toward politicization as well. The typical women's club of the 1880s began by holding weekly meetings for lectures, discussions, and book reports. Sometimes the group would choose a topic for the week, month, or season, devoting itself to ancient history or contemporary drama. These literary and cultural overtones provided clubwomen with a substitute for the higher education now open to their daughters. Like the college, the club was also an exclusionary society, defined as much by who was admitted and who was left out as by the novels or works of art that were discussed. By the turn of the century, however, the thrust of the clubs had shifted to civic affairs, a crucial change in direction. Clubwomen, explained the president of the General Federation of Women's Clubs (GFWC) in 1904, were abandoning the study of Dante's *Inferno* and beginning to "proceed in earnest to contemplate our own social order."

The social order was usually contemplated on a local level in a noncontroversial manner. Women's clubs raised funds for planting trees, establishing libraries, and building hospitals and playgrounds. They supported worthy projects, such as women's colleges, social settlements, and visiting nurse services, and pressured local governments for clean drinking fountains and better school facilities. After women's clubs federated in 1892, delegates to biennial meetings moved on to national issues, passing resolutions on those in which women, home, and family had a stake—such as protective laws, child labor laws, pure food and drug legislation, and finally, in 1914, woman suffrage. That year, GFWC official Mary Woods expressed the tone of the clubs when she claimed that "thosuands of towns, cities, and hamlets can bear testimony to the work of these organized women." No cause for social or moral uplift, said Woods, "has not received a helpful hand from the clubwomen."

If the women's clubs had influence, it often depended as much on who their members were as on what they did. In important clubs, such as the exclusive Chicago Woman's Club, which Jane Addams and Ellen Starr approached in 1889, members were the wives and daughters of wealthy men in prominent positions. Bertha Palmer, for instance, a great patron of Jane Addams and a frequent visitor at Hull-House, was married to a local tycoon who made his fortune during the Civil War, built up much of Chicago, and owned its grand hotel. Club member Louise Bowen, who served as a Hull-House trustee, was able to give the settlement three-quarters of a million dollars. The Chicago Woman's Club was a counterpart of the male power structure. It had access to funds and could generate support for all the projects it undertook, which meant that it could make or break any new venture on its own turf.

The GFWC, accordingly, was a superstructure of locally influential women, with outposts in every state. Like the WCTU, the women's club movement quickly spread throughout the South. North and South, clubwomen extolled similar benefits of association. One southerner described the women's club as a "university" in which women learned about themselves, other women, and men. "They have learned respect for their own opinions, toleration for the opinions of others and the necessity of cooperation for the successful accomplishment of all aims." Boston clubwoman Josephine Ruffin, a leader in the black women's club movement, contended that "We need to feel the cheer and inspiration of meeting each other, we gain the courage and fresh life that comes from the mingling of congenial souls, of those working for the same ends."

Whereas early women's clubs had been modeled on men's clubs, black women's clubs were modeled on white women's clubs, into which some black leaders had been admitted. Ruffin, wife of a Harvard-trained judge, was a

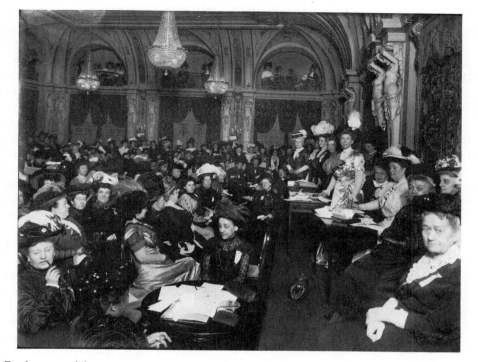

By the turn of the century, women's clubs had shifted their attention from cultural concerns to civic affairs. The delegates to a New York meeting of the General Federation of Women's Clubs around 1900, above, are ready to pass resolutions to protect the home, ensure child welfare, and improve community life. *(Brown Brothers)*

member of the prestigious New England Women's Club. She formed Boston's New Era Club for black women and organized a National Conference of Colored Women in 1895. Fannie Barrier Williams, a lawyer's wife in Chicago who was active in philanthropic projects, became the first and only black member of the selective Chicago Woman's Club in 1894, after over a year of debate on the issue. She then turned her attention to the National Association of Colored Women, a federation of clubs established in 1896 after a merger of two earlier federations, the National Federation of Afro-American Women, led by educator Margaret Murray Washington, wife of Tuskeegee's founder, and Mary Church Terrell's National League of Colored Women. But black clubs were not welcomed in the GFWC, as became clear in 1900, when Mary Church Terrell, representing the National Association of Colored Women, was denied seating at a GFWC convention.

Black women's clubs, therefore, occupied a truly separate sphere, rejected by white clubwomen but united by a sense of racial pride. According to Josephine Ruffin, the black women's club movement filled much the same function as the GFWC. Local clubs ran day nurseries, reading rooms, and welfare projects. The national federation, like the WCTU, set up "departments" to deal with major women's issues, such as suffrage, education, and women's employment. It also voiced concern about race-specific causes, such as "railroad conditions" and antilynching. Since the 1890s, pioneer clubwoman and suffragist Ida Wells-Barnett had run her own one-woman crusade against lynching. The black women's club movement, finally, adopted a distinctive mission, which Josephine Ruffin described as "the moral education of the race with which we are identified." By the turn of the century, these upper-rung black club leaders staked out their roles as moral beacons. Through the club movement, they intended to improve "home training" of children, provide racial leadership, and demonstrate that black women could form "an army of organized women for purity and mental worth." The last goal, in fact, contained a hidden agenda. A driving force behind black club formation, contends historian Gerda Lerner, was to protect black women from charges of moral looseness and from exploitation by white men.

The groundwork of organization laid by the temperance movement and women's clubs bore results in the progressive era, when "efficient combination among women," in the words of women's club leader Julia Ward Howe, took on massive proportions. By the end of the century, a vocal and visible woman's movement (or "the woman movement," as it was often called) had developed, with overlapping networks of local, state, and national organizations, united in the conviction that women, as women, had something distinctive and significant to contribute collectively to public life. For women of the progressive era, such social activism symbolized middle- and upper-class status. Simultaneously, changes in household technology also distinguished the lives of middle-class urban women from those of rural housewives as well as from those of their poorer neighbors in urban areas.

Educated Homemakers

By the turn of the century, the middle-class home had been transformed. "The flow of industry has passed and left idle the loom in the attic, the soap kettle in the shed," Ellen Richards wrote in 1908. The urban middle class could now buy a wide array of food products and clothing—baked goods, canned goods, suits, shirts, shoes, dresses. Not only had household production waned, but technological improvements rapidly changed the rest of domestic work. Middle-class homes had indoor running water and furnaces, run on oil, coal, or gas, that produced hot water. Stoves were fueled by gas, and delivery services provided ice for refrigerators. Electric power was available for lamps, sewing machines, irons, and even vacuum cleaners. No domestic task was unaffected. Commercial laundries, for instance, had done the wash for urban homes for decades; by the early 1900s, the first electric washing machines were on the market. One innovation after another changed the middle-class homemaker's responsibilities, each removing a different aspect of physical labor and household drudgery.

One impact of the new household technology was to draw a sharp dividing line among women according to class and region. Technological advances always affected the homes of the wealthy first, and then filtered downward into the urban middle class. But women who lived on farms were not yet affected by household improvements. Throughout the nineteenth century and well into the twentieth, rural homes lacked running water and electric power. Housewives had to haul large quantities of water into the house from wells or pumps for every purpose. Doing the family laundry, in large vats heated over stoves, continued to be a full day's work, just as canning and preserving continued to be seasonal necessities. Heat was provided by wood or coal stoves that left soot and ashes all over the house. In addition, rural women continued to produce most of their families' clothing. The urban poor, similarly, reaped few benefits from household improvements. Urban slum areas such as Chicago's nineteenth ward often had no sewers, garbage collection, or gas or electric lines; and tenements lacked both running water and central heating, to say nothing of any other conveniences that appeared in middle-class homes. Nor could poor urban women or rural housewives even attempt to meet the higher standards of cleanliness that middle-class women now adopted. At the turn of the century, variations in the nature of women's domestic work were probably more marked than at any time before.

Another impact of household technology was on its prime beneficiary, the middle-class housewife. By 1900, housekeeping—laundry, mending, cooking, cleaning—had become merely "daily tasks relating to food and cleanliness," wrote Ellen Richards, "the dull routine never done or only to be done over." The middle-class home had long lost not only its productive function but some of its personnel, including the large supply of servants, once a standard feature of domestic life. Improved technology reduced dependence on servants, although urban middle-class homes usually had domestic help. Employing a servant was a major female perquisite of middle-class status. Daughters, however, were no longer part of the household labor force; housekeeping was a one-woman responsibility. But what was the ultimate purpose, the social importance of such a vocation? During the late nineteenth and early twentieth centuries, women proposed various strategies to confront the labor crisis within the home.

A dominant strategy was ideological: to professionalize the homemaker's vocation, to elevate her role to the managerial level, to imbue her calling with value and significance. During the progressive era, housekeeping and child care became specialized missions that required commitment, talent, training, executive abilities, and professional skills. Domestic science, home economics, household engineering, and child psychology became arts and sciences that only an educated woman could master. High schools began to teach home economics, while college students could study chemistry, hygiene, domestic science, and psychology. Advice books, textbooks, and popular magazines, led by the *Ladies' Home Journal* (an influence since 1889), gave the woman at home some insight into the scope of her mounting obligations. New pressure groups, such as the National Congress of Mothers (1897) and the American Home Economics Association (1908), devoted themselves to the protection of the home and the ennoblement of the homemaker. Finally, as writers Barbara Ehrenreich and Deirdre

Urban middle-class homemakers were able to escape the physical labor involved in laundry, first by hiring laundresses, then by patronizing commercial laundries, and eventually by buying electric washing machines. But rural housewives, who lacked indoor plumbing or electricity, were likely to spend a full day of outside work doing the laundry. In order to wash, boil, and rinse one load of clothes, according to historian Susan Strasser, about fifty gallons of water had to be lugged from an outdoor pump to stoves and tubs. Clothes soaked in caustic substances, such as lye or lime, had to be scrubbed, rinsed, wrung, and rinsed again. Until well into the twentieth century, laundry remained the most strenuous of household jobs, even with the aid of such devices as the mechanical wringer, shown above. *(State Historical Society of Wisconsin)*

English have shown, academics and professionals began defining the home-maker's role.

The home had become a center of consumption, Marion Talbot explained in *The Modern Household* (1912), and it needed a trained executive to manage it. Her colleague Alice Norton told a home economics conference, held annually at Lake Placid, that "centrifugal forces" were working against the home, luring its members outside. It was the homemaker's job to make the home "a more interesting place . . . and the possibilities of doing this today are almost endless." If the middle-class homemaker had less menial work than her grandmother, her mental work had increased. Some tasks required special insight into science—such as the job of preventing family members from picking up germs in public places and spreading contagious diseases around the home, or of avoiding items made in contaminated sweatshops. The educated homemaker had to "keep the world clean," a housekeeping text proclaimed. She had to know how to buy appliances to foster efficiency, and to master techniques of scientific management, as explained by expert Christine Frederick in the *Ladies' Home Journal*. In addition to schedules and files of medical records and household expenses, she had to keep itemized lists of articles of clothing, birthdays, jokes, and quotations. And she had to adopt a self-critical posture, asking herself the questions proposed by Ellen Richards: "Can I do better than I am doing?" "Is there any device which I might use?" "Is my house right as to its sanitary arrangements?" "Is my food the best possible?" "Have I chosen the right colors and best materials for clothing?" "Can I make the best use of my time?"

The elevation of the homemaker to professional status had appeal in many quarters. It appealed to the *Ladies' Home Journal* readers who did housework anyway. New appliances such as the vacuum cleaner and the first, cumbersome washing machines had only recently appeared on the market; most homes were without them. The availability of new commercial food products hardly relieved homemakers from an endless round of food preparation. Even if servants were available to dust, sweep, wash, and scrub, it was still the housewife who bought everything the household needed, who decided how the home should be run. Her elevation to professional status appealed to the colleges, which established departments of domestic science and degree programs in home economics. It won applause in suffragist circles, ready to endorse any enhancement of women's status. The household arts, said an editor of the *Woman's Journal*, the suffrage movement's newspaper, in 1898, "should be as highly esteemed as medicine, law, theology." And professionalization of homemaking gained support from doctors. Domestic science, said the American Medical Association in 1899, would reduce infant mortality, disease, divorce, insanity, and pauperism, as well as "competition of labor between the sexes." The Home Economics Association, meanwhile, promoted domestic science extension courses for homemakers. It sent out syllabi to women's clubs, complete with vocabulary lists and annotated bibliographies. The home, as a spokeswoman declared at a 1902 Lake Placid meeting, was not a retreat from society but "a social workshop for the making of men. No home, however isolated, can escape the social obligations that rest upon it."

Not least of these obligations were those pertaining specifically to mothers, who, in the progressive era, received extremely favorable publicity. Child care, like housekeeping, had always been a central part of women's culture. But at the turn of the century, Ehrenreich and English emphasize, the child was "discovered" as the veritable centerpiece of society. With the birth rate at a new low, the middle-class child already received more attention than ever before. Although a large minority of the nation's children in 1900 were employed—in mines, cotton mills, canneries, and other factories—the offspring of middle-class urban families no longer served as either household laborers or family wage earners. Rather, they were the primary products of the home, its sole contribution to the world beyond. The decline of the father ("an earning mechanism," said sociologist Arthur Calhoun in the World War I era, "a tame cat") and the rise of the child left the mother in a strong position. The transformation of the child, as Ellen Key explained in her 1909 best seller, *The Century of the Child*, required "an entirely new conception of the vocation of mother."

During the progressive era, motherhood was described as not only a noble calling ("more important to the community than even the ablest man" as President Roosevelt said in 1908) but also a learned one. The competent mother, historian Sheila M. Rothman points out, now needed more "insight" than "instinct." She had to acquire expertise and sophisticated skills, preferably in college classes in child study and psychology, but in any case through conscious effort. The campaign for educated motherhood found an outlet in the 1890s in an outburst of "mothers' clubs" and, in 1897, in the formation of the National Congress of Mothers, a pressure group that would do for motherhood what domestic science enthusiasts did for housekeeping. By 1910, "mothers' clubs" had 50,000 members, and a decade later, over three times as many. In 1924, the National Congress of Mothers became the Parents Teachers Association.

The educated mother, like the educated homemaker, won quick approval from academics and experts. Here psychologist G. Stanley Hall was a pivotal figure. A regular participant in the National Congress's functions, Hall outlined the prerequisites of scientific motherhood, a status that only an educated woman could attain. The competent mother was a record keeper and rule follower who could learn techniques and instill habits. She had to understand each stage in the child's growth, to gear her responses to the child's changing needs, from infancy to adolescence, and to judge her own self-worth by how well she succeeded. "The heart and soul of growing childhood is the criterion by which we judge the larger heart and soul of mature womanhood," said Hall.

Like the educated housekeeper, the professional mother was an ideal that only the well-trained sophisticated middle-class woman could realize. She was also an agent of reform. Scientific motherhood, a mother announced at the National Congress of Mothers in 1897, would lead to "a grander, nobler race." It would reform the drunkard, criminal, and murderer; it would lead to "the abolition of asylums . . . the elimination of selfishness, the death of oppression . . . the uplifting of mankind." The National Congress of Mothers, moreover, intended not only to perfect middle-class motherhood but also to bring other mothers up to par. Heading the battery of reforms it proposed were kindergartens—to take lower-class children out of less fortunate homes and expose them to educated women who could instill proper values. The congress also supported the mother's right to legal guardianship of children, as well as playgrounds, foster home programs, juvenile courts, child labor laws, compulsory school attendance, and domestic science and child-study courses in the high school and college curricula.

But efforts to "professionalize" the vocations of mother and housekeeper were not the only facet of women's agenda for domestic reform. While advocates of home economics and the National Congress of Mothers ennobled the homemaker, some women created collective strategies to liberate the woman at home for a larger life outside it. As historian Dolores Hayden has shown, visions of cooperative housekeeping, food preparation, and even child care had a long history, dating back to soon after the Civil War. One early enthusiast, Melusina Fay Peirce, for instance, made elaborate plans for producers' cooperatives that would perform domestic work—cooking, baking, sewing, and laundry—collectively. Peirce organized such a cooperative in Cambridge, Massachusetts, in 1869 (the same year she chaired a large "women's parliament" in New York under the auspices of Sorosis, the pioneer women's club). The Cambridge collective fell apart after two years, since husbands, who were assessed for the women's services, objected to the new arrangements. But Melusina Peirce continued to endorse the virtues of "cooperative housekeeping," and other women persevered along similar lines. Hayden calls their tradition "material feminism."

Most proponents of collective efforts had experience in the left wing of social reform. During the 1880s, Marie Stevens Howland, former Lowell mill worker and communitarian, became involved in an American experimental community in Mexico and, with the collaboration of an architect and an engineer, drew up plans for community organization that incorporated cooperative housekeeping and child-care schemes. Other advocates of collective arrangements, more in the mainstream of the late-nineteenth-century woman's movement, were adventurous liberals. Reformer Mary Livermore, known for her work in the Sanitary Commission, the temperance crusade, and women's clubs, advocated cooperative laundries, kitchens, and eating facilities that utilized the services of "professional" household labor. Authorities such as Ellen Richards and Jane Addams endorsed more limited collective schemes, such as public kitchens for working mothers. As in much else, Hull-House was a pioneer in cooperative arrangements, whether in its Jane Club boardinghouse or in the residence plans and common dining facilities of the settlement itself. Finally, at the turn of the century, Charlotte Perkins Gilman became the best-known advocate of collectivist plans. Denouncing the isolated private home and its harmful effects on the human race, Gilman proposed new arrangements for cooperative housekeeping, cooking, and child care, utilizing the services of paid professionals in domestic work. Evoking widespread interest, Gilman's ideas inspired other enthusiasts through the 1920s.

Proponents of collective plans disagreed on major issues, such as *who* should do domestic work. According to Melusina Fay Peirce's scheme, former servants and their mistresses would labor side by side in producers' cooperatives. Others, among them Mary Livermore and Charlotte Perkins Gilman, envisioned paid staffs of domestic specialists. Most collectivists concentrated on plans for communal cooking and housework but some, such as Howland and Gilman, included child care as well. In all cases, significantly, collectivists viewed domestic work as women's realm. Throughout their visions of kitchenless homes, communal facilities, and cooperative strategies, moreover, ran several themes: Women should be paid for household work, spatial design of home and community should be reorganized to suit women's needs, and divisions between private household space and public space should be revised.

Plans for cooperative housekeeping and other collectivist ventures, how-ever, remained visions more than realities, domestic counterparts to socialist visions that flourished at the same time. At the turn of the century, the middle-class woman, who valued her individualism, was more likely to adopt the role of household executive and professional parent, as touted by the Home Econom-ics Association and the National Congress of Mothers. She also became a vital contributor to the progressive reform agenda. Capitalizing on her domestic expertise, inspired by a sense of shared feminine interests, and supported by a wide range of women's organizations, she was ready to take an active role in public life.

Social Housekeepers

During the progressive era, the ranks of women's organizations exploded. Besides the oldest and largest, the WCTU and the women's club movement, many new associations were formed—by homemakers, mothers, alumnae, pro-fessional women, charity workers, and reformers of all stripes. Some new organi-zations were special interest groups such as the Daughters of the American Revolution (1890) and the National Council of Jewish Women (1893). Others were professional associations—of doctors, nurses, educators, or settlement workers. Yet others carved out new public fiefs, such as the National Congress of Mothers (1897) or the Home Economics Association (1908). Many women's groups specialized in philanthropic works—such as the Young Women's Chris-tian Association, started soon after the Civil War, which aided young women who came to the city alone, or the Junior League (1901), which sponsored civic projects. On the left wing, new coalitions evolved to improve the lot of women workers, such as the National Consumers' League (1899), which sought to improve working conditions in factories and retail sales, and the Women's Trade Union League (1903), which spurred the formation of women's unions. Each club, society, and federation strove for specific goals, but all united behind the banner of women's special interests, interests that began to occupy more and more public space.

Here the women's clubs had set the tone. Women were enemies of vice, filth, corruption, ugliness, ignorance, and exploitation. Their special concerns were anything that involved children, home, family, education, health, hygiene, food, sanitation, and other women. However specialized their original goals, most women's associations turned into pressure groups and ended up tackling local officials and state legislators—for playgrounds, kindergartens, compulsory education laws, child labor laws, protective laws, pure food laws, juvenile courts, and other items on the progressive reform agenda. The rationale behind such efforts was so often repeated that it took on the aura of gospel. "The woman's place is in the home," a progressive wrote in a university bulletin in 1915. "But to-day would she serve the home, she must go beyond the home. No longer is the home encompassed by four walls. Many of its most important duties lie now involved in the bigger family of the city and the state." Capitalizing on a long tradition of female benevolence and combining it with a newfound interest in social science, middle-class women collectively embarked on the solution of urban problems. By the turn of the century, the new woman had become a social housekeeper, an active participant in civic affairs.

The settlement worker, a living bridge between traditional philanthropy and progressive reform, served in the front ranks of social housekeeping. The number of settlements multiplied rapidly, along with the number of women college graduates. According to historian Allen Davis, there were 6 settlements in 1891, 100 in 1900, 200 in 1905, and 400 by 1910. Although a national settlement movement began in the 1890s, dominated by Jane Addams, no formal organization was established until the National Federation of Settlements in 1911. By that time, the settlement had become a pivotal institution in both progressive reform and women's politics. Drawing on the talents of college-trained women, the settlement house was a more elite, selective outpost than either the women's club or any other voluntary society. It was also an avenue through which the educated women could make a tangible social contribution, by bringing the urban poor and foreign-born in contact with the "best in American life." Although neither settlement work nor settlement programs excluded men, women dominated the ranks of settlement residents as well as neighborhood participants. The women and children who joined settlement clubs and classes, such as those at Hull-House, were supposed to serve as carriers of values back to their homes. Moreover, most of the men in Chicago's nineteenth ward could not be lured into the Hull-House Men's Club or other settlement functions, whereas the children in the afterschool clubs, the working girls in the Jane Club, and the mothers with babies in the day nursery rushed to take advantage of the settlement's services.

The other beneficiaries, as Jane Addams always stressed, were the residents themselves. "I can see why life in a settlement seemed so great an adventure," wrote Alice Hamilton, who became a Hull-House resident in 1897. "It was all so new, this exploring of a poor quarter of a big city. The thirst to know how the other half lived had just begun to send people pioneering in the unknown part of American life." Vida Scudder, a settlement pioneer in Boston, had been "aimless and groping" after graduating from Smith in 1884, feeling suffocated by "the customs, the assumptions of my own class." Like Alice Hamilton, Vida Scudder had a "biting curiosity" about the "other half." "Were not the workers, the poor, nearer perhaps than we to the reality I was always seeking?" Few settlement pioneers made a lifetime career of it. Allen Davis shows that half of settlement workers married, and most of these spent less than five years in settlement work. But they were replaced by others equally capable of transmitting middle-class values and practices to newly arrived immigrants and the urban poor. Long-term residents, meanwhile, profited from the settlement's role as surrogate family.

The settlement house resembled not only an upper-class home—with its parlor, drawing rooms, library, and music room, its fireplaces and stuffed armchairs—but also the colleges from which most residents had recently graduated. One visitor described a settlement's atmosphere as that of a "college dormitory in the center of the urban slums." Like the college, the settlement was an "experiment," but one designed, in Addams's words, "to aid in the solution of the social and industrial problems which are engendered by the modern conditions of urban life." In the settlement context, educated women could preserve a collegial spirit while attempting to solve these problems. At the same time, settlement work was an opportunity for residents to apply their academic training, using the neighborhood as a social science "laboratory." Hull-House, for instance, became an outpost of the University of Chicago. Searching for the roots of poverty and crime, corruption and labor exploitation, residents collected evidence from daily life and worked it up into generalizations, reform proposals, and legislative remedies.

The settlement worker also had much in common with the educated homemaker, since she held the same values. The National Congress of Mothers in 1897 traced the roots of crime and disease to "inefficient homes," and the settlement worker gained access to those homes, or at least to their occupants. The women and children who participated in settlement programs learned thrift, cleanliness, orderliness, refinement, manners, culture, responsibility, and, above all, citizenship. "Almost daily contact with Jane Addams gave me an abiding faith in the true principles of Americanism," a young working woman at Hull-House recalled. Especially effective were the settlements' clubs, with their rites and rituals, regular meetings, and democratic procedures. Residents also brought the basic lessons of domestic science, or "right living," to the slums. The Italian girl who learned to cook, as Jane Addams explained, could "connect the entire family with American food and household habits." If she learned about child care, she could tell her mother why the baby had to be fed purified milk. The settlement's visiting nurse services meanwhile taught health and hygiene to neighborhood residents. While immigrant mothers learned household management, day nurseries and kindergartens exposed infants and toddlers to the best in educated child care, and instilled those habits that the tenement home was unable to provide. Even the Hull-House kitchen reflected Ellen Richards's latest precepts. Residents also extended good housekeeping into their community patrols by inspecting water supplies, garbage disposal, and sanitary conditions, reporting violations, and insisting on improved municipal services. The settlement was not only a "big brother" in the playground, as Addams described it, but also a female watchdog that barked whenever male government fell short.

Finally, settlement houses transformed their leading residents into civil servants and politicians. In 1912, for instance, when Jane Addams appeared at the Progressive party convention, Lillian Wald of the Henry Street Settlement served much the same function for the Democrats. A similar path was followed, on the state and local level, by other activists in the settlement movement. As experts in social welfare and spokeswomen for the "other half," settlement workers created a niche for themselves in government service and in political life. Leading spirits ended up as lobbyists who appealed to local governments for improved services and to state legislators for improved laws, especially those that affected women, children, and public welfare. Hull-House alumnae were the prime examples. Florence Kelley, the best known, moved on not only to government appointments, first as an agent for the Illinois Bureau of Labor

Statistics and then as a state factory inspector, but also to work as a lobbyist and reformer. The many causes that Kelley promoted included child labor laws, protective laws for women workers, and mothers' pension programs to support children in families that lacked breadwinners. After joining Lillian Wald's Henry Street Settlement in 1899, Kelley took a leading role in the National Consumers' League, another exemplary progressive women's organization.

Like the settlement movement, both the Women's Trade Union League and the National Consumers' League attempted to provide a women's bridge between social classes. While the settlement movement offered mutual benefits to both residents and neighborhood participants and the WTUL united "allies" and wage earners in common cause, the NCL cut across class lines by a campaign that would benefit middle-class homemakers and women workers. Started in New York in 1891 by Maud Nathan and Josephine Lowell, the Consumers' League became a national organization in 1899. It adopted the settlement technique of thorough investigation, inspecting factories and stores. Its "white label" was awarded only to workplaces with sanitary conditions—to ensure that germ-laden garments and food products would not infiltrate homes. "It is the duty of consumers to find out under what conditions the articles they purchase are produced and to insist that these conditions be at least decent," Maud Nathan said. The league also produced a "white list" of local retail stores, those where the wages, hours, and working conditions of women employees met their standards, and it urged the public to use "selective patronage." Protecting home and housewife, worker and consumer, the NCL was an exemplary social housekeeper. Like the WTUL, it was also a coalition of many state branches and urban groups, each committed to local vigilance.

The reform-minded spirit of the New Woman, as embodied in the settlement movement, the NCL, the WTUL, and other women's associations, succeeded on many fronts. One was legislative. During the first decades of the twentieth century, campaigns for child labor laws, protective laws, compulsory education laws, juvenile courts, mothers' pensions, and other causes sponsored by women often prevailed on the state and local level. Women's campaigns thus affected public policy for decades to come. There were national victories, too, such as the Pure Food and Drug Act of 1908 and the establishment of the Children's Bureau in the Labor Department in 1912. This would be followed, after World War I, by the establishment of the Women's Bureau, intended to guard the interests of women workers. The two bureaus served an important function as permanent female outposts in the federal government. Another success was purely institutional. The progressive era left in its wake hundreds of settlement houses and a spate of national women's organizations, most of them started in the 1890s. This outburst of association was not peculiar to women; many middle-class interest groups coalesced around the turn of the century. But it represented a peak of female activism. By the early twentieth century, the vital, energetic woman's movement had many bases—college, profession, settlement house, and a loose coalition of overlapping interest groups—all committed to women's causes, social service, and civic improvement.

A final success was political. The New Woman of the progressive era, vigorous, confident, and assertive, had left her mark on public life. Her political tendencies varied. Sometimes she tilted to the right, as in the turn-of-the-century WCTU and the women's club movement. Sometimes she tilted to the left, as in the WTUL or among converts to socialism such as Florence Kelley and Ellen Starr. Often she ended up in the progressive camp, as did Jane Addams, and sometimes in the suffrage camp as well. Her ideology, to be sure, centered more around female distinctiveness than sexual equality. But by the 1890s this was the thrust of the suffrage movement, too. By demonstrating her concern for social welfare and her ability to participate in public life, the New Woman contributed to the effectiveness of arguments for woman suffrage. The large, energetic woman's movement, moreover, provided a context in which the suffrage movement could thrive and prosper.

SUGGESTED READINGS AND SOURCES

CHAPTER 11

Allen F. Davis's biography, *American Heroine: The Life and Legend of Jane Addams* (New York, 1973), is the best starting point. Other important interpretations are Christopher Lasch, "Jane Addams: The College Woman and the Family Claim," in *The New Radicalism in America 1889–1963: The Intellectual as a Social Type* (New York, 1965); Jill Conway, "Jane Addams: An American Heroine," *Daedalus*, 93 (Spring 1964), 761–780; and Staughton Lynd, "Jane Addams and the Radical Impulse," *Commentary*, 32 (July 1961), 54–59. For the development of settlement work, see Allen F. Davis, *Spearheads for Reform: The Social Settlement and the Progressive Movement, 1890–1914* (New York, 1967), and Mary L. Bryan and Allen F. Davis, eds., *One Hundred Years at Hull-House* (Bloomington, Ind., 1990).

Christopher Lasch has edited a collection of Jane Addams's essays, *The Social Thought of Jane Addams* (Indianapolis, Ind., 1965). For Addams's autobiography, see *Twenty Years at Hull House* (New York, 1910) and *The Second Twenty Years at Hull House* (New York, 1930). Davis provides a cogent interpretation of the first volume in *American Heroine*, ch. 9. Addams's famous essays "The Subjective Necessity for Social Settlements" and "The Objective Value of a Social Settlement" are reprinted in the Lasch collection. Another major essay is "The College Woman and the Family Claim," *Commons*, 3 (September 1898), 3–7. Addams's most important books are *Democracy and Social Ethics* (New York, 1902), *The Spirit of Youth and the City Streets* (New York, 1909), and *A New Conscience and an Ancient Evil* (New York, 1912), on prostitution.

CHAPTER 12

For an overview of women's new roles in this era, see Sheila M. Rothman, *Woman's Proper Place: A History of Changing Ideals and Practices, 1870 to the Present* (New York, 1978), chs. 1–3.

Changes in family life are examined in Carl Degler, *At Odds: Women and the Family in America from the Revolution to the Present* (New York, 1979), chs. 7–13; Steven Mintz and Susan Kellogg, *Domestic Revolutions: A Social History of American Family Life* (New York, 1988), chs. 4–6; Elaine Tyler May, *Great Expectations: Marriage and Divorce in Post-Victorian America* (Chicago, 1980); and William L. O'Neill, *Divorce in the Progressive Era* (New Haven,

Conn., 1967). The concept of family life cycle is explained in Robert V. Wells, "Demographic Change and the Life Cycle of American Families," *Journal of Interdisciplinary History*, 2 (Autumn 1971), 272–282. On "voluntary motherhood," see Linda Gordon, *Woman's Body, Woman's Right: A Social History of Birth Control in America* (New York, 1976), part 2. See also James C. Mohr, *Abortion in America: The Origins and Evolution of National Policy, 1800–1900* (New York, 1978), and John D'Emilio and Estelle Freedman, *Intimate Matters: A History of Sexuality in America* (New York, 1988). For the underside of family life, see Linda Gordon, *Heroes of Their Own Lives: The Politics and History of Family Violence* (New York, 1988), and Elizabeth Pleck, *Domestic Tyranny: The Making of Social Policy Against Domestic Violence* (New York, 1987).

The social purity movement is examined in David J. Pivar, *Purity Crusade: Sexual Morality and Social Control 1868–1900* (Westport, Conn., 1973). Cynthia Eagle Russett, *Sexual Science: The Victorian Construction of Womanhood* (Cambridge, Mass., 1989) assesses scientists' assertions about sexual difference. Carl Degler, "What Ought to Be and What Was: Women's Sexuality in the Nineteenth Century," *American Historical Review*, 79 (December 1974), 1479–1490, describes the Mosher Report, the earliest survey of female sexuality. Daniel Scott Smith defines "domestic feminism" in "Family Limitation, Sexual Control, and Domestic Feminism in Victorian America," in Mary Hartmann and Lois Banner, eds., *Clio's Consciousness Raised* (New York, 1974), pp. 119–136. Relations between women are explored in Carroll Smith Rosenberg, "The Female World of Love and Ritual," *Signs*, 1 (Autumn 1975), 1–29; Blanche Wiesen Cook, "Female Support Networks and Political Activism: Lillian Wald, Crystal Eastman, and Emma Goldman," *Crysalis*, 1 (1977), 43–61; D'Emilio and Freedman, *Intimate Matters*, cited above; and Lillian Faderman, *Odd Girls and Twilight Lovers: A History of Lesbian Life in Twentieth-Century America* (New York, 1991), ch. 1. Helen Lefkowitz Horowitz discusses identity and sexuality in "'Nous Autres': Reading, Passion, and the Creation of M. Carey Thomas," *Journal of American History* 79 (June 1992), 68–95. In *Alice James: A Biography* (New York, 1980), Jean Strouse provides insights into female friendship, "Boston marriage," and the dynamics of an unusual late-nineteenth-century family.

The movement of women into higher education is examined in Patricia Albjerg Graham, "Expansion and Exclusion: A History of Women in Higher Education," *Signs*, 3 (Summer 1978), 759–773; Helen Lefkowitz Horowitz, *Alma Mater: Design and Experience in the Women's Colleges from their Nineteenth-century Beginnings to the 1930s* (New York, 1984); Barbara Miller Solomon, *In the Company of Educated Women: A History of Women and Higher Education in America* (New Haven, Conn., 1985); and Lynn D. Gordon, *Gender and Higher Education in the Progressive Era* (New Haven, Conn., 1990). For reactions to feminization in higher education, see Rosalind Rosenberg, "The Academic Prism: The New View of American Women," in Carol Ruth Berkin and Mary Beth Norton, eds., *Women of America: A History* (Boston, 1979), pp. 318–341. The roles of women graduates are discussed in Joyce Antler, "After College, What? New Graduates and the Family Claim," *American Quarterly*, 32 (Fall 1980), 409–435; Patricia Palmieri, "Patterns of Achievement of Single Academic Women at Wellesley College 1880–1920," *Frontiers*, 5 (Spring 1980), 63–67; and Roberta Wein, "Women's Colleges and Domesticity, 1875–1918," *History of Education Quarterly*, 14 (Spring 1974), 31–47. Martha H. Verbrugge explores physical education in several women's institutions in *Able-Bodied Womanhood: Personal Health and Social Change in Nineteenth-Century Boston* (New York, 1988). For the development of a black women's college, see Beverly Guy-Sheftall and Jo Moore Stewart, *Spelman: A Centennial Celebration, 1881–1981* (Atlanta, Ga., 1981). The work of black women educators is discussed in Gerda Lerner, "Black Women in the United States: A Problem in Historiography and Interpretation," in *The Majority Finds its Past* (New York, 1979), pp. 63–82, and Evelyn Brooks

Barnett, "Nannie Burroughs and the Education of Black Women," in Sharon Harley and Rosalyn Terborg-Penn, eds., *The Afro-American Woman: Struggles and Images* (Port Washington, N.Y., 1978), pp. 97–108. The multi-volume Schomburg Library of Nineteenth-Century Black Women Writers, ed., Henry Louis Gates, Jr., includes some relevant works. For instance, Anna Julia Cooper, *A Voice From the South,* int. by Mary Helen Washington (New York, 1988), an 1892 book by the pioneer educator, urges black women to assume leadership roles in racial advancement.

For women's efforts to enter traditionally male professions, see D. Kelley Weisberg, "Barred From the Bar: Women and Legal Education in the United States, 1870–1890," *Journal of Legal Education,* 38 (1977), 485–507; Nancy Gilliam, "Myra Bradwell's Fights to Practice Law," *Law and History Review,* 7 (1987), 105–133; and Regina Markell Morantz-Sanchez, *Sympathy and Science: Women Physicians in American Medicine* (New York, 1985). See also Regina Markell Morantz, "Feminism, Professionalism, and Germs: The Thought of Mary Putnam Jacobi and Elizabeth Blackwell," *American Quarterly,* 34 (Winter 1982), 459–478. For nursing see Susan Reverby, *Ordered to Care: The Dilemma of American Nursing, 1850–1945* (Cambridge, England, and New York, 1987). Barbara Melosh discusses the professionalization of nursing since 1920 in *"The Physician's Hand": Work Culture and Conflict in American Nursing* (Philadelphia, 1982). See also Darlene Clark Hine, *Black Women in White: Racial Conflict and Cooperation in the Nursing Profession, 1890–1950* (Bloomington, Ind., 1990). Joan Jacobs Brumberg offers insights into medical practice and women's lives in *Fasting Girls: The Emergence of Anorexia Nervosa as a Modern Disease* (Cambridge, Mass., 1988).

For women in science, see Sally Kohlstedt, "In From the Periphery: American Women in Science, 1830–1880," *Signs,* 4 (Autumn 1978), 81–96, and Margaret W. Rossiter, *Women Scientists in America: Struggles and Strategies to 1940* (Baltimore, Md., 1982). Rosalind Rosenberg examines academic women's careers in social science and psychology in *Beyond Separate Spheres: Intellectual Roots of Modern Feminism* (New Haven, Conn., 1982). Ellen Fitzpatrick explores the impact of social science training in *Endless Crusade: Women Social Scientists and Progressive Reform* (New York, 1990). Joyce Antler presents the innovative career of a married professional pioneer in *Lucy Sprague Mitchell, The Making of a Modern Woman* (New Haven, 1987). Dee Garrison describes the feminization of library work in *Apostles of Culture: The Public Libraries and American Society, 1876–1920* (New York, 1979). For teaching, see Nancy Hoffman, ed., *Woman's "True" Profession: Voices From the History of Teaching* (Old Westbury, N.Y., 1981). For social work, see Roy Lubove, *The Professional Altruist: The Emergence of Social Work as a Career, 1880–1930* (Cambridge, Mass., 1965). Barbara Harris surveys women's movement into the professions in *Beyond Her Sphere: Women and the Professions in American History* (Westport, Conn., 1978). Joan Jacobs Brumberg and Nancy Tomes assess disparities between professionalism and women's culture in "Women and the Professions: A Research Agenda for American Historians," *Reviews in American History,* 10 (June 1982), 275–296. For the professional man, see Burton J. Bledstein, *The Culture of Professionalism: The Middle Class and the Development of Higher Education in America* (New York, 1976).

The technological changes that transformed domestic labor are examined in Susan Strasser, *Never Done: A History of American Housework* (New York, 1982) and Ruth Schwartz Cowan, *More Work for Mother: The Ironies of Household Technology from the Open Hearth to the Microwave* (New York, 1983). The impact of household technology is also discussed in Susan J. Kleinberg, "Technology and Women's Work: The Lives of Working Class Women in Pittsburgh, 1870–1900," *Labor History,* 17 (Winter 1976), 55–72, and Cowan, "The 'Industrial Revolution' in the Home: Household Technology and Social Change in the Twentieth Century," *Technology and Culture,* 17 (January 1976), 1–23. See also Glenna

Matthews, *"Just a Housewife": The Rise and Fall of Domesticity in the United States* (New York, 1987). For the home economics movement and the National Congress of Mothers, see Rothman, *Woman's Proper Place*, ch. 3, and Barbara Ehrenreich and Deirdre English, *For Her Own Good: 150 Years of the Experts' Advice to Women* (New York, 1978), chs. 5 and 6. Dolores Hayden examines the "material feminist" tradition in *The Grand Domestic Revolution: A History of Feminist Design for American Homes, Neighborhoods, and Cities* (Cambridge, Mass., and London, 1981). Clifford E. Clark, Jr., *The American Family Home, 1800–1960* (Chapel Hill, N.C., 1986) explores changing vogues of home design. David M. Katzman discusses the relations of servants and employers in *Seven Days a Week: Women and Domestic Service in Industrializing America, 1865–1895* (New York, 1978). See also Norton Juster, *So Sweet to Labor: Rural Women in America, 1865–1895* (New York, 1979), an evocative collection of primary sources on domestic life.

Recent scholarship suggests a powerful feminist thrust in both the temperance and women's club movements. For the emergence of the temperance crusade in the early 1870s and the development of the WCTU, see Barbara Leslie Epstein, *The Politics of Domesticity: Women, Evangelism, and Temperance in Nineteenth-century America* (Middletown, Conn., 1981), chs. 4 and 5; Ruth Bordin, *Women and Temperance: The Quest for Power and Liberty, 1873–1900* (Philadelphia, 1980); Jack Blocker, *"Give Wind to Thy Fears"* (Westport, Conn., 1985); and Blocker, *American Temperance Movements: Cycles of Reform* (Boston, 1989). For an earlier interpretation, see Joseph Gusfield, *Symbolic Crusade: Status Politics and the American Temperance Movement* (Urbana, Ill., 1963). Paula Baker examines WCTU activism on the local level in *The Moral Frameworks of Public Life: Gender, Politics, and the State in Rural New York, 1870–1930* (New York, 1991), ch. 3.

In *The Clubwoman as Feminist: True Womanhood Redefined* (New York, 1980), Karen J. Blair contends that women's clubs promoted autonomy while providing a covert feminist agenda. For the women's city club, see Maureen A. Flanagan, "Gender and Urban Political Reform: The City Club and the Woman's City Club of Chicago in the Progressive Era," *American Historical Review*, 95 (October 1990), 1032–1050. Older histories of the club movement are Jennie C. Croly, *The History of the Women's Club Movement in America* (New York, 1898); Mary I. Woods, *The History of the General Federation of Women's Clubs* (New York, 1912); and Mildred White Wells, *Unity in Diversity: The History of the General Federation of Women's Clubs* (Washington, D.C., 1958). For the black women's club movement, see Gerda Lerner, "Early Community Work of Black Clubwomen," *Journal of Negro History*, 59 (April 1974), 158–167; Paula Giddings, *Where and When I Enter: The Impact of Black Women on Race and Sex in America* (New York, 1984), ch. 6; and Cynthia Neverdon-Morton, *Afro-American Women of the South and the Advancement of the Race, 1895–1925* (Knoxville, Tenn., 1989).

Marion Talbot and Lois Rosenberry describe the formation of the Association of Collegiate Alumnae in *The History of the American Association of University Women* (Boston, 1931). Women's philanthropic work is covered in Josephine Shaw Lowell, *Public Relief and Private Charity* (New York, 1884). For the YWCA, see Elizabeth Wilson, *Fifty Years of Association Work Among Young Women, 1866–1916* (New York, 1916). For the collective endeavors of churchwomen, see Joan Jacobs Brumberg, "Zenanas and Girlless Villages: The Ethnology of American Evangelical Women, 1870–1910," *Journal of American History*, 69 (September 1982), 347–371; Jane Hunter, *The Gospel of Gentility: American Women Missionaries in Turn-of-the-Century China* (New Haven, Conn., 1984); and Patricia R. Hill, *The World Their Household: The American Woman's Foreign Mission Movement and Cultural Transformation, 1870–1920* (Ann Arbor, Mich., 1985).

Allen F. Davis examines the settlement movement in his pioneer work, *Spearheads for Reform* (New York, 1967). See also Mina Carson, *Settlement Folk: The Evolution of Social*

Welfare Ideology in the American Settlement Movement, 1883–1930 (Chicago, 1990). For Hull-House and its personnel, see Kathryn Kish Sklar, "Hull House in the 1890s: A Community of Women Reformers," *Signs,* 10 (Summer 1985), 658–677; Barbara Sicherman, *Edith Hamilton: A Life in Letters* (Cambridge, Mass., 1984); Lela B. Castin, *Two Sisters for Social Justice: A Biography of Grace and Edith Abbott* (Urbana, Ill., 1983); Rivka Shpak Lissak, *Pluralism and Progressives: Hull House and the New Immigrants, 1890–1919* (Chicago, 1889); and, for a first-hand account, Hilda Satt Polacheck, *I Came a Stranger: The Story of a Hull House Girl* (Urbana, Ill., 1989). A history of the National Consumers League is Maud Nathan, *The Story of an Epoch-Making Movement* (New York, 1926). For the WTUL, see Nancy Shrom Dye, *As Equals and As Sisters: Feminism, Unionism, and the Women's Trade Union League of New York* (Columbia, Mo., 1980); Robin Miller Jacoby, "The Women's Trade Union League and American Feminism," *Feminist Studies,* 3 (Fall 1975), 126–140; and Gladys Boone, *The Women's Trade Union League in Great Britain and the United States* (New York, 1942). For the first decades of the federal Children's Bureau, see Molly Ladd-Taylor, *Raising a Baby the Government Way: Mothers' Letters to the Children's Bureau, 1915–1932* (New Brunswick, N.J., 1984).

The ground swell of association among women is examined by William L. O'Neill in *A History of Feminism in America* (2d ed., New Brunswick, N.J., 1989), ch. 3. O'Neill coins the term "social feminist" to describe activists in women's associations and reform movements who might support women's rights but "generally subordinated them to broad social movements they thought more urgent." Nancy F. Cott criticizes this concept in "What's in a Name? The Limits of 'Social Feminism,' or, Expanding the Vocabulary of Women's History," *Journal of American History,* 76 (December 1989), 809–829. In *Womanhood in America* (New York, 1975), Mary P. Ryan uses the term "social housekeeping" to describe women's reform work. Women's activism in reform has recently attracted abundant attention. See, for instance, Robyn Muncy, *Creating a Female Dominion in American Reform, 1890–1930* (New York, 1991); Noralee Frankel and Nancy S. Dye, eds., *Gender, Class, Race and Reform in the Progressive Era* (Lexington, Ky., 1992); and Anne Firor Scott, *Natural Allies: Women's Associations in American History* (Urbana, Ill., 1992). Important articles include Marlene Stein Wortman, "Domesticating the Nineteenth-Century City," *Prospects: An Annual of American Cultural Studies,* 3 (1977), 531–572, a study of "municipal housekeeping" in Chicago; Jill Conway, "Women Reformers and American Culture, 1870–1930," *Journal of Social History,* 5 (1971–1972), 164–177; Paula Baker, "The Domestication of Politics: Women and American Political Society, 1780–1920," *American Historical Review* 89 (June 1984), 620–647; Linda Gordon, "Black and White Visions of Welfare: Women's Welfare Activism, 1890–1945," *Journal of American History,* 78 (September 1991), 559–590; Gordon, "Social Insurance and Public Assistance: The Influence of Gender in Welfare Thought in the United States, 1890–1935, *American Historical Review,* 97 (February 1992) 19–54; and Suzanne Lebsock, "Across the Great Divide: Women and Politics, 1890–1920," in Louise Tilly and Patricia Gurin, eds., *Women, Politics and Change* (New York, 1990). Linda Gordon, ed., *Women, the State, and Welfare* (Madison, Wisc., 1990) is an important collection that traces women's influence on public policy. Theda Skocpol examines mothers' pensions in *Protecting Soldiers and Mothers: The Political Origins of Social Policy in the United States* (Cambridge, Mass., 1992). For a comparative perspective, see Sonya Michel and Seth Koven, "Womanly Duties: Maternalist Politics and the Origins of Welfare States in France, Germany, Great Britain, and the United States, 1880–1920," *American Historical Review* 95 (October 1990), 1076–1108. Estelle Freedman assesses the significance of separate women's institutions—colleges, associations, reform movements—in her important article, "Separatism as Strategy: Female Institution Building and American Feminism, 1870–1930," *Feminist Studies,* 5 (Fall 1979), 512–549.

Memoirs of women reformers include Frances Willard, *Glimpses of Fifty Years: The Autobiography of an American Woman* (Chicago, 1889); Mary Ashton Livermore, *The Story of My Life or the Sunshine and Shadow of Seventy Years* (Hartford, Conn., 1898); Julia Ward Howe, *Reminiscences, 1819–1899* (Boston, 1899); Mary Church Terrell, *A Colored Woman in a White World* (Washington, D.C., 1940); Alfreda Duster, ed., *Crusader for Justice: The Autobiography of Ida B. Wells* (Chicago and London, 1970); Lillian Wald, *The House on Henry Street* (New York, 1915); Vida Scudder, *On Journey* (New York, 1937); and Alice Hamilton, *Exploring the Dangerous Trades* (Boston, 1973). Biographies include Josephine Goldmark, *Impatient Crusader: Florence Kelley's Life Story* (Urbana, Ill., 1953); Ruth Bordin, *Frances Willard: A Biography* (Chapel Hill, N.C., 1986); and Deborah Pickman Clifford, *Mine Eyes Have Seen the Glory: A Biography of Julia Ward Howe* (Boston, 1979). For the careers of Maud Nathan, Lillian Wald, and other reformers, see Ellen Condliffe Lagemann, *A Generation of Women: Education in the Lives of Progressive Reformers* (Cambridge, Mass., 1979).

CHAPTER 13

❧

The Crisis of the NWSA

In January 1871, leaders of the National Woman Suffrage Association began arriving in the capital for their third annual Washington convention. A "call" had been issued months before, and ever since, the convention's organizer, Isabella Beecher Hooker, had been planning an array of sessions and speakers. Although the NWSA president, Elizabeth Cady Stanton, was off on a far-flung speaking tour and not expected to attend, Susan B. Anthony, the major power of the suffrage group, had interrupted her own lecture tour to appear in Washington. Other veterans of the old women's rights crusade, such as Paulina Wright Davis and Josephine Griffing, also helped with arrangements for the meeting, while newer recruits looked forward to defending the cause in a public forum.

Barely two years old, the NWSA was busy carving out a terrain for itself on the political scene. This involved several objectives. One was to distinguish itself from a rival organization, the American Woman Suffrage Association, formed at around the same time. Although the press often had difficulty telling one organization from the other, a gamut of personal and political differences separated the two. The "American," founded by Lucy Stone and her husband Henry Blackwell, was the more conservative. Not only did it support the Republican party, not only did it accept male officers, not only did it have a larger following, but it had won the allegiance of many luminaries from the old women's rights/abolitionist ranks. The "National," led by Elizabeth Cady Stanton and Susan B. Anthony, had a smaller constituency but a far broader range of goals, above and beyond enfranchisement. Through the vote, it hoped, women could create a political force to promote their own sexual and economic equality. The NWSA also rejected the tactics of its "American" rivals, who ran state campaigns for woman suffrage. This seemed a long-term, piecemeal approach. The "National," in contrast, claimed Congress as its turf. It was now embarked on a lobbying campaign for passage of a sixteenth amendment to the Constitution to permit woman suffrage in all of the states.

The Washington convention was a pivotal event in this campaign. In the 1870s, the convention was a political rite with many functions. First, it legitimized an association's very existence, by speeches, resolutions, audience, and applause. This was especially important in the case of the NWSA. Hostile to Republicans, the party currently in power, abandoned by leading abolitionists, and led entirely by women, it had to establish an independent identity in the political arena. Indeed, both suffrage associations had as many conventions a year as they could. Another function of the convention was as a publicity device. A convention drew attention to a cause, provided a podium for its advocates, and kept its claims before the public. Spectators, sympathizers, and curiosity seekers flocked to conventions, as did newspaper reporters, ever hungry for copy. On such occasions, the NWSA felt obliged to compete with its "American" rival. Always able to draw on the old antislavery network and assemble a gallery of notables, the AWSA ran conventions that it described as "orderly, harmonious, and effective." The NWSA, thus far, had less in the way of order and harmony. But Isabella Beecher Hooker was determined to run an impressive meeting. In addition, though only a recent convert to the cause, Hooker wanted to assume an important role in the suffrage movement.

The wife of a prominent Connecticut lawyer, Isabella Beecher Hooker was also the eleventh of the thirteen Beecher offspring. Her well-known older siblings included Catharine Beecher, famous proponent of women's education, Harriet Beecher Stowe, internationally acclaimed author, and Henry Ward Beecher, a prominent Brooklyn minister, who also enjoyed a national reputation. Henry currently served as president of the rival American Woman Suffrage Association. Isabella Hooker did not intend to be left in the shadow cast by her impressive siblings. Once disdainful of women's rights, she had become involved in the late 1860s, first by joining the New England Woman Suffrage Association, forerunner of the "American," and then by moving off to the NWSA camp, where her name and funds were welcomed. Her sisters had little praise for her new interest. Harriet Beecher Stowe was now going through her own women's rights phase, but no political activist, she was not involved in the suffrage movement. Catharine Beecher opposed woman suffrage. As she informed the AWSA in 1869, women had more than they could handle in their own sphere "and to add the civil and political duties of men would be deemed a measure of injustice and oppression."

But opposition from her brother and sisters only increased Isabella Hooker's commitment, both to the suffrage cause and to the NWSA. And she had thrown all of her energy into the Washington meeting. If the "American" rivals were able to involve prominent men in their gatherings, so was the "National." Isabella Hooker had been able to persuade five senators to chair the convention's various sessions, a coup that would clearly legitimize the cause. In addition, she had arranged for a surfeit of speakers, including members of Congress as well as NWSA activists. "Through this suffrage movement," Hooker told the press, "it is hoped to bring the sexes closer together." Finally, she had prepared a speech herself. But on January 11, just before the convention was about to begin and after all the arrangements had been made, the suffragists learned of alarming news.

Without any warning, at least to the organizers of the NWSA, Victoria Woodhull, a thirty-three-year-old New York stockbroker, had been invited to appear at a House Judiciary Committee hearing that very morning, to present a memorial in favor of woman suffrage. Though obscure in Washington, Woodhull was already very well known in New York. She and her younger sister, Tennessee Claflin, ran the first women's brokerage firm and published their own *Woodhull and Claflin's Weekly*, a universal reform sheet with a wide circulation. Often seen about town with gentleman companions, they provided boundless copy for newspaper reporters themselves. Attractive, audacious, and very voluble, the Claflin sisters relished attention and flourished in the spotlight. But Victoria Woodhull had not yet entered the public forum as an orator. No woman, in fact, had ever addressed a congressional committee. The Judiciary Committee, moreover, was of prime importance, since it had to approve all bills sent to the floor of Congress. Taken by surprise, the NWSA decided to postpone its own convention until the afternoon so that its leaders could attend the committee hearing.

The Judiciary Committee chamber that morning was unusually crowded. Ten committee members were present, some of them extremely prominent, such as Ben Butler of Massachusetts, a famous former Union general. They had been joined by other members of Congress and more than the usual claque of spectators and reporters. Finally, there was a delegation from the NWSA, including Susan B. Anthony, Isabella Hooker, Josephine Griffing, and Paulina Wright Davis, all of them curious about the new advocate. If suffragists were surprised by the large attendance, Victoria Woodhull's formal address proved even more of a surprise. As she later revealed, her speeches came to her through mystical voices, which were in this case extremely professional ones. Both her memorial and the accompanying remarks seemed to have been prepared by a lawyer. They cited state laws, cases before the Supreme Court, recent decisions, and the Constitution, on which the Woodhull case was based.

Victoria Woodhull argued that no further constitutional amendment was needed to give women the vote because they already had it. Women, she explained, were entitled to vote on the basis of the recently ratified Fourteenth and Fifteenth Amendments, which, designed to ensure the rights of black men, guaranteed civil and political rights to all citizens. Contending that women were citizens, and that the amendments applied to them, Woodhull insisted that all state laws enacted prior to the new amendments that prohibited woman suffrage were "null and void and of no effect." Congress, moreover, was now obliged to enforce the provisions of the Fourteenth Amendment and provide for woman suffrage by enabling legislation. To these contentions, embossed with many professional touches such as scriptural quotations and Latin terms, Woodhull, or her advisory voices, appended "natural rights" rhetoric, along with some reference to women's special responsibilities.

Women have the same invaluable right to life, liberty, and the *pursuit* of happiness that men have. Why have they not this right politically as well as men? Women constitute a majority of the people of this country—they hold vast portions of the nation's wealth and pay a proportionate share of the taxes. They are intrusted with the most holy duties and the most vital responsibilities of society; they bear, rear and educate men; they train and mold their character; they inspire the noblest impulses in men. . . . The American nation, in its march onward and upward, cannot publicly choke the intellectual and political activity of half its citizens by narrow statutes.

At first uncertain and almost inaudible, Victoria Woodhull soon gained confidence, presented her case with passion and conviction, and made an impression on everyone in the room. Her delivery impressed Congressman Butler, who had arranged for the presentation of the memorial and had probably contributed to its composition. He was subsequently to write the minority report recommending that Congress act on it. It impressed Congressman George W. Julian of Indiana, abolitionist stalwart, who had introduced the first woman suffrage bill in Congress in 1866. Julian, in fact, had presented the Woodhull memorial to Congress as well, a few weeks before. It even made a favorable impression on a majority of the Judiciary Committee members, though they

Victoria Woodhull in the early 1870s, when she ran a New York brokerage firm, published *Woodhull and Claflin's Weekly,* and appeared before the House Judiciary Committee. *(Sophia Smith Collection, Smith College)*

would soon agree to table the memorial and forget about it forever. Finally, the Woodhull presentation was very well received by delegates from the National Woman Suffrage Association.

At the outset, NWSA leaders had been suspicious about Woodhull, an interloper who had so unexpectedly invaded their turf and usurped the attention of congressmen and the press. But they quickly adopted a positive view. To Susan B. Anthony, Victoria Woodhull had great appeal. Anthony, who had already visited Woodhull at her New York brokerage office, was impressed with her success in business, as well as with her ability to gain the ear of congressmen. She felt that Woodhull would be a valuable ally and also a wealthy one. The NWSA needed money as well as advocates. Moreover, Victoria Woodhull had proposed an attractive new strategy for the suffrage movement. Were women to claim the vote at the polls, insisting that the right to suffrage was already theirs, the courts would be forced to consider their case. This tactic could be far more fruitful than the flagging attempt to amend the Constitution. At this point, in fact, the NWSA had nothing to lose by following the new strategy, or "new departure," as it would be called. Victoria Woodhull seemed to be a dynamic source of inspiration and funds.

Paulina Wright Davis agreed with Anthony. An abolitionist in the 1830s, a lecturer on physiology and women's health in the 1840s, and a frequent chairwoman of women's rights conventions in the 1850s, Davis had long been a Stanton-Anthony ally. She had also once published a women's rights newspaper, the *Una*, which gave her something in common with Victoria Woodhull. Isabella Beecher Hooker became another enthusiast. Like the others, Hooker had at first been dubious about Woodhull, but after the Judiciary Committee hearing, she emerged a loyal supporter. In fact, of all the NWSA leaders, Hooker was probably the most captivated. She would retain her allegiance to Victoria Woodhull for years to come. Isabella Hooker was also eager to capitalize on the Judiciary Committee triumph. NWSA leaders therefore invited Victoria Woodhull to join their convention that very afternoon and present her memorial again.

To Isabella Hooker's gratification, the NWSA convention was even more successful than she could have anticipated. A raft of congressmen appeared on the platform, including senators from Nevada, Utah, and Massachusetts, which gave the meeting an aura of authority, just as Hooker had intended. The lineup of speakers included Frederick Douglass, long a supporter of women's rights, Susan B. Anthony, some of the senators, and many of the newer faces who were rising to prominence in the NWSA, such as pioneer minister Olympia Brown and Washington journalist Lillie Devereux Blake. But the leading attraction of the NWSA's Washington convention was Victoria Woodhull, fresh from her appearance in the Judiciary Committee chamber. Woodhull once again captured the interest of the press. The suffragist mood was now "anthems to Woodhull," reported the New York *Times*. "There was an air of novelty about the proceedings indicating healthy life in the movement," said the *Republican*, a local newspaper. Most important, in a burst of enthusiasm, the NWSA adopted the Woodhull memorial and declared itself ready to pursue the new departure. Dropping the campaign for a sixteenth amendment, it would now encourage women to register and vote. In her own outburst of enthusiasm, Victoria Woodhull promised a large contribution to the NWSA coffers, and others seemed to follow her example.

The Washington convention, so well received in the press, marked the beginning of Victoria Woodhull's involvement with the NWSA as well as a period of complete acceptance by its leaders. Susan B. Anthony and Paulina Wright Davis voiced support for their new ally, while Isabella Hooker began an admiring correspondence, addressing Woodhull as "My Darling Queen." Elizabeth Cady Stanton, who had not been present in Washington, also offered a supportive voice. When she learned in February that the Judiciary Committee had tabled Woodhull's memorial, Stanton was outraged, especially since Republicans had signed the majority report. Stanton was already upset by "a general insulting tone in the press," as she wrote to Anthony, "and now by an open declaration by the most liberal one of the parties that we are 'not citizens.'" Stanton also rose to Woodhull's defense when the "American" rivals, critical of Woodhull's flamboyant demeanor in New York, especially her active social life, denounced her inclusion in suffrage activities. "When the men who make laws for us in Washington can stand forth and declare themselves unspoiled from all the sins mentioned in the Decalogue," Elizabeth Cady Stanton responded, "then we will demand that every woman who makes a constitutional argument on our platform will be as chaste as Diana."

But Elizabeth Cady Stanton, who had not yet met Victoria Woodhull, also urged caution about the new entanglement. She and Anthony had recently been involved with another wealthy enthusiast, handsome and unreliable George F. Train, whom they had met during an unsuccessful referendum campaign for woman suffrage in Kansas in 1867. Running out of funds and floundering for allies, Stanton and Anthony had welcomed the support of the charming young millionaire with political ambitions. Train hoped to run for President, found a national reform party, disfranchise the uneducated, and enfranchise women. For a brief period, he had financed Stanton and Anthony's feminist journal, *Revolution*, a vehicle for a broad range of women's rights arguments. But Train's commitment had been short-lived. By 1870 he had vanished from the women's camp as suddenly as he had entered it, leaving them and *Revolution* in the lurch and in debt. Generous and appealing, Train had been an unstable ally and, in the end, more of an embarrassment than an asset. Elizabeth Cady Stanton did not want to repeat such an experience.

Such remnants of caution, however, were overshadowed by the activist appeal of the new departure as well as by the appeal of Victoria Woodhull herself. As New Yorkers, Stanton and Anthony were well aware of Victoria Woodhull's wealth, success, and rapid rise to local attention. They were also aware of her radical views as voiced in *Woodhull and Claflin's Weekly*, views that had considerable allure. Like Stanton and Anthony's *Revolution,* the *Weekly* endorsed not merely votes for women but a far broader battery of women's causes. In fact, judging from the *Weekly*, Victoria Woodhull was an exceptionally liberal spirit, receptive to a wide variety of reforms. But Stanton and Anthony, at the beginning of 1871, were probably not acquainted with her exotic background. This background, as it turned out, had little in common with their own. A relative newcomer to public life, Victoria Woodhull had no connection with the inspirational world of antebellum reform, the rousing spirit of the antislavery crusade, or the early campaign for women's rights. Rather, she came from the world of the carnival and road show, the hoax and the swindle. Her background, moreover, involved the entire Claflin clan.

Victoria Woodhull was one of ten children of Roxana Claflin, former tavern maid and spiritualist, and Reuben Bucklin Claflin, who had run a traveling medicine show in the Ohio backwoods, telling fortunes, advertising cancer cures, and promoting a miraculous "elixir of life." Early in life, Victoria and Tennessee had become clairvoyants, spiritualists, mesmerists, and part of the family business. After Victoria married, at fourteen, Tennessee continued her own successful career as a magnetic healer in the Claflin enterprise. The sisters' upbringing in an atmosphere of quackery and theatrics had left its imprint. Both were imbued with a love of applause and a flair for getting attention. The whole Claflin family, as it soon became clear, were opportunists and publicity hounds, always ready to conjure up the spirits, promote the latest "elixir," or, as a last resort, defend their interests in court. As united as they were disputatious, the Claflins quickly joined Victoria and Tennessee in their New York triumph.

This triumph was impressive. Since their arrival in New York in 1868, Victoria Woodhull and Tennessee, or Tennie C., her current alias, had put on their most successful performance. Enterprising "Buck," their father, ever a promoter, had managed to introduce them to wealthy Cornelius Vanderbilt, now an elderly widower, who was interested in spiritualism and clairvoyance, the sisters' forte. While manipulating the spirits, the two sisters arranged to enter the world of finance. Their brokerage firm at 44 Broad Street, opened in 1870 with Vanderbilt's backing, was a great novelty. Its carpeted reception room, according to reporters, was something of a showplace, full of black marble counters, an array of wall safes, buckets of champagne, and scrapbooks of clippings about the sisters. The firm was also a startling success, whether because of the owners' ability, tips from friends, or advice from the spirits whom Woodhull contacted. She and Claflin soon announced themselves millionaires. Meanwhile, Victoria Woodhull's substantial talents emerged more fully.

One was for attracting the attention of important men, with whom her name was linked in the press. Another was for publicity, which she and Tennie C., skilled in road-show tactics, were able to generate. Both loved to talk to reporters, who descended like flies on any available news source. Full of compliments for the "fascinating financiers," journalists kept the sisters' activities in constant view. Victoria Woodhull quickly added to the outflow of newsprint. Soon after entering the world of finance, she became a columnist for James Gordon Bennett's *New York Herald*. Then, in May 1870, she and Tennie C. became publishers of *Woodhull and Claflin's Weekly*, a universal reform sheet that immediately claimed 20,000 readers.

Like the brokerage firm, the *Weekly* was unique. It supported so many causes that they spilled off the pages. The editors supported spiritualism, internationalism, free trade, currency reform, women's rights, woman suffrage, liberalized divorce laws, the licensing of prostitutes, and "a single standard of morality." The *Weekly* featured exposés of corrupt business practices, serialized a George Sand novel, and filled its columns with favorable, if not adulatory, correspondence from readers. It also appeared to cater to a male clientele. The advertisements were for brokerage houses, liquor dealers, and billiard parlors, along with medical cures and "personals." Nor was the *Weekly* Woodhull's only contribution to public life. She also served as head of Section 12 of the International Workingmen's Association, an American branch of the Marxist organization formed in 1864. Within just a few years, Victoria Woodhull had become a journalist, publisher, stockbroker, political activist, and public personality.

But if her achievements were unusual, so were her domestic arrangements. These did not receive a public airing until after Victoria Woodhull's career in the NWSA was well launched, but they would play a role in the fate of the suffrage movement. By 1870, the sisters lived in a mansion in fashionable Murray Hill, along with six servants and the crowd of Claflins who had hastened to join them. Their parents, unstable Roxana and showman "Buck," now introduced as a retired judge, were only the beginning. Other relatives and hangers-on also appeared, many of them laden with made-up ranks and titles, to which the Claflins were attracted. An older sister, Dr. Polly Spann, for instance, who practiced magnetism, was in residence with her husband and two children. Three other siblings, one with four children, also moved in. Claflin siblings were only part of the household. There was also Victoria Woodhull's first husband, Dr. Canning Woodhull, who had a genuine medical degree. Never a success, he was now a drinker and morphine addict. Two Woodhull children, Byron, aged sixteen and severely retarded, and Zulu Maud, aged eight, had always lived with Victoria. But that was not all. Although Victoria Woodhull had kept her first married name, she had divorced Canning Woodhull and now had a second husband. Colonel James Blood was a dashing young man whom she had met at a St. Louis spiritualist conference. He described himself not only as a spiritualist but as a communist, internationalist, free spirit, free lover, and all-around radical. His military rank, like most Claflin titles, was fabricated. The most crucial figure in the household, however, was neither of Woodhull's husbands but a more recent addition: Stephen Pearl Andrews, a well-known figure of prewar reforms, who had dropped in for a visit and stayed on for months.

Eccentric and erudite, Andrews was the driving force behind Victoria Woodhull's many enterprises. Former abolitionist and Fourierist, and now a philosophical anarchist, Andrews was an original. Master of twenty languages, he had invented his own. He was also the originator of pantarchy, a perfect state of society, and an exponent of stirpiculture, a scientific system of human breeding. Known as an advocate of labor reform as well as of free thought, free trade, and free love, Stephen Pearl Andrews had long been a center of radical circles in New York. During the 1850s and 1860s, he had organized a rash of societies that met to discuss utopian schemes, always attracting a wide range of activist women—from journalist Jane Croly, founder of Sorosis, the pioneer women's club, to health reformer Mary Gove Nichols. By 1870, Stephen Pearl Andrews also inspired Victoria Woodhull and Colonel Blood. His distinctive rhetoric permeated both the *Weekly*, on which he labored, and all of Woodhull's columns and speeches. Never at a loss for ideas, Andrews had cartons of unpublished essays at hand, for whatever purpose. But Victoria Woodhull was a far better publicist. She was magnetic and effective, as her dealings with the suffragists suggested. Her role was that of spokesperson. Here she also had some spiritual help. This was revealed in a dime-tract biography published in 1871 by yet another of Woodhull's admirers, young editor Theodore Tilton. Tilton was a protégé of Henry Ward Beecher and an adviser to Stanton and Anthony in the suffrage movement's formative years. According to his account of Victoria Woodhull's life, both Claflin sisters had been in touch with spirits since their earliest days in Homer, Ohio. As a child, Victoria had been visited by the ghost of the orator Demosthenes, who though silent in his first manifestations, later advised her to move to New York and continued to advise her thereafter.

With spiritual guidance and her new success as an orator in the Judiciary Committee chamber and at the NWSA Washington convention, Victoria Woodhull's scope was suddenly enlarged. While Colonel Blood managed the brokerage office and Stephen Pearl Andrews directed the *Weekly*, she began an ambitious career on the lecture platform, perfecting her technique of opening inaudibly and working her way up to passionate oratory. In February 1871, she again spoke in Washington on suffrage, accompanied by NWSA leaders Paulina Wright Davis and Isabella Beecher Hooker. "The lecture was a triumph," said the *Washington Chronicle*. Two weeks later, Woodhull appeared at New York's Cooper Union, and then in Philadelphia, extending her topics to cover capital and labor. Her speeches got longer and more elaborate, as more of Andrews's ideas were hauled out of the cartons. But her major effort came in the spring of 1871, at the May convention of the NWSA in New York. Labeled by the press "the Woodhull Convention," the May meeting at the Apollo Theatre represented the very peak of Woodhull's career in the suffrage movement.

For most of the proceedings, Victoria Woodhull sat still on the platform, between Elizabeth Cady Stanton, whom she had just met for the first time, and elderly Lucretia Mott. But when she gained the floor, she embarked on a long and exceptionally militant speech. If Congress refused women "the legitimate rights of citizenship," Woodhull told the convention, women would hold a constitutional convention and elect a new government. "We mean treason! We mean secession, and on a thousand times greater scale than that of the South!" she proclaimed. "We are plotting Revolution! We will overthrow this bogus republic and plant a government of righteousness in its stead." Afterward, Victoria Woodhull was able to sell 100,000 copies of her militant speech. Moreover, she still had the loyalty of the NWSA, in which she had now assumed a pivotal role. Elizabeth Cady Stanton found in her "the means of a grand development," a view endorsed by other leaders. Woodhull's dynamism had inspired the association, brought it to public attention, and set it off on a new activist tack. Susan B. Anthony still had hopes for some activist financing. "Go ahead, bright, glorious, young and strong spirit," she wrote to Woodhull from a midwestern lecture tour.

But Victoria Woodhull was not the only member of the Claflin clan to receive publicity in the spring of 1871. Perhaps, according to the family dynamic, she was receiving more than her share of it. In any event, soon after the "Wood-hull Convention," her mother, Roxana, who seemed to be well ensconced in the Murray Hill mansion, suddenly brought Colonel Blood to court, and charged him with threatening her life. The lawsuit was a commonplace Claflin tactic, though one usually employed against outsiders. But this time numerous Claflins testified in court about their unusual domestic arrangements, including the presence of two of Victoria's husbands. The lawsuit also drew attention to Stephen Pearl Andrews's moral philosophy. Victoria Woodhull believed in free love, the *Weekly* explained, "in the highest purest sense as the only cure for immorality." Theodore Tilton then published his dime-tract biography, describing Victoria's marriage to Dr. Woodhull and revealing the influence of Demosthenes. The *Weekly*, curiously, reprinted critical quotes from the national press accusing Victoria Woodhull of "shameless effrontery." "She is a suffrage advocate," said a Cleveland paper, "because being so made her notorious and her paper profitable."

As the publicity increased, so did Victoria Woodhull's addiction to it. Spurred by Blood, by Andrews, and by newsprint, crowds, cheers, and applause, she began to capitalize on the rising interest. That spring she was elected head of the American Spiritualist Association, and in the fall of 1871 she organized a march of the International Workingmen's Association. On election day, she led a group of thirty-one women to the polls in an attempt to vote. She also began public lecturing on her own, or Andrews's, social theories. The first such speech, entitled "The Principles of Social Freedom, Involving the Questions of Free Love, Marriage, Divorce, and Prostitution," drew a crowd of 3,000 to Steinway Hall, far more than had ever attended the most successful of suffrage conventions. Introduced by Theodore Tilton, always a link between Woodhull and the NWSA, Victoria Woodhull explained at length a whole barrage of Andrewisms. "Promiscuity in sexuality is simply the anarchical stage of development wherein the passions rule supreme," she told the crowd. "When spirituality comes in and rescues the real men or women from the domain of the purely material, promiscuity is simply impossible." In an impromptu declaration, beyond the text of the speech, Woodhull informed the audience of her inalienable right "to love whomever I may . . . to change that love every day if I please." After this performance, she took off on a midwestern lecture tour, stopping off in Washington for an end-of-the-year appearance. Victoria Woodhull had found her own "elixir of life."

While Woodhull became a one-woman media event, some of the NWSA membership began to express objections to linking their cause with hers. Upholding "promiscuity" seemed to be a precarious stance. But Stanton and Anthony defended her at the annual Washington Convention in January 1872 and insisted that she take the floor. In the months that followed, both refused to withdraw their endorsements. "I have thought much of Mrs. Woodhull and of all the gossip about her past," Stanton wrote to Anthony in April 1872, "and have come to the conclusion that it is great impertinence in any of us to pry into her private affairs. To me there is a sacredness in individual experience which it seems like profanation to search into or expose." (This was Andrews's position in the *Weekly*, too.)

The political cartoons of Thomas Nast were a leading attraction of *Harper's Weekly,* one of the most popular magazines of the late nineteenth century. This portrayal of Victoria Woodhull as "Mrs. Satan" appeared on February 17, 1872, after she had fully expressed her free love philosophy on the lecture platform and in the press. The woman in the background, who is carrying the burden of her drunken husband and children, is saying, "I'd rather travel the hardest path of matrimony than follow your footsteps." *(New-York Historical Society)*

Moreover, convinced that Woodhull was a capable speaker and writer, Stanton insisted that her appearance, manners, and conversation "all indicate the triumph of the moral, intellectual and spiritual." Above all, as she wrote to Anthony, she could not bear the condemnation of any radical woman.

> We have already women enough sacrificed to this sentimental, hypocritical prating about purity, without going out of our way to increase the number. Women have crucified the Mary Wollstonecrafts, the Fanny Wrights and the George Sands of all ages. Men mock us with the fact and say we are ever cruel to each other. Let us end this ignoble record and henceforth stand by womanhood. If this present woman must be crucified, let men drive the spikes.

There were other important reasons for the NWSA's receptivity to Victoria Woodhull. The small core of activists around Stanton and Anthony had little timidity about sexual issues such as those raised at Steinway Hall. On the contrary, free discussion of marriage, divorce, prostitution, and sexual relations was, they insisted, one of their major objectives. Moreover, though committed to women's enfranchisement, or to changing women's role in the public sphere, NWSA activists were also concerned with the private sphere. Throughout the pages of *Revolution*, even before Victoria Woodhull appeared on the suffrage scene, they had published their views on a panoply of social questions, with special attention to the "marriage relation." To be sure, leading NWSA members did not appear to endorse the free love doctrines Victoria Woodhull now expounded. Rather, they envisioned an improved type of marriage, cooperative and harmonious, that would promote women's sexual equality and freedom. Nonetheless, within the NWSA, there was wide support for free discussion of "social" topics, to which Victoria Woodhull contributed. And no NWSA leader was more committed to free discussion and to a broad range of feminist goals than Elizabeth Cady Stanton, whose support for Woodhull soon became crucial.

Since Seneca Falls, Stanton had developed an independent vision of reform, one that now began to veer away from that of colleagues in the suffrage movement. By the 1870s, Susan B. Anthony believed that suffrage should be the first step in women's emancipation. But Stanton, who had been the first to demand the vote, was never convinced. She had always been and still was committed primarily to a change of attitudes toward women, to an assault on what she called "aristocracy of sex," in all its guises—social, sexual, and psychological, as well as political. Her major conviction, moreover, was that any change of attitudes toward women must begin with the institution of marriage. "This whole question of women's rights turns on the pivot of the marriage relation," she had written to Anthony in 1853, and her view had not changed since. "The true relation between the sexes is the momentous question," Stanton wrote in an 1869 article. "Our low ideas of marriage, as set forth in our creeds and codes, making man master, woman slave, one to command and one to obey, are demoralizing all our most sacred sentiments and affections." Most important, Elizabeth Cady Stanton defended more liberal divorce laws as a vital step toward improving marriage and enhancing women's rights. Easier divorce was hardly a popular cause, even among fervent suffragists, since most women feared it would work to men's advantage. Moreover, to most Americans of the 1870s, there was little difference between easy divorce, as demanded by such radicals as Stanton, and Victoria Woodhull's defense of free love.

Elizabeth Cady Stanton, in fact, agreed with them, though she cautiously confined her views to friends, associates, and limited audiences. In 1870, before the suffrage movement had heard of Victoria Woodhull, Stanton had once expressed her libertarian sentiments on divorce and free love to a small private club of men and women. Defining marriage as "a compulsory bond enforced by the law," Stanton argued for "freedom from binding obligations involving impossibilities." Unlimited freedom of divorce, she advised her audience, could indeed be equated with free love. But lifelong marriage could be considered free love just as well as could "unlimited variety in promiscuity." Having redefined her terms, Stanton went on to defend free lovers as "among the most virtuous of women and men." Woman suffrage, moreover, she told her listeners, would be followed by social equality and indeed free love as she defined it. If its advocates, male or female, "wished to get out of the boat, they should for safety's sake get out now."

Fortunately for the newborn suffrage movement, Elizabeth Cady Stanton subsequently refrained from defining or defending "free love" in public, though she continued to support divorce reform. But women's right to sexual self-determination could be defended on another front. In 1869, just as the first suffrage societies were organized, Stanton began to carve out an independent career for herself on the lyceum circuit as a women's rights lecturer. Crossing the nation, from New England to the Midwest, in trains and coaches, meeting two engagements a day, nine months a year, the NWSA president used these occasions to campaign for her own brand of feminism.

Nothing could have been more different from Victoria Woodhull's campaign style than Elizabeth Cady Stanton's. Once her lyceum career was under way, Stanton devised the idea of special afternoon sessions, limited to women, who came to hear her expound on such topics as "Home Life" or "Marriage and Maternity." A mother of seven, Stanton was now a heavy-set woman in her fifties, with a headful of white curls and a pleasant, kindly manner. Always full of amusing tales and domestic anecdotes, Stanton was also a powerful evangelist, bent on bestirring an awakening. "This idea of mine of addressing women by themselves should produce rich fruitage in the future," she wrote to her cousin, Elizabeth Smith Miller, in 1871. "What radical thoughts . . . I could put into their heads." Stanton's thoughts covered the entire range of current feminist issues, from coeducation, one of her favorite causes, to more liberal divorce laws, a more controversial one. But her central theme was marital relations, or what she called "enlightened motherhood." And during her lectures, she used this theme to evoke responses from far more women than had ever been reached by *Woodhull and Claflin's Weekly*.

"Enlightened motherhood" was a rubric covering sex and conception, subjects on which Stanton was able to speak without scandal or controversy, though in guarded euphemisms, in the all-woman sessions. Her audiences, she discovered, were far more interested in these immediate topics than in the vaguely irrelevant issue of suffrage. "Oh, how they come to me with their sorrows," she wrote to Anthony. Woman's goal, Stanton told her listeners, was to be "absolute sovereign of herself," which meant control over sexual relations within marriage. Stanton urged her listeners to demand self-control from men and to engage in sexual relations not at men's insistence but only of their own volition, possibly only for purposes of conception. As Stanton explained to Elizabeth Miller, she was preaching "the gospel of fewer children and a happy, healthy maternity." Woman's right, she wrote, was "to become a mother or not, as her desire, judgment, and conscience may dictate."

The doctrine of "enlightened motherhood" (or "self-sovereignty" or "self-ownership," as other advocates described it) was wholeheartedly endorsed by women's rights advocates of the 1870s, as divorce was not. "Self ownership," wrote NWSA officer Lucinda Chandler in articles in *Revolution* and the Woodhull *Weekly*, would liberate women from male "lust of dominion and appetite."

Stanton's lectures, confirmed Paulina Wright Davis, created a "healthier tone of public sentiment on the marriage question." Enlightened motherhood seemed to have little connection with Victoria Woodhull's avowed policy of sexual freedom. But in Stanton's view, both she and Woodhull advocated female autonomy and a new degree of feminine power. Stanton, moreover, found great value in Woodhull's approach.

Hardly ready to leap onto the free love bandwagon because she was too circumspect a politician, Elizabeth Cady Stanton was not ready to repudiate it either. The current crop of free love advocates, she felt, served a worthwhile function. First, they brought issues of marriage, divorce, and sexual relations into the open. Second, as she told Anthony, they made suffragists seem more respectable by comparison. Finally, Stanton despised critics of free love who used it as a curse to hurl on radical women reformers. High on her list of enemies in 1871 were several prominent Beechers. Henry Ward Beecher, for instance, had denounced the NWSA for its involvement with Victoria Woodhull. Catharine Beecher, who had no use for the suffrage movement, had special animosity for Woodhull, to whom her sister Isabella had, disastrously, introduced her. Harriet Beecher Stowe, perhaps worst of all, was an ingrate. The year before, Stanton had praised Stowe's own contribution to free discussion, an exposé of the poet Lord Byron, whom Stowe accused of incest. Stowe, in return, published a novel that caricatured both Victoria Woodhull and Elizabeth Cady Stanton. The first appeared as Audacia Dangereyes, a free love advocate, and the second as Mrs. Cerulean, a large and enthusiastic social reformer.

Common enemies were not all that Elizabeth Cady Stanton shared with Victoria Woodhull. She also sympathized with another desire of the Woodhull-Andrews contingent—to form a party of reform that would press for sweeping social change. Stanton had long envisioned some sort of popular front, made up of liberal reformers and women of different backgrounds. In 1868, she and Anthony had tried to organize a Workingwomen's Association, which would, they hoped, involve women of all classes and serve as a base for a large reform party. After the association failed, Stanton and Anthony turned to the suffrage cause and its natural constituency, middle-class women. But still attracted to broader ideals, Stanton had not lost her vision of a universal reform party. This turned out to be the very next item on the Woodhull agenda. In May of 1872, while Susan B. Anthony was away on a lecture tour, the *Weekly* announced that a convention was called, under NWSA auspices, at Steinway Hall to form a new political party and nominate a candidate for President. NWSA leaders, meanwhile, sent Anthony their announcement of a preliminary meeting to consider a merger with Victoria Woodhull's International Workingmen's Association.

The proposed merger provoked a crisis in the Stanton-Anthony friendship, a friendship that had just survived several years of disagreements. Elizabeth Cady Stanton saw nothing but gain in the new alliance and in the adoption of a comprehensive program of reform. Suffragists, she wrote to Isabella Hooker, had "culture, refinement, social influence but no political power." The proposed merger with radical men would help to provide political clout. To Anthony, however, a coalition with the International Workingmen's Association would only hurt the suffrage movement and undercut its feminist goals. In Anthony's experience, even radical men, once in power, lost all interest in women's demands. Republican abolitionists were proof of this. There was little reason to think that the radical men attached to Victoria Woodhull or the International Workingmen's Association would be any more reliable. On the contrary, the Woodhull forces seemed to be using the suffragists for their own goals. Once alerted to the new development, Anthony immediately returned from her lecture tour to prevent it.

When the NWSA meeting opened Victoria Woodhull, predictably, proposed that her own contingent, devoted to universal reform, merge with the suffrage association. But Anthony seized the podium, took over the meeting, and refused to allow Woodhull to speak any further. For good measure, she turned out the lights, bringing the Woodhull ploy to a halt. "If she were influenced by *women* spirits, either in body or out of it . . . I might consent to be a mere sail-hoister for her," Anthony said, "but, as it is, she is wholly owned and dominated by *men* spirits." The next day Woodhull held a rival meeting of 500 admirers to form an Equal Rights party, which nominated her for President. The new party, said opponent Henry Ward Beecher, was "a motley crowd of disreputables and visionaries upon a crusade of egotism." Anthony, meanwhile, retained her grip on the NWSA and began to prepare its membership for an assault on the polls.

In the fall elections of 1872, following the thrust of the Woodhull memorial and contending that women were enfranchised by the Fourteenth Amendment, Susan B. Anthony mobilized a large contingent of supporters to attempt to vote. Elizabeth Cady Stanton was not among them. During the May NWSA meeting, she had resigned as president. Although ready to fuse with the Woodhull forces, Stanton, in the end, could neither follow her instincts nor betray Anthony. She was forced to remain aloof.

This stance turned out to be a fortunate one. By the end of 1872, Victoria Woodhull's career had completely collapsed. After her role in the suffrage movement capsized, her reputation fell as swiftly as it had risen. Her presidential campaign disintegrated, her finances were wrecked, and the whole Claflin clan was evicted from the Murray Hill mansion. Woodhull even had to stop, temporarily, publication of the *Weekly*, since wealthy contributors withdrew their support. Perhaps a final blow came from leaders of the Marxist International Workingmen's Association, who had long been irritated by the woman suffrage/free love views that had infiltrated Woodhull's section 12. They had section 12 expelled from the international organization in July 1872. But just when her career seemed to be reaching a nadir, Victoria Woodhull suddenly struck back with a public accusation that left both admirers and enemies speechless.

Henry Ward Beecher, she charged in a November issue of the *Weekly*, was having an affair with the wife of her longtime admirer Theodore Tilton. She had been told of this affair long before, either by Elizabeth Cady Stanton or, as she claimed, Paulina Wright Davis. In any event, it seemed to be common knowledge among Beecher relatives and Tilton associates, since all participants in the triangle told their stories widely. But Victoria Woodhull felt compelled to bring the triangle into public view, thereby heaving herself into the spotlight for what was to be the last time. She explained her motives at some length. Endorsing free love had brought her only condemnation, she contended, and made her a "scapegoat of sacrifice." But Beecher, who habitually practiced it, remained sanctimonious. In a dialogue in the *Weekly* with an anonymous reporter, Victoria explained why she endorsed free love and, at the same time, condemned Henry Ward Beecher.

Woodhull.—I believe that the marriage institution, like slavery and monarchy, and many other things which have been good or necessary in their day, is now *effete,* and in a general sense injurious, instead of being beneficial to the community, although of course it must continue to linger until better institutions can be found. I mean by marriage, in this connection, any *forced* or *obligatory tie* between the sexes, any legal *intervention* or *constraint* to prevent people adjusting their love relations precisely as they do their religious affairs in this country, in complete personal freedom; changing and improving them from time to time, and according to circumstances.

Reporter.—I confess, then, I cannot understand why you of all persons should have any fault to find with Mr. Beecher, even assumed everything to be true of him which I have hitherto heard only vaguely hinted at. . . .

Woodhull.—[because] he has permitted himself . . . to profess to believe otherwise than as he does believe, to help, persistently, to maintain, for these many years, the very social slavery under which he was chaffing, and against which he was secretly revolting, both in thought and in practice, and that he has, in a word, consented, and still consents, to be a hypocrite.

Although the accusation was to leave a trail of carnage, Victoria Woodhull was herself its first victim. She was quickly arrested at the instigation of vice crusader Anthony Comstock, who contended that the crucial issue of the *Weekly* condemning Beecher was obscenity. Woodhull spent a month in jail before her case was dismissed. Although she subsequently revived both the *Weekly* and her lecturing career, she had lost the public's avid interest and goodwill. The brief intersection of her flamboyant career with the central swirl of public events was suddenly over. But Woodhull's wide swath through public life, short as it was, involved an intricate web of entanglements, personal and political. It would also leave a tangible imprint on the woman suffrage movement.

The Beecher-Tilton scandal dragged on for three years, amid a barrage of songs and skits, jokes and burlesques. It finally culminated in a six-month trial in 1875, when Tilton sued Beecher for alienation of affection. The trial ended in a hung jury, thus exonerating Beecher, who had already been cleared by a church investigation. The major casualties were the Tiltons, whose marriage and lives were ruined. Beecher's reputation was not enhanced by the scandal either, but he was a survivor. Emerging relatively unscathed, Henry Ward Beecher continued to preach for the rest of his life. He was permanently estranged, however, from his sister Isabella Hooker, who remained committed to both Victoria Woodhull and the suffrage movement. During the scandal, Henry took every opportunity to denounce the NWSA and to declare that Isabella, who refused to desert it, was insane. But Isabella was a survivor as well. Snubbed by her siblings, who took Henry's side, she was now in touch with spirits introduced by Victoria Woodhull. Pouring her energies into the suffrage cause, she remained devoted to the goal of a federal woman suffrage amendment. Hooker outlived all her brothers and sisters.

The Claflin clan were, in their own way, survivors too. Victoria Woodhull managed to pick up the shreds of her career, but she was never able to regain the attention, or notoriety, she had achieved in the brief period of her New York success or her few years as a suffrage crusader. During the years of the scandal and trial, she went through some new metamorphoses. By 1876, Woodhull had found religion, denounced promiscuity, declared marriage a divine institution, and divorced the free-thinking, free-loving Colonel Blood for adultery. She denounced divorce as well. As Susan B. Anthony wrote in her diary after a visit, Victoria Woodhull now had "no connected train of thought." Like Victoria's reputation, the Claflin fortunes also declined. But after Commodore Vanderbilt's death, in 1877, the Claflin sisters and their enterprising father sued for a portion of the Vanderbilt estate. The suit seemed to bring results, although out of court. Woodhull and her sister soon sailed for England in grand style, followed by their parents. In England, Victoria Woodhull took to the lecture platform again, with Tennessee, now T. Celeste, in her wake. Within a decade, both sisters had married wealthy Englishmen, and they lived out their lives in considerable style. Woodhull published occasional articles on reform, granted interviews to reporters, and ran for President from time to time, from abroad. She lived until 1927, by which time she had claimed credit for the success of woman suffrage in the United States.

The suffrage movement, meanwhile, had to recover from the devastation Victoria Woodhull had wreaked and to recoup its losses. The American Woman Suffrage Association was only slightly affected, even though Henry Ward Beecher had been an officer. The AWSA had warned at the outset against Woodhull. It gave her scant coverage in its publication, the *Woman's Journal*, and formally denounced her at conventions. Throughout the Beecher-Tilton scandal and trial, the "American" tried to stay as aloof as possible. But the AWSA did not escape free and clear, since journalists and the public tended to confuse the rival suffrage associations and the NWSA had been deeply embroiled. Its connection with Victoria Woodhull, so promising at first, had been a tactical disaster and a close call.

Not only had the Woodhull forces attempted to use the NWSA for their own purposes, but Victoria Woodhull had provoked a serious split between its two major leaders. Although Susan B. Anthony managed to regain control of the NWSA and save it from merging and sinking with Woodhull's Equal Rights party, Elizabeth Cady Stanton, who resigned, was temporarily in limbo. She continued to offer words of support for Victoria Woodhull, even after the scandal broke, without resuming personal contact. Woodhull had been a very unstable ally. After 1872, the NWSA endured continual ridicule because of its involvement with her, as well as with various Beechers and Tiltons; the scandal had a terrible spillover effect. In 1874, Stanton admitted to Anthony that she should have been quieter in Woodhull's defense, especially out of loyalty to the woman's movement. "I feel obliged just now to take extra efforts to keep our ship off the rocks," she wrote. "We must not let the cause of women go down in the smash. It is innocent."

After her resignation, Stanton put her energies into her career on the lyceum circuit and into her talks to all-women audiences. Her lyceum efforts were so successful that she kept on the lecture trail until the mid-1880s. Soon reconciled with Anthony, she also rejoined the NWSA and once again became its president. Stanton's radicalism, temporarily in abeyance or under cover, was never completely submerged. She continued to envision a far broader scope of reform than that contained in the suffrage movement. Also, the Beecher scandal increased her mounting anticlerical sentiments, to which she gave voice in the 1890s. But Elizabeth Cady Stanton had been well into her reform career when the Woodhull debacle occurred, whereas the suffrage movement was only a few years old. Stricken in infancy, the movement learned a powerful lesson from its experience with Victoria Woodhull—one that hovered over it for the rest of the century and helped to determine its subsequent tactics, tone, and policy.

The lesson was that woman suffrage, and suffrage alone, was the only viable cause, as the AWSA had contended. To infuse or connect it with "outside" issues was foolhardy if not suicidal. Far from being the most radical and unacceptable of women's demands, as it had been in 1848, suffrage was now the central demand and the only one. To attain its goal, the suffrage movement would have to develop its own brand of politics, create its own constituency, and convert a substantial number of women to its cause. It would never be able to do so if confused with, or attached to, any radical platforms, left-wing coalitions, or flamboyant personalities who were, at bottom, committed to their own agendas of reform—especially if those agendas involved changing or challenging marriage or promoting sexual freedom. The suffrage movement could not afford to lend its name to risky allies or to squander its influence on comprehensive reform. It had to dissociate itself from rebels and radicals, hucksters and publicity hounds, trials and scandals, and the invisible influence of "men spirits," such as those that seemed to propel Victoria Woodhull. By the end of the century, this mission was accomplished. A united suffrage movement steered its course toward the calmer waters of benevolence and respectability. With a new rhetoric and a limited objective, it sought the endorsement of middle-class women and kept its sights fixed firmly on the vote.

14

FEMINISM
AND SUFFRAGE,
1860–1920

"So long as woman labors to second man's endeavors and exalt his sex above her own, her virtues pass unquestioned," Elizabeth Cady Stanton reflected in 1898, looking back on the early days of the suffrage campaign. "But where she dares to demand rights and privileges for herself, her motives . . . and character are subjects for ridicule and detraction." Victoria Woodhull's impolitic swath through public life in 1871–1872 increased the suffrage movement's share of ridicule at a crucial juncture. It was newly formed, small in size, divided into factions, and barely able to legitimize its existence, let alone affect public policy. But by World War I, woman suffrage was a mass movement, with membership in the millions and enough support to secure the Nineteenth Amendment in 1920. During the final stage of its fifty-year campaign, the suffrage movement became the pivot of women's politics, just as the vote became the symbol of women's rights.

The greatest testimony to the symbolic power of the vote, to both supporters and opponents, was the length of the fight to achieve it, longer than any comparable reform campaign and certainly longer than any other campaign for an electoral reform. But the very length of the suffrage campaign provided a major benefit. For three generations, the suffrage movement gave American women a separate sphere of political life, one with purpose, esprit, and continuity. It politicized existing networks of women, created new ones, and evoked their efforts in common cause—in conventions, addresses, memorials, manifestoes, petitions, resolutions, lobbies, and an endless round of state campaigns. The movement provided both a political context and a feminist community. One result was that women seemed to play a more forceful role in public life in the decades just before suffrage was won than after. Another was that the cause created a highly charged sense of feminist unity. "The Woman's Movement," wrote Charlotte Perkins Gilman in 1898, "rests not alone on her larger personality, with its tingling sense of revolt against injustice, but on the wide, deep sympathy of women for each other."

Just as the women involved in other causes were overwhelmingly middle- and upper-class women, so the suffrage movement was a middle-class crusade. "The plutocrats have organized their women," Mother Jones told an astonished gathering of clubwomen who had invited her to speak in the early 1900s. "They keep them busy with suffrage and prohibition and charity." Working-class women, more directly oppressed by economic inequities than by political exclusion, had little interest in the largely symbolic, remote vote. Nor indeed had most middle-class women, who were more likely to be involved with prohibition or charity than with the suffrage movement. Suffragists were usually politicized by some special factor, whether advanced education, professional status, or experience in another reform. Not only did the suffrage movement have a singularly middle-class appeal but its arguments began to reflect conventional middle-class values. During the progressive era, the movement adopted such values with a vengeance—to affirm its propriety, enhance its influence, and enlarge its constituency.

As a result, the suffrage campaign became more conservative in tone than its antebellum predecessor. In 1848 the Seneca Falls Declaration of Sentiments had encompassed a broad spectrum of grievances and demands, including the demand for a major shift of attitudes toward women. To antebellum women's rights advocates—an extremely small and marginal group—lack of the vote was part of a complex network of social and institutional oppression, involving marriage, family, employment, education, and religion, in addition to politics. Enfranchisement was widely viewed as the most farfetched of "women's rights," even by its supporters. After the war, women's rights activists dropped the broad spectrum of grievances to focus on the vote. "Social issues" soon fell by the wayside. And by the 1890s, demands for political equality had been replaced by claims about the good that woman, with her distinctive qualities, could do for society through the ballot. The new tilt of argument reflected the suffrage campaign's need to attract a broader base. In its final years, woman suffrage was no longer a fringe movement of "wild enthusiasts and visionaries," as women's rights advocates had been called in the 1850s, but a large, legitimate social cause, "bourgeois" (in its own words) and public spirited. As the movement's constituency expanded, in short, its goals contracted and its radicalism diminished.

By the progressive era, the suffrage movement had become a national umbrella for middle-class activists with different priorities. According to historian William L. O'Neill, some suffragists were committed, first and foremost, to gaining equal rights. Others were "social feminists," who turned to suffrage in order to further some other cause to which they were primarily devoted, whether the temperance movement, women's club activities, settlement work, consumer protection, or the organization of women in industry. Though not a term in use at the time, and currently a source of dispute, "social feminist" is a rubric that can be affixed to the majority of women's associations in the late nineteenth and early twentieth centuries and to the women who participated in them; that is, to women committed to public service, civic works, and social reform. It was by coopting such reformers, capitalizing on their achievements, and adopting their outlook and rhetoric that the suffrage movement finally managed to mobilize both feminine and popular support.

The campaign for the vote, however, was still a distinctive phenomenon, apart from the rest of the "woman's movement." All women activists may have challenged male domination, whether they ran colleges, organized temperance societies, or joined women's clubs, but only suffragists did so overtly. Assaulting the main bastion of male power, politics and government, the suffrage movement was a women's crusade to legitimize women's role in public life, a campaign to ensure that women could participate in society as individuals, rather than just as family members. Historian Ellen Dubois suggests that in demanding the vote, early suffragists were attempting to "bypass" the family and attain a direct relation to the state. Such a goal proved extremely elusive. Suffragists had to convince male voters, state legislators, and congressmen not only that woman suffrage would benefit society but that women wanted the vote; indeed, they had to convince women that they wanted the vote. This major hurdle, until the very last years of the campaign, remained insurmountable. American women seemed to view woman suffrage as tangential to their interests, irrelevant, useless, or threatening. "In the indifference, the inertia, the apathy of women, lies the greatest obstacle to their enfranchisement," wrote Susan B. Anthony and Ida H. Harper in 1902. In their view, as soon as women showed that they wanted the vote, they would get it—a view that turned out to be correct. The suffrage campaign was therefore a crusade in political education, by women and for women, and for most of its existence, a crusade in search of a constituency.

The search began immediately after the Civil War, when the old women's rights movement—a small battalion of antebellum activists centered around Stanton, Anthony, and Lucy Stone—reassembled itself. During the next decade these veteran crusaders established an independent woman suffrage movement and laid the groundwork for a half-century campaign.

An Independent Suffrage Movement

Between 1865 and 1869, when the issue of black male suffrage arose, woman suffrage became the focus of feminist aims. While the Fourteenth and Fifteenth amendments were debated and ratified, the small coalition of antebellum women's rights advocates, many of them long immersed in the abolitionist crusade, suddenly had hopes for themselves. Since the freedman's turn, the "Negro's hour," had come, woman suffrage seemed to loom on the horizon, an almost tangible goal.

Women's hopes were also raised, as historian Ellen Dubois points out, because some of their male colleagues in the now victorious abolitionist camp were tasting power for the first time and having an influence on Republican politics. But these old associates, once sympathetic to woman's rights, proved fickle allies. In their view, the fight for black suffrage was enough of a battle and woman suffrage was extra baggage. Prominent abolitionists now turned their efforts to defending the proposed Fourteenth Amendment, which would guarantee black rights—and injected the word "male" into the Constitution. After it was ratified in June 1868, abolitionist politicos began a campaign for the Fifteenth Amendment, to prohibit black disfranchisement. Anxious to preserve their influence among Republicans, they were more reluctant than ever to saddle themselves with feminist demands. "Women's cause is in deep water," Elizabeth Cady Stanton wrote to Susan B. Anthony.

The prospect of black male suffrage both inspired and provoked these veterans of antebellum reform. As Stanton pointed out, any extension of suffrage that excluded women only increased their powerlessness: "In proportion as you multiply the rulers, the condition of the politically ostracized is more hopeless and degraded." Universal manhood suffrage, indeed, brought women "to the lowest depths of political degradation." This nosedive in status caused an outburst of anger, against newly enfranchised freedmen as well as against rapidly retreating abolitionist allies. First, educated and enlightened women such as those who were prominent in antebellum reform felt more qualified to vote than either newly freed blacks or foreign-born men, "who do not know the difference between the monarchy and the republic," as Stanton wrote in 1869. Such an injustice was not the women reformers' only grievance. They also felt ignored by the nation in general and by abolitionists in particular. During the war, women's rights advocates had supported the Union effort by their patriotic National Women's Loyal League, which had won great praise, as Stanton pointed out, for patience, prudence, loyalty, and ability. But after the war, when these same women began demanding rights for themselves, she contended, they were "uniformly denounced as 'unwise' 'imprudent' 'fanatical' and 'impractical.'" Even old colleagues dismissed their claims. "All their transcendent virtues vanished like dew before the morning sun."

Despite early signs of abolitionist defection, women's rights advocates made one major effort to link their goals with those of their old allies by insisting that the causes of the black vote and the woman's vote went together, hand in hand. Their ploy, the Equal Rights Association of 1866, led by Stanton, Anthony, and Lucy Stone, was dominated by women. It involved at least some abolitionist men; committed Garrisonians such as Parker Pillsbury and Thomas Wentworth Higginson were consistently supportive. But it was eschewed by those with political influence. Petitioning and lobbying through 1866 and 1867, the Equal Rights Association took its major stand in Kansas, an old antislavery battlefield, where it hoped to remove the word "male" from the new state constitution and ensure the vote for women, as well as for blacks. Not only did the Kansas campaign fail (Kansas voters, as it turned out, rejected both woman suffrage *and* black suffrage) but it provoked a split within the Equal Rights Association. During the campaign, abolitionist organizations withdrew funds and support from the cause of the women's vote. At this point, with great resentment, the women activists had autonomy thrust on them. But the abolitionist desertion, to

Stanton and Anthony, was not without benefit. "Standing alone, we learned our power," they later concluded. "Woman must lead the way to her own enfranchisement and work out her own salvation."

During the Kansas campaign, Stanton and Anthony reached their summit of unity and friendship. After it, they embarked on a serious search for new allies, including the Democratic party, the newly formed National Labor Union, and, finally, working women. The Working Women's Association of 1868 was the most interesting of all these failed ventures. An attempt to unite women of all classes in common cause, it was part of Stanton's ambitious hope for a liberal, humane "party of reform," one in which feminists could join forces with other reformers. But as women's rights advocates discovered, working women were difficult to organize and generally disinterested in enfranchisement. When the Working Women's Association fell apart, Stanton and Anthony were left floundering, with only one route left: to seek a constituency of middle-class women. As they started to do so, a new conflict emerged, provoking a split in the small but embattled feminist camp.

This was the controversy, during the winter of 1869, over ratification of the Fifteenth Amendment, intended to ensure black male suffrage. The amendment battle divided woman suffragists into factions that lasted for decades. The radical wing—Stanton, Anthony, and their supporters—denounced the amendment. They were now completely disenchanted with the Republican party, which had failed to support woman suffrage. The more moderate faction—led by Lucy Stone, her husband, Henry Blackwell, and a galaxy of former antislavery stalwarts, such as Thomas Wentworth Higginson and Wendell Philips—were willing to support the amendment. They wanted to retain Republican allies, they counted on Republican support in the future, and they felt that universal manhood suffrage was a step in the right direction. Before the year was out, the rival factions, now competing for old supporters and new ones, split into rival suffrage associations.

The moderates were the first to organize. Their New England Suffrage Association, started in 1868, drew to its corner luminaries from the antislavery circuit, including Abby Kelley Foster and Paulina Wright Davis, though Davis subsequently defected to the radicals. It had also cornered a new leading light, nationally known Julia Ward Howe. Widely admired, Howe became a pivotal figure in women's politics, a leader of suffrage societies and women's clubs, and an invaluable asset. The death of her husband in the mid-1870s, moreover, liberated her for decades of activism. Meanwhile, the NESA burst into action all over New England, forming suffrage societies along old antislavery routes. In 1869, it became the American Woman Suffrage Association, devoted to pressing on the state level for the removal of the word "male" in the voting provisions of state constitutions (the radicals laid prior claim to the goal of a federal woman suffrage amendment). In 1870, the AWSA began publishing its *Woman's Journal,* an attractive, well-financed publication that lasted for the duration of the suffrage crusade.

The radical faction centered around Stanton and Anthony, who in 1869 founded the National Woman Suffrage Association. This was, in fact, the fourth association they had founded in six years. The radicals were far more belligerent and outspoken, especially in their opposition to the Fifteenth Amendment. Publicizing their views in *Revolution,* a weekly begun in 1868 and financed by the generous but unreliable George Train, the Stanton-Anthony faction had no hesitancy about denouncing Republican Reconstruction and all its works. The Fifteenth Amendment, said the NWSA, was a step backward for women, one that would only intensify male supremacy and sexual inequality. A *Revolution* reader repudiated the amendment, she claimed, because it asked her to attest to "the inferiority of women." Elizabeth Cady Stanton consistently argued that black men should not be elevated over "women of wealth, education, virtue, and refinement." (This point was made at AWSA meetings too.) She urged *Revolution* readers in 1869 to support woman suffrage "if you do not wish the lower orders of Chinese, Africans, Germans, and Irish, with their low ideals of womanhood, to make laws for you and your daughters." Suffrage, indeed, should be restricted to exclude the "lower orders of men."

But the notion of suffrage restriction was hardly *Revolution*'s only contribution nor was woman suffrage its only cause. Rather, the journal was a hot-bed of feminist issues. Denouncing unequal pay, unfair divorce laws, and clerical conservatism, *Revolution* continued to agitate for the broad spectrum of goals inherited from the Declaration of Sentiments. The vote was only one part of this spectrum and, in *Revolution*'s view, not the major one. "The ballot is not even half the loaf; it is only a crust, a crumb," wrote Laura Curtis Bullard, a loyal Stantonite, in an 1868 article. "Woman's chief discontent is not with her political, but with her social, and particularly, her marital bondage." Endorsing marriage reform and the principle of "self-ownership," *Revolution* writers agreed with Ballard that "the marriage question reaches down to a deeper depth in woman's heart, and more thoroughly constitutes the core of the woman's movement, than any such superficial and fragmentary question as woman suffrage." Indeed, it was the NWSA's interest in a wide range of "social" issues that made its leaders so receptive to Victoria Woodhull in 1871. Elizabeth Cady Stanton, moreover, lost no opportunity to reiterate demands for total equality. "The only revolution that we would inaugurate," she told the NWSA in 1870, "is to make woman a self-supporting, dignified, independent, equal partner with man in the state, the church, the home."

Despite the broad spectrum of goals endorsed by Stantonites and the outspoken *Revolution,* woman suffrage remained the most viable cause. Once political equality became a major national issue, women's demand for enfranchisement had been raised from marginality to preeminence. Indeed, the vote was now the only issue around which women could mobilize collectively. Like its Boston-based rival, the NWSA had no hesitancy about labeling itself a suffrage association. And like the AWSA, it began actively to seek out middle-class adherents.

NWSA strength began in New York, where it had a strong core group in New York City and a statewide network as well. It also had national ambitions.

While the "American" was basically a regional organization, relying on contacts from the old abolitionist network, the "National" began to recruit on a larger scale. In 1868, Stanton and Anthony had gone off on a mid-western campaign tour, spurring the formation of suffrage societies and gaining recruits. These women were usually newcomers to reform, with no abolitionist ties or split loyalties but, rather, with some Civil War experience, often in the Sanitary Commission. Unlike the Stantonites, they tended to view the vote as more important than "social" issues. Also, from the start, the NWSA was clearly an all-woman organization, with all-women officers. To be sure, the AWSA had coopted most of the sympathetic men. But female leadership was also a matter of principle. As Matilda Joslyn Gage later concluded, "Women can work more successfully for their own freedom than anyone else can work for them." Finally, the NWSA laid first claim to Congress, by announcing its intent to push for a federal woman suffrage amendment. The New Englanders, in response, leveled their charges at the states.

The division into rival groups in 1869 was an asset as well as a liability. It enabled the suffrage movement to involve a wider range of women nationwide than either the *Revolution*aries or the New Englanders would have reached alone. It also helped the movement survive the fiasco of Victoria Woodhull in 1871–1872. This debacle had many reverberations. It accentuated the acrimony between the two suffrage associations, increasing antagonisms that took years to heal. It also forced Elizabeth Cady Stanton to tone down her politics, despite her innate and unquenchable radicalism. When Stanton resumed NWSA leadership in 1876, she was willing to adjust to an era of single-issue politics and to steer clear of extraneous issues and risky associates, in the interest of the cause. Basically, Stanton was a congenial woman who disliked controversy. Woodhull's third legacy, of course, was the "new departure" she had proposed—for women to assault the polls, contending that they had been enfranchised by the Fourteenth and Fifteenth Amendments. This was the strategy that the NWSA adopted in the fall elections of 1872, when Susan B. Anthony mobilized more than seventy women to vote, nationwide.

"Women are citizens," said Anthony, "and no state has the right to make any new law or enforce any old law, which shall abridge their privileges or immunities." New York State, it turned out, had that right, since Anthony was herself indicted for voting. In 1873, she was tried, convicted, and fined. More important, the Supreme Court soon affirmed, in *Minor* v. *Happersett* (1875), that it was constitutional for a state to deny women the vote. Virginia Minor, a Missouri suffragist who had tried to vote in 1872, had brought suit with her husband (as a married woman she could not bring suit alone) against the registrar who had excluded her from the polls. When the case reached the Supreme Court, the Court declared that the Minors were wrong and that suffrage was not a privilege of citizenship. The Minor decision made it clear that the "new departure" had no future. After its failure, the NWSA once again turned to Congress to lobby for a federal amendment. By 1875, an independent suffrage movement had been established, but it entered the Gilded Age on a note of defeat, with divided ranks, limited adherents, and no leverage over male legislators.

Finding a Constituency

During the 1870s and 1880s, the rival suffrage organizations competed for members; each strove for a larger middle-class base. More regional and parochial, the AWSA directed its efforts toward excising the word "male" in state suffrage provisions. Better financed, and able to maintain its well-produced *Woman's Journal*, it remained the larger suffrage organization, at least until the mid-1880s. The New York-based NWSA depended mainly on its statewide feminist network but also took the nation as its recruiting ground. This effort was aided by Stanton and Anthony's far-flung lecture tours and the western suffrage networks they inspired. Both associations relied on small groups of activists who did all the work: testifying before legislative and platform committees, serving as emissaries to state and national party conventions, and running their own annual conventions. Both adopted a nonpartisan stance in politics, mainly by default, since neither party endorsed woman suffrage or paid much attention to its advocates.

The major feat of the divided suffrage movement in the 1870s and 1880s was survival in the face of almost perpetual rebuff. A sense of camaraderie-in-combat alleviated the indignity of such rebuff. Still, the rival suffrage associations met with one failure after another. First, neither was able to attract significant numbers of women constituents. The two groups combined had far fewer adherents than newborn reform associations, such as the popular women's temperance movement, white-badged and zealous. Abigail Duniway, an NWSA stalwart in Oregon, summed up some of the problems in attracting supporters. Inspired by Anthony, Duniway established a state Equal Suffrage Association in the 1870s and traveled widely on behalf of the cause, but her efforts in organization were often fruitless. A group of a dozen or so women might be convinced to form a suffrage society in one small western town or another. But they would soon spend their dues on some new worthy project and, not long after that, fade into the scenery. Duniway concluded that it was more profitable to agitate for the vote through her own suffragist newspaper, to harangue state legislators, and to convince male voters, than try to organize women.

Inability to attract a large female constituency was compounded by perpetual failure at both the state and federal levels. Between 1870 and 1890, suffragists were able to convince eight states to hold referenda on the issue and lost all eight. More often, they were unable to convince state legislators even to call for a referendum. In Massachusetts, the very crucible of AWSA efforts, woman suffrage campaigns were a highly organized but futile annual ritual. Every year, activists presented petitions to state legislators and testified at public hearings, without any results. And in 1895, when Massachusetts permitted women to vote in a state referendum on woman suffrage (an unusual move), the cause still lost, with far more men than women voting *for* woman suffrage. Agitation on the state level was by no means a total loss, however, since many legislators were willing to vote for a wide array of legal reforms affecting women—indeed, for virtually anything *except* suffrage. By 1890, thirty-three states had enacted married women's property rights laws, and by the turn of the century, according to Susan

B. Anthony, married women could keep their own earnings in two-thirds of the states. In a majority, they could make contracts and bring suit, and in some states they gained equal guardianship rights over children. As in the antebellum era, legal reform proved easier to accept than the highly charged vote. By 1890, nineteen states had granted women a limited form of suffrage; that is, the right to vote in school board elections or, in some cases, municipal elections. A modicum of "justice" was not beyond the comprehension of state legislators; it was the prospect of political equality that offended them.

NWSA efforts to make Congress enact, or even consider, a federal woman suffrage amendment were hardly more fruitful. In 1882, NWSA lobbyists convinced each house to create a committee on woman suffrage, and both committees sent bills to the floor. But when the issue finally reached a vote in the Senate in 1886, woman suffrage was defeated. After that, its prospects were even dimmer. Full woman suffrage, to be sure, had been enacted in two territories. In 1869 and 1870, independent of the suffrage movement, women were enfranchised in Wyoming and Utah. Both were extremely special cases. Wyoming was barely settled; indeed, there were very few women in it and a great many mining camps. To improve the area's uncivilized reputation and attract stable settlers, the tiny territorial legislature gave women the vote, which they retained when Wyoming was admitted to statehood in 1890. In Utah, in 1870, Mormon voters enacted woman suffrage in order to retain control and outvote non-Mormom settlers, mainly male. Although Congress revoked woman suffrage in Utah in 1887 in a bill that made polygamy illegal, when Utah became a state in 1896 it once again enfranchised women. During the 1870s and 1880s Wyoming and Utah remained anomalies. Suffragists had no success elsewhere. Still lacking broad support, they were unable to sway legislators. Moreover, since the vote itself was a prime tool of legislative pressure, scholar Steven M. Buechler points out, "the movement was in the paradoxical position of being denied a major method for seeking legislative change." Finally, Buechler suggests, "the relative exclusion of women from the public realm and existing structures of power meant that women had little institutional power to bring to their movement."

In the 1890s, however, changes occurred outside the suffrage movement that enabled it to expand and legitimize its role. By 1890, the middle-class woman was in motion. The high school population was female-dominated, and women attended the majority of American colleges. They constituted one-third of college students, and over one-third of professional workers. Most important, middle-class women were creating a large nexus of associations—women's clubs, temperance societies, and charitable and civic organizations of all types. By the 1890s, in short, a new world of organized women had sprung into existence, reflecting a shared desire to participate in public life beyond the home and family. As a result, the suffrage movement was no longer an isolated island of demanding women but part of a larger phenomenon—one of several national women's groups that held conventions, elected delegates, ran campaigns, and lobbied for causes. Although far outnumbered by women who were active in social reform and worthy projects, by women determined to extend woman's sphere, not to challenge it, suffragists benefited from the new context. The larger "woman's movement" testified to women's rising social consciousness and made their own efforts more legitimate and respectable.

One result of the new climate was the unification of the two wings of the suffrage movement in 1890. The National American Woman Suffrage Association (NAWSA) was part of a larger trend toward federation in other middle-class associations. It was also an attempt to take advantage of women's new social activism and unify as many women as possible under a single banner. This goal appealed especially to Susan B. Anthony, the major power of the NWSA, which had grown bigger than the AWSA. To be sure, animosities between the rival suffrage associations had not totally withered. But opposition to a merger came mainly from a minority of dissidents within the NWSA, such as Olympia Brown and Elizabeth Cady Stanton. In Stanton's view, both of the old suffrage groups had grown "political and conservative." Neither Anthony nor Lucy Stone, she felt in 1888, could see anything besides suffrage. "They do not see woman's religious and social bondage, neither do the young women in either organization."

The International Council of Women, founded in 1888, was an NWSA ploy to mobilize support for woman suffrage among delegates of leading women's organizations. Although the ploy failed, a group portrait of council participants commemorates the determination with which women entered the public sphere. Susan B. Anthony is seated in the front row, second from the left, and Elizabeth Cady Stanton, third from the right. NWSA activist Matilda Joslyn Gage, second from right, front row, joined with Stanton and Anthony to edit the *History of Woman Suffrage*. *(Library of Congress)*

Once the merger had reconciled survivors of the old guard, the new NAWSA streamlined its operations. It ran more formal conventions, attended by delegates from state organizations; it ended internal debate; and it became more professional, especially in tactics and propaganda. Dropping efforts to work for a federal amendment (after 1896, Congress no longer considered such amendments), the NAWSA agreed to direct all its efforts toward the state level. During the 1890s, state campaigns became more numerous and effective, especially as Carrie Chapman Catt, a forceful younger spirit, rose in the organization and spearheaded some of its major efforts. These campaigns usually failed—between 1896 and 1910 not a single state granted women the vote. But during the same period, the suffrage movement benefited from rising membership, new leadership, and a shift in argument.

Membership rose throughout the progressive era, as the NAWSA became a truly national movement. In the 1890s, it moved into the South, in the wake of the temperance movement and women's clubs. Although never powerful there, the NAWSA did acquire a corps of southern leaders, which certified its new national scope. In the South as elsewhere, the emergence of other women's groups was a great asset. Since club work and temperance work attracted large numbers of women, suffragists profited from a coattails effect. In the Midwest and West, for instance, a majority of suffragist leaders were also temperance activists. And in the Northwest, as Abigail Duniway testified, the women's club movement provided a "safety valve." It legitimized organized activity for more conservative women who were not politicized enough to support suffrage and often provided suffragists with an audience—an arena in which they strove for conversions. Suffragists profited from women's new social activism in other ways, too, especially when prominent women reformers lent their support.

There had always been a degree of overlapping affiliation among leaders of women's associations. Since the early postwar days, for instance, Julia Ward Howe had been a heroine of both the women's club and the suffrage movements. Frances Willard had converted the conservative Women's Christian Temperance Union to her own suffragist stance, though after her death it returned to single-interest politics. But during the late nineteenth century, there was more conflict than affinity between suffragists and other women reformers. First, the energies of some suffrage leaders, such as Howe and Mary Livermore, were diverted away from the suffrage movement and into other causes, such as clubs and temperance. Second, suffragists and other women reformers could rarely agree on priorities. When the NWSA invited leaders of many women's groups to attend an International Council of Women in 1888, hoping to gain support for the vote, reformers refused to adopt suffrage as a plank. And at the World's Columbia Exposition in Chicago in 1893, suffragists and reformers were again at odds, over the highly charged issue of whether to segregate women's achievements in a separate building (the reformers won and a Woman's Building was established). Suffragists hardly dominated the women's movement, nor was woman suffrage a goal to which large numbers of activist women were as yet committed.

During the progressive era, however, differences between suffragists and other reformers became less overt, and a new network of overlapping leadership evolved. The NAWSA now drew support of leaders in the National Consumers' League, the Women's Trade Union League, and the settlement movement—such as Jane Addams and Florence Kelley, both of whom served as NAWSA vice presidents. Indeed, Addams and Kelley held pivotal roles in a wide range of women's organizations, since between them they held posts in the NCL, WTUL, NFWC, and eventually in a new Woman's Peace party. By the twentieth century, the growth of women's reform organizations and overlapping leadership helped the suffrage movement attract a constituency. In 1893, the new NAWSA had only about 13,000 members—far less than the General Federation of Women's Clubs or the mammoth WCTU. But during the early twentieth century, the membership rolls began to climb, reaching about 75,000 (these figures were never precise) in 1910.

After 1900, moreover, historians point out, the rise of the progressive movement also favored the suffragist cause. In the context of the progressive reform agenda, woman suffrage was neither outlandish nor bizarre. Progressives endorsed a battery of electoral reforms and believed that all social problems could be solved by legislation. Woman suffrage meshed right into the progressive scheme and promised tactical benefits. Clearly, enfranchising women would double the middle-class, educated, fair-minded electorate who would support other progressive reforms. In addition, suffragists and progressives seemed to share the same vision of society, one run by educated citizens, without poverty, injustice, or corruption. The NAWSA house organ, the *Woman's Journal,* doubled its support for reform legislation, while influential women reformers, such as those at Hull-House, pressured legislators for a barrage of progressive bills—to clean up slums, sweatshops, sewer systems, food products, and local government. Women reformers declared themselves enemies of party bosses, ward politics, and political corruption, thereby enhancing their appeal as potential progressive voters.

Finally, a change of leadership enhanced the NAWSA's new legitimacy. For the first decade of unification, the old guard remained at the helm. Stanton, who presided over the 1890 merger, was never a very popular president. She retired two years later to agitate for divorce reform, resume her role as rebel, and publish her *Woman's Bible* (1895), an attack on organized religion's oppression of women. (The NAWSA, in convention, at once repudiated the *Bible,* by resolution.) Susan B. Anthony, who replaced Stanton, assumed office at age seventy-two and held it until 1900, when the second generation of suffrage leaders began to move in. Carrie Chapman Catt, who became prominent in the 1890s when in her thirties, was a master strategist of state campaigns. She served as president from 1900 to 1904 and again from 1915 to 1920. Anna Howard Shaw, ordained minister, physician, WCTU lecturer, renowned orator, and protégé of Anthony, held control from 1904 to 1915. The new leaders, both westerners and neither admirers of Elizabeth Cady Stanton, augured a new spirit. Now legitimate, larger, and unified, the suffrage movement shifted its arguments into terms that appealed to its expanding constituency.

From 1890 onward, while the suffrage movement gained cohesion and clout, it functioned mainly as an educational crusade, a propaganda machine. Its arguments, presented in resolutions, testimony at hearings, convention speeches, and suffrage publications, took on a new tone. Suffragists put less emphasis on demands for "equal" rights or on the "justice" of enfranchising women, and more stress on the special qualities women would bring to the polls and on the good they could do for the nation. The new arguments presented woman suffrage not in terms of a radical change in women's status but rather as a tool of female benevolence. As a result, movement propaganda reflected traditional ideas about woman's role, terms that would appeal both to middle-class men's views of women and to women's views about themselves. More of an amalgam of claims than an ideology, suffragist propaganda now aimed at attracting the largest possible base of female support and convincing the public of the suffrage movement's good intentions. It also responded to arguments against suffrage, which rose in volume as suffragist influence increased.

The Argument Over Suffrage

Antisuffrage sentiment was hardly a novelty, but when the suffrage movement was weak and ineffectual, it emerged only in the occasional congressional debate or state campaign. During the progressive era, however, antisuffragism took on new zest and organizational voice. Associations opposed to woman suffrage began to appear in the 1890s, mainly in states where the suffrage movement was strongest. These "anti" organizations included men but were run and led by women, the same type of women who joined the suffrage campaign—well-off, well-educated, and active in professions, charities, clubs, and reform. Their arguments against the vote now permeated state campaigns, legislative debates, and the press. To antisuffragists, as historian Aileen Kraditor points out, woman suffrage was an attack on traditional beliefs about sex roles and social organization. In defending these beliefs, Kraditor shows, antisuffragists posed the problems that suffragists had to solve.

Opponents of suffrage consistently asserted that the sexes had different functions, that each occupied a separate sphere, and that any perversion of this social division would have dire consequences. According to their arguments, men functioned in society as distinctive individuals, but women were all cut from the same mold—a mold defined by maternity and domesticity. While the state fell into the male realm, the female realm was the home. Suffrage would therefore be an illicit entry into man's province. Moreover, the basic unit of society was not the individual but the family, a unit on which social stability rested. From this premise, antisuffragists drew two contradictory conclusions. One was that women were virtually represented in politics by male family members—by a "household" vote. The other was that if enfranchised, women would vote against their husbands, destroy their homes and families, and bring society to the point of anarchy. Women, therefore, were represented by men but would vote against them if they had the chance.

Despite the inconsistency of these positions, antisuffragists lost no opportunity to stress the damage that woman suffrage would inflict on family and society. During a congressional debate in 1866, an Oregon senator expressed the classic antisuffragist case. Contending that women could exercise more influence on public affairs by their "elevated social position" than they could "coerce" through the ballot, the senator asserted that with the vote, women would oppose men, turn society "into a state of war, and make every home a hell on earth." This became a staple threat. Leaders of antisuffragist organizations argued that if women were enabled to vote against their husbands, they would "wreck our present domestic institutions." In the 1917 debate on woman suffrage in Congress, a southern representative reiterated that giving the vote to women would "disrupt the family, which is the unit of society, and when you disrupt the family, you destroy the home, which is the foundation of the Republic."

Besides destroying homes, opponents of suffrage contended, enfranchised women would harm themselves. A major antisuffragist point was that women were physically, mentally, and emotionally incapable of duties associated with the vote. Lacking rationality and sound judgment, they suffered from "logical infirmity of mind," as a minister argued in 1910. Idealistic and sentimental, they were likely to support wide, sweeping reforms. Unable to withstand the pressure of political life, they would be prone to paroxysms of hysteria. Female character, therefore, with its innate, implicit foolishness or "milder, gentler nature," as a senator put it in the 1860s, disqualified women "for the turmoil and battle of public life." They were not so much excluded from the vote as excused from it: Voting would ruin the purity and moral superiority they had always claimed. Woman suffrage, as Grover Cleveland explained to *Ladies Home Journal* readers in 1905, would have "a dangerous, undermining effect on the character of wives and mothers." By the twentieth century, antisuffragists conceded that women *did* have a viable role in public life, but not in what a congressman in 1915 called "the muck and mire of politics." Woman's role was in charity, philanthropy, and indirect influence over male voters.

Toward the end of the suffrage crusade, when the woman's vote loomed far larger as a real possibility, a gamut of pragmatic arguments were added to the antisuffrage arsenal. These addenda sometimes contradicted other "anti" tenets, but neither suffragists nor their opponents had a monopoly on inconsistency. Woman suffrage, antisuffragists claimed, would double the number of "undesirable" voters, giving the "unfit" a potential majority. (Suffragists went to some pains to answer this argument.) Also, their opponents pointed out, suffragists overestimated the impact of the vote. Woman suffrage would not produce any significant reforms because, if enfranchised, women would not vote as a bloc, but as their husbands or class did. Indeed, in states where women already voted, their votes made little difference. Finally (and this was the "anti" trump card), most middle-class women, the ones most qualified to vote, were not interested in their own enfranchisement anyway.

Suffragists sought to answer their opponents by fusing woman suffrage with traditional ideas about woman's role. Since the Civil War, the suffrage argument had always been a blend of natural rights and moral superiority. Demands for "justice" (women were entitled to vote) had always been combined with claims of "expediency" (women's votes would benefit the nation). During

Fear of role reversal was always an implicit part of the antisuffragist argument. With women in control, literally in the driver's seat, men would be reduced to sewing, laundry, and infant care. Such fear was also a telling comparison between the domestic sphere, limited and confined, and the public sphere. "The Age of Iron," Currier and Ives lithograph, 1869. *(Library of Congress)*

the progressive era, when the suffrage movement finally gained a constituency, the emphasis shifted to expediency. This was not a sharp break but rather a tilt, a reformulation. The tone of suffrage rhetoric now veered away from self-interest to altruism. Significantly, suffrage arguments were now based not on the equality of women, but on their difference. "It is because of the difference between men and women that the nineteenth century more than any other demands the enfranchisement of women," Carrie Chapman Catt contended in 1893. The woman's vote, in suffragist claims, would accordingly make a difference. It would purify politics, effect reforms, and outweigh the votes of less desirable and less competent voters.

A chasm of "difference" between men and women was not the only assumption suffragists shared with antisuffragists. They also assumed that women had special, shared interests and would vote together and that politics was a dirty business. Like antisuffragists, they often contended that the ignorant and foreign-born were unfit voters. But in the "anti" argument, the woman voter was depicted, sometimes explicitly, as foolish, hysterical, and destructive. In the suffrage argument, she appeared as a paragon—morally superior, intelligent, educated, competent, humane, and cooperative, with an eye for detail, a skill for management, and a passion for fairness. Suffragists argued that these qualities were needed in government and that the woman's vote would put them there. By such claims they transformed the image of the suffrage movement from a threatening, challenging group into a wise, compassionate, and service-oriented one. The woman voter would not be the destroyer of home, family, and society but their protector. The vote was not a violation of sphere but the consummation of motherhood. The women who asked for it were not a radical fringe but rather models of middle-class virtue. And the enemy, significantly, was no longer "man," as in the 1848 Declaration of Sentiments, but, implicitly and explicitly, specific men—lower-class men, the foreign-born, poor, black, and uneducated men, those with an affinity for the saloon, the slums, the party machine, and patriarchal habits.

A major tenet of the suffragist argument was female moral superiority, a claim that had long been present. Elizabeth Cady Stanton, like other early feminists, was once hesitant about the moral superiority claim, but she had adopted it in the 1860s (Stanton was a versatile logician). "The male element is a destructive force," she proclaimed in an 1869 speech, "stern, selfish, aggrandizing, loving war, conquest, acquisition, breeding . . . discord, disorder, disease, and death. . . . The need of the hour is . . . a new evangel of womanhood, to exalt purity, virtue, morality, true religion, to lift men into the higher realm of thought and action." Since suffragists asserted that female values would carry over into the polls, uplift was a consistent theme in their argument. "Everyone connected with the gambling house, the brothel, and the saloon works and votes solidly against the enfranchisement of women," Susan B. Anthony told the NAWSA convention in 1900, "and I say, if you believe in chastity, if you believe in honesty and integrity, put the ballot in the hands of women." Maternal influence was also cited to reinforce the need for woman's vote. "In so far as motherhood has given to women a distinctive ethical development, it is that of sympathetic personal insight respecting the needs of the weak and helpless, and of quick-witted flexible adjustment of means to ends," declared Anna Garlin Spencer, Unitarian minister and a frequent figure on the podium, in 1898. "Thus far has motherhood fitted women to give a service to the modern state which men cannot altogether duplicate."

Women's special qualifications for political life, and the consequent good their votes would do, were points picked up by women reformers who added their voices to suffragist claims. Hull-House veterans took the lead, each relying on her own field of expertise. Julia Lathrop, children's advocate, told a NAWSA convention that woman suffrage was "the next great service for the welfare and ennoblement of the home." Florence Kelley, in addresses to the NAWSA from 1898 onward, stressed that woman suffrage was needed to protect the working woman, who, unenfranchised, had lost the respect of the men in her family. (Lack of respect for women, like lack of sobriety, was attributed to the lower-class male.) And Jane Addams emphasized the need for women's contributions to urban government. In one of her standard speeches, presented to the NAWSA in 1906, Addams contended that "city housekeeping has failed recently because women, the traditional housekeepers, have not been consulted as to its activities." Men, said Addams, were as indifferent to civic management as they were to housekeeping tasks.

The very multifariousness and complexity of a city government demand the help of minds accustomed to detail and variety of work, to a sense of obligation for the health and welfare of young children and to a responsibility for the cleanliness and comfort of other people.

Women had traditionally cared for just such detail, Addams explained, before industrialization had transformed the home and society, but now, unable to vote, "they are losing what they always had." This was a powerful argument.

Social reformers also stressed that women's votes were needed to foster legislation to protect the family and to provide progressive reforms. This argument carried considerable weight since many of the women involved in clubs, temperance, and settlements strove to promote such legislation. In a 1910 article in the *Ladies Home Journal*, Addams reeled off all the problems afflicting modern life that begged for the woman's vote—unsanitary housing, poisonous sewage, contaminated water, adulterated foods, impure milk, infant mortality, smoke-laden air, ill-ventilated factories, juvenile crime, prostitution, and drunkenness. The electorate, Addams concluded, should logically be made up of "those who have in the past at least attempted to care for children, to clean houses, to prepare food, to isolate the family from moral danger." Modern problems, Addams contended, could not be solved by military or business expertise but from "the human welfare point of view."

One more claim bolstered the expediency argument: the votes of middle-class women would outweigh those of the lower classes, foreign-born, and blacks. This response to antisuffragists was really a reformulation of an old feminist contention, first voiced at Seneca Falls, that "man" deprived woman of rights "given to the most ignorant, degraded men—both native and foreigner." The old grievance was now adapted to the new argument. The 1893 NAWSA convention and subsequent ones resolved that with woman suffrage, literate women could outvote uneducated men and "settle the question of rule by illiteracy." There was an even better solution, as Carrie Chapman Catt told the convention the following year: "Cut off the vote of the slums and give it to women." Franchise restriction, moreover, had long been supported by Elizabeth Cady Stanton, who now advocated "educated suffrage," a proposal to give the vote to all educated citizens, men and women, and take it away from the uneducated.

Other important voices joined this chorus. Henry Blackwell, a founder of the AWSA, told the 1895 NAWSA convention that "in every state save one there are more educated women than all the illiterate voters, white and black, native-born and foreign." By outvoting the foreign-born, NWSA's Olympia Brown contended in 1889, women's votes could be used to maintain "our free institutions . . . Our Republican government." And as Mississippi suffragist Belle Kearney told the 1903 New Orleans convention (somewhat to the embarrassment of President Catt), "The enfranchisement of women would insure immediate and durable white supremacy, honestly attained." Since such sentiments were widely voiced, prominent black women expressed reservations about the suffrage movement, even when they supported the cause. "Personally," said Margaret Murray Washington, black clubwoman and educator, "woman suffrage has never kept me awake at night."

Black women, indeed, did endorse the suffrage cause, but they were generally excluded from the suffrage crusade. NAWSA leaders feared antagonizing southern members, whose support was worth more to the cause than that of black women, North or South. The NAWSA, for instance, rejected an application for admission from a federation of black women's clubs as late as 1919. On other occasions, suffrage leaders attempted to express unity of interest. In New Orleans in 1903, for instance, after Belle Kearney's speech, Susan B. Anthony paid an expedient visit to a local black women's club, where she was politely received. But this hardly made the NAWSA an integrated movement. A few integrated local societies existed; black women's clubs usually supported woman suffrage; and black club leaders sometimes addressed NAWSA conventions, as when Mary Church Terrell spoke in 1900. But the gist of Terrell's speech was to denounce prejudice in the suffrage movement. In general, the suffrage movement ignored black women, and the NAWSA took advantage of racist arguments when they were useful.

Racism and nativism were not, of course, peculiar to the suffrage movement. They were, rather, familiar middle-class sentiments. Desire for reform was often combined with similar antidemocratic ideas, as at the Progressive party convention of 1912. And it was by endorsing a wide gamut of middle-class values that the suffrage movement was winning its new, enlarged constituency. Only massive support among women could put enough pressure on male voters, state legislators, and congressmen even to consider enfranchising women. By capitalizing on moral superiority and domestic ideals, with which many women identified, suffragists could, simultaneously, combat their opponents, prove their respectability, and attempt to gain wider support. By 1917, when the suffrage movement reached its apogee, the *Woman Citizen* (the latest version of the NAWSA *Woman's Journal*) was able to describe the suffrage movement, triumphantly, as "bourgeois, middle class, a great middle-of-the-road movement."

In gaining respectability and constituency, of course, suffragists had long since discarded any traces of the radical feminism personified by Elizabeth Cady Stanton, whom the NAWSA had in fact repudiated in the 1890s. The crucial alliance of suffragism and progressivism, scholar Steven M. Buechler contends, "minimized the feminist content of the ballot demand." Unlike the coterie of women who had written for *Revolution* in the late 1860s, the progressive era suffrage movement did not demand changes in women's domestic, social, and economic roles. Nor did it resurrect sexual issues or attempt to reform the institution of marriage. As the Woodhull fiasco in 1872 suggested, the "marriage question" was best ignored when trying to create a unified, middle-class women's movement, and the NAWSA ignored it with a vengeance. But more radical themes never vanished from the larger woman's movement. Rather, they were picked up by more radical activists—some within the suffrage crusade, some on its periphery, and some outside it entirely.

Voices on the Left

The first two decades of the twentieth century saw a ferment of activism among women. The growing suffrage campaign was only one facet of this ferment, though by World War I it would be the dominant one. Throughout the era, however, a wide range of views emerged; the vitality of the woman's movement rested not on its unity of opinion but rather on its diversity. If the NAWSA, with its expedient arguments and progressive support, now occupied the middle of the road, to its left arose more radical voices, those of socialists, anarchists, and indeed "feminists"—a term that sprang into use after 1910. The new label represented a battery of demands exceeding that of the suffrage movement, although a smaller constituency. "All feminists are suffragists," one adherent explained in 1913, "but not all suffragists are feminists."

Infusing the feminist upsurge were women of the political left. Now at the peak of its influence, the Socialist party provided an ideological home for politicized women who looked on the NAWSA as a bourgeois bastion. Socialist women, historian Mari Jo Buhle points out, were involved in all phases of the woman's movement. They were often active advocates of woman suffrage, despite conflicting loyalties and nagging doubts about whether enfranchising women would accelerate proletarian revolution. They were also involved in other women's causes, such as settlement work and the WTUL; indeed, some prominent reformers like Florence Kelley were even drawn into the Socialist party. The woman's movement fostered a wide network of overlapping affiliations and many joint endeavors. But from left-wing perspectives, the "woman problem" assumed a different shape. The contributions of Charlotte Perkins Gilman, Emma Goldman, and Crystal Eastman, for instance, were hardly identical, either with one another or with the platform of the suffrage movement. Rather, they provided a counterpoint. Stressing the need for changing women's lives, economically, emotionally, and sexually, and for revamping male/female relations and attitudes, women on the left called attention to "social" issues that the NAWSA had left in limbo.

Though only tangentially connected to the suffrage crusade, Charlotte Perkins Gilman was the most influential feminist of the progressive era. Born the same year as Jane Addams, Gilman came from the same sort of social background as the middle- and upper-class suffragists. Her mother was a descendant of Roger Williams, and her father of the Beechers. Gilman, in fact, was the Beecher family's last and greatest contribution to American feminism. Her early life, as she described it, was one of financial and emotional impoverishment. But after a miserable first marriage, pregnancy, and breakdown, Gilman slowly worked her way back to integration, remarriage, and a successful career as a writer and speaker on the "woman problem." Throughout her career, she maintained contacts with many circles of activist women—socialists, social reformers, and suffragists. A speaker at several NAWSA conventions, Gilman supported the vote but thought it was unimportant. Her favored affiliations were with the Socialist party, with Heterodoxy, a New York feminist group formed in 1912, and later with the Woman's Peace party, started in 1915. But more important than these involvements were Gilman's original contributions to the ongoing debate over woman's role in society.

Her pivotal contribution, *Women and Economics,* published in 1898, was an argument for women's economic independence that won her a wide following; she reiterated its precepts in speech and print for two decades. Demolishing most of the major totems on which woman's sphere and indeed suffrage arguments rested, Gilman presented her own unique blend of evolutionary theory and utopian proposals, in a personal rhetoric full of striking images. The image of "woman" that emerged in her books and articles was hardly that of the paragon described on the NAWSA podium. On the contrary, Gilman described women, in their present oppressed state, as stunted, crippled, contaminated, and conse- quently malevolent. However, despite her visceral sense of disgust at traditional womanhood, Gilman's original brand of feminism was widely praised. Jane Addams hailed *Women and Economics* as a "masterpiece," and Florence Kelley considered it the first substantive contribution made by a woman to the science of economics.

Since woman was utterly dependent on man for survival, Gilman argued, over the centuries her personality had become distorted. Those characteristics that were needed to attract and retain male support had become overblown and exaggerated. "So utterly has the status of women been accepted as a sexual one," Gilman wrote, that women were not considered persons, except by the woman's movement. "We have come to consider most human attributes as masculine attributes." Having lost her ability to contribute to the larger society, beyond home and family, woman had evolved into a deformed and imbalanced being with only a sexual role and self-image.

In garments whose main purpose is unmistakably to announce her sex; with a tendency to ornament which marks exuberance of sex-energy, with a body so modified to sex as to be grievously deprived of its natural activities; with a manner and behavior wholly attuned to sex advantage, and frequently most disadvantageous to any human gain; with a field of action most rigidly confined to sex relations; with her overcharged sensibility, her prominent modesty, her 'eternal femininity,'—the female of genus homos is undeniably oversexed.

This grotesque creature, with her "feminine tricks and charms," had but a single option—marriage, "the one road to fortune, to life." But as wife, mother, and homemaker, her role had become pathological. First, said Gilman, she had become a nonproductive consumer who "in her unintelligent and ceaseless demands, hinders and perverts the economic development of the whole world." Her economic devastation was exceeded only by the damage she caused as a mother. Motherhood, Gilman contended, was ideally a sacred function; but like woman herself, it had become deformed and perverted. "Human motherhood is more pathological than any other, more morbid, defective, irregular, diseased," as she bluntly put it. "Human childhood is pathological." Children were stunted because mothers manipulated them, interfered with their lives, destroyed their privacy, and, in the end, produced even more monsters: "Idiots, imbeciles, cripples, defectives, and degenerates, the vicious and the criminal, as well as all the vast mass of slow-minded, prejudiced, ordinary people who clog the wheels of progress." Indeed, since woman was defined by "sex-function" and cut off from "all economic use," she became a disaster as both parent and progenitor: "The female segregated to the use of sex alone deteriorates in racial development and naturally transmits that deterioration to her offspring."

Not only did female pathology wreck the economy and future generations, but it was permanently institutionalized in the most deformed of institutions—the home. In a 1903 book entitled *The Home* (as well as in many articles in women's magazines, including the suffragist *Woman's Journal*), Gilman demolished yet another, fundamental female icon.

The Home, in its arbitrary position of arrested development, does not properly fulfill its own essential function, much less promote social ones. It hinders, by keeping woman a social idiot, by keeping the modern child under the tutelage of the primeval mother. . . . It hinders by its enormous expense; making the physical details of daily life a heavy burden to mankind. . . . They should have long since been reduced to a minor incident.

The home was both an economic disaster and a female prison. It wasted half the world's labor, "It maintains a low grade of womanhood, overworked or lazy; it checks the social development of men as well as women, and, most of all, children." Since the home was not the basis of civilization, but rather its antithesis, the woman who remained in it continued to be thwarted, diseased, and demented. Moreover, her domestic drudgery, which was in inverse relation to her economic status, diverted her from both her true maternal role and any chance to contribute to the larger society. "Only as we live, think, feel and work outside the home," Gilman wrote, "do we become humanly developed, civilized and socialized." Clearly, this assessment contradicted every tenet of nineteenth-century women's culture, which not only sanctified the home but also—according to Frances Willard, for instance—attributed to woman a higher evolutionary status and urged her to civilize and socialize men.

Charlotte Perkins Gilman's remedies for woman's plight were collectivist and futuristic. Economic independence would relieve women of the need to attract men for survival; but to achieve such independence woman had to be emancipated from the tyranny of home. Gilman's proposals included large apartment units, rather than wasteful separate houses, and communal arrangements for housekeeping and child rearing. Centralized nurseries could replace child care at home, and liberate women for "a far wider sense of love and duty" as well as for better parenthood. The mother would love her child more when not in constant contact with it, when she had her own life and could "give her mind another channel for her own part of the day." Cooperative kitchens, meanwhile, run by specialists, would enable her to fulfill her own specialized, productive role beyond the home. Gilman's remedies, in short, were intended to instill economic independence, redefine femininity, and apply socialist principles to domestic life. They had much in common with the ideas of her fellow socialist Edward Bellamy, whose utopian proposals had won wide popularity. They were also part of the collectivist tradition that can be traced back to Melusina Fay Peirce and her Cambridge cooperative in 1869.

While Charlotte Perkins Gilman had affiliations with various branches of the middle-class women's movement, anarchist Emma Goldman agitated outside it, although she too maintained a wide range of contacts with suffragists and reformers. Nor did Goldman express anything like Gilman's visceral animus toward middle-class femininity; though more radical politically, Goldman was a compassionate and sympathetic soul. But like Gilman's, her views were yet another counterpoint to the middle-of-the-road stance represented by NAWSA.

Born in Russia, Emma Goldman emigrated to New York as a teenager in 1885 and began her political career in 1889, when she became involved in anarchist circles. A magnetic personality, Goldman crossed the nation defending anarchism and free speech, throughout the progressive era, and published her views in her magazine *Mother Earth* (1906–1918). To Goldman, as to Gilman, woman suffrage was of little import. As an anarchist, Goldman viewed politics as profane, since they would always be dominated by business interests, whether women voted or not. There was no reason woman should not vote, Goldman said, but "to assume . . . that she would succeed in purifying something which is not susceptible of purification is to credit her with supernatural powers." Central issues of the "woman problem" therefore lay outside the voting booth, and while Goldman dealt with many other issues too, she had much to say on the "marriage question," and the nature of woman's "emancipation."

Like Charlotte Perkins Gilman, Emma Goldman rejected woman's role as mere "sex commodity," but she attacked "the conventional lie of marriage" as well. Marriage was primarily "an economic arrangement, an insurance pact," Goldman explained in a 1910 essay. "If, however, a woman's premium is a husband, she pays for it with her name, her privacy, her self-respect, her very life." While Goldman favored mutual affection outside marriage (in her own case, this proved an elusive goal, since she was usually torn between man and cause), she was not surprised that working girls accepted the first offer of marriage, "sick and tired of their 'independence' behind the counter, the sewing or typewriter machine." Never limited by a middle-class perspective, Goldman criticized contemporary feminist notions of "emancipation," in which she found an ascetic, asexual quality: The new, emancipated, independent woman had excluded men from her emotional life. "True emancipation begins neither at the polls nor in court," Goldman wrote. "It begins in a woman's soul."

Emma Goldman's ideal was the woman who could "direct her own destiny" in every way, who could fuse emancipation with romantic attachment. But she felt that contemporary feminists, especially when disdainful of men, had "failed to reach that great end."

The narrowness of the existing conception of woman's independence and emancipation . . . the fear that love will rob her of freedom and independence . . . the horror that
love or the joy of motherhood will only hinder her in the full exercise of her profession—all
these together make of the emancipated modern woman a compulsory vestal, before
whom life . . . rolls on without touching or gripping her soul.

In a statement oddly similar to one of Jane Addams's observations, Goldman
commented that "A goodly number of our grandmothers had more blood in their
veins, more humor and wit . . . than the majority of our emancipated, professional
women who fill the colleges, halls of learning and various offices." No "compulsory vestal" herself, Emma Goldman became an early advocate of birth control,
although arrested for lecturing on the subject in 1916. (Dispensing birth-control
information was illegal under both state laws and the Comstock law of 1873.)
Her efforts, however, inspired younger women on the left, such as Elizabeth
Gurley Flynn and Margaret Sanger, who began to crusade for birth control just
before World War I and provided their own counterpoint to middle-of-the-road
feminism.

Younger than Charlotte Gilman and Emma Goldman, socialist lawyer
Crystal Eastman represented a new generation of feminists who, at the end of
the suffrage crusade, formed its militant and radical wing. Moreover, through
her multiple affiliations and commitments, Eastman linked several aspects of the
woman's movement. A Vassar alumna, Crystal Eastman entered public life
through a "social feminist" route, by working at New York settlement houses
while earning a master's degree in sociology and attending law school. She then
moved into the field of industrial safety and in 1909 was appointed to a New
York State commission to draft workmen's compensation laws. In 1912, when
she was married and living in Wisconsin, Eastman joined that state's woman
suffrage campaign and became an activist in the suffrage movement. During the
next few years, back in New York, her combination of radical and feminist
interests emerged fully.

A member of the feminist group, Heterodoxy, as well as of New York's
radical and socialist circles, Eastman worked with Emma Goldman on causes of
mutual interest, such as birth control and free speech. Committed to women's
sexual emancipation, she shared Goldman's objections to marriage, although she
married twice. Unlike Emma Goldman, Eastman was primarily involved in the
suffrage crusade. By 1915, she had become a prominent leader in two new
developments. One was the National Woman's party, a militant offshoot of the
NAWSA, which split apart in 1916 and waged its own dramatic campaign for
the vote. Another was the Woman's Peace party, formed in 1915, which involved
a broad cross section of feminists, including NAWSA president Carrie Chapman
Catt, Charlotte Perkins Gilman, and Jane Addams. Defending the cause of peace
even after the United States entered World War I and most other suffragists had
retreated from pacifism, Crystal Eastman became ever more committed to her
own brand of radical feminism. In 1919, she helped to organize a Feminist
Congress in New York, where she advocated the battery of causes that had

become important to like-minded feminists, from economic independence and equal employment opportunities to birth control.

Crystal Eastman was often trapped between affiliations with different priorities, such as the conflict between the suffrage movement and the women's peace movement that emerged during World War I. She was also caught up in a conflict of interest between socialism and feminism, a conflict that left many left-wing women torn between ideologies that were difficult to fuse. Though sympathetic to woman suffrage, the Socialist party was not ready to support the type of complete emancipation endorsed by such radicals as Crystal Eastman. Therefore, though committed to both ideologies, Eastman clung above all to her feminist vision. "The true feminist, no matter how far to the left she may be in the revolutionary movement, sees the woman's battle as distinct in its objectives and different in its methods from the worker's battle," Crystal Eastman wrote in 1920.

> As a feminist she . . . knows that the whole of women's slavery is not summed up in the profit system, nor is her complete emancipation assured by the downfall of capitalism. If we should graduate into communism tomorrow . . . man's attitude to his wife would not be changed.

Crystal Eastman best represents the feminist wave that erupted in the last decade of the suffrage crusade. The onset of "modern feminism," historian Nancy F. Cott contends, was a crucial phenomenon, distinctive from both suffragism and the nineteenth-century woman's movement. Modern feminism embraced a panoply of goals, for economic, social, and sexual emancipation, or even, in one advocate's words, "complete social revolution." "None of its single tenets was brand new," Cott points out, "Not the claim for full citizenship, nor for equal wages for equal work, nor even for *equal work*, nor for psychic freedom and spiritual autonomy, nor even for sexual liberation, nor for wives' independence." But such demands "assumed intensity in constellation." Significantly, modern feminism embodied paradoxes, Cott points out. Its demands entailed recognition of sexual equality and sexual difference, individual freedom and sex solidarity, unity and diversity, gender consciousness and the elimination of gender roles. The impact of such paradoxes would emerge more fully in women's politics of the 1920s.

The ferment of feminism to which Gilman, Goldman, and Eastman contributed had an important impact on the suffrage crusade. First, these radicals changed the political climate of the woman's movement. By World War I, the cause of woman suffrage truly assumed a centrist stance between more conservative women reformers and left-wing feminists. The feminist left also helped to legitimize NAWSA demands by presenting far more radical ones. "What you ask is so much worse than what we ask," a suffragist once told Charlotte Perkins Gilman, "that they will grant our demands in order to escape yours." Finally, during World War I, when both socialism and pacifism fell into disrepute, woman suffrage was in fact the only major women's cause left. By then, it had come into its own.

Peace, War, and the Woman's Party

In 1910, the tide began to turn in favor of woman suffrage, slowly at first but then in a mounting crescendo. Signs of progress came in a rush at the outset, when the woman's vote was endorsed by the Progressive party, the General Federation of Women's Clubs, and a string of western states. Progressive endorsement in 1912 was especially gratifying. Although woman suffrage had long won support in progressive circles, the progressives had never been a national party nor mounted a presidential campaign. And neither Republicans nor Democrats had been inclined to support the "non-partisan" suffrage cause. But the national platform at the Progressive party convention of 1912 included a woman suffrage plank. Candidate Theodore Roosevelt, who supported the cause, was "not an enthusiastic advocate of it because I do not regard it as a very important matter," as he had written to a friend four years earlier. Unconvinced that woman suffrage would either improve woman's condition or produce any of the "evils feared," he was certain that women would get the vote whenever "women as a whole show any special interest in the matter."

This special interest emerged in 1914, when the huge General Federation of Women's Clubs finally resolved to support woman suffrage. The GFWC endorsement signified that woman suffrage had at last entered the mainstream of acceptability and respectability—clubwomen were hardly a radical fringe, as their rhetoric confirmed. "Women realize that we are living in an ungoverned world," said the GFWC magazine in 1917. "We know how much we are needed in the world's affairs." In addition to winning the approval of clubwomen, the suffrage movement also won a sudden cascade of western victories between 1910 and 1914. More state campaigns were lost than won during these years, but the rash of success in the West, after over a decade of steady failure, suggested that the suffrage campaign was finally having an impact.

The western trend had started slowly in the 1890s, when Wyoming, Utah, Colorado, and Idaho enfranchised women. After 1896, western successes came to a halt. But in 1910, when the state of Washington gave women the vote, a major new surge began. A well-mounted, well-publicized California victory in 1911 was crucial. By 1914, Oregon, Arizona, Kansas, Nevada, and Montana had granted women the vote; and in 1913, the Illinois legislature gave women the right to vote in presidential elections. In many states, final victory was hard-won. In Oregon, for instance, woman suffrage had been persistently defeated in five referenda before it was accepted. The western victories enfranchised only a small minority of American women. But they did make western congressmen responsible to women constituents, and they proved that woman suffrage would do little damage. The vote, it was observed, did not destroy the home and family in Colorado. Indeed, according to Helen L. Sumner's pioneer study, it seemed to have little impact there at all, except to suggest that few women would run for public office and that women voters would unite on few issues. But most important, the western victories gave the suffrage movement new impetus. By 1914, the stage was set for a change of leadership and a final surge of agitation.

Anna Howard Shaw, NAWSA president from 1904 to 1915, had not been known as an exceptional administrator and had never captivated the social feminists—the clubwomen, settlement workers, and labor reformers. She also had the reputation of disliking men. During her reign, massive energies had gone into state campaigns, but no efforts had been made with a federal amendment, which NAWSA had decided to ignore. Congress had considered no such amendment since 1896. Shaw's successor, Carrie Chapman Catt, was a different type of leader. Catt had already served as NAWSA president at the turn of the century and was by now a highly experienced politician. Since her rise to influence in the 1890s, as a strategist of state campaigns, Catt had shown great personal charm, political finesse, and organizational zest. As leader of the International Woman Suffrage Alliance, formed in 1902, she presided continually over conferences in European capitals and helped to create an international woman's movement. A well-educated westerner, Catt was the beneficiary of solvent marriages, the last of which included a contract that had given her half the year to work for suffrage and eventually made her a wealthy widow (her husband died in 1905). Like other reform-minded women, to whom she appealed, Catt believed that the vote would be a "first step" toward effecting a range of social reforms. She also maintained a wide range of affiliations among women—from the wealthy contributors who formed her new NAWSA board to Emma Goldman, with whom she discussed anarchism.

By the time Catt entered office in 1915, the NAWSA was shifting its tactics from "education" to more methodical modes of pressure, such as buttonholing legislators. A 1914 handbook for suffragists advised that no political meeting, convention, platform committee, or any appropriate gathering be spared a spate of suffrage demands. In New York, where a crucial victory was anticipated, suffrage clubs were organized on a precinct basis to coerce voters and politicos personally. Carrie Chapman Catt, moreover, had a master plan for victory. After converting President Wilson (this was accomplished by 1917) and winning the pivotal New York battle, the NAWSA would overcome congressional lethargy, win a proposed suffrage amendment, and wage state fights to get it ratified. Catt carried her plan into effect even faster than she had anticipated. But she also had to cope with two new developments that had not been part of the plan. One was the apostasy of dissident radicals within the NAWSA, which culminated in the formation of a rival suffrage organization, the National Woman's party, in 1916. The other was U.S. entry into World War I in 1917, which destroyed an impressive women's peace movement that many suffragists had supported. Both new developments changed the course of the suffrage campaign in its last, crucial years.

Rebellion within the NAWSA had begun before Catt took office. In 1913, a young Quaker activist, Alice Paul, arrived in Washington, fresh from a stint with English suffragists, who were known for their distinctive tactics. In England, suffragists marched through the streets, chained themselves to lampposts, starved themselves in prison, and attacked the "party in power," whatever it might be, for denying the vote to women. Contending that the Democrats were now responsible for failure to enact a woman suffrage amendment, Alice Paul organized a massive rally to protest President Wilson's inauguration. Such militant tactics evoked controversy, since the NAWSA prided itself on four decades of nonpartisan politics and less disruptive modes of pressure. But Alice Paul was evangelical and charismatic, especially among younger women in the suffrage movement—the third generation. She soon had a large, committed following, ranging from radicals such as Crystal Eastman, a pacifist and socialist, to imposing Alva Belmont, now ready to commit her funds and energy to the new faction. Forming their own contingent, the Congressional Union, Paul and her followers resurrected the long-dormant campaign for a federal amendment and created a determined congressional lobby.

In 1915, while the NAWSA began its final round of buttonholing, negotiating, and persuading, Alice Paul's Congressional Union rebelled. Leaving the NAWSA, the Congressional Union joined forces with western women voters to form the National Woman's party in 1916. Continuing to attack the Democrats, the NWP was not unlike the Stanton-Anthony faction of the 1860s, which had attacked the Republicans for failure to support a woman suffrage amendment. Indeed, to some old campaigners, such as Olympia Brown, it seemed to be a rebirth of the old radicalism. This time, however, the radicals attracted supporters in all of the states and mobilized them to oppose the Democrats locally. The Woman's party also spurred both houses of Congress to consider a federal woman suffrage amendment, which had been shelved since the 1890s.

The Woman's party proved an embarrassment to the NAWSA, which felt that it would only alienate sympathetic Democrats. The NAWSA also believed that the suffrage movement should be above party politics. But the Woman's party's dramatic mode of agitation also drew attention to the cause. Once again, the press was sometimes unable to distinguish between the two woman suffrage associations. Attention increased in 1917, when Alice Paul and her supporters began picketing the White House to condemn the "party in power" for failing to produce a woman suffrage amendment. Such militancy aroused both antipathy and interest, especially when the picketers were arrested and went on hunger strikes, the ultimate English tactic. Although the jailed suffragists were soon released, their arrests evoked attention and sympathy. All the women had done, as Alva Belmont told the press, was to stand there "quietly, peacefully, lawfully, and gloriously." Despite NAWSA objections to these new rivals, the militants probably had a positive impact. According to historians Ann Firor Scott and Andrew Scott, "nervousness about what the radical women might do next encouraged both Congress and the president to . . . embrace the more conservative suffragists as the lesser evil."

While the National Woman's party pressured Congress and attracted attention, Carrie Chapman Catt increased the tempo of her master plan. The crucial New York State referendum, won in 1917 (it had failed two years before), suggested that the "slum" vote was not the terror that the NAWSA had once imagined. A new light of tolerance entered the movement, though rather too late to affect its arguments. By now, tactics were more important than argument. In 1917, Catt announced that she did not know whether the vote was a right, a duty, or a privilege, but that "whatever it is, women want it." To ensure that they got it, the NAWSA had to capitalize on all the good works that American women were now contributing to the war effort. It also had to extricate itself from what had become an impressive and powerful women's plea for peace.

During the first two decades of the twentieth century, international peace had become a major theme in women's politics. Since 1869, suffragists had argued that peace-loving women would use the vote to overcome, or at least counteract, the male martial instinct. At the turn of the century, all major women's organizations had "peace" departments. By 1910, the cause of peace attracted a wide gamut of women leaders and activists, including Catt, Gilman, Addams, and younger radicals such as Eastman. In 1915, eighty-six delegates from all major women's groups attended the opening meeting of the Woman's Peace party in Washington, chaired by Catt, and drew up a pacifist platform representing the views of "the mother half of humanity." Within a year, the WPP had a membership of 25,000, drawing on the ample membership rolls of other women's associations.

But the WPP's hopeful future capsized almost immediately when the United States entered World War I—a move opposed by the first woman in Congress, Jeanette Rankin, a suffragist who had just been elected from Montana. During the war, a radical minority continued to agitate for peace. So did Jane Addams, true to her convictions and much to the detriment of her reputation. The National Woman's party also refused to support U.S. entry into the war. The NAWSA, however, unable to oppose the popular tide of patriotism, dropped the cause of peace. Instead, it attempted to profit from war. Indeed, during the war NAWSA membership doubled, reaching its peak of 2 million by 1919.

As historian William L. O'Neill points out, World War I added "a few strings to the suffrage bow." The war effort won favor among activist middle-class women, especially clubwomen, who plunged into volunteer war work—selling bonds, saving food, and organizing benefits for the troops. On the verge of victory, the NAWSA, with its membership rolls and popular support now at a peak, had too much to lose by ignoring the war effort or clinging to the cause of peace. Rather, it endorsed the war, mainly in rhetoric, since Catt did not want her troops to divide their efforts. During the war, indeed, the suffrage movement's great opportunity finally arrived. Half a century before, women's rights leaders had complained that all of women's contributions to the Union cause had gone unheeded and unappreciated. Now Carrie Chapman Catt asked for passage of the woman suffrage amendment as a "war measure." The fight for democracy began at home, Catt argued, in a brief revival of the "justice" argument. The war also presented an additional "expediency" argument: It was unwise to deprive women of the vote just when their war work was needed. Taking the latter position, President Wilson, a convert to woman suffrage since 1916, urged the Senate in 1917 and 1918 to pass a woman suffrage amendment. He contended that such a measure was "vital to the winning of the war." Despite the National Woman's party rebellion and despite, or because of, the interruption of war, Catt's master plan was paying off.

Influenced by the Wilson administration, by the NAWSA (which at last showed strength in numbers), and by favorable wartime public opinion, the House of Representatives finally passed a woman suffrage amendment on

In 1915, the newly formed Woman's Peace party sent a committee of delegates to the International Congress of Women in the Hague. The meeting had been organized by the International Suffrage Alliance, in which Carrie Chapman Catt was active, to demonstrate female friendship and solidarity in time of war. "The whole enterprise has about it a certain aspect of moral adventure," wrote Jane Addams (front row, second from left) to Lillian Wald. To Alice Hamilton, the mission felt like "a perpetual meeting of the women's club or the federation of settlements, or something like that." Although support for the new women's peace movement dwindled once the United States entered World War I in 1917, the movement was revived during the 1920s. *(Swarthmore College Peace Collection)*

January 10, 1918. The recalcitrant Senate approved it in June 1919. (Significantly, a prohibition amendment was ratified that year as well, suggesting that the major causes supported by women would triumph almost simultaneously.) Fourteen months after the Senate suffrage vote, on August 26, 1920, the thirty-sixth state ratified the woman suffrage amendment, and the woman's vote was finally legal nationwide.

The final months of state suffrage campaigns evoked more female participation, in marches, parades, speeches, and meetings, than had been mobilized for the past fifty years. Once victory was imminent, the woman suffrage movement finally achieved its long-sought momentum. Victory can be attributed to massive participation in the final round of ratification campaigns, to President Catt's organizational skill, to the NAWSA's redoubled efforts, and to the fortuitous interruption of the war. Some 26 million women were enfranchised in time for the presidential election of 1920, transformed, as Catt said, from "wards" of the nation into "free and equal citizens." One of the voters was Charlotte

After 1910, the suffrage parade became a leading NAWSA publicity tactic. White-clad suffragists, marching in formation, were an impressive sight on city streets, as in this New York City parade in 1913. Although a major referendum campaign failed in 1915, two years later New York became the first state east of the Mississippi to grant suffrage to women. *(Sophia Smith Collection, Smith College)*

Woodward, aged ninety-one, who had ridden with friends to the first women's rights convention in 1848. Then a teenaged farm girl, she had watched the proceedings from a back row and, at the end of the meeting, signed her name to the Declaration of Sentiments. Charlotte Woodward was the sole survivor of Seneca Falls.

Women and the Vote

When Carrie Chapman Catt wrote her "inner story" of the suffrage movement in the 1920s, she itemized the unparalleled string of efforts that had been needed to attain the vote. Over the past half-century, suffragists had waged fifty-six referenda campaigns and hundreds of assaults on state legislatures, state party conventions, and state constitutional conventions, as well as on Congress. No other electoral reform, said Catt, had ever been so expensive or aroused such antipathy. In the aftermath of their triumph, suffragists awaited the impact of the woman's vote on political life, social reform, and women's status. High expectations prevailed—on the part of both suffrage veterans, who envisioned the vote as a "first step," and the public.

Woman suffrage had an immediate impact. Polling places shifted from saloons and barber shops to schools and churches, to accommodate the newly enfranchised. In addition, state legislatures quickly enacted a small barrage of statutes. Twenty states, for instance, passed laws at once to enable women to serve on juries, and some states rushed through protective laws that women reformers had long demanded. Congress too seemed anxious to please women voters, at least for a few years. Its brief spurt of interest began with the Sheppard Towner Act of 1921, a plan to finance maternal education and child health-care programs, and ended in 1924 with passage of a federal child-labor amendment, which was never ratified. Throughout the decade, however, a Women's Joint Congressional Committee, representing major women's organizations, lobbied for passage of desired bills. And political parties at last began to cater to what was expected to be the "woman's vote." Both major parties welcomed women into their national committees. Finally, in a few localities (Chicago was one) there were signs that women did prefer the least corrupt and most reform-minded candidates and could influence the outcome of elections. But by mid-decade, it was clear that supporters and opponents of woman suffrage alike had overestimated the impact it would have on political life. The onus fell on the supporters. As Mother Jones once observed, suffragists expected that "kingdom come would follow the enfranchisement of women." During the 1920s, such millennial expectations—and even more modest ones—rapidly faded.

A main false assumption apparently shared by suffragists and antisuffragists alike was that women would vote as a bloc. Or at least their rhetoric implied such an assumption. Over the decades, suffragists had often contended that women's votes would purify politics and end war, imperialism, disease, crime, vice, and injustice. According to antisuffragists, women as a group would be carried away by sweeping reforms and wives would vote against husbands, contributing to domestic discord, excessive individualism, social anarchy, and the collapse of the state. But none of the claims had immediate relevance. As the 1920s showed, women voted in smaller proportions than men. (Isolated data suggest that where blacks were permitted to vote, black women seized the ballot in the same numbers as black men and in greater proportions than white women; but limited by state restrictions and intimidation, black suffrage remained too small to affect elections.) Not only did women in general vote in smaller proportions than men, but they voted the same way as male relatives—of course, some antisuffragists had predicted this too. Unable to affect the outcome of elections, women never rallied behind "women's issues"—any more than they rallied behind women candidates, of whom there were few. "I know of no woman today who has any influence or political power because she is a woman," said Emily Blair, a Missouri suffragist who became vice president of the Democratic National Committee in 1924. "I know of no woman who has a following of other women." As politicians soon realized, there would be no great influx of women candidates or officeholders. Women did not seem to share political goals, they were unable to demand an array of reforms, and they voted as individuals, not as a bloc. Moral superiority, in short, had not carried over to the voting booth; the "woman's vote" did not exist.

Suffragists were not the only reformers ever to fall short of their own expectations. Other electoral reforms of the progressive era, such as the referendum, the recall, and direct primaries, historian William E. Chafe points out, also had little impact. Despite progressive efforts to democratize the electoral process, voter turnout in the 1920s fell; only about half of eligible voters participated in presidential elections in the 1920s, for instance, compared to 80 percent in the late nineteenth century. Women alone could not be blamed for the decline, recent studies suggest, for male voter participation dropped as well. Jane Addams made this point at the time: When asked in 1924 by the *Woman Citizen,* "Is woman suffrage failing?" she replied that the question should be "Is suffrage failing?" Still, women took the blame. By the mid-1920s, articles proclaimed the "failure" of woman suffrage, and veterans of the suffrage movement analyzed what had gone wrong. Women were disappointed in politics, contended Carrie Chapman Catt in 1923, "because they miss the exaltation, the thrill of expectancy, the vision which stimulated them in the suffrage campaign. . . . They find none of these appeals to their aspiration in the party of their choice." Emily Blair, in 1931, found even deeper cause for activists' disappointment. Feminism, said Blair, "expressed the desire of women once more to have a part in the making of the world."

But it did not work out that way. The best man continued to win, and women, even the best, worked for and under him. Women were welcome to come in as workers but not as co-makers of the world. For all their numbers, they seldom rose to positions of responsibility or power. The few who did fitted into the system as they found it. All standards, all methods, all values, continued to be set by men.

Historian Chafe concludes that women "faced a no-win situation when it came to electoral politics." First, they had won the vote just when it declined in importance. Second, the two-party system, the lack of single-issue elections, and the varied class and ethnic interests of women voters precluded an independent women's constituency or bloc that could affect the existing parties.

Lack of political clout was only one part of a double blow for suffrage veterans in the 1920s. It was compounded, as Carrie Chapman Catt suggested, by the loss of a cause. For decades, suffrage had served as a focus of feminist energies and a source of continuum between generations. "Hundreds of women gave the accumulated possibilities of an entire lifetime," Catt wrote in 1926. "It was a continuous, seemingly endless chain of activity. Young suffragists who helped forge the last links of the chain were not born when it began. Old feminists who forged the first links were dead when it ended." Some women had even personified the general links—such as Harriot Stanton Blatch and Alice Stone Blackwell, daughters of suffrage leaders who both became leaders themselves. But once the umbrella of the cause vanished, the coalition of women that had gathered under it diminished and divided, often in factional disputes over protective laws and a newly proposed equal rights amendment. Indeed, the formation of the Woman's party in 1916 augured such disputes. Although organized women remained active throughout the 1920s, the inspiration of the suffrage campaign was difficult to recapture—or so its leaders suggested. "I am sorry for you young women who have to carry on the work in the next ten years," Anna Howard Shaw told Emily Blair, "for suffrage was a symbol and you have lost your symbol. There is nothing for women to rally around." Veteran suffragists especially regretted their inability to connect to the "rising generation," the post-World War I cohort of younger women, who took for granted what the suffragists had achieved and lacked interest in women's causes or institutions. The new generation seemed to be carried away by a new sense of individualism, although not the sort that either suffragists or their opponents had envisioned.

Feminist problems in the 1920s, says historian William L. O'Neill, were largely the feminists' fault. They should not have dropped the broad spectrum of demands of the antebellum era, ignored "social" issues, or shifted their arguments toward altruism and expediency. These moves, he contends, contained the seeds of failure, although this was not clear until after the vote was won and suffragist factions fell out of harmony. Mourning the loss of radical ideology, O'Neill also argues that social feminism drained off personnel from the suffrage movement and even prolonged the crusade for the vote. In response, other historians have pointed out that had feminists not narrowed their goals and broadened their constituency, they would have had even less success than they did. Nor is it clear that socialism, as O'Neill suggests, or any other sort of coalition on the left, would have provided solutions to the "woman problem" that women failed to achieve alone. During the progressive era, many women on the left, whether social reformers like Florence Kelley, ideologists like Charlotte Perkins Gilman, or radical suffragists like Crystal Eastman, were committed to socialism. The Socialist party appreciated the support of its women devotees and voiced concern about the "woman problem," but it had no plans for, nor means of effecting, any substantive changes in women's lives either. Without any broad consensus among women, such as that finally achieved by the suffrage movement, it is unlikely that even a grand coalition of feminists and socialists would have made much headway, had such a coalition been feasible.

Historian Nancy F. Cott challenges O'Neill's interpretation in a fundamental way by disputing the "failure" of feminism in all its particulars. Starting with electoral politics, Cott denies that suffragists had referred specifically to a future voting "bloc" of women or expected that women would form such a bloc. Nor, she contends, did the "woman's vote" fail. Rather, women's voting participation "varied greatly from place to place, group to group, issue to issue." Further, Cott refutes the contention that women's voluntary organizations, another vital aspect of political participation, capsized or diminished once the vote was won; rather, she contends, such groups grew in numbers and remobilized. Minimizing the role of 1920 as a turning point, Cott posits continuity over change in women's political behavior before and after 1920. Most important, she refutes the idea that suffragism was "the matrix of women's politics and also a proxy for feminism." Rather, the suffrage crusade and the eruption of modern feminism were separate phenomena. The latter, with its distinctive paradoxes, would determine women's politics in the decades ahead. "What historians have seen as the demise of feminism in the 1920s," Cott contends, "was, more accurately, the end of the suffrage movement and the early struggle of modern feminism."

Neither miscalculations about the "woman's vote" nor the nature of women's politics after 1920 ultimately suffices to assess the achievement of the suffrage crusade. One question that remains is, What contribution did the achievement of woman suffrage make toward attaining the overhaul of attitudes demanded in 1848 and toward assaulting "aristocracy of sex"? Since changes in social attitudes occur at a glacial pace, the question is a difficult one. Clearly, as Elizabeth Cady Stanton told her friend Theodore Tilton in the 1860s, lack of suffrage was a "symbol" of woman's degradation rather than a cause of it. Clearly, too, the achievement of woman suffrage redressed an inequity more than it bestowed political power. Its significance, however, can be suggested by turning to the elusive realm of attitudes as well as to the more concrete realm of involvement.

The first factor, attitude, was identified by Walter Lippmann in a *New Republic* article in 1915, when intense pressure for woman suffrage began to build. The vote itself would change nothing, Lippmann predicted, but the suffrage battle represented more than mere attainment of the vote. Rather, it represented "an infinitely greater change, a change in the initial prejudice with which men and women react towards each other and the world." As Lippmann observed, the change he was describing was almost "too subtle for expression." Women have to take part "in the wider affairs of life," he concluded. "Their demand for the vote expresses that aspiration. Their winning of the vote would be a sign that men were civilized enough to understand it." Historian Ellen Duboois suggests a related realm of significance: She stresses the implications of women's involvement in the suffrage movement, and thereby in what Lippmann called "the wider affairs of life." Winning the vote, says Dubois, proved that women could unite to affect public policy and change the course of history, to serve as an active agency of change. "It was women's involvement in the movement, far more than the eventual enfranchisement of women that created the basis for new social relations between men and women," Dubois contends. The five-decade suffrage movement, she points out, actually accomplished the very goal that three generations of suffragists expected from the vote. By acting "deliberately and collectively," suffragists were achieving equality and independence. The movement itself showed that "democratic participation in the life of the society was the key to women's emancipation," Dubois concludes. "Therein lay its feminist power and historical significance."

During the 1920s, women's organizations strove to maintain the collective spirit that had won the vote and to continue to act as an agency of change. But after World War I, new factors came into play. The new era was a politically conservative one, in which enthusiasm for reform dwindled and commitment to cause went out of style. The shift in political climate was accompanied by a major shift in social climate, one that had its most profound effect on middle-class women, the constituency of the woman's movement.

๛

SUGGESTED READINGS AND SOURCES

CHAPTER 13

Victoria Woodhull's distinctive career lends itself to popular biographies that capitalize on her flamboyance and notoriety. Three such biographies are Emanie Sachs, *The Terrible Siren* (New York, 1928); Johanna Johnston, *Mrs. Satan: The Incredible Saga of Victoria Woodhull* (New York, 1967); and M. M. Marberry, *Vicky: A Biography of Victoria C. Woodhull* (New York, 1967), which is the best. Madeline Stern, ed., *The Victoria Woodhull Reader* (Weston, Mass., 1974), has a good introduction and includes speeches given by, though not necessarily written by, Woodhull.

For the concerns of the NWSA, the goals of its leaders, and Victoria Woodhull's impact on the early suffrage movement, see Lois Banner's biography, *Elizabeth Cady Stanton: A Radical for Women's Rights* (Boston and Toronto, 1980), and the introductory sections of Ellen Carol Dubois, ed., *Elizabeth Cady Stanton/Susan B. Anthony: Correspondence, Writings, Speeches* (New York, 1981). See also Dubois, "On Labor and Free Love: Two Unpublished Speeches of Elizabeth Cady Stanton," *Signs,* 1 (Autumn 1975), 157–268. For Isabella Beecher Hooker and her siblings, see Jeanne Boydston, Mary Kelley, and Anne Margolis, *The Limits of Sisterhood: The Beecher Sisters on Women's Rights and Woman's Sphere* (Chapel Hill, N.C., 1988), and Clifford E. Clark, Jr., *Henry Ward Beecher: Spokesman for a Middle Class America* (Urbana, Ill., 1978). A recent study of the Beecher-Tilton scandal is Altina L. Walker, *Reverend Beecher and Mrs. Tilton: Sex and Class in Victorian America* (Amherst, Mass., 1982).

CHAPTER 14

Since the publication of Eleanor Flexner's *Century of Struggle: The Women's Rights Movement in the United States* (Cambridge, Mass., 1959), the history of feminism has enjoyed a revival. Three studies of the woman suffrage movement have been pivotal. For the origins of the movement, see Ellen Carol Dubois, *Feminism and Suffrage: The Emergence of an Independent Women's Movement in America 1848–1869* (Ithaca, N.Y., 1978). Aileen Kraditor analyzes the changing suffrage argument in *Ideas of the Woman Suffrage Movement 1890–1920* (New York, 1965). In *Feminism in America: A History,* 2d rev. ed. (New Brunswick, N.J., 1989), William L. O'Neill provides "an internal study of the woman movement." His account of women's politics in the progressive era is unsurpassed. For the new wave of feminism in the early twentieth century, see Nancy F. Cott, *The Grounding of Modern Feminism* (New Haven, Conn., 1988).

There are several excellent document collections, or, in some cases, combinations of narrative and documents. See Aileen Kraditor, ed., *Up From the Pedestal: Selected Writings in the History of American Feminism* (Chicago, 1968); William L. O'Neill, *The Woman Movement: Feminism in the United States and England* (New York and London, 1969); and Anne F. Scott and Andrew Scott, *One Half the People: The Fights for Woman Suffrage* (Philadelphia, 1975). For the Stanton-Anthony alliance, see Ellen Carol Dubois, ed., *Elizabeth Cady Stanton/Susan B. Anthony: Correspondence, Writings, Speeches* (New York, 1981), and Alice Rossi, ed., *The Feminist Papers* (New York, 1973), part 2. An important source book is Mari Jo Buhle and Paul Buhle, eds., *The Concise History of Woman Suffrage: Selections from the Classic Work of Stanton, Anthony, Gage, and Harper* (Urbana, Ill., 1981).

Scholarship on the suffrage movement has gained momentum in recent years. Alan P. Grimes, *The Puritan Ethic and Woman Suffrage* (New York, 1967), examines the early acceptance of woman suffrage in the western states. David Morgan, *Suffragists and Democrats: The Politics of Woman Suffrage in America* (East Lansing, Mich., 1972), traces the campaign for suffrage as part of the political process. Steven M. Buechler's insightful book, *The Transformation of the Woman Suffrage Movement: The Case of Illinois, 1850–1920* (New Brunswick, N.J., 1986), explores a regional suffrage movement and illuminates the changing direction of the national movement. Studies of suffragism at the local level include Ronald Shaffer, "The Problem of Consciousness in the Woman Suffrage Movement: A California Perspective," *Pacific Historical Review,* 45 (1976), 469–493; Sharon Hartman Strom, "Leadership and Tactics in the American Woman Suffrage Movement: A New Perspective from Massachusetts," *Journal of American History,* 62 (September 1975), 296–315; and Ellen Carol Dubois, "Working Women, Class Relations, and Suffrage Militance: Harriet Stanton Blatch and the New York Woman Suffrage Movement, 1894–1909," *Journal of American History,* 74 (June 1987), 34–58. Paula Giddings examines suffragism among black women in *When and Where I Enter: The Impact of Black Women on Race and Sex in America* (New York, 1984), ch. 7. Michael McGerr discusses suffragist campaign techniques in "Political Style and Women's Power," *Journal of American History,* 77 (December 1990), 864–885. For conflict within the suffrage movement in its final stage, see Christine Lunardini, *From Equal Suffrage to Equal Rights: Alice Paul and the National Woman's Party* (New York, 1986). Antisuffragism is examined in Aileen Kraditor, *The Ideas of the Woman Suffrage Movement,* cited above; Jane Camhi, *Women Against Women: American Anti-Suffrage, 1880–1920* (1974); and Susan E. Marshall, "In Defense of Separate Spheres: Class and Status Politics in the Anti-Suffrage Movement," *Social Forces,* 65 (December 1986), 327–351. Two views on the radicalism of the suffrage movement are Ellen Carol Dubois, "The Radicalism of the Woman Suffrage Movement: Notes Toward the Reconstruction of Nineteenth-century Feminism," *Feminist Studies,* 3 (Fall 1975), 63–71, and William L. O'Neill, "Feminism as a Radical Ideology," in Alfred F. Young, ed., *Dissent: Explorations in the History of American Radicalism* (DeKalb, Ill., 1968), pp. 273–300. For suffragist voices, see Sherna Gluck, ed., *From Parlor to Prison: Five American Suffragists Talk About Their Lives* (New York, 1976).

Other recent studies consider facets of suffragism and feminism. Late nineteenth-century suffragists are prominent in William Leach, *True Love and Perfect Union: The Feminist Reform of Sex and Society* (New York, 1980), which links strands of feminist thought to other intellectual currents. Mari Jo Buhle examines the role of socialist women in the suffrage campaign and a variety of women's causes, such as labor organization and sexual reform, in *Women and American Socialism 1870–1920* (Urbana, Ill., 1981). For women on the left, see also Margaret S. Marsh, *Anarchist Women, 1870–1920* (Philadelphia, 1981); June Sochen, *The New Woman: Feminism in Greenwich Village, 1910–1920* (New York, 1969); and Judith Schwartz, *Radical Feminists of Heterodoxy: Greenwich Village, 1912–1940* (Lebanon, N.H., 1982). Conflict between suffragists and other women reformers emerges in Jeanne Madeline Weiman, *The Fair Women: The Story of the Women's Building, World Columbia Exposition, Chicago, 1893* (Chicago, 1981).

Several valuable studies examines women's role in American politics. Paula Baker considers the long-term process of the politicization of women in "The Domestication of Politics: Women and American Political Society, 1780–1920," *American Historical Review,* 89 (June 1984), 620–647. Louise A. Tilly and Patricia Gurin, eds., *Women, Politics, and Change* (New York, 1990), presents many valuable articles on American women's political behavior from the late nineteenth century to the present. Suzanne Lebsock's essay on "Women and Politics, 1880–1920," pp. 35–61, is relevant to this chapter. The aftermath of the suffrage campaign is discussed in William H. Chafe, *The Paradox of Change: American Women in the 20th Century* (New York, 1991), part 1; William L. O'Neill, *Feminism in America,* cited above, ch. 8; Nancy F. Cott, *The Grounding of Modern Feminism,* cited above, ch. 3; and Cott, "Across the Great Divide: Women in Politics Before and After 1920," in Tilly and Gurin, eds., *Women, Politics, and Change,* cited above, pp. 153–176. For an astute analysis of the feminist predicament in the 1920s, see Estelle Freedman, "Separatism as Strategy: Female Institution Building and American Feminism, 1870–1930," *Feminist Studies,* 5 (Fall 1979), 512–529.

The suffrage movement is well documented because suffragists wrote their own histories. The major source is the six-volume *History of Woman Suffrage,* eds. Elizabeth Cady Stanton, Susan B. Anthony, et al. (Rochester, N.Y., 1881–1902, vols. 1–4, and New York, 1922, vols. 5 and 6). A massive compilation of speeches, reminiscences, convention reports, and press clippings, the HWS is a memorial to the historical self-consciousness of nineteenth-century suffragists, especially those in the NWSA who started the collection and dominated it until 1890. For highlights of the HWS, see Mari Jo Buhle and Paul Buhle, eds., *The Concise History of Woman Suffrage,* cited above. A history of NAWSA is Carrie Chapman Catt and Nellie Rogers Shuler, *Woman Suffrage and Politics: The Inner Story of the Suffrage Movement* (New York, 1926). For the National Woman's party, see Inez Hayes Irwin, *The Story of the Woman's Party* (New York, 1921), and Doris Stevens, *Jailed for Freedom* (New York, 1920). For the women's peace movement, see Mary Louise Degan, *History of the Woman's Peace Party* (Baltimore, Md., 1939). Another useful source for suffragism is "The Significance of the Woman Suffrage Movement," *Annals of the American Academy of Political and Social Science* (May 1910 supplement). Major suffragist publications are available on microfilm, including *Revolution* (New York, 1868–1871), *Woman's Journal* (Boston, 1870–1917), *Woman Citizen* (New York, 1917–1919), and *Suffragist* (Washington, D.C., 1914–1918). Also available on microfilm are the National Woman's Party Papers, ed. Anne Firor Scott and William H. Chafe (1989); the Collected Records of the Woman's Peace Party, 1914–1920, ed. by the Swarthmore College Peace Collection Staff (1988); the Papers of Elizabeth Cady Stanton and Susan B. Anthony, ed. Patricia G. Holland and Ann D. Gordon (1990).

Feminist autobiography and biography abound. For Stanton, besides Lois W. Banner, *Elizabeth Cady Stanton,* cited above, see Elizabeth Griffith, *In Her Own Right: The Life of Elizabeth Cady Stanton* (New York, 1984); Stanton, *Eighty Years and More: Reminiscences 1815–1897* (New York, 1898); and Theodore Stanton and Harriet Stanton Blatch, eds., *Elizabeth Cady Stanton as Revealed in Her Letters, Diaries, and Reminiscences* (New York, 1922). For Anthony, see Ida Husted Harper, *The Life and Work of Susan B. Anthony,* 2 vols. (Indianapolis, Ind., 1898 and 1908), and Kathleen Barry, *Susan B. Anthony: A Biography of a Singular Feminist* (New York, 1988). Feminist memoirs include Harriet Stanton Blatch and Alma Lutz, *Challenging Years: The Memoirs of Harriet Stanton Blatch* (New York, 1940); Olympia Brown, "Autobiography," *Annual Journal of the Universalist Historical Society,* 4 (1973), 1–73; Rheta Child Dorr, *A Woman of Fifty* (New York, 1924); Abigail Scott Duniway, *Pathbreaking: An Autobiographical History of the Equal Suffrage Movement in the Pacific Coast States* (Portland, Oreg., 1914); Belle Kearney, *A Slaveholder's Daughter* (New York, 1900); and Anna Howard Shaw. *The Story of a Pioneer* (New York, 1915). For a controversial assessment of Shaw, see James P. McGovern, "Anna Howard Shaw: New Approaches to Feminism," *Journal of Social History,* 3 (1970), 135–153. Ruth Barnes Moynihan examines western suffragism in *Rebel for Rights, Abigail Scott Duniway* (New Haven, Conn., 1983). For Alva Belmont, see Peter Geidel's Ph.D. Thesis, Columbia University, 1993.

For Crystal Eastman, see Blanche Weisen Cook, ed., *Crystal Eastman on Women and Revolution* (New York, 1978). For Charlotte Perkins Gilman, see *The Living of Charlotte Perkins Gilman: An Autobiography* (New York, 1935); Mary A. Hill, *Charlotte Perkins Gilman: The Making of a Radical Feminist, 1860–1896* (Philadelphia, 1980); Carol Ruth Berkin, "Private Woman, Public Woman: The Contradictions of Charlotte Perkins Gilman," in Carol Ruth Berkin and Mary Beth Norton, eds., *Women of America: A History* (Boston, 1979), pp. 150–176; Carl Degler, "Charlotte Perkins Gilman on the Theory and Practice of Feminism," *American Quarterly,* 8 (Spring 1956), 21–39; Dolores Hayden, *The Grand Domestic Revolution* (Cambridge, Mass., 1981), ch. 9; Polly Wynn Allen, *Building Domestic Liberty: Charlotte Perkins Gilman's Architectural Feminism* (Amherst, Mass., 1988); and Ann J. Lane, *To Herland and Beyond: The Life and Work of Charlotte Perkins Gilman* (New York, 1990). For Emma Goldman, see Goldman, *Living My Life,* 2 vols. (New York, 1931); Joseph Drinnon, *Rebel in Paradise* (Chicago, 1961); Alix Kates Shulman, ed., *Red Emma Speaks: Selected Writings and Speeches* (New York, 1972); Alice Wexler, *Emma Goldman in America* (Boston, 1984); and Wexler, *Emma Goldman in Exile: From the Russian Revolution to the Spanish Civil War* (Boston, 1989).

CHAPTER 15

Direct Action:
Margaret Sanger's Crusade

In 1912, Margaret Sanger, a twenty-nine-year-old mother of three, began to work as a public health nurse for the Henry Street Settlement's visiting nurse service on New York's Lower East Side. Her specialty was obstetrical cases. During her calls to crowded tenements, she saw the plight of working-class women, chronically pregnant, overburdened with youngsters, exhausted from "excessive child-bearing," or injured or dead from knitting-needle abortions. Unable to propose any "remedy," Sanger felt "helpless to avert such atrocities." The neighborhood women, she insisted, laughed when she mentioned withdrawal or condoms. But out of her experience on the Lower East Side, Margaret Sanger wove a personal myth—a dramatic story that revealed the urgent need for birth control, the cause that would occupy most of her life.

The drama began one summer day when she was called to the home of an immigrant family on Grand Street.

My patient was a small, slight Russian Jewess, about twenty-eight years old. . . . The cramped, three-room apartment was in a sorry state of turmoil. Jake Sachs, a truck driver scarcely older than his wife, had come home to find the three children crying and her unconscious from the effects of a self-induced abortion. He called the nearest doctor, who in turn had sent for me. . . .

The doctor and I settled ourselves to the task of fighting the septicemia. Never had I worked so fast, never so concentratedly. . . .

After a fortnight Mrs. Sachs' recovery was in sight. . . . As I was preparing to leave the fragile patient to take up her difficult life once more, she finally voiced her fears, "Another baby will finish me, I suppose?"

"It's too early to talk about that," I temporized.

But when the doctor came to make his last call, I drew him aside. "Mrs. Sachs is terribly worried about having another baby."

"She well may be," replied the doctor, and then he stood before her and said, "Any more such capers, young woman, and there'll be no need to send for me."

"I know, doctor," she replied timidly, "but," and she hesitated as though it took all her courage to say it, "what can I do to prevent it?"

The doctor was a kindly man, and he had worked hard to save her, but such incidents had become so familiar to him that he had long since lost whatever delicacy he might once have had. He laughed good-naturedly. "You want to have your cake and eat it too, do you? Well, it can't be done."

Then picking up his hat and bag to depart he said, "Tell Jake to sleep on the roof."

After the doctor had left, Sadie Sachs pleaded with Margaret Sanger for some kind of "self-protection," but Sanger, claiming ignorance, was unable to help. Still, the incident haunted her. "Night after night, the wistful image of Mrs. Sachs appeared before me. . . . Time rolled by and I did nothing." Three months later, Jake Sachs telephoned, begging her to come again, for the same purpose. By the time she arrived, it was too late.

Mrs. Sachs was in a coma and died within ten minutes. I folded her still hands across her breast, remembering how they had pleaded with me, begging so humbly for the knowledge which was her right. I drew a sheet over her pallid face. Jake was sobbing, running his hands through his hair and pulling it out like an insane person. Over and over again he wailed, "My God! My God! My God!"

That night, after she returned home, Margaret Sanger underwent the final throes of her conversion.

As I stood there the darkness faded. The sun came up and threw its reflection over the house tops. It was the dawn of a new day in my life also. The doubt and questioning, the experimenting and trying, were now to be put behind me. I knew I could not go back merely to keeping people alive.

I went to bed, knowing that no matter what it might cost, I was finished with palliatives and superficial cures; I was resolved to seek out the root of evil, to do something to change the destinies of mothers whose miseries were vast as the sky.

Margaret Sanger's emotional account of Sadie Sachs's death, with its aura of revelation, served several purposes. Like Jane Addams's bullfight conversion of the 1880s, it helped to sanctify her cause in incontrovertible terms. The story was potent; she had practiced it on countless audiences before this ghost-written version was published. The Sadie Sachs incident also helped to impose order on her chaotic and frenzied early career, an intricate tangle of causes, goals, and shifting affiliations. Margaret Sanger actually began her crusade several years after the Grand Street drama. But the battle for contraception, which she came to personify, had its own drama. It also had its own history, one that started long before Margaret Sanger became a public health nurse.

Over the past century, native-born middle- and upper-class women had been attempting to avoid pregnancy, with increasing success. Most methods in use—such as withdrawal, so unpopular on Grand Street—required male cooperation. So did continence and abstinence, the methods of birth control in widest use at the turn of the century. Limiting sexual relations to infrequent intervals— or only for "purposes of procreation," as advised in nineteenth-century health manuals—effectively limited pregnancies. So did abortion, although it was illegal in all states by the end of the century. But contraceptive devices were not unknown. Douches, sponges, and condoms had been recommended in the first contraceptive tracts of the 1830s. By the second half of the nineteenth century, some sorts of "womb veils," which covered the cervix, were also sold, though only by irregular or nonmedical sources. Until the 1870s, like other "remedies," quack and authentic, they were discreetly advertised in newspapers.

In 1873 such advertising ended. Congressional passage of the Comstock laws, and subsequent supportive state laws, classified contraceptive information and devices as obscenity and prevented their manufacture, sale, importation, mailing, or distribution. This legislation had widespread support. Doctors, for instance, usually viewed the prospect of contraception with suspicion. In their eyes, it violated nature's laws, bred immorality, damaged health, and threatened the sanctity of motherhood. Moreover, by the late nineteenth century, fears of "race suicide"—fears that native-born, well-off, white Americans were wiping themselves out by having too few children—added a new imperative to the contraceptive ban. Finally, middle-class women of the progressive era, not immune to class sentiments, had their own reasons for letting comstockery pass without challenge. Though anxious to limit or space their own pregnancies, they were not avid to legitimize contraceptive devices, since doing so would undercut widely shared goals: extending female authority, ending promiscuity, and containing male sexuality. As Carrie Chapman Catt, a sophisticated politician, was to write to Margaret Sanger in 1920, "No animal is so uncontrolled as the mass of men."

What support contraception had came from three sources, none of them strong enough to sway public opinion or combat the Comstock laws. One source was within the medical profession, where since the 1870s there were some, if few, proponents. Abraham Jacobi, for instance, an AMA president in the early twentieth century, and his wife, physician Mary Putnam Jacobi, supported contraception and decried its unavailability beyond the middle class. From 1903 on, William J. Robinson, an avid exponent and publicist, claimed that contraception would improve marriage, health, and the human race. None of these physicians' efforts was known to Margaret Sanger in 1912. Another source of support was eugenics. Some eugenicists stressed the need for "selective breeding" to weed out the poor and unfit from society. Contraception could prevent the prolific poor from increasing their numbers and stop venereally diseased parents from producing defective children. (Eugenics tilted both ways; other eugenicists feared that contraception would be used only by the middle class, thus hastening "race suicide.") A third source of support was political.

Throughout the nineteenth century, advocates of contraception could be found around the fringes of radical reform, in free thought, free love, and utopian circles—in short, in left field. This was true in the early twentieth century too. Socialists and anarchists, at the peak of their fervor and activism in the pre-World

War I era, ardently discussed a broad array of sexual reforms, including "voluntary motherhood." Margaret Sanger's conversion began not in a Grand Street tenement but in the inspirational left-wing circles she had entered in New York City, among socialists and anarchists, rebels and radicals. Between 1912 and 1915, when Sanger discovered the birth-control cause, she actively sought a leadership role, an arena in which to achieve recognition within the context of the radical left.

Before Margaret Sanger found this context, nothing in her career pointed to a leadership role. Born in 1879, she was the sixth of eleven children of Michael Higgins, an Irish Catholic stonecutter in Corning, New York, and his religious, tubercular wife Anne, who died at the age of forty-eight after eighteen pregnancies. Higgins, a radical and free thinker, lived to be eighty. Despite the deprivations of life in a large family at the bottom rung of the middle class, Sanger had a favored existence. Two older sisters sent her to a private preparatory school. She then taught school briefly, cared for her dying mother, and studied nursing in White Plains. After two years, without completing the nursing course, Margaret married William Sanger, a young architect and artist and, like her father, a radical. Despite tuberculosis, which kept her in and out of a sanitarium for a year, Margaret Sanger had a son, Stuart, in 1903 and resumed life with her family in Westchester. There another son, Grant, was born in 1908 and a daughter, Peggy, in 1910. The Sanger's political enthusiasms grew with their family. In 1911, they moved to Manhattan, where William Sanger, a long-time socialist, had contacts. Settling uptown, the Sangers began to participate in the thriving prewar left. Stuart was eight, Grant was three, and Peggy was one.

Although Margaret Sanger's interest in her marriage had started to wane, this was obscured by the lure of the left. The Sangers were both drawn into Greenwich Village social life and left-wing politics, and in these circles Margaret Sanger found a new field of interest. Her first affiliation was socialist. Then at its apogee, the Socialist party welcomed women as members and organizers; many locals had "women's committees." Margaret Sanger became a party member and a salaried women's organizer. But within the left, she moved quickly *to* the left. In 1912, she turned her allegiance to the IWW (Industrial Workers of the World), devoted to organizing industrial unions and mobilizing the working class to "do away with capitalism." Once again, Sanger took a paid position as an organizer. With her new comrades, she took part in IWW actions. She evacuated children from Lawrence, Massachusetts, during the bloody textile strike of 1912 and later supported the Patterson textile strike of 1913. Only after dropping both the Socialist party and IWW jobs did Sanger take on nursing cases, briefly, for the Henry Street service. One of her sisters, Ethel Byrne, a trained nurse, helped her find the post, and she remained in it for less than a year.

Throughout this period of rapidly shifting jobs and affiliations, Margaret Sanger absorbed new ideas on all sides. Her oldest son, Stuart, attended an anarchist school in Greenwich Village, where Margaret Sanger also took classes. She made further contacts at left-wing gatherings, especially in Mabel Dodge's white-walled apartment on lower Fifth Avenue, where notables of the left congregated. A wealthy young heiress, then in her thirties, Mabel Dodge was a pivotal center of New York cultural and artistic life. She provided a haven for ever-expanding circles of friends. Feminists and artists, socialists and Wobblies, as members of the IWW were called, met amid her crystal chandeliers and bearskin rugs to argue with one another and enjoy lavish meals. Lincoln Steffens remembered "poor and rich . . . strikers and unemployed, painters, musicians, reporters, editors, swells; it was the only successful salon I have ever seen in America." To Max Eastman, Crystal Eastman's brother, Mabel Dodge created a "magnetic field in which people became polarized and pulled in," engaging in arguments, debates, and entanglements, and then coming "back for more."

The guest list, moreover, included an impressive array of personalities. Eugene Debs had led the Socialist party since 1900; John Reed was a young revolutionary and reporter; his classmate, Walter Lippmann, another young radical, was writing his first book; Emma Goldman had long inspired fellow anarchists; her friend Alexander Berkman had been in prison for attempting assassination; Bill Haywood led the IWW; Elizabeth Gurley Flynn, who had become an IWW organizer at sixteen, magnetized picket lines. The Dodge salon in fact attracted a large coterie of radical women, among them socialist lawyer Jessie Ashley, Greenwich Village feminist Henrietta Rodman, and Elsie Clews Parsons, a young ethnologist who would later aid Margaret Sanger in some of her efforts. To this invigorating, radical context was added a new array of sexually revolutionary ideas. Dodge salon members were talking about Freud, who had recently lectured in America, about Swedish feminist Ellen Key, and about English sexual radical Havelock Ellis, all of whom were gaining an American audience.

Sanger's left-wing activism provided not only context and inspiration but role models. Emma Goldman, then in her forties and at the height of her career, was the most influential. As an anarchist lecturer and advocate of free speech, Goldman had long voiced her own views on women's rights and sexual emancipation, in speech and in print. Moreover, she had espoused contraception as woman's right for over a decade. As early as 1900, Goldman had investigated contraceptive methods in France and even smuggled some devices into the United States. By 1910, she was regularly defending contraception on her speaking tours. Women should not be forced to produce "a race of sickly, feeble, decrepit, wretched human beings," Emma Goldman told her audiences. They wanted, rather, "fewer and better children, begotten and reared in love and through free choice, not by compulsion, as marriage imposes." (In private, Goldman would give out contraceptive advice; she recommended douches, condoms, cervical caps, and diaphragms, or pessaries, as they were sometimes called. She even distributed a pamphlet on such devices.) Contraception was not only a woman's right, said Emma Goldman, but an anticapitalist tool: "Children glut the labor market, tend to lower wages, and are a menace to the welfare of the working class."

Goldman's arguments, stature, and fearless radicalism were inspirational. By the end of 1912, Margaret Sanger claimed, she had lost interest in "palliative" methods such as public health nursing. She had also lost interest in being another cog in the socialist wheel, another waver of the IWW banner. She now aspired to a heroic stance like that of Emma Goldman. To fill such a role required specialization in some aspect of radical politics, and Sanger, as a nurse and mother, quickly found her area of expertise: hygiene, health, sex education, venereal disease. By 1912, she was speaking to appreciative left-wing audiences on a gamut of sex-related subjects. She also published an excellent series of articles in the *Call*, the socialist weekly that covered the shirtwaist strike, entitled "What Every Girl Should Know." One article on venereal disease in February 1913 contained an explicit discussion of symptoms and their fearful implications. Four out of five married men in New York had gonorrhea, said Sanger, and more wives contracted venereal disease than did prostitutes. The *Call* article was banned by the Post Office as obscene under the Comstock laws, but the ban was rescinded. Sanger followed up with an equally risky series on sex education, "What Every Mother Should Know." Sex education was, at the time, a free speech issue and a popular cause on the left.

Neither series of articles gave advice on contraception, which would have been illegal, nor was Sanger yet committed to what was to become her crusade. She still sought a foothold in radical politics. In 1913, the Sanger family left for a year in France—an excursion long desired by Margaret Sanger and one in which William Sanger could further his career as an artist. In France, Margaret Sanger set forth to find out about contraceptive methods, as Emma Goldman had done a decade before. When she returned to New York (leaving William Sanger behind; this marriage was virtually over), she suddenly embarked on a new, independent course. In 1914, Margaret Sanger began to publish her own radical monthly, the *Woman Rebel*, and in so doing, engaged in a major piece of "direct action."

Direct action was a powerful IWW tactic. It meant violating a law and then, in the furor of arrests and trials that ensued, gaining publicity and support for the cause. When Margaret Sanger published seven issues of the *Woman Rebel* in 1914, working "day and night at making it as red and flaming as possible," she used direct action with enormous success. The Post Office quickly acted to quell the *Rebel* and indict Margaret Sanger, which served to put her firmly on the radical map. Edited in the Sanger apartment, the *Rebel* was produced single-handedly by Margaret, who kept the books, dealt with printers, canvassed for subscriptions, set the pages, and wrote most of the copy herself. The paper would strive, as the handbills announced, "for the advancement of WOMAN'S FREE-DOM." It would show woman's enslavement by "the machine, by wage slavery, by bourgeois morality, by customs, laws, and superstitions." The *Rebel* was aimed specifically at working-class women, to stimulate them "to think for themselves and build up a fighting character." (The masthead slogan "No Gods, No Masters" was borrowed from the IWW; Sanger also reprinted the IWW preamble in the first issue.)

Another announced purpose of the *Woman Rebel* was "to advocate the prevention of conception," or "birth control," a term first used in the June issue. Birth control was indeed a multifaceted weapon. Not only could it be used as a tool in the class struggle, as the *Rebel* contended, but it also had explicit feminist components. "A Woman's body belongs to herself alone," Sanger wrote in a *Rebel*

article. "It does not belong to the United States of America or any other government on the face of the earth." "Enforced motherhood," she told her readers, "is
the most complete denial of a woman's right to life and liberty." Birth control
also had expedient aspects. "Women cannot be on an equal footing with men
until they have full and complete control over their reproductive function."

The *Woman Rebel* had a long enemies list. In column after column, Sanger
attacked capitalism, religion, middle-class values, private property, and marriage, which made women "chattel." Denouncing meliorist efforts, she indicted
middle-class women who worked in charity, philanthropy, and settlements. The
"modern woman," said Sanger, was "a willing and efficient slave of the present
system." Full of fury and outrage, the *Woman Rebel* omitted only one thing:
contraceptive information. As a result, it was able to publish earnest letters from
working-class men and women, begging for the information that was left out. "I
am the mother of six children," wrote Mrs. J. S. from Chicago. "I am not well
enough to have any more and hardly strong enough to work for these. My
husband is sick too. . . . Will you please send me the information you speak of in
your paper, so I can prevent me having another child. Your [sic] doing a noble
work for women." "I write to ask you if you can give me the remedies you speak
of," wrote a Montana workingman. "My wife is pregnant again . . . and with
already three children. Perhaps it is illegal for you to send it, but in God's name
send us some knowledge of how to prevent this awful curse of too many
children." "Dear Comrade," wrote a New York workingman, once father of six,
"four still living to become slaves to capital. . . . I can see the good that will come
of your noble effort. . . . I would defy the law myself in a noble cause."

Despite the lack of contraceptive information, the Post Office recognized a
woman rebel. The March issue was declared unmailable, as were subsequent
issues from May to October. IWW comrades distributed the *Rebel* at meetings, as
did loyal Emma Goldman, who handed it out at her speeches. In August,
Margaret Sanger was indicted under nine counts of the Comstock laws. "The
very idea of birth control," she later wrote, "resurrected the spirit of the witch
hunts at Salem." On this occasion, however, none of the charges involved
contraception. Rather, they referred to *Rebel* articles that denounced marriage,
defended assassination, and discussed female physiology. Still, direct action had
succeeded, since Margaret Sanger had evoked attention and admiration on the
left. But she also faced a federal trial and after that, almost inevitably, jail. After
demanding several delays, she left the country instead, fleeing first to Canada
and then to England. She left behind her now-estranged husband, her children,
and a radical following. To the last she left a special legacy.

After the *Rebel* was first declared unmailable, Margaret Sanger wrote a
pamphlet containing all the contraceptive advice the newspaper had omitted.
She had 100,000 copies printed up for IWW colleagues to distribute while she
was in jail, as she then expected to be. *Family Limitation*, subtitled "A Nurse's
Advice to Women," was a flagrant violation of the obscenity laws and a masterful
model of direct action. In a covering letter to IWW comrades, Sanger asked them
to distribute the pamphlet to "poor men and women who are overburdened with
children." The first few pages made it clear that the pamphlet was meant for

working-class women, "especially wage workers, who should not have more than two children at most." The contraceptive methods contained in the pamphlet, Sanger explained, were already known to the middle class. "It is only the workers who are ignorant of the knowledge of how to prevent bringing children into the world to fill jails and hospitals, factories and mills, insane asylums and premature graves, and who supply millions of soldiers and sailors to fight battles for financiers and the ruling class." From this point of view, contraception *itself* was direct action. Working-class women could combat capitalism "by refusing to supply the market with children to be exploited, by refusing to populate the earth with slaves." They could also use birth control for personal as well as political goals, to help themselves and improve their lives, "today."

Above all, *Family Limitation* was a self-help manual that women could use themselves and then, as Sanger advised, pass the information on to others. The bulk of the manual described in detail the full array of known contraceptive methods and devices. It told when and how to use them and assessed their liabilities and advantages. Sanger did not endorse the time-tried method of withdrawal, which she claimed was inhumane to women. Rather, she gave formulas for douches and suppositories, explained the function of sponges and the virtues of condoms (the latter clearly required male cooperation) and recommended, most explicitly, pessaries, a middle-class favorite. The pessary, or diaphragm, required some knowledge of physiology but women could easily learn to use it, Sanger claimed. "Follow the directions given with each box," she wrote, and then added for good measure: "Any nurse or doctor will teach one how to adjust it; then women can teach each other." Assuring readers that the pessary would not get "lost," Sanger explained that it provided safe, effective contraception without ruining a sexual experience, as withdrawal did. Moreover, the pessary was under a woman's control; in fact "the man will be unconscious that anything is used." Dispelling quack remedies, such as lying on the left side during intercourse, Sanger proposed some equally ineffective ones, such as taking laxatives to induce menstruation. Nonetheless, *Family Limitation* was full of clear, comprehensive instructions, replete with assurance that "the satisfied sexual act . . . is health-giving and acts as a beautifier and tonic."

When Margaret Sanger left for England, her comrades, mainly women, distributed the pamphlets. Between 1914 and 1917 they managed to circulate over 160,000 copies of the first few editions. William Sanger, now back from France, helped to distribute the manual as well. Though estranged from Margaret Sanger, he seemed as devoted to her as ever. He also became a prime target. In 1915, William Sanger was entrapped and arrested by Anthony Comstock, leading agent of the New York Society for the Suppression of Vice, whose name had been attached to the 1873 laws. Accused of violating the obscenity laws, William Sanger conducted his own defense. When convicted he chose to serve a thirty-day jail sentence rather than pay a fine (another direct action precept). "People like you who go around circulating such pamphlets are a menace to society," the judge told William Sanger, adding, somewhat gratuitously, "If some of the women who are going around advocating equal suffrage would go around and advocate women having children, they would do a greater service."

Margaret Sanger, in England, had little gratitude for William's efforts and less sympathy for his current plight. William's troubles, she told her diary, were no greater than those of women who endured "involuntary motherhood" or died from abortion. During William Sanger's jail term, in October 1915, she finally returned to the United States to take charge of their three children. But by this time Margaret Sanger had gone through another crucial stage in her evolution as an advocate of birth control. During her year in England, she had been strongly influenced by the sexual psychologist Havelock Ellis and formed a friendship with him that lasted for decades.

Trained as a physician, a profession he never practiced, Havelock Ellis had found his mission early in life: to dispel Victorian taboos and find out all there was to know about sex. He had been doing so since the 1880s. Accomplished and eccentric, and now in his fifties, Ellis was amazingly prolific. He had written seven volumes of *Studies in the Psychology of Sex* and had just published *The Task of Social Hygiene*, which explained his eugenic and sexual philosophies. When Margaret arrived in England, he was revising *Sexual Inversion,* a pioneer study of homosexuality that appalled her. (*Sexual Inversion* was mainly about men. Ellis had little to report about women.) Since Ellis lived apart from his wife, Edith, who was then in America lecturing on "masculinism and feminism," marriage reform, and other topics, Margaret Sanger had a clear field. Ellis later claimed that he had never met a more "congenial companion" or any woman who had influenced him more. Meanwhile, he proved an inspirational adviser.

Havelock Ellis introduced Sanger to his own ideas. Some were "hygienic," that is, eugenic; Ellis believed in "selective breeding." The rest were sexual. An enemy of repression and an advocate of sexual emancipation, which augured "the glorious freedom of a new religion," Ellis invested sex with a spiritual quality. It bore, he said, "the wonderful possibility of mystical communion." A great liberator, Ellis was an ardent defender of female sexuality as well as a great admirer of women. But this did not mean that he was in the vanguard of feminism. Here he assumed a more conservative stance. Viewing the English suffragists as brash and unpleasant, Ellis reserved his eloquence for the joys of motherhood. He also liked to think of women as more childlike than men. "Their development must be along their own lines, not masculine lines," Ellis had written in the *Psychology of Sex.* "In a certain sense their brains are in their wombs." As a sexologist, clearly, he had his own ideas about sphere.

But Ellis's romantic and spiritual sexual enthusiasm could not help but reinforce Sanger's own views. In the 1912 *Call* articles, she too had explained "the beauty and wonder and sacredness of the sex function." She now incorporated Ellis's eugenic and sexual tenets into her defense of birth control. Contraception could, simultaneously, unleash female sexuality from repression, uplift sexual experience into mystical communion, and rid humanity of poverty and deformity. Ellis was also full of practical advice. He urged Sanger to focus on a single cause rather than dissipate her energies in left-wing crusades. He also urged her to study birth-control methods, especially in Holland. There, as in Germany, contraceptive centers where midwives gave advice to women had long been in operation.

Margaret Sanger's stay in Holland, at Ellis's suggestion, proved another pivotal stage in her development as a reformer. She attended classes for midwives under the direction of physician Johannes Rutgers (like Ellis, a Neo-Malthusian, or eugenicist), who taught her how to fit pessaries, as midwives did in Dutch clinics. Clearly public health nurses could do the same in the United States. But clearly, too, the very nature of contraception would affect the crusade to sanction it. In *Family Limitation,* Sanger had recommended a simple type of pessary, which, she claimed, women could easily learn to use and then teach each other. In Holland, she dropped the idea that pessaries could be used without professional instruction; Rutgers favored the Mensinga diaphragm, which had to be fitted by a professional. Sanger would later contend that all birth control should be under a physician's supervision. But since she had learned to fit the device herself, it seems likely that she believed then that nurses and midwives could do the job, as Dutch midwives did, and switched only later, for tactical reasons, to a "doctors only" policy.

During this second European trip, Margaret Sanger had not completely abandoned leftist goals or IWW rhetoric. In a lecture in London's Fabian Hall in 1915, she told her audience that the "master class" used "welfare capitalism" to "blind women to their slavery." Birth control, she declared, was a working-class weapon. But when she returned to the United States later that year, Sanger's radicalism had been channeled into new grooves; she had absorbed Ellis's eugenic goals and sexual romanticism. Although still bound to a left-wing context and left-wing tactics, she now had a single cause, as Ellis had advised. This, again, was a crucial turning point. For Margaret Sanger, 1915 marked the beginning of a gradual veering away from the left, soon to be accelerated by factors beyond her control.

If Sanger had changed, so had the scene she had left behind. By October 1915, when she arrived in New York, radical comrades were rallying to her support—spurred by William Sanger's conviction, Margaret's upcoming trial, and the pamphlet *Family Limitation.* Direct action had made an impact. Emma Goldman now spoke regularly on birth control and was arrested for doing so. Both Goldman and Elizabeth Gurley Flynn, moreover, collected funds for Margaret Sanger's defense. Another change had occurred too. Scorning formal organization, Sanger's loose coalition of left-wing supporters had never really formed one. But middle- and upper-class liberals had just coalesced into a National Birth Control League, led by Mary Ware Dennett, a former NAWSA officer and peace activist. The NBCL was the first formal link between the birth-control cause and middle-class women. Mary Ware Dennett and her followers disapproved of radical tactics like lawbreaking. Instead, they campaigned for the repeal of federal and state laws that categorized birth control as obscenity and prevented the free distribution of contraceptive information and devices.

By adopting a "free speech" stance, however, the NBCL had encroached on radical terrain and threatened Margaret Sanger's preeminence. Her irritation was overshadowed only by a genuine tragedy, her daughter Peggy's death of pneumonia at age five, a death to which Sanger could not help but think she had contributed, through her absence. In a real way, Margaret Sanger was now a martyr to her own cause. And she still had to face her *Woman Rebel* trial, intending to fill the role of martyr once again. But the government, it turned out, had no desire to contribute to her heroism or influence, and in February 1916, it suddenly dropped the charges against her. Liberated at last from the *Woman Rebel,* which had won her an enormous amount of publicity, Margaret Sanger now had an audience, a following, and a single-issue crusade. She would advocate removal of contraception from the category of obscenity, spread contraceptive information among working-class women, and spearhead a popular-support movement. With the encouragement of her left-wing comrades, Sanger now began her lifetime's work.

By the spring of 1916, Margaret Sanger was embarked on a three-month speaking tour through major midwestern and western cities, following a route carved out by IWW campaigners. She traveled through Chicago and St. Louis, San Francisco and Portland. "I can understand how restless the death of Peggy makes you," Havelock Ellis wrote from England. The speaking tour helped Sanger reach a national audience and spurred the activity of local birth-control leagues that had formed, usually under radical auspices. By now an experienced campaigner, Sanger made an impressive appearance, even more appealing to some audiences than Emma Goldman. Slight and beautiful, as Mabel Dodge described her, Sanger combined "a radiant feminine appeal with an impression of serenity, calm, and graciousness of voice and manner," all of which masked her "tremendous fighting spirit" and "relentless drive." Her talks, which invariably included the Sadie Sachs drama, were effective too. Calling for free speech and sexual emancipation, Sanger again denounced, in radical spirit, the remedial efforts of middle-class progressives to solve social problems. But her arguments now included some different planks as well. Birth control was presented no longer as an anticapitalist weapon but as an antipoverty one. Similarly, Sanger now stressed a eugenic goal: Birth control would prevent an increase in the number of defectives. Finally, during the 1916 tour, she contended that the medical profession should dispense contraceptive information and devices.

During this nationwide campaign, Margaret Sanger reached a new audience, beyond IWW and socialist networks. The working class still remained a primary target, however, according to Sanger, who claimed that she wanted to reach the women of the stockyards and factories. It also remained a primary target for women of the left. Elizabeth Gurley Flynn, for instance, *did* talk to women at stockyards and mills, where she handed out birth-control literature. The response, she said, was enthusiastic. Meanwhile, Margaret Sanger continued to be inundated with letters from working-class women requesting information and expressing support. "Even if women can't help much, don't know how to speak in public or write for the press etc.," wrote a St. Louis working-class woman in 1916, "yet they are awakening up all over the nation and waiting for someone to lead the way." But working-class women, despite the letters, remained difficult to reach. "It seems strange, but it is almost impossible to interest the workers," wrote Caroline Nelson, an IWW comrade on the west coast, who had started birth-control leagues in Portland and San Francisco.

> While they want to get contraceptive information in secret, they cannot discuss it in public without giggling and blushing. . . . How we are going to get [birth-control information] to the workers is the problem that I constantly harp on. They wouldn't know how to use it, is the answer I constantly get. They have no bathrooms, they are too tired after a day's work to get up and douche, they are too timid to ask for material in a drugstore, etc.

It was even harder to involve working-class women in birth-control agitation, as Caroline Nelson told Margaret Sanger: "Our league here consists mostly of professional people." Reform activism was overwhelmingly a middle- and upper-class prerogative, as Elizabeth Cady Stanton and Susan B. Anthony had discovered in the 1860s. During her 1916 tour, Margaret Sanger began reaching middle-class women, among whom she tried to broaden support for the cause.

Sometimes she succeeded. In Denver, for instance, a liberal young juvenile court justice, Ben Lindsey, chaired one of Sanger's lectures and was able to provide a large audience made up of the wives of businessmen and professionals. But gaining access to such well-off women was not always easy. The Chicago Woman's Club, where Jane Addams had once drummed up support, refused Margaret Sanger an opportunity to speak, as did Hull-House. Sanger concluded that Chicago was too much under the thumb of Addams and social workers. There was a real chasm of disagreement, however, between Sanger's goals and those of most middle-class women activists of the progressive era, such as those in the suffrage and settlement movements.

Since her *Woman Rebel* days, Sanger had denounced women reformers, such as settlement workers, for meliorism. By trying to remedy the defects of capitalism, they became its slaves. Suffragists, she contended, were apologetic, always trying to seem "harmless" and "respectable." These indictments were now returned. To social reformers in women's clubs and settlements, birth control undercut the progressive agenda; working-class families should be protected, not diminished. To suffragists, now in the last lap of their drive toward victory, there was little appeal in birth control, a controversial cause of left-wing origins. The suffrage movement had long since learned the virtue of "single-issue politics." Moreover, like many progressives, suffragists were nervous about "race suicide." In addition, their arguments stressed the significance of motherhood. Most of all, they feared that rampant birth control would only enhance the sexual freedom of men, who would be unbound by "consequences." Finally, the very focus on sexuality seemed counterproductive. Confronted with a birth-control appeal in 1916, a California feminist responded that she feared "more and more intercourse until life would consist of nothing else."

Not surprisingly, when Margaret Sanger and Elsie Clews Parsons solicited statements from fifty prominent women, endorsing birth control and stating they practiced it, they met with failure. But Sanger now succeeded, as she had in the past, with another attempt at direct action. In the fall of 1916 she opened the first American birth control clinic, in the Brownsville neighborhood of Brooklyn. Direct action, as usual, brought attention and acclaim, publicity and sympathy. It even brought a surge of middle-class support.

Brownsville was a working-class area—as Sanger described it, "dingy, squalid, peopled with hard-working men and women," mainly Jewish and Italian immigrants. But the two ground-floor rooms that she rented on Amboy Street were intended for larger purposes than helping the working-class mothers of Brownsville. Margaret Sanger hoped to achieve publicity by courting arrest, to overshadow Mary Ware Dennett's new birth-control league, and to challenge state obscenity laws, which prohibited distribution or sale of contraceptive information or devices. The New York law did provide that doctors could prescribe such devices to prevent venereal disease, but this clause was intended solely to protect the health of men. Moreover, the Brownsville clinic had no doctors. Like the clinics in Holland, it was staffed solely by women: Margaret Sanger; her sister, Ethel Byrne; and Fania Mindell, a Chicago recruit who could speak Yiddish. Sanger had tried to find a physician to supervise the clinic, but no one would do it. William J. Robinson, however, one of the few physicians who endorsed birth control, sent her lots of advice. Dispense only "hygienic advice," he warned, not "treatment," since treatment was the province of medicine. (This piece of advice was ignored.) "Have every woman who applies

MOTHERS!

Can you afford to have a large family?
Do you want any more children?
If not, why do you have them?
DO NOT KILL, DO NOT TAKE LIFE, BUT PREVENT
Safe, Harmless Information can be obtained of trained
Nurses at

46 AMBOY STREET
NEAR PITKIN AVE. — BROOKLYN.

Tell Your Friends and Neighbors.   All Mothers Welcome
A registration fee of IO cents entitles any mother to this information.

!מוטערס
?זיים איהר פערמעגליך צו האבען א גרויסע פאמיליע
?ווילם איהר האבען נאך קינדער
? אויב ניט, ווארום האם איהר זיי

.מעררערם ניט, נעהמט ניט קיין לעבען, נור פערהים זיך

זיכרע, אנשעדליכע אינסקינאמסט קענם איהר בעקומען פון ערפארענע נוירסעס אין

46 אמבאי סטריט ניער פיטקין עוועניר ברוקלין
מאכם דאם בקאנם צו אייערע פריינד און שכנות.   יעדער מומער איז ווילקאמען

.פיר 10 סענם איינשרייב-געלד זיינם איהר בערעכטיגט צו ריזיע אינפארמיישאן

MADRI!
Potete permettervi il lusso d'avere altri bambini?
Ne volete ancora?
Se non ne volete piu', perche' continuate a metterli al mondo?
NON UCCIDETE MA PREVENITE!
Informazioni sicure ed innocue saranno fornite da infermiere autorizzate a
46 AMBOY STREET   Near Pitkin Ave. Brooklyn
a cominciare dal 12 Ottobre. Avvertite le vostre amiche e vicine.
Tutte le madri sono ben accette. La tassa d'iscrizione di IO cents da diritto
a qualunque madre di ricevere consigli ed informazioni gratis.

A 1916 handbill advertising the services of the Brownsville clinic in English, Yiddish, and Italian. Since providing information about contraception violated New York law, Margaret Sanger and her two colleagues at the clinic were quickly arrested. *(Library of Congress)*

for advice sign a slip that says she is a married woman," Robinson continued, and "don't charge the people anything for advice." "If you do as I say," the physician concluded, the Brownsville clinic "might become the germ of thousands of similar clinics."

After plastering handbills all over the neighborhood, and after notifying the district attorney so as to ensure arrest, Margaret Sanger opened the clinic on October 16, 1916. In ten days, the three women saw 488 married women from the neighborhood, gave out both information and contraceptive devices, and sold copies of "What Every Girl Should Know." To no one's surprise, a policewoman was sent to entrap the clinicians ("A woman—the irony of it!" Sanger later wrote.) All three were arrested; their records and devices were confiscated. In her autobiography, Sanger described the scene of her arrest with the same sense of drama as that which pervaded the Sadie Sachs story.

Crowds began to gather outside. A long line of women with baby carriages and children had been waiting to get into the clinic. Now the streets were filled, and police had to see that traffic was not blocked. The patrol wagon came rattling through the streets to our door, and at length Miss Mindell and I took our seats within and were taken to the police station.

As I sat in the rear of the car and looked out on that seething mob of humans, I wondered, and asked myself *what* had gone out of the race. Something had gone from them which silenced them, made them impotent to defend their rights. I thought of the suffragists in England, and pictured the results of a similar arrest there. But as I sat in this mood, the car started to go. I looked out at the mass and heard a scream. It came from a woman wheeling a baby carriage, who had just come around the corner preparing to visit the clinic. She saw the patrol wagon, realized what had happened, left the baby carriage on the walk, rushed through the crowd to the wagon and cried to me: "Come back! Come back and save me!" The woman looked wild. She ran after the car for a dozen yards or so, when some friends caught her weeping form in their arms and led her back to the sidewalk. That was the last thing I saw as the Black Maria dashed off to the station.

When brought to trial, all three women were convicted. Ethel Byrne, whose case was considered first, was sentenced to a thirty-day stint in the workhouse on Blackwell's Island, where she went on a hunger strike until carried out on a stretcher. Margaret Sanger and Fania Mindell, tried next, entered a courtroom crowded with photographers, supporters, and spectators. Brownsville women, laden with children, had come to defend the clinicians' efforts, although their testimony was used by the prosecution. Fania Mindell was fined for selling a copy of "What Every Girl Should Know." The decision was later reversed. At the end of January 1917, Margaret Sanger, like Ethel Byrne, received a thirty-day sentence, but her fate was quite different from her sister's. Refusing to be fingerprinted, Sanger was sent off to the Queens County jail, where, exempt from work, she answered her mail and reaped the rewards of direct action. The clinic had brought intensive publicity, national recognition, and mounting sympathy—not least of all from well-off women, many of whom had attended the trial. Members of the New York Women's City Club, wealthy and prominent, now sought to raise funds for Sanger's crusade.

Finally, direct action soon bore judicial results. When the New York Court of Appeals reviewed Sanger's case in 1918, it upheld her conviction but opened the way for a broader interpretation of the law. Physicians, said the court, could give "help or advice to a married person to cure or prevent disease." This meant that the venereal disease clause had been extended to cover the provision of contraception to married women, as long as it was provided only by doctors and only under limited conditions.

During early 1917, as the nation moved toward entry into World War I, Margaret Sanger took new steps to proselytize and organize. In January, even before she went to jail, a new publication appeared. The *Birth Control Review* was run by Margaret Sanger and a new left-wing colleague, Frederick Blossom, an Ohio birth controller, socialist, social worker, and member of the IWW. Besides these credentials, Blossom was an effective and efficient campaigner who brought with him much radical support. Like the *Woman Rebel*, the *Birth Control Review* contained no specific contraceptive advice; unlike the *Rebel*, it adopted a calm, professional tone. Publicizing the activities of local birth-control leagues, it also published articles by such distinguished contributors as Socialist party leader Eugene Debs, physician William J. Robinson, and Havelock Ellis, who, ever generous, sent in a piece on "The Love Rights of Women." Most important, the *Review* supported "doctors only" bills that would enable physicians to

Margaret Sanger with supporters and admirers after the New York Court of Appeals decision in 1918. *(Planned Parenthood Federation of America)*

provide contraceptive information and devices to all women. Birth-control politics, meanwhile, became a three-way power struggle.

Since Mary Ware Dennett's NBCL had taken a "free speech" stance, by urging repeal of the obscenity laws so that contraceptive information could be freely distributed, Sanger and Blossom formed a rival group, the New York Birth Control League, which campaigned for "doctors only" bills. By a strange inversion, the Sanger-Blossom faction, self-proclaimed radicals, had adopted a more conservative, pragmatic approach, while Dennett's middle-class liberals demanded a far more radical change in the law. Rivalry within the birth-control movement, never free of rancor and dispute, was now compounded by rivalry within the radical wing. Frederick Blossom, it turned out, also wanted to lead the movement. In the spring of 1917, he took his own form of direct action by departing with *Birth Control Review* accounts, records, and some office furniture—and much of the radical support with which he had come. When Margaret Sanger pressed charges against him, she further alienated the left. Running to the district attorney struck some comrades as consorting with the enemy. Frederick Blossom had, in fact, damaged Sanger's radical credentials. By the time she was able to get the *Review* in operation again, in 1918, it was only with the support of wealthy women backers, whom she had recently acquired. These new allies bought shares of stock in the *Review*. Inch by inch, Margaret Sanger had shifted away from the left. And U.S. entry into World War I was to make the shift permanent.

The war era affected the birth-control movement in a variety of ways. First, during the war, the U.S. government waged a massive assault on venereal disease by distributing condoms to American troops. This had more impact on the future of birth control than did the Brownsville clinic. Curiously, the government also distributed, without attribution, Sanger's article on venereal disease (twice found to be obscene) from the 1913 *Call*. "What Every Girl Should Know" turned out to be what every soldier should know as well. World War I also brought a major crackdown on the left—which, whatever grief it had given Sanger, had consistently provided her with a base of operations. By the fall of 1917, this base was under assault. Socialists were threatened with prosecution for antiwar activities; the IWW was dismembered by government raids, confiscations, and arrests, and an even worse wave of repression followed in 1919. By the war's end, the left was dismantled. The interlocking networks of socialists and anarchists, rebels and radicals, who had once given Sanger inspiration and support were gone. Some were in jail, like Eugene Debs, some were deported, like Emma Goldman, and all were silenced. Once the left was demobilized, Margaret Sanger had to shift political gears and find a new constituency. Working-class women had never provided one. At the end of World War I, she was ready to enter the new decade as the spokeswoman for a middle-class movement.

Margaret Sanger's severance from the left had come in stages, and at each stage her personal power had increased. An early factor was her alienation from William Sanger, well in progress by 1914. As Margaret wrote in her journal that year, "The man who shouts loud about liberal ideas and thinks himself advanced finds the servile submission of his wife charming and womanly." Another factor was the influence of Ellis in 1914–1915. A sexual radical rather than a political one, Ellis had encouraged devotion to a single cause, as well as acceptance of his own ideals, eugenic and sexual. A third factor, after 1916, was Sanger's ability to win the support of wealthy New York women, who attended her trial, contributed to her cause, and later backed the *Birth Control Review*. A fourth factor was Sanger's fight with Frederick Blossom in 1917 for power within the birth-control movement, a fight that antagonized radical supporters in the Blossom camp. Another consideration, running through these years, was the ambivalence of the left. Although birth control had been forged in a left-wing cauldron, although Sanger had capitalized on left-wing networks, the left had actually been elusive. The Socialist party never formally endorsed birth control, and the IWW had its own priorities. The male leftist had "Marxist blinders and will not see," Sanger told her diary in 1919. Finally, during World War I and immediately after, the left was destroyed by waves of repression. By 1920, Margaret Sanger was free of her radical origins, which she thereafter minimized or ignored.

As the new decade began, she quickly reshaped her personal life and the birth-control movement for a "New Era." In 1920 the Sangers were divorced, and in 1921 Margaret married a multimillionaire, oil company president Noah Slee, who devoted massive funds to the cause. ("I should be rather nervous about marrying the Woman Rebel," Havelock Ellis wrote to a mutual friend.) In similar pragmatic spirit, Sanger shifted her goals and tactics. During the war, she had found support among women of means. In 1921, with their backing, she started a new organization, the American Birth Control League, which campaigned for the passage of "doctors only" bills. Hardly a group of radical agitators, the ABCL was a middle-class, highly professionalized reform organization. Under its auspices, direct action was replaced by an educational campaign like that of the suffrage movement. The ABCL intended to turn the tide of public opinion and, in particular, to solicit the support of the medical profession.

Family Limitation was similarly adapted, by strategic deletions and additions, to meet the changing times. In its last edition, in 1921, the manual no longer urged birth control as direct action or as an anticapitalist weapon; nor did it urge self-help among working-class women. Rather, it presented birth control as a tool to end misery and poverty, and urged women to get the advice of physicians. Doctors, indeed, would now be central to the birth-control cause. When Margaret Sanger next opened a birth control clinic, in 1923, physicians were in charge of dispensing contraceptive devices and information. And as Sanger wrote to a colleague six years later, "It was I who switched the birth control movement from the channels where I first claimed it belonged into the realm of the medical profession."

Once the left was invalidated as a political base, Margaret Sanger was also free to adjust her policies to suit the popular mood. As the 1920s began, she rearranged her armory of arguments. Birth control, she contended, would "limit and discourage the over-fertility of the mentally and physically defective." It would provide the nation with "wanted" children, not deformed or delinquent, but social assets. No man and woman, Sanger wrote in 1920, "have a right to bring into the world those who are to suffer from mental or physical affliction."

Not only would birth control foster eugenics, it would also promote "new ideals of sex." Birth control, Sanger explained, would transform sex from a merely "propagative act" or "biological necessity" into "a psychic and spiritual avenue of expression." It would liberate women from repression ("loathing, disgust, or indifference to the sex relationship") and contribute to their sexual satisfaction. With birth control, moreover, "the moral force of woman's nature will be unchained." It would rescue women from the role of "dominated weaklings in a society controlled by men," and it would foster the creation of "a human world by the infusion of the feminine element into all of its activities."

Before World War I, Margaret Sanger had taken direct action to liberate working-class women from "enforced motherhood." During the 1920s, she embodied and proclaimed the new ideal of sexual emancipation, just as it reached a nationwide, middle-class audience.

16

CROSS-CURRENTS:
THE 1920s

The movement for birth control appeared at a turning point in women's history. A dividing line between generations, it separated contrasting sets of middle-class ideals. The New Woman of the progressive era, who had carved out a space in public life, devoted herself to causes, reform, and collective action. Her most visible counterpart in the 1920s, a markedly younger model, was more involved in private life than in public affairs, more attuned to competition than coopera- tion, more interested in self-fulfillment than in social service. "This new girl, the modern flapper, with her lack of respect for the ideals of her predecessors," had an infectious influence, writer V. F. Calverton proclaimed at mid-decade. No longer a symbol of moral superiority, she seemed to adopt a provocative, even exhibitionist pose. "Cigarette in hand, shimmying to the music of the masses, the New Woman and the New Morality have made their theatric debut upon the modern scene."

The modern scene was urban, technological, commercial, and conservative. By 1920, half of Americans lived in towns or cities of 25,000 or more, with a growing concentration in large metropolitan areas. During the decade, middle- class urbanites were linked together by new technology and mass communica- tions—telephone, radio, phonograph, movies, and large-circulation magazines. The press, the screen, and the world of advertising helped to establish common values and standards. They spurred the growth of leisure-time interests and generated an air of prosperity and well-being. Above all, the modern scene was an apolitical one. After World War I and the demolition of the left, discontent, protest, and even reform became less acceptable. The progressive spirit, with which women's groups had long been allied, wavered in strength and declined. Old political divisions were now eclipsed by new generational ones, the sense that old and young, as the *Atlantic* put it in 1922, "were as far apart in point of view, codes, and standards, as if they belonged to different races." The flapper, with her aura of self-indulgence and independence, came to personify the "point of view" of her generation. She stood for a shift in middle-class sexual mores, of which birth control was a pivotal part. She signified a demand for equality, since she seemed to be adopting privileges and liberties once reserved for men. And she represented individualism, the keynote to modernity. Like the heroine of a *McCalls* story in 1925, her philosophy was "To live life in one's own way."

Despite her extensive publicity, the irrepressible flapper was hardly the only New Woman of the 1920s. On the contrary, she was more of a symbol of liberated attitudes or aspirations, constantly promoted in the movies and the press and vividly imprinted on the popular memory. The decade was in fact populated by a variety of New Women. There was the campus coed, now imbued more with hopes of marriage than with a sense of mission; the modern housewife, who adopted the role of companion and consumer; the new professional and businesswoman, who sought to integrate marriage and career; and the postsuffrage feminist, sometimes embroiled in battles over legal and constitutional change and sometimes preoccupied with the new ideal of economic independence. Indisputably, the decade was a crucible of contemporary middle-class roles. It was also a crossroads at which different themes of women's history overlapped and intertwined. During the 1920s, women embarked on two paths toward equality, though they tended to lead in different directions.

One path was personal. Diffuse, unorganized, and often nonideological, the movement toward individual liberation was overwhelmingly the province of the young—including young women in their twenties and thirties who had participated in or witnessed the last stages of the suffrage campaign. Another path was political. This was the province of organized women, spurred by the achievement of suffrage and full of ambition. As historian Nancy F. Cott has shown, the decades surrounding 1920 constituted "a period of crisis and transition" when the modern feminist agenda was shaped. During the 1920s, the feminist movement entered an intense phase of activism. But it also fought against the tide. Handicapped by the national retreat from reform and caught in a conservative undertow, it was splintered by internal conflict.

Feminists in Conflict

Tensions within the feminist camp emerged before the vote was won. At one time, all activists had been united under the suffrage umbrella; by World War I, the coalition had begun to collapse. Cleavage between more militant feminists and progressive reformers started when Alice Paul's Congressional Union split apart from the NAWSA. After 1920, the division expanded while the ranks of activists shrank. The NAWSA, resurrected after suffrage as the League of Women Voters, was one-tenth its former size. It had about 200,000 members. Working in tandem with the Women's Joint Congressional Committee, a watchdog agency made up of women's group representatives, and with the new federal Women's Bureau, formed during World War I, the league strove for new goals. It would educate the electorate, democratize political parties (by female infiltration), and support laws to protect women and children. The LWV, in short, represented the reform-minded mainstream of the suffrage movement.

The new National Woman's party, started in 1921, was a more militant but far smaller organization than the LWV, with a membership roll of only about 8,000. Defining itself as a third party, the NWP intended to support women candidates and women's causes, and to work "to remove all the remaining forms of the subjection of women." But its goals soon shrank to one. In 1923, the NWP proposed an Equal Rights Amendment to the Constitution, stating that "Men and women shall have equal rights throughout the United States and every place subject to its jurisdiction." Minimizing the achievement of suffrage, the NWP contended that women were still subordinate to men in all aspects of life; indeed over 1,000 state laws discriminated against women. The ERA would erase sex as a legal classification and make women equal in every arena, from property rights to divorce rights to employment opportunities. It would also, however, invalidate the barrage of protective laws for which women reformers had long campaigned. Once the NWP goal of equality was posited against the goal of protection, the stage was set for a divisive intramural feud.

The NWP based its arguments solely on justice. Defending the need for an ERA, it developed two lines of attack on protective laws. One was that these laws were paternalistic, discriminatory, and damaging to women. The landmark *Muller* v. *Oregon* decision, which sanctioned such laws to protect the woman worker's "physical structure and proper discharge of her maternal function," clearly assumed that women had inferior capacities, the NWP charged. Under protective laws, Crystal Eastman argued in 1924, women were classified with children and minors. Moreover, by ensuring different status for women, the laws actually protected men against female competition. Minimum wage laws, for instance, could exclude women from the job market; limits on overtime and maximum-hour laws made them less desirable employees. The eight-hour law, Gail Laughlin contended, meant "shutting the doors of opportunity to women." The laws did not protect women, claimed Harriot Stanton Blatch, but "crowded them into lower grades of work" or enabled male unions to keep them out of work. But another facet of the NWP argument sought to distinguish between the laws' protective and exclusionary impact. Denying that they were antilabor or opposed to worker protection, NWP activists contended that protective laws should not be repealed but extended to apply to both sexes. Men deserved protection too, as *Equal Rights,* the NWP journal, argued in 1923. Far from invalidating protective laws, Eastman claimed, the ERA would force their extension to men. (This was an unlikely outcome in the conservative 1920s, but *Equal Rights* staunchly insisted that "a righteous principle" would bring "good results.") In either event, whether protective laws were dismantled or extended, the ERA would "secure for woman complete equality under the law and in all human relationships."

Most activist women, however, defended protection on the basis of expediency. To the LWV and other women's organizations, an ERA would be a calamity. To Mary Anderson, director of the Women's Bureau, stronghold of reform convictions, the amendment was diabolical. In fact, said Anderson, militants voiced "a kind of hysterical feminism with a slogan for a program," and as Florence Kelley added, the ERA was a "slogan of the insane." Decrying the prospect of such an amendment, women reformers argued that equality was chimerical, that women were different, that protection was necessary, and that the NWP was an elitist saboteur of working women's interests.

The concept of legal equality, Mary Anderson contended, was a myth. The ERA dealt with "abstract rights, not real rights." Motherhood had indeed given woman a permanent disadvantage, Alice Hamilton argued in the *Woman Citizen* (the LWV journal), and this made protective laws a permanent necessity. "Women cannot be made men" by constitutional amendment, Florence Kelley contended, and would always need laws "different than those needed by men." More women benefited from protective laws than were injured by them, claimed ERA opponents. Moreover, the Women's Bureau confirmed, women were suited to special sorts of work and were therefore restricted in employment opportunity anyway, with or without laws. The ERA would only be used by exploitative employers to take advantage of women workers, as they had before protective legislation was enacted. Finally, reformers charged, the NWP had taken an elitist stance. It represented only the interests of its membership, professional and businesswomen, and had no sympathy for the average woman wage earner. The type of equality the ERA would impose was appropriate only for competitive professionals seeking career advancement, not for industrial workers. The NWP, in short, represented class interests, not women's interests. By insisting on an ERA, historian Mary Beard wrote to a friend in the NWP, the militants ran the risk of "forsaking humanism in the quest for feminism." And by clinging to the chimera of equality, reformers charged, the NWP was rejecting the spirit of cooperation that had long characterized the women's movement.

Conflict over equality and protection permeated women's politics through-out the decade. As battle lines hardened, the NWP withdrew its support from *all* women candidates, endorsing only those who supported the ERA. NWP members also proposed and campaigned for hundreds of measures in state legislatures, though to no avail. By 1930, the only equal rights clause was in Wisconsin's state constitution, and this was a compromise clause, worded to protect protective laws. Meanwhile, conflict among American feminists reached international dimensions. During the early 1920s, the NWP and LWV competed fiercely for preeminence within the International Alliance of Women, made up of European and American feminists. ("Feminists intuitively understand that they are citizens of the world," as *Equal Rights* declared.) In 1926, NWP rejection by the alliance created a major schism, causing the withdrawal of European "equal rights" advocates and seriously weakening the international woman's movement. The two American organizations, however, continued to vie for influence on the international front. While the LWV maintained its status within the alliance, and Carrie Chapman Catt created a new peace coalition, the NWP campaigned for an international equal rights treaty. By the end of the decade, conflict between feminist factions had alienated many women's leaders from one another. Antagonism among activists hardly caused feminist decline but, rather, accompanied it. Although the battle over the ERA continued into the 1930s, it hit its peak in the mid-1920s, when feminist fortunes began to falter. The year 1925 was a turning point.

Equality may have been a chimera, but so by now was the "woman's vote." Women had never formed a voting bloc that would support either women candidates or "women's issues." By mid-decade, political parties, which had at the outset wooed women voters, began to drop women from party committees. Congress, which never considered the ERA, became unresponsive to the demands of *all* women's groups. Retaining the allegiance of women constituents no longer seemed to involve an obligation to support women's causes. Moreover, all progressive reforms fell out of favor. This meant in effect that protective legislation now had as dim a future as the Equal Rights Amendment. A major obstacle was the Supreme Court. In 1923, in *Adkins* v. *Children's Hospital,* the Court declared a federal minimum wage law for women unconstitutional, and thereby undermined a major goal of women reformers. Such a law, said the Court, deprived a woman of the liberty to bargain directly with her employer, a position endorsed by the NWP. (In Florence Kelley's view, the Court had affirmed only "the inalienable right of women to starve.") Another blow was failure to attain a child labor law, a cause with much support. Congress passed child labor laws in 1918 and 1922, but in both instances the Supreme Court declared the laws unconstitutional. A final tactic was to strive for a child labor amendment, which Congress approved in 1924. But this too failed; by 1930, only six states had ratified it. In addition to such rebuffs, reform-minded feminists were defeated even in victory, as the strange fate of the Sheppard-Towner Act was to prove.

Immediately after suffrage was won, Congress made a few gallant blows to what it expected to be the "woman's vote." The most important gesture was the Sheppard-Towner Act of 1921, a welfare measure intended to reduce infant and maternal mortality. The first federally funded health care act, it provided states with matching federal funds to establish prenatal and child health centers, where expectant mothers could receive advice and where preventive health checkups would be provided for women and children. The centers would also send public health nurses out into homes. The act focused on rural areas, since urbanites were more likely to have the services of city welfare agencies or settlements, such as the Henry Street visiting nurse service in which Margaret Sanger had been briefly employed.

From the woman reformer's viewpoint, Sheppard-Towner was a major triumph. An expensive measure, it had been enacted by an overwhelming majority of congressmen, all anxious to curry favor with women constituents. Significantly, southern senators and legislators, never known for feminist sympathies, voted heavily in its favor. Moreover, the passage of Sheppard-Towner suggested that woman suffrage had opened a new era of humane, benevolent legislation. Not only would the law protect maternal and child health, but it would enlarge women's roles in the public sector. The centers, staffed by physicians (mainly women) and public health nurses, would be overseen not merely by the states but by the federal Women's Bureau. After passage of the legislation, indeed, Sheppard-Towner centers provided a great barrage of classes, literature, and health services, and reached thousands of pregnant women and millions of infants and children.

But Sheppard-Towner aroused opposition. The NWP disliked it, since it classified all women as "mothers." Margaret Sanger disliked it, too. She contended that Sheppard-Towner's "benevolence" was superficial, nearsighted, and "dysgenic." Women wanted to have fewer children, Sanger claimed, but the Sheppard-Towner centers "would teach them to have more." (Birth control was not one of the preventive health measures the centers espoused.) Most important, from the outset, the AMA opposed the law and mounted a vigorous campaign against it. Physicians objected to the interference of outsiders, such as federal officials and women reformers, in the health care business. Moreover, preventive health care, such as checkups of pregnant women and well children, was a potentially lucrative field. During the 1920s, preventive care was absorbed into private practice; the doctor's domain expanded to include the office visit for well patients. In 1929, capitulating to the AMA, Congress terminated the Sheppard-Towner program. The short-lived act did have an impact, although not the impact its supporters had envisioned: It forced physicians to take a stand on preventive health and enlarged the scope of medical practice.

Although the fate of Sheppard-Towner was unknown at mid-decade, women's reform organizations faced other setbacks. Like all progressive groups, they suffered from diminished size and influence, a part of the postwar retreat from reform. There were some new ventures. In the South, a new women's movement for interracial cooperation developed, followed in 1930 by the Association of Southern Women for the Prevention of Lynching. Founded by Texas suffragist Jessie Daniel Ames, the ASWPL, which drew on women's church networks, responded to a major concern of black women—one that had been voiced since the days of Ida B. Wells. But some important older women's institutions had started to wane. During the 1920s, the Consumers' League shriveled; Maud Nathan claimed its major goals had been achieved. The Women's Trade Union League, which had working-class leadership by 1919, still depended on upper-class funds. During the 1920s, these funds dried up and support fell off. Efforts to organize women workers capsized, although replaced by ambitious educational projects. The settlement movement also suffered. Many settlements had financial problems and could not recruit new residents; "social work" was now a career more than a cause. Other women's organizations gained new members but lost their reform thrust. The General Federation of Women's Clubs, conservative even in the progressive era, was an example. Still massive in size, it turned its energies to spreading the gospel of home economics and urging the use of electric appliances. Finally, the LWV joined the retreat from reform by concentrating on child welfare measures rather than on women's issues. "We are not feminists primarily," a league officer would declare in 1933. "We are citizens." The shifts and shrinkage of women's reform bastions reflected the "New Era's" conservative swing. They also reflected feminist inability to appeal to the next generation.

"My generation didn't think much about the place or the problem of women," playwright Lillian Hellman recounted in her autobiography. "[We]

Founded in 1920, the League of Women Voters represented the mainstream of postsuffrage feminism. Determined to promote child welfare, protect women workers, and educate the female electorate, it also attempted to shape the planks of party platforms. But to younger women of the 1920s, the LWV conveyed a staid, old-fashioned image. The long tradition of female association was losing its appeal. *(Library of Congress)*

were not conscious that the designs we saw around us had so recently been formed that we were still part of the formation." By mid-decade, the alienation of the young was clear. Young middle-class women appeared to have little interest in organized feminism, either in its militant egalitarian wing or in its social reform one. Moreover, they tended to associate feminism with "sex antagonism" or hostility to men. In 1927, psychologist Lorine Pruette suggested that women under fifty could be divided into three groups: those who had "struggled for independence of action . . . and never quite [lost] their bitterness towards men"; younger women who were less familiar with either bitterness or struggle; and still younger ones who were "likely to be bored" when feminism was mentioned. Women of the new generation took feminist gains for granted, an LWV member wrote in 1928. The rights won by the "old feministic movement" were accepted by the young as a matter of course. "'Feminism' has become a term of opprobrium to the modern young woman," writer Dorothy Dunbar Bromley confirmed in *Harper's* in 1927. Young women had contempt for those "who antagonize men with their constant clamor about maiden names, equal rights, woman's place in the world, and many another cause." And the youngest women, those growing up in the 1920s, said psychologist Phyllis Blanchard, equated feminism with being lonely and unmarried. Each year the generation gap among women seemed to take a harsher toll.

This toll was compounded by a falling off of commitment even among women who had recently been active in the last stages of the suffrage campaign. The NAWSA's 2 million members were not expected to continue the fight for women's causes once the vote was won; suffrage had generated singular momentum. But now even highly committed, militant young women withdrew—from feuds, politics, and collective action. Their withdrawal was reflected in the *Nation*'s "Modern Women" series in 1926–1927—a group of anonymous essays by independent, self-supporting, career-minded feminists. Most of the authors had, as one of them put it, "lost faith in the righteous cause of women." "I no longer work in movements," wrote a second, a former militant suffragist and demonstrator. "My energies are bent on achieving an income." Since the vote had been won, wrote a third, who had once been arrested in suffrage marches, her interests had become "broader and more human . . . especially in my belated recognition of the vital importance of economic independence for women."

Economic independence was in fact the new frontier of feminism in the 1920s. A change of direction from the service-oriented, progressive goals of the presuffrage era, it was also a shift of emphasis from public cause to private career, from society to self.

Aspiration and Career

In *Concerning Women,* a feminist primer of 1926, Suzanne LaFollette argued that sexual equality could be based only on economic independence. Women's main achievement had been their entry into the labor force—into factories, shops, schools, and professions, "invading every field that had been held the special province of men," LaFollette wrote. "This is the great unconscious and unorganized women's movement." After World War I, the aspiration for economic independence took on new visibility. The proportion of women in the labor force remained unchanged, about 25 percent. But the actual numbers of working women increased, more middle-class women became wage earners, and the types of work women did changed. During the 1920s, characteristically, change led in two directions at once.

On the one hand, fewer women worked at the rock bottom of the vocational ladder, as domestics, and more entered white-collar jobs, such as clerical and sales work. In addition, new vocations opened up in the business and professional worlds. Educated women, whose numbers constantly rose, surged into professional work. And many of these women attempted to combine careers and marriage, another major innovation. During the 1920s the proportion of women wage earners who were married rose 25 percent, with the greatest increase among women in their twenties and thirties. On the other hand, the decade's aspirations were matched by its limitations. Traditional male professions closed ranks against female entry. Most women were confined to "women's professions," and in the business world, to lower-level job categories. Disparities in pay between men and women increased in all fields as more women entered the labor market. Finally, the gains of the decade were all middle-class gains. In industry, where women were hampered by both protective laws and weakened unions, the situation was especially bleak.

World War I created no permanent jobs for women. During the war, women had worked in the iron, steel, and munitions industries, as well as in other traditionally male jobs, such as streetcar conductors, but these opportunities soon vanished. At the war's end, most emergency appointees were forced to retire, and new options in industry ended. During the 1920s, the woman worker's plight was dismal. Despite the decade's aura of prosperity, some industries—such as textiles, in which many women were employed—suffered setbacks, and unemployment rose. Women's unionization hit a new low of 3 percent. Although the labor movement as a whole lost ground, only one working woman in thirty-four was a union member, as opposed to one man in nine. Since the WTUL shifted its efforts from organization to education, and since the AFL, much weakened, had always been indifferent if not hostile to women workers, hopes for organization were slim. Efforts to form industrial unions had been wiped out when the left was demolished, and skilled workers of the AFL were concentrated in industries from which women were excluded. For most working-class women, work experience in a sex-segregated labor force remained less a source of economic "independence" than a confirmation of second-class status.

Not surprisingly, the exclusionary facet of protective laws abetted the income gap between men and women. Such laws did protect women in fields where they were already in a majority, such as in the garment industry, by regulating hours and improving working conditions. But they had an adverse impact in fields where fewer women worked, since limits on women's hours and functions made men more desirable employees. Moreover, they often excluded women completely, not only from heavy industry but also from the new leisure industries, such as bowling alleys, that required night work. Women reformers, meanwhile, concentrated their efforts on women who were already active unionists. One ambitious project was the summer school for women workers, started at Bryn Mawr in 1921 by M. Carey Thomas and WTUL member Hilda Smith, a social welfare professor. Intended to train working women for union leadership roles, the summer school inspired its participants and spurred similar programs at other colleges. But it had little impact on the average woman industrial worker who was unlikely to be a union member.

Neither protective laws nor progressive efforts had much impact on minority women workers. Mexican American women in northern Colorado had only limited opportunities, such as domestic work and agricultural labor, where they earned less than subsistence wages. By 1920, a small proportion of black women wage earners in urban areas had moved away from domestic work to industrial work or other service work, such as operating elevators. But the great black migration to northern cities that started during World War I increased the black female labor pool; women remained a majority of migrants. In New York City in the mid-1920s, for example, there were still about 85 men to every 100 women among native-born blacks; nearly three out of ten black women lived alone or as lodgers and most took domestic jobs. After World War I, indeed, once immigration was halted, black women began to dominate the domestic labor force in northern cities. During the 1920s, almost three out of four employed black women were domestic servants or laundresses. The white-collar worker, however, had many more opportunities.

The business world expanded in the 1920s, vastly increasing the need for office clerks, stenographers, typists, switchboard operators, and saleswomen. By 1930, 2 million women office workers—secretaries, typists, and file clerks—comprised one-fifth of the female labor force. Women's roles in the lower realms of the business world were widely acclaimed; the working girl had found her place at desk, counter, and switchboard. Even the *Ladies Home Journal,* which had once condemned the exodus of young women from home to office, discovered by 1916 that the secretary "radiated the office with sunshine and sympathetic interest." Female office help became part of the businessman's perquisites, in advertising offices, insurance companies, small firms, and large corporations. "The businessman begins to feel himself a success when he has a secretary," Lorine Pruette wrote in 1931. "A girl feeds his vanity. . . . The stenographer is wife and mother, child and mistress."

There were new vocational options, too, such as the cosmetics counter and beauty parlor—a bonanza for hairdressers, manicurists, cosmeticians, and the

Summer schools for women industrial workers were one of the WTUL's most idealistic enterprises. Under the pioneer Bryn Mawr program, financed by union funds, sixty or more women wage earners were brought to the campus for six to eight weeks of academic courses—economics, history, politics, or even creative writing. Although some participants resented the contrast between campus privilege and working-class lives, and others demanded courses that were critical of capitalism, the response was usually enthusiastic. "I believe that worker education will lead to a new social order," one student declared. The Bryn Mawr summer school ran from 1921 until 1938, when financial support dwindled. The wage earners above were part of a class in American civilization in 1929. *(Schlesinger Library, Radcliffe College)*

vocational schools that trained them. By 1930, over 40,000 beauty parlors were open for business in towns and cities across the nation. What had once been a private service performed at home for a well-off patron was now available to the average middle-class woman in any urban area. Women also entered other fields, such as real estate, retailing, and banking, although they were rarely promoted beyond the rank of buyer, cashier, or supervisor of other women. Still, a spirit of adventure pervaded the business world, since even a slight gain of occupational mobility was exhilarating. Throughout the decade, moreover, novel vocations for women won applause. The press liked to celebrate such advents as the nation's first woman kettle-drummer (1922) or deep-sea diver (1924), suggesting new heights of female emancipation. The most exciting frontier of the era, aviation, also attracted women, who joined in stunt flying and barnstorming, to the delight of reporters. Young Amelia Earhart, briefly a teacher and settlement worker, gained acclaim, as Charles Lindbergh did, first as a barnstormer and then, in 1927, by flying across the Atlantic as part of a crew of three. But neither "firsts" nor press coverage created vocations. Every business had special service jobs intended for women, and such jobs were geared, as always, to short-term employees receiving lower pay and doing lower levels of work.

The vanguard of vocational progress was the professions. During the 1920s, the number of women professionals increased by 50 percent and the percentage of women workers in professions rose from 11.9 percent to 14.2 percent. As historian Frank Stricker points out, the proportion of adult women that pursued careers in professions and business rose during the 1920s, as it would continue to rise after the Great Depression. Three out of four professional women entered "women's fields"—the space in the public sector that progressive women had carved out. And this space expanded too, especially in education and social welfare. By the 1920s, the upper-class settlement resident had been replaced by a trained, licensed, salaried social worker, usually a woman, although men held managerial posts, as they did in library work and education. Mass communications, another rapidly growing field, also provided new jobs. During the 1920s, the number of women editors, reporters, and journalists doubled. But in most competitive fields, women had to fight a rising tide of professionalism.

Professional men hoped both to increase their own status and to preserve traditional divisions of sphere; even during the progressive era, few doors opened more than a crack except in medicine and academic life. Medicine, which had started out with lower status than law or the ministry, rose the fastest. Since 1910, it had made major gains; the medical profession extended its influence, limited its practitioners ("fewer and better doctors" became AMA policy), and shut women out. Foundations poured money into prestigious medical schools, while lesser schools closed. Since prestigious schools kept strict quotas on women entrants and 90 percent of hospitals refused to appoint women interns, the proportion of doctors who were women began to decline—from 6 percent in 1910 to 5 percent in 1920 and 4.4 percent in 1930. And since the profession itself grew smaller, the number of women physicians dropped by a third. Medical rebuff was not caused by feminist decline; it had started when the suffrage movement was at its peak. Still, as Alice Hamilton pointed out in the 1920s, it was easier for women physicians when they could "count on the loyalty" of devoted feminists who would choose a doctor because she was a woman.

While medicine shrank, higher education expanded. In academic life, slower to respond to female presence, women capitalized briefly on progressive gains. Since 1910, the proportion of doctorates earned by women rose—from 10 percent that year to 15.1 percent in 1920 to 15.4 percent in 1930. The proportion of women in college teaching faculties rose too—from 18.9 percent in 1910 to 30.1 percent in 1920 to 32.5 percent in 1930. Clearly, women's advances had been most substantial in the decade 1910–1920, when the feminist movement gained momentum. "I find myself wondering whether our generation was not the only generation of women which ever found itself," wrote Marjorie Nicolson, a college graduate in 1914 and much later Columbia's first tenured woman professor. "We came late enough to escape the self-consciousness and belligerence of the pioneers, to take education and training for granted. We came early enough to take equally for granted professional positions in which we could make full use of our training." Here too the tide began to turn around 1920, when the proportion of women graduate students started to decline, in part a response to universities' tightened quotas. But during the 1920s, when women earned one-third of all graduate degrees, their numbers constantly rose. Significantly, many academic women of the decade made their mark in the behavioral sciences, fields to which progressive era women had been attracted.

Some of these anthropologists, psychologists, and social scientists were linked to pioneers of earlier generations, just as they became involved in the careers of woman scholars of the next one. Social scientist Katherine Bement Davis, whose survey of sexual attitudes was published in the 1920s, had once studied with Marion Talbot at the University of Chicago. During the prewar era she supervised the work of such Chicago graduate students as psychologist Jessie Taft, who became a leading figure in child welfare and social work education. Ruth Benedict began work in anthropology at the New School in 1919 with ethnologist Elsie Clews Parsons, an ally of Margaret Sanger's from the days of the Dodge salon. During the 1920s, as a lecturer at Columbia, Benedict helped inspire a new generation of graduate students, including Margaret Mead. Historian Rosalind Rosenberg has shown that these women scholars were part of a special tradition in social science that began around the 1890s. Encouraged and supported by a coterie of prominent academic men, from John Dewey to Franz Boas, they questioned traditional assumptions about sex differences, stressed the impact of cultural conditioning, and "formulated theories about intelligence, personality development and sex roles that . . . affected the whole course of American social science."

As social scientists, women scholars often saw themselves as participants in two cultures—a male culture of academic research and scientific rigor, and women's culture; as women, indeed, they were often relegated to the very periphery of academic life. But during the 1920s their vocations held great allure. New behavioral scientists often described their choice of field as a way to resolve quandaries about their roles or to understand women's place in society. For psychologist Phyllis Blanchard, a student of G. Stanley Hall, "the necessity of solving my own problems developed into a desire to understand all problems, and I turned to the social sciences." For Ruth Benedict, the discipline itself provided a mode of accommodation to her culture. Dissatisfied with conventional role limitations but unable to discard expected patterns of behavior, Benedict found in anthropology a reconciliation between scientific and humanistic inclinations, a resolution of what she viewed as a male/female dichotomy. Psychologist Lorine Pruette, another Hall student, found a different kind of accommodation through her career. "In general," she wrote, "all my old feministic revolt has been transferred from men to the condition of human existence."

Not all aspiring social scientists saw themselves as feminists. Young anthropologist Zora Neale Hurston, a leading figure in the 1920s Harlem Renaissance, was more involved in black culture than in women's culture. In 1927, as a Boas graduate student at Columbia, she embarked on a field trip to southern Florida to collect black folklore, a project intended to invalidate racial stereotypes. But Hurston's role as a black woman intellectual in the 1920s was atypical. Most young women academics of the decade, whether or not they shared a feminist identity, were informed by a feminist consciousness. Such consciousness was important in the career of Margaret Mead, another Boas student at Columbia. In 1925, she persuaded Boas to support her plans for field work outside North America, despite the objections of prominent men in the field who thought her sex a handicap. "Margaret's mother passed on to her the ideal of women's rights, and in the difficult process of persuading her father to let her go to college she learned who the 'enemy' was," Mead's first husband, anthropologist Luther Cressman, recalled a half-century later. "She had the firm conviction that she could establish and hold her place in the profession with men." A similar conviction inspired other young academic women of Mead's generation. However, like many women seeking careers in competitive fields, they had to confront a new array of problems.

During the 1920s feminist impulses veered from politics toward professional goals, but the loss of a cohesive woman's movement deprived professionals of a united body of support. Professional situations were competitive, not cooperative; individual achievement was more vital than collective action. Aspiring career women were more likely to join professional societies than women's societies, to strive for their own advancement rather than pave the way for others. "As soon as a woman has it for herself," Anna Howard Shaw told Emily Blair, "she will have entered a man's world and cease to fight as a woman for other women." Professional success was also likely to require accommodation more than militancy. "Any weakness is likely to be considered feminine," warned Elizabeth Kemper Adams in a 1921 study of women professional workers. Defending the woman professional, Adams explained that she worked not for profit but out of "intellectual and moral devotion." Still, she could expect to be judged more rigorously than a man and to "breathe an atmosphere of being on trial." In addition, the professional woman of the 1920s often tried to combine career and marriage, a novel, modern goal.

The married career woman was a major New Woman of the 1920s—a shift from the progressive era, when marriage and career had been viewed as mutually exclusive. Since 1910, the proportion of professional women who married had steadily increased—from 12.2 percent in 1910 to 19.3 percent in 1920 to 24.7 percent in 1930. During the 1920s, even the proportion of teachers who married doubled, despite the refusal of most school boards to hire married women. The new trend reflected not only the rapid increase in college-educated women and the rising rate of marriage among them but a shift of goals. The modern young woman as Dorothy Dunbar Bromley explained in her *Harper's* article, "Feminist-New Style," in 1927, believed that "a full life calls for marriage and children as well as a career." Freda Kirchwey, who edited the *Nation's* series on "modern women" claimed that the New Woman of the 1920s was "not altogether satisfied with love, marriage, and a purely domestic career." A Barnard graduate, former suffragist, and active supporter of birth control, Kirchwey enumerated the New Woman's goals. "She wants money of her own. She wants work of her own. She wants some means of self-expression, perhaps, some way of satisfying her personal ambition. But she wants a home, husband, and children, too."

The problem of welding marriage and career emerged as a theme in the *Nation* essays, whose authors, all working professionals, were mainly married—although few had children. "Marriage is too much of a compromise," wrote Sue Shelton White, NWP leader, lawyer, and Democratic politician. "It lops off a woman's life as an individual." But renouncing marriage was also a "lopping off," White wrote. "We choose between the Frying Pan and the Fire." Psychologist Phyllis Blanchard described a long struggle "between my own two greatest needs—the need for love and the need for independence." At first unable to reconcile the two or to abandon her "desire for personal autonomy," she eventually found, in marriage at thirty, both "love and freedom, which once seemed to me such incompatible bedfellows." But the *Nation* essayists' desire for autonomy and their low rate of childbearing did not impress those experts whose critiques were appended to the series of articles. Only Beatrice Hinkle, psychoanalyst and feminist, commended their struggles with "convention and inertia" and felt they signified "the birth of a new woman." Two male critics dissented. One, a prominent neurologist, thought the *Nation's* "modern women" revealed a low "sex-coefficient" and would make poor companions. He also regretted that they were not having five to ten children in the interest of eugenics.

Reconciling marriage and career meant more than pacifying such critics. Another goal was to reshape the home to suit women's needs, along the lines suggested by Charlotte Perkins Gilman. A pioneer attempt had been made in 1915 by Greenwich Village feminist Henrietta Rodman, a participant in the Dodge salon before the war. Rodman planned an apartment house with communal nursery, cooking, laundry, and housework, to free married women for productive work. A decade later, Smith College opened an Institute for Coordination of Women's Interests, directed by Ellen Puffer Howe, another *Nation* essayist. Its purpose was to resolve the "intolerable choice between career and home," to integrate family life with women's "continuous intellectual interest," and to provide models for combining marriage and career—through cooperative nursery, kitchen, laundry, and shopping arrangements. Neither project succeeded; Rodman's building was never built, and the Smith institute lasted only six years. But both were attempts to adjust the home to accommodate women, rather than the reverse.

Some feminists of the 1920s went even further by advocating a readjustment of the workplace, economy, and society. The Smith attempt to "modernize" the home was only a "temporary expedient," wrote Alice Beal Parsons in *Women's Dilemma* (1926). Parsons proposed part-time jobs, payments to mothers for child care, crèches (infant care centers), and day-care centers run by professionals. Suzanne LaFollette, similarly critical of the Smith institute, contended that sexual equality required "profound psychic and material readjustment" so that women could be equal participants in the economy. LaFollette insisted that woman was primarily an individual, not a wife or a mother. She denied "the assumption that marriage is the special concern of woman" or "that marriage and motherhood constitute her normal life and her other interests are extra-normal."

Individualism, as LaFollette defined it, had a vocal, optimistic coterie of support throughout the decade. Psychoanalyst Beatrice Hinkle, ever hopeful, claimed that women were moving toward "individual direction." "They have cast aside the maternal ideal as their goal and are demanding recognition as individuals first and wives and mothers second." The modern young woman, said Dorothy Dunbar Bromley, was no longer "a creature of instinct" but "a full-fledged individual who is capable of molding her own life." But individualism was not only the rallying cry of Bromley's new-style feminist. It was also a facet of the "new morality," the upshot of a long-term shift in sexual attitudes and behavior.

The New Morality

The sexual revolution of the early twentieth century was hardly an overnight coup, sending Victorian values into oblivion; rather, it was an evolutionary change in attitudes and practices that had been building since at least the 1890s. Its hallmarks were a positive view of human sexuality, acceptance of female sexuality, freedom in the discussion of sexual issues, looser moral standards, and new norms of sexual behavior. Shifts in all areas were well under way before the 1920s; some symptoms of change can be traced back to the last third of the nineteenth century. By the pre-World War I period, when Margaret Sanger took "direct action," middle-class mores were in transition. The flapper had made her first appearance; dance crazes caught popular attention; the press mentioned sexual issues such as venereal disease and prostitution; and readers besieged popular columnists with questions about the behavior of well-bred daughters. Beatrice Fairfax responded, with regret, that "Making love lightly, boldly, and promiscuously seems to be part of our social structure." ("Making love," in this context, meant some form of affectionate display, or what came to be labeled petting.) Dorothy Dix observed in 1913 that "the social position of women has been revolutionized since mother was a girl."

But changing sexual attitudes had their greatest impact in the 1920s. Before the war, liberated behavior, notably among young women, was regarded as a hazard. In the 1920s, while still controversial, the same behavior became a given rather than an omen. In the prewar era, sexual emancipation had had a narrow base of urban sophisticates. In the 1920s, it became a national concern, dividing the generations in small-town America as well as in the metropolis. In the prewar era, sexual revolutionaries such as Margaret Sanger and her Greenwich Village cohort were usually affiliated with the left. Their sexual rebellion was fueled by political fervor and linked to rejection of all middle-class values. After World War I, the new mood of sexual emancipation, like the birth-control campaign, was severed from its radical origins and became itself a middle-class attribute. During the 1920s, the new morality received a label. Defended by enthusiasts, celebrated in the media, and immortalized by youth, it was absorbed into popular culture.

The ideology of sexual revolution arrived full force in the prewar era, with the writings of Havelock Ellis, Ellen Key, and Freud; but it had at that time a limited audience, such as the radical New York vanguard. By the 1920s, "sexual enthusiasm," once a left-wing perquisite, had permeated the mainstream. Freud stressed the centrality of sex in human experience; his popularizers in the 1920s stressed the hazards of sexual repression. The "id" and "libido" became working concepts in common lingo. Key advocated free sexual expression for women, including "free motherhood" (without marriage). "The most sacred thing in life is individual desire," she wrote, "with special emphasis on sex-desire." Key contended, too, that love and motherhood were spheres for which women were best equipped; every woman should set aside a decade for having three or four children. Ellis's philosophy, which began arriving in the early 1900s, was widely popularized through Margaret Sanger's instigation in the 1920s. Ellis had long been a herald of female sexuality. In 1905, he had proclaimed that the "sexual impulse in women" existed apart from the "reproductive instinct." Presenting sexuality as ennobling, not destructive, and "restraint" as more dangerous than "excess," Ellis had urged a new morality based on greater freedom and self-expression.

During the 1920s, the ideology of sexual emancipation helped to sweep away old rules and introduce new ones. Now, sex was central to life, repression damaging to health and psyche. Lending support to changes in attitudes and practices already under way, the new morality legitimized a role reversal for women. Clearly, women's roles had undergone and were undergoing the most change. Men had always been assumed to have sexual natures, even if "restraint" had once been thought preferable to "indulgence." But the new morality proclaimed equality of desire. Discarding purity for sexuality, women could now claim a facet of male privilege. "The myth of the pure woman is almost at an end," one enthusiast, V. F. Calverton, proclaimed in 1928. "Women's demands for equal rights have extended to the sexual sphere as well as the social." Equal rights in the sexual sphere remained as elusive as they were undefinable. Nonetheless, there were two important, overlapping types of sexual revolution taking place at various points after 1910, both based on shifting attitudes toward female sexuality.

One was a sexual revolution within middle-class marriage. Indeed, middle-class married women were the unsung sexual revolutionaries of the early twentieth century. This gradual revolution had long-term repercussions, starting in the 1920s when marriage was redefined as a sexual institution. The other sexual revolution was the new behavior of "youth," especially of middle-class daughters. The revolution of youth took the form of dramatically revamped courtship customs, a modest but significant increase in premarital affairs, and a far larger increase in premarital sexual contact. Youthful rebellion had repercussions on the older generation, first, because it was widely publicized (as the revolution within marriage was not) and second, because youth was brief, and the young, single generation that seemed to dominate the decade quickly became an older, married one.

A major symptom of change in the 1920s was that middle-class women adopted a positive view of sexuality, though this was a change that had been in progress over the first two decades of the century. Its impact was revealed at the end of the decade when Katherine Bement Davis published her pioneer sexual survey. Carried out in 1918, Davis's survey was based on the responses of 2,200 middle-class women, married and unmarried, mainly college graduates, whose names had been taken from women's club membership rolls and alumnae files—indeed, it was quite an elite, upper-crust sample. Undertaken to further the cause of social hygiene and the social purity movement, the survey ultimately served another purpose: to document the importance of sexual experience in women's lives. The Davis survey actually caught women at an important *pre-*1920s junction in the shift of sexual attitudes and practices. Over half of the unmarried women, for instance, and three out of ten of the married women, had intense emotional relationships with women. One out of five of the entire sample had homosexual experiences, though few had premarital heterosexual relations. This aspect of the survey reflected the old morality. The married women Davis surveyed, however, most of whom used contraceptives, described sexual relations in positive, receptive terms like those Margaret Sanger used—"as an expression of love," "because it is a natural, normal relation," "for pleasure, satisfaction, development," "for mental and physical health." Since the average respondent was born around 1880, the Davis survey suggested that changes in middle-class women's attitudes toward sexual experience were well under way before the 1920s. Moreover, Davis was forced to conclude (contrary to her expectations) that frequency of intercourse could not be correlated with poor health or sterility, thereby supporting the sexual revolution within marriage.

Katherine Bement Davis's study, the first national survey of its type and the most comprehensive until the Kinsey report, was significant in another way, too. Earlier sexual surveys were usually carried out among prostitutes and delinquents to analyze "deviance." Davis was herself trained in such research. Only in the 1920s did researchers turn their attention to what was "normal." While Davis was interested in all facets of female sexual life, as well as in women's attitudes toward sexual experience (her respondents provided reams of commentary), most researchers were bent on tabulating loss of purity. Rising rates of (middle-class) premarital and extramarital intercourse were seen as the hallmark of sexual revolution, and surveys and studies of the 1920s and 1930s pointed to the decade after 1910 as a watershed of moral change. Later, using broader samples that more accurately measured the repercussions of changing mores (beyond the urban middle-class), Kinsey found that twice as many women born after 1900 had premarital experience as those born before 1900, putting the brunt of change in the 1920s. The gist of the research, during the 1920s and after, was that around the time suffrage was won, traditional morality had started to crack. Using premarital sex as a touchstone, male and female "morals" were starting to become more alike. The "single standard" of morality had materialized, said Beatrice Hinkle, and it was "nearer the standard associated with men."

The death of the double standard was of course wildly exaggerated. But even shifts toward a single standard were often bewildering, especially to women who had grown up with the old morality. "We were reared, educated, and married for one sort of life, and precipitated before we had a chance to get our bearings into another," Frances Woodward Prentiss wrote in *Scribners.* "Perhaps we cannot take sex as lightly as the young nor as calmly as the old." Nor were women who defended the new morality unaware of its liabilities. "Far more will be expected of sex when it is left free to express itself than under any repressive system," Elsie Clews Parsons had predicted in 1914. The interest of the 1920s, however, was neither in the reaction of women past youth nor in the rising expectations Parsons anticipated. Rather, it was in the newly emancipated young, especially young women, who seemed to be the prime movers in moral change.

To some observers, the sexual emancipation of young women seemed linked to economic independence. "In the great cities . . . where women can control their own purse strings, many of them are able to drift into casual or steady relationships which may or may not end in marriage," Alyse Gregory wrote in *Current History* in 1923. The self-supporting young woman "has her own salary at the end of the month and asks no other recompense from her lover but his love and companionship." Other observers agreed that once young women supported themselves, they were likely to develop behavior patterns more like those of men. The liberation of the young working woman had been in progress in urban areas for several decades. During the 1920s, self-consciously "modern" middle-class women began to adopt the life-style developed by working-class women around the turn of the century. But neither economic independence nor the emancipation of city life were seen as the main spurs of the new morality of the 1920s. "Youth" as a whole, even youth supported by their parents, seemed to be shifting moral gears, as reflected in endless articles with such titles as "These Wild Young People" and "The Uprising of Youth."

The phenomenon evoked alarm, concern, and, among its best-known analysts, acclaim. Enthusiasts were notably middle-aged men. One, for example, was Denver judge Ben Lindsey, who had helped Margaret Sanger in 1916 by providing entrée to a middle-class audience. Lindsey, now fifty-four, defended *The Revolt of Modern Youth* in 1925. Youth of the decade had been transformed, Lindsey wrote, by the modern environment—by its economy and culture, by science and technology; by the car, movies, and radio; and by the very speed of change. The world of the young was so different from that of their parents that old morals and standards had no significance. "Youth has always been rebellious; youth has always shocked the older generation," Lindsey said. "But this is different. It has the whole weight and momentum of a new scientific and economic order behind it. . . . These boys and girls can do what boys and girls were never able to do in the past." Lindsey was referring mainly to "tentative excursions into sex experience" and "sexual liberties," although he pegged the premarital sexual intercourse rate between 15 and 20 percent. Emancipated behavior, he felt, was preferable to outworn values, "the ragtag and bobtail of adult puritanism." Especially commendable was the modern young woman, "who makes her own living, votes, holds her own in competition with men [and] is capable of doing things her mother couldn't come within sight of." To defenders of the new morality, suffrage, self-support, self-assertion, and sexual emancipation were linked together in a modern package.

   To traditionalists, the rebellion of youth was a danger signal more than a cause for acclaim, and on this issue, feminists aligned with the traditionalists. Veterans of the last generation such as Jane Addams objected to the "astounding emphasis upon sex," and Charlotte Perkins Gilman opened fire on "selfish and fruitless indulgence." "It is sickening to see so many of the newly freed abusing that freedom in a mere imitation of masculine weakness and vice," she wrote in *Century Magazine* in 1923. Gilman was repelled by young women who gave way to "appetite and impulse," who adopted "a coarseness and looseness in speech, dress, manners, and habits of life," and who, instead of preparing for motherhood, were "enjoying preliminaries" or even "mastering birth control and acquiring experience." Clearly, progressive era feminism and sexual emancipation did not necessarily lead in the same direction; rather, they seemed to be at cross-purposes. Gilman was making a political as well as a personal critique. As historian Linda Gordon points out, feminist suspicions of sexual permissiveness were well-founded. Assertion of female sexuality did not of itself raise woman's status, nor did the new legitimacy of "indulgence" ensure women freedom, independence, or power. Rather, women had lost bargaining power, or the right of refusal, a crucial weapon in nineteenth-century sexual politics.

   Traditionalists, however, including the older generation of feminists, lost ground in the 1920s. Not only did the new morality enjoy extensive publicity, but its very emblem was the young woman, who until then was customarily one of society's most powerless and least influential members. Now, significantly, she was cast in the role of cultural symbol. From the outset, she was distinguished by her anonymity. "This nameless one, the American flapper," H. L. Mencken had labeled her in 1915. Urban and upper middle class, the prewar flapper had had a superficial sophistication. She had "forgotten how to simper," Mencken wrote. "She seldom blushes; it is impossible to shock her." She opposed the double standard, favored a law prohibiting it, and planned to read Havelock Ellis over the summer. Columnist Dorothy Dix confirmed that the prewar flapper was "a girl in good position in society" and defined her by her energy, spunk, and sportive esprit. She could "play golf all day, drive a car, offer first aid, and . . . is in no more danger of swooning than a man would be." Before the war, there was a certain looseness in flapper definition. After, the role became a mold, a style, a stereotype. "The flapper of fiction, plays, movies, and newspapers," said the *New*

Since the late nineteenth century, carnivals and mass circulation newspapers had used beauty contests as publicity devices, but the formal beach beauty contest came to characterize the 1920s. Like the winner and runners-up in this California contest in 1920, contestants were valued for their natural, unsophisticated qualities. They also personified the spirit of exhibitionism, competition, and novelty so prized in the flapper. Starting in 1921, the Miss America contest in Atlantic City made the beauty contest a national ritual. *(UPI/Bettmann)*

Republic in 1922, "offers a vivid pattern of modern young life and creates a certain bravado . . . the necessity for living up to current opinion."

The flapper of the 1920s, still distinguished by youth and class, was at once "boyish" and provocative. In dress, habits, and mannerisms, she assumed a dual role. On the one hand, she was a temptress, an aspect emphasized in movie stars who exuded sexual power and appeal, whether Gloria Swanson's upper-class heroines or Clara Bow's lingerie salesgirl in *It* (1927). On the other hand, the 1920s flapper was a pal and a sport, a challenger and competitor. This facet was revealed in other heroines of the decade such as Amelia Earhart and Gertrude Eberle, who broke boundaries and set records. In both cases, the flapper was characterized by assertion and defiance—of rules, traditions, and conventions, although defiance itself became a convention. Whether winning contests or smoking in public, she claimed privileges reserved for men, including the privilege of sexuality. According to the tabloids, she might even assume the role of sexual aggressor, as demonstrated by sixteen-year-old Peaches Browning, who ensnared her millionaire sugar daddy. The heroine of *Flaming Youth* (1923), a sensational best-seller soon made into a movie, was equally aggressive. Willful and capricious, this "dangerously inflammable" eighteen-year-old seduces a friend of the family, a married man of forty, who at last discards his wife to reward her efforts—with marriage. A new type of heroine, the fictional flapper had novel tactics but traditional goals.

The flapper was a vital economic symbol too. She was defined by the goods and services she was able to buy, whether silk stockings, bobbed hair, jazz records, or rouge compacts. Her attributes symbolized, at once, freedom, availability, and purchasing power. Clothes, the great liberator of the decade, were her major hallmark. While the styles of the 1890s had enabled women to ride bicycles and work in offices, the flapper's clothes advertised both equality and sexuality. During the 1920s, the ready-made women's clothing industry began to surpass "cloakmaking" as the mainstay of the garment trade. The flapper's cigarette was also a loaded symbol. It proclaimed equality with men, who conventionally smoked in public, while conveying an aura of suggestion and bravado. Between 1918 and 1928, production of cigarettes more than doubled. By the end of the decade, cigarette ads showed women, sometimes movie starlets, smoking or having their cigarettes lit by men. Cosmetics were another suggestive part of the flapper's equipment. A generation earlier, makeup was associated mainly with prostitutes. It now conveyed the intent to be provocative. By 1929, the flapper could choose from a grand array of cosmetics, another multimillion-dollar business. Temptress and challenger, she was also a consumer, an omnipresent advertisement for the clothing, tobacco, and beauty products industries.

Finally, the flapper was a great competitor. Her styles and affectations represented not only new freedoms—to wear, to do, to buy—but also new criteria for success. "Youth in this day and age," wrote sociologist Ernest Burgess, "are rated in terms of sex appeal," and the flapper sought a high score. Sometimes she competed with men, though only in a pallish, sportive, companionate way. More often, flappers competed with one another, and not only in dance contests and beauty pageants. Even Dorothy Dunbar Bromley's "feminist—new style" did not identify with other women or profess any "loyalty to women en masse." Rather, she was "a good dresser, a good sport, a good pal," who dealt with men on a basis of "frank comradeship." Dropping "sex-antagonism," she also discarded older traditions of female friendship, fellowship, and association. Once sexual expression was viewed as central to life, opportunities for same-sex relationships among women decreased, a change that did not escape notice. During the 1920s, men and women, husbands and wives, became "more than before . . . friends," wrote Floyd Dell, editor of the *Masses,* the vanguard magazine read by the Sangers' radical friends in the prewar era. "At the same time the intensity of friendship between people of the same sex seems to be diminishing." As romance was eroticized, the intense friendships between women that had characterized the Victorian era appeared to fade.

What, in fact, happened to same-sex relationships in the 1920s? Again, the currents of change flowed both ways, for as historian Lillian Faderman points out, elements of liberation and repression coexisted. New York sophisticates, for instance, attended drag balls as spectators; Greenwich Village bohemians, who embraced the unconventional, defended homosexuality and experimented with bisexuality; a working-class lesbian subculture began to evolve in big cities. Concurrently, among middle-class Americans, the pendulum swung in another direction. As sex became more visible and legitimate, same-sex relationships became less so. Once love between women was *seen* as sexual, such relationships no longer seemed harmless, but rather a hazard—a barrier to heterosexual happiness. With its promise of sexual equality, the new morality erased a facet of women's culture.

The young woman growing up in the 1920s was more likely to be influenced by national culture, by the media, and by her peers. Two particular influences, the campus and the movies, helped her to fuse the new morality with traditional roles.

"Pals" and "Partners"

During the 1920s, for the first time, over half of young people were enrolled in some sort of educational institution. The numbers of high school and college students surged upward. By 1930, over half of Americans of high school age attended high school, 12 percent of the college-aged went to colleges and universities, and many others were at "junior colleges" and normal schools. Although the proportion of women in the college population declined slightly during the decade, from a high of 47.3 percent in 1920 to 43.7 percent in 1930, women flocked to college at almost the same rate as men. During the 1920s, the pacesetting college woman was not the student at an elite woman's college, as had been the case in the 1880s and 1890s, but the coed at a large state college or university. In the college setting, where the authority of peers replaced that once held by parents and community, her role was shaped by the campus itself.

The campus context, as historian Paula Fass explains, provided "informal access" between the sexes. Such access promoted a new sense of equality and also encouraged "pronounced attention to sexual attractiveness." The coed of the 1920s, a product of the campus context, assumed the roles of "pal" and "partner," both defined in terms of her relationship to men. Her dual role rested on the assumption that equality meant assuming the privileges and mannerisms once monopolized by men. It carried an aura of experimentation and innovation, adventure and bravado. And it was gallantly defended by the men on campus, especially in the pages of college newspapers (men tended to dominate extracurricular activities while women students engineered social events). "The flapper is the girl who is responsible for the advancement of women's condition in the world," announced an Illinois editor in 1922, citing her "independent" and "pally" qualities. "The weak, retiring 'clinging' variety of woman really does nothing but cling." The coed was not inferior, claimed an Ohio editor, and therefore did not need special rules and regulations, "as if she were feeble-minded or insane." But there were new rules and regulations on campus, determined by the students themselves. The social rites and rituals that began in the 1920s were extremely important for the coed, whose marital future might well be decided in the campus arena (a "glorified playground" one educator

Gender roles were of prime concern to coeds of the 1920s. Sorority sisters at the University of Kansas surround the "Most Perfect Man," a title given annually to the coed judged most capable of "dressing and acting like a gentleman." *(Bettmann)*

called it). Moreover, college students were innovators and pacesetters. Their customs and manners affected the roles of women attending single-sex colleges, primarily on weekends, when they came in contact with men. Simultaneously, collegiate manners spread to students in high school, and thereby became staples of national youth culture.

"Dating" was a major innovation. Going out on dates was a marked change from the calls paid at home by suitors of an earlier generation, and suggested a more assertive, independent role for middle-class daughters; adult supervision had been banished. The main architects of the dating system, historian John Modell contends, were middle-class girls. They had more to gain, he suggests, because the new version of the double standard that dating put in place "was considerably less restrictive than the one it replaced." On the other hand, historian Beth Bailey points out, dating shifted power *from* women *to* men; courtship no longer took place in the home, a female domain, but in the world beyond. The dating phenomenon clearly invites varied interpretations. Still, dating had indisputable influence on women's roles. It provided practice in the paired activities that would later be a way of life—basic training in the roles of "pal" and "partner." Also, the coed who went out on dates four nights a week had less opportunity for the single-sex fellowship of an earlier day. The sense of sisterhood shared by Jane Addams's class at Rockford was now replaced by competition for dates. By the mid-1920s, Bailey explains, dating had almost completely replaced the system of "calling," and in so doing, had transformed American courtship. The rite of dating was abetted by the automobile, which replaced the front porch—although it was hardly a "house of prostitution on wheels," as labeled by a juvenile court judge in Middletown (Muncie, Indiana, whose residents were studied in the 1920s by sociologists Helen and Robert Lynd). Still, the car served as a vehicle of liberty, both for campus couples already removed from the authority of home and for small-town couples who, the Lynds reported, could now drive off to the next town.

The custom of dating contributed to a second innovation in social rituals—"petting," another warm-up for future roles. Like dating, petting was a significant change but not a total rejection of custom and convention. It was attached to the old framework of courtship, since marriage was still the ultimate goal. In a survey of young women's attitudes, Phyllis Blanchard and Carolyn Manasses reported that their subjects viewed petting as "an end in itself . . . a substitute for more advanced sexual activity." Moreover, campus surveys suggested, students' attitudes had become far more liberal than their practices. The "wild and reckless and radical" aspect of youth was exaggerated, a campus editor at Duke University observed in 1927, "a lot of lashing and lather on the surface with miles of unmoved depths below."

But early training in paired relationships, Blanchard and Manasses suggested, could be an advantage. "The girl who makes use of the new opportunity for freedom is likely to find her experiences have been wholesome," they wrote in 1931. "She may be better prepared for marriage by her playful activities than if she had just clung to a passive role of waiting for marriage before giving an expression to sex impulses." Like campus editors, the surveyors contrasted the "active" role of the 1920s girl with the "passive" role of her grandmother. They also added that in young men's views, purity was not as important in a potential wife as were compatible qualities, such as "congenial tastes" and "ability to take an interest in the husband's work." Margaret Sanger, however, in her marriage manual of 1926, urged premarital purity for women and sexual "experience" for men (some of her colleagues found the book hypocritical). Men did not value an easy conquest, Sanger warned, and preferred women who were "playfully elusive."

The coed's preparation for her future included not only social but extra-curricular activities. These centered around the sorority—a popular college institution of the 1920s modeled on the fraternity, which had appeared in the mid-nineteenth century. The first sororities, founded in the late nineteenth century, had served a special function at coeducational schools by providing a separate space for women students as well as practice in the types of social service work appropriate for middle-class women. During the 1920s, fraternities and sororities served to impose social order on a rapidly expanding, heterogeneous college population. Sororities proliferated so rapidly that most big coed colleges had about fifteen or twenty, and they radiated down to the high school level, where they affected an even larger student population. For the coed of the 1920s, historian Sheila Rothman points out, the sorority replaced the social service club and college suffrage league of the last generation. It also served a different purpose than its nineteenth-century antecedent. An exclusionary institution, the sorority now fostered a competitive spirit more than a sororal one. The qualities it favored for admission were the same as those appreciated by men in dating relationships: attractiveness, amiability, and compatibility. By cultivating such attributes, and by setting standards on appearance, social behavior, and even sexual conduct, the sorority promoted the role of "pal" and "partner."

Finally, the college itself also took a hand in preparing women students for future roles. As college populations grew, luring thousands of middle-class students who would not have been there a decade earlier, business and home economics provided new arenas for male and female specialization. During the 1920s, men and women were educated together in larger numbers, but they were expected to follow different paths after graduation. Home economics, which pervaded both high school and college curriculums, was financed at state colleges and universities by the federal Smith-Lever Act of 1914, a follow-up to the Civil War Morrill Act. Unlike women's schools of the 1890s, the colleges now produced housewives rather than moral leaders, and the trend influenced women's colleges too. At Vassar, for instance, after 1925, students were exposed to the new interdisciplinary School of Euthenics, devoted to the development and care of the family. Here again, there was a contrast with the previous generation. When Marion Talbot began her department of "sanitary science" at the University of Chicago in the 1890s, the curriculum included physics, chemistry, physiology, political science, and modern languages. The goal was to prepare experts in modern urban life. But the new school at Vassar carried such courses as "Husband and Wife," "Motherhood," and "The Family as an Economic Unit." Like the expanding home economics programs in state colleges, it fostered accommodation to traditional roles.

While campus activities, curricular and extracurricular, shaped women's goals, the new era of mass communications also had an influence. A major influence, setting standards and ideals, molding dreams and fantasies, was the movies. Few could attend Vassar's School of Euthenics, but the impact of the screen was universal, affecting the values of small-town girl and housewife as well as college student. By the end of the 1920s, 115 million Americans each week were exposed to the wiles of a new gallery of movie heroines. Since 1910, the innocence and purity of Mary Pickford had been succeeded by Theda Bara's dangerous vamp, who in turn gave way to such sex symbols as Clara Bow, the "slam-bang kid" of 1927, full of vitality and appeal. Idols were not all the screen offered to women growing up in the 1920s. Movies gave graphic lessons in social behavior. They taught how to look, talk, and behave, and how to compete in the marital marketplace. As one college woman observed, the movies provided "a liberal education in the art of making love."

Movies of the decade, historian Mary P. Ryan points out, conveyed advice on sexual tactics. Film heroines, significantly, followed Margaret Sanger's advice about elusiveness and preserved their virginity until marriage, whatever their allure, dazzle, and sex appeal. Screen women also knew where to be—in places where the sexes were in close proximity. And they knew how to assert themselves, since captivating a man was no longer a passive proposition. Alarmingly, considerable animosity arose between the sexes on screen; plot construction often made heroes and heroines adversaries. But women in the movies had even more animosity toward one another. Since relations with men were central, female friendships were casual and insubstantial; interchanges between women tended to be snide. Sexual conquest, the movies suggested, was a competitive vocation—whether for the well-off heroine in furs, jewels, and the latest styles or for the humble white-collar worker, the salesgirl or secretary who escaped her job (so much for economic independence) by finding a man. The arch success was that of the gold digger, like Anita Loos's Lorelei Lee, who captured the richest bachelor in America. With pluck, daring, and know-how, a girl might marry a millionaire.

At the same time, the movies offered lessons in consumption. They showed what merchandise to buy, from makeup and lingerie to bathtubs and furniture. Clothes, clearly, were the screen star's forte. In a 1920 film, Gloria Swanson retained her husband's affection by buying an exotic flapper wardrobe and revamping her image. Movies also revealed the latest in household technology and home decor. They enabled the viewer, as one woman wrote to a fan magazine, "to observe the better way of living." "Here [at the movies]" wrote another, "I learn what to wear, how to dress, how a refined home should look." A third fan revealed that she returned from the theater and rearranged her home "like I have seen at the movies." The woman of Chicago's nineteenth ward in 1900 might have learned "right living" from the settlement, but her daughter saw it on the screen. And like the campus, the movies steered a young woman toward traditional goals—man, marriage, and domestic life.

After the turn of the century, more women married and they married younger. Even women college graduates, by the 1920s, were wed at near the rate of the general female population. This was not a sudden shift but one that had been building, with a turning point around 1910. In the latter part of the nineteenth century, about half the graduates of women's colleges had remained single (coeds were always more likely to marry). By the 1920s, the pattern had changed. Of those who graduated between 1919 and 1923, 80 percent married. In 1923, a survey of Vassar graduates revealed that 90 percent wanted to marry, and an even higher percentage shared that ambition in other schools surveyed.

Younger women were similarly inclined, especially as the decade wore on. When Lorine Pruette surveyed the ambitions of teenage girls in the early 1920s, the results were mixed. Of her sample of young women aged between fifteen and seventeen, 35 percent wanted careers and were willing to give up marriage and family for them. Pruette found their goals unrealistic since they tended to envision glamorous jobs. Even more teenagers wanted to combine career and marriage, perhaps an equally unrealistic goal. By the end of the decade, Blanchard and Manasses found that among young women eighteen to twenty-six years old, few were willing to forgo marriage for a career. Their survey revealed that young women of the 1920s, at least those in their middle-class sample, had fused liberal attitudes with traditional goals. Almost all favored divorce, for instance, if marriage failed; and over half expected marriage to provide sexual satisfaction even more than economic security. Most important, young women of the 1920s had high expectations tinged with egalitarian hopes. They envisioned marriage as "a perfect consummation of both personalities that would involve all phases of mutual living."

Companions and Consumers

During the prewar decade, radical spirits proposed all sorts of marriage reform. In the Greenwich Village enclave the Sangers had joined, matrimony was often rejected, along with other middle-class values. Like Margaret Sanger, Dodge salon members were influenced by the sexual radicals whose books they read. Havelock Ellis contended that the "artificial restraints of marriage" should be replaced by "natural monogamy." Ellen Key, whose tributes to Havelock Ellis were published in the *Birth Control Review*, recommended "free motherhood." Edith Ellis, during her American tour of 1914, explained the virtues of "semi-detached" marriage, like her own; and Margaret Sanger adopted this pattern in her second marriage, to Noah Slee. The 1920s were not without innovative ideas either. In 1927, Judge Lindsey proposed a form of trial marriage, based on contraception. "Companionate marriage" could be easily dissolved at the initiative of either spouse if no children had been born. But marriage was neither discarded nor legally reformed during the 1920s, along Lindsey's lines or any other. Rather, it was redefined.

The new ideal of marriage in the 1920s was a romantic-sexual union, with a primary focus on the relation between husband and wife rather than on the family as a unit. The role of the wife was that of sexual partner and agreeable companion, an extension of the qualities valued in dating relationships. The new ideal of marriage was always described in egalitarian terms—compatibility, reciprocity, and mutuality—that reflected women's raised expectations. The New Woman of the 1920s expected more of marriage, Dorothy Dunbar Bromley wrote in 1927. She wanted to be satisfied in her role "as a lover and companion" and expected *more freedom and honesty within the marriage.*" Elsie Clews Parsons confirmed that women demanded "more of marriage than in the days when they had little to expect but marriage." Young middle-class women, according to Blanchard and Manasses, expected to attain through marriage "a fuller and richer life." They envisioned "sharing joys and sorrows with a mate who will be not merely a protector and provider but an all round companion." Companionate qualities were now defined by experts—sociologists, psychologists, psychiatrists, and physicians. Their views appeared in college texts, marriage manuals, advice columns, and mass-circulation magazines. Reflecting changes that had already occurred, at least within the middle class, descriptions of marriage now combined egalitarian hopes with a new set of prescriptions.

Sexuality was primary to companionate marriage of the 1920s. Sociology texts explained that women were sexual beings and that marriage was both a romantic and sexual institution. Ernest Burgess declared that the "highest personal happiness comes from marriage based on romantic love." Ernest Groves and William Ogburn, in their textbook on marriage and the family, confirmed that modern matrimony was a "fellowship of love." Birth control advocates added their own message to the marriage literature. Physician Ira Wile, who had begun aiding Margaret Sanger before the war, posited a new criterion for the success of marriage: the sexual satisfaction of the partners. In a text on the family in the early 1930s, sociologist and birth control advocate Joseph K. Folsom contended that sex served to "intensify, beautify, and sanctify love." During the 1920s, proponents of birth control also began to enter the marriage manual market. One of the first was Margaret Sanger, who published an advice book in 1926. Her manual, *Happiness in Marriage*, revealed that marital sex was elevating, romantic, and pivotal. Both partners must realize "the importance of complete fulfillment of love through the expression of sex," Sanger wrote. "Sex expression, rightly understood, is the consummation of love, its completion and consecration."

Although the literature usually presented sexual-romantic marriage as a medley of passion, friendship, and equality, the role of "companion" assumed the same ambivalence it had had in the late eighteenth century. This became clear in the popular press, where companionship, realistically, involved unequal obligations. The responsibility of amiable companionship fell on the wife, who had to keep romance and friendship alive. From metropolis to Middletown, women received the same message: to "keep the thrill in marriage," wives had to maintain a high level of sex appeal. They also had to "keep up"—their appearance, interests, and contacts. The successful wife was no longer primarily industrious or thrifty; nor did she have to make lists of birthdays and clothes items, or scour the home for germ-laden articles. Rather, she had to be able to propose enjoyable joint activities, and she had to be attractive, agreeable, and available. Such goals were not achieved without effort. Even the birth of a child could imperil a marriage. It could drain a woman's energy, make her less interesting, and sabotage sexual mutuality. (The white fertility rate, which had steadily declined since 1800, took a precipitous plunge in the 1920s.) Other women were also a hazard. The married woman needed survival tactics to meet the competition—whether from the next generation of flirts and flappers, with access to offices and husbands; from family friends, as in *Flaming Youth;* or from married peers. Almost 300 movies in the 1920s dealt with the theme of infidelity, and their lessons were obvious. The companionate wife would have to work at it.

Companionate marriage took another toll too, belying the egalitarian rhetoric used to describe it. As Suzanne LaFollette explained in *Concerning Women,* marriage was still a "state" for men, but for women it was a "vocation," a calling. The domestic dictum of the 1920s, contrary to the aspirations of the "feminist—new style," was that marriage was a woman's primary role. Work or career, if she had any, would be confined to the interval, if there was one, between school and marriage. This axiom had a new corollary. Now that women were imbued with sexual natures, marriage alone could satisfy all needs; outside activities were secondary, if not perilous, to the health of the union. Women had to be willing, as was one Vassar student in a survey of goals, "to pay whatever price the companionship costs." Surveys among college students clearly reflected division of opinion over what companionate marriage meant. One issue of contention was whether wives should work, even in the early (childless) years of marriage. Men rejected the idea, women supported it. The "abyss of disagreement," as one researcher called it, extended to decision making within marriage. Male students expected their future wives to contribute only to certain types of decisions, those affecting "the family as a whole," while women nurtured more egalitarian expectations. But equality and companionship were not necessarily compatible. Sexual-romantic marriage, according to the surveys, seemed most viable if the wife lacked individual goals or forceful opinions. Companionate potential could best be realized if she was willing to assume a subordinate role, and preferably a domestic one.

The lure of domesticity emerged in the press, especially in such mass-circulation magazines as the *Ladies Home Journal* and *McCalls*. Since 1889, editor Edward Bok had steered the *Journal*, which led the field, to unparalleled success. Sometimes adopting a muckraker role, as in its campaigns against adulterated food and venereal disease, the *Journal* maintained a conservative stance. After opposing woman suffrage, it began the 1920s by condemning jazz and all it represented ("a bolshevik element of license"). In 1923, Bok revealed in his autobiography that he neither liked women nor understood them; nor had he any wish to. Nonetheless, the *Journal* and its competitors understood what women at home liked to read. By the end of the decade, the magazines articulated what historian William H. Chafe calls "an elaborate ideology in favor of home and marriage." The *Journal*, for instance, urged a "return" to femininity and found homemaking an "adventure." Positing the fulfilled homemaker against the unfeminine, sex-deprived career woman, women's magazines urged their readers to renounce careers and strive for "an executive position in the home."

A major part of this position was as purchaser. "Where income permits," wrote Elsie Clews Parsons, "the wife continues to be the consumer." Since 1910 the magazines women read had become heavy with ads for devices that would save time and energy—for cleaners, polishers, refrigerators, sewing machines, washing machines, stoves—and products such as canned soup that would liberate wives from "constant drudgery." During the 1920s, the volume of advertising doubled, the range of household products increased, and the electric appliance industry boomed. Between 1921 and 1929, the total output of electrical goods tripled in value. The Lynds reported from Middletown that household appliances had invaded middle-class homes and that the physical labor of housework had decreased, although rising standards kept housewives just as busy. (Poorer families also invested in household improvements—such as linoleum and running water.) Electrical companies urged women to give up sweeping, buy a vacuum cleaner, and "delegate to electricity all that electricity can do." New products, such as electric toasters and irons, were necessary to run a successful home, keep up with the social whirl, and remain attractive enough to retain a man's interest. "Time for Youth and Beauty! Time for Books and Plays!" a Middletown laundry advertised. Shopping could even be an enjoyable companionate activity. The cover of the Sears Roebuck catalog of 1927 depicted an attractive, well-dressed young couple, intertwined on a settee, making mail-order selections. While the wife takes the lead in pointing out items, the attentive, affectionate husband looks on, engrossed. Modernity was translated into romance, home, and consumption.

The final message received by the middle-class wife of the 1920s was the need for adjustment. Women's magazines advised her not to reject femininity but to enjoy it, to approach domesticity with a positive outlook. Their message

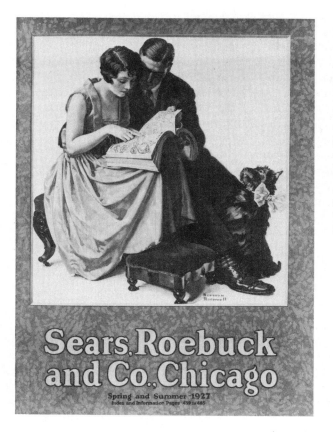

The Sears-Roebuck catalog cover of 1927, by Norman Rockwell, promoted both the joy of consumerism and the ideal of romantic marriage. The modern, companionate, middle-class couple is absorbed in a future of prospective purchases. The leading illustrator of the *Saturday Evening Post* since 1916, Rockwell was able to capture the way a large audience of Americans wish to see themselves. *(Sears Roebuck and Company)*

became more forceful as the decade wore on, since clearly it had opposition. Throughout the 1920s, articulate feminists waged a counterattack. Suzanne LaFollette, for instance, assaulted the consumer mentality. Influenced by advertising, leisure, and luxury, she claimed, women were living "without ideas, without ideals." Alice Beal Parsons contended that Havelock Ellis had pointed the way to "limitations" not liberation. Sex was not a panacea, she insisted; productive work was preferable to "getting everything out of some man that one can." Beatrice Hinkle praised the development of women "as individuals, in contradistinction to the collective destiny that has exclusively governed their lives." By 1931, Lorine Pruette, a consistent critic, sounded a note of desperation. Most women, she wrote, led "contingent lives." They preferred "to work through another person and to find their own joys and compensation in the success of another. This is not so self-sacrificing; generally, it appears to be the easier way."

Some psychological advisers of the 1920s also took issue with the glorification of domesticity in the popular press. The "nervous housewife," wrote Abraham Myerson, a prominent neurologist, suffered from an increasing desire "for a more varied life than that afforded . . . by a life of housework." Indeed, said

Myerson, much female neurotic behavior seemed to be connected to isolation within the home. To career-minded feminists, the solution lay in employment, aspiration, and individualism. To Myerson, the cure was "adjustment . . . fortitude . . . patience . . . fidelity to duty," and community activities. Still, he identified a real discrepancy: The "modern" housewife played a premodern role. But this was a minority view. Freudianism, parceled out into popular advice, had a double-barreled message for women of the 1920s. One part was that sexual repression was harmful. The other was that it was healthy to adjust to familial roles and domestic vocations.

By providing the latest in science, psychological advisers supported the message of advertisers who displayed the latest in technology. Modern women were to find fulfillment in traditional roles, now enlivened by a sexual dimension. Eschewing maladjustment and neurosis, aspiration and ambition, they were to seek satisfaction in romance, marriage, and sexual expression.

Needless to say, it was another type of technology, contraception, that underlay the new ideal of sexual-romantic marriage. Throughout the decade, birth control changed middle-class moral standards, courtship customs, and marital ideals while these very changes simultaneously made birth control all the more imperative. Contraception had created its own dynamic.

Contraceptive Politics

"Whether or not birth control is eugenic, hygienic, or economic," Walter Lippmann wrote in his 1929 *Preface to Morals*, "it is the most revolutionary practice in the history of sexual morals." During the 1920s, the impact of contraception became visible. It legitimized female sexuality, as no tract or argument could do. It contributed to the establishment of new sexual norms. Without contraception, the dictum that repression was unhealthy would hardly have been viable. It promoted premarital experimentation, although not to the extent that traditionalists feared. It enabled couples to marry earlier, since the economic burden of children could be postponed. Most decidedly, contraception transformed marital ideals. Separating sex from procreation, it released the companionate potential of marriage. Liberating women from "involuntary motherhood," it transformed marital sex from "obligation" to "communication." At the same time, contraception facilitated the new desire to merge marriage and career. It is fair to say that throughout the 1920s, contraception was at once the crux of the new morality, the opening wedge of "economic independence," and the most crucial change in women's lives.

The brunt of its impact was of course on middle-class women. Contraception had long been a common middle-class goal, but during the 1920s it received mounting approval and acceptance. Widespread use of the pessary (or diaphragm), meanwhile, made it even more effective. Middle-class women, who favored this method, were able to obtain the device from private physicians, although doctors were legally required to look for "indications" and prescribe contraceptives only to "cure or prevent disease." But indications were broadened in private practice, just as birth control advocates argued that they should be broadened in law. Meanwhile, illegal importation of contraceptive devices expanded, creating a lively underground traffic. At mid-decade, one researcher estimated that up to six out of ten American women used contraceptives. Surveys of middle-class women more than supported such claims. Blanchard and Manasses found that 80 percent of their sample of young women planned to use contraception when they married. Of the unmarried women interviewed by Katherine Bement Davis, 85 percent believed contraception should be practiced in marriage and less than 8 percent disapproved. About 75 percent of the married women in Davis's sample avowed belief in the principle of contraception, and almost all of this group practiced it.

Although contraception remained a middle-class perquisite, there were some ramifications beyond. During the prewar years, birth control activists had sometimes expressed the fear that they would never convert the working class. "Dilettante Birth Control Leagues may help as the workers take their morals from the upper class," Caroline Nelson had written to Margaret Sanger in 1915. "But they will not go far, they will not reach the bottom." After Sanger published *Women and the New Race* in 1920, she received thousands of letters from working-class women expressing resentment that contraception was a class privilege. "The rich don't seem to have so many children, why should the poor who can't afford to?" asked one correspondent. "I cannot see why it's always the poor that's got to suffer," wrote another. During the 1920s, contraception did not "reach the bottom" but its use was broadened, as much as a result of the World War I campaign against venereal disease as of the birth control crusade. Working-class use never reached the middle-class high. For instance, one research project in 1925 suggested that among young married women aged twenty-five to twenty-nine with one child, about 80 percent of the well-off but only 36 percent of poorer women used contraception. In Middletown, the Lynds reported, contraceptive use presented "the appearance of a pyramid." "Relatively efficacious" methods were in almost universal use at the top, among the "business group," but then declined as one descended the social scale, "sloping down from this peak until the base of ignorance is reached."

During the 1920s, the birth control crusade never became either a working-class movement or a feminist movement. Both wings of organized feminism, in fact, ignored the issue of contraception. Before the war, when Margaret Sanger had tried to drum up suffragist support, she was told to wait until the vote was won. But after 1920, there was no support in the feminist camp. In 1927, the NWP rejected a birth-control plank, and three years later the LWV refused to study the issue. There were of course supportive individuals. Physician Alice Hamilton, for instance, endorsed birth control as a cure for poverty. As she wrote in the *Birth Control Review* in 1925, the poor should have "the knowledge and power which has long been in possession of those who need it least." But leading feminists remained suspicious or ambivalent. When Sanger appealed to Carrie Chapman Catt in 1920 to support the cause, Catt's reply epitomized feminist equivocation. "Please be assured that I am no opponent even though I do not stand by your side," she wrote.

In my judgment you claim too much as the result of one thing. Most reformers do that. Your reform is too narrow to appeal to me and too sordid. When the advocacy of contraception is combined with as strong a propaganda for continence (not to prevent conception but in the interest of common decency), it will find me a more willing sponsor. . . . There will come some gains even from the program you advocate—and some increase in immorality through safety. The gains will slightly overtop the losses however, so I am no enemy of you and yours.

Charlotte Perkins Gilman would later endorse birth control too, but in the 1920s she was a more formidable critic than Catt. Gilman voiced her objections in the *Birth Control Review,* where she attacked Sanger's defense point by point. She denied that sex was the ultimate in spiritual communion or self-expression, that "indulgence" was necessarily an improvement over "repression," and that new prescriptions were better than old ones. Birth control, Gilman contended, would not improve marriage but transform it into "unromantic, dutiful submission to male indulgence." Finally, she pinpointed a double standard of expectations. "When men talk of sex, they mean only intercourse," Gilman wrote. "For women it means the whole process of reproduction, love, and mating." Both Gilman and Catt suspected that birth control would bolster an old form of male tyranny, forcing women into male-ordained sexual roles. Significantly, neither viewed contraception as an individual "right" or a form of "protection," but, rather, as a new factor in sexual politics.

Without a feminist base, a working-class base, or a left-wing base, the birth-control movement of the 1920s created its own constituency. Margaret Sanger had embarked on this effort during the war when she began to win the allegiance of well-off women. During the 1920s she turned to professional men. The aim of the American Birth Control League was to alter both medical opinion and popular opinion, which meant winning the endorsement of influential opinion makers—especially physicians, but also academics, eugenicists, and other experts. A related thrust was the ABCL campaign for "doctors only" bills. For the first half of the decade, this policy was controversial. Mary Ware Dennett's faction, now called the Voluntary Parenthood League, was still fighting to repeal the obscenity laws. The "doctors only" policy, it contended, would result in "special privilege class legislation," since only the well-off had access to doctors, (The VPL argument resembled the social reformers' assault on the NWP.) But by mid-decade, the Dennett faction had capsized and disbanded. "Doctors only" was now the thrust of the birth-control movement. The ABCL's goals were to evoke medical support and to broaden, not repeal, the obscenity laws so that physicians could legally prescribe contraception for healthy women. The physician became the key to contraceptive progress.

This policy of course affected birth-control clinics, which the ABCL now established. Here physicians took charge, as had not been the case at the Brownsville clinic in 1916. During the 1920s, clinic doctors could prescribe contraceptives either by stretching "indications" or by sending healthy patients to private physicians who would do so. Birth control was still a precarious business. Clinics appeared in twenty-three cities in twelve states, but many were short-lived. At the decade's end, some thirty to fifty were in operation, though their numbers would increase rapidly during the depression. Significantly, the clinics had more of a eugenicist goal than a feminist one. By 1919, Margaret Sanger argued that birth control would produce "more children from the fit, less from the unfit," and this theme became a dominant one. During the 1920s, Sanger stressed the movement's mission to eliminate the illiterate and degenerate. Birth control would not only protect women from pregnancy, it would also protect society from decay. "A high rate of fecundity," Sanger wrote in 1922, "is always associated with the direst poverty, mental defects, feeble-mindedness, and other transmissible traits." Eugenic arguments helped to win support from doctors, professionals, and well-off contributors. The last was vital, since clinics were expensive. They needed salaried doctors, salaried staff, medical backing, community backing, and operating funds. A new branch of philanthropy, the clinics were also a eugenic mission of social control.

While organizing the clinic movement, the ABCL turned much of its attention to physicians, seeking their support for contraception. During the 1920s, medical views were in transition. Doctors had already sanctioned a first wave of sexual revolution, or evolution, by rejecting continence as a moral and medical ideal. Support had shifted to moderate "indulgence." Sanction of birth control was a next logical step. Moreover, physicians were suspicious of "indiscriminate" distribution of contraceptives by outsiders, just as they were hostile to the encroachment of Sheppard-Towner outsiders on medical turf. By mid-decade, the medical profession had formally shifted ground. In 1925, contraception won AMA support. Physicians preferred to control birth control themselves. "Conjugal hygiene" now became a part of the medical curriculum, a topic at professional conferences, and the province of an AMA committee. Margaret Sanger's pragmatic campaign for medical support had proved effective.

Though successful with the AMA, the ABCL had far less impact on the law. During the 1920s, obscenity laws were neither broadened nor repealed. Contraception for the healthy remained illegal until a federal court decision of 1936. The law, clearly, had not caught up with the new morality. This was evident in the case of Mary Ware Dennett, still an opponent of the obscenity laws and a crusader for "free speech." Dennett advocated free dispersal of sex education material and contraceptive information without interference. But in 1929 she was arrested and convicted under the obscenity laws for mailing out copies of a published sex education essay, describing reproduction. Upholding her conviction in 1930, a federal court of appeals contended that Dennett's motive, an educational one, was irrelevant, since the information conveyed was "clearly indecent." Unlike Mary Ware Dennett, Margaret Sanger continued to profit from whatever controversy she created. When her prize New York City birth-control clinic, run by physician Hannah Stone, was raided by the police in 1929, Sanger's courting of the medical profession paid off. Physicians now supported her cause. During the 1920s the birth-control movement succeeded not only in converting physicians but in converting itself—into a respectable middle-class reform movement.

Whereas organized feminism, diminished in strength and divided in policy, had difficulty adapting to the New Era, the birth-control movement had done so with alacrity and finesse. The ABCL quickly became a centralized, professional organization. With its appeal to doctors, its eugenic thrust, and its aura of science and technology, it was able to survive and prosper in an apolitical, antireform, and increasingly antifeminist era. In many ways, the ABCL had more in common with the Sanitary Commission of the 1860s than with the feminist movement that had evolved in the interim. Although Sanger remained dominant, the birth-control movement was supported and guided by professional men. In 1926, the ABCL reached a peak membership of 37,000 native-born, well-off supporters, mainly from the North and Midwest. Almost nine out of ten were women volunteers who devoted their time to the league's multifaceted campaigns. But professional men assumed the managerial, influential roles. Margaret Sanger, meanwhile, recruited among the prominent, speaking to women's clubs and social service groups, which she had once denounced as capitalist tools. While paid field workers organized local leagues and health professionals ran clinics, Sanger, using her now extensive private funds, hired a physician to address medical societies. The one-time radicalism of the birth-control movement had been modernized, professionalized, and mainstreamed.

In the 1914 *Woman Rebel,* Margaret Sanger had declared that "Women cannot be on an equal footing with men until they have full and complete control over their reproductive function." During the 1920s, equal footing emerged as an ideal—for supporters of the ERA, for women striving for "economic independence," for women combining careers and marriage, and for "pals" and "partners" with romantic hopes of companionate relationships. New aspirations, from individualism to equal rights in the "sexual sphere," permeated the middle class. Throughout the decade, sexual rules were changing, but social, economic, and political rules remained much the same. Neither the vote nor contraception, alone or together, ensured equal footing. In the 1930s and 1940s, two national emergencies, depression and war, provided a new combination of liabilities and opportunities.

SUGGESTED READINGS AND SOURCES

CHAPTER 15

Linda Gordon, *Woman's Body, Woman's Right: A Social History of Birth Control in America* (New York, 1976), is an invaluable study of the movement for birth control since the mid-nineteenth century. Chapter 9, on the prewar birth-control movement, assesses Margaret Sanger's political shifts and birth-control arguments. David M. Kennedy, *Birth Control in America: The Career of Margaret Sanger* (New Haven and London, 1970), a study of the birth-control movement since 1914, thoroughly explores Sanger's entanglements with law, medicine, and religion. James Reed, *From Private Vice to Public Virtue: The Birth Control Movement and American Society Since 1830* (New York, 1977), examines the contributions of major advocates of contraception, including Margaret Sanger. Joan M. Jensen, "The Evolution of Margaret Sanger's 'Family Limitation' Pamphlet, 1914–1921," *Signs,* 6 (Spring 1981), 548–557, which includes the 1914 edition of the pamphlet, traces Sanger's movement away from the left. For the eugenics movement, see Daniel Kevles, *In the Name of Eugenics: Genetics and the Uses of Human Heredity* (New York, 1985).

An outstanding biography of Sanger is Ellen Chesler, *Woman of Valor: Margaret Sanger and the Birth Control Movement in America* (New York, 1992). Madeline Gray, *Margaret Sanger: A Biography of the Champion of Birth Control* (New York, 1980), describes Sanger's chaotic personal life. For an adulatory biography, see Lawrence Lader, *The Margaret Sanger Story* (Garden City, N.Y., 1955). Sanger's relationship with Ellis is discussed in Phyllis Grosskurth, *Havelock Ellis: A Biography* (New York, 1980).

Margaret Sanger published two versions of her life story, *My Fight for Birth Control* (New York, 1931) and *An Autobiography* (New York, 1938); Kennedy calls them ghost-written campaign biographies. Alex Baskin, ed., *The Woman Rebel* (New York, 1976), is a reprint of Sanger's 1914 periodical. For Sanger's publications in the 1920s, see *Women and the New Race* (New York, 1920) and *The Pivot of Civilization* (New York, 1922), which contain her revised, eugenic defense of birth control; *Happiness in Marriage* (New York, 1926), a manual; and *Womanhood in Bondage* (New York, 1928), which contains letters written to Sanger, mainly by working-class women, asking for birth-control information. The *Birth Control Review* (New York) was published from 1917 to 1940.

CHAPTER 16

General discussions of women in the 1920s include William H. Chafe, *The Paradox of Change: American Women in the 20th Century* (New York, 1991), chs. 1–5; Lois W. Banner, *Women in Modern America: A Brief History,* 2d ed. (New York, 1984), ch. 4; Peter Gabriel Filene, *Him/Her/Self: Sex Roles in Modern America,* 2d ed. (Baltimore, Md., 1986), ch. 5; Sheila M. Rothman, *Woman's Proper Place: A History of Changing Ideals and Practices, 1870 to the Present* (New York, 1978), chs. 4 and 5; and Rosalind Rosenberg, *Divided Lives: American Women in the Twentieth Century* (New York, 1992), ch. 3. Dorothy M. Brown surveys the decade in *Setting a Course: American Women in the 1920s* (Boston, 1987).

Feminism in the 1920s is examined in Nancy F. Cott, *The Grounding of Modern Feminism* (New Haven, Conn., 1987); William L. O'Neill, *Feminism in America,* rev. ed. (New Brunswick, N.J., 1989), chs. 7 and 8; Susan D. Becker, *The Origins of the Equal Rights Amendment: Feminism Between the Wars* (Westport, Conn., 1981); J. Stanley Lemons, *The Woman Citizen: Social Feminism in the 1920s* (Charlottesville, Va., 1990); Lois Scharf and Joan M. Jensen, eds., *Decades of Discontent: The Women's Movement, 1920–1940* (Boston, 1987); Christine A. Lunardini, *From Equal Suffrage to Equal Rights* (New York, 1986); and Wendy Sarvasy, "Beyond the Difference versus Equality Policy Debate," *Signs* 17 (Winter 1992), 329–362. Elaine Showalter, ed., *These Modern Women: Autobiographical Essays from the 1920s* (Old Westbury, N.Y., 1978), contains the series of articles by feminists published in the *Nation* in 1926–1927. Joan G. Zimmerman explores the intersection of women's politics and constitutional law in "The Jurisprudence of Equality: The Women's Minimum Wage, the First Equal Rights Amendment, and *Adkins v. Children's Hospital,* 1905–1923," *Journal of American History,* 78 (June 1991), 188–225. An important article on the fate of feminism in the 1920s is Estelle B. Freedman, "Separatism as Strategy: Female Institution Building and American Feminism, 1870–1930," *Feminist Studies,* 5 (Fall 1979), 512–529. See also Freedman, "The New Woman: Changing Views of Women in the 1920s," *Journal of American History,* 61 (September 1974), 372–393.

Felice D. Gordon explores the impact of woman sufffrage in *After Winning: The Legacy of the New Jersey Suffragists, 1920–1947* (New Brunswick, N.J., 1986). See also Nancy F. Cott, "Across the Great Divide: Women in Politics Before and After 1920" in Louise A. Tilly and Patricia Gurin, eds., *Women, Politics, and Change* (New York, 1990), pp. 153–176.

Elizabeth Israels Perry examines the life of a unique political figure in *Belle Moscowitz: Feminine Politics and the Exercise of Power in the Age of Alfred E. Smith* (New York, 1987). Joyce L. Kornbluh and Mary Frederickson present the workers' education movement in *Sisterhood and Solidarity: Workers' Education for Women, 1914–1984* (Philadelphia, 1984). For the Bryn Mawr summer school, see the film *The Women of Summer* (1984), by Suzanne Bauman and Rita Heller, in which former students tell how the school affected their lives.

Anne Firor Scott discusses the activism of southern women in "After Suffrage: Southern Women in the 1920s," *Journal of Southern History*, 30 (August 1964), 298–315, and Scott, *The Southern Lady: From Pedestal to Politics, 1830–1930* (Chicago, 1970), ch. 8. For the women's interracial movement and the development of the ASWPL, see Jacquelin Dowd Hall, *Revolt Against Chivalry: Jessie Daniel Aymes and the Women's Campaign Against Lynching* (New York, 1979). Kathleen M. Bree provides a counterpoint in *Women of the Klan: Racism and Gender in the 1920s* (Berkeley, Calif., 1991).

Maureen Weiner Greenwald discusses women's wartime employment in *Women, War, and Work: The Impact of World War I* (Westport, Conn., 1980). See also William J. Breen, "Black Women and the Great War: Mobilization and Reform in the South," *Journal of Southern History*, 44 (1978), 421–440. For women in the labor force, see Leslie Woodcock Tentler, *Wage-earning Women: Industrial Work and Family in the United States, 1900–1930* (New York, 1979), which reconstructs the experience of early twentieth-century working-class women in manufacturing, sales, and service jobs; Alice Kessler-Harris, *Out to Work: A History of Wage-Earning Women in the United States* (New York, 1982), ch. 8; and Claudia Goldin, *Understanding the Gender Gap: An Economic History of American Women* (New York, 1990). Sarah Deutsch discusses changes in Hispanic women's work roles in the Southwest in the 1920s in *No Separate Refuge* (New York, 1987), ch. 6. Frank Stricker assesses women's advances in the professions and business in "Cookbooks and Lawbooks: The Hidden History of Career Women in Twentieth-Century America," *Journal of Social History*, 10 (Fall 1976), 1–19. See also Barbara Harris, *Beyond Her Sphere: Women and the Professions in American History* (Westport, Conn., 1978), ch. 5. Daniel J. Walkowitz explores the development of the social work profession in "The Making of a Feminine Professional Identity: Social Workers in the 1920s," *American Historical Review*, 95 (October 1990), 1051–1075. Studies of professional women include Joyce Antler, *Lucy Sprague Mitchell: The Making of a Modern Woman* (New Haven, Conn., 1987); Robert E. Hemenway, *Zora Neale Hurston: A Literary Biography* (Urbana, Ill., 1977); Sara Alpern, *Freda Kirchwey: A Woman of "The Nation"* (Cambridge, Mass., 1987); Judith Schachter Modell, *Ruth Benedict: Patterns of a Life* (Philadelphia, 1983); Margaret M. Caffrey, *Ruth Benedict: Stranger in this Land* (Austin, Tex., 1989); Robert C. Bannister, *Jessie Bernard: The Making of a Feminist* (New Brunswick, 1991); and Jane Howard, *Margaret Mead: A Life* (New York, 1984). For Mead's memoir, see *Blackberry Winter: My Earlier Years* (New York, 1972).

A most valuable source for the 1920s is Paula S. Fass, *The Damned and the Beautiful: American Youth in the 1920s* (New York, 1977). Fass assesses changes in the family as well as the values, mores, and behavior of middle-class collegiate youth. The problem of finding the origin of changes in sexual behavior is suggested in Daniel Scott Smith, "The Dating of the American Sexual Revolution," in Michael Gordon, ed., *The American Family in Social and Historical Perspective*, 2d ed. (New York, 1978), pp. 426–438. James P. McGovern offers evidence of a new morality in the prewar era in "The American Woman's Pre-World War I Freedom in Manners and Morals," *Journal of American History*, 55 (September 1968), 315–333. Kenneth A. Yellis considers aspects of the flapper in "Prosperity's Child: Some Thoughts on the Flapper," *American Quarterly*, 21 (Spring 1969), 44–64. For the dating system that flourished from the 1920s through the 1950s, see Beth L. Bailey, *From Front Porch to Back Seat: Courtship in Twentieth-Century America* (Baltimore, Md., 1988) and John L. Modell, *Into One's Own: From Youth to Adulthood in the United States, 1920–1975* (Berkeley, Calif., 1989). Lillian Faderman describes currents of sexual experimentation and repression in *Odd Girls and Twilight Lovers: A History of Lesbian life in Twentieth-Century America* (New York, 1991), ch. 3. Joanne Meyerowitz discusses the emancipation of young middle-class wage earners in the 1920s in *Women Adrift: Independent Wage-earners in Chicago, 1880–1930* (Chicago, 1988), ch. 6.

Rosalind Rosenberg examines the pioneer work of women social scientists as surveyors of sexual behavior in *Beyond Separate Spheres: Intellectual Roots of Modern Feminism* (New Haven, Conn., 1982), ch. 7. For the birth control movement in the 1920s, see Linda Gordon, *Woman's Body, Woman's Right,* ch. 10, and David M. Kennedy, *Birth Control in America,* both cited above. For changes in childbirth, see Judith Walzer Leavitt, *Brought to Bed: Childbearing in America, 1750–1950* (New York, 1986), ch. 10. Mary P. Ryan suggests the impact of the movies in "The Projection of a New Womanhood: The Movie Moderns in the 1920s," in Jean E. Friedman and William G. Shade, eds., *Our American Sisters: Women in American Life and Thought,* 2d ed. (Boston, 1976), pp. 366–383, and Lary May, *Screening Out the Past: The Birth of Mass Culture and the Motion Picture Industry* (Chicago, 1980). For beauty contests, see Lois W. Banner, *American Beauty* (New York, 1983), ch. 12. Sarah Stage, *Female Complaints: Lydia Pinkham and the Business of Women's Medicine* (New York, 1979), ch. 8, offers interesting remarks on the 1920s.

Women who lived through the 1920s, a self-conscious decade, provide an abundance of commentary. For feminism, see Suzanne LaFollette, *Concerning Women* (New York, 1926); Lorine Pruette, *Women and Leisure: A Study of Social Waste* (New York, 1924); Pruette, *Why Women Fail* (New York, 1931); Charlotte Perkins Gilman, "The New Generation of Women," *Current History,* 18 (August 1923), 735–736; Gilman, "Van Guard, Rear-Guard, and Mud-Guard," *Century Magazine,* 104 (1922), 349–350; and Nancy F. Cott, ed., *A Woman Making History: Mary Ritter Beard Through her Letters* (New Haven, Conn., 1991). Of special interest is Dorothy Dunbar Bromley, "Feminist—New Style," *Harper's,* 155 (October 1927), 552–560. Women's status is examined in Elizabeth Kemper Adams, *Women Professional Workers* (New York, 1921); Sophonisba P. Breckinridge, *Women in the Twentieth Century: A Study of Their Political, Social, and Economic Activities* (New York, 1933); and *Annals of the American Academy of Political and Social Science,* 142 (May 1929), on "Women in the Modern World."

A classic of the decade is Helen Merrill Lynd and Robert S. Lynd, *Middletown: A Study of Contemporary American Culture* (New York, 1929). See also the textbook by Ernest R. Groves and William F. Ogburn, *American Marriage and Family Relationships* (New York, 1928). For new morality, see V. F. Calverton, *The Bankruptcy of Marriage* (New York, 1928); Freda Kirchwey, ed., *Our Changing Morality* (New York, 1930); Phyllis Blanchard and Carolyn Manasses, *New Girls for Old* (New York, 1930); Floyd Dell, *Love in the Machine Age: A Psychological Study of the Transition from Patriarchal Society* (New York, 1930); Ben Lindsey and Wainright Evans, *The Revolt of Modern Youth* (New York, 1925); Lindsey and Evans, *The Companionate Marriage* (New York, 1927); and Katherine Bement Davis's 1918 survey, *The Sex Life of Twenty-Two Hundred Women* (New York, 1929). Two popular contemporary novels are Warner Fabian, *Flaming Youth* (New York, 1923), and Percy Marks, *The Plastic Age* (New York, 1924). The classic novel about a woman's experience in small-town America is Sinclair Lewis, *Main Street* (New York, 1920). See also Dorothy Parker's short stories of the 1920s and 1930s, available in *The Collected Dorothy Parker* (New York, 1973), and Marion Meade's biography, *Dorothy Parker: What Fresh Hell Is This?* (New York, 1988). For the aesthetic antecedents of the 1920s "New Woman," see Martha Banta, *Imaging American Women: Ideas and Ideals in Cultural History* (New York, 1987), ch. 1.

CHAPTER 17

Humanizing the New Deal, 1933

"The century-old White House wore a startled air today as its new mistress took over," Associated Press reporter Bess Furman announced on the front page of the nation's newspapers, dateline March 4, 1933. As soon as the inauguration was over, Eleanor Roosevelt welcomed 75 Roosevelt relatives to the White House and served tea to 3,000 guests in the Dining Room and East Room. She also gave an interview to another AP reporter, Lorena Hickok. (The two women retreated to the bathroom in order to get some quiet.) An interview with the press at such a time, or any time, was a rare event. The former First Lady, Lou Hoover, had granted only one interview in four years, and that was during the 1932 campaign. But Eleanor Roosevelt had already made it clear that she would be a trendsetter. Within two days, she set yet another precedent by holding her own White House news conference. "Never before in White House history has the wife of a President agreed to talk freely with newspaper people for publication," exclaimed correspondent Emma Bugbee in the *New York Herald Tribune*. Moreover, as the Washington press corps had just learned, the conferences would be closed to all but women reporters.

"We had it in the Red Room," Eleanor Roosevelt wrote to Lorena Hickok afterward. "Thirty-five came and of course there weren't enough chairs to go around so some had to sit on the floor." Armed with a box of candied fruit, which she passed around, Eleanor confronted the roomful of women. She knew very few besides the AP's Bess Furman and Ruby Black of the United Press. The press, however, was overwhelmed. Mrs. Roosevelt "entered breezily, with outstretched hand offered informally to those she recognized personally," Emma Bugbee recounted in the *Herald Tribune*, and after that she "chatted with her customary vivacity on the practical problems of handling the news." The conferences would be limited to women, an idea suggested by Lorena Hickok, to help save them from unemployment. People were being fired all over, Eleanor

Roosevelt recalled, and "unless women reporters could find something new to write about, the chances were that some of them would lose their jobs in a very short time." Not only would the women's press conferences provide something new to write about but they would also cover subjects of "special interest and value to the women of the country and that the women might write up better than the men." Most important, these subjects would never "encroach on the field of politics," as Emma Bugbee told *Herald Tribune* readers. Nor would they touch on what Eleanor Roosevelt called "my husband's side of the news." Government policy and political issues would be banned from the women's sessions.

"It really wasn't so bad," Eleanor confided to Lorena Hickok. "I think I'll continue them." But the new institution evoked mixed reactions. Not everyone present liked the women-only policy. Reporter May Craig, covering the White House for a chain of Maine newspapers, insisted that men be admitted because she believed in sexual equality. She also feared that, in reprisal, women reporters might be banned from other Washington press sessions. (In Eleanor's opinion, May Craig was "so well established that at no time was her job in jeopardy.") There were objections from other quarters too. "Many thought it was unbecoming of a President's wife and might embarrass the President," UP reporter Ruby Black revealed. Others feared that since politics were banned, "the press conferences would produce nothing but stories about her clothes, her parties, her menus, and the charity benefits she might aid." Newspaper editors, in fact, predicted that the press sessions would last no longer than six months.

At the early conferences, Eleanor Roosevelt managed to adhere to her own political ban. She told about her daily schedule, discussed the prints on the White House walls, explained the use of homegrown herbs, and gave out recipes. With the help of a dietician, she even offered low-cost menus for depression households ("Tuesday lunch: hot-stuffed eggs, tomato sauce, mashed potatoes, prune pudding, coffee," Bess Furman wrote in her notebook.) But women reporters wanted what Bess Furman called "an appropriately newsworthy answer." How did Mrs. Roosevelt feel, they kept asking, about a government policy to fire women from federal jobs when staff reductions were made? Everyone had a right to her job, said Eleanor, but in an emergency anyone with another means of support might give up a job "or share it with another who needed it more."

As reporters prodded, the Red Room sessions broadened their scope. Soon Eleanor Roosevelt began to talk about "whatever she might have on her mind at the moment," Bess Furman recalled. "No newspaperwoman could have asked for better luck." The President's wife turned out to be, first of all, an advocate. "She was always ready to lash out earnestly at sweatshops, to demand a changed system of education," Furman wrote. She was also unable to avoid "politics." By the end of the year, according to Ruby Black, Eleanor Roosevelt was defending low-cost housing, the subsistence homestead program, the need for women's jobs, equal pay for equal work under the National Recovery Administration, old age pensions, and the minimum wage. She also discussed "whether or not women will be employed in the United States embassy in Soviet Russia," with whom diplomatic relations, severed in 1918, were just being reestablished.

"Nearly all these subjects had something to do with pending legislation or administrative policies," said Ruby Black. Even casual mention of a subject, Bess Furman added, "usually meant that something was really up which would bear looking into." Eleanor soon told the newswomen that she liked to introduce controversial topics in order to get them talked about and thought about.

Moreover, to the delight of the press, she began to introduce special guests, such as foreign notables who had come to visit the White House, along with their families. But most of the special guests were women. Before a year was out, the Red Room reporters had met Secretary of Labor Frances Perkins, who proposed special camps for unemployed women, and Ellen Woodward, the head of women's projects at the Civil Works Administration, who described women's work-relief programs, and Mary Harriman Rumsey, of the National Recovery Administration consumers' advisory board, who explained efforts to fight rising prices, and Mary W. (Molly) Dewson, head of the Women's Division of the Democratic National Committee, who described women's new clout in the Democratic ranks. "Previously, a President's wife acted as if she didn't know that a political party existed," wrote Ruby Black. Reporters soon looked for tips about New Deal policies, and as the conferences ranged further into "politics," interest in them grew. No newspaper chain, press association, or major newspaper, said Lorena Hickok, could afford to ignore them.

Women reporters in Washington, meanwhile, were ecstatic. During the Hoover administration, Bess Furman had had to rely on secret servicemen, ushers, secretaries, and florists for White House news tips. Once she had disguised herself as a girl scout (the Girl Scouts were Mrs. Hoover's major interest) in order to report on a White House reception. But after Eleanor Roosevelt began her press conferences, stories were routinely available every week. Some reporters, like the *Tribune*'s Emma Bugbee, sent to cover the inauguration, were kept on in Washington months longer than planned; by April, Bugbee's press conference stories appeared on page one. "Tea Pouring Items Give Way to Big News," wrote Ruby Black. "The unprecedented idea of having two news personalities in the White House still has Washington slightly groggy—or, maybe agog." Moreover, the press conferences, said Black, brought a "New Deal for newswomen," in the form of new jobs, increased pay, and higher status. Of course, some stories written by women and about women might still be relegated to the woman's page or even thrown in the wastebasket, but no longer did editors feel that "a male correspondent would have a better chance to have a close White House contact than a woman." However, the most distinctive facet of the press conferences, reporters noted, beyond their all-woman composition, was that Eleanor Roosevelt created a nationwide schoolroom. "She conducts classes on scores of subjects," wrote Bess Furman, "always seeing beyond her immediate hearers to 'the women of the country.'"

Eleanor Roosevelt's Red Room classes were much in character. When she moved into the White House, she was not only an experienced politician but also a veteran activist in the woman's movement. Her activism had early roots. As a debutante at the turn of the century, Eleanor had worked at the Rivington Street Settlement and joined the National Consumers' League, then led by Florence

Eleanor Roosevelt surrounded by reporters at one of her Monday morning press conferences. *(Franklin D. Roosevelt Library Collection)*

Kelley. After her marriage in 1905, such intensive involvement ended. Between 1906 and 1916, Eleanor had five children and settled into the role of upper-class matron and sometime volunteer. During World War I, when Franklin Delano Roosevelt was assistant secretary of the navy, she organized a Washington canteen, managed a recreation room in a naval hospital, and began a household food-saving program, which was written up in the newspapers. But after World War I and the campaign of 1920, when FDR ran unsuccessfully for Vice President, she actively sought a public outlet. Through women's organizations and Democratic politics, she quickly became "a much more ardent citizen and feminist than anyone about me would have deemed possible."

Eleanor had not voted in 1917, when New York first gave women suffrage. As a young woman she considered politics "a sinister affair" and avoided both the suffrage movement, which FDR had supported since 1912, and the antisuffrage movement, which her cousin Alice Roosevelt had joined. After 1920, however, she had new motives to find a role in public life. First, she had just learned of her husband's affair with Lucy Mercer, a young Washington socialite who had been working as Eleanor Roosevelt's social secretary, a trauma that spurred her to seek her own sphere of action. In 1921, moreover, after FDR was stricken by polio, the Roosevelts' resident political adviser, former newspaperman Louis Howe, urged Eleanor to take an even larger role in public affairs in order to keep her husband's name in the news. In cousin Alice's view, FDR's infidelity was the turning point. "After the Lucy Mercer affair, which hurt her very badly, and Franklin's illness, Eleanor came into her own," Alice wrote. "She developed a tougher side of her character, which was admirable, even though it didn't bring much enjoyment to anyone, least of all herself." (Cousin Alice, a formidable rival, was always critical.) For Eleanor Roosevelt, political activity was a way to assert herself as an individual and, simultaneously, a way to make herself invaluable to FDR. Just after suffrage was won, moreover, there was still a separate world of women's politics, partisan and nonpartisan, into which she had easy entry.

In 1920, she joined the newly formed League of Women Voters. The league, said its president, Maud Wood Park, would "promote reforms in which women will naturally take an interest in a greater degree than men," such as protection of children and working women, education, public health, and "the care of the dependent and delinquent classes." Eleanor Roosevelt's high social position aided her swift rise in league politics, but so did her talent for application. She was asked at the outset to serve on the LWV's New York State board. She was also assigned to monitor the legislature, where her husband had served, noting bills of interest. With the help of suffragist lawyer Elizabeth Reid, Eleanor learned about legislative pressure politics. Soon she was listening to speeches by Carrie Chapman Catt, talking out at league conventions, and addressing league chapters and women's clubs about the need for welfare legislation. Within a year, Eleanor's extremely tall figure was a familiar sight on lecture podiums. Handicapped at first by a fear of public speaking, a high-pitched voice, and "a nervous habit of laughing when there was nothing to laugh at," she overcame these obstacles with Louis Howe's help. Ever encouraging, Howe told her how to speak from the floor in public meetings: "Have something to say, say it, and then sit down."

In 1922, Eleanor also joined the Women's Trade Union League, that liberal enclave on the left wing of the woman's movement, full of what Roosevelt relatives called "parlor socialists"—and real socialists too. Eleanor had first met WTUL leaders such as Rose Schneiderman and Mary Anderson at a Washington tea in 1919. During the 1920s, WTUL activists became her friends and associates. An industrious fund-raiser, Eleanor ran evening classes for working women (the WTUL had given up "organization" for "education"), gave Christmas parties in her home for the children of WTUL members, learned about trade unionism, and campaigned for maximum-hour and minimum-wage laws for women. Soon she divided her efforts among the LWV, the NCL, the WTUL, the New York Women's City Club (the socially prominent group that had raised funds for Margaret Sanger in 1917), and the peace crusade, where she promoted U.S. entry into the World Court. "As my activities and work broadened and reached out . . . I never tried to evade an issue," she told journalist Cissy Patterson in a *Washington Herald* interview in April 1933. "When I found I had to do something, I just did it."

During the mid-1920s, much of what she had to do involved Democratic politics. All informed reporters, said UP reporter Ruby Black in 1933, knew that

Eleanor Roosevelt "had been the major worker in organizing New York Democratic women from 1922 on." By 1924, Eleanor had an office in the Women's Division of the Democratic state committee. That year she addressed the platform committee at the Democratic state convention on behalf of thirty women's groups, demanding a child labor law, an eight-hour day, and minimum wages for women. Not only did she oppose the National Woman's party call for an Equal Rights Amendment, but she viewed its proponents as "reactionaries." At the Democratic national convention of 1924, Eleanor waited all night outside the room of the platform committee, from which women were excluded, accompanied by a group of Democratic women and armed with an unread list of women's demands, which "some kind gentleman" finally took in. The proposals, said Bess Furman, who later looked them up in the *New York Times,* "practically forecast the New Deal"—conservation, the eight-hour day, collective bargaining, a federal employment agency, equal pay for equal work, federal aid for maternal health and child welfare, and "educational work to eradicate venereal disease."

But that was not all. In the New York gubernatorial race that year, Eleanor campaigned for Al Smith and against a Roosevelt cousin. She stumped rural districts again in 1926, and in 1928 headed women's efforts to elect Smith as President. In this capacity, she worked with a Women's Division colleague, Nellie Tayloe Ross, who had taken over her late husband's job as governor of Wyoming. When AP reporter Lorena Hickok first met Eleanor Roosevelt during the 1928 campaign, the most important woman in Democratic politics was New York social worker Belle Moscowitz, Al Smith's right arm, whom Hickok labeled "the real power" at Democratic headquarters. Eleanor took charge of mobilizing women campaign workers. "I knew little about her," said Hickok, who watched Eleanor towering over male politicians at the state convention at Rochester, "although she had for several years been very active among the women and was better known to politicians around the state than her husband was."

In 1928, Eleanor Roosevelt's hard work paid off when FDR became governor of New York. "What a First Lady you will make," wrote Democratic national committeewoman Emily Newell Blair after the election, "and how splendid it is to have one in that place with the political acumen and feeling for women that you have." (Since 1920, the Democratic National Committee included one committeewoman from each state; Blair represented Missouri.) As governor's wife, Eleanor cultivated a routine of constant activity, vindicating her desire "to do things on my own, to use my own mind and abilities for my own aims." She ran the executive mansion, taught history at the Todhunter school in New York, of which she was part owner, began a series of radio speeches, and edited a popular magazine about babies. She also edited a party publication, the Women's Division's *Democratic News,* and worked with the women on the Democratic state committee. Both as party activist and as governor's wife, she supported the appointment of Frances Perkins, then a New York social worker, to the post of state industrial commissioner. FDR was extremely receptive to the idea of a woman appointee, though he had refused an administrative position to Belle Moscowitz, whom Eleanor and Franklin Roosevelt regarded as an overly domineering personality.

By this time, Eleanor Roosevelt had become the pivot of a group of politically active women, including Molly Dewson, Nancy Cook, Marion Dickerman, and Caroline O'Day, in the New York State Women's Division. She was also the center of a group of reformers in the WTUL and often served as an intermediary between her friends and her husband. She had other irons in the fire too. When depression struck, Eleanor, Nancy Cook, and Marion Dickerman set up a furniture factory on the Roosevelt estate, to employ local people who had lost their jobs; the crafts movement was always popular among women reformers, who generally shared an anti-industrial bent. Finally, in the late 1920s, Eleanor Roosevelt expounded her own combination of philosophy and advice to women readers. "Home comes first," she advised American mothers in *Success* magazine in 1927. But they should also develop "lives, interests, and personalities of their own apart from their households." Above all, Eleanor stressed the value of service. "If any one were to ask me what I want most out of life, I would say—the opportunity for doing something useful, for in no other way, I am convinced, can true happiness be obtained."

When Lorena Hickok was assigned to cover FDR in the 1932 presidential campaign, an assignemnt which was, for a woman reporter, "something of a novelty," she convinced the AP's New York bureau to let her cover Eleanor as well. This too was novel. "Candidates' wives in those days were supposed to be seen and not heard," Hickok recalled. "They went along on their husbands' trips, but their activities were limited to teas and luncheons in their honor—at which, of course, they did not utter a word for the public to hear." Reporters assigned to such events were limited to describing watercress sandwiches, orchid corsages, and what the candidate's wife was wearing. FDR's wife, it was noted, wore tweedy suits, white blouses, and hats that looked, someone observed, though not in print, "as though she rushed in and bought them while waiting for the traffic light to change." But Eleanor Roosevelt's role during the campaign was more unusual than her hats.

Not only did she talk freely to Lorena Hickok, whereas Bess Furman of the AP's Washington bureau had eked one interview out of Mrs. Hoover, but she worked throughout the campaign with the Democratic party's Women's Division. Now headed by Molly Dewson, the Women's Division served as a propaganda machine, inundating the country with Roosevelt fliers. "Eleanor and I made the same amount of money go twice as far as the men," Molly Dewson told Bess Furman after the election. "We carried on a huge correspondence with precinct workers and our letters were really personal." By the time of the innovative March 6 press conference, newswomen knew that Eleanor was not only an old hand at politics but a natural crusader. The new First Lady, Emma Bugbee wrote, had "an instinct for civic and social reform."

At no time was such an instinct more appropriate. During the winter of 1932–1933, the depression became even worse. Since 1929, national income had been cut in half, 9 million savings accounts had been wiped out, and 15 million workers had lost their jobs. When FDR was inaugurated, up to a thousand homes were foreclosed every day, local governments were unable to meet relief payments, and thirty-eight states had closed their banks. From the outset, Eleanor

Roosevelt viewed the depression as a moral more than an economic failure—the result of a national preoccupation with material gain. But during the 1932 campaign and throughout 1933, she began to assess its lessons for Americans. The depression showed, she explained, the need to rebuild moral fiber and to unite families, communities, and nation in common cause. In times of difficulty, Eleanor wrote in 1933, family members must draw together. "They have to depend on each other and they have to do things with and for each other, and the result is that the clan spirit grows." The need for unity extended beyond the family to society at large. In a 1932 radio speech, Eleanor expressed her hope that depression would teach Americans the lesson of "interdependence." ("One part of the country or group of countrymen cannot prosper while the others go downhill.") Above all, she voiced the hope that the depression might engender a feeling of community, a spirit of cooperation, and a sense of mutual responsibility. "If we can get back the spirit that we are responsible for each other, these years of depression would have been worthwhile."

In March 1933, as soon as FDR was inaugurated, Eleanor Roosevelt began to display the sense of responsibility she urged on others. She became at once a visible fount of concern. When the second bonus army of unemployed veterans arrived at the capital, they were provided with food at government expense and settled in an old army camp across the Potomac. There they were visited by Louis Howe and Eleanor Roosevelt, who led a round of World War I songs. (During the summer of 1932, under the Hoover administration, the first bonus army had been greeted by four troops of cavalry and a column of infantry, which burned their shacks and chased them out of Washington.) The Monday morning press conference heard next about Eleanor's visit to the capitol's black slums, where she started a campaign to get rid of decrepit and unhealthy alley dwellings. Sixty percent of Washington crimes, she told the newswomen, could be traced to the alleys, as could the city's highest tubercular rates. "She took all the cabinet wives on the alley tour," Bess Furman wrote. To reporters, Eleanor Roosevelt's "visiting" seemed incessant. It extended to the air, when she went on a flight with Amelia Earhart, and to the halls of Congress, where she sat in the spectators' gallery to hear Frances Perkins make a speech. But her major role as an intermediary between the administration and its constituency depended not so much on personal appearances as on the bulging mail sacks that began to be delivered to the White House. Through mail alone, in 1933, Eleanor Roosevelt was becoming what Ruby Black called "a major factor in humanizing the New Deal."

In Eleanor's view, the number of incoming letters served as a barometer of suffering. When conditions improved, her mail dropped off; she later observed, "but if anything disturbed the public it immediately increased." The year 1933 was the acme of public disturbance. By the end of the year, the President's wife had received 301,000 pieces of mail, sometimes arriving at a rate of 400 a day. In prior administrations, similar mail had been answered mainly by form letter. But Eleanor Roosevelt's small staff dealt with it differently, the press conference learned. As many as 50 letters a day received personal answers. The letters were mainly from people with problems, some overwhelmingly pathetic and a few fraudulent, as Eleanor was soon to discover, when desperate cases were checked out. Much of the mail contained requests, for jobs, advice, relief, even funds, and many letters contained complaints—about the unfairness of employers, land-lords, local officials, or relief agencies.

Eleanor passed the requests along to her own contingent of friends and allies, some federal administrators, some Democratic party workers, some social reformers—such as Mary Anderson at the Women's Bureau, Harry Hopkins at the Federal Emergency Relief Administration, Pauline Newman at the WTUL, or National Democratic Committeewomen, like Emma Guffey Miller of Pennsyl-vania. Sister of a senator and leader within the Women's Division, Emma Miller proved an energetic collaborator. She methodically investigated the letters of request that Eleanor passed on, finding eighty-six valid relief cases in the 1933 mail from Pennsylvania. By responding to the onslaught of mail and taking action to resolve individual problems, Eleanor became an intermediary between the New Deal and the depression victim, a quasi-official agency of appeals for the evicted, excluded, disabled, unemployed, and forgotten. Her "one passion," Ruby Black confirmed in 1934, "is human beings and their happiness, comfort, and security."

That Eleanor often relied on co-workers such as Emma Guffey Miller, Mary Anderson, or Pauline Newman was significant. Throughout the 1920s, women who had been involved in such organizations as the Women's Trade Union League, the League of Women Voters, or the Women's Division of the Demo-cratic party developed personal friendships and overlapping circles of links and contacts. They relied on each other to get things done, as Eleanor Roosevelt and Molly Dewson had during the 1932 campaign. Once Eleanor was installed in the White House, she and Molly Dewson at once began a new crusade. Women who had been active in the 1932 campaign, they insisted, must be granted the same desserts of political patronage that men received—appointments to high-level posts in the New Deal. Molly Dewson had already won a monumental victory, through her nationwide campaign in support of Frances Perkins as labor secre-tary. FDR had been inundated with letters solicited by Dewson and had read many favorable articles about Perkins planted by Dewson in newspapers and magazines. "I have always felt that it was not I alone who was appointed to the Cabinet, but that it was all the women in America," Frances Perkins announced in a 1933 speech. After that, Dewson and Eleanor continued to work as a team to win even more women's appointments.

In Molly W. Dewson, Eleanor Roosevelt had not only an ambitious ally but one with a similar background and outlook. Before they had met in the early 1920s, when both were officers of the New York Women's City Club, Molly Dewson had been a social worker, probation officer, and suffragist. During the 1920s, she rose to leadership in the National Consumers' League, where she had long been active as a lobbyist for the minimum wage (her initials were said to stand for "Minimum Wage" Dewson). In 1928, she shifted her energies to Democratic politics, and when the 1932 campaign began, she served as head of the party's Women's Division.

In Democratic circles, Molly Dewson became known as a battler for equal power for women (her initials were now said to stand for "More Women"

Dewson). And as a Democratic politician, she continued to share with Eleanor Roosevelt a basic commitment to their own wing of the woman's movement, which was more interested in protecting women's special interests, through such measures as the minimum wage, than in demanding equal rights, through such proposals as the Equal Rights Amendment. Like Eleanor Roosevelt, Dewson believed that women had both special interests to protect and a distinctive contribution to make to public life. She also believed that women would make superior public servants because they were more interested in social service than in gaining power or personal distinction. "I don't claim many women are competent to fill these high positions," Dewson told Bess Furman in a 1933 interview. "But when a woman does emerge, she frequently proves to be a more valuable public official than any man that could be chosen." Women's appointments, Molly Dewson insisted, also had a political value. "I feel that the women's vote is going to be important four years from now," she had written to Eleanor Roosevelt in 1932.

All patronage appointments in 1933 depended on James Farley, postmaster general and party leader, whom the two women soon besieged. In April, Eleanor Roosevelt convinced Farley to upgrade the Women's Division into a more vital part of the Democratic national committee. Soon thereafter, Molly Dewson arrived in Washington with a select list of perhaps 100 women who deserved federal jobs. The list itself was an innovation. Until 1933, Dewson told Bess Furman, women's recognition within the party had been based on money, looks, or "their late husband's service." Now it was based on their own achievements and their own service. Heading the list was Judge Florence Allen of the Ohio Supreme Court, whom Democratic women had slated for a Supreme Court appointment. (Allen was "one in the tradition of Mrs. Catt, if you get what I mean," Committeewoman Emily Blair had written to Molly Dewson in 1932.) After Florence Allen, the list was graded by rank, from women who deserved "imperative recognition" to those who were worthy of "lesser distinction." Since Eleanor Roosevelt's opinions carried particular weight with James Farley, Dewson urged her to make her weight felt. Continuous pressure would have to be applied "on behalf of one woman today and another woman another day," Molly Dewson warned, since men wanted the jobs too.

By June 1933, seven appointments had been made from the list, but the pace was too slow to suit Dewson. "The nicest of men are slippery as eels," she told Eleanor. Over the summer, Molly Dewson was still embroiled in battle, consulting with Eleanor and pressuring James Farley, who admired her persistence. "I am going to paddle right along and wring as many jobs out of the men as I can," she wrote to Emily Blair in July. Six months later, she still persisted. "Mary Dewson is back on my neck," a presidential aide complained to Farley. By 1935, according to Bess Furman's AP report, at least fifty women had been appointed to high-level posts in the New Deal. "The steady increase of woman's influence," Eleanor told writer Martha Gellhorn, "tends to ameliorate bad social conditions."

But even before the end of 1933, a pattern of upper-rank women's appointments was clear. Women could be most easily appointed to jobs concerned with women and children; to advisory boards, where they had no direct power; and to newly formed agencies, where men would not have to cede control. Within the executive departments, Frances Perkins's Labor Department was a special bastion, since it included both the Women's Bureau, headed by WTUL stalwart Mary Anderson, and the Children's Bureau, under Hull-House veteran Grace Abbott. Most women's appointments, however, were in agencies that had just been created to administer the New Deal—such as the NRA consumers' advisory board, which Frances Perkins described as "an afterthought of my own," or in new federal relief agencies, like the Federal Emergency Relief Administration (FERA), where Ellen Woodward, a former Mississippi legislator and social welfare leader, headed women's projects. Like Eleanor Roosevelt and Molly Dewson, the women appointed in 1933 were invariably both active Democrats and longtime activists in woman's organizations, with friendships and contacts in the WTUL, NCL, LWV, social welfare work, and the Women's Division of the Democratic party. Bess Furman felt she was witnessing a "New Deal women's movement of impressive proportions." The movement was "completely out in the open," Furman wrote. "Yet it was so ignored by many masculine politicians that it might as well have been underground."

Unable to find appointments for everyone on her list, Molly Dewson sometimes paid off loyalists with jobs for their husbands, part-time work at the Women's Division, or honorary posts ("No pay but good chance"). Meanwhile, Eleanor Roosevelt convinced Postmaster Farley to give out 4,000 postmasterships to women, raising the female proportion of postmasters from 17.6 percent under Hoover to 26 percent after 1933. "You are at the center of it all," Carrie Chapman Catt wrote to Eleanor, "the beginning of a grand display of stateswomen we are going to have after a time." To women in office, Eleanor was also a pivotal figure. "I felt much closer to the White House because of Mrs. Roosevelt's interest and friendship," wrote Mary Anderson of the Women's Bureau. "I felt that working women everywhere could turn to her for help and support and through her could find the kind of sympathetic interest from the President that would be very helpful." To pressure groups outside of government, Eleanor seemed the person to reach in order to get a woman a job. "The only way the Negro is going to get fair treatment is for you to see that a strong, capable Negro woman is appointed," insisted the Negro Press Association in 1934.

The "women's movement" spirit that Eleanor generated in 1933 included not only women in top-level appointments but also cabinet wives, newswomen, and all women who worked in the executive branch. Within this group, she had certain preferences. "For women who held jobs and made their own way in the world she had an admiration that amounted almost to awe," Lorena Hickok wrote, and this admiration seldom extended to cabinet wives. With the exception of Eleanor Morgenthau, an old friend and frequent companion, cabinet wives resisted Eleanor Roosevelt's example of activism "because their husbands would not approve," Eleanor later wrote. They seemed to prefer to limit themselves to social duties, "which they felt safe and correct." Nonetheless, in 1933 she used her personal influence to forge a women's constituency in Washington.

Since the President and male cabinet officers were traditionally entertained by newsmen at their annual "Gridiron dinner," from which Frances Perkins was excluded, Eleanor Roosevelt at once established a new rite, the annual "Gridiron widows dinner," for cabinet wives, women reporters, newsmen's wives, and prominent women officials. At the first such occasion, held in Frances Perkins's honor, news was created when an overly enthusiastic White House guard dog bit Senator Hattie Caraway of Arkansas, who had recently been elected to her late husband's seat. Eleanor also began to hold elaborate teas and garden parties for cabinet wives and women who worked in the executive branch. "A fine gesture," said Mary Anderson, since women in government service "had never before been particularly recognized by the White House or by other government officials." Some congresswomen, however, declined to attend; they disliked being lumped together with secretaries and wives. Bess Furman, meanwhile, started an elaborate system of file folders in order to keep track of Eleanor's "constant companions and co-workers." Added to such files as "Jaunts and Journeys," "Education Theories," and "World Court" came new ones labeled "Cabinet Wives," "Congress gals," "Women Peacers," "Women Patrioteers," "Women's Clubbers," and "White House Lore."

What kept reporters really busy and drove Bess Furman into low-heeled shoes were Eleanor Roosevelt's causes—evidence of what Emma Bugbee called her "instinct" for social reform. By the middle of 1933, her major cause was the 400,000 unemployed women who had lost their jobs since depression struck. Federal programs such as FERA, CWA, and the Civilian Conservation Corps had been started both to provide relief and to "meet some of the people's need to work," as Eleanor explained in a 1933 radio speech. But as she told her civics class at the New York Junior League that fall (and Emma Bugbee reported in the *Tribune*), "Most of the re-employment-relief measures have been directed towards men." In her new crusade to create women's jobs, Eleanor Roosevelt used all of the tactics available, including personal pressure, the press conference, and a new device, the White House conference.

In November 1933, she organized a White House Conference on the Emergency Needs of Women to discuss "better handling the needs of unemployed women." Attended by fifty social work leaders, including the core of women appointees and social reformers that had coalesced around Eleanor, the conference induced a reporter to observe that the White House was becoming "Hull-House on Pennsylvania Avenue." "Either a certain number of jobs must be found for a certain number of women or . . . a certain amount of money must be allocated for giving women work," Eleanor told the conference. After Harry Hopkins, head of relief efforts, announced his hope to provide work for 3,000 to 4,000 women, Ellen Woodward, head of women's projects at FERA and CWA, suggested the types of work that women could do, such as sewing, canning, clerical work, public health work, emergency nursery schools, musical programs, and historical research. By the end of the year, 100,000 jobs (out of 2 million) had been allocated to women under FERA and CWA. Ellen Woodward, an enthusiastic collaborator, told Eleanor that thirty-five states had appointed women directors to head women's projects. "Keep at it, Sister Woodward," Molly Dewson wrote at the beginning of 1934.

Eleanor Roosevelt, meanwhile, pursued a related goal. "June 1, 1933," Bess

Furman wrote in her journal, "an endless, wrecking, dizzying day. Mrs. Roosevelt and Frances Perkins give out joint statement on women's camps." Addressing the women-only press conference, the two women proposed female counterparts to the CCC camps, in which "unattached young women would do lighter horticultural tasks in reforestation," Furman reported. The proposed camps, labeled "She, She, She" by the press, never materialized. Frances Perkins, reporters learned, had been deluged with telegrams condemning the idea of taking women from their homes. But Eleanor Roosevelt persisted, calling for another White House conference, this time on Resident Schools for Unemployed Women. Soon some women's camps were set up as joint federal-state agencies under FERA. The first, at Bear Mountain, New York (later called Camp Jane Addams), became Eleanor's special interest. By the end of 1934, twenty-eight such camps had been established under the direction of Hilda Smith, who had run Bryn Mawr's summer school for women in industry. Young single women from needy families attended the camps for a summer term and were given small allowances—although not wages, as were men at CCC. Once installed, they attended programs in handicrafts, home economics, health education, workers' education, and vocational guidance; afterward, some even found jobs. The women's camps were a special triumph, but like the women's work-relief projects, they also turned out to be a token effort. "The boys get the breaks, the girls are neglected," Hilda Smith later told Eleanor.

By the time Camp Jane Addams was established, some ambiguity was developing between Eleanor Roosevelt's roles as public leader and private citizen. When applying pressure or campaigning for a cause, she often claimed to be acting merely as a "private citizen." Even the press conferences were held only by a private citizen, Eleanor claimed, since were she a public official she would have to open the conferences to all reporters, not just women. Nor did she stress her own leadership role. "She is careful to point out that she merely cooperates with officials," confirmed Ruby Black, "that she does not and cannot direct." To others, of course, Eleanor seemed to be something of a meddler. "The way Eleanor buzzed about like a fly annoying you was fairly characteristic of her then," said Walter Lippmann, later an admirer. But she was unable to avoid causes, since "each thing I saw proved so fascinating, that I found myself going more and more, farther and farther." And once involved in a cause, she was usually unable to avoid leadership. This proved to be the case at the end of 1933, when Eleanor became involved in one of the New Deal's most adventurous experiments.

By June of 1933, AP reporter Lorena Hickok was no longer able to cover so close a friend as Eleanor Roosevelt. Since their friendship had formed on the 1932 campaign trail, Hickok and Eleanor had written to each other incessantly and talked on the phone every night. "You have grown so much to be a part of my life that it is empty without you even though I'm busy every minute," Eleanor wrote in March 1933, before the first press conference. "My pictures are nearly all up and I have you in my sitting room where I can look at you most of my waking hours," she told Hickok a few days later. When Lorena Hickok came to Washington in the spring for a newswomen's party given by Bess Furman, she stayed in the White House. During the summer, the two women had finally driven off to the Gaspé Peninsula for a month's vacation, evading reporters entirely. But for Lorena Hickok, the friendship became a professional hazard. "A reporter should never get too close to the news source," Louis Howe told her. So leaving her successful AP career behind, Hickok took a job with Harry Hopkins, head of relief efforts.

Her assignment was to "travel around the country," as she described it, "watching what was happening to people on relief, physically, mentally, and socially." During these travels, Lorena Hickok sent long confidential reports to Harry Hopkins and daily letters to Eleanor Roosevelt, telling of her experiences from the Dakotas to Appalachia. The most dire reports came from West Virginia, where, Hickok found, unemployed miners were living with their families in decrepit huts; children were sleeping on bug-ridden rags; everyone drank polluted water from sewage-filled gullies; and disease was rampant. "Not a county or city hospital with a free clinic in the whole state," she wrote to Eleanor.

This was not the first Eleanor Roosevelt had heard of West Virginia's problems. The WTUL had channeled funds into the area, and the American Friends Service Committee was already at work on the scene. At the Friends' invitation, Eleanor drove down to inspect the area around Morgantown. She was able to spend the day with a social worker, visiting miners' homes, "without anyone discovering who I was or that I was even remotely connected with the government." What she saw only confirmed Hickok's reports. "There were men in that area who had been on relief for three to five years and who had almost forgotten what it was like to have a job. . . . There were children who did not know what it was like to eat a proper meal." On Scott's Run, near Morgantown, "some of the company houses, perched on hills on either side of the run, seemed scarcely fit for human habitation," Eleanor wrote. Kitchens were equipped with only a few cracked cups and plates; families were in debt to company stores; outbreaks of typhoid fever and diphtheria were prevalent; and the whole place was black with dust. "You felt as if the coal dust had seeped into every crack in the house and it would be impossible to get them or the people clean."

Cleaning up the area around Scott's Run became at once a preoccupation. At first, Eleanor served on an advisory committee to find jobs for local residents, but this was merely a stepping-stone. "Soon our press conference was hearing of plans for a pioneer subsistence homestead project for some of the stranded miners' families," Bess Furman wrote. The goal of the new Subsistence Homestead Act, then under the auspices of the Department of the Interior, was to enable the rural poor to buy their own federally built homes over a thirty-year period, while farming their own plots and working in local industry. "I liked the theory of trying to put people to work to help themselves," Eleanor wrote. She also liked putting the theory into practice. Once a federal homestead community was established near Morgantown, her enthusiasm was boundless. Arthurdale, the first of thirty-four planned communities, was built on a 1,200-acre run-down estate. When the first fifty families moved in, Eleanor Roosevelt led newswomen around on a tour. By then she was well embarked on what Bess Furman called "a marathon of devotion" to Arthurdale.

The homestead community was in fact a social reformer's field day. Plans for Arthurdale involved arrangements for homes, education, health, and culture, and Eleanor was involved in every aspect of planning, injecting her own ideas, standards, and personnel. She wanted to establish, for instance, a progressive education system, exemplary public health services, consumer cooperatives, a handicraft business, and cultural programs to preserve the Appalachian heritage. To Eleanor Roosevelt, the planned community meant not just constructing houses but also teaching residents "how to live" and infusing them with a communitarian ethos. Before long, old friends and new ones, notably progressive educators, were hired at her insistence to manage Arthurdale's institutions. Meanwhile, she was busy choosing homesteaders, organizing a children's clinic, selecting appliances for the federally built homes, and raising funds for the school and craft programs. In 1934, when she resumed radio talks, her broadcast earnings were contributed to Arthurdale.

The press had a field day too. News photos showed the President's wife addressing groups of homesteaders, meeting infant Franklins and Eleanors, and joining in Arthurdale square dances. But since the community was viewed as Eleanor's project, Bess Furman explained, it was "doomed to political stress and storms from the outset." Not only did critics view the homestead program as

From 1933 on, Eleanor Roosevelt was a constant visitor at Arthurdale, where she often participated in community activities. Below, a square dance in 1938. *(AP/Wide World Photos, courtesy FDR Library)*

creeping socialism and an attack on free enterprise, but Arthurdale in particular was widely held up as a bungled effort. Everything that could go wrong seemed to do so, starting with the houses, which at first did not fit the foundations. It was "one big headache . . . from the beginning," Interior Secretary Ickes wrote in his diary. "We are spending money down there like drunken sailors." Neither agricultural subsistence nor local industry ever succeeded; a communal ethos never evolved; and Arthurdale residents proved especially hostile to progressive education. Most of the families remained on work relief until World War II, when the aircraft industry finally lifted the community out of the depression. By then it had cost $2 million. In Eleanor's opinion, however, Arthurdale was hardly a failure. People had been saved from sanitariums, insane asylums, and jails. They had been "restored to usefulness and given confidence in themselves," she wrote. "The human values were most rewarding even if the financial returns to the government were unsatisfactory."

"Human values" were, after all, the pivot of the reformer's creed that Eleanor Roosevelt had adopted during her early efforts in settlement work and the NCL, and later in the LWV and the WTUL. If neither the women's residence camps nor subsistence homesteading were ultimately marked successes, Eleanor had, throughout 1933, proven a champion of women's interests and provided a model of social concern. She had created a "New Deal for newswomen," insisted on women's appointments to high-level posts, defended the interests of unemployed women, increased women's clout in the Democratic party, created a "women's movement" on Capitol Hill, and touted women's projects and achievements at the Monday morning press conferences. She had inaugurated a campaign for the end of alley slums, aided thousands of correspondents who wrote to her, supported the cause of the World War I veterans, and organized a program to rescue the families of West Virginia miners. Before the year was out, she had also published a personal and political manifesto. *It's Up to the Women*, which appeared in November 1933, called on women to use the depression to assert traditional feminine strengths, both as "inspirations of the home" and as activists in public life.

The book was in fact a manual of housekeeping, domestic and civic. It moved methodically, as the press conferences had, from the home outward. Eleanor began with advice to the homemaker—on menus, budgets, clothes buying, time allocation, baby care, child psychology, and family health. She included a medley of domestic tips, from recipes for vegetable stew, a depression standby, to commonsense reminders ("Sleep with the windows open"). From these she moved steadily outward to jobs, causes, and public life. *It's Up to the Women* was stuffed with injunctions about the importance of outside affiliations, whether volunteer ("Work with some civic group or some active piece of work for the community") or remunerative. Paid employment, Eleanor stressed, satisfied a woman's need to find out that "she is still able to do something which expresses her personality even though she may be a wife and mother. . . . Of course, her first duty is to her home, but her duty to her home must not of necessity preclude her having another occupation."

The occupations she recommended were teaching, nursing, and social work, but the highest calling was public service, an arena in which she had great expertise. Women had not yet used the vote or political rights to change the way government worked, Eleanor posited, but "the attitude of women towards change in society is going to determine to a great extent our future in this country." She advised women first to join nonpartisan organizations and do some political work on a local level—such as "helping the assistant chairwoman bring people in on election day to the polls"—before trying to move on to elective or appointive office.

Once in office, a woman's obligations multiplied. She would have to evoke civic consciousness among other women by pointing out how government "affected their homes, building, and working conditions, the water they drink, the food they eat, their children, the schools, the public health, the recreations." She would have to act as a trailblazer for others. "During the next few years every woman in public office will be watched far more carefully than a man holding a similar position, and she will be acting as a pioneer preparing the way for many other women who will follow in her footsteps." She would have to fulfill higher standards than men. Like Frances Perkins, the woman who held political office "must be very excellent in her job." Above all, she would have to be a new type of disinterested public servant, again exemplified by Frances Perkins, who pursued her career "not because she will gain anything materially . . . but because she sees an opportunity to render a public service to the general happiness of the working man and woman in their families."

Women had special obligations in public life, Eleanor Roosevelt stressed, whether as educators, pacifists, consumers, or political watchdogs. But the most important of these special obligations was to protect the interests of wage-earning women, a tenet that served as a dividing line between such organizations as the LWV or the WTUL, which supported protective laws, and the National Woman's party, which demanded an Equal Rights Amendment. Eleanor espoused the principle of equal pay for equal work, "but also special legislation regarding special conditions of [women's] work." Wage-and-hour laws, she contended, were needed until both men and women "had equal pay and were assured a living wage." Women workers were not yet "as well organized or able to negotiate for themselves" as men, she explained, and therefore the state was obligated to protect them. Indeed, "it must concern itself with the health of the women because the future of the race depends on their ability to produce healthy children." The NWP was wrong to insist on the ERA, Eleanor concluded, because "Women *are* different from men. They are equal in many ways but they cannot refuse to acknowledge their differences. Not to acknowledge them weakens their case. Their physical functions in life are different and perhaps in the same way the contributions which they are to bring to the spiritual side of life are different."

Although hardly a runaway best-seller, *It's Up to the Women* moved along briskly, as Eleanor's publisher informed her. It also met with mixed reviews, especially from feminists. To Suzanne LaFollette, who had promoted the cause of "economic independence" in the 1920s, the tone and content of Eleanor Roosevelt's tract seemed silly. "*It's Up to the Women* isn't likely to be very helpful to the wives of miners or steel workers, who probably won't read it anyhow,"

LaFollette wrote in the *Saturday Review* at the end of 1933. "It may be helpful to the middle-class woman who needs to be told that two and two are four." But historian Mary Beard, reviewing the book in the *Herald Tribune,* was more receptive. Hardly from the same camp as Eleanor, Mary Beard was in fact an NWP member, although one who could never bring herself to renounce protective laws. In her review, she tried to identify the virtues of both book and author. Eleanor Roosevelt, she pointed out, had become a national advice giver, replacing such authorities as Dorothy Dix and Beatrice Fairfax. She offered "inspiration to the married, solace to the lovelorn, assistance to the homemaker, menus to the cook, help to the educator, direction to the employer . . . and deeper awareness of its primordial force to the 'weaker sex.'" Eleanor's model of activism had also transformed the White House into a last stop of solace. "This suffering generation may bring its more complex problems to the center of the nation."

The year 1933 was only the beginning of Eleanor Roosevelt's long career in national life. Through depression and war, she remained a model of social concern at the center of power. As lobbyist, publicist, moralist, and partisan, she filled an unprecedented space in public affairs, especially as an advocate for the underrepresented—whether women, blacks, youth, or the unemployed. Once she was installed in the White House, moreover, her perpetual motion was highly visible. Touring the coal mines or visiting the troops, as recorded in newsreels and news photos, or reaching the public through her magazine articles, newspaper columns, radio talks, or lecture tours, Eleanor Roosevelt was constantly in the public eye. As time went by, she no longer confined her efforts to issues of "special interest and value to the women of the country," as she had attempted to do at her early press conferences. Indeed, the more she became involved with national affairs, the less involved she was with women's affairs. By the end of the 1940s, she had become a major fixture in Democratic politics and the nation's representative at the newly formed United Nations. The first woman to achieve such a powerful national presence, Eleanor Roosevelt was also the most prominent alumna of the woman's movement, which had provided her with both a social philosophy and a training ground for public life.

18

⚬∾⚬

EMERGENCIES:
THE 1930S AND 1940S

While Eleanor Roosevelt rose to national prominence, women's history was reshaped by national events. The Great Depression and World War II were disruptive "emergencies" that changed women's roles, at home, at work, and in public life.

The emergencies affected, first of all, women's participation in the labor force. In both the 1930s and the 1940s, women were advised to adapt their roles to suit the nation's economic needs. When depression struck, they were urged to remain at home and leave what jobs there were for male "breadwinners." During World War II, they were exhorted to assume paid jobs, especially in the war industries, to relieve the nation's manpower shortage. Throughout both emergencies, however, women's participation in the work force rose, slowly during the 1930s and rapidly during World War II, when a record number of women started to work. Both emergencies, moreover, drew married women into the labor market. The new opportunities provided by war were temporary; at demobilization, women's jobs in the millions were lost. But by the end of the 1940s, when the female segment of the labor force began again to expand, its composition changed. Unlike wartime welders and riveters, the average new worker in the postwar era was likely to enter a traditional "woman's field," not heavy industry. But like the war worker, and indeed like many new wage earners of the 1930s, she was apt to be married and middle-aged. She was also more likely to be middle class than the average working woman before the depression. The emergencies set the stage for the contemporary female labor force.

The long-range change in women's work patterns was not connected to a national shift in ideas about what woman's role in society should be. On the contrary, the emergencies confirmed a shared conviction that in the best of times as in the worst of times woman's place was in the home. Almost two decades of crises only underlined a desire for stable and secure American families, with paychecked fathers and caring mothers who devoted themselves to domestic life. Throughout the 1930s and 1940s, domestic ideals showed tremendous resilience. Vindicated in depression and retained through the war, they emerged full-blown and stronger than ever in the postwar era. World War II, which brought great disruption of family life, was a turning point. By the end of the 1940s, a vigorous cult of domesticity had emerged, more strident in tone than earlier versions. The emergencies of the 1930s and 1940s did not pave a path to sexual equality, at least ideologically. Rather, they laid the groundwork for a conservative division of gender roles, an apparent retreat from public affairs, and a pronounced antifeminist mood.

Feminist decline was another theme of the 1930s and 1940s. During the 1920s, the woman's movement had been beset by strains, internal and external, but full of fight as it reorganized for the postsuffrage era. The sequence of emergencies, however, did not provide a favorable climate. Egalitarian hopes were an early casualty. New aspirations of the expansive 1920s, for economic independence and individualism, were quenched by depression, which made them, quite quickly, irrelevant luxuries. The minority National Woman's party, committed to egalitarian goals, soon assumed a marginal role. "Social feminism," a larger and more hardy specimen, faded away gradually. During the early New Deal, as Eleanor Roosevelt's experience suggests, veterans of progressive reform made an impact on federal policy. But women's activism in politics and government during the New Deal was more a last gasp of progressive energy than an omen of future trends. "Human values" held sway only briefly.

By the late 1930s, all varieties of postsuffrage feminism declined and world war, once again, was a turning point. By the end of World War II, the liberal, social reform wing of the woman's movement was gone. Its functions had been supplanted by New Deal welfare policies, labor laws, and the emergence of a strong labor movement. The government social worker had long since replaced the settlement-house reformer. Large surviving groups such as the General Federation of Women's Clubs, now apolitical, and the civic-minded League of Women Voters had melted into the suburban scenery. Although the battle over an Equal Rights Amendment continued into the early 1950s, feminism was now a marginal force. By the postwar era, the energetic world of women's politics, through which Eleanor Roosevelt had once entered public life, no longer existed. A major blow came at the outset, when the Great Depression began.

Depression Families

"I have watched fear grip the people in our neighborhood around Hull-House," Jane Addams wrote in 1931, "men and women who have seen their small margin of savings disappear; heads of families who see and anticipate hunger for their children before it occurs. That clutch of cold fear is one of the most hideous aspects." During the 1930s, the clutch of cold fear transformed family life, not only for the families of the 25 percent of workers who were unemployed by 1933, such as the Morgantown miners, but also for those middle-class families whose incomes were so drastically reduced that they fell from a state of relative security into a limbo of uncertainty and panic. For the family as for the economy, the depression provided an interruption in the rapid movement toward modernity of the 1920s, with its ever-expanding, upwardly mobile, individualistic and consumerist thrust. The retreat from modernity affected many aspects of American life: Migration to cities, for instance, halted or even reversed itself, as urban areas became pits of unemployment rather than centers of opportunity. For women, the depression brought a sudden end to the aspirations of the 1920s. Sometimes it reinforced traditional roles. More often it demanded new emergency roles, appropriate to the dire situation.

Ideologically, the depression gave new currency to the dogma that woman's place was at home, that women who worked did so mainly for "pin money," and that jobs should be reserved for male "breadwinners." In 1930, when Frances Perkins denounced the "pin-money worker" as a "menace to society, a selfish and short-sighted creature who ought to be ashamed of herself," she was expressing a widely held view. The wage-earning wife, it appeared, committed an antisocial act by taking away a man's salary and, implicitly, depriving another family of income. As unemployment rose and family income sank, government, business, labor, and public opinion reinforced the need to exclude married women from the work force.

Federal law, from 1932 to 1937, prohibited more than one family member from working in the federal civil service. Although women's groups, including both the LWV and especially the NWP, mobilized to repeal Section 213 of the National Economy Act, they had no success. Women were three-quarters of those federal workers forced to resign. (Eleanor Roosevelt, who denounced Section 213 forcefully, hoped such resignations would be "voluntary" and "temporary," not a "permanent concession.") States, too, rejected married women from government posts, and local governments instituted similar policies. In half the states, bills were proposed to prohibit the hiring of married women in *any* job, but a women's lobby led by the LWV defeated these measures. Still, bias against wives was extensive. In 1931, three out of four school boards surveyed by the National Educational Association would not hire married women teachers, and most dismissed women teachers who married. Private businesses discouraged women from competing with men for jobs, while women's colleges urged their graduates not to take paid work. Organized labor joined the campaign as well. Married women workers with employed husbands, said the executive council of the AFL, "should be discriminated against in the hiring of employees."

Public opinion reinforced antipathy to the working wife, and during the 1930s public opinion became a tangible entity. The public opinion poll replaced the sexual survey as the latest contribution to social science. In 1936, when the Gallup poll asked whether wives should work if their husbands had jobs, a resounding 82 percent of all respondents (and 75 percent of women respondents) said no. The same year, *Fortune* revealed that 85 percent of male readers and 79 percent of female readers thought that *no* wife should work outside the home; in 1937, over half of all Gallup respondents (and 42 percent of female respondents) agreed. And in 1938, the *Ladies' Home Journal* reported that although 75 percent of its readers believed that husbands and wives should make decisions together, 90 percent thought that the wife should give up work if the husband wished her to remain at home. Despite the variety of samples and the consistent differential between male and female views, the weight of the polls did not support the working wife.

But public animosity to married women wage earners was counteracted in practice by family need. During the depression the proportion of married women in the work force rose. Indeed, most new workers were married women—precisely those who were urged to remain at home. (The proportion of single women who worked declined.) The working wife who contributed her wages to family support had little connection with those hopes for individualism and economic independence that had been voiced in the expansive 1920s. "Feminists—new style" of the 1930s who sought to combine marriage and career did not publicize their endeavors; aspiration had gone out of vogue. Now wage work could be defended only as an extension of the traditional task of family sustenance. Historian Lois Scharf contends that the depression caused "an erosion of feminist rhetoric and thought," one that would long outlive the 1930s. This erosion damaged the credentials of the National Woman's party, which steadfastly championed women's right to work outside the home. If the 1920s had proved unsympathetic to "equal rights," Scharf points out, the 1930s provided an even more hostile climate.

While many married women assumed new roles as wage earners, often in temporary or part-time work, most retained traditional roles as homemakers. But their contributions to the household economy became more significant. Clearly, home management assumed new importance as family resources dwindled. The thrifty, inventive housekeeper was once again crucial to family survival. Eleanor Roosevelt set the pace by instituting 7-cent meals in the White House, as revealed at a 1933 press conference. (Some noted that only FDR could be forced to eat these concoctions, since no one else would.) The White House example was timely. The successful homemaker of the 1930s was one who could "make ends meet." As household budgets fell, women also began to sew their own clothes and can their own food, reversing the trend of the 1920s toward ever more consumer goods. In addition, housewives once again took in paid work, such as laundry, boarders, or dressmaking, and even started small household businesses—whether running kitchen beauty parlors or selling baked goods or clothes items. "In the South, if you were a lady, you sewed," recalled a Chicago widow, southern-born and once well-off, who had gone into the negligee business with a friend.

Home industry was not the only retreat to traditionalism. During the 1930s, the family often expanded to include marginal members, old or young, who sometimes doubled up with another generation. New York public health nurses sometimes found twelve people in three rooms, which did not necessarily enhance the "clan spirit" that Eleanor Roosevelt envisioned. At the bottom of the depression, in fact, family life seemed to disintegrate, a matter of enormous concern. While divorce declined, due to the expense, desertion increased and marriage was postponed. After 1929, the marriage rate plunged, and it did not start to rise again until 1934. "Do you realize how many people in my generation are not married?" a Chicago educator asked Studs Terkel in *Hard Times,* his oral history of the depression. "There were young men around when we were young but they were all supporting mothers." Available men were likely to disappear, as her own prospect did when he lost his job: "It hit him like a ton of bricks and he just vanished."

While the marriage rate took a sudden fall, the birthrate continued its long-term decline. Births per 1,000 women of child-bearing age plunged from 97.4 to 75.7 in the nadir of 1933. "The drop has been precipitous," *Harper's* announced in 1935. Overall, the birthrate fell less in the 1930s than it had in the 1920s. Still, contraception gained new popularity, especially among men. "Before the depression I never gave a thought to birth control," one father told sociologist Mirra Komarovsky. "Had we been able to foresee the depression, we would have felt differently about it." Birth-control clinics, which had dwindled in number by the time of the 1929 stock market crash, suddenly boomed. By 1931, eighty-five clinics gave out advice to alleviate "mental and physical suffering." During the depression, birth-control clinics also provided counseling for married and engaged couples, and the *Birth Control Review* shifted its stress from eugenic arguments to "marriage and family guidance." Birth-control proponents, meanwhile, attempted to incorporate contraception into New Deal programs. By the end of the decade, the birth-control movement had won its major victory. After a 1936 federal court decision, it was finally legal for doctors to distribute contraceptive information and devices except where prohibited by state law, as in Massachusetts and Connecticut.

While the marriage rate fell and the birthrate drooped, the depression family withdrew into itself, as reported by the small army of sociologists that examined it. Study after study showed that husbands and wives tended to drop social friendships and outside connections because of fear of snubs, suspicion of others, or inability to meet the expenses of socializing. Family members now relied on one another for company. "The unemployed man and his wife have no social life," Mirra Komarovsky wrote in 1934, and for months at a time the family had no social contacts with outsiders. "The only visitors that they have are their married children with their families." In some cases, social withdrawal was accompanied by sexual withdrawal, as in Komarovsky's sample of bottom-rung middle-class families hit by depression, where sexual activity often came to a halt. In only one of fifty-nine cases was increased activity reported. When a husband proved unable to provide for the family, sociologist Eli Ginzburg observed, "his wife frequently lost her balance." Such lack of balance was exemplified by Mrs. Wolfe, who revealed "a changed attitude toward intercourse":

> When her husband was working and supporting her, she supposed it was his right to have sexual relations and she therefore acquiesced. Now she avoids it. She has limited sexual relations to once a week and even tried to get out of this. . . . She saw no reason [to use] contraception just to give her husband pleasure.

If Mrs. Wolfe appeared unbalanced, or at least a poor sport, this was because woman's traditional role was to provide psychological sustenance, especially for men who were humiliated by loss of work. In times of crisis, Eleanor Roosevelt wrote in 1933, women had "more strength of a certain kind than men . . . a certain kind of vitality which gives them a reserve which at times of absolute necessity they can call upon." Since the obligation of "breadwinner" fell on men, they became desperate when jobs vanished. "Like searing irons, the degradation, the sheer terror and panic which loss of job brings, the deprivation and the bitterness have eaten into men's souls," an officer of a District of Columbia welfare agency wrote in 1931. In some cases women shared this despair; they withdrew from life and retreated into "dreary little worlds of their own," psychologist Lorine Pruette reported in 1934. More often, she found, they "triumphed over their difficulties." Protected by gender roles, women did not suffer the same humiliation from loss of work that afflicted men. Married women, moreover, who were less likely to have jobs to lose, continued in their old routines and often took on expanded responsibilities. They also assumed increased authority, while husbands' wages and power declined. "When Mr. Raparka lost his job in the fall of 1933, he dominated the family," Wight Bakke observed in *Citizens Without Work.* "Two years later it was Mrs. Raparka who was the center of authority."

Not all households studied were transformed by the depression. During the mid-1930s, sociologist Margaret Hagood traveled throughout the Southeast, interviewing the wives of tenant farmers, whose lives remained much the same. Caring for large families, doing field work, farm work, and housework, in impoverished circumstances, poor rural women retained traditional and subordinate roles. But most researchers focused their attention not on the families of migrant workers nor on families that had always been poor but rather on middle-class families that had suffered a sudden decline in status. In such families, wives often moved in to fill a power vacuum. The Burtons, described in a University of Michigan study, were a good example. The father, once a successful wholesale merchant in Saginaw, lost his business and took a salesman's job in Ann Arbor. This meant, at the outset, a loss of community ties and far lower pay. His income dropped from $10,000 to $3,000 a year. After the move, Mr. Burton lost energy, became nervous, and was afflicted by strain. But Mrs. Burton, once a conventional housewife whose outside affiliations extended only to the wives of her husband's associates and a church auxiliary, catapulted into the ascendancy. In Ann Arbor, she earned most of the family's income by taking in boarders. Although she never made any new outside connections, she quickly became, in the case analyst's words, "the family heroine."

She remains healthy, ambitious, vivacious, while doing all the housework for her own family and looking after the rooms for eight students, as well as doing their washing and ironing. . . . She has given up all her former activities. She finds her life completely within the home. Now and then she wishes for her old life but is on the whole contented.

Families that were well-adjusted, like the Burtons, sociologists stressed, were able to survive the depression in better shape than those that were not. In

While sociologists of the 1930s concentrated their attention on urban families, photographer Dorothea Lange, who worked for the Farm Security Administration, documented the Great Depression's impact on rural Americans. During the years 1936–1938, working with sociologist Margaret Hagood, she traveled through the South and the Dust Bowl, where bad weather and crop failures had forced farmers off the land. This picture of a migrant mother and her children was taken on a Texas roadside in 1936. *(Dorothea Lange, Library of Congress)*

fact, in less well-integrated families, children rather than mothers moved into control, an even more drastic form of role reversal. This was the case with the Riley family in the Michigan study. Mr. Riley, a never-too-successful lawyer but a big spender, neglected his practice and slid swiftly downhill in the early 1930s, taking to the local poolroom where he played cards with "riff-raff" and became very nervous. His wife was "little concerned by either his mental decline or financial problems." But twenty-four-year-old Winifred, a musical performer, emerged triumphant. "As her father's income went steadily down, that of his daughter went steadily up, so that she became the chief breadwinner," the case analyst reported. "Winifred became a family leader."

Young people such as Winifred often resented being put into "breadwinner" positions, according to *The Survey*, a magazine for social workers, in 1935. Once the "emergency" became a "permanency," employed offspring, especially working teenagers, protested against "the hardships of supporting unemployed fathers, brothers, sisters, and others living in the home." Depression role reversals, whether parent/child or husband/wife, came to be associated with negative causes—poverty, misfortune, and downward mobility. Underlining the depression's impact, such role reversals only enhanced a desire for the traditional family of more prosperous times, where authority rested with the male "breadwinner." Still, once crisis struck, women's significance at home seemed to increase (relative to that of men), transforming even inconspicuous housewives like Mrs. Burton into "heroines." Ironically, women sometimes fared better than men as wage earners as well. For despite injunctions to remain at home, the depression actually had a dual message for women workers.

Working Women

During the 1930s, contradictory pressures affected women: Public attitudes urged them not to work, but economic circumstances both spurred wage labor and in some circumstances made jobs available. Not surprisingly, public policy and public opinion took a toll on female employment. Women professionals were especially hard hit. By the end of the 1930s, the proportion of women in professional work had dropped, as men sought jobs in such fields as social work and education. The teaching force, which had been 85 percent female in 1920, was only 78 percent female in 1940. Other women lost jobs in business, as bookkeepers and insurance agents, for instance, and moved downward in the occupational scale. By 1938, one-fifth of the female work force was unemployed. But wage-earning women were still less likely than men to be forced out of the work force entirely. Throughout the depression, women's overall participation in the labor force increased, to a higher level than ever before. Women entered the labor force at twice the rate of men, the number of women workers rose 25 percent, and the proportion of married women who worked rose as well. In 1930, only 29 percent of women wage earners were married, but in 1940, 35 percent. Even in some professions, the numbers of women grew.

The increase of women in the work force was not due solely to a rise in "need"—though as the Women's Bureau contended in a steady stream of publications, women *did* work out of need and not for "pin money." Rather, the depression's impact on women workers was minimized because sexual segregation in the labor force provided some insulation. Women workers were concentrated in "women's fields," such as sales, clerical, and service occupations, and these were less hard hit than the areas of heavy industry—autos, steel, construction—where few women were employed. In some states, at the depths of the depression, male unemployment was as much as four times as great as female unemployment. Similarly, the sectors that employed the most women tended to recover most rapidly. Moreover, government measures to revive the economy created more women's jobs, especially in clerical and sales work.

Finally, segregated occupational patterns held fast. Beyond some encroachment into "women's professions," men did not seek "women's work"—althought a *Harper's* article in 1935 suggested that a young man who became a stenographer could, with ambition and aggressiveness, rise to a "semi-executive post." In theory, as sociologist Ruth Milkman points out, women were a reserve labor force to be pushed out of the labor market when times were bad. In practice, however, they were protected to an extent by division of labor within the work force. In addition, while all wages fell, women's wages actually rose proportionally until they were 63 percent of men's wages. (Ordinarily, any increase of women workers means a drop in their relative wages.) In many ways, therefore, women wage earners were relative beneficiaries of economic crisis, or at least some of their disadvantages were transformed into assets. A major beneficiary was the woman worker in industry, whose status at the outset was the most desperate.

The end of European immigration in the 1920s should have gradually expanded opportunities for women in industry, but the onset of depression wiped out or at least postponed any hope of such expansion. By the early 1930s, the status of the woman industrial worker had reached a nadir. If still employed, she was likely to work for reduced pay, which sometimes dropped to abysmally low levels. Southern textile workers, for instance, earned less than 5 cents an hour, and in some garment shops, the Massachusetts Consumers' League reported, women were hired as "apprentices" for no pay only to be fired when their "apprenticeship" ended. Like all factory labor, a woman worker was apt to confront layoffs or speed-ups as companies reduced production or cut back on costs, but she was less likely to be organized, except in a company union. The mid-1930s, however, brought the beginnings of change. New Deal policies were prolabor, prounion, and geared toward protection. And women workers, worst off to begin with, had the most to gain.

From the outset, the Roosevelt administration sought labor support and cooperation and acted to improve the worker's status, especially through wage and hour regulation, a cause for which women reformers had campaigned throughout the 1920s. First, the National Industrial Recovery Act (1933) gave the government the power to establish industrywide codes that included wage and hour provisions. (The Supreme Court had rejected a federal minimum wage law in 1923 and continued to do so until 1937, when it reversed itself.) After the NIRA was invalidated by the Court in 1935, Congress passed the Fair Labor Standards Act of 1938, which established maximum hours and minimum wages, starting at 25 cents an hour, in industries involved in interstate commerce. "Everyone claimed credit for it," said Labor Secretary Frances Perkins, though in her view credit belonged to FDR and herself. The FLSA also helped to improve sweatshop working conditions. It provided minimum wages for women doing piecework at home and, like the defunct NRA codes, prohibited child labor in factory work. (The child labor amendment never made any progress.) During the New Deal, in short, the federal government began to fulfill both women reformers' goals and those endorsed by the National Woman's party in the 1920s—extending "protection" to both male and female workers.

This protection was not always extended in an egalitarian way. Recovery, not equality, was the major New Deal aim. Just as federal work-relief programs either excluded women, as in the case of the Civilian Conservation Corps, or gave men preference and paid them more, as in the case of CWA and the Public Works Administration, labor regulations too reflected sexual preference. While work relief programs focused on heads of household, usually men, labor regulations excluded women in other ways. The NRA codes covered only some industries, and excluded some with large proportions of women workers, like the textile industry. Of the short-lived codes, 75 percent included provisions for equal pay to women workers, which Mary Anderson claimed as a Women's Bureau victory. But the 25 percent that set lower minimum wages for women than for men covered industries with large proportions of women workers, such as cloakmaking, electronics, and commercial laundries. Ten women's organizations, led by the WTUL and NCL, protested against the discriminatory aspects of the NRA codes but to no avail. The FLSA was more effective than the poorly enforced NRA codes and did affect most women in factory work, although clearly it had no impact on other large categories of women wage earners, such as those in sales, service, domestic, or agricultural work.

Whenever protection was provided and enforced in laws or codes, however, women tended to benefit more than men because they were concentrated in unorganized industries and in the lowest paid work. Even the minimum wage often meant a hefty salary hike for women workers, though not enough to make men seek their jobs. There were other benefits from New Deal laws, too. Owners of some types of factories, such as cigar factories, were able to receive government assistance for technological improvements to transform their plants to assembly-line production, which created more low-paid work for women (indeed, this was the very sort of transformation skilled craftsmen had always feared). Finally, in a major shift from policies of the 1920s, the New Deal spurred the formation of labor unions, which benefited all industrial workers.

Depression had weakened the union movement, and women's union membership had accordingly dropped, but an upswing began in 1933. Section 7A of the NIRA protected the right of unions to organize and required employers to bargain with union representatives. As soon as the law went into effect, union membership began to rise. The ILGWU, which had hit a low point, increased its size four times over in 1934 alone. After the NIRA was invalidated, the National Labor Relations Act of 1935 again protected the right of labor to organize and, since it included provisions for enforcement and barred company unions, served as an even more effective spur to union growth. The most important advance for the woman worker, usually neither in skilled crafts nor organized, was the industrial union. These began to form in 1935, first under the industrial union committee of the AFL and then, after 1937, under the new Congress of Industrial Organizations. Although the main focus of the CIO in the late 1930s was in heavy industry with predominantly male employees—such as mining, steel, and automobiles—it also moved into factories where many women worked, such as northern textile plants, and the West Coast canning industry, where many young Mexican American women held jobs. Entering the union was "like joining a great big family," one woman worker recalled. "I loved it." Between 1930 and 1940, women's union membership tripled, reaching 800,000 by the end of the decade.

Like the NRA codes and the FLSA, the union movement of the late 1930s had no impact on the majority of women in the labor force who were outside of factory work. "In the thirties, there was no union," a former salesclerk told interviewer Jeane Westin. "Any woman lucky enough to have a job better not complain about conditions." Nor did the union movement ensure equality to the woman industrial worker. In industries where the majority of workers were men, unions approved contracts with unequal pay for women and men doing the same jobs and also created separate seniority lists for women, which perpetuated inequality in union ranks. Not surprisingly, women were not well represented in union leadership, for reasons that had long been recognized by the WTUL. "Women had an awfully tough time in the union because the men brought their prejudices there," remembered Stella Nowicki, an organizer in the Chicago meat-packing plants in the 1930s and also a "colonizer" for the Communist party, which sent its emissaries into the shops to organize. "The fellows couldn't believe that women in the union were there for the union's sake," Nowicki recalled in Staughton and Alice Lynd's oral history, *Rank and File:*

> The women felt the union was a man's thing because once they got through the day's work they had to take care of their one to fifteen children and the meals and the house and all the rest. . . . The union didn't encourage women to come to meetings. They didn't actually want to take up the problems that women had. . . . The union had so many things to work for—the shorter work day, improved conditions—so many things that they couldn't worry about these things in relation to women.

The great surge in women's organization and CIO growth was yet to come, during World War II, when women provided over a third of the work force and when the meat-packing industry and others were at last successfully organized. Still, the 1930s marked the start of a new era for the woman factory worker. At the same time, the major gains of the New Deal era—such as minimum wage laws, maximum hour laws, child labor prohibitions, and the spurt of unionization—also marked the beginning of the end of the woman's movement to protect women workers. During the 1930s, the WTUL was active but waning. Its budget shrank and the last of its Washington lobbyists resigned. During World War II, when the numbers of women in unions shot upward, the WTUL began to fold its wings, and it finally dissolved in 1950.

While the WTUL's role in labor organization faded, that of the Communist party grew. Party membership doubled in the early 1930s and continued to grow; in 1933, one out of every six members was a woman and by the end of the decade, more than one out of three. Although Communist women never organized autonomously, as socialist women had before World War I, and relatively few assumed key roles on party committees, mere involvement held attraction. For some women on the left, communism seemed to exert the same appeal that feminism had a generation earlier. The party, moreover, made efforts to engage women members. Through a staffed women's commission, women's publications, and a *Daily Worker* column, it addressed "women's issues." It also provided political space for long-time radicals like Elizabeth Gurley Flynn, once Margaret Sanger's colleague in the IWW, or Ella Reeve Bloor, another veteran of prewar socialism, labor organization, and the birth-control crusade. Throughout the decade, women members were active in party campaigns, whether sit-ins, protest marches, factory agitation, or mobilizing the relatives of male workers, as at the Flint Auto strike of 1937. And like colonizer Nowicki, they participated in efforts to organize industrial workers.

The woman factory worker of the 1930s was almost always white. The black working woman was less likely to benefit from either the growth of unions or New Deal labor laws. Women in general faced discrimination in the labor market, the Women's Bureau contended in 1938, but "such hardships have fallen upon Negro women with double harshness." Married or unmarried, black women had always been a disproportionate part of the female labor force and had long worked for family support, a position new to many white middle-class women in the 1930s. The black woman worker had never been accused of working for "pin money." More important, she was customarily excluded from most occupations open to white women, such as white-collar work or industrial work, and relegated to the lowest-paid and most menial jobs, a situation that remained unchanged by depression.

In 1930, according to the Women's Bureau, 90 percent of black women workers were domestics or farm laborers, occupations uncovered by either the NRA codes or the FLSA. In 1938, only 10 percent of black women workers were employed in industry and mainly in such bottom-level categories as laundry work (under the NRA, the 30,000 black women working in power laundries were granted a 14-cent minimum wage, but it was never enforced). Finally, in the North or the South, married or single, the black woman worker was more likely than a white woman to be unemployed and less likely to be included in a federal work-relief program.

Throughout the depression, black women suffered a disproportionately high unemployment rate. Over half lost their jobs, compared to three out of ten working white women. The depression severely cut into domestic employment, especially in the South. A Kentucky study of 1933 noted that over half of black women in domestic service were unemployed, and federal data confirmed such reports. In 1934, FERA surveys of persons on relief in urban centers showed that two-thirds of women once employed as domestics were out of work, with the greatest concentrations in southern cities. Since white women began to take more domestic jobs, competition for work increased. In large cities such as New York, black women would congregate at streetcorner "slave markets" early in the morning, seeking a day's work and bargaining with customers for rates as low as 10 cents an hour. While blacks of both sexes had higher unemployment rates than whites in the 1930s, the differences were pronounced between men and women as well as between blacks and whites. In Chicago in 1931, for instance, 43.5 percent of black men were unemployed and 29.7 percent of white men; 58.5

percent of black women were unemployed and 19.4 percent of white women. (Unemployment rates, of course, covered only persons who had once been in the labor force, a category that included a far larger proportion of black women than white women.) Clearly, occupational segregation by sex, which provided something of a cushion against job loss for white women in white-collar work, was of no benefit to black women.

Relief rolls reflected the high unemployment figures. Between 1930 and 1935, the proportion of the black population on relief doubled. Although a higher percentage of blacks than whites received federal aid, a smaller percentage of unemployed blacks benefited from work-relief programs, which tended to aid the "temporary" poor, those who had recently fallen in status. The National Youth Administration (NYA) had a relatively good record in warding off discrimination, but blacks were often at a disadvantage in other New Deal work-relief agencies, and black women were likely to be excluded entirely, especially in the South. Women's greatest complaints were about programs administered by state personnel, such as the PWA and WPA. They voiced their grievances in a trail of letters to FDR, Eleanor Roosevelt, and the heads of federal agencies. "Mr. Hopkins, colored women have been turned out of different job projects to take us other jobs and white women were hired & sent for and given places that colored women was made to leave or quit," wrote a North Carolina woman in 1937 in a letter indicting the WPA. Other correspondents echoed these grievances. "I has no mule, no wagon, no feed, no grocery," a Georgia widow with seven children told the secretary of agriculture, "and these women and men that is controlling the civil work for the government won't help me."

On the eve of World War II, black women retained their disproportionate share of the female work force. Thirty-eight percent of black women were employed and 24 percent of white women, while the proportion of black married women that worked was more than double the proportion of white married women. But the decade of the 1930s had provided little to improve the black woman's status as a wage earner. The white woman worker, however, survived the crisis in better shape than her male counterpart. Although the depression effectively limited options, sanctioned demotions, and quenched aspiration, it also provided hidden advantages and drew even more women into the work force. At the same time, what seemed like throngs of women assumed administrative posts on the federal level. During the early 1930s, when the New Deal was in its experimental phase, an experienced group of women reformers had an impact on politics and government.

Women's New Deal

During the 1920s, to many observers, women's political clout had contracted, not expanded. At mid-decade, once the "woman's vote" had failed to materialize, women's welcome in political parties flagged and women's groups' proposals for reform were ignored. By the end of the decade, woman suffrage was widely proclaimed to have made no impact on political life. "Ten years of suffrage have proved that women have become the tools of party leaders just as men have," claimed muckraker Ida Tarbell in 1930. Democratic national committeewoman Emily Blair told an interviewer that women had accomplished little with the vote, while reporter Emma Bugbee pointed out in the *Herald Tribune* that few women candidates had won office; most women elected to Congress in the 1920s were in fact widows who succeeded their husbands. But the 1920s had been a period of reaction, whereas the early New Deal was, to an extent, an era of reform. The 1930s brought a rise of women in Democratic ranks, an influx of women into New Deal posts, and a brief revival of female "influence."

To social reformers especially, the New Deal seemed a major triumph, even a vindication of the now defunct Sheppard-Towner act, since New Deal legislation incorporated measures for which women activists had long campaigned. Child labor, for instance, was prohibited under the NRA codes in 1933; the Social Security Act of 1935 provided maternal and child welfare benefits; and the Fair Labor Standards Act of 1938 ensured minimum wages and maximum hours. Most important, the New Deal proved that the federal government could act to promote human welfare, aid homes and families, protect women workers, and take responsibility for what Jane Addams called "our unfortunate fellow citizens." (A long-time Hoover supporter, Addams became a New Deal defender, especially after the NRA financed some large slum clearance projects near Hull-House.) Moreover, once Eleanor Roosevelt entered the White House, her wing of the woman's movement gained an advocate and exemplar. Eleanor Roosevelt appeared to increase her influence not by discarding traditional roles but by extending them. By the end of the decade, she had assumed an array of strategic functions.

As presidential assistant, Eleanor Roosevelt was in constant transit around the country, a visible spokeswoman who reported to the White House. As political strategist, she ran the 1935 campaign, acting as an intermediary between FDR in the White House and James Farley and Molly Dewson at Democratic headquarters. As resident guardian of "human values," she served as an ombudsman for the disadvantaged, a link between depression victims and the administration. And as outspoken liberal, she steadily took stands to the left of FDR, especially in her contacts with the National Association for the Advancement of Colored People, pacifist groups, and the American Youth Congress. Such liberalism not only captivated her own constituency but spared the President, who was uninvolved, some assaults from the left. Whether acting as a public figure or as a "private citizen," Eleanor Roosevelt's campaigns never ceased. She persistently defended the homestead program; she testified before legislative committees on migratory workers and on discrimination in the armed forces; and she became entrenched in the administration of relief agencies, notably the NYA and WPA.

Some of her causes had only "token" success, like the resident camps for women; others became controversial, like Arthurdale; and others failed completely, such as her demands for compulsory health insurance, a child labor amendment, and an anti-lynching law. But Eleanor Roosevelt succeeded as a political presence. Federal officials vied for her attention, pressure groups besieged her, newswomen trailed her, and voters admired her. "I am sure, Eleanor dear, that millions of people voted with you in their minds also," Rose Schneiderman wrote after the 1936 election. In 1939, 67 percent of a Gallup poll approved her conduct as First Lady, with more enthusiasm among women than among men. In the 1940 campaign, Republican women confirmed her impact with large campaign buttons that said "We Don't Want Eleanor Either."

During the 1930s, Eleanor Roosevelt was also at the center of a female upsurge in politics and government. A vocal publicist for women's projects, as at the press conferences, she served as a White House liaison for women's groups and a lobbyist for women reformers' causes. In 1939, for instance, when the LWV urged Children's Bureau head Katherine Lenroot to pressure the House Appropriations Committee to fund improved social services for the District of Columbia, Lenroot asked the President's wife to hold a White House conference. When this proved impossible, Eleanor Roosevelt waged a personal campaign. She addressed the House committee, conferred with its chairman, and even after victory continued to pressure members of Congress with letters demanding the appointment of a district coordinator of child care—adding that she was acting "simply as a private citizen." Not surprisingly, women in government such as Katherine Lenroot and Mary Anderson relied on Eleanor Roosevelt as an advocate. So did the LWV and the WTUL.

While Eleanor Roosevelt capitalized on her personal influence, Molly Dewson mobilized women within the Democratic party. A superb administrator, Dewson won impressive victories. At the Democratic national convention of 1936, there were 219 women delegates, compared to 60 at the Republican convention, and 302 alternates; women made eight seconding speeches. Moreover, Dewson gained for women equal representation on the platform committee, which Eleanor Roosevelt had been unable even to address in 1924. In addition, under Dewson's leadership, the Women's Division played a crucial role in Democratic campaigns. In 1936, Dewson's troops of Democratic women explained New Deal policies door-to-door, a tactic she called "mouth to mouth" campaigning. The Women's Division's *Democratic News,* meanwhile, vastly expanded its audience. By the start of FDR's second term, when the administration rewarded Molly Dewson with an appointment to the Social Security Board, women were seen as part of the new Democratic coalition.

Finally, during the New Deal, women made unprecedented inroads on appointive offices, a triumph symbolized by Frances Perkins's appointment as labor secretary. Women appointees were not distributed evenly throughout the executive branch. Rather they were concentrated in the Labor Department, where Anderson and Lenroot headed the Women's and Children's Bureaus, and in newly created federal agencies and advisory boards, where they would not encroach on traditional male fiefs. New Deal agencies, in short, literally provided new space for women in the federal bureaucracy. Emily Blair, Mary Harriman Rumsey, and suffragist lawyer Sue Shelton White, for instance, served on the NRA consumers' advisory board (Frances Perkins's "afterthought"); Rose Schneiderman served on the NRA labor advisory board; Ellen Woodward and Hilda Smith held administrative posts under FERA and WPA; Mary McLeod

Bethune, a leading black educator, was chosen at Eleanor Roosevelt's instigation to head black programs at NYA; and after 1935, White, Woodward, and Dewson were appointed to the Social Security Board. A smaller group of women appointees moved into other areas. Nellie Tayloe Ross was appointed to the Treasury Department; Florence Jaffrey Harriman and Ruth Bryan Owen became the first women diplomats; and Ohio judge Florence Allen, who had headed the list of nominees drawn up by Molly Dewson and Eleanor Roosevelt, became the first woman appointed to a federal court of appeals.

Most of the New Deal's high-level women appointees, like their sponsors, Dewson and Roosevelt, shared backgrounds in women's organizations and social welfare. Frances Perkins's career was significant. A Mount Holyoke graduate, Perkins had been drawn to social service after hearing Florence Kelley give a college talk. She then worked in settlement houses and in the New York Consumers' League before becoming New York State's industrial commissioner under FDR in 1928. Other women installed in federal posts in 1933 had similar backgrounds, as did later appointees. Florence Allen had left law school midway through to work for the New York League for the Protection of Immigrants and the College Equal Suffrage League, while living at the Henry Street Settlement. Florence Harriman, a founder of New York's Colony Club, had served on President Wilson's Federal Industrial Relations Committee and, during the 1920s, had led NCL opposition to the ERA.

Long-time Democratic activist Emily Blair found it "enlightening" that the first woman cabinet member achieved her position "by way of social welfare work" rather than through traditional routes of party service. A leadership role in social welfare, she contended in 1933, did not offend men's prejudices "as to the proper sphere of women." Rather it seemed "merely an extension of woman's traditional job of helping the unfortunate." But the type of affiliations shared by women in New Deal posts had further significance. Historian Susan Ware has identified a network of twenty-eight women, linked by a history of "personal friendship and professional interaction," who moved into jobs in politics and national government in the 1930s. The network included not only federal appointees but activists in the Democratic party's Women's Division, such as Emma Guffey Miller, and elected officials, such as representatives Mary T. Norton of New Jersey and Caroline O'Day of New York. Long in existence, the network had roots in suffrage, progressivism, and social reform. Born around 1880, network members were usually well-off and well educated; two-thirds were married. They knew each other from the WTUL, the NCL, and politics. During the 1920s most had been active in Democratic campaigns. Significantly, about half of network members were, like Eleanor Roosevelt, daughters, sisters, or wives of male politicians. Ellen Woodward and Katherine Lenroot, for instance, were senators' daughters; Emma Guffey Miller was a senator's sister; and Ruth Bryan Owen was the daughter of William Jennings Bryan.

During the New Deal, Ware contends, women officeholders used their longtime network to "maximize their influence in politics and government." Though committed to the advancement of women, most network members avoided the label of "feminist," which was now reserved for National Woman's party members. They identified themselves as social reformers. Like Molly Dewson, network members believed that women's goals in politics differed from men's, just as they believed that women's special role in office was to "humanize" government policy. They agreed with Eleanor Roosevelt's view, as expounded in *It's Up to the Women,* that women officials should measure their achievements not by material gain but by the social improvements they made. Finally they also felt that women in office had special interests to protect. As Ellen Woodward stated in a 1939 speech, "Whether we are actively engaged in homemaking or not, we are family conscious." The New Deal network was not completely monolithic. Two of its members, Sue Shelton White and Emma Guffey Miller, supported the ERA. But despite such internal disagreements, network members consistently provided one another with help and support. "Those of us who worked to put together the New Deal," Frances Perkins later told Molly Dewson, "are bound by spiritual ties that no one else can understand."

Within the women's network, Frances Perkins was the most powerful figure, next to Eleanor Roosevelt. Her Labor Department, moreover, was responsible for the Social Security Act of 1935 and the Fair Labor Standards Act of 1938—permanent reforms that incorporated a raft of protective measures long endorsed by women reformers. The Social Security Act, for instance, provided unemployment compensation, old age pensions, and care for the disabled. It also included many measures prepared by Grace Abbott and Katherine Lenroot of the Children's Bureau such as grants to the states for the care of homeless, destitute, delinquent, or crippled children, as well as for public health services, maternal care, and infant care. Aid to Dependent Children (ADC), though a minor part of the 1935 law, has special significance. Replacing the mothers' pension programs that had been enacted by some forty state legislatures in the progressive era, ADC provided funds to families where male breadwinners were dead, absent, or incapacitated. Under ADC, as under the pension plans, states could judge the "suitability" or "propriety" of the recipient parent (most of the aid went to widows). In 1950, ADC became Aid to Families with Dependent Children (AFDC), the crux of the current welfare system. In retrospect, a combination of progressive measures, promoted by women reformers and etched into New Deal legislation, provided the core of the modern welfare state.

Always held up by Eleanor Roosevelt as an exemplary public servant, Frances Perkins also exemplified the tenets of the reform-minded branch of the woman's movement, as opposed to the egalitarian National Woman's party. Since the days of the crusade for woman suffrage, which she never viewed as of primary importance, Perkins had always been "more deeply touched by the problems of poverty, the sorrows of the world, the neglected individual." She defined feminism as "the movement of women to participate in service to society" and clung to the goal of service to others throughout her career. When accepting her cabinet appointment, she had "more of a sense of obligation to do it for the sake of other women than I did for any other thing."

But Frances Perkins's post was the New Deal's hot seat. Not only were labor bills always at the center of controversy, but as the first woman cabinet member, Frances Perkins was suspect from the outset. When she arrived in Washington, no one save Grace Abbott and Mary Anderson sent notes of welcome; the Gridiron celebrants excluded her; and on formal occasions, when cabinet members were seated by rank, Perkins was usually placed with their wives. Congress called on her endlessly to testify, far more so than any man in the executive branch. Organized labor suspected her, since she had never been a union leader or even a union member. Mary Anderson criticized her for lack of partiality to working women. (During Perkins's tenure, the Women's Bureau remained small, while the Children's Bureau grew.) According to Anderson, Perkins "leaned over backwards" not to favor women and "did not want to be thought of as a woman too closely identified with women's problems." Setting a precedent for women officeholders under such circumstances was a major achievement.

Another precedent setter was Mary McLeod Bethune, head of "Negro affairs" at NYA from 1935 to 1943 and a leader of FDR's shifting "black cabinet." Bethune envisioned "dozens of Negro women coming after me, filling positions of high trust and strategic importance," as she told *Ebony* magazine in 1949. Though not a member of the women's network identified by Susan Ware, Bethune was closely connected to Eleanor Roosevelt, who urged her appointment and found in her a kindred spirit. An educator and women's club leader, Bethune had been president of Bethune-Cookman College, a Florida vocational school she founded herself, and an officer of the National Association of Colored Women. In 1935, she became the first president of the National Council of Negro Women, a coalition of black women's organizations. Bethune saw herself as a black advocate rather than a woman's advocate. As an administrator, however, she was often unable to take stands on racial equality as strong as those of such pressure groups as the NAACP and the Urban League.

Her tiny office, staffed by an assistant and a few secretaries, was hardly a power base. Lines of authority had never been clearly established, so it was unclear whether Bethune or state NYA directors would shape black programs, just as it was unclear whether state NYA advisory boards would be segregated or integrated. Bethune pressed for integrated boards, for black training projects in skilled work, for black project supervisors, and for black participation in NYA policymaking. Effective with both black and white audiences, she persistently urged that other high-level jobs be given to blacks. "It is impossible for you to enter sympathetically and understandingly into the program of the Negro, as the Negro can do," she told the predominantly white national advisory committee of the NYA in 1939.

The mood of reform that brought women such as Perkins and Bethune into New Deal posts had peaked by 1936. Once social welfare policies required defense and the climate of experiment cooled, women's influence began to wane and access to important jobs diminished. But the New Deal still had a permanent impact on women's role in public service. The 1930s saw an expansion of federal agencies and in particular a marked growth of opportunity for social workers. After the federal government initiated welfare and relief measures, the social work profession, which remained two-thirds female throughout the decade, grew by leaps and bounds. Not only did social welfare leaders work throughout New Deal agencies, serving on advisory boards and helping to draft new legislation, but jobs also opened up down the line—on the federal, state, and county levels.

Social work was already in transition. During the early twentieth century, as graduate programs emerged, the social worker gained a professional identity. In the 1920s, when the casework method became popular, her attention shifted from social reform to individual "adjustment." Finally, during the depression, the social worker changed from an agent of assimilation, who helped immigrants adapt to American life, to a middlewoman between the depression family and the public purse. "My studies at school didn't prepare me for this," recalled a new county caseworker who had graduated from college in 1933, in Studs Terkel's *Hard Times*. "We were still studying about immigrant families. Not about mass unemployment." In her research trips for Harry Hopkins, Lorena Hickok found that social workers had been trained to deal with "problem families," not with "respectable citizens, who, through no fault of their own, were obliged to have some help from the federal government." Carrying large caseloads and adapting to the welfare bureaucracy, new social workers often resented the insensitivity their roles demanded. "We're under pressure to give as little help as possible," a caseworker complained in 1934.

But the New Deal era also brought the social worker rewards. In Eleanor Roosevelt's view, she gained "the satisfaction of feeling that she has entered the lives of innumerable families and left them better off than she found them." A more tangible reward was that she was able to get a job, at a time when others were losing them. The creation of large-scale government relief programs had another impact too. Once the volunteer settlement worker was permanently replaced by the trained, salaried government employee, another rung of the woman's movement broke. This process was under way in the 1920s, but the New Deal was a turning point. Afterward, social welfare was a government function and no longer an extension of "woman's sphere," as it had been for over a century. The social worker, however, was not the career woman most in the public eye during the 1930s. This was probably the woman reporter, suddenly elevated to the status of culture heroine.

"Front Page Woman"

Mass culture had become an important force in the 1920s. During the 1930s, despite the depression, the power of the media dramatically increased. Drops in theater attendance only spurred new ingenuity from the movie industry, while huge newspaper chains competed for readers, and the number of radio sets doubled. During the media blitz of the 1930s, women emerged in assertive roles—the ambitious career girl, the gutsy entertainer, the sophisticated socialite, the blond seductress, and, leading the list, the worldly wise reporter. Though hardly cut from a single mold, women in mass culture exuded vitality. Dynamic, aggressive, even flamboyant, they provided a respite from the apathy or panic that seemed to characterize real life. The new publicity for female assertiveness was not always favorable; the depression was not a feminist era. But the headstrong heroines of the 1930s, real and invented, provided a repository for some of the lost aspirations of the 1920s.

During the depression, misery loved company. The universality of domestic woes was explicit in the new radio soap opera. Daytime serials (thirty-eight of them by 1938) revealed predicaments with which entire homebound families, but mainly homebound women, could identify. Indeed, the formula for serials required that each episode begin and end with severe troubles. Soap operas also provided a mode of escape. The most popular of them centered around women who had recently moved, upward or downward, to a new status, whether *Backstage Wife* (the girl who married a Broadway idol), *Our Gal Sunday* ("Can a girl from a little mining town in the West find happiness as the wife of a wealthy and titled Englishman?"), or *The Romance of Helen Trent* (an older woman, once-married, who now made her own way in the world). Surveys concluded that the more complex a listener's problems the more serials she followed. Escape literature served a similar function. The fatter the novel, the bigger the bargain— whether the beleaguered protagonists were Chinese peasants or antebellum aristocrats. Pearl Buck's *The Good Earth,* a novel about the rise of a Chinese family from peasantry to wealth, was the most widely read book of 1932, while Margaret Mitchell's *Gone With the Wind* (over a thousand pages) sold a million and a half copies by 1937 and became a movie in 1939. That selfish, aggressive Scarlett evoked far more sympathy than frail, good Melanie typified the 1930s. In the world of mass culture, meekness, passivity, and even virtue had gone out of style.

The reader seeking adventure and excitement could also turn to real life as depicted in the daily press. Newspapers flaunted sensational stories, offering public disasters—such as the Lindbergh kidnapping or Amelia Earhart's disappearance in flight or Bonnie Parker's bullet-ridden body—as distractions from private ones. As ballast, the press also presented comic diversion, such as Chic Young's *Blondie,* who in 1930 began maneuvering the inept Dagwood through domestic and vocational crises. At the outset, Blondie had been a gold-digging flapper and Dagwood a millionaire's son. But the Bumsteads adapted to changing times and became an everyday troubled family, like everyone else. By 1940, Brenda Starr, girl reporter, joined Dagwood and Blondie in popularity. Her vocation was significant. For women readers, the press provided a new type of role model.

The woman reporter took on large dimensions in public life in the 1930s, whether Anne McCormick and Dorothy Thompson reporting from Europe or Ruby Black and Bess Furman reporting from the White House. The great upsurge in the number of women journalists had in fact occurred in the 1920s; during the depression, however, their number continued to increase. And for those who had already gained a foothold, in major chains or press associations—like Hickok, Bugbee, Furman, and Black—the syndicated column and national byline were major boons. Eleanor Roosevelt's press conferences, meanwhile, gave Washington newswomen excellent publicity. Significantly, the First Lady joined them herself, by becoming a member of the Newspaper Guild, the journalists' union, and starting a media blitz of her own. Before her first term in the White House ended, Eleanor Roosevelt had become a radio personality in major-network, commercially sponsored talks. She had also embarked on well-paid lecture tours, continued her articles for women's magazines, and started "My Day," a syndicated column for United Features.

First appearing in December 1935, "My Day" was at once a success. In 1936, it appeared in sixty-two newspapers, reaching an audience of up to 4 million. By the end of the decade, 136 papers printed the column. Newspaper readers of the 1930s were likely to know more about Eleanor Roosevelt than about any other figure in public life. They shared her experiences—White House entertaining, royal receptions, family dinners, far-flung trips—just as they absorbed her housekeeping tips, child-care advice, educational theories, and social causes. Like the press conferences, "My Day" started out in a personal, domestic vein likely to appeal to women readers. But it rapidly enlarged its scope, delving into politics and promoting New Deal policies. Before the 1930s were over, Eleanor Roosevelt had a $70,000 annual income from radio talks, lectures, articles, and columns, most of which she gave away to such favored organizations as the WTUL and the American Friends Service Committee.

As a columnist, Eleanor Roosevelt did not lack competition. Dorothy Thompson's syndicated column, "On the Record," appeared in 140 papers in 1936 and even more at the end of the decade. Since 1920, Thompson had worked her way up from unpaid correspondent to European bureau chief for the Curtis chain, which included the *Philadelphia Inquirer* and the *New York Evening Post*. During the 1930s, unhampered by her failing marriage to Sinclair Lewis, Dorothy Thompson won a national reputation. She reported from Europe, took on a heavy lecture schedule, broadcast over NBC as a regular commentator, reached millions of readers through "On the Record," and in 1937 began a monthly column for the *Ladies' Home Journal*. An exemplar of the ambitious, successful career woman, Thompson embodied the aspirations of the 1920s. Once depression struck, few could follow Thompson's example—or that of Bugbee, Black, Furman, and Craig. But aspiration was not yet quenched. During the 1930s, the enterprising career woman was alive and well on the movie screen.

The woman reporter, in particular, cut a wide swath through a succession of celluloid city rooms. As film historian Marjorie Rosen has shown, the movie stars of the early 1930s often portrayed working women who survived by their wits in assertive and competitive roles. While female unemployment rates rose, Bette Davis appeared as a stenographer and political campaigner in 1932, as a copywriter, insurance probator, and government agent in 1934, and as a reporter (*Front Page Woman*) in 1935. Joan Crawford, Loretta Young, and Jean Arthur were similarly at home in the working world. Resourceful go-getters, the movie careerists competed with men, stole their stories, met their deadlines, and hogged the screen. The clothes they popularized—man-tailored suits with broad, padded shoulders—signified their competitive intent. Though competent, confident, and full of ambition, the movie career women had their limits; they were willing to give up their jobs for the right man. Jean Arthur's reporter married the boss, while Bette Davis in *Front Page Woman* ensnared a competitor from a rival paper. (In real life, Bess Furman married a fellow journalist and kept on working for the AP. During the 1940s, she ran an independent news service, worked for the Office of War Information, and replaced Eleanor Darnton as the Washington "woman interest" reporter for the *New York Times*.)

Cleverness and assertiveness were not limited to the city room in the 1930s films. The woman reporter was only one of a gallery of enterprising heroines. Moviegoers could also watch Greta Garbo as a spy, Myrna Loy as an amateur detective, or Joan Blondell as an ambitious chorus girl in *Gold Diggers of 1933*. Throughout the depression, high society held great fascination. Sophisticated comedies in upper-class settings provided a vehicle for Katherine Hepburn, who radiated intelligence and independence. (A Bryn Mawr graduate, Hepburn was indeed upper class. Her mother, moreover, was one of Margaret Sanger's lieutenants in the birth-control crusade.) Low society had equal appeal. Mae West provided a powerful aggressor who controlled her own plots and manipulated men. "It's not the men in my life but the life in my men that counts," said Mae, who described herself as "the woman's ego."

But Mae West's movies, usually period pieces, were set in a personal fantasy land; Mae was a joke more than a threat. The movies of the 1930s also revealed a harsh, mean antiwoman streak. Headstrong heroines who dominated the screen were often meddlesome, manipulative, selfish, or dangerous. Jean Harlow's characters, low-life or high-life, were faithless, immoral, conniving, and scheming. In a steady spate of underworld movies, gun molls and girlfriends were mauled, discarded, and pushed in the face. There were other inauspicious notes as well. The malicious gossip of spoiled socialites in Clare Boothe Luce's *The Women* (1939) conveyed disgust with the entire sex. To make this clear, each member of the all-woman cast was introduced, at the film's start, by comparison to an appropriate animal—cow, sheep, tiger, or weasel.

By the end of the 1930s, the ambitious career woman with 1920s aspirations faded. "Men demand and need in marriage the full emotional power of the women they love," Dorothy Thompson told *Journal* readers in 1939, stressing the dangers of career and success. "I should hate to see most women exteriorize their lives as I have," she exhorted in 1940. Thompson reflected the tone of the times. The working woman of 1940s movies sometimes retained her zest, competitiveness, and career. Katherine Hepburn, for instance, in her movies with Spencer Tracy, was, successively, an athlete, lawyer, and reporter. But during World War II, a new type of wage-earning heroine appeared as well. Though embarked on a job for the course of the war, she was usually waiting for a man to come home.

Like the depression, the war had a dual message for women. A sudden demand for female labor vastly expanded women's economic options, as the depression era had not. But the woman war worker was also a hazard. Lured into factories and praised for her patriotism, she inspired a backlash that hit full stride at demobilization.

The Impact of World War II

During the depression, the federal government joined with local government, school boards, and private business to exclude married women from the work force. A decade later the policy was reversed. By 1942, the War Department was inviting women into defense plants, urging women to enter government offices, and pressuring employers to utilize "the vast resource of womanpower." War created a tremendous labor shortage, both in the rapidly expanding defense industry and in the private sector, as millions of men (seven times as many as in World War I) joined the armed services. The national work force was quickly transformed. During World War II, over 6 million women took jobs for the first time, which increased the number of working women by 57 percent. In 1940, women were under 25 percent of the labor force; by July 1944, 35 percent. The number of married women holding jobs doubled, the age of the female labor force rose, and the number of unionized women surged from 800,000 in 1940 (9.4 percent of unionized workers) to 3 million in 1944 (21.8 percent of unionized workers.) "Almost overnight," wrote Mary Anderson, "women were reclassified from a marginal to a basic labor supply." During the war, said Eleanor Roosevelt, women became "an indispensable part of the life of the country."

The greatest need for "womanpower," as government propaganda made clear, was in war industry. At defense plants, which absorbed 2 million female workers, women made airplane frames, engines, propellers, parachutes, gas masks, life rafts, artillery, munitions, and electrical equipment. They loaded shells, assembled machine guns, cleaned spark plugs, wired instrument panels, and operated hand drills, turret lathes, rivet guns, and band saws, and learned their jobs in two to six months. The aircraft industry, a prime example, quickly adapted to female labor. By 1943, at major factories like Boeing's huge Seattle plant, half the workers were women. The aircraft worker was joined by the woman keel binder, toolmaker, foundry worker, stevedore, and die cutter; bans against women in heavy industry were discarded. Many states modified their protective laws or temporarily removed restrictions against women doing night work or overtime, or lifting heavy weights. During the war, as publicity features and personal testimonials suggested, there was no job a woman could not fill. "Today I had a good job," wrote Nell Giles, a Boston reporter who went to work in a defense plant. "It was to bore twenty holes in an aluminum disk, which is part of one of the instruments we make."

While the number of women employed in the defense industry rose 460 percent, the number of women in other manufacturing rose too. By the war's end, it had doubled. Government bureaucracy expanded as well. Over 2 million new women workers found jobs in offices, half of them in the federal government. By 1945, the nation's clerical work force had doubled. There was spillover into the professions, as ranks of male competitors were depleted. In Washington, D.C., for instance, the number of women journalists tripled. Finally, after a major shift of government policy, thousands of women joined the armed services, filling the ranks of the Women's Army Auxiliary Corps, quickly formed after Pearl Harbor. By 1943, women pilots, or WASPs, tested planes, ferried them from base to base, and flew other noncombat missions. Women volunteers, meanwhile staffed the Red Cross, ran bond drives, served on ration boards, and worked on civil defense. Eleanor Roosevelt and Florence Kerr, Ellen Woodward's successor at WPA, worked out a plan to use volunteer "womanpower" in civil defense. But once the

In August 1943, a corps of Women Airforce Service Pilots (WASPs) was formed to meet the wartime pilot shortage. Until then, women pilots with civilian status had provided aircraft ferrying service. WASPs, too, did noncombat jobs, mainly ferrying bomber and fighter planes from factories to airbases and embarkation points. They also towed targets for anti-aircraft gunnery practice and flew engineering missions, did instrument flight checks, and flew test flights of modified plane models. Although the presence of WASPs often evoked antagonism from male pilots on army bases, the women pilots captured the imagination of press and public. By the end of 1944, when the critical shortage of male pilots ended, the House of Representatives narrowly defeated a proposal to make the WASPs part of the Army Air Froces. The corps of women pilots was disbanded without military status or veterans' benefits, an injustice not remedied until 1979. *(Smithsonian Institution)*

program was approved, Eleanor Roosevelt refused to take a place at its helm; she preferred to exercise influence indirectly and thereby cause less controversy.

During the war, the woman worker had not only a new range of job possibilities but a new opportunity to move up the vocational ladder, or at least off its bottom rungs. Defense work was the most attractive option, since pay was 40 percent higher in war plants than in factories making consumer goods. Many women migrated to such war production centers as Detroit, Seattle, and Baltimore in order to take these well-paid jobs. High wages, moreover, easily lured working women away from jobs as waitresses and laundry workers, which now went begging. Significantly, during wartime, the number of women in domestic service fell rapidly. By the war's end, the proportion of black women workers in domestic jobs had dropped to 48 percent, while 18 percent were employed in industry—about twice as many as before the war. But as in the depression, when they were the first to be fired, black women were the last line of emergency workers, hired for nondomestic jobs only when both white workers and black men were unavailable. Although they enjoyed a rise in options, few black women

By the end of World War II, over 4,000 black women had enlisted in the Women's Army Corps, other were admitted to the WAVEs, and a small number served as officers, in both army and navy. But racially segregated units were the rule, for women as for men. The 500 black nurses who served in the Army Nurse Corps were assigned to hospitals serving only black men. Above, newly trained army nurses await disembarkment in Scotland. *(UPI/Bettmann)*

could get more than low-level jobs in manufacturing, while entry into white-collar fields, such as sales and clerical work, was still limited. Only a tiny proportion were accepted either in the Women's Army Corps or as army nurses. For black women, racial barriers remained in effect more than they were discarded. Many, however, joined a new wave of migration from the rural South to northern cities, one that would continue through the 1950s.

Still, the need for women workers during World War II dramatically changed the nature of the female labor force. For the first time, the majority of women workers were married, as were three out of four new women workers. The proportion of wives who held jobs, which had risen from 12 percent to 15 percent during the 1930s, now shot upward. By 1945, one out of four married women worked. At the same time, the age of the female labor force rose. Three out of five new workers were former housewives over thirty-five. Not only was the new woman worker likely to be older and married, but one-third of the new female work force had children under fourteen at home. Objections to working wives and mothers temporarily faded. As a result, the war era accelerated a trend toward wage-earning wives that had begun before the depression, continued throughout it, and would pick up again in the 1950s. According to historian William H. Chafe, World War II was a "watershed in the history of women at work."

Rapid absorption of women into the work force, however, testified to the extent of the emergency rather than to any sudden shift in opinion about gender roles. During World War II, behavior changed more than convictions. Indeed, as historian Karen Anderson has shown, war itself reinforced traditional beliefs about family life and woman's place. First, the war enhanced the significance of men while diminishing their supply, especially for women in their early twenties. During the war, the sex ratio for those aged twenty to twenty-four, for instance, fell to new depths; there were two women for every man. But scarcity of men appeared to increase male value rather than female autonomy. Young women felt a "sense of urgency regarding marital prospects," and early marriages abounded. Meanwhile, stresses on family life such as wartime separations increased, which spurred concern about the maintenance of traditional roles. Rising divorce rates, for instance, were often attributed to new work options for women. There was also much anxiety about women abrogating domestic responsibilities, rejecting their families, neglecting their children, and fostering juvenile delinquency. Finally, fearful that wartime breakdowns of traditional channels of authority would encourage a wave of promiscuity, the government waged a special campaign to end "sex delinquency" among young women in war production areas. Such responses to wartime changes, Karen Anderson contends, "were important in shaping Americans' values and behavior in the postwar era."

Nor did temporary acceptance of Rosie the Riveter reflect a change of view about "woman's place" in the work force. Although 60 percent of respondents polled by Gallup during the war believed wives should work in war industry, sexual equality was never an issue for workers, employers, or the federal government. At the start of the war, both government and industry hesitated to hire women workers, especially married ones. By 1942, once men were unavailable, reluctance diminished, but hostility to women in policymaking continued. Running the home front, like running the war, was seen as a man's job. The Women's Bureau, Mary Anderson complained, was never consulted about women's employment policies. A Women's Advisory Commission was finally created, under pressure, as a counterpart to the War Manpower Commission, but the advisory board, a New Deal tactic, was now wearing thin. Advisory committees, said Mary Anderson, were "not really allowed to have a voice in formulating policy." Resentment about wartime inequity, however, was muted. Women war workers appreciated their options for better jobs and higher pay though men were earning more. The National War Labor Board stipulated equal pay for equal work, but it also provided loopholes by which women workers could be placed in different job categories and paid less for the same work—both in war industry and in the private sector.

One issue that illustrated the government's attachment to traditional ideas about woman's role was its resistance to creating child-care centers for women employed in defense work, despite an absentee problem among working women with young children at home. War-torn England, with an even larger percentage of women in the work force, provided a rash of special services, such as hot meals to take home after work and child-care facilities. But the American government was reluctant to enter the child-care arena, and Perkins, Anderson, and Lenroot at the Labor Department shared this reluctance. "A mother's primary duty is to her home and children," the Children's Bureau said. "This duty is one she cannot

Following Office of War Information guidelines, advertisers attempted to spur women into the civilian labor force while reinforcing sex-role stereotypes. Typically, as above, wartime ads appealed to traditional female qualities, and emphasized women's loyalty to home, men, and nation. *(Life, January 18, 1943.)* Fear of role reversal, however, lurked beneath the surface. Usually a subliminal theme, it emerged in one of Norman Rockwell's most impressive covers for the Saturday Evening Post on May 29, 1943 (right). Here a muscle-bound Rosie the Riveter, wearing her propaganda buttons like medals and her mask tilted back like aviator glasses, is armed with a pneumatic riveting machine. Proud, self-contained, and self-satisfied, this young amazon appears immovable, especially from her well-paid wartime job. *(Curtis Publishing Company)*

lay aside, no matter what the emergency." Women wage earners, significantly, also suspected institutionalized child care. They associated it with public welfare and preferred to leave children with friends or relatives. "I guess I'm not the only woman who's raising a second batch of children, now that the country needs the young women to make munitions," said Grandmother Saunders in *McCalls* in 1942. In 1943, funds were finally allotted to establish federal child-care centers, under the Lanham Act, but since these centers were under the auspices of seven agencies, their administration was not a model of efficiency. Only 10 percent of defense workers' children were enrolled, and by 1946 federal funding for the centers had ended.

Traditional convictions about woman's place also emerged in the government's campaign to lure women into the work force. At the head of this effort was the Office of War Information, run by advertising men. Throughout the war,

the OWI, the War Manpower Commission, and the War Advertising Council gave guidelines and suggestions for the press, radio networks, and advertisers. Newsreels, posters, billboards, feature articles, and such radio shows as "Commando Mary" reflected their efforts. The propaganda campaign was a hard sell. Whenever Bess Furman, now a disgruntled employee of OWI, opened the newspaper, read a magazine, or listened to the radio, she heard "the pitch." And the pitch had its purpose. Wartime propaganda, as historian Leila M. Rupp has shown, sought to ensure that women's war work would be only a temporary response to an emergency, with no permanent effects on either the work force or women's status. By portraying the woman war worker as an attractive wife and mother who sacrificed home life to patriotism, wartime propaganda minimized the war worker's challenge to traditional roles. Changes in behavior, propaganda suggested, reflected only the "emergency," not any basic change in attitudes.

Attempts to attract women into defense work therefore appealed to such qualities as altruism and affection, rather than the base motive of high pay. Contributing to the war effort, propaganda suggested, would shorten the war and protect family members from death on the battlefield. Each bullet that the war worker produced, said a National Association of Manufacturers pamphlet, might "avenge her son." War work was also shown to be glamorous, sometimes by featuring movie stars in the propaganda campaign. Hollywood joined in by showing stars engaged in an array of wartime jobs—Ann Sothern as an aircraft worker, Lucille Ball in a defense plant, Claudette Colbert as a welder, Jennifer Jones as a nurse's aid, and Lana Turner, variously, as a war correspondent and a WAAC. An army photographer, meanwhile, discovered Marilyn Monroe, then eighteen-year-old Norma Jean Dougherty, assembling target airplanes in a California factory. The picture appeared in a feature on women war workers in *Yank* magazine.

Propaganda often stressed the similarity between industrial work and "women's work" in an avalanche of similes. Munitions making, for instance, was compared to running a sewing machine or a vacuum cleaner. "If you've used an electric mixer in your kitchen, you can learn to run a drill press," read a billboard sign in 1943. An underlying assumption was that women had a special proclivity for tedious, repetitive work, whether on the assembly line or in the household. The assumption became explicit in business magazines, which praised women's ability to work in small spaces and adapt to factory life. The female personality, *Nation's Business* confirmed in 1942, was ideally suited to industrial work, since women had less initiative, were "creatures of habit," and "don't get bored as easily." But altruism, vanity, and affinity for boring tasks were not reflected in the letters women wrote to the OWI. "The major inducement is money!" one woman wrote. Women also reported other benefits, such as getting out in the world and away from the home, as well as personal satisfaction.

A major government goal, however, even before the end of the war was in sight, was to ensure that women's work would be temporary and that women would not replace men in the labor force, crowd the market, force wages down, and destroy family life. Like role reversals in the depression family, the new role represented by the woman welder caused mounting anxiety and underscored a desire to return to traditional arrangements where the economy did not depend on women. "What About Women After the War?" the *New York Times Magazine* asked as early as 1943. Answers varied. Women war workers, the Women's Bureau found, had originally intended to take jobs only for the "emergency" but by the end of the war, in a survey of major defense industry areas, three out of four women workers who had taken jobs for the first time wished to remain at them. This sentiment, however, was strongest among older, married war workers who had already raised families. It did not seem to be shared by all women workers, many of whom viewed their war jobs as temporary and identified with the domestic images prevalent in wartime propaganda. ("I think a woman's place is in the home—except when there's a war on," a discharged war worker in Detroit was quoted in the press in 1945.) Nor was it shared by public opinion, employers, or the Labor Department.

"We should immediately start planning to get these women back where they belong," a correspondent wrote to OWI in 1943, "amid the environment of home life." "Too many women should not stay in the labor force," the chairman of the National Association of Manufacturers confirmed in 1945. "The Home is the basic American institution." Before the war ended, the Labor Department began to issue recommendations to sever women from wartime jobs, provide work for returning veterans, and ensure a smooth transition. The Women's Bureau, meanwhile, faced a predicament. Frieda Miller, who replaced Mary Anderson in 1944, expressed resentment that public opinion was tilting against the woman worker. The war, she contended, had proved women's capacities and they should not be forced to "return to their proper sphere—the kitchen." On the other hand, Miller also sought to assuage public opinion. "Women workers do not want to get ahead at the expense of the veterans," she said in 1944. "In fact, they have never regarded their own work as a substitute for that of men." The ambivalent stand of the Women's Bureau seemed to reflect the mixed views of women war workers.

When millions of veterans were demobilized in 1945, women were again called upon to alter their roles to suit the nation's economic needs. As war production plants closed and large industries like aircraft and shipbuilding laid off workers, the number of women in heavy industry dropped. In the auto industry, which had made tanks, jeeps, and trucks during the war, women's share of the work force plunged from 24 percent in 1944 to 7.5 percent in mid-1946. Layoffs were greatest in the high-paid industries that had customarily employed men, but spread further as well. Comparing women's experiences in auto production and the electric industry, traditionally a big employer of women, economist Ruth Milkman finds similarities. In both cases, a prewar pattern of sexual division of labor was disrupted by war but not eliminated. During the war, most women worked in predominantly female departments or job classifications; boundaries changed but did not vanish. After the war, management revived prewar sex-typing of jobs, laid off women, and took on men, both veterans and others—though hiring experienced women and new women workers would have cost less, Milkman contends. Labor efforts helped reinforce old patterns. In auto plants, male unionists supported sex discrimination in seniority to preserve men's monopoly of jobs; in the electric industry, men endorsed elimination of sex discrimination in wages to reduce the prospect of female competition and replacement. Distinctions arose among types of women employees. "Let's keep the single girl on the job and put the married woman back in the kitchen," declared the leaflet of an electrical workers' local.

By the end of 1946, 2 million women had left the labor force and another million were laid off. Black women, the last line of emergency workers, were among the hardest hit by the postwar loss of jobs. So were those riveters and welders whose images had once filled wartime propaganda. And so were older women whom the war had drawn into the work force. Although other women moved into jobs at the same time, the proportion of women who worked plummeted from 36 percent at the war's end to 28 percent in 1947. Moreover, the high pay and new options that had once attracted women to wage earning vanished, as did the public approval the war had briefly engendered.

World War II's impact on American women, historian Susan M. Hartmann suggests, was a mixed one that precludes sweeping generalizations about war and social change. Obviously, the war had different effects on different women. The experience of the wartime welder, WASP, or professional woman differed from that of the 50,000 Japanese women who were interned in West Coast relocation camps, guarded by armed sentries. The war also had mixed effects on women in general. On the one hand, Hartmann points out, it provided unprecedented employment opportunities, higher wages, public recognition of the woman worker, and an easing of restrictions in some areas. On the other hand, it also contained "powerful forces which put checks upon women's aspirations and options." Indeed, since traditional attitudes about gender roles were sustained throughout the war, some historians contend continuity to be a more important theme than change. The attitudes that seemed least changed by war, in the end, were those toward the married wage earner.

Once the war was over, the woman worker was no longer a symbol of patriotic ardor but rather a threat to social and economic security. Eighty-six percent of Americans, said the Gallup poll, now opposed the employment of married women. But the anxiety created by the woman war worker remained. It soon emerged in a new barrage of propaganda extolling the virtues of traditional roles.

Postwar Prospects

"What's Become of Rosie the Riveter?" asked the *New York Times Magazine* in May 1946. By now she had lost her acetylene torch and her well-paid job in war industry. She was, presumably, readjusting to life at home; the postwar era brought a swing back to private life. During 1946, more marriages occurred than in any other year. And in 1947, the birthrate accelerated. This extended a trend of the war years and reversed the trend of over a century to smaller and smaller families. The postwar era also brought inflation ("a spend-thrift masculine-looking spiral," Bess Furman wrote), an expanding economy, and new hopes of social mobility. The end of the 1940s revealed, finally, the distinctive themes of women's history in the coming decade: a growing number of women wage earners, an orchestrated outburst of domestic ideology, and a large space where the woman's movement once had been.

American feminism had not survived the emergencies intact. Since suffrage was won, feminists had been battered by a series of blows; but during the 1930s and 1940s, the organizations that once had made up the woman's movement fell by the wayside—by shrinking, folding, or losing their feminist thrust. During the early New Deal, to be sure, women's pressure groups were still in operation, warily monitoring government policy. The NWP, the LWV, and the dwindling WTUL joined forces to combat Section 213 and other offensive developments, such as discrimination against women in federal relief projects. But the tone of reform changed during the 1930s. As historian Lois Scharf points out, idealists were more interested in revising the economic system than in enhancing individual rights. The cause of women's rights, in particular, became peripheral. During World War II, women's pressure groups were pushed even further toward the margins of public life, and after the war, their marginality increased. Feminism, traditionally, was a middle-class movement with upper-class leadership. By the postwar era, a growing middle class no longer shared those common class interests that had propelled the suffrage and progressive movements. No umbrella issue, like the vote, could now appeal to a wide range of middle-class women for whom, on the whole, family mobility was now more important than women's causes.

Feminists had no leadership either. Most New Deal survivors, who had entered public life early in the century, had now retired or been absorbed into the recesses of the federal bureaucracy. More important, there were few followers. No major women's institutions had been formed since the vote was won and the old ones no longer served as training grounds for public life; the generation gap of the 1920s was now a chasm. Once the woman's movement had decomposed, the media took over as women's representatives in public life. And in the media, since the late 1930s, serious statements about women took on an underground quality, appropriate to a hostile environment. "Women must become more conscious of themselves as women and of their ability to function as a group," Eleanor Roosevelt wrote in *Good Housekeeping* in 1940. "At the same time they must try to wipe from men's consciousness the need to consider them as a group, or as women, in their everyday activities, especially as workers in industry or the professions." This indeed was an archetypical feminist dilemma. It was also a double bind.

The most visible tension between "women as individuals" and "women as a group" was the prolonged conflict over the Equal Rights Amendment that accompanied feminist decline in the 1930s and 1940s. During the New Deal years, social reformers had trounced the National Woman's party, which was further weakened by its own internal schisms. Most women prominent in political life, such as Frances Perkins and Eleanor Roosevelt, viewed the ERA as anathema, and their opposition carried weight. Still, the amendment made progress. In the late 1920s it had been endorsed by women's business and professional groups, and during the 1930s it gained support among male politicians. No man in public office wanted to be considered an opponent of "equal rights," Mary Anderson complained. In 1936, a House subcommittee endorsed the ERA; in 1938, the Senate Judiciary Committee reported it to the floor. In 1940, the Republican party, rarely at the forefront of social change, endorsed the amendment. So did the conservative General Federation of Women's Clubs, though opponents of the ERA claimed that only a handful of club leaders really supported it. In 1944, the amendment finally won the endorsement of the Democratic party as well, after a vigorous campaign by Emma Guffey Miller, who then assumed a leading role in what remained of the NWP.

ERA opponents now mobilized their forces. In 1945, the Women's Bureau described National Woman's party members as aging suffrage veterans, militant and leisure class, who resented "not having been born men." Legal change could only harm women, the bureau claimed, by depriving them of such benefits as alimony. "This doctrinaire position," Frances Perkins told Florence Armstrong, head of the NWP, would make it difficult to pass laws "to improve the condition of . . . working sisters." Trade unions joined the opposition as well. In 1945, a coalition of forty-three organizations united to defeat the "Unequal Rights Amendment," including the League of Women Voters, the American Association of University Women, the Young Women's Christian Association, the New York branch of the Women's Trade Union League, the National Congresses of Catholic and Jewish Women, and twenty-five trade union groups. The amendment was opposed by Carie Chapman Catt, Alice Hamilton, Mary McLeod Bethune, Freda Kirchwey, Frances Perkins, and Frieda Miller; Eleanor Roosevelt had avoided taking a stand on the issue at the time of the 1944 Democratic party convention. When the ERA reached the Senate in July 1946, it did not win the needed two-thirds majority; thirty-eight senators were in favor and thirty-five opposed. "Motherhood cannot be amended," said the *New York Times*. In 1950, the Senate approved an ERA with a rider excluding protective laws from its impact, and it repeated this effort in 1953. But by now the issue seemed dead. And so, by and large, did the woman's movement, which had argued about it since the 1920s. Pockets remained in the LWV, which monitored the electoral process; the remnant of the NWP; and the Women's Bureau, a small bastion in the federal bureaucracy.

By the time the ERA finally capsized, the number and nature of "working sisters" was changing. The postwar economy provided new space for women wage earners, and in 1947, the number of working women began to climb. By the end of the decade, the proportion of women in the work force had risen to 31 percent and kept rising; this quickly made up the losses of the immediate postwar slump. Women no longer entered heavy industry, where they had made inroads during the war, nor did they surge into the professions. Rather, they took jobs in traditional "women's fields"—office work, sales, and services—which rapidly expanded. The postwar female work force, however, retained important wartime characteristics. It was predominantly married, older, and middle class, a trend that had started in the 1920s but was not noticeable until World War II. The postwar era even provided a new justification for the middle-class working wife. As historian William H. Chafe points out, a second income was needed to maintain a middle-class life-style. Inflation, not "individualism," spurred the married wage earner. During the 1930s, depression had served the same purpose.

Wage earning in the late 1940s did not necessarily provide a rise in status, either outside the family or within it. First, in 1946, Congress failed to act on an Equal Pay bill, one supported by both women's organizations and labor unions (which feared the replacement of male wage earners by cheap female labor). Second, in the view of sociologists, ever vigilant, the postwar family was settling into a staunchly traditional shape. According to the *American Journal of Sociology* in 1947, the modal type of family was now the "semi-patriarchal form in which a dominant husband 'brings in the bacon' and a submissive woman plays a traditional wife-and-mother role." Not only had the companionate model of marriage waned, but men sought spouses who had less education than they did and were less qualified to make decisions. Moreover, even if both spouses worked, the wife's wages, which were less than the husband's, were regarded as minor. A similar trend toward hierarchy within the family had been noticed even earlier in the decade. Sexual equality was threatened by changing attitudes, sociologist Joseph K. Folsom had warned in 1943, when he prophesied a "resubjection of women." Not only were younger women attracted to traditional domestic roles but they were urged into these roles, as opposed to careers, by a great barrage of "adroit publicity."

The full-scale revival of domestic ideology in the postwar era hardly materialized out of the blue. Rather, it reflected currents that were present throughout the depression, when wage-earning women seemed to threaten "breadwinners," and throughout the war, when working women loomed as a threat to social stability. After the war, the threat of the married wage earner was reduced to a personal problem. Conflict between traditional roles and outside involvements was the "American woman's dilemma," said *Life* magazine in 1947. Should she work outside the home or should she devote her time and energy solely to household and family?

The issue was discussed that year in the prestigious *Annals of Social and Political Science* in a special issue, "Women's Opportunities and Responsibilities," which revealed the anxiety that was brewing over women's roles. Clearly, there were two sides. Frieda Miller of the Women's Bureau rose to the defense of women's work and aspiration. "Intermingled . . . with the necessity for self-support is the desire for self-expression, the need to make a contribution to society in a field adapted to one's individual personality," said Miller. "The same aspiration has been engendered in both men and women . . . the desire to choose a field of endeavor suited to one's psychic need." Some women, she contended, found work in office, store, factory, school, or hospital more satisfying than work at home. Pursuing a career, she suggested, was no longer an "act of heroism," nor restricted solely to single women. "It may very well be that we are approaching a period when for women to work is an act of conformism."

But by 1947, Miller's interpretation of "psychic need" was out of date. A WTUL activist since World War I and a protégé of Frances Perkins, Miller represented the old guard. The latest insights into women's needs were now provided neither by the Women's Bureau nor by the National Woman's party but by psychiatry, a profession that had made great strides during World War II. Conflict between home and career, psychoanalyst Marynia Farnham pointed out in the 1947 *Annals*, could lead a woman into psychological purgatory. She might want a career as "a source of prestige," but this required "a great deal of drive, self-assertion, competition, and aggression," while fulfillment of her biological function through marriage and childbearing called for qualities "that can best be classified as protective or nurturing, passive and receptive." The disparity between such contradictory demands made women harassed and even psycho-logically ill, "hostile, aggressive, and perpetually at odds with their environment."

The popular press of the late 1940s dealt with the "dilemma" by throwing its weight on the side of passivity. Since the end of the war, advice literature had urged women to assume feminine roles and to remember that veterans expected "admiration, or at least submissiveness"; the postwar campaign to keep women home was soon as strong and well organized as if it had been run by the Office of War Information. Articles with such titles as "Isn't a Woman's Place in the Home?" were supported by fiction extolling the advantages of romance over career. Prominent journalists contributed to the vogue. "Women Aren't Men," Agnes Meyer told *Atlantic* readers. "God protect us from the efficient, go-getter business woman whose feminine instincts have been completely stifled." *Redbook* in 1947 contended that divorce was "less an expression of our freedom than a new indication of failure to adjust." Not surprisingly, as an article in the 1947 *Annals* confirmed, "Girls of today apparently accept the feminine role with less rebellion than their mothers did." Such acceptance appeared in the question submitted to Eleanor Roosevelt's question-and-answer column—first in the *Ladies' Home Journal* and then, starting in 1949, in *McCall's.* "I am a rather young housewife who for four years has been working to help my husband make a down payment on a little home," wrote a reader. "Do you think I could safely quit my job now and keep house as I have wanted to do all my life?" A youngster was more to the point. "Do you agree that a girl should hide her intellectual side if she's going to be popular with boys?"

The new propaganda for domesticity and passivity may have made little impression on educated women who had embarked on careers in the 1920s and 1930s and advanced in them during World War II. But it did have an impact on young middle-class women who were deciding what to do with their lives. Betty Friedan remembered 1949 as "the year the feminine mystique really hit us." Recently out of college, Friedan was part of the cohort most severely hit. "In 1949, nobody had to tell a woman that she wanted a man, but the message certainly began bombarding us from all sides; domestic bliss had suddenly become chic, sophisticated. . . . It almost didn't matter who the man was who became the instrument of your feminine fulfillment." Injunctions to reject masculine values and standards and to find fulfillment as wives, mothers, and homemakers were not without their advantages. "The feminine mystique," said Friedan, "made it easier for a woman to retire smugly, avoiding conformity and competition as men could not."

Although the postwar version of domestic ideology had ample precedents, starting in the 1920s, there was one overwhelming difference. Now, in the late 1940s, since feminist pressure groups had faded or folded, countervailing arguments received small publicity. Domestic ideology, however, received ample publicity. In *Modern Woman: The Lost Sex*, a best-seller of 1947 written by psychoanalyst Farnham and sociologist Ferdinand Lundberg, the "independent woman" was labeled a contradiction in terms. Denouncing feminism as a lethal sickness, the authors urged women to find mental health in domestic roles. The vehemence of their attack exceeded the paternal advice given to "the nervous housewife" in the 1920s and differed with the goals set forth by Eleanor Roosevelt in *It's Up to the Women* in 1933. An extremist tract, *Modern Woman* drew critical scorn ("dogmatic and sensational") but reached a wide audience.

Feminism, said Farnham and Lundberg, was a neurotic reaction to natural male dominance. It made women reject their instincts and try to become men, as illustrated in the sad career of Mary Wollstonecraft. The symptoms of feminist psychological disorder were hatred of father, rejection of motherhood, and unpleasant, aggressive behavior. The true woman, on the other hand, was characterized by self-acceptance, dependence on men, and passive fulfillment in sex and motherhood. Proposing government measures to spur such fulfillment, such as subsidies for childbearing and payments for therapy for maladjusted feminists, Farnham and Lundberg demanded that feminine women "reclaim the home as their proper domain."

Modern Woman was a final legacy of World War II and of the resistance toward women wage earners that had built up during both depression and war. But the war left other legacies too: economic recovery, higher wages, higher living standards, a market bulging with goods and services, and a national rise in expectations. During the 1950s, more Americans had access to middle-class status than ever before. Within the growing middle class, women were impelled by two forces, not unlike those that pervaded the "emergencies." One was a search for domestic security, a goal that had intensified during the 1930s and 1940s. Another was a thrust toward wage earning, once again fostered by family need and expanding employment opportunities. The emergencies left a legacy of apparent contradictions.

⌒⌒⌒

SUGGESTED READINGS AND SOURCES

CHAPTER 17

Blanche Wiesen Cook presents Eleanor Roosevelt's early career in *Eleanor Roosevelt: Volume One, 1884–1933* (New York, 1992). See also Joseph P. Lash, *Eleanor and Franklin* (New York, 1971), Tamara K. Hareven, *Eleanor Roosevelt: An American Conscience* (Chicago, 1968), and Joan Hoff-Wilson and Marjorie Lightman, eds., *Without Precedent: The Life and Career of Eleanor Roosevelt* (Bloomington, Ind., 1984). Eleanor Roosevelt wrote two autobiographies, *This Is My Story* (New York, 1937) and *This I Remember* (New York, 1947). For her stance as a reformer, see *It's Up to the Women* (New York, 1933), and her columns in the *Woman's Home Companion* (New York) from 1933 to 1935. For the friendship between Eleanor Roosevelt and Lorena Hickok, see Doris Faber, *The Life of Eleanor Hickok: Eleanor Roosevelt's Friend* (New York, 1980), and Lorena Hickok's memoir of Eleanor Roosevelt, *Reluctant First Lady* (New York, 1962). Bess Furman recalls a newswoman's career in Washington during the New Deal in *Washington By-Line* (New York, 1949). Ruby Black describes the impact of Eleanor Roosevelt's press conferences in "New Deal for News Women in Capitol," *Editor and Publisher* (February 10, 1934), 11. Maurine Beasley, ed., *The White House Conferences of Eleanor Roosevelt* (New York, 1983), presents the notes of reporters Martha Strayer, Bess Furman, and Ruby Black. Interviews with women reporters who covered the press conferences are available at the Oral History Center, Columbia University.

The careers of women who held high-level positions in the federal government and in the Democratic party are examined by Susan Ware in *Beyond Suffrage: Women in the New Deal* (Cambridge, Mass., 1981), which draws on a wealth of personal correspondence.

CHAPTER 18

For overviews, see William H. Chafe, *The Paradox of Change: American Women in the 20th Century* (New York, 1991); Lois W. Banner, *Women in Modern America: A Brief History,* 2d ed. (New York, 1984), ch. 5; Peter Gabriel Filene, *Him/Her/Self: Sex Roles in Modern America,* 2d ed. (Baltimore, Md., 1986), ch. 6; and Rosalind Rosenberg, *Divided Lives: American Women in the Twentieth Century* (New York, 1992), ch 4. Two surveys are Susan Ware, *Holding Their Own: American Women in the 1930s* (Boston, 1982), and Susan M. Hartmann, *The Home Front and Beyond: American Women in the 1940s* (Boston, 1982). Both present cogent syntheses and extensive bibliographies.

Sociologists of the 1930s and 1940s provide a wealth of studies on the depression's impact on family life. See, for instance, Ruth S. Cavan and Katherine H. Ranck, *The Family and the Depression: A Study of One Hundred Chicago Families* (Chicago, 1938); Mirra Komarovsky, *The Unemployed Man and His Family: The Effects of Underemployment upon the Status of Men in Fifty-Nine Families* (New York, 1940); Winona L. Morgan, *The Family Meets the Depression: A Study of a Group of Highly Selected Families* (Minneapolis, Minn., 1939); Robert S. Lynd and Helen Merrill Lynd, *Middletown in Transition: A Study in Cultural Conflict* (New York, 1937); Wight Bakke, *Citizens Without Work* (New Haven, Conn., 1940); and Eli Ginzburg, *The Unemployed* (New York, 1943). The case studies of the Burtons and the Rileys are in Robert Cooley Angell, *The Family Encounters the Depression* (New York, 1936). "The Modern American Family," an issue of *Annals of the American Academy of Social and Political Science,* 160 (March 1932), includes articles on homemaking and welfare services. For contemporary sources on women wage earners, see Lorine Pruette, *Women Workers Through the Depression* (New York, 1934), a study of white-collar employment, and the steady stream of publications from the Women's Bureau (Washington, D.C.) in the 1930s. Margaret J. Hapgood, *Mothers of the South: Portraiture of the White Tenant Farm Woman* (Chapel Hill, N.C., 1939), describes women's work and family roles in the rural South.

Lois Scharf's important book, *To Work or to Wed: Female Employment, Feminism, and the Great Depression* (Westport, Conn., 1980), examines women's roles in the labor force and family, with attention to the experience of married working women. Scharf's bibliography is an excellent guide to the 1930s. Ruth M. Milkman, "Women's Work and the Economic Crisis: Some Lessons from the Great Depression," in Nancy Cott and Elizabeth Pleck, eds., *A Heritage of Her Own* (New York, 1979), pp. 507–541, suggests the effect of sexual segregation in the workplace on women's employment. Winifred D. Wandersee Bolin, "The Economics of Middle-Income Family Life: Working Women During the Great Depression," *Journal of American History,* 65 (June 1978), 60–74, examines the increase of married women in the 1930s labor force. See also Wandersee, *Women's Work and Family Values, 1920–1940* (Cambridge, Mass., 1981), and Alice Kessler-Harris, *Out to Work: A History of Wage-Earning Women in the United States* (New York, 1982), chs. 9 and 10. Wandersee and Kessler-Harris show that significant changes in married women's employment patterns began before the 1940s. Staughton Lynd and Alice Lynd examine labor organization in *Rank and File: Personal Histories of Working Class Organizers* (Boston, 1973).

For the problems of black women wage earners, see Jean Collier Brown, *The Negro Woman Worker,* Bulletin 165 of the Women's Bureau (Washington, D.C., 1938), and

Jacqueline Jones, *Labor of Love, Labor of Sorrow* (New York, 1985), ch. 6. Letters of protest about racial discrimination appear in Rosalyn Baxandall, Linda Gordon, and Susan Reverby, eds., *America's Working Women* (New York, 1976), pp. 248–251, and Gerda Lerner, ed., *Black Women in White America: A Documentary History* (New York, 1976), pp. 398–405. For southern migrants, black and white, of the 1920s and 1930s, see Jacqueline Jones, *The Dispossessed: America's Underclasses from the Civil War to the Present* (New York, 1992), chs. 7 and 8. Evelyn Nakamo Glenn examines work roles in the 1930s and after in *Issei, Nisei, Warbride: Three Generations of Japanese American Women in Domestic Service* (Philadelphia, 1976). For the experience of Hispanic women in the depression and after, see Julia Kirk Blackwelder, *Women of the Depression: Caste and Culture in San Antonio, 1929–1939* (College Station, Tex., 1984); Rosalinda M. Gonzolez, "Chicanas and Mexican Immigrant Families 1920–1940: Women's Subordination and Family Exploitation," in Lois Scharf and Joan M. Jensen, eds., *Decades of Discontent: The Women's Movement, 1920–1940* (Boston, 1987), pp. 59–84; Virginia E. Sanchez Korrol, *From Colonia to Community: The History of Puerto Ricans in New York City, 1917–1948* (Westport, Conn., 1983); and Vicki L. Ruiz, *Cannery Women, Cannery Lives: Mexican Women, Unionization, and the California Food Processing Industry, 1930–1950* (Albuquerque, N. Mex., 1987).

Social histories of the depression include Caroline Byrd, *The Invisible Scar: The Great Depression and What It Did to American Life, From Then Until Now* (New York, 1966); Studs Terkel, *Hard Times: An Oral History of the Great Depression* (New York, 1970), a collection of reminiscences from a broad cross section of Americans; and David H. Kennedy, ed., *The American People in the Depression* (West Haven, Conn., 1973), a short sourcebook. Jeane Westin, *Making Do: How Women Survived the 30s* (Chicago, 1976), is a lively collection of interviews.

Susan Ware, *Beyond Suffrage* (Cambridge, Mass., 1981), examines the women's "network" that moved into posts in the federal government and Democratic party in 1933. For some network members' comments on women's political roles, see Mary T. Norton, "What Politics Has Meant to Me," *Democratic Digest* (February 6, 1938), 18; Emily Newell Blair, "Women and Political Jobs," *New York Herald Tribune Magazine,* April 23, 1933, p. 4; and Eleanor Roosevelt, "Women in Politics," *Good Housekeeping,* 110 (March 1940), 45. Women's careers in major New Deal posts are described in Mary Anderson, *Woman at Work* (Minneapolis, Minn., 1951); George F. Martin, *Madame Secretary: Frances Perkins* (Boston, 1976); Frances Perkins, *The Roosevelt I Knew* (New York, 1946); Susan Ware, *Partner and I: Molly Dewson, Feminism, and New Deal Politics* (New Haven, Conn., 1987); James T. Patterson, "Mary Dewson and the American Minimum Wage Movement," *Labor History,* 5 (Spring 1964), 135–152; Rackham Holt, *Mary McLeod Bethune: A Biography* (New York, 1964); B. Joyce Ross, "Mary McLeod Bethune and the National Youth Administration: A Case Study of Power Relationships," *Journal of Negro History* 60 (January 1975), 1–28; and Bethune, "My Secret Talks with FDR," *Ebony,* 4 (April 1949), 42–51. For the origins of the welfare state, see Linda Gordon, ed., *Women, the State, and Welfare* (Madison, Wisc., 1990), and Theda Skocpol, *Protecting Soldiers and Mothers: Political Origins of Social Policy in the United States* (Cambridge, Mass., 1992).

Feminism in the 1930s is explored in Susan D. Becker, *The Origins of the Equal Rights Amendment: American Feminism Between the Wars* (Westport, Conn., 1981), a study of the National Woman's party; Lois Scharf and Joan M. Jensen, eds., *Decades of Discontent: The Women's Movement, 1920–1940* (Boston, 1987); Susan Ware, *Beyond Suffrage;* and Lois Scharf, *To Work or to Wed.* For social work, see Clarke A. Chambers, *Seedtime of Reform: American Social Service and Social Action, 1918–1933* (Minneapolis, Minn., 1972), and Grace Abbott, *From Relief to Social Security: The Development of the New Public Welfare Services and their Administration* (Chicago, 1941). Women's activism in the Communist party is discussed in Susan Ware, *Holding Their Own,* ch. 5. See also the reminiscences collected by Vivian Gornick in *The Romance of American Communism* (New York, 1977).

For women's careers in journalism, see Agnes E. Meyer, *Out of These Roots: The Autobiography of an American Woman* (Boston, 1953); George Martin, *Cissy: The Extraordinary Life of Eleanor Medill Patterson* (New York, 1979); Peter Kurth, *American Cassandra: The Life of Dorothy Thompson* (Boston, 1990); Richard Lowitt and Maurine Beasley, eds., *One Third of a Nation: Lorena Hickok Reports on the Great Depression* (Urbana, Ill., 1983); and Ishbel Ross, *Ladies of the Press: The Story of Women in Journalism by an Insider* (New York, 1936). For the career of a radical journalist and novelist, see Elinor Langer, *Josephine Herbst: The Story She Could Never Tell* (Boston, 1983). Women's roles in 1930s movies are described in Marjorie Rosen, *Popcorn Venus: Women, Movies, and the American Dream* (New York, 1971); June Sochen, "Mildred Pierce and Women in Film," *American Quarterly,* 30 (Spring 1978), 3–20; and Andrew Bergman, *We're in the Money: Depression America and Its Films* (New York, 1971). See also Maureen Harvey, "Images of Women in the *Saturday Evening Post,* 1931–1936," *Journal of Popular Culture,* 10 (1976), 352–358. For Margaret Mitchell's career, see Claudia Roth Pierpont, "A Study in Scarlett," *New Yorker* 68 (August 31, 1992), 87–103, and Darden Asbury Pyron, *Southern Daughter: The Life of Margaret Mitchell* (New York, 1991). For fictional renditions of the 1930s, see Tess Slesinger, *The Unpossessed* (New York, 1934), a novel about the left; Mary McCarthy's short stories in *The Company She Keeps* (New York, 1942); and McCarthy, *The Group* (New York, 1963), a novel about the Vassar class of 1933. Also of interest are Mary McCarthy, *Intellectual Memoirs: New York, 1936–1938* (New York, 1992); recent biographies of McCarthy, such as Carol Gelderman, *Mary McCarthy: A Life* (New York, 1988), and Carol Brightman, *Writing Dangerously: A Critical Biography of Mary McCarthy* (New York, 1992); and Paula Rabinowitz, *Labor and Desire: Women's Revolutionary Fiction in Depression America* (Chapel Hill, N.C., 1991). For murals and plays of the 1930s, see Barbara Melosh, *Engendering Culture: Manhood and Womanhood in New Deal Public Art and Theater* (Washington, D. C., 1991).

William H. Chafe presents World War II as a watershed in the history of women's employment in *Paradox of Change,* chs. 7–9. Chafe's interpretation has been challenged or modified by recent studies, such as Karen Anderson, *Wartime Women: Sex Roles, Family Relations, and the Status of Women During World War II* (Westport, Conn., 1981), an examination of the war's impact on women's lives in three major defense production areas; Ruth Milkman, *Gender at Work: The Dynamics of Job Segregation During World War II* (Urbana, Ill., 1987), which explores the experience of women workers in the electrical and auto industries; and Amy Kesselman, *Fleeting Opportunities: Women Shipyard Workers in Portland and Vancouver During World War II and Reconversion* (Albany, N.Y., 1990). Sherna Berger Gluck, ed., *Rosie the Riveter Revisited: Women, the War, and Social Change* (Boston, 1987), presents ten oral histories of war workers.

For studies of women's war work from the 1940s, see Laura N. Baker, *Wanted: Women in War Industry* (New York, 1943); Helen Baker, *Women in War Industries* (Princeton, N.J., 1942); Eva Lapin, *Mothers in Overalls* (New York, 1943); and Katherine Glover, *Women at Work in Wartime* (New York, 1943). For demobilization, see Frieda S. Miller, "What's Become of Rosie the Riveter?" *New York Times Magazine,* May 3, 1946, pp. 21ff. Among Women's Bureau publications, see *When You Hire Women,* Bulletin no. 14 (Washington, D.C., 1944), a list of suggestions to employers; *Changes in Women's Employment During the War,* Bulletin no. 20 (Washington, D.C., 1944), and *Women in Ten Production Areas and Their Post-War Employment Plans,* Bulletin no. 249 (Washington, D.C., 1946). Available on microfilm are Anne Firor Scott and William H. Chafe, eds., *Records of the Women's Bureau of the U.S. Department of Labor, 1918–1965, Part II: Women in World War II.* Elizabeth Faulkner

Baker describes the labor that women performed in war industry in *Technology and Women's Work* (New York, 1974).

D'Ann Campbell surveys women's wartime experiences in *Women at War With America: Private Lives in a Patriotic Era* (Cambridge, Mass., 1984). For aspects of women's lives during the war, see Karen Anderson, "Last Hired, First Fired: Black Women Workers During World War II," *Journal of American History*, 69 (June 1982), 82–97; Leila M. Rupp. *Mobilizing Women for War: German and American Propaganda, 1939–1945* (Princeton, N.J., 1978); Sheila Tobias and Lisa Anderson, "What Really Happened to Rosie the Riveter?" *Ms*, 1 (June 1973), 92–94; and Susan M. Hartmann, "Prescriptions for Penelope: Literature on Women's Obligations to Returning World War II Veterans," *Women's Studies*, 5 (1978), 223–239. For the Japanese-American woman's wartime experience, see Deborah Genensway and Mindy Roseman, *Beyond Words: Images from America's Concentration Camps* (Ithaca, N.Y., 1987); Ronald Takaki, *Strangers From a Different Shore: A History of Asian Americans* (Boston, 1989); and Valerie Matsumoto, "Japanese American Women During World War II," *Frontiers*, 8 (1984), 6–14, which is reprinted in Ellen Carol DuBois and Vicki L. Ruiz, eds., *Unequal Sisters* (New York, 1990), pp. 373–386. Eleanor Straub assesses the problem of the Women's Advisory Committee in influencing policymaking, in "United States Government Policy Toward Civilian Women During World War II," *Prologue*, 5 (Winter 1973), 240–254. For women's military roles, see Hartmann, *The Home Front and Beyond*, ch. 3, and D'Ann Campbell, "Women in Uniform: The World War II Experiment," *Military Affairs*, 51 (July 1987), 137ff. Important interpretations of the war experience include John Costello, *Virtue Under Fire: How World War II Changed our Social and Sexual Attitudes* (Boston, 1985), and Alan Berube, *Coming Out Under Fire: The History of Gay Men and Women in World War II* (New York, 1990). See also Lillian Faderman, *Odd Girls and Twilight Lovers: A History of Lesbian Life in Twentieth-Century America* (New York, 1991), ch. 5. The impact of war on gender roles is explored in Margaret Randolph Higgonet, Jane Jensen, Sonya Michel, and Margaret Collins Weitz, eds., *Behind the Lines: Gender and the Two World Wars* (New Haven, Conn., 1987). Beth Bailey and David Farber reveal a cauldron of cultural change in *The First Strange Place: The Alchemy of Race and Sex in World War II Hawaii* (New York, 1992).

Attitudes toward women in the late 1940s are discussed in Chafe, *Paradox of Change*, ch. 9, and Betty Friedan, *It Changed My Life* (New York, 1977), pp. 26–37. See also *Annals of the American Academy of Political and Social Science*, 251 (May 1947), on "Women's Opportunities and Responsibilities"; Ferdinand Lundberg and Marynia Farnham, *Modern Women: The Lost Sex* (New York, 1947); Agnes Meyer, "Women Aren't Men," *Atlantic*, 186 (August 1950), 32–36; Joseph K. Folsom, *The Family and Democratic Society* (New York, 1943); and Reuben Hill, "The American Family: Problem or Solution," *American Journal of Sociology*, 53 (September 1947), 125–130. For the political mood at mid-century, see Elaine Tyler May, *Homeward Bound: American Families in the Cold War Era* (New York, 1988), and Leila Rupp and Verta Taylor, *Survival in the Doldrums: The American Women's Rights Movement, 1945 to the 1960s* (New York, 1987), ch. 7. Studies of women in politics include Ralph G. Martin, *Henry and Clare: An Intimate Portrait of the Luces* (New York, 1991), and Ingrid Winther Scobie, *Center Stage: Helen Gahagan Douglas, A Life* (New York, 1992). For women and world affairs, see Edward P. Crapol, ed., *Women and American Foreign Policy: Lobbyists, Critics, and Insiders* (Westport, Conn., 1987), chs. 5 and 6.

CHAPTER 19

Turning Points:
The Early Sixties

During the last week of the spring semester in 1963, Anne Moody, a senior at Tougaloo College in Mississippi, joined a sit-in at the Woolworths lunch counter in Jackson, the state capital. The local branch of the National Association for the Advancement of Colored People, which organized the sit-in, "had a rough time finding students who were in a position to go to jail," she wrote. "I had nothing to lose one way or the other." By 11 o'clock in the morning, when the event was supposed to begin, Capitol Street in downtown Jackson was lined with reporters, alerted by the NAACP, as well as with local police. While other students created a diversion by picketing stores on Capitol Street, Anne Moody and two Tougaloo classmates, Memphis and Pearlena, entered Woolworths through the rear entrance. At 11:15, as prearranged, just when the picketers down the street were being arrested, they sat down at the lunch counter reserved for whites at the front of the store.

There they began a tense and interminable wait. After trying to redirect them to the black lunch counter at the back of the store, the waitresses quickly vanished, along with all the other customers. The Woolworths manager then roped off the rest of the lunch counter to prevent the arrival of more demonstrators, and a substantial crowd gathered around—newsmen and cameramen, hecklers and bystanders. Anne even recognized one hostile antagonist from a previous encounter at a Jackson bus station. An hour later, when a crowd of white high school students arrived, "they were sort of surprised," she remembered. "They didn't know how to react." But the teenagers soon made a noose out of the Woolworths rope and began to insult the demonstrators. Suddenly the three Tougaloo students were thrown off their seats. Memphis was knocked down, kicked, and beaten by a man in the crowd ("A burly ex-cop dragged Memphis Normon, 21, off his stool, slugged him to the floor," *Time* magazine would report), while a United Press photographer took a picture of the scene. Memphis was arrested, along with his attacker, and charged with disturbing the peace. When the two black women got back up on their seats, they were joined by a white Tougaloo student, Joan Trumpauer.

"Which one should I get first?" a big husky boy asked.

"That white nigger," the old man said.

The boy lifted Joan from the counter by her waist and carried her out of the store. Simultaneously, I was snatched from my stool by two high school students. I was dragged about thirty feet towards the door by my hair when someone made them turn me loose. As I was getting up off the floor, I saw Joan coming back inside. We started back to the center of the counter to join Pearlena. Lois Chaffee, a white Tougaloo faculty member, was now sitting next to her. So Joan and I just climbed across the rope at the front end of the counter and sat down. There were now four of us, two whites and two Negroes, all women. The mob started smearing us with ketchup, mustard, sugar, pies, and everything on the counter. Soon Joan and I were joined by John Salter [Anne Moody's social studies teacher, a white NAACP activist] but the moment he sat down he was hit on the jaw with what appeared to be brass knuckles. Blood gushed from his face and someone threw salt on the wound. Ed King, Tougaloo's chaplain, rushed to him.

Then the four women at the lunch counter were joined by two young men, a Congress of Racial Equality field worker and a black high school student, whose shirt was immediately sprayed with paint by the mob. Harassed by the crowd, the counter sitters remained in their seats for three hours, although about ninety policemen had lined up outside Woolworths and were watching the sit-in through the store windows. But no one else was arrested. The store finally closed, and the president of Tougaloo College led out the small group of demonstrators, separated from the mob outside by a line of policemen. Tougaloo's chaplain, Ed King, drove them off to NAACP headquarters in Jackson. "After the sit-in, all I could think of was how sick Mississippi whites were," Anne Moody wrote. "Before the sit-in I had always hated the whites in Mississippi. Now I knew it was impossible for me to hate sickness."

By the time of the Jackson sit-in, Anne Moody was a committed activist in the southern movement for civil rights. When freedom rides and sit-ins started in 1960, Anne was a student at a black junior college in Natchez. Her involvement began when she entered her junior year at Tougaloo, a leading black private college near Jackson. The NAACP was starting a voter registration drive in Hinds County and needed canvassers. Recalling a minister who had been run out of her hometown for merely mentioning the NAACP in a sermon, she had no doubts about becoming a member. "The more I remembered the killings, beatings, and intimidations, the more I worried what might possibly happen to me and my family if I joined the NAACP," Anne Moody wrote. "But I knew I was going to join anyway." At the end of the school year she became involved with the Student Non-Violent Coordinating Committee, founded during the first sit-ins of 1960. Joan Trumpauer, who lived in her dormitory and later joined her at the Jackson sit-in, had introduced her to SNCC (Tougaloo, unlike most black colleges in Mississippi, had many white teachers and some white students). Over the summer of 1962, Anne Moody joined a SNCC voter registration drive in the Mississippi Delta.

The Delta campaign was a turning point both for Anne and for the southern civil rights movement. It was concentrated in seven towns, all of them in LeFlore County, which had 50,000 people, two-thirds of them black. But the blacks owned only about 10 percent of the land, and only 2 percent were registered to vote, compared to 95 percent of voting-age whites. In order to raise voter registration, all the civil rights groups in Mississippi—older ones, such as the NAACP and CORE, and newer ones, such as the Southern Christian Leadership Conference and SNCC—combined their efforts under a new statewide coalition. The Delta campaign was led by Bob Moses of SNCC, a young black New York school-teacher, whom Anne Moody, like other field workers, regarded as "Jesus Christ in the flesh." Like Anne, most of the field workers were black students or former students; the majority were men.

Anne stayed at first, together with three other young women, with a local family and then in the Greenwood "Freedom House," filled with students. At the beginning, the Delta campaign made little headway. Mass rallies were poorly attended, and when SNCC workers started to speak at black churches, congregations remained at home. "Most of these old plantation Negroes had been brainwashed so by the whites, they really thought that only whites were supposed to vote," Anne Moody reflected. But as the Delta campaign continued, "people began to come around." The more success field workers had with voter registration, however, the more local blacks lost their jobs or were evicted from the plantations where they lived. Many were left without resources. Soon SNCC workers were distributing food, clothing, and money collected on northern campuses. "That summer I could feel myself beginning to change," Anne Moody wrote. "I knew I was going to be a part of whatever happened."

The civil rights assault in the Delta continued for over a year; then field workers who had congregated in Greenwood spread out all over the state. Anne Moody returned to Tougaloo in the fall of 1962 to finish college. Jackson, however, soon became "the hotbed of demonstrations in the South." After the Woolworths sit-in, widely reported in the national press, the pace of local civil rights demonstrations increased and so did Anne Moody's commitment. "Something happened to me as I got more and more involved in the Movement," she wrote. "I had found something outside myself that gave meaning to my life." Like the sit-in, most demonstrations involved younger blacks, college students, and high school students who were willing to run the risk of physical abuse and arrests. Anne helped conduct workshops for student demonstrators, showing them how to protect themselves in confrontations with angry crowds or with the police.

Inevitably, she was arrested too, at a demonstration in front of a Jackson post office, along with some Tougaloo friends, a group of black ministers, and 400 high school students. "Most of the ministers were scared stiff," wrote Anne, whose esteem for the clergy was diminishing. "I thought they would cry any minute and here they were, supposed to be our leaders." In Anne's group, twelve women were arrested, and since the jail was racially segregated, she was separated from her Tougaloo companions and put in a cell with young black women from Jackson State College. She regarded this institution, like other state-supported black colleges, as an "uncle Tom" school. Anne Moody resented the separation from her white co-workers. "Here we were going to school together, sleeping in the same dorm, worshipping together, playing together, even demonstrating together [and] they were rushed off to some cell designated for whites."

But if Anne was upset by segregation in the Jackson jail, her family was more upset by her activism. Since 1962, news of her involvement had reached her relatives in Centreville, a small town in the southwest corner of Mississippi, on the Louisiana border, as had the civil rights literature that Anne had sent. "Please don't send any more of that stuff here," wrote her mother, after a visit from the local sheriff. "I don't want nothing to happen to us here. If you keep that stuff up you will never be able to come home again."

In June 1963, civil rights leader Medgar Evers was shot in the back and killed outside his home in Jackson. Anne Moody moved on to a CORE voter registration drive in Canton, Mississippi, despite the objections of Tougaloo chaplain Ed King, who thought the Canton campaign was too risky for women. In Madison County, with 29,000 blacks and 9,000 whites, blacks owned 40 percent of the land, far more than in the Delta. But only 200 blacks were registered to vote, and of these, only half did. Despite the efforts of CORE workers to mobilize the black community, the campaign in Canton was even more difficult than that in the Delta, where so many field workers had been concentrated. The only black support at first came from one local family and forty or fifty teenagers. By September, when Anne Moody was put on the CORE payroll by project leader Dave Dennis, the Canton campaign was wearing her down. Even a summer trip to the March on Washington made little impact. While Martin Luther King made his "I Have a Dream" speech, Anne "sat there thinking that in Canton, we never had time to sleep much less dream."

Occasionally, the "Movement spirit" seemed to be on the rise, as CORE workers spoke at churches, distributed food and clothing, and pleaded for voter registration, but obstacles and disasters abounded. Anne Moody was angry at older blacks, especially middle-class blacks, who cautiously avoided the field workers. Her fear mounted too, despite what she felt was the overprotective attitude toward women field workers. She had seen her picture on a Mississippi Klan leaflet, along with those of civil rights leaders and martyrs. In addition, she was unable to go home to Centreville, as her mother had predicted. Her county was so hostile to black protest that no civil rights organization would go near it, and under such circumstances, she was loath to put her family at risk. But worst of all were the Birmingham bombings in the fall of 1963, when four black children were killed in church. After that, the Canton campaign became demoralized. Most black ministers in Madison County, Anne observed, seemed to be taking off on expeditious trips to Africa. More important, she had to confront what appeared to be a loss of faith. "God didn't seem to be punishing anyone" either for the Birmingham bombings or for any other acts of violence committed against blacks in the South. "It seemed to me now that there must be two Gods, many Gods, or none at all."

In the spring of 1964, one year after the Jackson sit-in, Anne Moody returned to Tougaloo to get her degree. The oldest of many children, she was the first member of her family to graduate from college. When she was back in Jackson, Ed King told her about the Mississippi Summer Project, then being organized by civil rights workers. Over 1,000 college students from all over the country were expected to arrive in the state over the summer to work on voter registration, run "freedom schools," and organize community centers. The project was already generating tremendous excitement in the black community, and the excitement seemed contagious. When Anne arrived at the project's headquarters on Lynch Street in Jackson, she was overwhelmed. Amidst shipments of books and clothes, mattresses and mimeograph machines, a group of about thirty students had just arrived to work on the summer project. Many were young women, recruited on northern campuses—the first large group of white women to become civil rights field workers in the South. "For once in the history of Civil Rights work in Mississippi," Anne Moody thought, "something was actually going to be accomplished."

In Canton, however, the "freedom summer" started inauspiciously. A large "Freedom Day" rally, the first in the county, had just ended in a rout. Feeling as though "the walls of Mississippi were closing in on me," Anne Moody raced out of Canton and back to Jackson. There, a bus full of civil rights workers was leaving for Washington to testify about their activities. Just as the next groups of white college students were heading South for the Mississippi summer project, Anne Moody sat in the northbound Greyhound, looking out at the landscape, with "images of all that happened crossing my mind." As she thought about the church bombings, jail sentences, and violence of the past few years, the civil rights workers were singing "We Shall Overcome." Anne Moody was still dubious. "I wonder, I really wonder."

～✑✎～

"Gradually, without seeing it clearly for quite a while, I came to realize that something is very wrong with the way American women are trying to live their lives today," wrote magazine journalist Betty Freidan in 1963.

> I sensed it first as a question mark in my own life, as a wife and mother of three small children, half-guiltily and therefore half-heartedly, almost in spite of myself, using my abilities and education in work that took me away from home. . . . There was a strange discrepancy between the reality of our lives as women and the image to which we were trying to conform, the image that I came to call the feminine mystique. I wondered if other women faced this schizophrenic split and what it meant.

In the spring of 1963, while the civil rights movement escalated, another type of protest was brewing, though visible only in women's responses to a widely read new book. In *The Feminine Mystique,* Betty Friedan revealed the hazards of a popular ideology that limited women's aspirations, deprived them of self-esteem, and presented them with a "problem that has no name." Since the end of the war, Friedan contended, women had been "told that they could desire no greater destiny than to glory in their own femininity," to find fulfillment as wives and mothers. Urged homeward by experts and educators, advertisers and women's magazines, Freudian psychologists and functionalist social scientists, women had become the victims of the feminine mystique. It confined them to the home, "a comfortable concentration camp"; it prevented them from assuming adult roles, as independent individuals; indeed, it deprived them of a sense of self, a feeling of identity.

Encouraged by the mystique to evade their identity crisis, permitted to escape identity altogether in the name of sexual fulfillment, women once again are living with their feet bound in the old image of glorified femininity. And it is the same old image, despite its shiny new clothes, that trapped women for centuries and made the feminists rebel.

Devoid of purpose and laden with problems, Friedan insisted, the postwar housewife was neither a good wife nor a good mother; nor was she a fulfilled human being, as documented by an array of personal testimony. "I've tried everything women are supposed to do," one of the mystique's victims revealed, "but I'm desperate. I begin to feel that I have no personality." "By noon I'm ready for a padded cell," said another homemaker. The feminine mystique, Friedan concluded, had "succeeded in burying millions of women alive." And women themselves were in part responsible for their own predicament. After World War II, "the American woman made her mistaken choice," Friedan accused. "She ran back home to live by sex alone, trading in her individuality for security." Security had temptations, she conceded (and these seemed to resemble the lures of "contingent living" revealed by psychologist Lorine Pruette three decades before). "It is easier to live through husband and child," Betty Friedan wrote, "than to make a road of her own in the world."

A revivalist tract, crammed with telling anecdotes and references to her personal experience, *The Feminine Mystique* was not without remedies. Education and employment, Betty Friedan contended, would liberate the housewife from the suburban home and enable her "to find herself, to know herself as a person by creative work of her own." Revised educational policies would steer her toward a career; a "new life plan" would enable her to mesh family role and vocational goals; a national education program similar to the GI Bill would allow women to resume their education and "commit themselves to professions." But the power of *The Feminine Mystique* was not in its remedies, which seemed quite meager compared to the enormity of the conspiracy against women that Friedan described. Rather, it was in the revelation of the "mystique" itself. And this was a revelation that Betty Friedan had recently experienced.

When Friedan reexamined her own life, a process that was central to *The Feminine Mystique,* she began at a personal turning point, 1942. This was the year she graduated from Smith College and won a graduate fellowship in psychology. "I thought I was going to be a psychologist," she told readers of the *Mystique.* "But if I wasn't sure, what did I want to be? I felt the future closing in and I could not see myself in it at all. I had no image of myself stretching beyond college." Nonetheless, she studied psychology at the Berkeley campus of the University of California for a year until, lacking a sense of professional identity, she gave up her fellowship and graduate school. She then worked for a small labor news service in New York, a job she eventually lost to a returning veteran. In the interim, Friedan married another returning veteran and soon had a baby, whom she left with a nurse while working as a reporter. When she became pregnant again, she was fired. "I was certainly not a feminist then," Betty Friedan recalled three decades later. "None of us were a bit interested in women's rights."

By the early 1950s, the Friedans had moved from a Queens housing project to the New York suburbs, where they had a third child. For the rest of the decade, Betty Friedan continued to work, although not as a labor reporter. She now was a writer for women's magazines, including *Cosmopolitan, McCall's,* and *Mademoiselle.* Producing such articles as "Millionaire's Wife" and "I Was Afraid to Have a Baby," she became a successful propagandist for what she would later define as an antifeminist ideology. In retrospect, however, the pieces she wrote themselves provided a catalyst: they made her wonder what she was writing about. "I started to write *The Feminine Mystique* because the very articles I was writing for women's magazines no longer rang true to me," Friedan later revealed, "though I—as other women in America—was living my personal life according to its assumptions." But her magazine articles were not the only catalyst.

In 1956–1957, Betty Friedan prepared a long survey of her classmates at Smith. She spent the year devising an elaborate questionnaire—"of inappropriate and unnecessary depth," she later felt—about the feelings and experiences of the Smith class of 1942 in the fifteen years since graduation. Her inquiries seemed a dress rehearsal of the themes that would permeate *The Feminine Mystique.* "What difficulties have you found in working out your role as a woman?" Friedan asked. "What are the chief satisfactions and frustrations of your life today? What do you wish you had done differently? How do you visualize your life after your children have grown?" When formulating the questions, she hoped the responses would disprove the then prevalent belief that higher education destroyed women's femininity and caused "unnecessary conflict and frustration." But the survey and its answers only opened a new bag of questions.

Of the 200 women who responded (less than half the class and perhaps a self-selecting sample to whom the questionnaire appealed), 97 percent had married, usually within three years of graduation. Only 3 percent had been divorced, and 89 percent were housewives, caring for an average of 2.94 children. Ten percent felt "martyred" as mothers; 60 percent did not find the occupation of homemaker "totally fulfilling." To be sure, few revealed the drive that had spurred Betty Friedan to work as a reporter after she had a child or to keep on writing articles after she moved to the suburbs and had two more. But none of Friedan's classmates admitted to more dire symptoms of "occupation: housewife" either. According to the responses, they did not watch daytime television, read women's magazines, or play bridge. The Smith class of '42, in fact, seemed to inhabit a sort of middle ground—a way station between domestic concerns and total involvement in outside interests. Four out of five were active in their communities—running libraries or nursery groups, working on school desegregation, curriculum revision, or museum programs; and three out of five planned to continue their education or go to work after their children had grown up. Nonetheless, four out of five regretted not having planned to use their education in professional work, and some had serious grievances. "If only it were possible to combine career and motherhood," one classmate wrote. "Never have decided what kind of woman I am," wrote another. "Wish I'd studied more science, history, government." "Still trying to find a rock to build on," wrote a third. "Wish I'd finished college. I got married instead." "Wish I'd developed a deeper and more creative life of my own," wrote a mother of six. "Having expected the ideal in marriage, it was a shock to find out this isn't the way it is."

Betty Friedan concluded that the problems faced by her classmates were not caused by their education but by "not planning to put it to serious use." Their answers, however, raised "such strange questions about the role we were all embracing." Like Jane Addams, Friedan had a knack for generalizing from her own experience to that of others. But the process also worked in reverse: Many of the responses of her college classmates mirrored her own as yet unarticulated ones. These Smith graduates of 1942 did not seem "to fit the image of the modern American woman as she was written about in women's magazines," an image that Friedan felt had taken shape after the war. Like Friedan, however, they seemed to lack a "life plan," a lack that in retrospect had pervaded her days as a graduate student and then as a reporter. Her own discarded ambition, in fact, proved a final catalyst.

Above all, what drove me to consciousness was the fact that—with all my high-powered education and brilliant promise as future psychologist or journalist—I too embraced and lived that feminine mystique. Determined that I find that feminine fulfillment that eluded my mother, I first gave up a psychology fellowship and then even newspaper reporting jobs. I lived the life of the suburban housewife that was everyone's dream at the time. . . . I could sense no purpose in my own life . . . until I finally faced it and worked out my own answer.

By the time her work on the Smith questionnaire was completed, Betty Friedan had formulated her ideas about the "feminine mystique" and started to explore its origins. She was also interested in the mystique's impact on women "who lived by it or grew up under it." "If I was right, the very assumptions on which I and other women were basing our lives and on which the experts were advising us were wrong." Besides delving into current studies about women, which seemed to be framed to support the mystique, and into new work in psychology on identity problems, Friedan held rafts of interviews. She talked to educators at women's colleges, to editors and former editors of women's magazines, to experts in advertising, to specialists in family life, and to a gamut of psychologists, psychiatrists, anthropologists, and sociologists. She also interviewed eighty women in different stages of the life cycle—high school students, college students (including the Smith class of '59), young housewives and mothers, and women of her own age, about forty, "who provided the most damning indictment of the feminine mystique." As a result, the book was filled with women's voices, though all, like the respondents to the Smith questionnaire, tended to speak a Friedanesque language. Finally, with research still in progress, Betty Friedan started to test the waters of publication, by writing an article conveying the gist of the "feminine mystique."

Unfortunately, most of the women's magazines that had previously printed Friedan's pieces disliked her critical view of "occupation: housewife." The article she wrote was turned down by *McCall's* as "unbelievable." It was rewritten by the *Ladies' Home Journal,* "to deny its evidence so I wouldn't let them print it." And it was rejected by *Redbook* as something with which "only the most neurotic housewife could possibly identify." But *Good Housekeeping* ran a piece by Friedan in September 1960 called "Women Are People, Too." "Is there more to modern woman's role than being a good wife and mother?" asked the magazine. "The author's answer may surprise and even shock you!"

"Women Are People, Too" laid out Friedan's new ideas in the simplest possible manner, supported by many quotations from her recent interviews with women. Two months later, a rash of replies were published in *Good Housekeeping.* One was unreceptive. "So Betty Friedan talked to hundreds of women?" wrote a housewife. "Well, one of the hundreds she didn't talk to was *me.*" But most of the letters expressed a shock of recognition. "Now that I am not alone the future seems brighter," wrote an appreciative homemaker. "It struck at the very heart of something that has caused me many hours of discontented soul searching," wrote another. "My own turning point came two weeks ago when I decided to start studying to become a doctor," wrote a third. The responses convinced Friedan that the "problem that has no name" was not confined solely to graduates of such colleges as Smith, whose class of '42 never read women's magazines. They also provided a preview of the responses that would inundate Friedan after the publication of *The Feminine Mystique.*

Once the book appeared, in the spring of 1963, it quickly took on a life of its own. Despite Friedan's denunciation of conventional attitudes, most reviewers were enthusiastic, with only an occasional gripe about the "drilling insistence of the style." Excerpts were also published simultaneously—in major women's magazines, some of them the same magazines that had rejected her earlier article. Paradoxically, of course, these were also the same magazines that Friedan attacked for promoting "the feminine mystique." Nonetheless, the *Ladies' Home Journal, Good Housekeeping,* and *McCall's* now brought Friedan's message to an even larger audience (five times as many as the 3 million who actually bought the book, she estimated). The women's magazines were not complete converts. A year later, *McCall's* ran a short story called "The Feminine Mystique" in which a fortyish housewife-heroine, mother of three, was confronted by a pollster whose questions made her feel obsolete, as if she had outlived her usefulness and was "going to seed." In response, the heroine sent bills to her family for services rendered, provoking a burst of hilarity, affection, and appreciation from husband and children. The housewife was still needed and loved, *McCall's* assured its audience.

Readers of *The Feminine Mystique,* meanwhile, responded directly to Betty Friedan. "In the weeks and months after the publication of *The Feminine Mystique,* I and other women knew we were not alone," one woman wrote. "It was a great relief to realize how many others had come up with the same painful questions in trying to live the mystique."

The flood of correspondence Friedan received expressed both gratitude and antagonism. Few angry letters came from men; indeed many wrote to say that they had bought the book for their wives. But among women, there appeared to be a chasm between negative and positive reactions, both of which, curiously, served to document the impact of the "feminine mystique." "I happen to love the rewards of being completely passive," wrote a California housewife. "I don't want to compete with my husband, I want to respect and admire him." Other negative responses, from similarly infuriated women, contended that Betty Friedan needed psychiatric help. There were also, overwhelmingly, positive responses. "It struck at the center of my being," wrote an Iowa woman. "I feel like I am on the threshold of a new life." Significantly, many of the appreciative letters, which confirmed Friedan's thesis in its entirety, were filled with negative feelings—guilt, shame, resentment, despair—and negative self-images. Women described themselves variously as mops, zombies, sissies, drudges, and freaks, "I have been trying for years to tell my husband of my need to do something to find myself—to have a purpose," wrote a Florida mother of four. "All I've ever achieved was to end up feeling guilty about wanting to be more than a housewife and mother." Younger women expressed a different kind of guilt. "I feel like an appliance," wrote a young Michigan mother of three. "My brain seems dead and I am nothing but a parasite."

"I did not set out consciously to start a revolution when I wrote *The Feminine Mystique* but it changed my life, as a woman and a writer, and other women tell me that it changed theirs," Betty Friedan wrote a decade later.

For me it began in the 1950s, with the gradual realization, that my own life, and those of other women, didn't fit, couldn't even be understood in the abstract terms of conventional or sophisticated thought which then defined women and by which we defined ourselves. The unraveling of what I called the feminine mystique from the actual fabric of women's life was my personal consciousness raising. . . .

In a sense it was almost accidental—coincidental—that I wrote *The Feminine Mystique* and in another sense my whole life prepared me to write that book; all the pieces of my own life came together for the first time in the writing of it.

⚬⚬⚬

"You are very much in our thoughts today," wrote commission members to their ailing chairman, Eleanor Roosevelt, in October 1962. One year before, while Betty Friedan was interviewing suburban housewives, President Kennedy, newly elected, had created a President's Commission on the Status of Women. The last project ever headed by Eleanor Roosevelt, the commission was the first federal body devoted to examining women's rights and roles. It was supposed to "develop plans for fostering the full partnership of men and women in our national life." But the new commission was also inspired by political motives. And like Betty Friedan's *Feminine Mystique,* it was to have unexpected results.

Apparently a low-cost effort to retain the "woman's vote," the Commission on the Status of Women was not a response to demands voiced by women's groups. During the 1950s, few women's organizations sought to exert political pressure; there was no longer a visible feminist movement. Rather, the commission had been proposed by Esther Peterson, the recently appointed head of the Women's Bureau and assistant secretary of labor. A former labor lobbyist and active Kennedy campaigner, Peterson was also the highest-ranking woman appointee of the Kennedy administration, indeed one of very few high-level woman appointees. And Esther Peterson had specific goals. The Women's Bureau was interested in equal pay legislation, in maintaining protective laws, and in urging women into the labor force. It was also interested in ending arguments about the Equal Rights Amendment, first proposed in 1923. A new commission on women's status, Peterson wrote to labor secretary Arthur Goldberg in 1961, could "substitute constructive recommendations for the present troublesome and futile agitation about the equal rights amendment." At the same time, it could promote the interests of women workers and "genuine equality of opportunity."

But Esther Peterson's concern for equality of opportunity was not enough to explain why President Kennedy had agreed to her proposal. Since the late 1940s, similar proposals for commissions on women's status, supported by the Women's Bureau and major women's organizations, had been rejected by previous Presidents. The Kennedy administration, however, had its own problem to face. Democratic women seemed to be extremely irked at the paucity of women's appointments to important federal jobs. And since the beginning of 1961, they had been complaining about it.

Neither of the Presidents who had immediately preceded Kennedy, Truman and Eisenhower, had outstanding records on women's appointments either. But each had appointed a woman cabinet member, as Kennedy had not. Moreover, politicized women appeared to expect more from Kennedy than from his predecessors. As soon as he took office, Eleanor Roosevelt, in the tradition of Molly Dewson, presented him with a long list of women whom she favored for high federal posts—though with few results. Another New Deal veteran, Democratic national committeewoman Emma Guffey Miller, was even more vociferous. Berating the President for failing to appoint enough women, Miller warned of "disastrous" consequences. Other prominent Democratic women voiced grievances as well, and under these circumstances, Esther Peterson's proposal for an advisory commission devoted to women took on new appeal. From the administration's point of view, the commission offered a way of recognizing women who were active in public life, of voicing interest in women's issues (women were now over half the electorate), and of compensating for the lack of high-level women's appointments. Finally, the commission itself might serve as a political substitute for an ERA—an amendment that was strongly opposed by the labor movement, to whom the new administration was indebted. Conceivably, a successful commission on women's status could bring this divisive and bothersome issue to an end.

Although an ERA had not been considered by Congress for almost a decade, many still had strong feelings about it. The amendment was opposed not only by the Women's Bureau and the labor movement but by all large women's organizations, such as the League of Women Voters and the General Federation of Women's Clubs. Nor was there any noticeable groundswell of popular support. But demands for an ERA had been included in both major party platforms since 1940. In addition, the amendment was still endorsed by at least some women's groups, such as the National Federation of Business and Professional Women's Clubs and the remnant of the National Woman's party—the only organization devoted solely to extending women's rights. Even within the Women's Bureau, long committed to protective laws, there were signs of mixed sentiments. Some important opponents, moreover, had switched their stance or at least, like Eleanor Roosevelt, hedged their bets. "Many of us opposed the amendment because it would do away with protection in the labor field," Eleanor Roosevelt was quoted as saying in the *New York Times* in 1961. "Now with unionization, there is no reason why you shouldn't have it if you want it."

Clearly, the new commission would have to contend with the divisive issue of the ERA, as turned out to be the case. "We were up against that awful Equal Rights Amendment situation," Esther Peterson later told an interviewer. But the commission was also an unparalleled opportunity to increase public awareness of women's issues and promote Women's Bureau goals. And it was securely under Women's Bureau auspices, since all commission appointments were approved jointly by Peterson and Labor Secretary Goldberg. Thirteen women served on the commission, representing leading women's associations, educational institutions, religious affiliations, and organized labor. So did eleven men, among them five cabinet members. Scores of additional women and men served as consultants to the commission's seven investigatory committees, supported by a backup staff of Women's Bureau personnel. Indeed, since the commission as a whole met infrequently, the bureau did most of the work. And Esther Peterson, commission vice-chairman and guiding spirit, directed most of its activities, especially after Eleanor Roosevelt's death in November 1962.

When the Commission on the Status of Women reported to the President on October 11, 1963 (the anniversary of Eleanor Roosevelt's birth), it had completed its investigations of women's employment, education, and legal status. And it was ready, according to the President's original order, to propose services that would "enable women to continue their roles as wives and mothers while making a maximum contribution to the world around them."

As expected, the commission report rejected the idea of an ERA. Few commission members were associated with pro-ERA organizations, and only one, Marguerite Rawalt, prominent attorney and president of the NFBPWC, was an ardent advocate. "Since the commission is convinced that the Constitution now embodies equality of rights for men and women, we conclude that a constitutional amendment need not now be sought in order to establish this principle," the commission reported. (Rawalt had insisted that the last "now" be injected.) An ERA was unnecessary, the commission explained, since women's equality was guaranteed by the Fifth and Fourteenth amendments, although "definitive court pronouncements are needed to invalidate laws that discriminate against women." In the end, the commission had managed to support the goal of equality while rejecting the proposed means—a constitutional amendment. An impressive report by Yale law school fellow Pauli Murray had helped effect this compromise, in committee. But ERA rejection was only one part of the commission's report. The most comprehensive document about women ever produced by the federal government, it also identified issues with which women would be preoccupied for the next decade. While Betty Friedan was uncovering the feminine mystique, the Commission on the Status of Women had started to create a new agenda of women's demands, most of which came directly from the Women's Bureau.

Women, said the commission, had primary responsibility for family life, just as men had primary responsibility for family support. And in their families, women were "the transmitters of the central values of their culture." At the same time, the commission insisted that "aspiration must be fostered, beyond stubbornly persistent assumptions about 'women's roles' and 'women's interests.'" Priding itself on its moderation, the commission rejected more drastic modes of fostering aspiration. It did not want to discard protective laws, or to treat sexual discrimination in the same manner as racial discrimination or to institute policies of "temporary discrimination" in order to increase women's numbers in high-level federal posts. On the other hand, it pointed out a wide array of injustices and proposed a long list of remedies.

Legal inequities, such as bars against jury service and restrictions on married women's rights, should be ended, the commission urged. Joint guardianship of children should be recognized under law. New community services were needed so that women could maintain dual roles, as family members and employees. The commission backed day-care programs, supported by both voluntary and federal funds; tax deductions for the child-care expenses of working mothers; continuing education programs for women; and an end to sexual inequities in social security benefits and unemployment insurance. Endorsing equal opportunity in employment, the report also proposed more part-time work, paid maternity leaves, state equal pay laws, increased vocational training, and promotion of women to upper-level federal jobs. The federal government, indeed, ought to provide a "showcase" of equal employment opportunity. Moreover, the commission insisted, since women were so under-represented in public office, "increasing consideration should continually be given to the appointment of women of demonstrated ability and political sensitivity to policy-making positions." Finally, the federal government must continue its efforts on women's behalf. Peculiarly, in the absence of any organized feminist movement, the Commission on the Status of Women had come up with an extremely long list of demands (or "recommendations").

Relatively few of the commission's recommendations evoked much friction within it. There were battles over dismissal of an ERA, and also some disagreement about protective laws. But a lively conflict did erupt at a special consultation, "Images of Women in the Media," where feelings seemed to run as strong as those about an ERA. Chaired by commission member Margaret Hickey, an editor of the *Ladies' Home Journal,* the discussion centered on the unrealistic ways in which women were portrayed in the media ("never as a serious partner or breadwinner"). Many of the women who participated in the session appeared to be unusually enraged. Playwright Lorraine Hansberry contended that the media depicted women primarily as "objects." Writer Marya Mannes added that the media presented only the "middle-class home-bound housewife with children" and neglected "the full-time working wife, the wife who supports the family, the single working woman, the career woman with husband and family, the professional intellectual, the Negro woman." Finally, writer Betty Friedan, who had the most to say, assaulted women's magazines for "not projecting a new horizon for women" as they had done, she claimed, in the 1930s. Magazine fiction, Friedan insisted, must stress "the image of a heroine who is using herself for some purpose or goal." Others, however, contended that women's magazines were "raising the standards of living and taste."

The session on media images had not originally been one of the commission's assignments; it was scheduled as an afterthought. Another afterthought was a consultation devoted to "The Problems of Negro Women," chaired by commission member Dorothy Height, president of the National Council of Negro Women. Black women had been mentioned throughout the commission report. Lack of opportunity for black men, it contended, "forced women to assume too large a share of family responsibility"; if married with young children, they were twice as likely as white women to seek employment. The special consultation reiterated this view.

Traditionally, Negro families have been more matriarchal than white families. The tendency has continued because of the inability of Negro men to get a decent job and earn a sufficient wage to carry the responsibilities of family life. Thus the Negro wife is forced into the labor market where she often earns more than her husband and sometimes becomes the only earner for the family. Therefore, not by choice, she may become the head of household.

The progress of the black woman, the session concluded, "her advancement and that of the whole family—is inextricably bound to the improvement of opportunities for the Negro male."

"Like a solid, protective wall," anthropologist Margaret Mead later wrote, "the Commission's report divides the past, with its limitations and difficulties, from a future in which it may be expected that these hindrances will be overcome." But the report of the Commission on the Status of Women attracted almost no attention in 1963. At the time it was presented to the President, Americans were far more interested in the visit of Madame Ngo Dinh Nhu of South Vietnam and with increased strife over civil rights in the South. The report was rarely mentioned in the press, except when Esther Peterson attempted to explain to readers of *McCall's,* in the simplest of language, that the report had been "Mrs. Roosevelt's legacy." Nonetheless, during the time the commission was at work, federal attempts to remedy some of the inequities it would reveal were already under way.

By the end of 1963, Congress had passed an Equal Pay Act, the first federal law against sex discrimination, and had also provided the first federal funds for day care since World War II. In addition, President Kennedy had issued a directive to executive agencies prohibiting sex discrimination in hiring and promotion, another "first." As soon as the commission disbanded, a permanent Citizens' Advisory Council on the Status of Women was formed, to serve as a federal watchdog agency. Moreover, even before the commission presented its report, many states had created their own commissions on the status of women, which began to spur inquiry into women's issues on a state level. Within a year, thirty-two states had formed such commissions.

"In the atmosphere of protest which prevails today, it is hard to recall the spirit of the times when President Kennedy created his status of women commission and the way we worked to implement 'full partnership,'" presidential commission member Caroline Ware wrote in a public letter to the National Organization of Women a decade later.

> I think we were all surprised that our suggestion that states establish status of women commissions should have met with such widespread response throughout the country. When the state commissions began to meet together, it became apparent that some of them . . . were prepared to penetrate more deeply into the factors limiting women's status.

Women's involvement in the civil rights movement, the publication of *The Feminine Mystique,* and the creation of the President's Commission on the Status of Women were disparate responses to different situations—a century of racial segregation, several decades of feminist stagnation, and a need to retain the "woman's vote." But in retrospect, all were turning points; they connected the apparently placid and conservative decade of the 1950s with a new era of political activism, social reform, and feminist revival.

20

❦

HIGH EXPECTATIONS: 1950–1975

The decade of the 1950s, when Betty Friedan began to trace the origins of the "feminine mystique," is remembered as a conventional and complacent one. But in women's history it was also a decade of tremendous change. Postwar America was characterized by an expanding economy, a growing middle class, and an abnormally high birthrate that rose for about a decade. This demographic reversal was accompanied by a new outburst of domestic ideology, a vigorous revival of traditional ideals of woman's place. At the same time, the postwar economy provided vocational space for women workers, who moved into the labor force in record numbers. During the 1950s, women's expectations shifted in two directions, simultaneously.

As a result, the decade had a split character; or, rather, it had an overt agenda, the return to domesticity, and a hidden one, a massive movement into the labor market. The first, though temporary, was more visible. The 1950s were an affluent era, when upward mobility seemed within reach; a consumerist era, when goods and services flooded the market; a conservative era, when voices of protest were muted or silent; and a period of consensus, when goals and aspirations were widely shared. The much-publicized domestic ideal of the decade, a vital part of this picture, appeared to be the most widely shared goal of all. "The suburban housewife was the dream image of the young American woman," Betty Friedan wrote in 1963. "She was healthy, beautiful, educated, concerned only about her husband, her children, her home. She had found feminine fulfillment."

Suburban Housewives

In *Life's* special issue "The American Woman" in 1956, the largest amount of picture space was devoted to a suburban housewife, aged thirty-two and mother

493

of four. A high school graduate who had married as a teenager, *Life*'s major subject, described as "pretty and popular," was a hostess, volunteer, and "home manager," who sewed her own clothes, entertained 1,500 guests a year, and was supported by a husband whose annual income was $25,000. "In her daily round she attends club or charity meetings, drives the children to school, does the weekly grocery shopping, makes ceramics, and is planning to learn French," *Life* revealed, as it followed the housewife from domestic chores to social gala. "A conscientious mother, she spends lots of time with her children, helping with their homework . . . listening to their stories or problems." That *Life*, which monitored the national pulse, chose the housewife as woman of the hour in 1956 was no surprise. During the 1950s, woman's sphere received extensive publicity.

The domestic ideology that permeated the 1950s was hardly new. It had been popular for over a century. The image of woman as homemaker and child rearer, more passive and less competitive than man, had never lacked a following. Though challenged by a feminist gust in the early twentieth century, the domestic ideal had gained ground since the 1920s. After World War II, it was cloaked in modern garb, bolstered by experts, and widely promoted. In part antifeminist, domestic ideology incorporated the backlash against women and the fear of female competition that had followed the war. In part anti-elitist, it posited fulfillment within the family as a goal to which women of all classes and backgrounds might aspire. Most important, during the 1950s, the domestic ideal won a fresh constituency: women who had grown up during depression and war and looked forward to stable, traditional roles in secure and prosperous environments. Domestic ideology did not reign unquestioned, as historian Joanne Meyerowitz points out; mass culture in fact reflected a variety of views. Still, the domestic ideal drew support from the dominant trends of postwar life—a consumer economy, an expanding middle class, a tremendous spurt of suburban growth, and a fifteen-year baby boom.

The 1950s were a decade of early marriages and young families. After the war, the average marriage age for women dropped to twenty. By 1951, one woman in three was married by nineteen, and in 1958, more women married between fifteen and nineteen than in any comparable age span. The postwar rush to matrimony was followed at once by a surge in the birthrate that continued for a decade, far longer than minor postwar baby booms in other modern nations. The American birthrate did not peak until 1957, when it reached a high of 25.3 per thousand people. The birthrate among college-educated women, moreover, was only slightly lower than that of the general female population. Since more young women were taking care of more young children than at any time in recent memory, domestic ideology had a captive audience. But that ideology rested on a built-in demographic flaw. Postwar childbearing was usually compressed into the teens and twenties; the average mother might expect to have her last child by the age of thirty. Within a decade after that, all her children would be in school if not starting to go off on their own. More than half her adult life would be spent neither having children nor taking care of them. The discrepancy between domestic ideology and the female life cycle was obscured, however, by the appeal and demands of suburban life.

The domestic passion of the 1950s coincided with a massive exodus to the suburbs, the ideal place for raising families. Suburbs had evolved in the 1890s and had grown again in the 1920s, but their rapid expansion was a post-World War II phenomenon: A large number of Americans could now afford homes, cars, and early marriage. During the 1950s alone, two-thirds of American population growth occurred in suburbs. Federal policy supported such growth. Young couples in search of suburban havens were aided by low-interest mortgages, veterans benefits, and federal support for highway construction. The same policies promoted domestic ideals, since suburban life, for women, meant commitment to home and family, to house care and child care. For the college-educated housewife later described by Betty Friedan, this commitment was a "mistaken choice," a step backward into traditional roles. But for the typical new postwar housewife, it was a step upward into the middle class, into normalcy, though it was a "normalcy" that had never existed before. After World War II, the proportion of Americans who were middle class approximately doubled. The postwar middle class, wrote journalist Agnes Meyer at midcentury, had been "augmented by seepage from above due to the decline of big fortunes and by seepage from below, due to the rise in wages, the improvement of educational opportunities, and technological progress."

Born in the depression, the new homemaker appreciated her security, life-style, and rising standard of living. Sociologist Herbert Gans, who lived in a New Jersey Levittown in the early 1960s, recorded a high level of satisfaction

A baby shower in the 1950s. Abetted by suburbanization, the total fertility rate of American women soared to over 3.6, higher than that of 1910. In tune with the times, planned parenthood clinics adapted to the baby boom. They developed sexual counseling programs and stressed the value of birth control as a tool to create enduring sexual relationships in marriage. *(Suzanne Szasz)*

among his suburbanites, male and female, who came from lower-middle- or working-class origins. For Levittowners, suburban life was not a "retreat into localism and familialism" but rather a continuation of it. "Most Levittowners grew up in the Depression and remembering the hard times of their childhood, they wanted to protect themselves and their children from stress," Gans wrote. So did the new suburban housewife of the 1950s. Neither a college graduate nor a career woman manqué, she was a survivor.

Unlike the urban, middle-class homemaker of the progressive era, who was active in women's organizations, the new suburban housewife of the 1950s rarely assumed a leadership role in community affairs. She might serve as a volunteer and join the PTA, but she avoided policymaking positions, which were filled by men. Her commitment to family life over community life was hardly unique. On a national level, women did not seem to play a large part in public affairs in the 1950s—with such notable exceptions as Margaret Chase Smith, who entered the Senate in 1948. Women also remained active as volunteers in political campaigns and in the movement against nuclear armament. But the general sentiment was that they had won equal rights in 1920 and chose to enjoy them by staying at home.

Major women's organizations, like the League of Women Voters, remained in the background. They opposed an Equal Rights Amendment, supported child welfare, and avoided controversy. By 1960, the LWV was half the size it had been in the 1920s. Feminism, now seen as either foolish or deviant, was mocked in the press if mentioned at all. (Describing the "emancipated" woman of an earlier generation, Cornelia Otis Skinner noted that "the first shackle from which she emancipated herself was charm.") Most important, the assertiveness needed to pursue any course in public affairs was in low repute in the 1950s, when domestic ideals held sway. But the housewife was not excluded from the nation's economic life. In an era of mass consumerism, she became once again an important consumer.

After World War II, items that had once been relative luxuries were, like the suburban home itself, now within reach for cash or credit. Over a million new homes a year needed appliances, decoration, and upkeep, creating a huge new household market. Housewives, who made 75 percent of family purchases, bought electric mixers and sewing machines, chose among floor waxes and detergents, and selected food and clothes for five or six people. The technology of housework had, by now, passed a fail-safe point. It decreased the heavy labor once associated with housewifery while increasing the range of products needed to find fulfillment in homemaking, as urged in the ads of mass-circulation women's magazines. The power of a woman, never undervalued by the *Ladies' Home Journal* or its competitors, was not moral power but purchasing power. "The buying of things," as an advertising expert told Betty Friedan, could provide a "sense of identity, purpose, creativity . . . self-realization." During the 1950s, aspiration assumed material shape. A Gallup poll run for the *Journal* in 1961 revealed that most young women aged sixteen to twenty-one could define their goals, beyond four children, with graphic precision—built-in ovens, formica counters, finished woodwork, and "a split-level brick with four bedrooms with French provincial furniture." Women's buying power had not been celebrated to such an extent since the 1920s.

Advertisers were not the only promoters of domestic ideals after World War II. So were the experts, who occupied a large sector of public space, offering scientific, medical, and psychological counsel. In postwar America professionals assumed new authority, filling roles that in earlier days had been filled by the clergy. Femininity itself was now defined by specialists, psychiatrists and psychoanalysts, whose messages filtered into magazines, movies, and marriage manuals. The drift of such messages was inescapable. Women, said the experts, found fulfillment in passive roles. The basic tenets had been set forth right after the war.

The feminine woman, psychoanalyst Helene Deutsch had written in 1946, "leaves the initiative to the man and out of her own needs, renounces originality, experiences her own self through identification." Unlike the "masculine" woman—intelligent, aggressive, and bent on achievement, due to some mishap in her psychological development—Deutsch's "ideal life companion," a more fortunate individual, abandoned ambition, avoided competition, and relied on intuition, "God's gift to the feminine woman." Women's needs, as Marynia Farnham and Ferdinand Lundberg confirmed in their 1947 best-seller, were "a wish for dependence, inwardness, a wish to be protected and made secure, a strong desire for passivity and compliance." The more women emulate men, they exhorted, "the less are their capacities for satisfaction as women." Moreover, the more education they had, the greater their chances of "sexual disorder." (This was a tenet that Betty Friedan set out to disprove when she surveyed her classmates at Smith.) Clearly the experts supported traditional roles, where passivity, dependence, and noncompetitiveness were expected. Their warnings, moreover, echoed through the 1950s, positing two alternatives: femininity or disaster. "Psychiatrists who studied the causes of our disturbing divorce rate," according to *Life* in 1956, "note wives who are not feminine enough."

If passivity was recommended for marital success, another type of passivity was urged on mothers. During the 1950s, child-rearing manuals came into their own. The market of middle-class mothers was now enormous. Dr. Spock, the most popular manual writer, reached one million readers a year between 1946 and 1960. But the mother's authority as guardian of youth had diminished. She was expected, instead, to act as a conduit between expert and child. Above all, she was exhorted to avoid two assertive attitudes that the experts deplored: rejection and overprotection. The working mother, for instance, escaped responsibility, leaving behind an abandoned, deprived, and potentially delinquent child. Dr. Spock cautioned mothers who wanted to leave young children for paid work to seek psychological or social counseling; it was best to leave home only for a trip to the beauty parlor, to see a movie, buy a new hat or dress, or visit a good friend. The overprotective mother, recently discovered, was another hazard. During the war, many army recruits had been given psychiatric discharges due to maladies doctors attributed to overdependence on their mothers. Powerful and grasping, the overprotective mother was now described as a saboteur, who attempted to keep her children emotionally immature and bound to her forever, thereby ruining their lives. Aware of the dangers of both rejection and overprotection, the postwar mother was supposed to be primarily a constant presence—nonassertive, available, and able to follow professional advice. If she had a problem, as did the thousands of mothers who wrote to Dr. Spock each year, she was likely to attribute it to her personal defects—in one mother's words, "my own emotionalism and lack of control."

The passivity urged on wives and mothers in the postwar era affected younger women too. The college woman, always a useful barometer, was hardly immune to domestic ideals. Indeed, the rush to matrimony took on new urgency. "Girls feel hopeless if they haven't a marriage at least in sight by commencement time," the *New York Times* reported in 1955. The Vassar woman no longer expected to make "an enduring contribution to society," a visitor observed in 1962. "Her future identity is largely encompassed by the projected role of wife and mother." During the 1950s, authorities and educators often reinforced the college woman's new traditionalism. When Adlai Stevenson spoke at Smith's commencement in 1955, he assured the graduate that her role would be to guide and influence the men in her life, to "inspire in her home a vision of the meaning of life and freedom." Educators at some women's colleges, meanwhile, found new value in vocational training for domesticity. Colleges should not treat women as "men in disguise," the president of Mills urged in 1950, but rather provide a "distinctively feminine curriculum," centered around a course in the family, that would not cut women off from their domestic destinies. Even in traditional courses, social science students were likely to learn that current ideals of gender roles served a functional purpose in society. Not surprisingly, college women adjusted their sights to cultural demands. In *Women and the Modern World* (1952), Barnard sociologist Mirra Komarovsky analyzed their modes of adjustment.

Komarovsky had a bias. She labeled demands for feminine curricula as "neo-antifeminist," linked such demands to the baneful rise of psychoanalytic influence, and even found fault with the ideal feminine woman Deutsch had described. ("At her worst, she risks a self-abased subjection to tyranny and a deterioration of personality.") The students she had surveyed during the previous decade, however, seemed to favor traditional goals. All but a handful anticipated marriage and motherhood, although most intended to work between graduation and marriage. "Work experience is beneficial because it gives some insight into the husband's world," a student observed. Beyond these general areas of agreement, aspirations were divided. Twenty percent of the college women were determined careerists who hoped to marry and have families as well; 30 percent were "middle-of-the-road" types who anticipated employment after ten or fifteen years of homemaking and child rearing. But half looked forward to lifelong domestic careers after marriage, contending "that it is natural for a woman to be satisfied with her husband's success and not crave personal achievement"; "that a woman who worked cannot possibly be as good a mother as one who stays home"; and "that a husband is naturally superior in certain spheres but that he requires constant and watchful encouragement on the part of the wife to maintain his superiority."

Komarovsky contended that students defended traditional roles "all the more passionately" because they felt tempted by "other goals." Conflict between individual inclinations and traditional roles emerged in some of the seniors' responses. "I am a natural leader," one student wrote. "But I know that men fear bossy women, and I always have to watch myself on dates not to assume 'the executive role.'" "Quite frankly, I am afraid to go into some kind of business career because I have a feeling that I would cheat myself out of marriage," said another senior. "I may be wrong, but I am just old-fashioned enough to believe that men (at least the type I want to marry) still want their wives to be feminine, domestic, dependent, and just a little inferior mentally."

The domestic ideology that Komarovsky's college students revealed remained alive and well for a decade after her book was published. Its impact was reflected again in 1962, in the responses to a massive 209-question Gallup poll, as reported in the *Saturday Evening Post*. "Our study shows that few people are as happy as a housewife," the pollsters, George Gallup and Evan Hill, concluded after interviewing 2,300 women. "Apparently the American woman has all the rights she wants." Supporting this assertion, 96 percent of those surveyed declared themselves extremely happy or very happy. The comments they offered, which more than fulfilled Farnham and Lundberg's requirements, also supported the pollsters' conclusions. "Being subordinate to men is part of being feminine," an Arizona mother volunteered. "A woman's prestige comes from her husband's opinion of her," a Portland housewife declared. "Women who ask for equality fight nature," said a New Jersey mother of three, formerly a career woman. Asked to identify the "most satisfying moments" of their lives, nine out of ten women voted for childbirth. "The most thrilling moment of Eleanor's life came when she watched her children being born, and being a good mother is the goal she considers most important," Gallup and Hill reported. "I want to be the kind of woman who gives her children emotional security," Eleanor explained. "That's one of the reasons why I don't think a mother should work." She was also bent on "broadening my interests so I won't bore Jim." Interviewing thousands of women was not without its lighter moments, though these also revealed a facet of traditional roles ("Why, you talk to my wife as if you thought she knew what she was talking about," a husband told the researchers). But the Gallup poll also provided a few downbeat notes. Most women interviewed wanted their daughters to have more education and marry later, and 90 percent hoped that their daughters would not "lead the same kind of life they did."

Gallup and Hill's testimonial to the 1950s domestic ideology was, ironically, one of its first obituaries. A second and more important one appeared in 1963, when Betty Friedan revealed the hazards of the "feminine mystique." The influence of her book was unanticipated. Like Jane Addams, Friedan was able to transform a personal problem first into a social problem, then into a public cause, and ultimately into political capital. Clearly, Friedan's message of 1963 was geared to the educated or highly educable woman like herself, capable of "creative work" and "professional achievement," who appeared to be the mystique's major victim. The remedies she proposed—such as the "new life plan"—were mainly individual solutions, not social solutions; Friedan did not urge the creation of a new women's movement. Nonetheless, the "problem that has no name" was one that women readers immediately recognized. From the outset, Friedan's polemics had more impact than her proposals. Her revelations, finally, were extremely well timed.

By 1963, when *The Feminine Mystique* appeared, the phenomenon it assaulted had started to lose its foundations. The birth rate was dropping, the marriage age was rising, and the conservative social climate was starting to change. Moreover, since the late 1940s, when (according to Friedan) the "feminine mystique" struck, middle-class women had been moving steadily into paid employment.

Working Mothers

When Gallup and Hill surveyed the views of "the American woman" in 1962, they paid scant attention to working wives. But after World War II, the female work force dramatically increased and the woman wage earner became a standard part of middle-class life. Before the war, only one out of four women over sixteen years old worked. But in 1960, two out of five held jobs, twice as many in number as in 1940. Women's proportion of the work force continued to grow. During the 1960s, two-thirds of new employees were women; and by the end of the decade, almost half of adult women earned wages. The new woman worker of the 1950s and 1960s, moreover, was likely to be married, middle-class, and middle-aged. And with each year that passed, she was more likely to be a mother with children under seventeen at home.

The advent of the working wife was the first major structural change of the postwar era. By 1950, married women made up over half the female work force, and each year their proportion rose. In 1940, only 15 percent of wives worked; in 1950, 21 percent; in 1960, 30 percent; in 1970, over 40 percent; and by 1980, over 50 percent. Once married women surged into jobs after the war, the age of the female work force also rose. The largest segment of new women workers in the 1950s were those in their forties or older; by 1960, the median age of the working woman was forty-one. Throughout the 1950s, the social status of the woman worker also rose; women from middle-class families entered the labor force faster than any other group. The new woman worker was also more likely to be a parent. In 1948, when the postwar female work force was just starting to expand, only one out of four women with school-age children, between six and seventeen years old, held jobs, but by 1960, two out of five of such women were at work. By the end of the 1960s, over half of all mothers of school-age children were in the labor force. Unlike the baby boom, which hit its peak in 1957 and then declined, the movement of wives and then mothers into paid employment steadily gathered momentum. The greatest increases, ironically, were during the 1950s, when domestic ideals held sway.

The figures cited here are somewhat overblown, since they include women who took on temporary, part-time, or seasonal work, as well as full-time wage earners. Moreover, the female work force continued to include a large proportion of "traditional" wage earners—women supporting themselves and their families, such as single women, widows, a growing number of separated and divorced women, and women married to low-income men. During the 1950s, two out of five women wage earners came from low-income families. Still, it can be fairly said that the "New Women" of the postwar era were middle-class working wives and, in ever growing numbers, working mothers. They had replaced older offspring as the providers of supplementary incomes.

The working wife had been denounced as anathema in the 1930s when jobs were scarce (though her numbers increased), and she was only reluctantly and temporarily accepted during World War II, when men were scarce. But during the 1950s a new set of circumstances not only spurred her entry into the labor force but quietly legitimized it. As the economy rapidly expanded, demand for low-paid qualified workers in such occupations as sales, service, and office work grew. Clerical jobs multiplied so quickly that by 1960, one of three women wage earners held one. Elementary school teachers were needed as well, as school systems started to expand to accommodate the baby boom. At the same time, the pool of available young, single women diminished. Birthrates had been low in the 1920s and 1930s and now, in the 1950s, young women married earlier and had children. The short supply of young women workers created vocational space for older, married women, whom employers welcomed. The wages earned by the married woman, meanwhile, were welcomed by her family. Since inflation was constant, a second income was often needed to maintain a family's middle-class status and higher living standards, as well as to pay for college education that would ensure the prospects of children. The decade of the "feminine mystique," therefore, was also one in which married women workers were much in demand and when their income (on the average about one-quarter of family income) was needed in middle-class homes.

Vocational space and family needs were not the only factors that legitimized wage earning for middle-class women. So did the types of jobs women took. The new woman worker of the 1950s and 1960s did not challenge traditional gender roles because she was likely to enter a sex-typed occupation. "Most of the jobs women hold are still in traditional fields," *Life* announced in 1956. "Household skills take her into the garment trades; neat and personable, she becomes office worker and sales lady; patient and dexterous, she does well on competitive, detailed factory work; compassionate, she becomes teacher and nurse." *Life* did not ignore professional women: The "homemaker-lawmaker" and "housewife-architect" were shown in their kitchens. But clearly these were rare compared to the anonymous hordes of middle-aged office workers, garment workers, and saleswomen captured by the magazine's photographer. Women workers of the 1950s did not surge into prestigious professions. After World War II, the professions, and also technical and managerial fields, expanded so rapidly that the proportion of women in them steadily fell. During the 1950s, the proportion of women dropped even in the "women's professions," such as elementary school teaching, librarianship, and social work. But the *number* of women in the professions steadily rose.

During the 1950s, an expanding economy and a rapidly growing service sector provided a vast increase of jobs for women in traditional fields, such as office work and retail sales. Like these Macy's saleswomen in 1956, preparing for the Christmas rush, new women workers tended to be middle-class and middle-aged. Although sales work may not have provided a sense of identity, as later recommended in *The Feminine Mystique*, it was often part-time or seasonal and easily fused with family roles. And it did provide a second income, which in turn provided household appliances, automobiles, television sets, and middle-class status. *(Eliot Elisofon, Life Magazine)*

Since working women moved mainly into traditional types of white-collar work, they received traditional low rates of pay, yet another factor that legitimized their wage earning. Therefore, as the female work force expanded, so did the disparity between male and female wages. In 1955, the median income of full-time workers was 63.9 percent that of men; but by the time of the Kennedy commission report, it had dropped to 60 percent, and it continued to fall thereafter. The disparity was even larger in fields that absorbed large numbers of women, such as sales work, where in 1960, for instance, the median wage of women was only 40 percent that of male workers. Postwar women, in short, contributed to the economy by providing an expanding pool of inexpensive labor.

This pool of female labor quickly became an essential part of the economy. And during the 1950s, the Labor Department and especially the Women's Bureau made efforts to increase it. No longer preoccupied solely with protective laws, though of course in favor of them, the Women's Bureau urged employers to take advantage of "womanpower" and encouraged women to enter the worker-hungry labor market. Significantly, the Women's Bureau, a vestige of the old "woman's movement," was also the only agency inside or outside government to represent the interests of working women, a group that now included a hefty segment of middle-class women. In this capacity, the bureau collected complaints about sex discrimination in employment, though little could be done about them. In addition, it steadfastly supported new policies to aid working women, such as paid maternity leaves, day-care facilities, and equal pay legislation—measures later endorsed by the Kennedy commission. While *McCall's* promoted family "togetherness," therefore, a speaker at the 1955 White House conference on "Womanpower," sponsored by the Women's Bureau, urged the acceptance of women in all occupations as well as women's "rights as achievement-oriented individuals."

Despite the factors that favored women's entry into the work force, the postwar working wife received mixed signals about her legitimacy as a wage earner. Although she could easily find a job in a traditional field, her role as a worker was still socially suspect. Domestic ideals, moreover, affected her attitudes and expectations. She was likely to defend paid work in terms of family need, not personal aspiration or individualism. (This was one of the depression's lasting legacies.) She was unlikely to plan ahead, seek special training, or expect vocational advancement. She rarely objected to sex-typing of occupations or wage discrimination, which were seen as part of the rules of the game. She was especially apt to feel guilty if she had children at home; the largest segment of new workers in the 1950s, accordingly, were older women with presumably less child-care responsibility or none at all. By shaping her work role around the family, often by entering the work force in middle age, the new working wife of the postwar era adjusted her sights to cultural demands. So had the great majority of married wage earners since the 1920s.

Working mothers were nonetheless a major concern in the 1950s. Their numbers rose every year, and their absence from home, critics alleged, led to child neglect, emotional ailments, and juvenile delinquency. Researchers of the 1950s voiced surprise that such ill effects were not borne out in their surveys. "Broken homes" more than working mothers seemed to injure children's prospects; the only significant differences between working and nonworking mothers seemed to be that the former lived in cities, were better educated, and had more anxiety because of their dual roles. During the early 1960s, the working mother rose into even greater favor with sociologists. She did have an impact on family structure and child rearing, they said, and this impact was a positive one: Work outside the home increased her influence within it. She was likely to assume a greater role in decision making and to encourage self-reliance and independence in her children. According to such studies, the working mother appeared to change the "neo-patriarchal" family structure that had been described in the late 1940s, just as she diminished the hazards of "overprotection" that psychiatrists had identified during World War II. "Employment emancipates women from domination by their husbands, and secondarily, raises their daughters from inferiority to their brothers," wrote sociologist Robert O. Blood in 1965. As a result, "the male-dominated, female-serviced family is being replaced by a new symmetry."

The prospect of such symmetry had greatest appeal to the college-educated middle-class woman of the 1950s and 1960s, who, if unemployed, was most likely to feel overtrained and undervalued at home and outside it. "Certainly today's homemaking chores are no great challenge to such a woman," said Women's Bureau head Esther Peterson in the early 1960s. "Her sense of frustration is likely to heighten as her children go to school and there is even less need for her in the home." The forty-year-old homemakers interviewed by Betty Friedan only confirmed such conclusions. Working-class and lower-middle-class wives did not share this sense of discontent with domestic roles. Among blue-collar wives in the 1950s, Mirra Komarovsky wrote, there was "little evidence of status frustration." Lower-middle-class wives, Herbert Gans reported from Levittown in the 1960s, were not so sure as upper-middle-class women "that life ought to be more than raising a family." But educated women, measuring their lives against those of educated men, were more likely to feel deprived of status, a deprivation for which domestic ideology did not compensate. On the other hand, since they accepted the primacy of their roles as child rearers, their options for achieving vocational status in professions or "creative work" were limited. While the New Women of the 1920s had been preoccupied with fusing marriage and career, the preoccupation of educated women of the 1960s was how to combine children and career.

This theme surfaced in a special issue of *Daedalus* in 1964, most of which concerned the problems of the educated woman and her need to mesh traditional and modern roles. Since women would probably continue to be primarily responsible for child rearing, sociologist Alice Rossi pointed out, ways must be devised "to ease the combination of home and work responsibility." Unlike Betty Friedan's *Feminine Mystique,* which urged women to liberate themselves from "occupation: housewife" through private routes, Rossi began with the premise that sexual equality was a positive good and that social measures were needed to effect it. Training a corps of wage-earning substitute mothers, she contended, would enable women to pursue careers; so would a national network of day-care centers. A new type of quasi-urban residence, between suburb and city, Rossi proposed, would facilitate employment for married women. Most important, she stressed, was the need to avoid sex-typing, both in educational institutions, where children were socialized, and in occupations themselves. Sexual equality would not exist, she posited, "until women participate on an equal basis with men, in politics, occupations, and the family."

Although Alice Rossi's concerns were novel in 1964, they would soon gain currency. By the early 1960s, moreover, public policy reognized the working woman. Here, President Kennedy's Commission on the Status of Women was a turning point. Significantly, the commission was both instigated and dominated by the Women's Bureau, a vestige of the old woman's movement and the only federal agency concerned with women's issues. Like World War II advisory commissions, this new one was not expected to do very much beyond preventing resurrection of an ERA and compensating for the lack of high-level women's appointments. But it was not without larger impact.

First, the presidential commission spawned state commissions on women's status, thirty-two by 1964 and fifty by 1969, which began compiling data on sexual inequities. Not only did the state commissions "penetrate more deeply into the factors limiting women's status," in Caroline Ware's words, but state commission members began meeting together, and thus created a new communications network on women's issues. Almost inadvertently, the federal government had helped lay the groundwork for both a feminist agenda and, before long, a new women's movement. Second, the Kennedy administration, whatever its paucity of women's appointments to federal posts, took the lead in initiating a federal policy against sexual discrimination. A major gesture was the Equal Pay Act of 1963, a federal law requiring equal pay for equal work that was enacted while the presidential commission was still at work. First proposed in 1945, the new law had long been urged by the Women's Bureau. Like the Fair Labor Standards Act, to which it was attached, the Equal Pay Act left large categories of women workers, such as domestic workers and farm workers, unaffected. Nor did it oblige employers to hire women workers in the first place. Finally, it was unenforceable. Still, the Equal Pay Act was the first federal law against sex discrimination. Its passage was also the first occasion since World War II on which Congress recognized women's status as wage earners.

In retrospect, the Equal Pay Act of 1963 and the publication of Betty Friedan's *Feminine Mystique* that year represented the tension that had developed since the end of the war between domestic ideals, which limited women to traditional roles, and the actual context of women's lives, which were now more likely to include some combination of domestic role and paid employment. The two events also marked a hiatus between the dominance of domestic ideology and the rise of the women's movement, which would soon challenge it. But the decade of the 1960s itself set the scene for feminist revival. The 1960s provided an enlarged supply of educated women, the prime movers in the new feminism; a liberated social climate, with a growing emphasis on personal fulfillment; and finally a new political climate, characterized by protest, activism, and militancy.

Mixed Signals

During the 1960s, women's roles reached a point of precarious balance. By the end of the decade, about half of American women were employed, as were almost half of mothers of school-age children and a quarter of the mothers of preschoolers. The steady surge into the work force was accompanied by a decline in the birthrate, which had been falling since 1957; a slight rise in the marriage age; and a new fragility in the institution of marriage, since the divorce rate increased by 80 percent. In addition, as the proportion of young adults in the population started to bulge, college enrollments expanded, the number of single persons almost doubled, and a new wave of sexual revolution rolled in. The decade in which feminism reappeared was also one in which a modern aura of individualism and competition began to undercut the traditional expectations of the 1950s.

If the working mother was a major New Woman of the 1960s, so was the educated daughter. During the 1960s, the number of women college students doubled, and the college, once an elite enclave, became the major institution in which large numbers of young women congregated. The impact of college attendance was, as always, significant, especially since it was part of a long-term development. Right after World War II, women's proportion of the college population took a nose dive. In 1940, women were 40 percent of college students, but by 1950, they had dropped to 31 percent and earned only 25 percent of bachelor's degrees. The relative decline of women graduates came at a time when overall college attendance vastly increased. Between 1940 and 1950, a decade of great social mobility, the proportion of the college-age population attending college rose from 14 percent to 27 percent; between 1945 and 1950 alone, college enrollment doubled. Most new students were men, and many were veterans (98 percent male) who entered college under the GI Bill. The immediate postwar education gap between men and women was only temporary, however. During the 1950s, when college enrollment continued to expand, the proportion of women students grew as well. By 1960, women earned 35 percent of college degrees; and by 1970, when almost 44 percent of the college-age population went to school, one-third of college-age women were enrolled and women students once again earned 41 percent of B.A.s.

College in the 1950s and 1960s was not the community of mission Jane Addams had found in the 1880s. Clearly, as college attendance became an increasingly "average" part of life, the aspirations of college women tended to become average as well. But college was still a community of experience, one that extended individualism through the late teens. It was also a singularly egalitarian experience, since college made approximately the same demands on men and women, provided both with the same sort of life-style, and conferred on both, at graduation, the same reward—certification of middle-class status. Despite calls in the 1950s for distinctively "feminine" curricula, such drastic changes were not widespread. Both coeducational universities and major women's colleges continued to provide academic programs, not preparation for domesticity; even in the 1950s, some educators had attempted, somewhat forlornly, to nurture professional expectations in women students. College, in short, remained a world apart, where men and women were more equal than elsewhere. In 1961, collegiate equality was even carried over to a new federal agency, the Peace Corps, which drew on recent college graduates and accepted women volunteers on an equal basis with men. Not surprisingly, the college community provided not only a breeding ground for social activism in the 1960s but also a constituency for the new feminism—a core of young women with egalitarian ideals, high expectations, and little investment in traditional roles.

The woman college student of the 1960s, however, received mixed signals. Her academic experience might be relatively egalitarian, but the social cues she absorbed were not. One type of cue made it difficult for her to plan ahead, the same problem that affected Betty Friedan in 1942. The average college girl viewed her future "through a wedding band," *New York Times* reporter Marilyn Bender observed in 1962. "Despite compelling evidence that she will be working by 35, today's 21-year-old has difficulty looking beyond [the ceremony of] her own marriage." Even if she harbored what Mirra Komarovsky had labeled "middle-of-the-road" goals—to join the work force after a hiatus for child rearing—it was difficult to be either ambitious or specific about such goals. As writer Caroline Bird pointed out in 1968, "Most girls find it hard to plan what they are going to do when they have reared children whose fathers they have not yet met."

A related handicap was the tendency to discard ambition, avoid competition, and minimize achievement, so as to keep the field clear for an appropriate marriage. In 1972, psychologist Matina Horner described a "fear of success" revealed by 80 percent of the college women in her samples of the late 1960s, who felt that any kind of achievement, in college or career, would undercut their attractiveness and limit their options. Young women, said Horner, had incorporated society's attitudes "that competition, success, competence, and intellectual achievements are basically inconsistent with femininity." Such internalized cues, feminists of the late 1960s contended, were reinforced by external ones. Caroline Bird pointed to an "invisible bar that keeps women down." It started early in life and continued at home and school as well as through graduate school, professional school, employment interviews, first jobs, and lost chances for promotions or assuming administrative positions. "Fear of looking aggressive" could be as great a handicap for the employed woman as "fear of success" was for the college student.

Another source of mixed signals in the 1960s was an increasingly liberal social climate and, especially, the latest blast of sexual revolution—well underway by mid-decade and extremely well publicized. The rules of the game had been shifting throughout the twentieth century, but during the 1960s, as in the 1920s, the pace of change seemed to accelerate. A new enthusiasm for casual "relationships," uninhibitedness, open discussion, self-fulfillment, and sexual free enterprise came into vogue, both among the unusually large cohort of youth and among adults finding a second youth in the sexual marketplace. The origins of the new vogue of self-indulgence remain elusive. According to writer Barbara Ehrenreich, a "male revolt" against domestic ideology had been building since the 1950s, characterized by a flight from commitment, responsibility, and breadwinner roles. Men, in short, were the first to demand "liberation." The media and press of the 1960s, however, depicted freedom from traditional values and behavior as a universal desire. By the end of the decade, surveys among college students revealed a pronounced rise in premarital sex, notably among women, along with widespread acceptance of liberal sexual attitudes. National magazines, movies, surveys, and exposés proclaimed extramarital sex a national pastime ("80 unfaithful wives and husbands reveal their secret lives," read the cover of a 1969 paperback, *The Affair*). A new array of advice literature appeared, with its own lingo of personal fulfillment. *Open Marriage: A New Life Style for Couples*, by Nena and George O'Neill, for instance, dispensed with "antiquated ideals" and "romantic tinsel" by endorsing equal-opportunity infidelity as the modern route to intimacy, trust, and "identity."

Sexual liberation of the 1960s had its own landmarks. The Supreme Court gave a final sanction to contraception, *Griswold* v. *Connecticut* (1965), though this was more a follow-up to the last wave of sexual revolution than a trailblazer.

More important was the marketing of birth-control pills in the early 1960s, so that antiquated modes of contraception could be tossed away with the romantic tinsel. This extraordinary breakthrough was not without potential health hazards for women, though these were not immediately revealed. William Masters and Virginia Johnson's *Human Sexual Response* (1966) was an equally significant landmark. If Alfred C. Kinsey (1948 and 1953) had confirmed the existence of female sexuality, Masters and Johnson testified to the equality, or even superiority, of female sexual responsiveness and invalidated long-held convictions about female sexual passivity. Masters and Johnson, moreover, surpassed all previous sex researchers by relying not on questionnaires but on scientific observation. Performance now took priority over "attitudes."

The celebration of female sexuality coincided with a new wave of sexual availability. The 1960s saw the influx of a generation of "singles," whose ranks were soon swollen by the first of the baby boom cohort, a group that seemed at least to triple the national supply of sexual energy. And as in the 1920s, "economic independence" also played a role. The decade began with a rash of publicity for the Single Girl, as advertised by editor Helen Gurley Brown, first in *Sex and the Single Girl* (1962), which Brown called an "upward and onward" book, and subsequently in the pages of *Cosmopolitan,* destined for the young singles market. Not unlike one of the New Women described in the 1920s, the Single Girl supported herself in an urban environment, worked in an office ("A job gives a single woman something to be," said Helen Gurley Brown), and moved in the realm of men. The Single Girl also had "relationships," and challenged the homebound housewife as a boring antique. "Her world is a far more colorful world than the one of P.T.A., Dr. Spock and the jammed clothes dryer," Brown wrote. "She is engaging because she lives by her wits." To be sure, the Single Girl wanted above all to get married—no simple assignment, since single women far outnumbered eligible men in the office world. Many "possibles," moreover, might turn out to be weird, dull, undesirable, or vocational failures. However, all men had their uses, Brown advised, including the occasional married man ("While they are using you to varnish their egos, you're using *them* to add spice to your life"). Finally, with determination and "quiet, private, personal aggression," the Single Girl could reach her goal of marriage. But in the interim, which might be a long one, she was both engaging and available.

The arrival of the Single Girl and a well-publicized single standard of morality had a dual impact. By the late 1960s there was genuine confusion between the new vogues of sexual liberation and women's liberation, which were often assumed to be the same thing. Liberated sexual attitudes played a major role in the feminist movement, since sexual grievances were openly discussed and sexual orientation became an allied cause. But the new vogue of license, as feminists revealed, was a mixed blessing. By the end of the 1960s, women's role as what feminists called a "sexual object" had visibly increased. Moreover, the new premium on availability changed the tone of the sexual marketplace. For young political activists who joined the civil rights and New Left campaigns of the early 1960s, as described by historian Sara Evans, "the double standard collapsed into a void." Striving for autonomy while seeking stable "relationships" with male counterparts often proved a source of frustration. Expanded options for sexual encounters and "relationships," young women discovered, were not in the end egalitarian. Moreover, men had a built-in demographic advantage. Not only were marriageable men outnumbered by available women in all age brackets, but male leverage increased with age. Once liberated from marriage, men were better able to dive downward into the pool of young singles, where available women were now in abundant supply. The latest blast of sexual revolution created a new atmosphere of lifelong sexual competition, with more liabilities for women than for men, as feminists would soon point out. "The Sexual Revolution and the Women's Movement are at polar opposites," a *Ms* article declared in 1972. "Women [have] been liberated only from the right to say 'no.'"

Finally, throughout the 1960s, the political climate changed. Change had been simmering since the middle of the 1950s. After the *Brown* v. *Board of Education* decision of 1954, a new civil rights movement emerged, setting the tone for the next decade. From the Montgomery bus boycott and battles over school integration through the "freedom summer" of 1964, civil rights activists created a mood of protest and a new receptivity to social change. By the mid-1960s, both student rebellion and protests against the Vietnam War contributed to the escalation of unrest. Once American policies at home and abroad came under assault, the stage was set for yet other reforms. Feminist revival in the mid-1960s began in the wake of freedom rides, voter registration drives, campus upheavals, teach-ins, sit-ins, and antidraft demonstrations. But it was the civil rights movement, above all, that paved the way for feminist resurgence.

Black Women in Postwar America

While suburbanization and its ramifications affected much of postwar history, black history followed another trajectory. The mechanical cotton picker reduced the need for southern field labor, sharecropping ended as a way of life, and waves of black migrants, mainly young, left the rural South for northern cities. The exodus began around 1940 and continued into the 1960s; by midcentury, one-third of blacks lived outside the South. Simultaneously, black population movement changed the South. By 1960, almost three out of five southern blacks lived in towns and cities, with a concentration in metropolitan areas. Large-scale urban migration spurred rising aspirations, soon manifest in the postwar civil rights movement, and often promoted social mobility. It also magnified the problems associated with urban ghetto life. In all instances, it affected the experience of black women, which in significant respects differed from that of the white majority.

Elements of continuity characterized the black female labor force. One was limited opportunity. Demobilization after World War II afflicted black women workers more severely than white women, for wartime jobs were not immediately replaced by new ones in industry or offices. Mechanized farming, meanwhile, cut the proportion of black women who worked in agriculture to one in ten. At midcentury, 60 percent of black working women held service jobs, either in private households or in restaurants or offices. Young women who migrated to cities might find work on the margins of the urban economy. Ruby Daniels Haynes, for instance, featured in Nicholas Lemann's study of the postwar migration, moved from Clarksville, Mississippi, to Chicago in the late 1940s. Over the next two decades, she worked variously in a janitorial job, a laundry, an awning factory, and as a barmaid, hotel maid, and office cleaner. During these years she raised eight children, sometimes with the aid of welfare payments.

Throughout the postwar era, the heyday of the "feminine mystique," black women remained major contributors to family support. They sought employment in higher proportions than did women as a whole, worked more continuously through the life cycle, and often combined paid employment with child rearing. As among white women, the role of wives and mothers in the work force increased. In 1950, three out of ten black married women worked, compared with 19 percent of white wives. A decade later, over 40 percent of nonwhite women living with husbands had joined the labor force, and in the thirty-five- to forty-four-year-old age bracket, about half. The black female work force changed in other ways, too. During the 1950s and 1960s, the proportion of black women in professional and white-collar work kept rising. At midcentury, black women constituted well over half of black college graduates and 58 percent of all black professionals. In 1960, over a third of black women workers held professional, sales, or clerical jobs, compared with under a fifth in 1940. Indeed, in 1960, more black women than black men held college degrees, advanced degrees, and professional status, mainly because women constituted the bulk of black teachers. Black women's incomes bolstered the growth of the black middle class. Between 1947 and the late 1960s, the income of black households more than doubled. Only 10 to 15 percent of the black population was considered middle class before 1960, but up to one-third had that status two decades later.

The prominent role of black women in the work force, however, drew negative attention from postwar sociologists. Reviewing the literature of the field in 1966, sociologist Jessie Bernard referred to the "superiority" of black women—compared with black men—as measured by education, ability to find work, and familiarity with white society. In 1960, for instance, black women had an average of 8.5 years of schooling as against 7.9 years for black men; typically they could expect to marry less-educated men. They could usually find employment, as black men could not, "even a higher kind of work than that available to Negro men; if not, [their] services were always wanted in the home." Black women also had superior "contacts with the white world," Bernard contended. "More doors—back doors to be sure, but doors, have opened for them. . . . Even in their contact with social work agencies, and the world of bureaucracy, they have known their way around." Summarizing the researchers' conclusions, Bernard observed that black men and women "tended to live in somewhat [different] worlds," that "Negro women fell into a higher class," and that the disparity between the sexes "may be destructive to both."

National Council of Negro Women president Dorothy Height's "consultation" reiterated such conclusions in its remarks about "matriarchy" to the

Kennedy commission in the early 1960s. The black woman, the consultation contended, had been "forced" into the labor market, "where she often earns more than her husband and sometimes seems the only earner for the family." The black periodical press, which catered to a middle-class audience, occasionally echoed this concern. *Ebony*, points out historian Jacqueline Jones, applauded the postwar return to black homes (as opposed to white ones). At the same time, it "presented working wives and mothers in a positive and frequently heroic light," and championed black women who entered male occupations. In other instances, however, the black press voiced anxiety about wage-earning women by linking their "independence" to the mounting rates of divorce and separation. Historian Paula Giddings cites two apposite articles. In one, on "Why Men Leave Home," Roosevelt University social scientist St. Clair Drake asserted, "When they [black men] have a chance to become solidly middle class, desertion rates will stop." A *Negro Digest* article on "Why Women Leave Home," by author Gwendolyn Brooks, contended that "Some working women leave home when they discover their husbands are gold-diggers."

The black press mentioned another factor of concern: an imbalanced black sex ratio in cities. Since 1910, the urban black sex ratio hovered around 90 men to every 100 women. In 1962, for the twenty-five- to forty-four-year-old age group, this ratio was 88. Attributed in part to the traditional undercount of urban black men, the disparity now seemed linked to their dangerous, marginal, or shortened lives. Attorney Pauli Murray, who played a pivotal role in the Kennedy Commission on the Status of Women, discussed the problem of sexual disparity in a 1963 speech to an NCNW conference. More than 600,000 "excess" black women might never marry, Murray said; the black woman could not necessarily "look to marriage for either economic or emotional support," and this deprivation injured her. "As long as . . . she must compete fiercely for a mate, she remains the object of sexual exploitation, and the victim of all the social evils which such exploitation involves," Murray observed. "How much of the tensions and conflicts traditionally associated with the matriarchal framework of Negro society are in reality due to the imbalance and the pressures it generates?" In *Black Metropolis,* a 1945 study of Chicago's black community, St. Clair Drake and Horace Cayton also cited a lack of leverage. "Most lower-class [black] women have to take love on male terms," they commented. "The men . . . are strongly tempted to take advantage of such a situation and to trade love for a living."

Growing black communities in northern cities, characterized by public housing, underemployment, and active street life, now absorbed researchers' attention. How were families affected? A few black migrant families, contends historian Jacqueline Jones, "managed to parley the slimmest of means into a stable and relatively privileged existence." Sociologists of the 1960s focused on less auspicious trends. In 1960, studies suggested, instability among black families in urban areas, especially central cities, exceeded that in rural areas. The hallmarks of such instability were rising numbers of female-headed households and mounting illegitimacy rates. By the end of the 1950s, 25 percent of black families were headed by women. During the 1950s, for instance, female-headed black families declined by 48 percent on farms but rose 58 percent in urban areas. In 1960, one out of three black adult women was divorced or, more likely, separated. Separation rates for black women exceeded those for white women by 400 percent. Simultaneously, the numbers of out-of-wedlock births surged, most significantly among women who were already mothers. Between 1947 and 1962, the black illegitimacy rate doubled. The strain on the black urban family emerged in Daniel P. Moynihan's 1965 report on *The Negro Family*. Moynihan's remarks about "pathology" and "instability" in the black family evoked fury from black opponents and liberal critics—a response that silenced discussion of the subject for almost two decades—yet the trends he identified were significant. As Nicholas Lemann points out, the report's "dire predictions about the poor black family all came true."

Rapid urbanization of postwar blacks, finally, affected political life: It abetted the eruption of the civil rights movement, in which black women played a major role. The movement began in 1955, a year after the *Brown* v. *Board of Education* decision, when Rosa Parks, a seamstress in a Montgomery, Alabama, department store, refused to cede her seat on a bus to a white passenger. A longtime NAACP member and local activist, Parks seized the opportunity to take

Rosa Parks being fingerprinted in Montgomery in 1956. *(AP/Wide World Photos)*

a political stand. The Montgomery Improvement Association, an organization of local ministers, soon led by Martin Luther King, generated a new protest movement, to which women made vital contributions. Household servants who boycotted the buses, for instance, disrupted employers' lives. Analyzing the reasons for black women's extensive participation in the new movement, historian Jacqueline Jones points out that women had a longtime custom of informal leadership in southern black communities. They were also the traditional bulk of congregations in Baptist and Methodist churches, whose religious rhetoric suffused the campaign.

Black women had long been active in such organizations as the NAACP, and from the outset the new civil rights movement welcomed their support. Over the next decade, their efforts reached new peaks. They participated in boycotts, demonstrations, acts of civil disobedience, sit-ins, and voter registration drives, and inspired other civil rights workers. According to civil rights leader Ella Baker, "The movement of the fifties and sixties was carried out largely by women." Some were women already prominent in black organizations. Daisy Bates, president of the NAACP chapter in Little Rock, Arkansas, for instance, took a leading role in the school integration struggle of 1957. After the freedom rides of the early 1960s, the newly militant southern civil rights movement made increasing use of women. Students like Anne Moody served as field workers, canvassers, and demonstrators. In some instances, women had a special edge of effectiveness. At the Jackson sit-in, for instance, they were able to keep the protest going, since most of the violence was directed at men. At the time of the freedom summers, 1964–1965, many black women activists were young, like Rubye Doris Robinson, a Spelman College student and former freedom rider, who assumed a prominent role as SNCC's executive secretary. Some were older women, such as Fannie Lou Hamer, a former sharecropper who lost her job and home when she attempted to vote. Hamer became active in the SCLC citizenship program, served as SNCC field secretary, and helped form the Mississippi Freedom Democratic party in 1964.

Ella Baker, who exemplified women's leadership role in civil rights organizing, also linked the pre-1960s and post-1960s civil rights movements. Born in Norfolk, Virginia, in 1903, Baker grew up in rural North Carolina, the granddaughter of slaves. In 1927, after graduating from Shaw University in Raleigh, North Carolina, she moved to New York City and organized consumer cooperatives. In the 1930s, she worked in consumer affairs for the Federal Works Project Administration and began twenty years of work for the NAACP, where she became national director of local branches. During World War II, she directed the New York City branch, served as an adviser for the Office of Price Administration, and ran unsuccessfully for the New York State Assembly on the Liberal party line. In the mid-1950s, Baker worked in the South as a field organizer for the NAACP, and after the founding of the SCLC in 1957, served as its national director. In 1960 she organized a conference that created the Student Nonviolent Coordinating Committee, and in 1964, with Fannie Lou Hamer, founded the Mississippi Freedom Democratic party, made up of blacks who were barred from the Mississippi delegation at the Democratic party convention.

Fannie Lou Hamer, left, and Ella Baker at the Democratic National Convention in Atlantic City in 1964, when the Mississippi Freedom Democratic party attempted to unseat the all-white regular Mississippi delegation. Hamer, a former sharecropper who lost her job in 1962 for registering to vote, became a SNCC field secretary and well-known civil rights activist. Formerly a WPA worker, Baker had long been active in the NAACP. Now head of the SCLC office in Atlanta, she also participated in the formation of SNCC.
(Ebony Magazine)

The civil rights movement culminated in the Civil Rights acts of 1964 and 1965 to integrate the workplace and protect voting rights. The movement played a vital role in women's history. Besides creating a climate of protest, it provided an immediate model for feminist activists. Challenging both racist ideas and segregationist practices, the civil rights movement posited equality as a positive good. It provided new models of militant, effective pressure groups such as CORE and SNCC, whose activities were well publicized. Through confrontation tactics like the Jackson sit-in and public events like the 1963 March on Washington, it captured the attention of the media and the sympathy of the public. Not least of all, it established a precedent for ending discrimination under law. Civil rights goals, tactics, and rhetoric were soon adapted to new purposes by activist women. By the end of the 1960s, feminists had created a two-pronged movement, calling both for legal equity and for the restructuring of gender roles and social institutions.

Civil Rights and Women's Liberation

Like the civil rights movement that preceded it, the feminist outburst was spurred by a specific federal act. In the case of civil rights, that act had been the Supreme Court's 1954 decision declaring segregation of schools by race unconstitutional. In the feminists' case, the spur was the Civil Rights Act of 1964, Title VII of which prohibited discrimination in employment on the basis of race. In an apparent effort to ensure the bill's defeat, eighty-one-year-old Virginia representative Howard W. Smith proposed an amendment to Title VII that would prohibit discrimination in employment on the basis of sex. Smith's motives were in fact complex. To be sure, he opposed civil rights; thus, to many, his proposal seemed facetious. Still, a long-time ally of Alice Paul and of the National Woman's Party, Smith had sponsored an ERA in congress for many years. In late 1963, expecting debate on the civil rights bill, NWP leaders decided to push for an amendment to end sex discrimination; two Virginia members of NWP had urged Smith to propose it. Whether the congressman intended to defeat civil rights or to fight sex discrimination, or both at once, remains a moot point. Several women involved in the battle that ensued felt that his act was a gesture of southern chivalry to white women.

Whatever Smith's motives, his maneuver caused havoc. The proposed amendment delayed passage of the bill and evoked great controversy. Liberal groups opposed it, as did Esther Peterson at the Department of Labor and women's organizations such as the LWV. These critics did not want to endanger the cause of black civil rights by adding a new one. (The Kennedy Commission on the Status of Women had also vetoed the idea of treating race discrimination and sex discrimination in the same manner.) In addition, as Brooklyn Congressman Emmanuel Celler contended in a speech in the House, equality of the type the amendment presaged might "endanger traditional family relationships" and even deprive women of such hard-won privileges as alimony and child custody. Celler's line of argument would often be repeated in the decade ahead, when other equity measures were proposed. But the Johnson administration mobilized support for the civil rights bill, as did Democratic Congresswoman Martha Griffiths, another NWP member, and Republican Senator Margaret Chase Smith. The bill was passed in the summer of 1964, its provision against sex discrimination in employment intact, and went into effect one year later.

The new law provided that employment discrimination complaints could be sent for investigation to the Equal Employment Opportunities Commission, which was soon besieged with women's grievances about sex discrimination. Viewing such discrimination as less serious than racial discrimination, the overworked commission followed up only class action complaints. It ignored individual complaints and in general paid little attention to women's grievances. Indeed, the commission had little motivation to pursue such grievances without the insistence of public pressure groups such as those that demanded civil rights. Unequal treatment at the EEOC soon spurred the rudiments of feminist organization. While representative Martha Griffiths charged in the House that the EEOC was depriving women of legal rights, a core of activist women tried to press the commission into action. But this feminist nucleus, in which Betty Friedan was prominent, was unable to evoke support for its demand from existing women's groups, such as the LWV, the American Association of University Women, or even the Citizens' Advisory Council on the Status of Women, which had been set up at the request of the Kennedy commission. Thus rebuffed, the new feminist nucleus felt compelled to create a civil rights organization for women. The National Organization for Women was formed by twenty-eight women in 1966 "to take action to bring American women into full participation in the mainstream of American society *now.*"

Unlike the group of New Deal women that coalesced around Eleanor Roosevelt in 1933, the founders of NOW had no longtime network of communication and cooperation. Nor did they have much connection with survivors of the last feminist wave. "Most of us were the kind of women who never had any patience with League of Women Voters teas," Friedan later told a NOW conference. Rather, the NOW founders were politicized, professional women, some of them veterans of state commissions on the status of women or even of the Kennedy commission, others union leaders from the United Auto Workers. The tone they adopted in the NOW "statement of purpose" of 1966 was not that of the LWV but rather that of the current civil rights movement. Decrying "tokenism," NOW demanded "a fully equal partnership of the sexes, as part of the worldwide revolution of human rights." NOW did not limit its demands to remedies for professional inequities, disparity of pay, and educational discrimination. It called also for a new concept of marriage, integration of women into political life, and changes in "the false image of women now prevalent in the media."

Like Seneca Falls feminists, NOW founders pointed to the psychological impact of sex discrimination by opposing "all policies and practices [that] not only deny opportunities but also foster in women self-denigration, dependence, and evasion of responsibility, undermine their confidence in their own abilities and foster contempt for women." In the pacifist spirit that then pervaded the civil rights movement, NOW denied enmity to men, who were also victims of "half-equality" and would benefit from complete equality. Unlike the supporters of woman suffrage, NOW denied that men and women had different roles or responsibilities in society. "We reject the current assumption that a man must carry the sole burden of supporting himself, his wife, and family . . . or that marriage, home and family are primarily woman's world and responsibility," NOW declared. "We do not accept the traditional assumption that a woman has to choose between marriage and motherhood, on the one hand, and serious participation in industry or the professions on the other." Finally, presenting self-interest as human interest, NOW contended that women's problems were society's problems. "Above all, we reject the assumption that these problems are the unique responsibility of each individual woman, rather than a basic social dilemma which society must solve."

A political pressure group, NOW was from the outset a formal organization with elected officers (Betty Friedan was its first president), dues-paying members, and state branches. Its resolutions demanded changes in public policy, such as equal opportunity legislation, a national network of day-care centers, and retraining programs for women who had retired from the work force to care for children; the voice of Friedan ran through NOW proposals. But as NOW's membership expanded, rising from about 1,000 in 1967 to 15,000 in 1971, so did its reform agenda. NOW's goals were soon affected by the emergence of a younger, more radical feminist wing, which, with singular zest and originality, launched its own assault in 1967–1968. Another by-product of the 1960s, radical feminism arose out of contradictions faced by young women who were active in New Left groups and in the civil rights movement. Within the context of these campaigns, devoted to ending social, economic, and racial discrimination, women had developed a new consciousness of sexual inequity.

During the early 1960s, hundreds of college-age women activists had participated in voter registration drives in the South, under the aegis of SNCC, and in community organizing projects in the North run by Students for a Democratic Society, the central organization of the New Left. Their experiences on the "cutting edge" of social protest, as described by historian Sara Evans, were expansive and exhilarating, especially in the South. During the "freedom summers" of 1964 and 1965, women made up almost half of the contingent of northern civil rights volunteers. Running freedom schools and libraries, canvassing for voters, living with violence, risk, and fear, and sharing in egalitarian goals, they grew in self-confidence and self-esteem. In addition, they were exposed to role models of impressive black women activists. For a brief interlude, the civil rights movement provided both a new arena for integrated effort and a new space for female activism, though not without cross-currents of racial and sexual tensions.

But by 1965, the space on the left created by white activist students was contracting. When SNCC turned its focus from civil rights to black power and excluded white participants, the "movement" turned its energies toward antidraft protests, in which, inevitably, men were pivotal and women marginal. "Girls say yes to guys who say no," read a movement slogan. More important, throughout the civil rights and SDS campaigns, women claimed, they were customarily excluded from decision-making roles and expected to assume traditional ones—as typists, clerical workers, and sexual companions to male activists. According to Evans, the movement played a dual role for the young women involved in it. It "provided women with a particular kind of social space within which they could grow in self-confidence," but at the same time it "exhibited the same sexism characteristic of American society."

Resentment over sexual inequality began simmering within civil rights circles in the early 1960s, spurring analogies between racial and sexual discrimination. In a SNCC "position paper" of 1964, for instance, activist Casey Hayden contended that "assumptions of male superiority are as widespread and deeply rooted and every much as crippling to the woman as the assumptions of white superiority are to the Negro." Antipathy to male dominance within the movement finally erupted at a Chicago Conference for New Politics in 1967, when dissatisfied women, whose grievances had been ignored, announced their intent "to organize a movement for women's liberation." Politicized by their recent personal experience, the New Left feminists soon unleashed a torrent of activism. Since radical protest was at its apogee, movement networks provided a ready-made constituency for feminist discussion groups. By 1968, the small contingent of Chicago dissenters had counterparts in other cities and college communities across the nation. Adapting New Left techniques to feminist ends, radical women's groups now embarked on the novel mission of "consciousness raising."

Consciousness raising was at once a recruitment device, an initiation rite, and a resocialization process aimed at transforming group members' perceptions of themselves and society. Originally intended to raise the political consciousness of oppressed communities such as ghetto blacks, the technique proved far more successful with middle-class women. By sharing personal experiences, as feminist Jo Freeman explained, a group would learn to regard personal problems as "common problems with social causes and political solutions." In consciousness raising, said Susan Brownmiller, "a woman's experience at the hands of men was analyzed as a *political* phenomenon." While engaged in this process of self-discovery and social analysis, group members would also gain in self-esteem and, ideally, benefit from mutual support and group solidarity. Usually, a series of questions helped to elicit shared experiences. ("Discuss your relationships with men. Have you noticed any recurring patterns?" was part of a list of consciousness-raising topics proposed by the Radical Feminists, a New York group. "Discuss your relationships with other women. Do you compete with women for men? Growing up as a girl, were you treated differently from your brother?") "Three months of this sort of thing," said feminist Shulamith Firestone, "is

A new left technique, consciousness raising contributed to a revival of the tradition of female association, which had been fading since the 1920s. During the early 1970s, when widely publicized in the media, it created hundreds of pockets of feminism across the nation. Below, a consciousness-raising group meets for the first time in New York City's Women's Liberation Center, December 5, 1970. *(Bettye Lane)*

enough to make a feminist of any woman." Moreover, a raised consciousness, group members discovered, permanently altered their social vision. "It makes you very sensitive—raw, even—this consciousness," wrote Robin Morgan in *Sisterhood Is Powerful* (1970). "You begin to see how all-pervasive a thing is sexism—the definition of and discrimination against half the human species by the other half."

Once the conversion process was complete, a group might move to some form of action, such as organizing a women's health collective or a day-care center, forming an abortion counseling center or a theater troupe, making a film or publishing a newsletter. Group projects reflected the range of topics that had contributed to consciousness raising—from sexual relationships and reproduction to child care and housework. ("[Men] recognize the essential fact of housework right from the beginning," wrote Pat Mainardi in a widely distributed position paper. "Which is that it stinks.") Sexual reform projects also became part of the feminist agenda. Rape, wife battery, sexual harassment, and child abuse, feminists claimed, were feminist issues and political ones. By the mid-1970s, alumnae of the discussion groups were running rape crisis centers, shelters for battered women, and vigorous campaigns against pornography and sexual violence. But women's liberation's greatest contribution to the new feminism, beyond its new issues and projects, was the critique of sexism that grew out of it, one that quickly infiltrated far less radical feminist groups and rhetoric as well.

Discrimination against women, feminists postulated, permeated society. Sexism was institutionalized in the family and in government, in the schools and in law. It pervaded religion, the economy, and social life. It assigned to men and women different character traits, personalities, and social roles, which were methodically instilled from infancy. Sexism ensured that men would be the primary, most valuable members of society, and that women would assume a secondary, subordinate place. They would depend on men, define themselves in relation to men, have poor self-images and low self-confidence, and devalue other women as well. The elimination of sexism, like the elimination of racism, therefore called for a drastic transformation. It meant changing values and attitudes, behavior and institutions. Getting rid of sexism, according to the ideology of women's liberation, meant both a massive awakening and fundamental social change or "revolution." Such goals and rhetoric might not have surprised some imaginative activists of the early National Woman Suffrage Association. The women's movement, Paulina Wright Davis had declared in 1870, "was intended from its inception to change the structure, the central organization of society."

Women's liberation groups often disagreed on how to combat the oppression of sexism. Some groups maintained New Left affiliations, others discarded them; some attempted to transform relations with men, while others contended that heterosexual relationships locked women into second-class status. "It is the primacy of women's relations to women . . . which is at the heart of women's liberation and the basis of cultural revolution," wrote the Radicalesbians. But despite the variety of political and sexual stances, divisions among groups did not hamper the growth of the movement. A structureless phenomenon, women's liberation had no formal organization, policy, headquarters, elections, officers, or, ideally, leaders. Lack of structure, at the outset, promoted diffusion. Between 1968 and 1970, feminist discussion groups splintered and multiplied, permeating city, campus, and suburb. "It's not a movement, it's a State of Mind," writer Sally Kempton was quoted in the *New York Times* in 1970.

Consciousness raising, moreover, had enormous appeal, well beyond radical circles. NOW, which organized nationwide networks of feminist discussion groups, adopted and promoted it. Radical feminists, meanwhile, evoked media attention by staging happenings—crowning a sheep at the Miss America Pageant of 1968, putting a hex on Wall Street, or invading an all-male New York bar. (Such public theater was more reminiscent of the tactics used by moral reformers of the 1830s than of civil rights sit-ins; feminist demonstrators expected neither violence nor arrests.) During 1970, women journalists staged their own rebellion at such major publications as *Time, Newsweek,* and the *Ladies' Home Journal.* By August 26, 1970, when thousands of women mobilized for a march to commemorate the suffrage victory of 1920, there was interaction between the diverse array of women's liberation groups and the more "moderate" feminists of NOW.

Considerable friction existed, however, between the two distinctive feminist wings. Some NOW founders considered the radicals a "lunatic fringe" whose "antics" would only injure the cause. Many radical feminists of New Left origins viewed Betty Friedan as a bourgeois conservative and NOW's equity goals as minor and meliorist, in view of the enormity of sexism. Others conceded similarities. Both factions of feminists were "achievement-oriented," radical feminist Anne Koedt contended, one in the professions, the other in the radical movement. "From both ends we were fighting a male power structure that prevented us from achieving." Friedan, too, avowed mutual interests, explaining to NOW that younger women from the ranks of women's liberation could provide feminist "troops." Since 1966, moreover, NOW had been transformed by its growing membership and, accordingly, had enlarged its demands to suit its constituency. Whereas the progressive era suffrage movement had moved to the right to secure a following, NOW shifted to the left.

In 1967, NOW resurrected the Equal Rights Amendment, shelved by Congress since the early 1950s and ostensibly put to rest by the Kennedy commission. The ERA was supported by National Woman's party veterans, although labor representatives in NOW at first objected to it. NOW also demanded the repeal of abortion laws—a popular cause within radical ranks, a controversial one outside them, and one that perplexed NWP veterans. "As far as I can see, ERA has nothing whatsoever to do with abortion," eighty-seven-year-old Alice Paul told an oral history interviewer. Finally, in 1971, NOW again catered to radical views by acknowledging "the oppression of lesbians as a legitimate concern of feminism." NOW's shift to the left was not without controversy. Some founding members departed, only to form new women's rights organizations. Feminist politics were pervaded by disagreements, both within and between the two wings. But diversity of views served to enlarge the feminist constituency. By the start of the 1970s, the two wings of feminism had assumed a complementary posture. Neither the "egalitarian ethic" nor the "liberation ethic," Jo Freeman

While sit-ins and street actions brought women's liberation to national attention, the Women's Strike for Equality on August 26, 1970, suggested a unity of feminist interests. Commemorating the victory of woman suffrage in 1920, the Strike for Equality was the largest women's rights demonstration ever. Since organized mainly by local chapters of NOW, the strike stressed the issues of day-care, abortion rights, and equal employment opportunity. But feminist solidarity was the major theme. Divisions among activists were temporarily suspended, as thousands of women across the nation joined marches and demonstrations. Above, New York women march down Fifth Avenue. *(Bettye Lane)*

declared in 1971, could succeed without the other. Indeed, liberation voices seemed to fulfill the traditional role of left-wing reform—making the centrist position more acceptable.

The women's movement that emerged in the 1960s had much in common with earlier outbursts of feminism. Like the antebellum women's rights movement and the progressive era suffrage crusade, the new feminism of the 1960s arose in and profited from an era of reform. Like earlier feminist movements, too, it was created by ambitious, educated, middle-class women, those with the highest expectations. Not surprisingly, neither black nor working-class women of the 1960s viewed the feminist campaign with much enthusiasm. For most black women, race remained a greater source of oppression than sex. As black feminist lawyer and Kennedy commission contributor Pauli Murray explained, black women were "made to feel disloyal to racial interests if they insisted on women's rights." Nor did black women feel that they had a "feminine mystique" to combat. Rather, they had a reputation for female dominance, a source of both pride and stress. "If the Negro woman has a major underlying concern, it is the status of the Negro man," National Council of Negro Women head Dorothy Height had stated when the Kennedy commission met in 1963, and civil rights activists of the 1960s reiterated this view. "We don't want anything to do with that feminist bag," a young woman in SNCC told Betty Friedan in 1966. The important thing for black women, Friedan was informed, was "for black men to get ahead." Such reluctance to enter feminist ranks was in fact part of a long tradition; black women had always viewed race discrimination as more oppressive than sex discrimination. As Aileen Fernandez, the president of NOW in 1974, herself black, told an annual conference, "Some black sisters are not sure that the feminist movement will meet their current needs."

White working-class women were similarly alienated from the feminist crusade, though for different reasons. According to historian Susan Estabrook Kennedy, the white working-class housewife of the 1960s felt threatened by "the independent, assertive, self-determined, equal role put forward for the liberated woman." She valued her role as a homemaker, a role that was devalued by women's liberation rhetoric; she viewed this role as more liberating than the alternatives, factory work or service work; and she had little interest in entering either all-male bars or men's jobs. "If your husband is a factory worker or a tugboat operator, you don't want his job," explained Congresswoman Barbara Mikulski. Attracted to, not repelled by, domestic ideals, the white working-class housewife saw feminist attacks on sexism as an assault on her life-style. Women's liberation seemed an elitist, self-interested, and suspiciously radical cause. Moreover, it seemed allied to other suspicious causes, such as school integration, civil rights militance, and antiwar protest.

But despite its middle-class identity, which made it similar to the earlier women's movements, the new feminism of the 1960s was also distinctive. Unlike suffragist predecessors in the 1860s, new feminists were immediately free to find a middle-class following. They had no male allies, or former allies, to break away from, since neither the civil rights movement nor the New Left had ever been committed to feminist concerns. New feminists were independent from the outset, and they had a large potential constituency. Second, they were not bound to a single goal, like the vote, on which the fate of the entire movement rested. The new feminism was characterized by an amalgam of goals, a gamut of grievances, and an extremely diffuse structure. Third, and perhaps most important, new feminists abdicated the traditional domestic power base and rejected all claims to special character traits and the perquisites that went with them. NOW, for instance, spurned "the idea that mothers have a special child-care role that is not to be equally shared by fathers," while radical feminists seemed to find anything connected with home, child care, or conventional roles demeaning. Finally, unlike the earlier woman's movement, the new feminism of the 1960s depended on a large core of highly educated young women with political experience, well-developed faculties of social criticism, and zealous attachment to ideology. Usually the least powerful members of society, young women now assumed a pivotal role. Their influence was felt through the 1970s, when feminism caused significant shifts in attitudes and opportunities.

Legitimizing Feminism

By the early 1970s, the feminist movement had generated both an ideology and an agenda, encompassing a spectrum of issues and goals. As commonly perceived, feminist demands fell between two poles, a "moderate" call for equity laws and a "radical" cry for abolishing gender roles. "The aims of the movement range from the modest, sensible amelioration of the female condition to extreme and revolutionary visions," *Time* announced in 1972. But antipathy to sexism was the common theme that ran throughout both moderate and radical demands. It permeated the central agenda endorsed by NOW—calling for an ERA, a national child-care system, abortion law repeal, and equal opportunity legislation—just as it permeated radical feminist ideology. "Revolutionary visions" were indeed a vital part of the feminist campaign, if only because they made more moderate demands seem reasonable and legitimate by comparison. The feminist agenda was further legitimized during the early 1970s by an outburst of organization, by media dissemination of feminist issues, and by a new direction in public policy.

A visible sign of momentum was the proliferation of feminist groups, which seemed to increase at a geometric rate. By 1973, a national women's newsletter provided a directory of several thousand. While NOW's membership tripled between 1971 and 1975, new national groups joined the equity campaign. The Women's Equity Action League (WEAL), a 1968 split-off from NOW, pressed for ending discrimination in employment and education; the National Women's Political Caucus, started in 1971, supported women candidates and raised "women's issues at all levels of government and in campaigns"; the Women's Action Alliance created *Ms* magazine; the Women's Lobby campaigned for ERA; Human Rights for Women pursued sex discrimination and abortion cases; a Professional Women's Caucus was formed in 1970; and by 1973, a National Black Feminist Organization had been founded. To these new pressure groups, which often had overlapping directorates, were added hundreds of projects and collectives that had been started by women's liberation cadres, including research libraries, publishing centers, and clinics. New feminist alliances, simultaneously, emerged within church associations and professional associations, among airline stewardesses, secretaries, and federally employed women. The vast spurt of organization in the early 1970s created a ferment of activism and provided a gamut of routes to participation in the feminist movement, thereby broadening the cause's constituency and generating support for the central core of feminist goals.

Consciousness raising, meanwhile, became a public undertaking, through an inundation of books, articles, and media attention. Although hostile to the initial rounds of women's liberation, the media by the early 1970s found the subject irresistible. Between 1970 and 1972, every national network and major publication devoted time and space to the women's movement, and made the new vocabulary of feminism—"sexism," "male chauvinism," "sisterhood," "sexual object"—a part of common parlance. While national magazines published special issues on women's status, such as the *Ladies' Home Journal* supplement of

August 1970 and *Time*'s edition of March 10, 1972, the movement's most successful media coup, *Ms.* magazine, edited by Gloria Steinem, provided an ongoing
forum for feminist issues. With a subscription of almost 200,000 by 1973 and a
hefty array of advertisers, *Ms.* was a novel propaganda organ. The name itself
was significant. A major feminist goal was to erase sexual discrimination from
language, and "Ms.," which made no distinction between married and unmarried women, quickly gained wide currency. The publication was significant, too.
Unlike women's liberation newsletters, which were limited to a readership of
insiders, *Ms.* extended the movement's message to a wider audience of unaffili-
ated sympathizers. A 1973 poll of subscribers revealed that almost three-quarters
of the respondents were not members of feminist organizations. Still, the *Ms.*
audience suggested an identifiable feminist constituency. Almost 90 percent
were college-educated; 75 percent worked part-time or full-time, and two-thirds
of these were in professional, technical, or managerial occupations; half were
married, and 72 percent were under thirty-five.

Public consciousness raising in the early 1970s did not depend solely on the
media, however. Feminist authors also burst into print, providing a steady
stream of propaganda, polemical and fictional. "Our society, like all other
historical civilizations, is a patriarchy," wrote Kate Millett in *Sexual Politics* (1969),
a book that set the tone for the feminist assault. "The fact is evident at once if one
recalls that the military, industry, technology, universities, science, political
office, and finance—in short, every avenue of power within the society, is entirely
within male hands." Like Friedan and Steinem, Millett was soon regarded as a
feminist spokesperson, as were radical feminists Robin Morgan and Shulamith
Firestone, both articulate alumnae of the New Left. In *The Dialectic of Sex: The Case
for Feminist Revolution* (1970), Firestone presented the ultimate of "revolutionary
visions"—a society in which gender, class, and family would play no role, in
which women would be freed from "the tyranny of their reproductive biology
by every means available," and in which "humanity could finally revert to its
naturally 'polymorphously perverse' sexuality." Radical feminism might
frighten off the faint-hearted, but feminist fiction had insidious appeal. Starting
with Sue Kaufman's *Diary of a Mad Housewife* in 1967 and continuing through the
1970s with the novels of Alix Kates Shulman, Marge Piercy, and Marilyn French,
among others, the case against male chauvinism reached ever widening circles
of readers. Poetry too was mobilized in the cause, as suggested by the attention
paid to Sylvia Plath, a suicide in 1962, and to feminist poet Adrienne Rich. The
new feminism became a literary crusade as well as a political one.

If organization and publication helped to legitimize feminism in the early
1970s, changes in federal policy did so even more. Between 1970 and 1975, a spate
of congressional laws, court decisions, executive orders, and Labor Department
directives gave official sanction to feminist demands. Once again, the civil rights
movement had paved the way. In many cases, the federal policy of nondiscrimi-
nation on the basis of race was simply extended to include sex. In 1967, for
instance, President Johnson extended an executive order prohibiting racial discrimination by federal contractors to prohibit sex discrimination as well; by the
end of 1970, the Labor Department had issued "affirmative action" guidelines to

all federal contractors in order to ensure nondiscriminatory hiring. Enforcing such directives for affirmative action proved far more difficult than issuing them. Still, the federal government in a few years made more efforts to end sex discrimination than in the entirety of the nation's history. The new direction in federal policy was accompanied by a surge of women candidates for political office; by massive pressure from feminist interest groups; and by a burst of feminization in the Democratic party. This was evident at its 1972 national convention, when the delegates were 40 percent women, and when the party platform endorsed federally funded day-care and an ERA. The new direction in federal policy was also supported by the efforts of women in government—such as representatives Bella Abzug and Martha Griffiths, who sought to attach amendments against sex discrimination to federal bills at every opportunity. The impact of feminist political clout was symbolized by congressional passage of the ERA in 1972.

Since 1964, the Senate Judiciary Committee had reported the amendment favorably, but both trade unions and the Women's Bureau viewed it as a threat to protective laws. Once a feminist movement emerged, the tide turned dramatically. By 1970, federal courts voided protective laws as sexually discriminatory, and thus swept away historic objections to an ERA. In 1969, the Women's Bureau switched its stance, followed in short order by the labor movement, the Citizens' Advisory Council on the Status of Women, and finally the LWV. "The President has publicly supported this amendment," Nixon adviser Chuck Colson wrote to another White House staff member in early 1970. "Fortunately the good sense and ultimate wisdom of Congress has always kept this ridiculous proposal from being enacted." But Congress would soon change its mind. Approved by the House in 1970 and 1971, the ERA became the new feminism's most prominent cause. In 1972, both houses of Congress passed the ERA by huge majorities, 354 to 23 in the House and 84 to 8 in the Senate. The amendment stated that "Equality of Rights under the Law shall not be denied or abridged by the United States or any State on the basis of sex," which meant that it would preclude sex discrimination only on the part of the government, its agencies and officials, or any institutions closely tied to the government. By the time Congress passed the ERA, sixteen states had their own equal rights provisions, fourteen of them enacted since 1969. After the amendment was sent to the states for ratification, it was approved by twenty-eight within a year. The ERA's initial success served a vital function for the feminist movement. Generating widespread interest in feminist issues, it also created what Martha Griffiths called "a moral climate for reform."

This climate reached its peak in the early 1970s in Congress and in the courts. Between 1971 and 1974, Congress enacted an unparalleled barrage of equity laws. It prohibited sex discrimination in medical training programs, enabled middle-income families to claim income tax deductions for child care if both spouses worked; extended employment benefits for married women in federal government jobs; prohibited creditors from discriminating on the basis of sex or marital status; extended coverage of the 1963 Equal Pay Act by an Education Amendments Act; and passed a Women's Equity Act, which supported training and counseling programs for women. Such equity statutes usually required only minimal federal funding or minor inconvenience to the institutions they affected. Federal court decisions complemented congressional concern for equity. While lower courts voided protective laws, challenged sex labeling of jobs, and reaffirmed the principle of equal pay for equal work, equity cases began to appear on the Supreme Court calendar. During the early 1970s, for instance, the Court invalidated a state law giving preference to men as executors, banned the press from referring to sex in "help wanted" ads, and invalidated an armed forces regulation denying dependents of women members the same benefits as those of male members. Finally, in *Roe* v. *Wade* (1973), the Court upheld women's constitutional right to abortion—a major feminist triumph, coming close on the heels of congressional passage of the ERA.

Since the 1960s, the right to abortion had proved the most controversial cause in the feminist arsenal. Moreover, like contraception in the early twentieth century, it seemed to involve a battery of complex legal, medical, and moral issues. State antiabortion statutes in effect in the 1960s had been enacted at the end of the nineteenth century, in the wake of the 1873 Comstock law. Most state laws prohibited abortion except for preservation of the mother's life, and it could be obtained only with medical certification of a life-threatening situation and with the approval of a board of doctors. Illegal abortion, as a result, was a thriving business. In 1972, according to one estimate, over 2,500 such abortions were performed every day. But during the 1960s, a movement to liberalize abortion laws had been growing. In 1962, the American Law Institute recommended revised abortion laws, to cover cases of rape and incest and those where fetal deformity was suspected, and in 1967, the American Medical Association endorsed such proposals. By 1972, sixteen states and the District of Columbia had liberalized their abortion laws.

Once feminists organized, however, their cause was abortion law repeal, not reform. Abortion on demand, they contended, was a woman's right—the same claim Margaret Sanger had made for birth control in 1914. The decision to abort was hers alone, not that of the AMA or the state. In 1970, three states repealed their abortion laws, and in 1973, in *Roe* v. *Wade* the Supreme Court confirmed the feminist stance by invalidating a state antiabortion law. For most of the nineteenth century, Justice Blackmun pointed out in the majority decision, "Woman enjoyed a substantially broader right to terminate a pregnancy than she does in most states today." *Roe* v. *Wade* immediately affected the lives of millions of women. Maternal deaths from illegal abortions dropped. The choice of abortion now became an option open to all women; before abortion became legal in New York State in 1970, for instance, therapeutic abortions had been granted almost exclusively to white women. *Roe* v. *Wade* had immediate political repercussions, too. Opponents at once proposed a "right-to-life" amendment and started an antiabortion campaign that burgeoned for the rest of the decade. As of 1973, however, the Supreme Court's decision helped to legitimize feminism: The federal government had endorsed a large chunk of the feminist agenda.

In only one instance did feminists meet a monumental roadblock. A Comprehensive Child Development Bill, which would have provided a nationwide network of day-care centers, was vetoed in 1972 by President Nixon, who denounced the "communal approach to child-rearing" and the "family-weakening implications" of the bill. Day care was hardly a simple equity measure. It required extensive federal funding and it hit an invisible boundary, where women's aspirations appeared to take precedence over child welfare. The prospect of day care in fact evoked considerable opposition within the child-guidance community, indeed within the middle-class community. The major postwar precedent for day care was the Johnson administration's Head Start program, intended to provide remedial training for very young children from culturally deprived homes. But Head Start was child-centered, whereas day care was clearly mother-centered. "It's Fine for Mother, but What About the Child?" asked the *New York Times* in 1973. The feminist agenda had been sabotaged at its weakest link, where family role and vocational role intersected.

Despite the day-care setback, feminist momentum of the early 1970s seemed unimpaired. The feminist movement finally won legitimacy by its own success, especially by its rapid and widespread impact on education and employment. By 1975, for instance, textbooks were scanned to eliminate sexist stereotypes; primary and secondary schools revised their curricula so that boys and girls were not segregated into shop or cooking classes; athletic allotments started to be channeled into girls' sports as well as boys' sports. Opportunities for higher education expanded as women were admitted to all-male schools, among them the U.S. Military Academy and Ivy League strongholds. (Such conversions to coeducation were expedient, at least for private colleges, in light of the shrinking applicant pool; as in the period during and after the Civil War, colleges needed women students.) Several women's colleges, however, followed a different route, and found new pride in single-sex status. Women's studies courses, which began in the late 1960s in the wake of black studies courses, became permanent institutions on college campuses. By 1974, 500 colleges offered an array of 2,000 women's studies courses; a decade later, there were 30,000 such courses. Academic disciplines, meanwhile, were reexamined and revised to include female experience—whether in history, psychology, religion, literature, or the social sciences. By creating new areas of expertise and women's studies programs, feminists carved out separate space for women on campuses. (During the progressive era, home economics programs had served a similar function.) Finally, during the 1970s, higher education was indeed feminized. The number of women students rose by over 60 percent, and by 1979, more women were enrolled in college than men.

By the mid-1970s, the feminist movement also made a major impact on women's employment. Some changes were a direct result of feminist pressure and federal policy. After a WEAL class action complaint in 1970, for instance, colleges and universities, threatened with loss of federal contracts, had to turn personnel files over to the Department of Health, Education, and Welfare for judgments as to whether affirmative action or sex discrimination was in effect. In 1972, a sex discrimination suit against American Telephone and Telegraph was settled out of court, with a multimillion-dollar payment to women workers and a plan to use both men and women in such formerly sex-typed job categories as linemen and operators. The AT&T decision suggested that equity measures would benefit the average woman worker, not merely the college graduates and professionals who appeared to dominate the feminist movement. Federal enthusiasm for utilizing "womanpower," meanwhile, even carried over to items not on the feminist agenda. By 1979, the armed forces, which had been racially integrated under President Truman, were once again integrated, this time with women. The Women's Army Corps, created during World War II, was abolished. Though expediency was the motive behind integration (once the draft ended in 1973, the all-volunteer army faced manpower problems), acceptance of women suddenly transformed the military into an equal opportunity employer and forced it to confront an unending list of equity problems.

The mounting number of equity suits, class action complaints, and sex discrimination charges, and the new shift in federal policy, did not end the concentration of women workers in women's fields or decrease income disparities between women and men. Nor was feminism alone responsible for the vast rise in female labor force participation of the 1970s, when the numbers of women who worked or sought work rose 47 percent—compared to 21 percent for men. Women had been entering the work force in steadily growing numbers since the late 1940s. But during the 1970s, economic and cultural factors seemed to reinforce each other: feminism legitimized female wage earning in a way that family need had not. And as the new women's movement gained momentum, significant changes in employment became visible, most markedly in prestigious professions—a major focus of feminist energy.

Between 1971 and 1981, for instance, according to the Labor Department, the proportion of lawyers and judges who were women rose from 4 percent to 14 percent; of doctors, from 9 percent to 22 percent; and of engineers, from 1 percent to 4 percent. The proportion of professional students who were women rose even more drastically. During the first half of the 1970s alone, the proportion of Ph.D.s awarded to women almost doubled, jumping from 11 percent to 21 percent, while by 1977, women students were earning one out of five law degrees and one out of six medical degrees. At the same time, radio and television networks rushed to move women into visible positions as anchor persons and news reporters; women seminary graduates, ordained as ministers, took over congregations; and women executives, the press reported, were being appointed to high-level jobs in banking and finance, business and government. Women's new mobility in business and the professions was not without widespread consequences, especially since the nation's teaching force began to lose a captive labor pool of educated women on which it had drawn for over a century. By the early 1980s, attention would be focused on the lower quality of teachers and the need for higher salaries to attract better ones. Equal opportunity had hidden costs that were not often evident in the early 1970s, when employment patterns began to change.

The aspirations of educated women seemed to change as well. In 1972, the *New York Times* revealed that Smith graduates of the class of 1955, who had been advised at commencement to devote their lives to home and family, were entering the job market. Public opinion polls of the early 1970s, meanwhile, suggested that the feminist movement caused a shift in women's attitudes, most clearly among the educated, employed, and young. By 1975, 63 percent of women respondents on a Harris poll, for instance, supported "efforts to strengthen and change women's status in society"; a majority had disapproved of such efforts four years earlier. Gallup polls in the early 1970s showed a similar tilt toward approval of the feminist agenda—day care, abortion rights, and equal employment opportunity. Young women appeared especially receptive to feminist goals. According to Yankelovitch surveys among college students in the early 1970s, a large majority endorsed the new ideas of the women's movement and rejected the statement that "woman's place is in the home." Polls that included men also reflected an egalitarian turn, especially among the young. A 1973 poll, for instance, revealed that 65 percent of respondents approved a wife's working even if her husband's income was "sufficient," a view shared by 80 percent of respondents under thirty. The feminist "state of mind," polls suggested, had made an impact.

Newly liberalized attitudes did not always reflect a willingness to change behavior. As Alice Rossi had observed in 1964, "Many people . . . espouse belief in sex equality but resist its manifestations in their personal lives." Male Ivy League students, Mirra Komarovsky discovered in the early 1970s, often accepted the intellectual equality of women but clung nonetheless to traditional expectations. ("It is only fair to let a woman do her own thing if she wants a career," one student said. "Personally, though, I would want my wife at home.") Nor did feminist visions win universal acclaim. During the early 1970s, when feminism made rapid legislative gains, "women's liberation" evoked powerful attacks from conservative critics, such as Midge Decter's *The New Chastity* (1972) and George Gilder's *Sexual Suicide* (1973). By the end of the decade, the term "liberation" had faded from the vocabulary of the women's movement, as it was now called, while more tangible equity goals took precedence. But it was also clear that a decade of feminism had evoked a hostile reaction among a vocal contingent of American women.

Although all major women's organizations had lined up in support of the ERA, and although national polls in the late 1970s showed that a majority of Americans supported the amendment, many women remained suspicious of it, while others opposed both the ERA and the entire thrust of the new feminist movement. Some distrusted feminist rhetoric, which seemed both to urge gender pride and to deny it. "Without saying so, most feminists have accepted the male model of the good life in sex, work, marriage, and parenthood," psychologist Judith Bardwick pointed out. "The most visible goals of mainstream feminists are status, power, money, and autonomy—all historically associated with men." Other women objected to the feminist movement's apparent rejection of *them*— by devaluing their contribution to family life, or scorning them for not having careers, or demeaning them as oppressed victims. Others were wary about the androgynous ideals that had been advocated in feminist literature. And some suspected that feminist goals, like the ERA, would undercut women's traditional role in the family and thereby bring more losses than gains. Conflict between traditional family values and feminist values had been evident in 1972, when President Nixon cited the "family-weakening implications" of day care. During the late 1970s, the conflict became more visible. Not only did opponents of feminism coalesce under a "pro-family" banner, but a conservative shift in political mood appeared to threaten feminist plans. After a decade of extraordinary achievement, the women's movement entered an era of contention and consolidation.

SUGGESTED READINGS AND SOURCES

CHAPTER 19

Anne Moody's autobiography is *Coming of Age in Mississippi* (New York, 1968). Early SNCC campaigns are described in Howard Zinn, *SNCC, The New Abolitionists* (Boston, 1964). For a history of SNCC, see Clayborne Carson, *In Struggle: SNCC and the Black Awakening of the 1960s* (Cambridge, Mass., 1981). Sara Evans examines women's participation in the southern civil rights movement in *Personal Politics: The Roots of Women's Liberation in the Civil Rights Movement and the New Left* (New York, 1979).

Betty Friedan discusses the background of and reactions to *The Feminine Mystique* (New York, 1963) in *It Changed My Life* (New York, 1976), pp. 21–51. The results of her alumnae survey are described in "If One Generation Can Ever Tell Another," *Smith Alumnae Quarterly* (Winter 1961). Friedan's first article expressing her thesis is "Women Are People, Too," *Good Housekeeping*, 151 (September 1960), 59. For reader responses, see *Good Housekeeping*, 151 (November 1960), 118. Friedan has reviewed her experience, the impact of her book, and the progress of feminism at regular intervals in the *New York Times Magazine*. See, for instance, "Feminism Takes a New Turn," November 18, 1979, p. 40; "Feminism's Next Step," July 5, 1981, p. 13; and "Twenty Years After the Feminine Mystique," February 27, 1983, p. 35. Joanne Meyerowitz provides an illuminating interpretation of Friedan's contribution in "Beyond the Feminine Mystique: A Reassessment of Postwar Mass Culture, 1946–1958," *Journal of American History* 79 (March 1993), 1455–1482.

The Kennedy commission's report was published as *Report of the President's Commission on the Status of Women and Other Publications of the Commission* (New York, 1965). For the commission's formation and significance, see Cynthia E. Harrison, "A 'New Frontier' for Women: The Public Policy of the Kennedy Administration," *Journal of American History*, 67 (December 1980), 630–646; Harrison, *On Account of Sex: The Politics of Women's Issues, 1945–1968* (Berkeley, Calif., 1988), chs. 7 and 8; and Judith Hole and Ellen Levine, *Rebirth of Feminism* (New York, 1971), ch. 1.

CHAPTER 20

For an interpretation of women's experience since World War II, see William H. Chafe, *Women and Equality: Changing Patterns in American Culture* (New York, 1977).

A prime source for the 1950s is Betty Friedan's exposé, *The Feminine Mystique* (New York, 1963). Pillars of that mystique include Marynia Farnham and Ferdinand Lundberg, *Modern Woman: The Lost Sex* (New York, 1947); Lynn White, Jr., *Educating Our Daughters* (New York, 1950); and Helene Deutsch, *The Psychology of Women* (New York, 1944), 2 vols. The impact of domestic ideology is suggested in Ashley Montagu, "The Triumph and Tragedy of the American Woman," *Saturday Evening Post*, 231 (September 27, 1958), 13–15; "The American Woman," a special issue of *Life*, 41 (December 24, 1956), and George Gallup and Evan Hill, "The American Woman," *Saturday Evening Post*, 235 (December 22, 1962),

15–32. Mirra Komarovsky discusses the attitudes and goals of college women in *Women and the Modern World* (New York, 1952).

For the domestic life of postwar Americans, see Elaine Tyler May, *Homeward Bound: American Families in the Cold War Era* (New York, 1988). Eugenia Kaledin surveys women's roles in *Mothers and More: American Women in the 1950s* (Boston, 1984). For suburbanization, see Herbert Gans, *The Levittowners* (New York, 1967), and John Modell, "Suburbanization and Change in the American Family," *Journal of Interdisciplinary History*, 8 (Spring 1977), 621–646. Histories of suburbia since the nineteenth century include Kenneth T. Jackson, *Crabgrass Frontier: The Suburbanization of the United States* (New York, 1985), and Margaret Marsh, *Suburban Lives* (New Brunswick, N. J., 1990). Nancy Pottishman Weiss discusses changes in child-care manuals and the responses they evoked from readers in "Mother, The Invention of Necessity: Dr. Benjamin Spock's 'Baby and Child Care,'" *American Quarterly*, 29 (Winter 1977), 519–546. See also Barbara Ehrenreich and Deirdre English, *For Her Own Good: 150 Years of the Experts' Advice to Women* (New York, 1977), ch. 7; Sheila M. Rothman, *Woman's Proper Place* (New York, 1978), ch. 6; and Stephanie Coontz, *The Way We Never Were* (New York, 1992).

For the sexual revolution of the 1960s, see *Annals of the American Academy of Political and Social Science*, 376 (March 1968), issue entitled "Sex and the Contemporary American Scene"; William H. Masters and Virginia Johnson, *Human Sexual Response* (New York, 1966); Mary Jane Sherfey, *The Nature and Evolution of Female Sexuality* (New York, 1966); and Paul A. Robinson, *The Modernization of Sex: Havelock Ellis, Alfred Kinsey, William Masters, and Virginia Johnson* (New York, 1966). The mood of the 1960s is conveyed in William L. O'Neill, ed., *Coming Apart: An Informal History of America in the 1960s* (New York, 1971); Sara Davidson, *Loose Change* (New York, 1979); Nena O'Neill and George O'Neill, *Open Marriage: A New Life Style for Couples* (New York, 1972); and Helen Gurley Brown, *Sex and the Single Girl* (New York, 1962). Barbara Ehrenreich posits a "male revolt" against 1950s ideology in *The Hearts of Men: American Dreams and the Flight from Commitment* (New York, 1983). John D'Emilio and Estelle B. Freedman assess the sexual revolution and its impact in *Intimate Matters: A History of Sexuality in America* (New York, 1988), chs. 13 and 14. Rickie Solinger, *Wake Up Little Susie: Single Pregnancy and Race Before Roe v. Wade* (New York, 1992) examines attitudes toward unwed mothers, black and white, in the postwar era.

The roles of educated women in the 1960s are examined in Robert J. Lifton, ed., *The Woman in America* (Boston, 1965), and Eli Ginzburg and Alice M. Yohalem, *Educated Women: Life-Styles and Self-Portraits* (New York, 1966). Alice Rossi's 1964 article, "Equality Between the Sexes: An Immodest Proposal," is reprinted in the Lifton volume. For women's politics in the postwar decades, see Cynthia Harrison, *On Account of Sex: The Politics of Women's Issues, 1945–1968*, cited above, which traces the conflict over ERA, and Leila J. Rupp and Verta Taylor, *Surviving the Doldrums: The American Women's Rights Movement, 1945 to the 1960s* (New York, 1987), which focuses on the National Women's Party. Susan M. Hartmann examines political behavior in *From Margin to Mainstream: American Women and Politics Since 1960* (New York, 1989). Blanche Linden-Ward and Carol Hurd Green survey politics, education, and other topics in *American Women in the 1960s: Changing the Future* (New York, 1993).

For women's entry into the labor force after World War II, see Alice Kessler-Harris, *Out to Work* (New York, 1982), ch. 11, and Claudia Goldin, *Understanding the Gender Gap: An Economic History of American Women* (New York, 1990). Valerie Kincaid Oppenheimer assesses the causes of change in the postwar female work force, in *The Female Labor Force in the United States: Demographic and Economic Factors Governing Its Growth and Changing Composition* (Berkeley, Calif., 1970). Victor R. Fuchs examines married women's motives for entering the labor force in *How We Live: An Economic Perspective on Americans from Birth to Death* (Cambridge, Mass., 1983), ch. 5. See also Lois Waldis Hoffman and Ivan Nye, *Working Mothers* (San Francisco, 1975) and Robert O. Blood, "Employment of Married Women," *Journal of Marriage and the Family*, 27 (February 1965), 43–47. Studies of women's vocations include Louise Kapp Howe, *Pink Collar Workers: Inside the World of Women's Work* (New York, 1977); Rosabeth Moss Kanter, *Men and Women of the Corporation* (New York, 1979); Cynthia F. Epstein, *Woman's Place: Options and Limits in Professional Careers* (Boston, 1970); and Barbara Melosh, *"The Physician's Hand": Work Culture and Conflict in American Nursing* (Philadelphia, 1982). For housewives, see Helen Z. Lopata, *Occupation: Housewife* (New York, 1971), a study of urban homemakers, and Rae Andre, *Homemakers: The Forgotten Workers* (Chicago, 1981).

The experience of working-class women since World War II is examined in Lee Rainwater, Richard P. Coleman, and Gerald Handel, *Workingman's Wife: Her Personality, World, and Lifestyle* (New York, 1959); Mirra Komarovsky, *Blue Collar Marriage* (New York, 1964); Lillian Rubin, *Worlds of Pain: Life in the Working-Class Family* (New York, 1976); and Nancy Seifer, *Nobody Speaks for Me: Self-Portraits of American Working-Class Women* (New York, 1976). For a historical perspective, see Susan Estabrook Kennedy, *If All We Did Was to Weep at Home: A History of White Working-Class Women in America* (Bloomington, Ind., 1979).

Black women's roles in the 1950s and 1960s are discussed in Jacqueline Jones, *Labor of Love, Labor of Sorrow* (New York, 1985), chs. 7 and 8, and Paula Giddings, *When and Where I Enter* (New York, 1984), part 3. See also *Ebony*, 21 (August 1966). For higher education, see Jeanne L. Noble, *The Negro Woman's College Education* (New York, 1956). The impact of postwar population movement is discussed in Nicholas Lemann, *The Promised Land: The Great Black Migration and How It Changed America* (New York, 1991), and Jacqueline Jones, *The Dispossessed: America's Underclasses from the Civil War to the Present* (New York, 1992), chs. 7 and 8. Jessie Bernard surveys the sociology of black family life as of the early 1960s in *Marriage and Family Among Negroes* (Englewood Cliffs, N.J., 1966). See also St. Clair Drake, "Folkways and Classways Within the Black Ghetto" *Daedalus*, 94 (Fall 1965), 771–814, and Lee Rainwater, "Crucible of Identity: The Negro Lower-Class Family," *Daedalus*, 95 (Winter 1966), 172–216. The classic study of Chicago by St. Clair Drake and Horace Cayton, *Black Metropolis* (New York, 1945), was enlarged and reissued in the 1960s (New York, 1963). LaFrances Rodgers-Rose describes demographic trends in "Some Demographic Characteristics of the Black Woman, 1940–1975," in Rodgers-Rose, ed., *The Black Woman* (Beverly Hills, Calif., 1980). For the "Moynihan Report," see Daniel P. Moynihan, *The Negro Family: The Case for National Action* (Washington, D.C., 1965). For response to the report, see Lee Rainwater and William L. Yancey, *The Moynihan Report and the Politics of Controversy* (Cambridge, Mass., 1967). William H. Chafe draws an analogy between the experience of women and blacks since World War II in *Women and Equality* (New York, 1977), chs. 3 and 4. Major themes in black women's history are discussed in Gerda Lerner, *The Majority Finds Its Past* (New York, 1979), chs. 5–7, and Angela Y. Davis, *Women, Race, and Class* (New York, 1983).

For the postwar civil rights movement and women's part in it, see Taylor Branch, *Parting the Waters: America in the King Years* (New York, 1988); Jo Ann Gibson Robinson, *The Montgomery Boycott and the Women Who Started It* (Knoxville, Tenn., 1987); Vicki Crawford, Jacqueline Ann Rouse, and Barbara Woods, eds., *Women in the Civil Rights Movement: Trailblazers and Torchbearers, 1941–1965* (New York, 1990); and the acclaimed television series *Eyes on the Prize*. Clayborne Carson, ed., *The Eyes on the Prize Civil Rights Reader* (New York, 1991) includes short pieces by, or interviews with, Rosa Parks, Ella Baker, Daisy Bates, Fannie Lou Hamer, and others. Autobiographies include Daisy Bates, *The Long Shadow of Little Rock: A Memoir* (New York, 1962); Charlayne Hunter-Gault, *In*

My Place (New York, 1992); Mary King, *Freedom Song: A Personal Story of the 1960s Civil Rights Movement* (New York, 1987); and Pauli Murray, *Pauli Murray: The Autobiography of a Black Activist, Feminist, Lawyer, Priest, and Poet* (Knoxville, Tenn., 1987). Also of interest is Murray's family memoir, *Proud Shoes: Story of an American Family* (New York, 1956). Catherine Clinton discusses Ella Baker's career in J. G. Barker-Benfield and Clinton, eds., *Portraits of American Women* (New York, 1991), pp. 581–597. See also Kay Mills, *This Little Light of Mine: The Life of Fannie Lou Hamer* (New York, 1993). Mary Aicken Rothschild discusses the experience of civil rights workers in "White Women Volunteers in the Freedom Summers," *Feminist Studies*, 5 (Fall 1979), 466–494. Donald Allen Robinson examines conflict and cooperation between activists in the civil rights and feminist movements in the 1960s and 1970s in "Two Movements in Pursuit of Equal Opportunity," *Signs* 3 (Spring 1979), 413–433. Doug McAdam follows women civil rights volunteers into the 1970s in *Freedom Summer* (New York, 1988). Carl M. Brauer reveals the origins of the amendment to the Civil Rights Act of 1964 in "Women Activists, Southern Conservatives, and the Prohibition of Sex Discrimination in Title VII of the 1964 Civil Rights Act," *Journal of Southern History* 49 (1983), 37–56.

For the development and ideology of the new feminism, see Sara Evans, *Personal Politics: The Roots of Women's Liberation in the Civil Rights Movement and the New Left* (New York, 1979); Jo Freeman, *The Politics of Women's Liberation: A Case of an Emerging Social Movement and Its Relation to the Public Policy Process* (New York, 1975); Judith Hole and Ellen Levine, *Rebirth of Feminism* (New York, 1971); Barbara Sinclair Deckard, *The Women's Movement: Political, Socioeconomic, and Psychological Issues* (New York, 1975); Anne Koedt, Ellen Levine, and Anita Rapone, eds., *Radical Feminism* (New York, 1973); Gayle Graham Yates, *What Women Want: The Ideas of the Movement* (Cambridge, Mass., 1971). Marcia Cohen, *The Sisterhood: The True Story of the Women Who Changed the World* (New York, 1988); and Alice Echols, *Daring to be Bad: Radical Feminism in America, 1967–1975* (Minneapolis, Minn., 1989). For the lesbian feminist experience of the 1960s and 1970s see Lillian Faderman, *Odd Girls and Twilight Lovers* (New York, 1991) chs. 8 and 9.

Some of the classics of the new feminism, besides Friedan's *Feminine Mystique,* are Alice Rossi, "Equality Between the Sexes: An Immodest Proposal," in Lifton, *Woman in America,* pp. 98–143; Caroline Bird, *Born Female: The High Cost of Keeping Women Down* (New York, 1969); Kate Millett, *Sexual Politics* (New York, 1969); Shulamith Firestone, *The Dialectic of Sex: The Case for Feminist Revolution* (New York, 1970); Robin Morgan, ed., *Sisterhood Is Powerful: An Anthology* (New York, 1970); Vivian Gornick and Barbara K. Moran, eds., *Women in Sexist Society: Studies in Power and Powerlessness* (New York, 1971); Shulamith Firestone and Anne Koedt, eds., *Notes From the Second Year: Major Writings of the Radical Feminists* (New York, 1970); Boston Women's Health Collective, *Our Bodies, Ourselves* (New York, 1971); Germaine Greer, *The Female Eunuch* (New York, 1972); and Susan Brownmiller, *Against Our Will: Men, Women, and Rape* (New York, 1975). See also Jane Howard, *A Different Woman* (New York, 1973), and Elizabeth Janeway, *Man's World, Woman's Place: A Study in Social Mythology* (New York, 1970). For Gloria Steinem's articles since the 1960s, see *Outrageous Acts and Everyday Rebellions* (New York, 1983).

Articles about the new feminism in the 1970s include Jane Kramer, "Founding Cadre," *New Yorker,* 46 (November 28, 1970), 51–139, on the formation of a women's liberation group; Susan Brownmiller, "Sisterhood Is Powerful," *New York Times Magazine,* March 15, 1970, p. 27; Sally Kempton, "Cutting Loose: A Private View of the Women's Uprising," *Esquire,* 74 (July 1970), 54–57; Gerda Lerner, "The Feminists: A Second Look," *Columbia Forum* (Fall 1970), 24–30; Jane O'Reilly, "Click! The Housewife's Moment of Truth," *The Girl I Left Behind* (New York, 1980), pp. 23–58; and Joseph Adelson, "Is Women's Lib a Passing Fad?" *New York Times Magazine,* March 19, 1972, p. 26, a thoughtful, critical assessment. For opinion polls, see Louis Harris, "Changing Views on the Role of Women," *The Harris Survey*, May 20, 1971, and December 11, 1975. Mirra Komarovsky examines the reactions of college students to changing social norms in "Cultural Contradictions and Sex Roles," *American Journal of Sociology*, 52 (November 1946), 164–189, and 78 (January 1973), 873–884. For feminist fiction of the 1970s; see, for example, Alix Kates Shulman, *Memoirs of an Ex-Prom Queen* (New York, 1972); Marge Piercy, *Small Changes* (New York, 1973); and Marilyn French, *The Women's Room* (New York, 1977). Two early critiques of radical feminism are Midge Decter, *The New Chastity and Other Arguments Against Women's Liberation* (New York, 1972), and George Gilder, *Sexual Suicide* (New York, 1973).

The impact of the new feminism is discussed in Cynthia Fuchs Epstein, "Ten Years Later: Perspectives on the Women's Movement," *Dissent*, 22 (Spring 1975), 169–176; Judith M. Bardwick, *In Transition: How Feminism, Sexual Liberation and the Search for Self-Fulfillment Have Altered America* (New York, 1979); William H. Chafe, *Women and Equality*, ch. 5; Jane Sherron De Hart, "The New Feminism and the Dynamics of Social Change," in Linda Kerber and Jane Sherron De Hart, eds., *Women's America: Refocusing the Past*, 3rd ed. (New York, 1991), pp. 493–521; Elizabeth Janeway, *Cross Sections from a Decade of Change* (New York, 1983); Janet Giele, *Women and the Future: Changing Sex Roles in Modern America* (New York and London, 1978), and Winifred D. Wandersee, *On the Move: American Women in the 1970s* (Boston, 1988). Marian Faux examines the Supreme Court's pivotal 1973 decision in *Roe v. Wade: The Untold Story of the Landmark Supreme Court Decision that Made Abortion Legal* (New York, 1988).

For black women's response to feminism in the 1970s see Pauli Murray, "The Liberation of Black Women," in Mary Lou Thompson, ed., *Voices of the New Feminism* (Boston, 1970), pp. 87–102; Gerda Lerner, ed., *Black Women in White America: A Documentary History* (New York, 1972), pp. 585–614; Toni Cade, ed., *The Black Woman: An Anthology* (New York, 1970); and Gloria T. Hull, Patricia Bell Scott, and Barbara Smith, *But Some of Us Are Brave: Black Women's Studies* (Old Westbury, N.Y., 1982). Diane K. Lewis assesses educational and occupational changes of the 1960s and 1970s in "A Response to Inequality: Black Women, Racism, and Sexism," *Signs*, 3 (Winter 1977), 339–361. Cynthia Fuchs Epstein examines the status of black professional women in "Positive Effects of the Multiple Negative: Explaining the Success of Black Professional Women," *American Journal of Sociology*, 78 (January 1973), 912–935. Carol B. Stack discusses black ghetto women's kinship and friendship networks in *All Our Kin: Strategies for Survival in a Black Community* (New York, 1974). Bonnie Thornton Dill posits a distinctive historical model of black womanhood in "The Dialectics of Black Womanhood," *Signs*, 4 (Spring 1979), 543–555. For black women's concerns in the 1970s, see *The Black Scholar*, 6 (March 1975).

For feminist impact on the social and behavioral sciences in the 1970s and early 1980s, see, for instance, Michelle Zimbalist Rosaldo and Louise Lamphere, eds., *Women, Culture and Society* (Stanford, Calif., 1974); Bernice A. Carroll, ed., *Liberating Women's History: Theoretical and Critical Essays* (Urbana, Ill., 1976); Nancy Chodorow, *The Reproduction of Mothering: Psychoanalysis and the Sociology of Gender* (Berkeley, Calif., 1978); and Carol Gilligan, *In a Different Voice: Psychological Theory and Women's Development* (Cambridge, Mass., 1982). The development of feminist scholarship also spurred new work on sex, sexuality, and same-sex relationships. For an example of multidisciplinary effort, see *Signs*, 5 (Summer 1980), and *Signs*, 6 (Autumn 1980), two issues devoted to "Women—Sex and Sexuality." Lillian Faderman examines declining acceptance of same-sex relationships in *Surpassing the Love of Men: Romantic Friendship and Love Between Women from the Renaissance to the Present* (New York, 1981). John D'Emilio traces the evolution of the contemporary gay subculture in *Sexual Politics, Sexual Communities: The Making of a Homosexual Minority in the United States, 1940–1970* (Chicago, 1983).

CHAPTER 21

The Thomas Hearings: Responses to Anita Hill, 1991

On October 11, 1991, Anita Hill, a thirty-five-year-oid law professor at the University of Oklahoma, rose before the Senate Judiciary Committee to explain her charges of sexual harassment against Judge Clarence Thomas, a nominee to the Supreme Court. The incidents of harassment, she said, began in 1981, when she worked as an assistant to Thomas, then an official at the Department of Education.

After approximately three months of working there, he asked me to go out socially with him. What happened next, and telling the world about it are the two most difficult things—experiences in my life. . . .

I declined the invitation to go out socially with him, and explained to him that I thought it would jeopardize at—what at the time I considered to be a very good working relationship. . . .

I thought that by saying no and explaining my reasons, my employer would abandon his social suggestions. However, to my regret, in the following few weeks, he continued to ask me out on several occasions.

He pressed me to justify my reasons for saying no to him. These incidents took place in his office, or mine. They were in the form of private conversations, which not—would not have been heard by anyone else.

My working relationship became even more strained when Judge Thomas began to use work situations to discuss sex. . . . After a brief discussion of work, he would turn the conversation to a discussion of sexual matters. His conversations were very vivid. He spoke about acts that he had seen in pornographic films involving such matters as women having sex with animals and films showing group sex or rape scenes.

He talked about pornographic materials depicting individuals with large penises or large breasts involving various sex acts.

On several occasions, Thomas told me graphically of his own sexual prowess.

Because I was extremely uncomfortable talking about sex with him at all, and particularly in such a graphic way, I told him that I did not want to talk about this subject. I would also try to change the subject. . . .

During the latter part of my time at the Department of Education, the social pressures, and . . . his offensive behavior ended. I began both to believe and hope that our working relationship would be a proper, cordial and professional one.

When Judge Thomas was made chair of the EEOC [Equal Economic Opportunity Commission], I needed to face the question of whether to go with him. I was asked to do so, and I did. . . . At that time it appeared that the sexual overtures which had so troubled me had ended. I also faced the realistic fact that I had no alternative job. . . .

For my first months at the EEOC, where I continued to be an assistant to Judge Thomas, there were no sexual conversations or overtures. However, during the fall and winter of 1982 these began again. The comments were random and ranged from pressing me about why I didn't go out with him to remarks about my personal appearance. . . .

He began to show displeasure in his tone and voice and his demeanor and his continued pressure for an explanation. He commented on what I was wearing in terms of whether it made me more or less sexually attractive. The incidents occurred in his inner office at the EEOC.

Anita Hill's charges culminated a chain of events that began in July 1991, when President Bush had nominated Thomas, age forty-three, to succeed retiring justice Thurgood Marshall on the Supreme Court. A member of the U.S. Court of Appeals for the District of Columbia, Thomas had risen swiftly in government jobs. Born in a small town in Georgia, he had grown up in Savannah, where he had attended parochial schools. After graduating from Holy Cross College and Yale Law School, he had worked for John C. Danforth in the Missouri attorney general's office, then for the Monsanto Company, and then again for Danforth as an aide in the Senate. In 1981 Thomas moved to the Office of Civil Rights at the Department of Education, and in 1982 he became head of the EEOC. Appointed to the federal bench in 1990, he was one of a handful of high-level black judges committed to the Reagan-Bush agenda.

Opposition quickly mounted to a conservative nominee, who would presumably help to dismantle *Roe* v. *Wade*. As a conservative, moreover, Thomas rejected affirmative action, criticized the civil rights movement, voiced antipathy to welfare, and seemed skeptical about integration. Critics charged that he had little judicial experience and lacked a scholarly reputation; that while he dismissed government efforts to redress racial injustice, he had benefited from similar efforts, such as admission to Yale under a minority recruitment program; and that his nomination was a cynical ploy, because Democratic senators would hesitate to reject a black nominee and thereby offend black constituents. By the end of July, NOW, the NAACP, the AFL-CIO, and the Black Congressional Caucus had joined the opposition. At the end of August, the American Bar Association gave Thomas the lukewarm rating of "qualified," as opposed to "well-qualified;" two committee members found him "unqualified."

When Judge Thomas began his testimony before the Senate Judiciary Committee on September 10, many anticipated that he would face rigorous questioning but would ultimately be confirmed. The committee, led by Democratic Senator Joseph Biden of Maryland, comprised six Republicans, who were expected to support Thomas, and eight Democrats, who were expected to challenge him. Thomas, however, eluded his questioners. Stressing his life story—a rise from humble origins to prominence—he skirted controversial topics, backed away from positions he had previously voiced, and refused to discuss abortion, the most disputed issue that the Court would confront. Thomas claimed that he had "no opinion" on *Roe* v. *Wade*. Supported throughout the hearings by his old mentor, Danforth, now senator from Missouri, Thomas seemed to bypass the pitfalls. On September 27, the committee deadlocked seven to seven on the Thomas nomination; one Democrat, Dennis DeConcini of Arizona, joined the six Republicans in favor of Thomas. Senator Biden had decided to send the nomination to the Senate floor for a vote when a strange news story erupted.

On October 6, the media first reported Anita Hill's allegations. According to stories released by Nina Totenberg of National Public Radio and Timothy Phelps of *Newsday,* Hill alleged that Thomas had sexually harassed her a decade earlier when she worked as his aide. Hill's charges came to light only through a circuitous route. She had first mentioned the harassment when questioned by an employee of the Senate Judiciary Committee, and had requested that her name not be used. After the FBI interviewed her, a portion of the interview had been leaked to the two reporters, who subsequently refused to reveal their sources. Whether committee members were familiar with Hill's allegations and had decided not to pursue them—and to respect her request for anonymity—remained a moot point; the sudden revelation in the press forced Hill to present her case.

On October 7, at a news conference, Anita Hill defended her accusation and contended that the Judiciary Committee had ignored it. The following day, Thomas denied the allegations. Calls now flooded the Senate switchboard. Seven congresswomen, mobilized by Louise Slaughter of New York and Patricia Schroeder of Colorado, marched to the Senate to demand a postponement of the Senate vote. Under intense pressure, especially from women's groups, the committee scheduled a continuation of its hearings in order to consider Hill's charges. This unusual turn of events brought Anita Hill to the committee hearing room in Washington.

Anita Hill's background in many ways resembled that of Judge Thomas. Born in a small rural community near Tulsa, Oklahoma, one of thirteen children, she too had risen from plain origins through talent and perseverance. Class valedictorian of her high school, she had gone to Oklahoma State University. Like Thomas, she attended Yale Law School, from which she graduated with honors in 1980. After working briefly for a law firm in Washington, Hill served as special counsel to Clarence Thomas at the Office for Civil Rights in the Department of Education; here, she claimed, he first made advances. A year later, in 1982, when Thomas became chairman of the EEOC, Hill moved with him as his assistant. In 1983 she left her job, after hospitalization for stomach pains that she said were stress related. She then became a law professor, first at Oral Roberts University and in 1986 at the University of Oklahoma. Her specialty was commercial law.

When the televised committee hearings continued on October 11, for a twelve-hour session, a nationwide audience sat spellbound. Before Anita Hill

Anita Hill at her news conference in Norman, Oklahoma, on October 7, 1991. *(Scott Anderson/NYT Pictures)*

presented her charges, quoted above, Clarence Thomas was given a chance to deny them, which he did with conviction:

The first I learned of the allegations by Professor Anita Hill was on September 25, 1991, when the FBI came to my home to investigate her allegations. When informed by the FBI of the nature of the allegations and the person making them, I was shocked, surprised, hurt, and enormously saddened. I have not been the same since that day. . . .

This is a person that I have helped at every turn in the road since we met. She seemed to appreciate the continued cordial relationship we had since day one. She sought my advice and counsel, as did virtually all of the members of my personal staff.

During my tenure in the executive branch, as a policy maker and as a person, I have adamantly condemned sex harassment. There is no member of this committee or this Senate who feels stronger about sex harassment than I do. As a manager, I made every effort to take swift and decisive action when sex harassment raised or reared its ugly head.

The fact that I feel so very strongly about sex harassment and spoke loudly about it at EEOC has made these allegations doubly hard on me. I cannot imagine anything that I said or did to Anita Hill that could have been mistaken for sexual harassment. But with that said, if there is anything that I have said that has been misconstrued by Anita Hill or anyone else to be sexual harassment, then I can say that I am so very sorry and I wish I had known. If I did know, I would have stopped immediately. . . .

But I have not said or done the things that Anita Hill has alleged. . . .

Though I am, by no means, a perfect person—no means—I have not done what she

California Representative Barbara Boxer leads women members of Congress to the Senate side of the Capitol on October 8, 1991, to demand a delay in the vote on the Thomas nomination. *(Paul Hosefros/NYT Pictures)*

has alleged. And I still don't know what I could have possibly done to cause her to make these allegations. . . .

No job is worth what I've been through. . . . No horror in my life has been so debilitating. Confirm me if you want. Don't confirm me if you are so led. But let the process end. Let me and my family regain our lives. . . .

I will not provide the rope for my own lynching, or for further humiliation. . . .

After Hill's testimony, to which Thomas said he did not listen, he again denied the allegations, which, he said, "play to the worst stereotypes we have about black men in this country."

Both protagonists then faced interrogation by committee members, but Anita Hill met the sharper questions; Republican senators assumed the roles of prosecutors. Orrin Hatch of Utah, a former trial lawyer, accused Hill of collusion with liberal "interest groups" and "slick lawyers," and fastened on details of obscene remarks that she claimed Thomas had made. Arlen Specter of Pennsylvania, another former trial lawyer, pursued the points of why Hill had decided to follow Thomas from the Education Department to the EEOC, why she had remained in touch with him afterward ("I did not feel that it was necessary to cut off all ties or burn all bridges"), why she had made eleven phone calls to him over six years, why she continued to receive recommendations from him, and whether she really expected her charges, at the outset, to remain anonymous.

Citing variations in her answers to questions about contacts with Judiciary Committee investigators, Specter accused her of "flat-out perjury." Senator Alan K. Simpson of Wyoming announced that his office had been flooded with letters and calls saying that Professor Hill had a flawed character ("statements from people that know her. . . . saying 'Watch out for this woman.'")

When the senatorial questions had ended, panels of witnesses testified on behalf of Thomas and Hill. Anita Hill's four witnesses, all lawyers, either friends or associates, praised her character and corroborated her testimony—she had told them about her experiences on previous occasions, in most cases, a decade earlier. Not only had Hill never lied, said Susan Hoerchner, a judge from California, but "I have never known Anita Hill to even exaggerate." A second panel of witnesses, all women who had worked with Clarence Thomas at the EEOC, praised *his* character and his sensitivity to female colleagues. In their testimony and responses to questions, panel members suggested that Hill might be a scorned woman, a disturbed person, a victim of fantasy, or just a hard-boiled careerist. J. C. Alvarez, who contended that Anita Hill wanted to be "the Rosa Parks of sexual harassment," challenged her demeanor before the Judiciary Committee—her "role of a meek, innocent, shy, Baptist girl from the South":

> I don't know who she was trying to kid, because the Anita Hill that I knew and worked with was nothing like that. She was a very hard, tough woman; she was very opinionated, she was arrogant, she was a relentless debator, and she was the kind of woman who always made you feel that she was not going to be messed with. . . . She was aloof, she always acted as if she was a little bit superior to everyone, a little holier than thou. . . . She definitely came across as someone who was ambitious and watched out for her own advancement . . . someone who looked out for herself first. . . . The Anita Hill I knew before was nobody's victim.

After three days of intense examination by senators of a series of witnesses, Senator Biden suddenly brought the hearings to a close; they had exploded into a spectacle that no one had anticipated. In major cities, since Anita Hill began her testimony, the hearings had eclipsed other televised programming, including a Sunday night National League playoff between the Atlanta Braves and the Pittsburgh Pirates. Ratings for PBS soared; commercial networks that broadcast the hearings lost an estimated $15 million to $20 million in advertising income.

As the Judiciary Committee sessions came to an end, public opinion research suggested that Thomas's defense carried more weight than Hill's allegations—among both men and women. According to a *Los Angeles Times* survey, 44 percent of women said they tended to believe Judge Thomas compared with 35 percent who said they tended to believe Anita Hill. National polls suggested that 55 percent of men and 49 percent of women found Thomas more believable than Hill. A *New York Times*-CBS News poll revealed that respondents favored Judge Thomas's confirmation by a margin of two to one. Fifty-eight percent said that they believed Thomas, compared with 24 percent (26 percent of women and 22 percent of men) who said they believed Hill. Significantly, over 40 percent of respondents believed that *neither* Thomas nor Hill told "the entire truth." Overall, views about confirmation at the end of the hearings did not differ greatly from views expressed in earlier polls, before Anita Hill's testimony, with two important differences: First, the proportion of respondents who were "undecided" fell markedly. Second, black support for Thomas leapt from about half to over 70 percent.

With the poll results in mind, the Senate met on October 15 to vote on the Thomas nomination. Deluged with telegrams and phone calls, and with pressure from lobbyists, many senators faced a problem: However they voted, they might alienate either black or women constituents. Most planned to vote along party lines, as they had before Hill's testimony; still, her charges had raised the political stakes. As they debated the nomination, many senators sought to minimize risk and ward off retribution.

Those who supported confirmation devoted most of their time to praise of Judge Thomas's character. While voicing staunch opposition to sexual harassment, they sought to attack Anita Hill's credibility. Republican Charles E. Grassley of Iowa, for instance, charged that Hill's corroborating witnesses had "collaborated with special interest groups." Democrat Jim Exon of Nebraska, who said that he had been disappointed by many of Thomas's statements, voiced doubts about Hill's story, too—especially about "how she could have brought herself to follow Judge Thomas so faithfully and so long in her career given the sordid remarks allegedly made to her." Arlen Specter renewed his charge that Anita Hill had perjured herself. Republican Nancy Kassebaum of Kansas, one of only two women in the Senate, refused to "vilify and disparage Anita Hill," or to accept the claims that Hill was "mentally unstable," "inclined toward fantasy," or part of "some dark conspiracy," but voiced several other doubts:

> Is it possible that Professor Hill, an experienced attorney and law professor, believed that Judge Thomas's appointment could be killed in secret? Was she led to believe that mere raising of these charges could force the judge to withdraw his nomination with no full explanation to the full Senate and the public. . . . there are real questions now about whether she was used by others in an attempt to subvert the Senate's confirmation process. . . . Three weeks ago, I spoke in support of Judge Thomas's confirmation. . . . I believe it would be manifestly unfair for the Senate to destroy a Supreme Court nominee on the basis of evidence that finally boils down to the testimony of one person, however credible. . . .
>
> I have to assume that many of my male colleagues are offended by the notion that they cannot begin to understand the seriousness of sexual harassment or the anguish of its victims. On the question before us, some women suggest that I should judge the nomination not as a Senator but as a woman. I reject that suggestion.

Opponents of confirmation, almost all Democrats, stressed their original objections to Judge Thomas, and added praise of Anita Hill or remarks about the injustice done to her. Majority leader George J. Mitchell, Democrat of Maine, for instance, charged that President Bush had established a "litmus test" for a potential nominee: "that person's position on abortion;" that the nominee had refused "to discuss those views publicly;" that the Senate was not required to "rubber stamp" the President's choice; that the nomination process had become a political campaign; and that Judge Thomas was neither the best-qualified American to serve on the Court nor the best qualified African American. The sexual harassment charge, which added to his doubts, had not been the deciding factor:

But what happened to Professor Hill, unfortunately, if unchallenged, sends a clear and chilling message to women everywhere: If you complain about harassment you may be doubly victimized. We must not let that message stand unchallenged.

Other Democrats supported this critique of Hill's experience. Barbara A. Mikulski of Maryland attacked Hill's treatment by Republicans on the Judiciary Committee:

The same people who gave us the worst of racial stereotypes in political campaigns—the Willie Horton ad—have now smeared Anita Hill. Much is said about ruined reputations, but what about Anita Hill?

At age 35, a professor of law, a Yale graduate, goes back to what? There is much said about her mental health, that she was delusioned, had fantasies. Maybe she was deluded in the fact that if she came forward and was a good citizen, she would be protected. Maybe she had fantasies about the fairness of a process she thought she would get in the United States Senate.

Senator Robert C. Byrd of Virginia, who had previously indicated an inclination to vote for confirmation, made a unique and startling announcement: He believed Anita Hill.

I believe what she said. I watched her on that screen intensely. . . . I did not see on that face the knotted brow of satanic revenge. I did not see a face that was contorted with hate. . . . I saw an individual who did not flinch, who showed no nervousness, who spoke calmly throughout, dispassionately, and who answered difficult questions.

Aside from believing Anita Hill, I was offended by Judge Thomas's stonewalling the committee. . . .

He wanted to clear his name. He was given the opportunity to clear his name. But he didn't even listen to the principal witness, the only witness against him. He said he was tired of lies. What kind of judicial temperament does that demonstrate? . . .

[He] mounted his own defense by charging that the committee proceedings were high-tech lynching of uppity blacks. Now . . . that was an attempt to shift the ground. That was an attempt to fire the prejudices of race hatred, shift it to a matter involving race. . . . Why give him the benefit of the doubt? . . . A credible charge of the type that has been leveled at Judge Thomas is enough, in my view, to mandate that we ought to look for a more exemplary nominee.

When the Senate finally voted, Judge Thomas's margin of victory (it was estimated that he had about 60 votes a week earlier) had narrowed. Three Democratic Senators who had backed Judge Thomas before Hill testified now voted against him. Three other Democrats who had seemed to be leaning toward confirmation now opposed it. But eleven Democrats, seven from southern states, joined the Republicans, of whom all save two voted for confirmation. The Senate confirmed Judge Thomas by a vote of 52 to 48. "We have to put these things behind us and go forward," said Thomas. In Norman, Oklahoma, Anita Hill taught her law school classes and said she was glad that national awareness of the sexual harassment issue had been heightened.

Throughout the Thomas hearings, the media indeed provided a national seminar on sexual harassment. This form of behavior had only recently become a crime, largely due to the efforts of another Yale Law School graduate, Catharine MacKinnon, author of *Sexual Harassment of Working Women* (1979). MacKinnon, who began to bring cases to the federal courts in the late 1970s, had campaigned to make sexual harassment a form of sex discrimination and thus prohibited by Title VII of the Civil Rights Act of 1964. A practice was discriminatory, she contended, if it "participates in the systemic social deprivation of one sex because of sex." MacKinnon had won several crucial victories. One was at the EEOC. In 1980, two years before Thomas arrived there, the commission adopted three tests for deciding whether "unwelcome verbal or physical conduct" violated the Civil Rights Act. Under EEOC guidelines, the conduct in question had to be (1) "quid pro quo" behavior that made submission to sex an explicit or implicit condition of advancement, (2) behavior that "unreasonably interferes with an individual's job performance," or (3) behavior that creates an "intimidating, hostile, or offensive working environment." The Supreme Court endorsed both the concept of sexual harassment as sex discrimination and the "hostile environment" test in *Meritor Savings Bank* v. *Vinson* (1986), a landmark case brought by a bank employee, Mechelle Vinson, against a supervisor.

Was the type of behavior that Anita Hill had recounted, which involved neither physical contact nor explicit threats, a bona fide case of sexual harassment? "If Professor Hill's account is true, it's certainly sexual harassment, in that it created a hostile environment for her to work in," said Catharine MacKinnon, now a law professor at the University of Michigan. The conduct Hill described, revealed a *New York Times* article by Tamer Lewin on October 8th, in fact typified many cases that had come to the federal courts in the past decade. It involved unwelcome advances, undesired conversations, and an implicit threat that if she did not tolerate such behavior, her career would suffer. To be sure, Hill's case had some unusual twists: First, if her charges were true, as a NOW lawyer noted, Thomas "personally ignored the law he was supposed to be enforcing." Second, had Hill sought to press charges at the time, she would have had to appeal to an agency headed by the very person she accused. Still, Anita Hill's account embodied several crucial features of sexual harassment complaints.

First, the "hostile environment" claim was the most subtle and controversial part of sexual harassment law. In such cases, an employee found it difficult to work because of a pattern of sexual overtures or remarks, or even the display of pornographic pictures. EEOC guidelines, however, drew no firm line between allowable and illegal behavior, since what constituted harassment depended on what a particular individual found offensive. Men and women, apparently, might interpret a specific type of conduct—a risqué joke, for instance—in different ways; indeed, one woman might interpret it in a different way than another did.

In practice, it was up to the victim to identify offensive behavior by her response to it. A lawyer for the Women's Legal Defense Fund explained, "If the employee shows that the behavior is unwelcome, by telling the harasser to stop, or filing a formal complaint, or, in some cases, by not responding, and the behavior continues, it is harassment." The crime, therefore, was defined neither by the perpetrator's intent nor by the conduct per se, but by the victim's reaction. In another recent landmark case, the Court of Appeals in California set a slightly tighter standard: how a "reasonable woman" would have responded.

A second peculiarity of sexual harassment, researchers revealed, was that it was more concerned with power than with sex. In MacKinnon's words, sexual harassment referred to an "unwanted imposition of sexual requirements in the context of a relationship of unequal power." It was an abuse of power, a way to make women employees feel vulnerable, and a tactic to devalue their role in the workplace. Less than 5 percent of harassment cases involved a bribe or threat for sex. Most were attempts to control or intimidate victims. Significantly, sexual harassment occurred most frequently in occupations or workplaces where women were new or in a minority, and where they filled jobs that men had traditionally held. In blue-collar work, employees such as construction workers, for example, were most at risk. Among professionals, too, some researchers claimed, women in fields that were dominated by men, such as stockbrokers or neurosurgeons, were targets of harassment. A *National Law Journal* survey reported that 60 percent of women lawyers in 250 top firms had reported harassment. In all of these instances, women had entered what until recently had been male preserves; harassment challenged their presence. "It's not just someone grabbing you and pushing you in a closet," explained *Wall Street Journal* reporter Susan Faludi, author of a new book, *Backlash* (1991). "It's more the subtler form of making women uncomfortable by turning the workplace into a locker room and then telling them, 'What's the matter, you can't handle it? You wanted equality, I'm going to give it to you with a vengeance.'"

Other studies, however, suggested that women in white-collar work, such as secretaries and office employees, were the most frequent targets. Government studies in the 1980s found that 42 percent of women employed in federal agencies had experienced sexual harassment, mainly unwelcome sexual remarks, leers, suggestive looks, and pressure for dates. (So had 14 percent of men in the agencies.) Few of these employees, however, complained of the offensive conduct—a third peculiarity of sexual harassment. Researchers indicated that only 3 percent of those who felt victimized complained or pressed charges. Some women blamed themselves; they might believe that their own conduct or appearance had invited unwelcome attention. Many feared that they would not be believed, that retaliation would follow, or that they would lose their jobs, close off their options, or ruin their careers. One study, in which none of the respondents sought recourse, revealed that only 22 percent had even told another person of their experiences.

Such caution seemed in some ways warranted, lawyers explained, for those who brought sexual harassment charges were likely to endure yet a second bout of humiliation, including queries into their private lives, social habits, or mode of dress. Women plaintiffs often had to "prove their innocence," a lawyer contended, and, as in rape cases, a double standard might prevail. Women who were single or dressed attractively were at a disadvantage. Another disadvantage—again, as in rape cases—was that sexual harassment charges were difficult to prove, especially if a long period of time had passed since the alleged incidents or if there were few corroborating witnesses. Lawyers commented that the Senate hearings illustrated what a woman might expect if she filed a sexual harassment suit. In the wake of the hearings, the *Wall Street Journal* revealed on October 18th, the EEOC reported a pronounced rise in harassment complaints; the agency's Chicago office found that they tripled. In private cases, however, some plaintiffs' lawyers reported that their clients had retreated in order to avoid the vilification "likely in a public trial."

Such mixed responses, it turned out, typified reaction to Anita Hill's testimony. During and after the Thomas/Hill hearings, as sexual harassment received detailed attention, responses to Anita Hill and Clarence Thomas surged through the media—in the press, on television, on radio call-in shows. On one level, the hearings evoked a chorus of condemnation—for the Judiciary Committee, for the Senate, for the injuries done to both parties, and for the entire spectacle, the "ugly circus." On another level, the Thomas/Hill testimony elicited revealing insights into race, class, gender, the workplace, and politics.

The responses of black Americans assumed heightened importance: The hearings had been, unintentionally, a showcase of successful black professionals—apparently of conservative bent—in major and minor roles. Yet to many, as to Yale law professor Stephen L. Carter, the Thomas/Hill conflict had been a "double tragedy, one that might have been avoided had the committee held a closed hearing." From the outset, the Thomas nomination had split the black community and black organizations. The NAACP opposed it; the SCLC supported it; and the Urban League remained neutral. Black critics objected to Thomas's rejection of the civil rights agenda and to his conservative views. Supporters admired his achievements and commitment to self-help. They also stressed the need to maintain a black presence on the Supreme Court and the certainty that were Thomas not confirmed, the President would replace him with a white conservative. If one supported Clarence Thomas, "one opposed the black agenda," as an editor of the *Black Scholar* later explained. "On the other hand, if one opposed Clarence Thomas for his record, it might very well mean sacrificing black representation on the Supreme Court for years to come."

Anita Hill's allegations seemed to increase both black support for Thomas and the level of controversy. Strong black endorsement no doubt influenced the seven southern Democratic senators who voted to confirm Thomas; it also suggested that race counted more than political ideology. Some black observers responded to Thomas's denunciation of the second round of hearings as a "high-tech lynching," and objected to Anita Hill's intervention in the committee proceedings. "There's a high level of anger among black men," Harvard psychiatrist Alvin F. Poussaint explained, "that black women will betray them; that black women are given preference over them . . . that white men are using this black woman to get another black man." Others, however, including the Black Con-

gressional Caucus, contended that the hearings concerned solely sexual harassment, not race. Nor did Anita Hill lack support: Black Women in Defense of
Ourselves, an ad hoc organization, ran an advertisement in the *New York Times*
to protest her treatment.

A series of comments published in *Essence* suggested the diverse views
among black opinion makers. Some contributors resented that "a Black woman
was used to bring down a Black man." Some challenged the nature of sexual
harassment charges. "The brothers are all over the place on the question of sexual
harassment," wrote political scientist William Strickland.

Some believe that he did what she said but they don't consider it sexual harassment
because he promoted her and did not demand sexual favors in return for her keeping her
job. . . . If one sticks to the definition that anything that makes a woman subjectively
uncomfortable is harassment, then that is an impossible standard. Black men and woman
have to sit down and define this stuff. Because otherwise the system will try to manipulate
us.

Other contributors expressed receptivity to Anita Hill. "If this man did what she
said he did, she had every right to seek some redress and tell what she knows,"
wrote sociologist Joyce Ladner. "Being supportive does not mean that you have
to support every Black man, regardless," noted political consultant Donna Braz-
ile. Historian Nell Irvin Painter objected that Thomas "wrapped himself in
lynching and Black history. . . . That tears at Black women's racial identity
because it affirms the pre-existing feeling that when it comes to racial issues, men
represent the race."

Two responses published in the *New York Times* sought to interpret the roles
of Hill and Thomas in the context of black history and culture. *New York Times*
editor Rosemary Bray stressed the singular predicament of black women, torn
between loyalties of gender and race:

The parallel pursuits of equality for African-Americans and for women have trapped
black women between often conflicting agendas for more than a century. Despite the bind,
more often than not we choose loyalty to the race rather than the uncertain loyalty of
gender. As difficult as the lives of black women often are, we know that we are mobile in
ways black men are not—and black men know that we know. . . . We have convinced even
ourselves that no sacrifice is too great to insure what we view in a larger sense as the
survival of the race. There are those who believe that the price of solidarity is silence. It
was that commitment [to the race] that trapped Anita Hill. . . . Anita Hill put her private
business in the street and she downgraded a black man to a room filled with white men
who might alter his fate—surely a large enough betrayal for her to be read out of the race.

Prim and reserved Anita Hill, Bray contended, fit no popular stereotype of black
women. Most people who saw her "had no context in which to judge her." The
context Bray suggested was Harriet Jacobs's *Incidents in the Life of a Slave Girl,* a
revelation of sexual harassment from the nineteenth century.

Harvard sociologist Orlando Patterson also offered readers insights into
black culture—in particular, insights into Clarence Thomas's alleged behavior.

Condemning "the trap of neo-Puritan feminism," Patterson offered a distinctive interpretation of what might have happened. "One revealing feature of these hearings," Patterson wrote, "is the startling realization that Judge Clarence Thomas might well have said what Prof. Anita Hill alleges and yet be the extraordinarily sensitive man his persuasive female defenders claimed."

How is this possible? . . . nearly all African Americans except their intellectually exhausted leaders have already come up with the answer. He may well have said what he is alleged to have said, but he did so as a man not unreasonably attracted to an aloof woman who is esthetically and socially very similar to himself, who had made no secret of her admiration for him.

With his mainstream cultural guard down, Judge Thomas on several misjudged occasions may have done something completely out of the frame of his white, upper-middle-class work world, but immediately recognizable to Professor Hill and most women of southern working-class backgrounds, white or black, especially the latter. . . . I am convinced that Professor Hill perfectly understood the psycho-cultural contest in which Judge Thomas allegedly regaled her with his Rabelasian humor (possibly as a way of affirming their common origins), which is precisely why she never filed a complaint against him.

Raising the issue 10 years later was unfair and disingenuous: unfair because . . . there is no evidence that she suffered any emotional or career damage. . . .

If my interpretation is correct, Judge Thomas was justified in denying making the remarks, even if he had in fact made them, not only because the deliberate displacement of his remarks made them something else but on the utilitarian moral grounds that any admission would have immediately incurred a self-destructive and grossly unfair punishment.

Unlike the majority of commentators, black and white, who condemned the hearings as a circus, Patterson found them to be "a riveting civic drama." They brought Americans to "a greater awareness of the progress in racial and gender relations already achieved by this country." They vitiated "superficial liberal stereotypes of blacks as victims or bootstrap heroes" and revealed, instead, "a diverse aggregate . . . with all the class differences, subcultural and regional resources, strengths, flaws, and ideologies we find in other populations." Indeed, for black Americans, said Patterson, the hearings had been "a ritual of inclusion."

Responses to the hearings also threw a spotlight on the workplace, where women's presence had recently increased, where men and women interacted, and where a majority of adults spent most of their time. As Patterson noted, "most of our relationships, including intimate ones, are initiated in the workplace." Concern with workplace relationships elicited a chorus of concern from men. How, they asked, would the recent criminalization of sexual harassment affect such relationships? Was office romance imperiled? Were they guilty in the past of some forms of behavior that now seemed to be illegal? According to a national poll on October 9th, 53 percent of men stated that at some point at work they had "done or said something" that a woman co-worker might have interpreted as sexual harassment. On the other hand, men asked, could they expect to be subject to wild accusations from women employees whose career ambitions had been thwarted or whose advances *they* had rejected? Finally, why did liberation for some (women who entered the workplace, for instance) seem to curtail the liberation of others (themselves)?

One response to the potential hazard of sexual harassment charges appeared in an editorial in the *New Republic,* traditionally a bastion of liberal causes. By limiting speech, the editors contended, the "hostile environment" provision seemed a radical exception to the First Amendment axiom that free speech cannot be punished just because it is offensive. "It is scary to suggest that the rights of expression (including the right to ask for dates) should be less protected at work than at home," the editorial claimed. "Work is where most Americans spend most of their waking hours; they must be free to express themselves verbally without fear of prosecution." Free speech, the editors implied, should not be limited by what any woman, even a "reasonable" woman, found offensive. By so doing, the "hostile environment" clause trivialized all sexual harassment charges. It also brought up a profound question: Did some people have the right *not* to be offended by others?

Behavior in the office, moreover, some men suggested, now seemed to be governed by extremely vague and uncertain rules. As Patterson observed, new types of gender relationships are "invariably ambiguous." Writer Warren Farrell, for instance, found the line between sexual harassment and courtship to be "thin as a razor's edge." William Broyles, Jr., a former editor of *Newsweek,* expressed the implications of ambiguous rules:

Sex arrived in the workplace when women did, and, ever since, men have been unsure just what women believe the boundaries are. . . . . . . What is offensive to one woman may be obnoxious, amusing, or even endearing to another. Where men and women are together, there is misunderstanding and mystery. Respectable women imagine relationships that do not exist and contrive harassment charges to revenge other slights or to advance themselves. . . . One troubling aspect of the Thomas hearings was that they put on display the private rituals by which men and women come together. . . . The rules of sexual harassment are not objective but determined by the reaction of the woman involved. Each woman makes her own law. Women want to be treated equally but don't want to be considered sexless. They want to be sexually attractive but only to the right man and only with the proper approach. That leaves considerable possibility for error.

Broyles concluded with an assault—one bound to enrage Hill's defenders—against the concept of sexual harassment. Recently, he pointed out, women had become police officers and firefighters; they had carried arms into combat: "If they are tough enough [to handle these jobs], they are tough enough to handle a dirty joke or a clumsy flirtation without rushing to join the women who are truly victims."

Women, however, like men, were hardly united in their views on victimization, or on Anita Hill. As the polls suggested, at least half of women respondents believed Thomas rather than Hill. One division was political: In contrast to a liberal outpouring of female sympathy for Hill, conservative women disparaged her. Reiterating challenges to her testimony, they sought to sever themselves from feminist views. "Feminists are asking to have it both ways," said Phyllis Schlafly. "They have spent twenty years preaching that there isn't any difference between men and women, and now they want to turn around and claim sexual harassment if somebody says something that they don't like." The sexual harassment issue was patronizing, Schlafly contended; it suggested that women were weak and that they had to rely on the government. Writer Midge Decter charged that women were now infringing on men's rights and that no man, however sensitive, "could know what the rules of the game are." Former Reagan speechwriter Peggy Noonan noted a "perceptual split" on Anita Hill between the "chattering classes," who supported her, and "normal humans . . . a class division, in a way, between clever people who talk loud in restaurants and those who serve them."

Other divisions of opinion among women, apparently less ideological, indeed reflected class and vocation. *Time* reported a split of opinion in offices: Secretarial workers supported Thomas while employers (male and female) supported Hill. To office workers, many of whom claimed to have been harassed themselves, Hill's charges often seemed either fabricated or an exaggerated response to a commonplace occurrence. Some sympathized with the testimony of J. C. Alvarez (who claimed to have been a victim of sexual harassment herself, twice), when she described Hill as aloof and ambitious; others seemed to recall their own contacts with women careerists, or perhaps the recent movie "Working Girl," in which the working-class secretary-heroine ensnared the boyfriend and job of her elitest, ambitious employer. Respondents to polls and surveys sometimes cited their own work experience when they challenged the veracity of Hill's testimony. One young Delaware woman who was interviewed after the *Times*-CBS poll, for instance, felt that if Thomas had harassed Hill, he would have harassed her co-workers, too; she concluded that Hill "might have thought some of this stuff up in her head."

Reporter Felicity Barringer, who surveyed the opinion of Baltimore women during the hearings, found that poor women, black and white, in low-rent neighborhoods responded to Hill with "incredulity spiced with contempt." So did blue-collar workers, nurses, and many other employees. "It's unbelievable that a woman couldn't stop something like that at its inception," a retired teacher said. In other instances, even the experience of sexual harassment did not turn into support for Hill. "I was harassed, and I nipped it in the bud," a worker at a battered women's shelter said. Lawyers, legislators, social workers, and other managers, however, voiced support for Anita Hill. "A number of things were hauntingly true in her testimony," a business executive commented. "The man was not seeking a date, he was seeking to intimidate and control her. Sexual harassment is not an act of lust or a compliment. . . . It's an act of control."

A particular point of contention was why Hill had neglected to press charges in 1982 and had followed Thomas to a new job. In many office workers' view, Hill's inability to respond to Thomas's alleged conduct, by either ending it or leaving, seemed unbelievable. Women were constantly harassed in the workplace but able to react, they contended; a Yale graduate could have easily found another job, had she wished to do so. Professional and executive women, however, sympathized with Hill's predicament. "She was afraid of losing a career track, a person who would be a valuable resource to her networking," the Baltimore business executive explained. Harvard psychologist Carol Gilligan, who in a widely acclaimed book *In a Different Voice* (1982) had shown how gender affected moral choices, similarly found Hill's reluctance to complain plausible. "It amazed me that no one understood the underlying logic of what she did," Gilligan said.

Her basic assumption was that you live in connection with others, in relationship with others. Now, her experience of that relationship was one of violation; it was offensive to her. But she was making the attempt to work it through in the relationship; trying to resolve conflict without breaking connection.

Writer Barbara Ehrenreich, in *Time,* explained Hill's decision in the context of power relationships:

Men and women do not yet meet on what is exactly a level playing field. Nine times out of ten, it's the male who has the power, the female who must flatter, cajole, and make an effort to please. If she turns him down, her career may begin to slide. She won't get the best job assignments. He might not be around when she needs help some day—as Hill apparently did—in getting a job or a grant.

An underlying point at issue was whether Hill had told the truth. A surfeit of commentary in the press suggested that a great many women believed that she had. In a column published right after the Senate vote, *New York Times* writer Anna Quindlen spoke out for those who accepted Hill's allegations. Quindlen reviewed how Anita Hill—"intelligent, composed, unflappable, religious"—had testified; how "as soon as she left the room, she was portrayed as a nut case, romantic loser, woman scorned, perjurer;" how black women were asked to choose "the race card versus the gender card;" how Thomas had exploited "the fact that the liberal guilt about racism remains greater than the guilt about the routine mistreatment of women;" and how Hill exhibited "the tranquility of a person who has done the right thing." Why had she done what she did? Quindlen could find only one explanation. "The explanation is that she was telling the truth and he was not. Simple as that. She got trashed and he got confirmed. Simple as that."

A vocal portion of Anita Hill's sympathizers, moreover, responded to the all-male Senate Judiciary committee, and to the almost all-male Congress; only 2 percent of senators and 29 out of 434 representatives were women. "Watching Anita Hill cruelly attacked strikes close to our self-respect," wrote Ann Lewis, former political director of the Democratic National Committee. "We wonder how different the process might have been had women been on the panel." Lewis predicted "a surge of support for women candidates in 1992—not good news for incumbents, including male Democrats." Eleanor Smeal, former president of NOW, had a similar response: "The Senate did more in one week to underscore the critical need for more women in the Senate than feminists have been able to do in twenty-five years." Within a week of the hearings, potential women candidates began to assess their options and women's political fund-raisers started to note a surge in contributions. "Sisterhood may not be powerful now," an official of the Women's Campaign Fund told reporter Jane Mayer, "but it's going to be a hell of a lot more powerful soon."

A few weeks after the hearings, Congress passed a new Civil Rights bill, sponsored by John Danforth, which for the first time awarded compensatory damages to victims of discrimination, including sexual harassment. In an interview in Norman, Oklahoma, after the Senate vote, Anita Hill reflected on her experience, thanked her supporters, and offered a few words of advice to victims of sexual harassment. "Try to find somebody you can trust and tell them . . . somebody who can help make you feel that you are not at fault . . . because you can't take it all out on yourself, you can't internalize it."

22

IN SEARCH OF EQUALITY: SINCE 1975

By the start of the 1980s, the women's movement had made a significant impact on American life. Laws, aspirations, and institutions had been transformed. Federal policy had been revised, new coalitions of women's organizations had been formed, and women's issues became national issues. But women's changing status in society brought with it new conflicts—between political factions, between women and men, and, indeed, among women with competing interests. It also raised new questions about public policy. Could legislation ensure sexual equality, for instance, when structural inequality persisted? Were policies that addressed sexual difference needed to provide equal opportunity? To what extent, moreover, could the state regulate the workplace and family? At issue in the 1980s and 1990s was the elusive goal of "gender justice," and the challenge of how to achieve it.

Feminism at Stalemate

"It was not the cause, or its rhetoric, or any single issue that emboldened or exhilarated us," Betty Friedan wrote in 1982. "It was the movement itself, the process, the activity of taking control of one's own destiny." By the 1980s, however, the conjunction of reform mood and feminist ground swell that had characterized the late 1960s had vanished. During the 1970s, an antifeminist backlash erupted, as evidenced in the "Stop ERA" campaign, led by Phyllis Schlafly, an experienced right-wing activist, and the "right-to-life" movement, which sought to reverse federal abortion policy. The role of women became a major issue in national politics, one around which the conservative right could organize; indeed, the feminist campaign fueled a battle between liberals and conservatives that had been brewing since the 1960s. Opposition to feminism now

552

evoked the commitment of thousands of women, to whom the women's movement represented an assault on women's interests and traditional values. With
the same zeal as that shown by feminists, their opponents assaulted state legislatures, ran for public office, and mobilized support for "pro-family" policies.

The defeat of the ERA in June 1982, only three states short of ratification,
was less a tribute to women's efforts to "Stop ERA" than to the solid South, since
no southern state legislature ratified the amendment. Southern hostility in fact
represented a long tradition; the South had never favored either feminist demands or federal encroachment on states' rights. The ERA defeat exemplified as
well the difficulty of the amending process, especially the ratification procedure.
The decade-long battle over ERA, however, was a revealing one. On both sides,
women measured the perils of legal equality, such as increased liability to the
draft, against the benefits; the threatened loss of now traditional rights, whether
to support in marriage or to child custody and alimony in divorce, against the
gain of relatively unknown rights. The ERA was once again a stacked deck, as it
had been at the Kennedy commission meetings in the 1960s, since it forced
women to balance hypothetical gains against hypothetical losses, and roles as
individuals against roles as family members.

Like woman suffrage, the ERA also became a highly charged symbolic
issue. Some experts contended that the amendment would make little difference
to women's lives or women's rights. By the end of the campaign, even some
sympathizers conceded doubts about ERA's potential for ensuring an egalitarian
society. To opponents, however, it represented an assault on womanhood and
family life. An ERA, wrote Phyllis Schlafly, would free men from family support
obligations, force women into the labor market, and cause "radical loosening of
the legal bonds that tend to keep the family together." To ERA defenders, the
battle over the amendment became a referendum on feminism. Defeat, said
Eleanor Smeal, NOW president, in 1978, "might give a false message to the courts
and state legislatures that the country does not want to have a policy on sex
discrimination." After the ERA capsized in 1982, the next Congress reconsidered
it. In November 1983 the House rejected the ERA by six votes.

The cumbersome process of constitutional amendment, while a handicap
in the ERA campaign, turned to feminists' advantage in the case of abortion.
Opponents of *Roe* v. *Wade* had proposed a "right-to-life" amendment that would
prevent the federal government and the states from "depriving any human being
of life." Contending that life began at conception, the right-to-life movement
began a massive antiabortion campaign that burgeoned in the late 1970s. When
Congress held hearings on when life began, women assumed leading roles on
both sides of the issue. Right-to-life advocates contended that abortion should
not be allowed under any circumstances. Feminists, Planned Parenthood, and
liberal pressure groups defended the option of abortion as a woman's constitutional right. By the start of the 1980s, an antiabortion amendment seemed
stymied. In June 1983, the Supreme Court reconfirmed women's constitutional
right to abortion by upsetting an array of city ordinances that limited access to
it. A few weeks later, the Senate defeated the Hatch amendment, intended to
make abortion unconstitutional.

But the battle had only begun. Throughout the 1980s, well-organized right-to-life groups picketed abortion clinics, intimidated doctors who performed abortions, and, in some areas, ensured that "choice" was virtually unavailable. By the end of the decade, the Supreme Court had assumed a more conservative cast. President Reagan had added three new appointees: Sandra Day O'Connor, the first woman to sit on the Court, in 1981; Antonin Scalia in 1986; and Anthony Kennedy in 1988. In *Webster* v. *Reproductive Health Care Services* (1989), by a five to four majority, the Court upheld a Missouri statute that contained twenty provisions designed to limit a woman's right to choice. Before approving abortions, for example, physicians were supposed to perform tests to determine whether a fetus estimated at over twenty weeks was "viable;" no such fetus could be aborted except to preserve a woman's life or health. Nor could public facilities or employees be used to perform abortions except under the same circumstances. Four justices indicated that they were ready to overturn *Roe* v. *Wade,* but Justice O'Connor, who had voted with the majority to uphold the Missouri law, contended that the *Webster* case did not require a reconsideration of the 1973 decision. In his majority opinion, Chief Justice Rehnquist stated that "politically divisive" issues should be decided by state legislatures.

This possibility seemed imminent in the spring of 1992, when the Court began consideration of a Pennsylvania law that regulated access to abortion. With yet one more Bush appointee, Clarence Thomas, on the Court, the conser-

Supporters and opponents of abortion gather outside the United States Supreme Court building on July 3, 1989, to await the decision on the *Webster* case. *(Jose R. Lopez/NYT Pictures)*

vatives had a firm majority. Many now expected the justices to take the next opportunity to overturn *Roe* v. *Wade,* and turn the abortion battle back to the states. Instead, in June 1992, in a five to four ruling, the justices upheld the 1973 decision. In *Planned Parenthood* v. *Casey,* the Court allowed most of the limits on abortion that the Pennsylvania law imposed. Such restrictions as a 24-hour waiting period or the requirement that a teenager gain the consent of a parent or judge did not impose an "undue burden" on a woman seeking an abortion, the decision stated. At the same time, the Court upheld the constitutional right to abortion. Justices O'Connor, Kennedy, and Souter joined the Court's two liberals, justices John Paul Stevens and Harry A. Blackmun, to defend the "essence" of *Roe* v. *Wade.* According to the majority opinion, written jointly by the members of the new centrist bloc, "The essential holding of *Roe* v. *Wade* should be retained and again affirmed." Although further state limitations on abortion were antici-pated, *Roe* v. *Wade* now seemed likely to endure.

What was public opinion on this controversial issue? A 1991 poll found that 40 percent of Americans believed "abortion should be generally available to those who want it;" 19 percent thought "it should not be permitted;" and 39 percent felt it should be "available but under stricter limits than it is now." Excepting a technological breakthrough, the fight over abortion seemed destined to continue. Such a breakthrough was perhaps in the offing. The mislabeled "day after" pill, RU-486, developed by a French physician, if taken within around six weeks of conception, could create the condition of a miscarriage by preventing an egg's implantation in the uterine wall. Barred from the United States by the Bush administration, RU-486 was in use in France, England, and China. At the start of 1993, when President Clinton lifted the ban on importing RU-486, the use of that drug or similar ones became more likely in the United States as well.

If the dispute between "choice" and "life" seemed insoluble, so did another conflict that evolved concurrently: the battle over pornography. As in the cases of ERA and abortion, women campaigned on both sides, but in this instance, feminists broke ranks. Ironically, since the start of the women's movement, pornography production had mushroomed; new technology—the VCR—and liberalization of obscenity statutes abetted its growth. By the late 1980s, pornog-raphy was a $7 billion a year industry; profits rolled in from videotapes, X-rated cable stations, phone services, and numerous publications. Lawyer Catharine MacKinnon and writer Andrea Dworkin, who joined forces at a law school seminar in 1983, spearheaded a feminist antipornography crusade. Adhering to feminist Robin Morgan's dictum, "Pornography is the theory; rape is the prac-tice," MacKinnon and Dvorkin argued that pornography involved violence against women. Moreover, they stated, pornography was not a free speech issue but a civil rights issue. (MacKinnon had similarly argued that sexual harassment was a form of sex discrimination that violated civil rights law.) The two women sponsored a Minneapolis ordinance that classified pornography as sex discrimi-nation and gave victims a chance to complain at the local civil rights commission. Approved by the city council, the ordinance was vetoed by the mayor. A similar law, enacted in Indianapolis the following year, was struck down by a federal judge. When a panel of judges of the U.S. Court of Appeals reviewed the

Using demonstrations, boycotts, petitions, and propaganda, the anti-pornography campaign protested "writing or imagery that objectifies, degrades, and brutalizes a person, usually a woman or girl, in the name of sexual stimulation or entertainment." Above, "tabling," or petition-signing, on a New York street corner during the summer of 1983. A cover of *Hustler* magazine is tacked to the poster. *(Leonard Speier)*

ordinance in 1985, they found that it violated freedom of speech but accepted MacKinnon's premise that pornography was "central to creating and maintaining sex as a basis of discrimination."

The feminist crusade against pornography, however, allied the crusaders with conservative opponents of pornography. Other feminists objected to this odd alliance. Some questioned the thesis that pornography "inspires negative attitudes and actions toward women" as unproven. Some stressed a civil libertarian approach: Objectionable as it might be, they argued, pornography was protected by the First Amendment and had to be tolerated. "Without free speech we can have no feminist movement," two leaders of NOW responded to MacKinnon in 1991. Others defended women's right to freedom of sexual expression, decried the posture of victim that the antipornography campaign imposed, and claimed that the campaign reinforced sexual stereotypes. MacKinnon "seemed to me . . . another voice reducing us, one saying we are creatures mainly acted upon," a critic charged. Still others sought to distinguish between pornography and erotica. More than any other feminist issue, legal historian Joan Hoff points out, the irresolvable pornography conflict was destined for longevity.

The dispute over pornography represented an upsurge of attention among feminists to forms of aggression that victimized women, such as sexual abuse in the home, sexual harassment in the workplace, wife battering, and rape. Response to the Thomas hearings illustrated the swirl of controversy that such issues elicited. The dispute over pornography also fueled another feud among feminists concerning "cultural feminism" or relational, transformative, or essentialist feminism—all rubrics for lines of thought that acknowledged and celebrated gender difference.

A trend within feminism since the early 1970s, cultural feminism affirmed and championed women's unique nature and qualities. It challenged the women's movement's current emphasis on equal rights; stressed women's links to one another, and their differences from men; and argued for distinctive female perceptions, skills, and abilities. Cultural feminists protested not the existence of gender roles, but the negative connotations of those roles and their devaluation in a male-dominated culture. They capitalized, for instance, on psychologist Carol Gilligan's influential book, *In a Different Voice* (1982), which argued that men and women had different moral sensibilities; agreed with Catharine Mac-Kinnon's assertion that "the engendered nature of law privileges men;" and appreciated linguist Deborah Tannen's best-seller *You Just Don't Understand* (1990), which analyzed gender differences in communication. "Pretending that men and women are the same hurts women, because the ways they are treated are based on the norms for men," Tannen contended. Opponents, however, charged cultural feminists with withdrawing into female culture or returning to a Victorian value system. "The question of whether feminism entails the transcendence of gender or the affirmation of femaleness has become the new feminist faultline," historian Alice Echols observed in 1988.

By the start of the 1990s, feminism remained a powerful force in public life, but as a political movement it clearly faced obstacles. Young, educated, professional women of the self-defined "postfeminist" generation, for instance, often took the achievements of the women's movement for granted, resented the status of oppression that it seemed to confer, or voiced little interest in affiliation with a militant crusade. "Feminists are losing the second generation because of this incredible bitterness we can't identify with," a young woman told a reporter in 1982. To some, emancipation meant independence from feminism, and the ability to get ahead on one's own. Other women claimed "feminist fatigue" after years of striving for feminist ideals that seemed elusive, if not unobtainable. Critiques from within also generated debate. In *The Second Stage* (1982), Betty Friedan urged the women's movement to pay more attention to issues involving the family. In *A Lesser Life* (1986), economist Sylvia Ann Hewlett assailed the feminist preoccupation with equal rights and contended that feminism had failed because of its reluctance to consider women's continuing child-care concerns. Perhaps most important, the political climate took a toll. The Reagan-Bush years saw massive cuts in social programs, a verbal emphasis on "family values" without any legislation to support such values, and official hostility to feminist messages. In

1991, journalist Susan Faludi issued a broadside, *Backlash,* that cited the many ways in which movies, the media, industry, the government, the right wing, and assorted revisionists had undercut or sabotaged feminist gains in the 1980s.

At the same time, the goals of the women's movement seemed to have been broadly diffused. Many women, for instance, participated in vocational associations that promoted women's issues or grassroots efforts to protect women's rights. In Norman, Oklahoma, to cite one example, Anita Hill served on the board of directors of the Women's Resource Center, a group that ran a shelter for battered women and a rape-crisis hotline. In other instances, the goals of the women's movement were privatized. "The people I hang out with or socialize with aren't hard-core card-carrying feminists," a woman police detective in Raleigh, North Carolina, told a *New York Times* reporter in 1987. "But there are women's issues they take sides with." Achieving equality after 1975 became as much an individual battle as an organizational crusade. Several preoccupations of the 1980s—achieving vocational success, weighing career against motherhood, coping with the dual stress of child rearing and employment—suggested that many facets of the search for equality had converged in a specific arena, the workplace.

Women in the Workplace

A massive influx of new women workers since the 1960s had transformed the workplace and the labor force. Women had penetrated the professions and prestigious occupations, entered new semiprofessional fields, and moved into the growing service industries, as well as into jobs once dominated by men. By 1980, for instance, women were the majority of insurance adjusters, bill collectors, and real estate agents, and almost half of all bus drivers and bartenders. By 1990, 58 percent of women were in the labor force, where they held about 45 percent of all jobs. During the 1980s, indeed, women filled four out of five new jobs. As the female work force expanded, its nature changed as well. By the end of the 1980s, about two-thirds of married women held jobs, as did 68 percent of women with children. The working wife—indeed the working mother—became the norm.

Concerns of women workers now reflected both the impact of the women's movement and the changing composition of the female labor force. A major change since the 1960s was the increase of employment among mothers of preschoolers. In 1991, almost 60 percent of mothers with children under six held jobs, compared with 20 percent in 1960. Many working parents left their very young children with relatives or in informal, unlicensed child-care arrangements. Others hired private caretakers, often recent immigrants, legal or illegal. One facet of the child-care problem received publicity at the start of the Clinton administration when the President's first nominee for attorney general was forced to withdraw because she had hired an illegal alien to care for her child, thus violating immigration law. At the end of the 1980s, one-quarter of young children attended day-care centers. Still, day care remained a minimum-wage

By the mid-1980s over 150 day-care chains ran centers around the country. Typically, they paid employees the minimum wage. Pictured is a day-care center in Montgomery, Alabama, in 1984. *(Mark Chesnutt/NYT Pictures)*

industry, with low-paid personnel and high turnover. "Quality care," if available, meant substantial expense. Surveys reported that working women's major goals were "helping balance work and family" and "getting government funding for programs such as child care and maternity leave." Among industrialized nations, the United States remained one of the few without subsidized day care and the only one with no statutory maternity leave.

The latter seemed elusive. The Federal Disability Law of 1978 barred discrimination against prospective mothers, and a California law went further. It required unpaid leave of several months for pregnant women, who would be guaranteed their original jobs when they returned. In 1987, the Supreme Court upheld the measure in *California Savings and Loan Association* v. *Guerra*. But the case evoked a dispute about "preferential treatment." NOW, for instance, attacked the California law. To regard women under law as a different class of workers, NOW asserted, would foster sexist stereotypes and increase discrimination against women. A compromise solution might be "parental" leave, available to either parent. By the end of the 1980s, seven states had enacted parental leave laws. In 1990, President Bush vetoed a "family leave" bill that would have provided unpaid leave to workers with family obligations. Although he favored the policy, the President contended, it should be voluntary and not obligatory on the part of employers. In early 1993, President Clinton signed a family leave bill that provided a family member with twelve weeks of unpaid leave, job retention, and continuation of health benefits.

Wage differentials between male and female workers also remained a major concern. By the end of the 1980s, the average earnings of full-time women workers were 70 percent those of men, and young women earned yet higher proportions of male wages. In occupations traditionally dominated by men, such as professional, managerial, and technical jobs, a federal spokesman explained, "the male-female wage gap . . . is narrowing." Overall, however, the wage gap continued. Women were predominant among newcomers to the job market, and the lower wages earned by new women workers lowered the average for all women employees. Experts offered other explanations, too: Women were less likely than men to work in unionized occupations; if they had families, they might prefer convenient or flexible work to higher pay; or they may have met discriminatory treatment. A lobbyist for the Women's Equity Action League blamed wage differentials on "sex discrimination, the old boys' network, and massive stereotyping of women's work."

To combat sex discrimination in employment, women relied on the government and the courts, specifically Title VII of the 1964 Civil Rights Act, the antidiscrimination policy the federal government started in the 1960s, as enforced by the Equal Employment Opportunity Commission. In 1987, in *Johnson* v. *Transportation Agency,* the Court extended its affirmative action thrust by ruling six to three that employers might sometimes favor women and minorities over better-qualified men and whites to correct "a conspicuous imbalance in traditionally segregated job categories" and to bring its work force into line with the makeup of the labor market. The decision enlarged an earlier one: In 1978, in *Steelworkers* v. *Weber,* the Court had ruled that private employers might sometimes give job preference under voluntary affirmative action plans "to break down old patterns of race segregation and hierarchy." In the *Johnson* case, the Court rejected a suit by a man whom the Santa Clara, California, County Transportation Agency had passed over in promotion to the job of dispatching road crews in favor of a woman with a slightly lower score in a competitive interviewing process. Supporters of the decision predicted an increase of women in jobs historically held by men. Opponents charged that the ruling would encourage employers to discount merit and reduce their risk of "reverse discrimination" suits. Justice Scalia said that the decision completed the conversion of the 1964 antidiscrimination law into an "engine of discrimination" against men and whites, especially the "unknown, unaffluent, and unorganized."

Not all affirmative action suits succeeded, as illustrated by the drawn-out Sears case. In 1979, the EEOC sued Sears Roebuck and Co., the first major retail chain to adopt an affirmative action plan, for sex discrimination in hiring, promotion, and pay. Not enough women had been given jobs in commission sales—the vending of such big-ticket items as automotive parts and aluminum siding—the EEOC charged. Sears claimed that it had met reasonable standards

After the United States armed forces turned from conscription to a volunteer force in 1973, the number of women recruits mushroomed. By 1987, over 225,000 women served in the armed forces. They constituted 10.2 percent of military personnel, compared to 1 percent twenty years earlier. *(J. P. Laffont/Sygma)*

for hiring women, that it had a commendable record on affirmative action, and that women had been less interested in and less qualified for commission sales. In 1987, a federal judge supported Sears's claim that it lacked discriminatory intent, and criticized the statistical evidence presented by the EEOC, which had never produced a witness to testify to discrimination. The case was less important for its results, since the EEOC case was faulty, than for the testimony of two expert witnesses, both prominent historians, who debated whether factors other than sex discrimination were likely to have limited women's aspirations to big-ticket sales positions. Alice Kessler Harris claimed that women workers strove for the highest wages and that only employer discrimination barred them from nontraditional jobs. Rosalind Rosenberg contended that historically men and women had different job preferences and that women's cultural conditioning could have led them to avoid competitive sales jobs at Sears.

Affirmative action cases such as the *Johnson* and *Sears* cases affected only women who entered, or sought to enter, fields dominated by men or nontraditional jobs. But despite the inroads that women had made in higher-paid and nontraditional occupations, most women of the 1980s and 1990s, as before, faced a segregated job market, or "massive stereotyping of women's work." Three out of five women workers in the 1980s held pink-collar jobs, and, as a census department official explained, "Working in an occupation that has a high proportion of women has a negative effect on earnings." The segregated job market fostered a demand for "pay equity" or "comparable worth," a campaign to raise pay levels in occupations in which women predominated. A clerical worker, for instance, pay equity advocates claimed, should receive the same pay as a truck driver working for the same employer.

The premise of pay equity was that the "worth" of a job could be reasonably determined, based on such factors as skill, training, effort, and responsibility. Critics contended that the concept took no notice of "market forces," or the demand for a certain type of worker. Supporters, too, voiced qualifications. A study in the *Harvard Law Review* suggested that comparable worth, though desirable, defied implementation by the courts and would have only a negligible impact on women's wages. A study of pay equity among public employees in Minnesota, which adopted the policy in the mid-1980s, suggested that it remedied low wages but increased managerial power. For many feminists, still, pay equity remained an attractive cause. If implemented, it would affect large numbers of ordinary wage earners rather than those professionals who had thus far reaped the vocational profits of feminist breakthroughs.

Pay equity, however, was unlikely to alter the changing structure of the economy, which itself posed problems for women workers in traditional fields. Since 1970, the rise of service industries and the impact of advanced technology had created many new jobs that women now held. But new options often entailed new liabilities. Computers, for instance, which had transformed the nature of office work, may have also devalued the labor of clerical employees, to whom repetitive data-processing tasks resembled piecework. "Automation is producing the sweatshops of the 1980s," an official of Nine To Five, a secretarial union, declared. Part-time work presented problems, too. As women surged into the labor market, employers increasingly relied on temporary or part-time workers. In the mid-1980s, over half of women wage earners worked part-time or for only part of the year. Less costly to employers, such "contingent" workers lacked the benefits available to full-time employees, such as health care insurance or pension plans. Women's need for "flexible" jobs—plus their massive entry into paid work and employers' desire for cheap labor—could create a class of second-class workers.

Upscale employees in the business world, meanwhile, voiced other grievances. One was a "glass ceiling" that barred advancement beyond middle management. Another was the sacrifice that the fast track, or even the middle management track, imposed. By the mid-1980s, 30 percent of managerial personnel were women. A slew of advice books on "The Right Moves" and "Feminine Leadership" offered strategies for success in business circles. But studies of women executives revealed "ambivalence," "burnout," and a feeling that "something's missing." Success in the higher ranks of business or the professions, the press suggested, seemed to exact a toll in personal life. In 1989, Felice Schwartz, president of a research group that focused on women in business, proposed in the *Harvard Business Review* that employers avoid the cost of high turnover among women executives by creating a two-track plan. "Career-primary" women managers, said Schwartz, needed an unimpeded "path to the top." However, "career-and-family" managers would benefit from a different track, one that involved maternity leave, flexible scheduling, part-time work, job-sharing, lower pay, and slower advancement. Such a plan would accommodate both women managers and business, said Schwartz, which "needs all the talented women it can get." The "mommy track," a term coined by opponents of the plan, evoked a storm of protest. One critic charged that it would "perpetuate a cycle in which generations of women have been depreciated, divided, and weakened." Schwartz replied that she was urging employers to "create policies that help mothers balance career and family responsibilities" and "eliminate barriers to productivity and advancement."

The debate aroused by the "mommy track" in part reflected Schwartz's assertion that "The cost of employing women in management is greater than the cost of employing men." It also illuminated some disparities that had increased in the decades since 1970. As women's rates of job holding increased, economist Juliet B. Schor, points out, men's fell. Moreover, among employees, the numbers of hours worked annually increased for men by 98 and for women by 305. Those most affected by "elastic" working hours were salaried—managerial and professional—workers, among whom women's numbers had steadily risen. Employers, however, enjoyed a structural advantage in the labor market, Schor points out, since more candidates existed for managerial and professional jobs—those that provided "job satisfaction"—than there were openings. With candidates competing for high-status employment and willing to endure the "work marathon," employers gained advantages. Typically, they favored cost-cutting measures, disliked work-sharing or part-time arrangements among managerial staff, and preferred to extract longer hours. Employers, apparently, did not yet share Felice Schwartz's contention that measures to retain trained women managers would lower costs. In 1992, only 10 percent of large companies had adopted flexible scheduling or other programs to aid workers with families. Even if employees wanted more time for themselves, as many claimed they did, Schor suggests, few could "reconcile the conflicting demands of employer and family." Women with families who entered competitive occupations were likely to be caught in a crunch between employer demands and private lives.

Advocates of equity for women workers therefore faced a variety of considerations, under less than favorable circumstances. Would demands concerning "family" issues, such as day care or parental leave, dilute demands for equal rights in the workplace? Would any acceptance in law or custom of gender distinctions foster discrimination against women workers and leave them at a competitive disadvantage? Would insistence on absolute equality limit the options for "flexible work" and "balance" that many women workers demanded, and also leave them at a competitive disadvantage? Would sex-neutral policies always work in women's interests? Or would they help some women and harm others? The search for equality in the workplace seemed to revive the issue of "difference" versus "equality" that had plagued the women's movement in the 1920s. It also involved another set of factors—changing expectations about family life.

Families in Transition

While politicians relentlessly endorsed "family values," the "traditional" family of postwar America swiftly faded. During the 1980s, the Census Bureau and social scientists issued a rash of messages about delayed marriage, unwed cohabitation, single parenthood, and mounting illegitimacy. Ironically, the impact of feminism coincided with significant shifts in domestic life, and the beneficiaries of the new developments did not appear to be women or children. The new woman of the "postfeminist" generation might well be the working wife in an upwardly mobile two-career family. But she might also be a single mother, deserted spouse, impoverished family head, or, by choice or circumstance, a woman living alone.

An acceleration of change began in the 1970s, when the marriage age started to climb. In 1960, the average marriage age for men was 22.8 and for women 20.3; thirty years later, it was 26.1 for men and 23.9 for women, about the same as in the 1890s. In 1960, again, only 28 percent of women aged twenty to twenty-four were single; in 1985, over 58 percent. Part of the increase of young single women reflected a proliferation of cohabiting unwed couples, whose numbers increased in the 1970s and rose again, by 80 percent, in the 1980s. Not all such couples, indeed, were heterosexual. Quasi-legitimization of gay life-styles spurred an increase in homosexual households in the 1970s and 1980s, especially in urban areas.

"Living together"—a relationship that resembled Ben Lindsey's plan for "companionate marriage" in the 1920s—had tentative connotations. But when a woman married legally, her security as family member became more tentative, too. In the 1950s, the divorce rate declined slightly, but between 1960 and 1980 it more than doubled. During the 1980s, almost one out of two first marriages ended in divorce; by 1990, the divorce rate had tripled since 1970. If separated or divorced when young, a woman was as likely as a man to remarry, but as she aged, her odds for remarriage dwindled. A census study in the mid-1980s revealed that among those aged thirty-five to forty-four, for instance, there were 84 eligible men to every 100 eligible women. For those aged forty-five to fifty-four, the odds dropped to 54 men to every 100 women. In her late forties, a woman was only half as likely as a man to marry again. The 1980 census reported 50 percent more separated or divorced women than men, as well as a 90 percent rise, since 1970, in the number of women living alone, and the trend continued into the 1990s.

Interpretation of trends in the marriage market offered fuel for conflict. In 1986 a team of social scientists from Harvard and Yale released dire predictions about educated women's options for marriage, based on a study of census data. College-trained women who had not married by twenty-five had only a 50 percent chance of doing so, the study said. At thirty, the odds dropped to 20 percent, at thirty-five to 5 percent, and at forty, to one percent. According to the social scientists, "marriage deferred is translating into marriage forgone." Census Bureau figures, cited above, mitigated the scope of decline in marriage odds for women in the population at large, and for educated women as well. Still, to many women, the warnings reflected experience. When asked about the Harvard–Yale study, young professional women suggested that diminished options reflected heightened selectivity more than male scarcity. "If you're college-educated and pursuing a career and trying to achieve something, right away half the men in the world are no longer interesting to you," a Yale graduate told a reporter. "I think women are much less frightened of going out and being alone," a young stockbroker added. "They get so much satisfaction from other parts of their lives that they don't rely so heavily anymore on the man in their life."

Another controversy involved the impact of "no-fault" divorce laws, enacted in forty-three states by the mid-1980s. Under no-fault divorce, a court held neither party responsible for the breakup of the marriage or subject to punitive charges; rather, the court divided a couple's property equitably between the parties. In *The Divorce Revolution* (1985), sociologist Lenore Weitzman argued that divorce impoverished ex-wives, especially older wives, and their children. Using a small sample of divorces in Los Angeles County, Weitzman contended that in the first year after divorce, ex-wives experienced a 73 percent drop in their standard of living, and husbands experienced a 42 percent rise. Other studies reported a less dire differential. Still, the upshot of the divorce studies—and the marriage market studies—was a general impression that women faced structural disadvantages; notably, as they aged, their options and leverage shrank, as men's did not. A built-in, and quite traditional, gender gap affected social life.

If marriage options had changed since the 1960s, so had expectations of motherhood. In 1981 the birth rate was 15.7 per thousand people compared with 18 in 1970 and 25.3 at the height of the baby boom in 1957. One census study in 1980 predicted a total fertility rate of 2.06 children per woman, under the 2.2 needed for a no-growth population birthrate. Even lower future birthrates were suggested by the responses of young single women, one-fifth of whom expected to have no children at all. If she had children, the young woman of the 1970s and after was likely to have them later than her mother had done. During the 1970s, fertility dropped precipitously among women in their early twenties, although it increased among women a decade older. At the start of the 1990s, some experts suggested that the birthrate had bottomed out and would shortly rise. Still, the era of the baby boom and "togetherness" seemed ancient history.

Women of the 1990s, however, were likely to be the primary caretakers of children, despite NOW's 1966 contention that child care should be "shared equally by fathers." During the 1970s and 1980s, to be sure, as women surged into the labor force, the fraction of married women who were full-time housewives fell from 30 to 15 percent of the adult female population. Men with families, meanwhile, spent increased hours at domestic tasks, including child care. Men's annual hours of household labor, economist Juliet B. Schor estimates, rose by 151, while women's fell. ("The more work women do for pay, the less they do without it.") By 1990, men did almost 60 percent as much domestic work as women. Still, women shouldered the bulk of home-care–child-care responsibilities. Similarly, they bore most of the burden of caring for the aged. Finally, they were increasingly likely to face these responsibilities alone. During the 1970s, when the women's movement had its greatest surge, the number of one-parent families doubled, and most such families were headed by women—divorced women, separated women, and unmarried women. Between 1970 and 1981, the number of families headed by never-married women increased four times over.

The rise of the female-headed family generated a "feminization" of poverty. In 1980, two-thirds of female-headed families received child welfare and two-thirds of the long-term poor were women. No doubt poverty had always been feminized, but its new visibility invited analysis. The rising failure rate of marriages and the low income of many women who were separated or divorced contributed to the "feminization" trend. Even more so did a massive rise in the number of babies born to unwed mothers, especially teenagers. During the 1970s, half of all out-of-wedlock births involved teenagers, and 16 percent of all births were to teenage women. If uneducated, unskilled, and unfinanced, the unwed mother was likely to turn to public support. The Aid to Families with Dependent Children (AFDC) program, which began as a temporary pension for mothers who were widowed or married to unemployed or disabled men, reflected the rise of the single mother and the female-headed household. Between 1955 and 1987, the number of women receiving AFDC benefits rose 600 percent. Among AFDC recipients in 1987, 52 percent were unwed mothers, compared with 31 percent in 1973. Among women entering the AFDC program for the first time, according to 1992 figures, 16 percent would be in it for less than a year, and 44 percent for six years or more.

The feminization of poverty was also disproportionately black, although the numbers of white unwed teenage mothers had increased at a faster rate. By the start of the 1980s, almost 55 percent of all black children were born out of wedlock, compared with 15 percent in 1940; 85 percent of black teenage mothers were unmarried; and 47 percent of black families were female-headed, compared with 8 percent in 1950. As the decade progressed, the trend continued. Among all women who had children in 1991, the Census Bureau reported, nearly one out of four and 57 percent of all black women were unmarried; two-thirds of teenage mothers and 90 percent of black teenage mothers were single. By the early 1990s, 26 percent of children under eighteen lived with a single parent, as did more than 60 percent of black children. According to Marian Wright Edelman, founder of the Children's Defense Fund, the high black illegitimacy rate "practically guarantees the poverty of the next generation of black children."

The escalating rate of black out-of-wedlock births and the rise of the female-headed household precipitated discussion of a "crisis" in the black family. Since Daniel P. Moynihan had warned of impending crisis in 1965, when only a quarter of black families were female-headed, fear of regenerating racism had stifled discussion of the issue. By the mid-1980s, discussion surfaced, both within the black community and at large. "With the exception of drugs and crime, the biggest crisis facing the black community today is the plight of the single mother," declared an article in *The Crisis*, an NAACP publication, in 1988. "Why are female-headed households multiplying now, when there is less discrimination and poverty than a couple of generations ago, when black family life was stronger?" asked Eleanor Holmes Norton, Georgetown law professor and former EEOC head, in a *New York Times* article in 1985.

Answers increasingly focused on dwindling numbers of eligible black men and rising unemployment among black men. An Urban League study in 1984 attributed the black family's problem to "steady attrition in the numbers of black men who can support a wife and children." The Labor Department confirmed that black male employment had steadily dropped from 74 percent in 1960 to 55 percent at the start of the 1980s. At an NAACP Civil Rights Institute in 1985, one panel revealed that among blacks aged twenty to twenty-four, there were only 45 eligible men for every 100 women, due to the impact of such factors as unemployment and incarceration. Among black men in the next age category, twenty-five to thirty-four, in 1987, only 39 percent were married and living with wives (as were 62 percent of white men, whose commitment to marriage had also fallen off). Women's responses to scarcity received less attention. "It is the news but no one with clout will explain it," wrote a journalism professor who regretted her daughter's dwindling options. "It is better to have no man than a no-good man," a Chicago divorcee told a reporter for *The Crisis*.

Several analysts sought long-term causes. "At the heart of the crisis lies the self-perpetuating culture of the ghetto," Eleanor Holmes Norton contended. "This destructive ethos began to surface 40 years ago with the appearance of permanent joblessness and the devaluation of working-class men." As the nation's postwar economy had helped to produce a black middle class, Norton concluded, it had also destroyed "the black working class and its family structure." The source of the black family crisis, she said, lay not with women and children, but "with working-class black men whose loss of function in the post–World War II economy has led directly to their loss of function in the family." In *The Truly Disadvantaged* (1987), scholar William Julius Wilson argued that deindustrialization of the American economy, which started in the early 1970s, and the movement of jobs to the suburbs left unskilled young men increasingly unemployable and undesirable as marriage prospects. The exodus of middle- and working-class blacks from the inner cities, meanwhile, left ghettos filled with the poor and unemployed, plagued by joblessness and lawlessness.

The scarcity of men, however, affected black communities beyond the inner city as well. Among educated black women, for instance, a marriage crisis loomed in proportions similar to that experienced by white college graduates a century earlier. By the end of the 1980s, studies reported, an educational gender gap emerged: Sixty percent of black college students were women (as opposed to about half of all students), and the numbers of black women exceeded black men in most forms of professional training. Black women, the American Council on Education predicted, would be better educated, have more prestigious jobs and higher incomes than black men, and hold more leadership positions. The president of the United Negro College Fund pointed out that there had always been more black women than men in college because there was more family pressure to save themselves from careers as maids. Joyce Ladner, sociology professor at Howard, said that the message of the educational gender gap for black women was "that the pool of eligible black men for them gets smaller and smaller the further they go up the educational and career ladder."

Since the start of the civil rights and feminist movements, many reports suggested, black women had made impressive and indeed disproportionate strides. In 1987, for instance, black women who completed college earned slightly more than white college-trained women; black college men, however, earned 78 percent of white men's incomes; among all workers that year, black median income was 57 percent that of whites. Black women held two-thirds of all professional jobs held by blacks (and white women 48 percent of white professional jobs). The proportion of black professionals that was female seemed destined to increase. The number of black men entering medical school, for instance, dropped 23 percent between 1971 and 1990, while the number of black women rose. As black women's vocational status rose, their likelihood of marriage fell. In 1987, only 48 percent of black professional women were married, compared with 62 percent of white professional women.

The gender gap among blacks—educational, vocational, social—might be viewed as an extension of trends that permeated relations between the sexes in the population at large. Illegitimacy, rising divorce, the female-headed family, and the scarcity of eligible men were not solely black developments. Social scientist Andrew Hacker, for instance, cited convergence of trends and experiences among blacks and whites. Still, black women's experiences after 1975 reflected circumstances that affected blacks in particular. One notable circumstance was the apparent split among blacks between an upwardly mobile middle class and a downtrodden urban "underclass," a term whose pervasive use itself incurred criticism.

Not surprisingly, black women sought a distinctive stance as feminists. "Black feminist thought," according to sociologist Patricia Collins, "sees three distinctive systems of oppression as being part of an overarching structure of domination . . . a system of interlocking race, class, and gender oppression." Nor was white feminism necessarily an appropriate model. "One of the problems with white feminism is that it is not a tradition that teaches white women that they are capable," author Alice Walker told a reporter in 1984. "Whereas my tradition *assumes* that I'm capable. . . . I have cleared fields, I have lifted whatever, I have *done* it." In the 1980s, Walker coined the term "Womanism" to represent black feminism. Womanism was "a word that is organic, that really comes out of the culture, that really expresses the spirit we see in black women," she said. "You know, the posture with the hand on the hip, 'Honey, don't you get in my way.'" Black feminist commentary reflected a growing emphasis on diversity. To consider women's status in the 1980s and 1990s meant paying attention to differences of race, class, and ethnicity—and in view of rising immigration since the 1960s, to the roles of women in the fastest-growing ethnic groups.

Immigration, Ethnicity, and Diversity

The new immigration that followed the Immigration Act of 1965 rapidly increased the numbers of foreign-born Americans, especially those of non-European origin. Between 1960 and 1990, 45 percent of immigrants came from the

Western Hemisphere and 30 percent from Asia. Several features marked the new immigration. First, women migrants outnumbered men, an uncommon pattern in recent international migration. In 1979, the sex ratio among adult migrants to the United States was 87 (87 men to every 100 women), and among those of certain groups, such as Filipinos, Koreans, and non-Communist Chinese, far lower. Second, immigrant women typically joined the labor force. Many single women came to the United States, as men had in the past, to seek employment; others, who arrived as family members, did the same. New York City demographers found that many women preceded their families because it was easier for them than for men to find work. Active labor force participation affected women's experience as immigrants and increased their importance in the economic life of their ethnic groups.

Working immigrant women were especially visible on the East and West Coasts, where they often congregated in distinct sectors according to ethnicity—many Filipino and Korean women, for instance, became medical personnel; Latin American, Mexican, and Asian women found jobs in the garment industry; and women from many nations took work in private households, thus expediting the exodus of other women to the job market. For some women, immigration entailed downward occupational mobility, as was the case for many white-collar workers from Cuba in the 1960s who took blue-collar jobs. Among Soviet emigrés of the 1970s and after, many former professionals faced similar downgrading. For most women, however, immigration provided vocational opportunity. A skilled nurse, for instance, might earn more by working one day with overtime in an American city than she would in a month in Manila. Trained or untrained, women immigrants expected better options, higher pay, and higher living standards than in their countries of origin.

Women's work roles were significant among the largest groups of newcomers, those of Hispanic and Asian descent. Each contingent, Hispanic and Asian, represented numerous nations; each encompassed its own diversity of class, education, and wealth. New arrivals in both groups often joined ethnic communities that had been established for decades or generations. In both cases, women might experience tension between their traditional roles in ethnic families and contemporary American women's roles, and often viewed their achievements as wage earners as contributions to the family economy.

Asian Americans, a rapidly expanding group, accounted for more than 40 percent of total immigrants since 1975. During the 1980s, the Asian American population grew by 80 percent. Arriving from China, Taiwan, Hong Kong, Vietnam, Cambodia, Japan, the Philippines, and South Korea, newcomers valued their specific national identities over their common Asian heritage. Disproportionately professional, Asian immigrants and their children proved upwardly mobile. Immigration law favored relatives of U.S. citizens and "persons with professional skills needed in the U.S. economy;" well trained in their countries of origin, many Asians arrived ready to compete for middle-class careers. Still, class distinctions provided varied experiences.

Japanese Americans, less affected than other groups by the new immigration, set a standard of economic achievement. By the 1990s, Japanese income exceeded the national per capita income, and women's occupations reflected the upward trend. Before the new immigration, women of Japanese origin had been employed mainly in craft, factory, and service jobs; in the 1970s and 1980s, their daughters became technicians, professionals, and managers. But not all new immigrants arrived prepared for upward mobility. Among Chinese immigrants, historian Ron Takaki shows, different class backgrounds led to the formation of a "bi-polar Chinese American community—a colonized working class and an entrepreneurial middle class." Nearly half of Chinese immigrants between 1966 and 1975, mainly newcomers from Taiwan and Hong Kong, had professional and technical occupations. But 80 percent of New York's Chinatown at the end of the 1980s—often immigrants from mainland China—were low-wage laborers, either service workers or factory workers. These included many women seamstresses in garment shops, whose experience resembled that of women garment workers at the turn of the century.

The "bi-polar" quality pervaded the new Asian immigrant community. Like the professionals from Taiwan and Hong Kong, many Asian American women arrived with extensive education. Among Filipino immigrants, who were predominantly female, for instance, 65 percent had professional and technical occupations. Overproduction of doctors and nurses in Korea also sent an influx of women professionals to the United States. Immigrants from Southeast Asia, less exposed to educational opportunities at home, fell into the lower-paid ranges of occupations. Still, as among other Asian immigrants, a high proportion of women entered the labor force. Among Vietnamese refugees in the late 1970s, one study suggests, 42 percent of women found work, compared with 64 percent of men. "Some women can get jobs in factories, and those with a high school education can go for vocational training," a resettlement worker among Southeast Asians explained. "So in many families, the woman has become the breadwinner. They not only make more money than the husband, they often have better jobs."

Asian American women's reflections on ethnic identity, typically written by second- or third-generation women of Chinese or Japanese origin, describe strong family traditions, intergenerational tension, and conflict between ethnic and American culture. In her memoir, *The Woman Warrior* (1976), Maxine Hong Kingston gives an example of cultural conflict from her American childhood. "Normal Chinese women's voices are strong and bossy," she wrote. "We American-Chinese girls had to whisper to make ourselves American-feminine." In a 1970s essay, Magoda Marayoma, a third-generation Japanese American from California, cited a contrary example. "My parents urged me, unconsciously I am sure, to perpetuate the stereotype of the quiet, polite, unassuming Asian," she wrote. "But survival in American society requires one to speak up vociferously to defend one's rights and gain recognition." Recognition of cultural differences, however, impeded neither ethnic pride nor upward mobility. Nor did it impede intermarriage, a trend first noted among Japanese American women and subsequently among other Asian American women. "In general in the American culture, if you're a professional Asian woman . . . you're extremely acceptable," a third-generation Korean American woman from Hawaii commented. "In fact,

I think it has become fashionable for white men to marry Asian women. Chinese American women married to white men are really pervasive. You don't see the reverse as much . . . for Asian men, it is more difficult."

Americans of Hispanic origin, the fastest-growing ethnic group, similarly encompassed people of varied nations and backgrounds. In 1960, before the new immigration, 85 percent were American-born; some traced their American ancestry back to the seventeenth century. By the end of the 1980s, however, over half of Hispanic Americans were foreign-born or children of immigrants. As immigration from the Western Hemisphere grew, so did the proportion of women among migrants. Among entrants from Mexico, men had traditionally predominated; by the early 1990s, half of Mexican immigrants who settled in the United States were women. Many families headed by women arrived from Mexico as well as from war-torn Central American or Latin American countries. Spanish-speaking Americans usually followed the assimilation patterns of other immigrant groups. However, 20 percent of Mexicans and 30 percent of Puerto Ricans remained below the poverty line. At the end of the 1980s, 74 percent of Hispanic families were two-parent families, as were 80 percent of white families. Out-of-wedlock births constituted 29 percent of Hispanic births, compared with 17 percent of white births and 62 percent of black births.

Hispanic women's work roles might reflect their immigrant status. A study of Mexican women migrants in Los Angeles County in the early 1980s shows that undocumented women found work in factories, restaurants, and private homes; legal immigrants were more likely to take white-collar jobs in offices and public institutions. The higher women's skills and knowledge of English, the more easily they could transfer their skills to the new economy. Their attitudes toward work might reflect both class differences and a tradition of male domination, as seen in Yolanda Prieto's study of Cuban women in New Jersey. Among these immigrants of the 1960s, mainly middle class, over half of women joined the work force. Although they considered work necessary for family mobility, they voiced other motives as well. "I work to help my family," one woman stated, "But besides that I couldn't stand the loneliness if I stayed home." One university graduate, formerly a professor in Cuba and now a teacher, merged her work role with her traditional family role:

I have always been very independent, that is why I have always worked. . . . I am so used to having my job that I want to continue working. Of course, I think that a woman should *never compete* with her husband. Women's role is fundamentally the family. But if a woman is intelligent and knows how to combine work and family she shouldn't have any problems.

Sociologist Norma Williams, who studied second- and third-generation Mexican American families in Austin and Corpus Christi, Texas, in the 1980s, elicited similar responses from "professional-class" working women. Although male domination was "modified" among her urban respondents, she notes, it persisted, and women had to deal with it. One way for women to minimize the role strain between demands of job and family, Williams notes, was "to 'compartmentalize' their lives and give priority to motherhood over their careers." One respondent, for instance, "reshaped her role to minimize conflict with her husband and the threat to his identity":

I started to work and get involved with civic issues. His pride began to show, and we started to argue. I guess he was jealous because I really enjoy my work. It wasn't easy for me, and I don't want you to think that it was.

Williams cites a difference, however, between women in professional families and those in working-class families. Professional-class women were likely to take an "independent" identity for granted, whereas working-class women sought it. Although both groups saw themselves as "twice a minority," Williams concludes, socioeconomic status affected their attitudes. "Working class women conceive of ethnicity as a more compelling issue than gender; professional women typically perceive gender issues as more salient than ethnicity."

Do gender issues become more salient for most women as social class rises? Significantly, Williams challenges assumptions of hegemony, specifically "the assimilationist model that has been so prevalent among social scientists." Noting that "generalizations about family life and women's gender roles have often been based on the white middle class" and that "the assimilationist world view looks on the social order from the top down," she observes that "certain role-making patterns among Mexican-American working-class and professional women do not conform to those in the privileged sector of Anglo society." Do women share commonalities that transcend ethnic boundaries? Williams, uncertain, concludes that "differences between privileged Anglo women and women of color may be greater than the similarities."

The attitude of new immigrants and other ethnic Americans to diversity was complex. Most new immigrants looked forward to assimilation and upward mobility. As a result, they had less impulse to define themselves as oppressed minorities than did native-born blacks, and less affinity to the 1960s mode of political pressure that spawned the civil rights movement and the women's movement. Women of ethnic groups also faced particular tensions. In a recent book on women immigrants, historian Maxine Seller points to "apparent contradictions between the traditional, submissive sex roles dictated by their ethnic cultures, and the assertive, egalitarian behavior dictated by the women's movement." Many felt "that their first loyalty should be to their ethnic group." Current research suggests that generalizations about women's roles may be subject to class and ethnic variations and need to be qualified. Generalizations about women in politics have recently demanded revision as well.

The Gender Gap

In the early 1980s, an unexpected trend developed. A "women's vote" had appeared—or at least a "gender gap" in political views, as revealed in election data and political polls. And as suffragists had once contended, the "women's vote" seemed to be a reform-minded vote that defied conservative trends in national politics. According to the polls, more women than men opposed Republican policies, high unemployment, ending federal support for human services, and large expenditures on nuclear weapons.

Until the late 1970s, polls showed that political opinions were undifferentiated by sex except on questions involving the use of force, which women tended to oppose more than men. In the 1980 presidential election, however, differences began to appear. Women provided far larger proportions of the vote for Democrat Jimmy Carter (58 percent), who lost the election, than of the vote for victor Ronald Reagan (49 percent). Moreover, as subsequent polls confirmed, women, who now voted for the first time in the same proportion as men, differed from men on major issues. In mid-1982, polls showed that greater proportions of women than men favored Democratic policies on employment, inflation control, and avoiding war. Curiously, there were no significant differences of view on the major women's issues, the ERA and abortion; indeed, men were slightly more favorable to both. The new gender gap on economic and military issues emerged again in 1982 election races and 1983 opinion polls, when almost one-third more men than women approved President Reagan's performance in office. Among Republicans alone, a similar trend emerged: Eighty-six percent of men and only 62 percent of women supported the President for a second term.

Significantly, wage-earning women contributed more to the gender gap than women who were not employed. According to some analysts, women's precarious vocational status and concentration in lower-income jobs were major determinants of their political values. Since women under forty-five, who were rapidly entering the labor force, now voted in higher proportions than men, the gender gap could be expected to continue and increase.

In 1984 Democrats sought to capitalize on the new development. Democratic presidential nominee Walter Mondale chose New York representative Geraldine Ferraro as his running mate at the 1984 convention. Describing herself as a "housewife from Queens," Ferraro had spent three terms in Congress and had headed the 1984 Democratic Platform committee. Several circumstances led to her candidacy. First, there were no self-evident competing choices for the nomination. Second, NOW applied pressure by threatening withdrawal of support for the Democrats if a woman were not chosen. Third, as Betty Friedan suggested, selecting a woman represented a commitment to expansion of opportunity for all, a theme that the Democrats wished to emphasize. Fourth, among the possible women candidates, Ferraro seemed the most promising because of her potential appeal to an ethnic, working-class vote, as well as to other traditional Democrats. The daughter of Italian immigrants, Ferraro had worked her way up in the world as a teacher, lawyer, and public prosecutor. Finally, the Mondale camp felt the need of a bold, unconventional step, both to energize the campaign and to prove that the candidate could take strong, decisive action.

Ferraro's nomination generated widespread excitement, drew an outpouring of volunteers, and represented a triumph to feminists. Republicans criticized the nomination as tokenism. "I would like it better if she were a candidate, and not a woman candidate," said former senator Margaret Chase Smith of Maine,

New York Representative Geraldine Ferraro, just selected as the Democratic nominee for Vice President, and presidential candidate Walter Mondale greet crowds in July 1984. *(AP/Wide World Photos)*

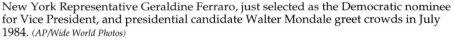

the first woman to serve in both houses of Congress, when interviewed in retirement. "Now, I was never a woman candidate." As soon as the campaign began, a furor erupted over whether Ferraro would reveal all of her family finances beyond the income tax statements required by law. To do so, as the press demanded, meant exposure not only of her own finances but those of her husband, a possible source of irregularities (as later turned out to be the case). No comparable concern over a spouse's finances had arisen before a woman ran for Vice President. Ferraro finally released the information that the press demanded, handled the situation with poise, and won applause. But the controversy jarred the Democratic campaign.

On election day, the gender gap seemed to have all but vanished. President Reagan, who won 59 percent of the popular vote, garnered 57 percent of the women's vote as opposed to 42 percent for Mondale. (The men's vote was 61 percent for Reagan to 37 percent for Mondale.) All nine women challengers for Senate seats lost, as did thirty-nine of forty-one women challengers for House seats. "I think we can consider the gender gap closed," said Reagan's new Secretary of Transportation, Elizabeth Dole. Recriminations abounded in the Democratic camp. "The party got a gun put to its head . . . to choose a woman for Vice President," a Mondale staffer told the press. "They didn't bring in anything. Women vote for President just like men do." Feminists were "remote from the women's vote," a top Democratic consultant charged. "These people can't deliver their sisters." With an eighteen-point chasm between the candidates, Democratic women pointed out, the gender gap could not be expected to provide a victory. "We didn't invent defeat," said Ann Lewis, political director of the Democratic National Committee. "White men have been losing elections for years." Defeating Reagan at the height of his popularity, Ferraro later said, "would have required God on the ticket."

In the wake of the election, feminists considered Ferraro's liabilities. "We should try to choose someone who already has a national image," said Gloria Steinem. Some Democratic strategists resented the influence of feminists and women's groups. "We can't afford to have a party so feminized that it has no appeal to men," said a leading Democratic consultant. "I am the first to admit that were I not a woman, I would not have been the Vice Presidential nominee," Ferraro wrote four years later. "Cynics will say it was strictly a political move playing to the gender gap. I agree. But . . . I can say it was equally important to [Mondale] to right a wrong; he removed gender as a disqualification for national office."

The gender gap survived 1984 and played a major role in 1986, when women's votes enabled Democrats to recapture a majority of Senate seats after six years of Republican control. In seven states, where a majority of men supported the Republicans, only the Democratic women's vote ensured victory. In two other states, where men were equally divided, women again provided the margin of victory. Women were now over half of voters. In a 1987 article, analysts suggested that peace was the crucial women's issue: Compared to men, women were more opposed to military involvement, military spending, capital punishment, and nuclear power, and more supportive of arms control and gun control. One pundit noted that the ideal Republican candidate would be a woman and the ideal Democratic candidate a general.

As the 1988 presidential campaign began, Republicans felt free to ignore the gender gap, while Democrats muted their appeal to the women's vote. Instead of stressing equality issues—the ERA, pay equity, abortion rights—they mentioned less divisive issues: day care, education, jobs, and health care. Much of the women's political lobby in the 1980s, similarly, shifted its emphasis from equity issues to women's economic and family issues. Such issues would "reach women across a broad range of classes," a poll taker said, and "not seem to address women at the expense of men." Tactical changes, however, reflected continued concern with women voters. Women assumed high posts on political staffs, which Ann Lewis termed "the last locker room." Most prominent was law professor Susan Estrich, campaign manager for Democrat Michael Dukakis. "Virtually every issue in this campaign is a woman's issue," Estrich declared. Candidates also shifted some scheduled speaking stops from factories and construction sites to hospitals and banks, where many women worked. Although a gender gap persisted, George Bush defeated Michael Dukakis, with 53 percent of the popular vote.

As evidence about a gender gap accumulated, women who ran for elective office made major strides, especially on the local level. By the mid-1980s, 15 percent of state and local officials were women. In 1991, 1,359 women (18.2

percent) served in state legislatures, compared with 362 (4.8 percent) in 1971. The number of women mayors in cities over 30,000 rose to 151 (17.1 percent) in 1991, compared with 7 (1.1 percent) twenty years earlier. Bipartisan women's fund-raising groups, such as the Women's Campaign Fund and the National Women's Political Caucus, aided women candidates, as did EMILY's List ("Early Money is like Yeast"), which supported pro-choice Democratic women candidates in the early stages of their campaigns. As the 1990s began, a new question arose: Would a rising number of women candidates and the gender gap in women's voting patterns converge?

The Year of the Woman

When the nation watched the Thomas/Hill hearings in 1991, many women complained that there were no women on the Judiciary Committee and only two in the Senate: Nancy Kassebaum of Kansas, a member of the pro-choice faction of Republican women, and Democrat Barbara Mikulski of Maryland, a longtime women's rights advocate who had been elected in the Democratic sweep of 1986. Angered by the treatment of Anita Hill in the Thomas hearings, a record number of women decided to run for office in 1992. In Illinois, Carol Moseley Braun, a black lawyer with a local political job, captured the Democratic senatorial nomination from Alan Dixon, a two-term incumbent who had voted to confirm Clarence Thomas. In Pennsylvania, Democrat Lynn Yeakel challenged Republican Senator Arlen Specter, who had led the interrogation of Anita Hill in the committee hearings. "If it hadn't been for those hearings," Yeakel announced, "it would never have occurred to me to run." In California, candidates in Senate races cited Anita Hill's experience. "The sense of rage I felt as I watched what they did to Anita Hill has not subsided with the passage of time," wrote former San Francisco Mayor Dianne Feinstein in a fund-raising letter. Five-term Representative Barbara Boxer, who had joined women colleagues to demand a delay in the Senate vote on the Thomas nomination, also recalled the Senate hearings. "If there had been only one woman on the Judiciary Committee," Boxer declared, "things would have been different."

By the spring of 1992, twice as many women had entered contests for congressional seats as had done so in 1990. Women's political fund-raising groups reported that since the Thomas hearings, contributions had doubled over those of two years earlier and support had surged. By the summer of 1992, EMILY's List membership had leapt from 3,000 before the hearings to 15,000. Eighteen women, mainly Democrats, now contended for Senate seats, and over 150 women, 95 Democrats and 59 Republicans, for House seats. The Thomas-Hill hearings and the performance of the Judiciary Committee, wrote columnist Elizabeth Drew, turned out to have been "radicalizing events that galvanized women to run for office."

Public opinion polls suggested that women candidates had special advantages. They were expected to benefit from an antiincumbent mood among voters, a surge of favor for political "outsiders," the thawing of the Cold War, and the consequent emphasis on domestic policy. They were also expected to gain from redistricting, retirement, scandals involving officeholders, and stereotypes that worked in their favor. According to the polls, voters viewed women candidates as more honest, moral, and responsive to constituents; they would be more likely than men to attend to health care, family issues, and education, and more apt to conduct public business in public rather than in secret. In instances when women failed to meet such high expectations, said the polls, public judgment would be harsher. Still, the increase of women candidates and the support they aroused led the press to proclaim 1992 the "Year of the Woman."

Women's roles also rose into view as a campaign issue. One point in dispute was the woman careerist. Women were "tired of hearing that they have to have careers," said a Republican campaign official, "and if they give them up they're somehow not as good." At the party convention, the wives of the nominees, Barbara Bush and Marilyn Quayle, spoke on "family values." Marilyn Quayle said that Democrats denigrated women who preferred to stay home. "Most women do not want to be liberated from their essential natures as women," she told the delegates. Republican strategists targeted Hillary Clinton, wife of the Democratic nominee, as a liability. A corporate lawyer in Little Rock, Hillary Rodham Clinton had long been active in public life. She had proposed educational reforms in Arkansas, worked on the Children's Defense Fund, and led the American Bar Association's commission on women. Under media scrutiny, Hillary Clinton modified her campaign style. The Democratic nominee sought the votes of working women. Bill Clinton presented himself as "the grandson of a working woman, the son of a single mother, the husband of a working wife," and told the voters, "I have learned that building up women does not diminish men." The campaign, wrote columnist Anna Quindlen, showed "how we feel about smart women, professional women, new women."

To what extent did such feelings affect the election results? A three-way race, the 1992 presidential election was the first in which suburbanites and babyboomers constituted a majority of voters. So did women, now 54 percent of the electorate. Since 1988, their numbers had risen 13 percent, while men's rose only 4 percent. Clinton won 41 percent of white women voters (and 37 percent of men) and 86 percent of black women voters (compared with 77 percent of men). Women candidates, who attracted increased funding, notably from women's political fund-raising groups, profited from a predicted rise in support. During the campaign, surveys showed that if all other factors were equal, both major political parties were more competitive by six to eight percentage points when they chose women candidates. The number of women doubled in the House, tripled in the Senate, and rose in state and local office.

Forty-seven women won House seats, compared with 28 in 1988. Few were true "outsiders": Three out of five new members had experience in local government or state legislatures. Among the six women senators were four Democratic newcomers: Braun, Feinstein, Boxer, and Patty Murray of Washington. Feinstein and Braun quickly won seats on the Judiciary Committee. The new administration appointed a record number of women to Cabinet posts and high-level advisory offices, thereby setting a standard to be matched by future administrations. It also resolved some longstanding issues. Within a few weeks of assuming office, the President signed a family leave bill, removed the ban on importing RU-486, and ended a gag rule on publicly-financed clinics to make information on abortion available. In June 1993, after Justice Byron White's retirement, Clinton named to the Supreme Court federal judge Ruth Bader Ginsburg, who had argued landmark sexual equality cases in the 1970s. A generation after the start of a new women's movement, the "women's vote" seemed to carry political weight.

The "Year of the Woman" also had a subplot, one that surfaced at intervals throughout the presidential campaign. Women's rise in the political polls accompanied a rise in attention to sexual harassment. In September 1992, the EEOC reported a 50 percent surge in harassment complaints since the Thomas-Hill hearings. Reported incidents of harassment filled the press: Assaults on women at a convention of the Tailhook Association, a group of naval aviators, led to the resignation of the Secretary of the Navy and the reassignment of an admiral; a series of sexual harassment accusations descended upon public officials, including two senators; a professor of neurosurgery at Stanford resigned to protest decades of harassment and sexism in academic medicine. Anita Hill's allegations seemed to have unleashed a torrent of complaints. Indeed, a new rash of books explained exactly how to file such complaints.

Meanwhile, "sensitivity" became the catchword of response. Several Republican senators, who had either implied disbelief of Anita Hill or ignored her allegations, commented on a national rise in "awareness" about sexual harassment and heightened "sensitivity" to it. Women executives demanded sensitivity training for their colleagues. Employers, now liable for damages of up to $300,000 to victims of job discrimination, including sexual harassment, under the Civil Rights Act of 1991, began to hire such sensitivity trainers. Network television raised viewer sensitivity by explaining the hazards of a "hostile environment" in the workplace. Finally, a year after the hearings, Anita Hill's credibility seemed to ascend in the public opinion polls; half or more of respondents now found her allegations truthful. Among women voters, surveys revealed, even those who didn't necessarily believe Anita Hill voiced dismay at her treatment by members of the Judiciary Committee. Among supporters, Hill became a champion of women's rights. During the presidential campaign, in a speech before a meeting of the American Bar Association, at which Hill appeared, Hillary Clinton declared that "All women who care about equality of opportunity, about integrity in the workplace, are in Anita Hill's debt."

At her infrequent public appearances, Anita Hill returned to aspects of her experience before the Judiciary Committee, including the personal costs, the outpouring of support she had aroused, and the contention that sexual harassment was an act of power. In a paper at the Georgetown Law Center a year after the hearings, Hill introduced another aspect of her experience: Her predicament as an outsider, whose message eluded comprehension. "Not only did the Senate fail to understand or to recognize me because of lack of attachment to certain institutions, like marriage and patronage," she contended, "they failed to relate to my race, my gender, my race and gender combined, and in combination with my race, my career choice, and my demeanor."

In her roles as career woman, complainant, and "outsider," and in her analysis of her experience, Anita Hill reflected themes that pervaded both the electoral campaign and contemporary women's issues. A major theme was empowerment. The theme of empowerment had emerged in many issues of the past decade—from glass ceilings and wage equity to reproductive rights and pornography. It emerged again when Hill testified before the Judiciary Committee. The controversy over the Thomas hearings "wasn't about her or him," Senator Biden told a columnist during the campaign. "It was about a fundamental issue of power: The way women are treated." The theme of empowerment emerged yet again, in the wake of the hearings, in the rise of attention to harassment in the workplace, and again in the campaign, when resentment against the all-male Judiciary Committee gained force and the numbers of women candidates surged. In the end, the "Year of the Woman" raised new questions about women, politics, and empowerment. What confluence of factors had fostered the unparalleled success of women's political fund-raising organizations and of women candidates? How would women's gains as officeholders change the lives of women constituents? To what extent would women's issues and the feminist agenda affect public policy?

For more than a decade, historian Elizabeth Fox Genovese contends, contemporary feminism had wrestled with contradictions. "For some, feminism necessarily means the promotion of equality between women and men; for others, it just as necessarily means the celebration of differences between women and men." This tension, she points out, had pervaded feminism since its origins. Women politicians of the 1990s often capitalized on one or the other strands of the feminist debate. In some instances, they contended that they filled the same roles as men. As Nancy Kassebaum explained before the Senate vote on Clarence Thomas, she rejected the suggestion that she "vote not as a Senator but as a woman." In other instances, they cited the theme of difference. Men could not "hear with a woman's ear or process information through a woman's experience," said Governor Ann Richards of Texas. "We pick up different nuances and bring valuable skills to the process." As the twentieth century entered its last decade, it seemed likely that tensions inherent in feminism and conflict over women's rights and roles would remain prominent features of political debate and public life.

❧

SUGGESTED READINGS AND SOURCES

CHAPTER 21

Anita Hill's appearance before the Senate Judiciary Committee in October 1991 was widely covered in national newspapers and magazines. I have used the *New York Times* coverage of the Thomas hearings, and special issues of publications that devoted extensive attention to the hearings, such as *The Wall Street Journal* (October 18, 1991) and *Time* (October 28, 1991). Among the *New York Times* sources cited, Rosemary Bray's article, "Taking Sides Against Ourselves," appeared in the *New York Times Magazine,* November 17, 1991, 56ff; Orlando Patterson's op-ed piece appeared on October 20, 1991; William

Broyles, Jr.'s op-ed piece appeared on October 16, 1991; Felicity Barringer's article appeared on October 18, 1991; and Anna Quindlen's column appeared on the op-ed page on October 16, 1991. For black responses to the Thomas hearings and Anita Hill, see "A House Divided," *Essence* 22 (January 1992), 58–59ff., and *The Black Scholar* 22 (Winter–Spring 1992). For Catharine MacKinnon, see MacKinnon, *Sexual Harassment of Working Women: A Case Study of Discrimination* (New Haven, Conn., 1979), and Fred Strebeigh, "Defining Law on the Feminist Frontier," *New York Times Magazine* (October 6, 1991), pp. 28 ff. For a televised debate on sexual harassment at the time of the Thomas hearings, see the "MacNeil-Lehrer Report," October 9, 1991.

Recent books on the Thomas hearings include Timothy M. Phelps and Helen Winternitz, *Capitol Games: Clarence Thomas, Anita Hill, and the Story of a Supreme Court Nomination* (New York, 1992); Paul Simon, *Advice and Consent: Clarence Thomas, Robert Bork, and the Intriguing History of the Supreme Court's Nomination Battles* (Washington, D. C., 1992); Toni Morrison, ed., *Race-ing Justice, En-gendering Power: Essays on Anita Hill, Clarence Thomas, and the Construction of Social Reality* (New York, 1992); and Robert Chrisman and Robert L. Allen, eds., *Court of Appeal: The Black Community Speaks Out on the Racial and Sexual Politics of Clarence Thomas vs. Anita Hill* (New York, 1992). Controversy over the Hill–Thomas episode continues. In *The Real Anita Hill: The Untold Story* (New York, 1993), journalist David Brock challenges Anita Hill's credibility. Journalists Jane Mayer and Jill Abramson, authors of a forthcoming book on the same subject, challenge Brock's credibility in "The Surreal Anita Hill," *The New Yorker* 69 (May 24, 1993), 90–97.

Chapter 22

For surveys of recent women's history, see William H. Chafe, *The Paradox of Change: American Women in the 20th Century* (New York, 1991), ch. 12, and Rosalind Rosenberg, *Divided Lives: American Women in the 20th Century* (New York, 1992), ch. 7.

Significant recent books on feminism include Betty Freidan, *The Second Stage* (New York, 1982); Sylvia Ann Hewlett, *A Lesser Life: The Myth of Women's Liberation in America* (New York, 1986); Elizabeth Fox-Genovese, *Feminism Without Illusions: A Critique of Individualism* (Chapel Hill, N. C., 1991); Naomi Wolf, *The Beauty Myth* (New York, 1991); Susan Faludi, *Backlash: The Undeclared War Against American Women* (New York, 1991); and Carol Tavris, *The Mismeasure of Woman* (New York, 1992). Discussions of feminist ideas include Hester Eisenstein, *Contemporary Feminist Thought* (Boston, 1983); Elizabeth V. Spelman, *Inessential Women: Problems of Exclusion in Feminist Thought* (Boston, 1989); and Jean Bethke Elshtain, *Power Trips and Other Journeys: Essays in Feminism as Civic Discourse* (Madison, Wisc., 1990). For feminism in the early 1980s, see Benjamin R. Barber, "Beyond the Feminine Mystique," *New Republic,* 189 (July 11, 1983), 26–32; Susan Bolotin, "Voices from the Post-Feminist Generation," *New York Times Magazine,* October 11, 1982, p. 28ff; Sarah Stage, "Women," *American Quarterly,* 35 (Spring/Summer 1983), 169–190; and Jean Elshtain, "Feminism, Family, and Community," *Dissent* 29 (Fall 1982), 442–449. Betty Friedan comments on feminist history at intervals in *New York Times Magazine* articles, including "Feminism Takes a New Turn," November 18, 1979; "Twenty Years After the Feminine Mystique," February 27, 1983; and "How to Get the Women's Movement Moving Again," November 3, 1985. Vivian Gornick reflects on the 1960s generation of feminists in "Who Says We Haven't Made a Revolution: A Feminist Takes Stock," *New York Times Magazine,* April 15, 1990.

For women's opposition to feminism, see Phyllis Schlafly, *The Power of the Positive Woman* (New York, 1978); Andrea Dworkin, *Right Wing Women* (New York, 1983); Susan Harding, "Family Reform Movements: Recent Feminism and Its Opposition," *Feminist*

Studies, 7 (Spring 1981), 57–75; Linda Gordon and Allen Hunter, "Sex, Family, and the New Left: Anti-Feminism as a Political Force," *Radical America,* 11 (November 1977–February 1988), 9–25; and Rebecca Klatch, *Women of the New Right* (Philadelphia, 1987). For the ERA, see Jane J. Mansbridge, *Why We Lost the ERA* (Chicago, 1986); Mary Frances Berry, *Why ERA Failed: Politics, Women's Rights, and the Amending Process of the Constitution* (Bloomington, Ind., 1986); Joan Hoff-Wilson, ed., *Rights of Passage: The Past and Future of the ERA* (Bloomington, Ind., 1986); and Donald G. Mathews and Jane Sherron De Hart, *Sex, Gender, and the Politics of ERA: A State and the Nation* (New York, 1990), which focuses on the conflict over ERA in North Carolina. For the abortion controversy, see Kristin Luker, *Abortion and the Politics of Motherhood* (Berkeley, Calif., 1984), and Faye D. Ginsburg, *Contested Lives: The Abortion Debate in an American Community* (Berkeley, Calif., 1989).

For feminist discussions of sexuality, see Christine Stansell, Ann Snitow, et al., *Powers of Desire: The Politics of Sexuality* (New York, 1983). Positions on the pornography issue are presented in Laura Lederer, ed., *Take Back the Night: Women on Pornography* (New York, 1980); Susan Griffeth, *Pornography and Silence: Culture's Revenge Against Nature* (New York, 1981); Linda Williams, *Hard Core: Power, Pleasure, and the "Frenzy of the Visible"* (Berkeley, Calif., 1989); and Dorchen Leidholdt and Janice G. Raymond, eds., *The Sexual Liberals and the Attack on Feminism* (New York, 1990). Joan Hoff discusses the pornography controversy and other contemporary legal issues in *Law, Gender, and Injustice: A Legal History of U.S. Women* (New York, 1991). Recent studies that convey the theme of sexual difference include Carol Gilligan, *In a Different Voice: Women's Conception of the Self and Morality* (New York, 1982); Carroll Smith-Rosenberg, *Disorderly Conduct: Visions of Gender in Victorian America* (New York, 1985); Suzanne Gordon, *Prisoners of Men's Dreams* (Boston, 1991); and Deborah Tannen, *You Just Don't Understand* (New York, 1990). Catharine MacKinnon's books are *Sexual Harassment of Working Women,* cited above; *Towards a Feminist Theory of the State* (New York, 1989); and *Feminism Unmodified: Discourses on Life and Law* (Cambridge, Mass., 1987).

For recent issues in women's education, see Mirra Komarovsky, *Women in College: Shaping New Feminine Identities* (New York, 1985); Nadya Aisenberg and Mona Harrington, *Women of Academe: Outsiders in the Sacred Grove* (Amherst, Mass., 1988); Elizabeth Minnich, Jean O'Barr, and Rachel Rosenfeld, eds., *Reconstructing the Academy: Women's Education and Women's Studies* (Chicago, 1988); and Dorothy Holland and Margaret A. Eisenhart, *Educated in Romance: Women, Achievement, and College Culture* (Chicago, 1990). The link between single-sex colleges and female achievement is discussed in M. Elizabeth Tindall, "Perspectives on Academic Women and Affirmative Action," *Educational Record,* 54 (Spring 1973), 130–135, and Joy K. Rice and Annette Hemmigs, "Women's Colleges and Women Achievers: An Update," *Signs,* 13 (Spring 1988), 546–559. For the contemporary debate on coeducation, see David Tyack and Elisabeth Hansot, *Learning Together: A History of Coeducation in American Public Schools* (New York, 1992), ch. 9.

Victor Fuchs examines the development of the female work force since the 1960s in *Women's Quest for Equality* (Cambridge, Mass., 1988). Sylvia Ann Hewlett explores the conflict between career and child rearing in *A Lesser Life,* cited above. Andrew Hacker surveys recent issues connected with female employment in "Women vs. Men in the Work Force," *New York Times Magazine,* December 9, 1984, pp. 124ff, and "Women at Work," *New York Review of Books,* (August 14, 1986), 26–32. Felice Schwartz's controversial proposal, "Management Women and the New Facts of Life," appeared in the *Harvard Business Review* 67 (January–February 1989), 65–82. For a defense of the proposal, see Felice N. Schwartz with Jean Zimmerman, *Breaking With Tradition: Women and Work, The New Facts of Life* (New York, 1992). For the *Johnson v. Santa Clara County* case of 1987, see Melvin I. Urofsky, *A Conflict of Rights: The Supreme Court and Affirmative Action* (New York, 1991).

Other important court cases of the 1980s include *California Savings and Loan* v. *Guerra*, 758 F.2nd 390, and *Equal Employment Opportunity Commission* v. *Sears, Roebuck, & Co.*, 628 F.Supp. 1286. For the Sears case, see Alice Kessler-Harris, "EEOC v. Sears, Roebuck & Co.: A Personal Account," *Radical History Review*, 35 (Spring 1986), and Thomas Haskell and Sanford Levinson, "Academic Freedom and Expert Witnessing: Historians and the Sears Case," *Texas Law Review*, 66 (1989), 1629–1659.

Anita Shreve discusses "The Working Mother as Role Model," in the *New York Times Magazine* (September 9, 1984), pp. 39ff. For the impact of pay equity, see Paul Weiler, "The Wages of Sex: The Uses and Limits of Comparable Worth," *Harvard Law Review* 99 (June 1986), 1728–1807; Sara M. Evans and Barbara J. Nelson, *Wage Justice: Comparable Worth and the Paradox of Technocratic Reform* (Chicago, 1989), a study of Minnesota employees; and Linda M. Blum, *Between Feminism and Labor: The Significance of the Comparable Worth Movement* (Berkeley, Calif., 1991). Recent studies of women at work include Kathleen Gerson, *Hard Choices: How Women Decide About Work, Career, and Motherhood* (Berkeley, Calif., 1985); Aileen Jacobson, *Women in Charge: Dilemmas of Women in Authority* (New York, 1985); Rosanna Hertz, *More Equal Than Others: Women and Men in Dual Career Marriages* (Berkeley, Calif., 1986); Sarah Hardesty and Nehama Jacobs, *Success and Betrayal: The Crisis of Women in Corporate America* (New York, 1986); Arlie Hochschild, *The Second Shift: Working Parents and the Revolution at Home* (New York, 1989); and Lise Vogel, *Mothers on the Job* (New Brunswick, 1993). For women's roles in the armed services, see Helen Bogan, *Mixed Company: Women in the Modern Army* (Boston, 1981), and Judith Hicks Stiehm, *Arms and the Enlisted Woman* (Philadelphia, 1989). Useful surveys of women's work roles include Ruth Milkman, ed., *Women, Work, and Protest: A Century of U.S. Women's Labor History* (New York, 1985), and Claudia Goldin, *Understanding the Gender Gap: An Economic History of American Women* (New York, 1990). Juliet B. Schor offers insights on the past two decades of economic change in *The Overworked American: The Unexpected Decline of Leisure* (New York, 1991).

For discussions of the contemporary family, see Mary Jo Bane, *Here to Stay: Families in the Twentieth Century* (New York, 1976); Christopher Lasch, *Haven in a Heartless World* (New York, 1979); Brigette Berger and Peter L. Berger, *The War Over the Family: Capturing the Middle Ground* (New York, 1983); Andrew Hacker, "Farewell to the Family?" *New York Review of Books*, 29 (March 18, 1982), 37–44; Philip Blumstein and Pepper Schwartz, *American Couples: Money, Work, Sex* (New York, 1983); and Anne Taylor Fleming, "The American Wife," *New York Times Magazine*, October 26, 1986, pp. 28ff. Barbara Katz Rothman discusses medical, legal, and social issues in *Recreating Motherhood: Ideology and Technology in a Patriarchal Society* (New York, 1989). Leonore J. Weitzman assesses the impact of no-fault divorce in *The Divorce Revolution: The Unexpected Social and Economic Consequences for Women and Children in America* (New York, 1985). For a critique of Weitzman's thesis, see Susan Faludi, *Backlash,* cited above, pp. 19–25.

For the feminization of poverty, see Ken Auletta, *The Underclass* (New York, 1982), and Ruth Sidel, *Women and Children Last: The Plight of Poor Women in Affluent America* (New York, 1986). A follow-up to the Moynihan Report of 1965 is Daniel Patrick Moynihan, *Family and Nation: The Godkin Lectures, Harvard University* (New York, 1986). Discussions of changes in black family life include Norman Riley, "Single Motherhood," *The Crisis* (November 1988), 18–22ff., and Eleanor Holmes Norton, "Restoring the Black Family," *New York Times Magazine,* June 2, 1985, 43ff. Recent discussions of race with attention to women's changing roles include Andrew Hacker, *Two Nations: Black and White, Separate, Hostile, Unequal* (New York, 1992), and Christopher Jencks, *Rethinking Social Policy: Race, Poverty, and the Underclass* (Cambridge, Mass., 1992). For the perspective of black feminists, see Bell Hooks, *Ain't I a Women: Black Women and Feminism* (Boston, 1981), and *Talking*

Back: *Thinking Feminist, Thinking Black* (Boston, 1989); Patricia Collins, *Black Feminist Thought: Knowledge, Consciousness, and the Politics of Empowerment* (Boston, 1990); Alice Walker, *In Search of Our Mothers' Gardens* (San Diego, Calif., 1983); and the novels of Alice Walker, notably *The Color Purple* (New York, 1982). For women's relation to the welfare state, see Linda Gordon, ed., *Women, the State, and Welfare* (Madison, Wis., 1990).

Women's experience as immigrants in the 1970s and 1980s is discussed in "Women in Migration," a special issue of *International Migration Review,* 18 (Winter 1984); a special issue of *Migration World,* 14(1/2) (1986); Rita James Simon and Caroline Betrell, *International Migration: The Female Experience* (Totowa, N.J., 1986); and Maxine Schwartz Seller, ed., *Immigrant Women* (Philadelphia, 1981), which includes useful introductions and bibliography. For the impact of ethnic diversity on women's history, see Ellen Carol Dubois and Vicki L. Ruiz, eds., *Unequal Sisters: A Multicultural Reader* (New York, 1990). Recent considerations of immigration and ethnicity include David Reimers, *Still the Golden Door: The Third World Comes to America* (New York, 1985); Lawrence H. Fuchs, *The American Kaleidoscope: Race, Ethnicity and the Civil Culture* (Middletown, Conn., 1990); and Ronald Takaki, *A Different Mirror: A History of Multicultural America* (Boston, 1993). An excellent sociological study is Norma Williams, *The Mexican American Family: Tradition and Change* (Dix Hills, N.Y., 1990). For the East Asian immigration, see Takaki, *Strangers from a Different Shore* (Boston, 1989), and Joann Faung Jean Lee, ed., *Asian American Experiences in the United States* (Jefferson, N.C., 1991). Fiction by Asian-American women includes Jade Snow Wong's classic, *Fifth Chinese Daughter* (New York, 1950); Maxine Hong Kingston, *The Woman Warrior: Memoirs of a Girlhood Among Ghosts* (1976); and Amy Tan, *The Joy Luck Club* (1989).

Women's political roles are explored in Susan M. Hartmann, *From Margin to Mainstream: American Women and Politics Since 1960* (New York, 1989), and Ethel Klein, *Gender Politics: From Consciousness to Mass Politics* (Cambridge, Mass., 1985). For the 1984 election, see Geraldine A. Ferraro with Linda Bird Franke, *Ferraro: My Story* (New York, 1985); Jane Perlez, "Women, Power, and Politics," *New York Times Magazine,* July 24, 1984, pp. 23ff; Elizabeth Drew, "A Political Journal," *New Yorker,* 60 (August 13, 1984), 34–44; and Maureen Dowd, "Reassessing Women's Political Role: The Lasting Impact of Geraldine Ferraro," *New York Times Magazine,* December 30, 1984, pp. 18ff. For the concept of gender justice, see David L. Kirp, Mark G. Yadof, and Marlene Strong Franks, *Gender Justice* (Chicago, 1986); Susan Moller Okin, *Justice, Gender, and the Family* (New York, 1989); and "Women and Rights," *Dissent,* 38 (Summer 1991), 369–405. Legal issues are discussed further in Joan Hoff-Wilson, *Law, Gender, and Injustice,* cited above; Deborah L. Rhode, *Justice and Gender: Sex Discrimination and the Law* (Cambridge, Mass., 1989); and Susan Gluck Mezey, *In Pursuit of Equality: Women, Policy, and the Federal Courts* (New York, 1992).

APPENDIX

1 Life Expectancy, by Sex and Race, for Persons Surviving to Age 20, 1850–1990

Year	White		Nonwhite	
	Male	Female	Male	Female
1850	60.1	60.2	—	—
1890	60.7	62	—	—
1900	62.2	63.8	55.1	56.9
1910	62.7	64.9	53.5	56.1
1920	65.6	66.5	58.4	57.2
1930	66.0	68.5	56.0	57.2
1940	67.8	71.4	59.7	62.1
1950	69.5	74.6	63.7	66.8
1960	70.3	76.3	65.8	70.1
1970	70.2	77.2	64.4	71.9
1980	72.2	79.4	67.6	75.9
1990	72.6	79.3	68.4	76.3

Sources: Historical Statistics of the United States Colonial Times to 1970. Part 1, Bicentennial Edition, Bureau of the Census, U.S. Department of Commerce, 1975. *Information Please Almanac, 1983* (New York: A & W Publishers, 1983), *World Almanac,* 1992.

NOTE: Data for nonwhites, 1900–1930, relate to blacks only.

2 Birthrate by Race, 1800–1990

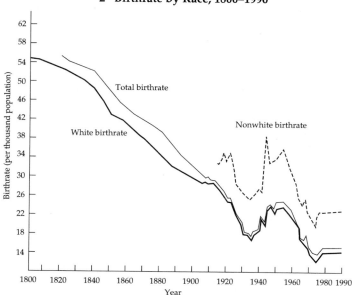

Sources: Historical Statistics of the United States, Colonial Times to 1970. Part 1, Bicentennial Edition, Bureau of the Census, U.S. Department of Commerce, 1975. *Perspectives on Working Women: a Databook.* Bulletin 2080, Bureau of Labor Statistics, U.S. Department of Labor. *Final Natality Statistics, 1978,* Monthly Vital Statistics Report, National Center for Health Satistics. *Statistical Abstract of the United States.* Bureau of the Census, U.S. Department of Commerce, 1981 and 1992.

NOTE: The birthrate is the annual number of births per 1,000 population. Figures for nonwhites were not computed until World War I.

3 Total Fertility Rate by Race, 1800–1989

Year	Total Fertility Rate	Whites	Nonwhites
1800	—	7.04	—
1810	—	6.92	—
1820	—	6.73	—
1830	—	6.55	—
1840	—	6.14	—
1850	—	5.42	—
1860	—	5.21	—
1870	—	4.55	—
1880	—	4.24	—
1890	—	3.87	—
1900	—	3.56	—
1910	—	3.42	—
1920	3.26	3.22	3.56
1930	2.53	2.51	2.73
1940	2.23	2.18	2.62
1950	3.03	2.94	3.58
1960	3.61	3.51	4.24
1965	2.88	2.76	3.66
1970	2.43	2.34	3.00
1975	1.80	1.71	2.32
1979	1.86	1.76	2.40
1989	2.01	1.81	2.46

Sources: "Fertility Tables for Birth Cohorts by Color: United States, 1917–73," U.S. Department of Health, Education, and Welfare, National Center for Health Statistics, Rockville, Md., April 1976. *Statistical Abstract of the United States,* Bureau of the Census, U.S. Department of Commerce, 1983 and 1992. Ansley J. Coale and Melvin Zelnick, *New Estimates of Fertility and Population in the United States* (Princeton, N.J.: Princeton University Press, 1963).

NOTE: The total fertility rate is the number of children born to a woman experiencing the average fertility for each year of her reproductive life. Figures for nonwhites were not computed until World War I.

---

4 Marriage and Divorce Rates, 1890–1990

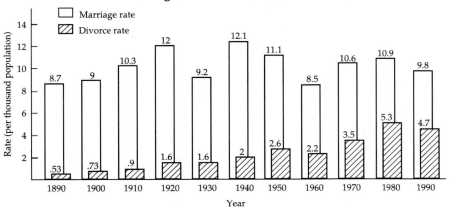

Sources: Marriage and Divorce, 1887–1906, Bulletin 96, Bureau of the Census, Department of Commerce and Labor, 1908. *Historical Statistics of the United States, Colonial Times to 1970,* Part I, Bicentennial Edition, Bureau of the Census, U.S. Department of Commerce, 1975. *Statistical Abstract of the United States,* Bureau of the Census, U.S. Department of Commerce, 1983. *World Almanac,* 1992.

NOTE: The marriage and divorce rates are the annual number of marriages and divorces per 1,000 population.

5 Women's Education, 1870–1990

Year	Percent of 17-Year-Olds Who Graduated From High School	Percent of High-School Graduates Who Are Female	Percent of 18- to 21-Year-Olds Enrolled in College	Percent of Under-graduates Who Are Female	Percent of Bachelor's or First Professional Degree Granted to Women	Percent of Doctorates Granted To Women	Percent of University Faculty That Is Female
1870	2.0	56.3	1.68	21.3	14.7	0	12.0
1880	2.5	54.2	2.72	32.7	19.3	5.6	36.4
1890	3.5	56.8	2.99	35.9	17.3	1.3	19.6
1900	6.4	60.0	3.91	35.9	19.1	6.0	19.8
1910	8.8	59.6	4.99	39.6	22.7	9.9	20.1
1920	16.8	60.5	7.88	47.3	34.2	15.1	26.3
1930	29.0	55.0	11.89	43.7	39.9	15.4	27.2
1940	50.8	52.7	14.49	40.2	41.3	13.0	27.6
1950	59.0	52.4	26.94	30.3	23.9	9.6	24.5
1960	65.1	51.8	31.27	35.3	35.3	10.5	22.0
1970	75.7	50.4	43.73	40.5	41.5	13.3	25.0
1980	73.6	50.9	(25.6)	50.9	47.3	29.7	33.4
1990	74.1	50.1	(30.3)	55.0	54.0	37.0	32.3

Sources: Historical Statistics of the United States: Colonial Times to 1970, Part 1, Bicentennial Edition, Bureau of the Census, U.S. Department of Commerce, 1975. Patricia A. Graham, "Expansion and Exclusion: A History of Women in Higher Education," *Signs,* 3 (Summer 1978), 766. W. Vance Grant and Leo J. Eiden, *Digest of Education Statistics,* National Center for Education Statistics, 1982. Thomas D. Snyder, *Digest of Education Statistics, 1990.*

NOTES: 1990 figures cover 1988–1991; 1980 and 1990 figures in 18- to 21-year-old column cover 18- to 24-year-olds.

6 Women and the Labor Force, 1800–1990

Year	Percent of All Women In the Labor Force	Percent of the Labor Force That Is Female
1800	4.6	4.6
1810	7.9	9.4
1820	6.2	7.3
1830	6.4	7.4
1840	8.4	9.6
1850	10.1	10.8
1860	9.7	10.2
1870	13.7	14.8
1880	14.7	15.2
1890	18.2	17.0
1900	21.2	18.1
1910	24.8	20.0
1920	23.9	20.4
1930	24.4	21.9
1940	25.4	24.6
1950	29.1	27.8
1960	34.8	32.3
1970	42.6	36.7
1980	51.1	42.6
1990	57.5	45.4

Sources: W. Elliot Brownlee and Mary M. Brownlee, *Women in the American Economy: A Documentary History* (New Haven: Yale University Press, 1976). *Historical Statistics of the United States: Colonial Times to 1970,* Part 1, Bicentennial Edition, Bureau of the Census, U.S. Department of Commerce, 1975. "Marital and Family Characteristics of Workers," March 1983, U.S. Department of Labor. *Statistical Abstract of the United States,* Bureau of the Census, U.S. Department of Commerce, 1983 and 1992.

7 Women in the Labor Force by Race, 1890–1990

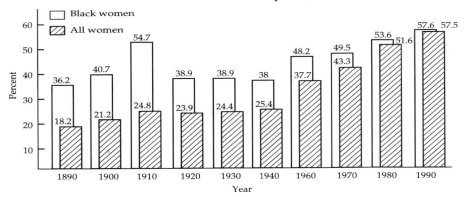

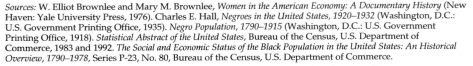

Sources: W. Elliot Brownlee and Mary M. Brownlee, *Women in the American Economy: A Documentary History* (New Haven: Yale University Press, 1976). Charles E. Hall, *Negroes in the United States, 1920–1932* (Washington, D.C.: U.S. Government Printing Office, 1935). *Negro Population, 1790–1915* (Washington, D.C.: U.S. Government Printing Office, 1918). *Statistical Abstract of the United States,* Bureau of the Census, U.S. Department of Commerce, 1983 and 1992. *The Social and Economic Status of the Black Population in the United States: An Historical Overview, 1790–1978,* Series P-23, No. 80, Bureau of the Census, U.S. Department of Commerce.

NOTE: Figures for black women in 1960, 1970, and 1980 also include those for other nonwhite women.

8 Women in the Labor Force by Marital Status, 1890–1990

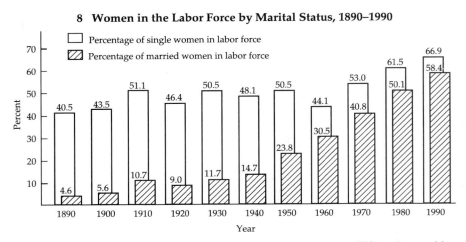

Sources: Historical Statistics of the United States: Colonial Times to 1970, Part I, Bicentennial Edition, Bureau of the Census, U.S. Department of Commerce, 1975. *Statistical Abstract of the United States,* Bureau of the Census, U.S. Department of Commerce, 1983 and 1992.

NOTE: Statistics from 1890 to 1930 are given for persons 15 years and older, from 1940 to 1950 for persons 14 years and older, and thereafter for persons 16 years and older. Figure for single women in 1920 includes both widowed and divorced women. Figures for married women in 1940, 1950, 1960, 1970, 1980, and 1990 denote only those married women with husbands present.

9 Women's Participation in the Labor Force by Age, 1890–1990

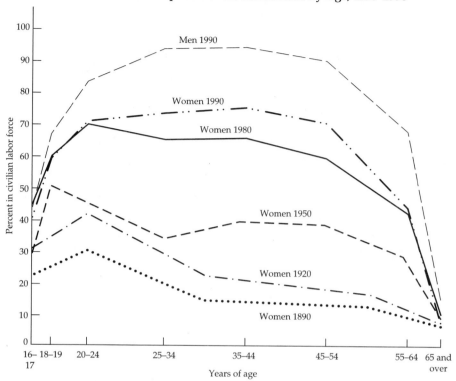

Sources: Historical Statistics of the United States: Colonial Times to 1970, Part 1, Bicentennial Edition, Bureau of the Census, U.S. Department of Commerce, 1975. "Handbook of Labor Statistics, 1978" and "Employment and Earnings," January 1981, Bureau of Labor Statistics, U.S. Department of Labor. *Statistical Abstract of the United States*, Bureau of the Census, U.S. Department of Commerce, 1992.

10 Women's Occupations, 1900–1980

Occupation Group	Percent Distribution of Employed Women by Major Occupational Group				
	1900	1920	1940	1960	1980
Professional and Technical Workers	8.2%	11.7%	12.8%	12.4%	16.8%
Managers and Administrators (except farm)	1.4	2.2	3.3	5.0	6.9
Sales Workers	4.3	6.3	7.8	7.7	6.8
Clerical Workers	4.0	18.7	21.5	30.3	35.1
Craft, Operative, and Kindred Workers	25.2	21.4	20.6	16.2	12.5
Nonfarm Laborers	2.6	2.3	1.1	0.4	1.2
Private Household Workers	28.7	15.7	18.1	8.9	2.5
Other Service Workers	6.7	8.1	11.3	14.8	17.0
Farm Workers	19.0	13.5	4.0	3.7	1.2

SOURCES: *Historical Statistics of the United States: Colonial Times to 1970*. Part 1. Bureau of the Census, U.S. Department of Commerce, 1975. "Employment and Earnings," Bureau of Labor Statistics, U.S. Department of Labor, January 1981.

11 Women in Selected Professional Occupations, 1910–1991

Occupation	Percentage of All Workers, Year								
	1910	1920	1930	1940	1950	1960	1970	1982	1991
Lawyers	1.0	1.4	2.1	2.4	3.5	3.5	4.7	14.0	19.0
College professors and instructors	19.0	30.0	32.0	27.6	23.0	19.0	28.3	35.4	40.8
Physicians	6.0	5.0	4.0	4.6	6.1	6.8	8.9	14.3	20.1
Nurses	93.0	96.0	98.0	98.0	98.0	97.0	97.4	95.6	94.8
Social workers	52.0	62.0	68.0	67.0	66.0	57.0	62.8	66.4	68.0
Librarians	79.0	88.0	91.0	89.0	89.0	85.0	82.0	83.4	83.0

Sources: Cynthia Fuchs Epstein, *Woman's Place: Options and Limits in Professional Careers* (Berkeley and Los Angeles: University of California Press, 1970). *Employment and Earnings,* Bureau of Labor Statistics, U.S. Department of Labor, January 1983. *The Female-Male Earnings Gap: A Review of Employment and Earnings Issues,* Report 673, Bureau of Labor Statistics, U.S. Department of Labor, September 1982. *1970 Census of Population: Detailed Characteristics, United States Summary,* Bureau of the Census, U.S. Department of Commerce. *Statistical Abstract of the United States,* Bureau of the Census, U.S. Department of Commerce, 1992.

12 Female-Headed Households by Race, 1940–1990

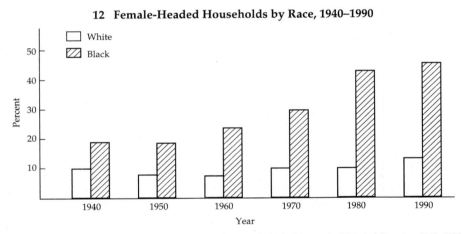

Sources: *The Social and Economic Status of the Black Population in the United States: An Historical Overview, 1790–1978,* Series P-23, No. 80, Bureau of the Census, U.S. Department of Commerce. *Statistical Abstract of the United States.* Bureau of the Census, U.S. Department of Commerce, 1983 and 1992.

NOTE: Female-headed households are presented as a percentage of all families.

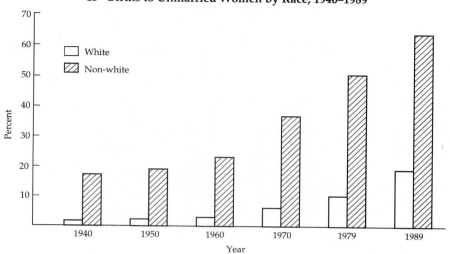

13 Births to Unmarried Women by Race, 1940–1989

Sources: The Social and Economic Status of the Black Population in the United States: An Historical Overview, 1790–1978, Series P-23, No. 80, Bureau of the Census, U.S. Department of Commerce. *Statistical Abstract of the United States,* Bureau of the Census, U.S. Department of Commerce, 1983 and 1992.

NOTE: Births to unmarried women are presented as a percent of all births.

14 Woman Suffrage Before the Nineteenth Amendment

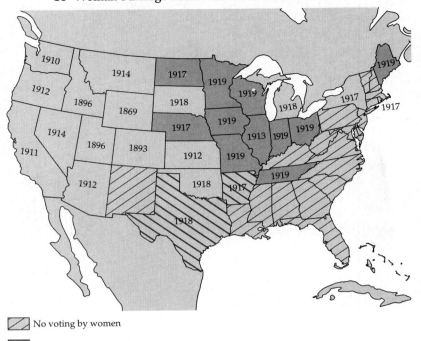

- ▨ No voting by women
- ▨ Women voting in presidential election
- ▨ Women voting in primaries
- ▢ Complete voting rights for women

Source: Richard N. Current, T. Harry Williams, and Frank Freidel, *American History: A Survey*, 4th ed. (New York: Random House, 1975), p. 577.

15 States Ratifying the Proposed Equal Rights Amendment to the U.S. Constitution by June 1982

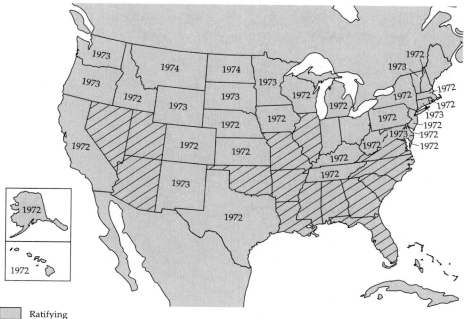

<table>
<tr><td>■</td><td>Ratifying</td></tr>
<tr><td>▨</td><td>Not ratifying</td></tr>
</table>

BIBLIOGRAPHICAL NOTE

Suggestions for further reading in American women's history may be found at the end of each pair of chapters. The suggestions below include journals, reference books, surveys, anthologies, and demographic sources.

Current journals in women's history include *Signs: Journal of Women in Culture and Society, Journal of Women's History, Feminist Studies,* and *Women's Studies.* Articles on women's history also appear in many historical journals, such as *American Quarterly, Journal of American History, Journal of Interdisciplinary History, Journal of Social History,* and *William and Mary Quarterly.* Occasional special issues devoted to women are especially useful—for example, "Women and Religion," *American Quarterly,* 30 (Winter 1978), and *American Historical Review,* 89 (June 1984).

A major resource is *Notable American Women 1607–1950: A Biographical Dictionary,* eds., Edward T. James, Janet Wilson James, and Paul S. Boyer (Cambridge, Mass., 1971), 3 vols., and a companion volume, *Notable American Women: The Modern Period,* eds., Barbara Sicherman and Carol Hurd Green (Cambridge, Mass., 1980). For black women, see Jessie Carney Smith, ed., *Notable Black American Women* (Detroit, 1992), and Darlene Clark Hine, ed., *Black Women in America: An Historical Encyclopedia,* 2 vols. (Brooklyn, N.Y., 1993). For bibliography, see Jill Ker Conway, *The Female Experience in Eighteenth- and Nineteenth-Century America* (New York, 1982), and *The Female Experience in Twentieth-Century America* (New York, 1986). Gerda Lerner, *Teaching Women's History* (Washington, D.C., 1981), an American Historical Association publication, includes bibliographical footnotes. Patricia K. Ballou, *Women: A Bibliography of Bibliographies,* 2d ed. (Boston, 1986), describes reference tools published since 1970 and cites bibliographical articles in many disciplines. For women's studies, see also Barbara Haber, *Women in America: A Guide to Books,* rev. ed. (Boston, 1981), which covers books published from 1963 to 1979, and Catharine R. Loeb et al., *Women's Studies: A Recommended Core Bibliography, 1980–1985* (Littleton, Colo., 1987). Angela Howard Zophy and Frances M. Kavenik, eds., *Handbook of American Women's History* (New York, 1990) includes bibliographies.

Specialized bibliographies include Bernice Redfern, *Women of Color in the United States: A Guide to the Literature* (New York, 1989); Andrea Timberlake et al., *Women of Color and Southern Women: A Bibliography of Social Science Research, 1975 to 1988* (Memphis, Tenn., 1988, with annual supplements); Rayna Green, *Native American Women: A Contextual Bibliography* (Bloomington, Ind., 1983); Mari Jo Buhle, *Women and the American Left: A Guide to Sources* (Boston, 1983); Nancy Sahli, *Women and Sexuality in America: A Bibliography* (Boston, 1984); Francesco Cordasco, *The Immigrant Woman in North America: An Annotated Bibliography of Selected References* (Metuchen, N.J., 1985); Cynthia D. Kinnard, *Antifeminism in American Thought: An Annotated Bibliography* (Boston, 1986); Cheryl Cline, *Women's Diaries, Journals, and Letters: An Annotated Bibliography* (New York, 1989); and Karen J. Blair, *The History of American Women's Voluntary Organizations, 1810–1960: A Guide to Sources* (Boston, 1989). For recent articles on theory and methodology, see Connie Miller with Corinna Treitel, *Feminist Research Methods: An Annotated Bibliography* (Westport, Conn., 1991), ch. 6.

For manuscript research, the major resource is Andrea Hinding, ed., *Women's History Sources: A Guide to Archives and Manuscript Collections in the United States* (New York, 1979). For catalogs of the major women's history archives at Radcliffe College and Smith College, see *The History of Women in America: Catalog of the Books, Manuscripts, and Pictures of the Arthur and Elizabeth Schlesinger Library* (Boston, 1983), 10 vols., and *The Author, Subject, and Manuscript Catalogs of the Sophia Smith Collection (Women's History Archive)* (Boston, 1983), 7 vols.

Surveys of American women's history include Mary F. Ryan, *Womanhood in America: From Colonial Times to the Present,* 3d ed. (New York, 1983); Glenda Riley, *Inventing the American Woman: A Perspective on Women's History,* 2 vols. (Arlington Heights, Ill., 1986); and Sara Evans, *Born for Liberty: A History of Women in America* (New York, 1989). Anthologies of articles include Nancy F. Cott and Elizabeth H. Pleck, eds., *A Heritage of Her Own: Toward a New Social History of American Women* (New York, 1979); Jean E. Friedman and William G. Shade, eds., *Our American Sisters: Women in American Life and Thought,* 4th ed. (Lexington, Mass., 1987); Nancy A. Hewitt, ed., *Women, Family, and Communities: Readings in American History,* 2 vols. (Glenview, Ill., 1990); Louise A. Tilly and Patricia Gurin, eds., *Women, Politics, and Change* (New York, 1990); Ellen Carol Dubois and Vicki L. Ruiz, eds., *Unequal Sisters: A Multi-Cultural Reader in U.S. Women's History* (New York and London, 1990); and

Kathryn Kish Sklar and Thomas Dublin, eds., *Women and Power in American History: A Reader*, 2 vols. (Englewood Cliffs, N.J., 1991). Anthologies of articles plus historical sources include Carol Ruth Berkin and Mary Beth Norton, eds., *Women of America: A History* (Boston, 1979); Linda K. Kerber and Jane Sherron DeHart, eds., *Women's America: Refocusing the Past*, 3d ed. (New York, 1991); and Mary Beth Norton, ed., *Major Problems in American Women's History: Documents and Essays* (Lexington, Mass., 1989). Collections of primary sources include Nancy F. Cott, *Root of Bitterness: Documents of the Social History of American Women*, 2d ed. (Boston, 1986); Gerda Lerner, ed., *Black Women in White America: A Documentary History* (New York, 1972); Lerner, ed., *The Female Experience: An American Documentary*, 2d ed. (New York, 1992); Susan Ware, ed., *Modern American Women: A Documentary History* (Belmont, Calif., 1989); and Nancy Woloch, ed., *Early American Women: A Documentary History* (Belmont, Calif., 1992). For legal history, see D. Kelly Weisberg, ed., *Women and the Law: A Social Historical Perspective*, 2 vols. (Cambridge, Mass., 1982), a collection of essays; Marlene Stein Wortman and Judith A. Baer, *Women in American Law*, 2 vols. (New York, 1985 and 1991); Deborah L. Rhodes, *Justice and Gender* (Cambridge, Mass., 1989); and Joan Hoff, *Law, Gender, and Injustice: A Legal History of U.S. Women* (New York, 1991). Other specialized surveys, anthologies, and source collections are mentioned in the suggested readings that follow the chapters.

Two sources of demographic data are Cynthia Taeuber, ed., *Statistical Handbook on Women in America* (Phoenix, Ariz., 1991), and Linda Schmittroth, ed., *Statistical Record of Women Worldwide* (Detroit, Mich., 1991). Useful sources for statistics in women's history include *Statistical Abstract of the United States* (Washington, D.C., issued annually); *Historical Statistics of the United States: Colonial Times to 1970* (Washington, D.C., 1975), which is republished periodically; publications of the U.S. Department of Labor; *The Social and Economic Statistics of the Black Population of the United States: An Historical View 1790–1978*, U.S. Department of Commerce, Bureau of the Census, Current Population Reports, No. 80 (Washington, D.C., 1978); and W. Vance and Leo J. Eiden, *Digest of Educational Statistics*, National Center of Educational Statistics (Washington, D.C., 1982). For fertility rates, see Ansley J. Coale and Melvin Zelnik, *New Estimates of Fertility and Population in the United States* (Princeton, N.J., 1963). For demographic history, see Robert V. Wells, *Revolutions in Americans' Lives* (Westport, Conn., 1982); Marcia Guttentag and Paul F. Secord, *Too Many Women? The Sex Ratio Question* (Beverly Hills, Calif., 1983); Suzanne Bianchi and Daphne Spain, *American Women in Transition* (New York, 1986); and Stephen D. McLaughlin et al., *The Changing American Woman* (Chapel Hill, N.C., 1988).

Two early essays proposing an examination of women's history are Arthur M. Schlesinger, "The Role of Women in American History," *New Viewpoints in American History* (New York, 1992), pp. 126–159, and, forty years later, David Potter's 1962 essay on American women and "National Character" in Edward Saveth, ed., *American History and the Social Sciences* (New York, 1964), pp. 427–448. Recent articles on women historians include Katherine Kish Sklar, "American Female Historians in Context, 1770–1930," *Feminist Studies*, 3 (Fall 1975), 171–184; Jacqueline Goggin, "Challenging Sexual Discrimination in the Historical Profession," *American Historical Review*, 97 (June 1992), 769–802; and Joan Scott, "American Women's History, 1884–1984," in her recent book, *Gender and the Politics of History* (New York, 1988), pp. 178–198.

INDEX